Comparative Grand Strategy

Comparative Strategy

A Framework and Cases

Edited by
Thierry Balzacq
Peter Dombrowski
Simon Reich

OXFORD
UNIVERSITY PRESS

Great Clarendon Street, Oxford, OX2 6DP,
United Kingdom

Oxford University Press is a department of the University of Oxford.
It furthers the University's objective of excellence in research, scholarship,
and education by publishing worldwide. Oxford is a registered trade mark of
Oxford University Press in the UK and in certain other countries

© Oxford University Press 2019

The moral rights of the authors have been asserted

First Edition published in 2019

Impression: 4

All rights reserved. No part of this publication may be reproduced, stored in
a retrieval system, or transmitted, in any form or by any means, without the
prior permission in writing of Oxford University Press, or as expressly permitted
by law, by licence or under terms agreed with the appropriate reprographics
rights organization. Enquiries concerning reproduction outside the scope of the
above should be sent to the Rights Department, Oxford University Press, at the
address above

You must not circulate this work in any other form
and you must impose this same condition on any acquirer

Published in the United States of America by Oxford University Press
198 Madison Avenue, New York, NY 10016, United States of America

British Library Cataloguing in Publication Data
Data available

Library of Congress Control Number: 2018968022

ISBN 978-0-19-884084-8 (hbk.)
ISBN 978-0-19-884085-5 (pbk.)

Printed and bound by
CPI Group (UK) Ltd, Croydon, CR0 4YY

Links to third party websites are provided by Oxford in good faith and
for information only. Oxford disclaims any responsibility for the materials
contained in any third party website referenced in this work.

ACKNOWLEDGMENTS

Large, collaborative projects always require an abundance of goodwill to achieve their goals. That becomes even more emphatic when the project attempts to develop a novel research program rather than address questions in the more comfortable intellectual confines of a well-established one. Sponsors require just a little more faith in allocating funds. Participants have to demonstrate a little more intellectual flexibility and dexterity when they ask questions like "what is the working definition of a grand strategy?" and the organizers' answer is "well, it depends." And administrators must show an even greater amount of patience dealing with the requisites of people assembled in a truly global project when they are drawn from four continents.

Under these circumstances, we, the organizers, have been very fortunate. We found generous sponsors who were willing to support two workshops, held on two continents, in the same year, and a set of scholars willing to move beyond their comfort zones in exploring the relationship between international relations theory and area studies in a new way.

The first workshop held in Namur, Belgium in June 2017, was convened by Thierry Balzacq. Thierry wishes to acknowledge the Research Council of the University of Namur, and specifically both Christine Culot (Director of the Research Council) and former Vice-Rector Martine Raes who provided a generous grant to fund the workshop. The Francqui Foundation, the Faculty of Economics, Social Sciences and Management, and the Department of Social and Political Science also offered financial assistance. Thierry also thanks Benjamin Puybareau, Nicole Desneux, and Karin Derochette for their invaluable logistical support in organizing that gathering of scholars. Finally, Thierry acknowledges the Asia-Pacific College of Diplomacy at the Australian National University for hosting him during his sabbatical in 2017–18, which enabled him to undertake the co-editorship of the volume in ideal circumstances.

Peter Dombrowski convened the second workshop at the US Naval War College (NWC) in Newport, Rhode Island in October 2017. Peter wishes to thank the Naval War College Foundation, the Strategic and Operational Research Department (SORD), and the Center of Naval Warfare Studies (CNWS) for their support. Andrew "Drew" Winner and Jacquelyn Schneider moderated panels, while colleagues from across the NWC shared insights from their own experience and research. Among the many individuals who worked behind the scenes to make the second workshop a success were Mike Sherlock, John Odegaard, and Wendy Skinner. As always the NWC leadership from Rear Admiral Jeff Harley, Provost Lewis Duncan, CNWS Dean Tom

Culora, to SORD chair Andrew Winner provided expert leadership. Most importantly, Rachael Shaffer labored long and hard to coordinate arrangements for participants and guests from across the NWC, the United States, and the world; she also expertly edited multiple versions of the entire manuscript. Peter would like to thank his fellow editors Simon and Thierry, and Ariane Chebel d'Appollonia for hosting several visits to New Jersey, and, of course, Ann Martino for her unwavering faith.

Simon Reich wishes to thank both Peter and Thierry for relieving him of the task of organizing the two workshops, the Gerda Henkel Foundation for its generous support of his work on this project, the Institute for Strategic Research (IRSEM) in Paris for hosting him while working on this project during his sabbatical in 2018, and Ariane Chebel d'Appollonia for providing him with all the perspective he needed on the significance of his work.

Finally, in addition to two workshops, the editors also organized a series of panels at the International Studies Association Annual Meetings, beginning in 2016. Participants, in addition to the contributors to this volume, included Robert Art, Hal Brands, Shaun Breslin, Colin Dueck, Steven F. Jackson, Bruce Jentleson, and Andrew Ross. They asked important and probing questions, forcing the editors and authors to refine their ideas and better articulate the issues critical for thinking about Comparative Grand Strategy.

With contributions from
Andrew S. Erickson
C. Christine Fair
Daniel Fiott
Ghaidaa Hetou
Robert Johnson
Céline Marangé
Carlos R. S. Milani
Tiago Nery
Wendy Ramadan-Alban
Norrin M. Ripsman
Eitan Shamir
Luis Simón

CONTENTS

LIST OF CONTRIBUTORS ... ix

1 Introduction: Comparing Grand Strategies in the Modern World ... 1
   Thierry Balzacq, Peter Dombrowski, and Simon Reich

PART I MAJOR POWERS

2 The United States of America ... 25
   Peter Dombrowski and Simon Reich

3 Russia ... 50
   Céline Marangé

4 China ... 73
   Andrew S. Erickson

5 France ... 99
   Thierry Balzacq

6 United Kingdom ... 123
   Robert Johnson

PART II PIVOTAL POWERS

7 Brazil ... 149
   Carlos R. S. Milani and Tiago Nery

8 India ... 171
   C. Christine Fair

9 Iran ... 192
   Thierry Balzacq and Wendy Ramadan-Alban

10 Israel ... 217
   Eitan Shamir

11 Saudi Arabia ... 239
   Ghaidaa Hetou

12 The European Union ... 262
   Daniel Fiott and Luis Simón

13 Conclusion: The Emerging Sub-field of Comparative Grand Strategy ... 284
   Norrin M. Ripsman

BIBLIOGRAPHY ... 303
INDEX ... 339

LIST OF CONTRIBUTORS

Editors

Thierry Balzacq is Professor of International Relations at Sciences Po Paris and Professorial Fellow at CERI-Sciences-Po. He was formerly a Visiting Fellow at the Asia-Pacific College of Diplomacy at the Australian National University (2017–18). In 2016, he was awarded a Francqui Research Chair (Belgium's highest academic title) and elected Visiting Professor at the London School of Economics and Political Science. He was the Scientific Director of the French Ministry of Defense's research center (2014–16). A former Postdoctoral Fellow at Harvard, Balzacq held an Honorary Professorial Fellowship at the University of Edinburgh, where he was also Fellow for "outstanding research" at the Institute for Advanced Studies in the Humanities. In 2015, he was awarded a Tier 1 Canada Research Chair in Diplomacy and International Security. "Tier 1 Chairs are for outstanding researchers acknowledged by their peers as world leaders in their fields." His articles have been published in *Review of International Studies, Security Studies, European Journal of International Security, International Studies Review, Cooperation and Conflict, European Journal of International Relations, Security Dialogue, International Relations*, and the *Journal of Common Market Studies*. He is author/editor of over twelve books in English and French. He has held visiting positions at various universities, including McGill, the Diplomatic Academy of Vietnam, the National University of Singapore (NUS), The International Relations Institute of Cameroon (IRIC), Aberystwyth, and the University Abdou Moumouni of Niamey (Niger). He is currently co-editing (with Ronald Krebs) *The Oxford Handbook of Grand Strategy*. Balzacq holds a PhD from the University of Cambridge and completed his Postdoctoral studies at Harvard in 2004.

Peter Dombrowski is a Professor of Strategy in the Strategic and Operational Research Department as well as the Director of the Cyber and Innovation Policy Institute at the Naval War College. His prior positions include Chair of the Strategic Research Department, Director of the Naval War College Press, editor of the *Naval War College Review*, co-editor of *International Studies Quarterly*, Associate Professor of Political Science at Iowa State University, and defense analyst at ANSER, Inc. He has also been affiliated with research institutions including the East-West Center, The Brookings Institution, the Friedrich Ebert Foundation, and the Watson Institute for International Studies at Brown University. Dr Dombrowski is the author of over sixty books, monographs, articles, book chapters, and government reports. Dombrowski's awards include a Chancellor's Scholarship for Prospective Leaders from the Alexander von Humboldt Foundation, the Navy Meritorious Civilian Service Medal, and the Navy Distinguished Civilian Service Medal. He received his BA from Williams College and an MA and PhD from the University of Maryland.

Simon Reich is a Professor in the Division of Global Affairs and Department of Political Science at Rutgers, Newark and a Chercheur Associé at the Centre de Recherches Internationales (CERI), Sciences Po (Paris). Reich is author, coauthor and editor of eleven books and over sixty articles or book chapters. Reich's work has been translated into Chinese, Dutch, French, German, Japanese, and Turkish. His most recent book (with Peter Dombrowski) is entitled *The End of Grand Strategy: Maritime Operations in the 21st Century* (Cornell, 2018). Reich also previously served as Director of Research and Analysis at the Royal Institute for International Affairs (Chatham House) in London and the inaugural Director of the Ford Institute for Human Security at the University of Pittsburgh.

Contributors

Andrew S. Erickson is Professor of Strategy in, and a core founding member of, the US Naval War College (NWC)'s China Maritime Studies Institute. Erickson also serves on the *Naval War College Review*'s Editorial Board. He is an Associate in Research at Harvard University's John King Fairbank Center for Chinese Studies and a member of the Council on Foreign Relations. Erickson has taught courses at NWC and Yonsei University. During 2014–15 he helped to establish, and to escort the first iteration of, NWC's first bilateral naval officer exchange program and field studies class in China, which he continues to support. In 2013, while deployed in the Pacific as a Naval Postgraduate School Regional Security Education Program scholar aboard the flagship aircraft carrier USS *Nimitz*, he delivered twenty-five hours of lectures. In 2012 the National Bureau of Asian Research awarded him the inaugural Ellis Joffe Prize for PLA Studies. Erickson received his PhD and MA in politics from Princeton University. Proficient in Mandarin Chinese and conversant in Japanese, he has traveled extensively in Asia and lived in China, Japan, and Korea. Erickson is the author of the book *Chinese Anti-Ship Ballistic Missile Development*. He is coauthor of two other books: *Gulf of Aden Anti-Piracy and China's Maritime Commons Presence* and *Assessing China's Cruise Missile Ambitions*. His research has been published widely in English- and Chinese-language edited volumes and in such peer-reviewed journals as *International Security*, *China Quarterly*, and *Journal of Contemporary China*. It may be accessed via http://www.andrewerickson.com.

C. Christine Fair is a Provost's Distinguished Associate Professor in the Center for Security Studies within Georgetown University's Edmund A. Walsh School of Foreign Service. She previously served as a senior political scientist with the RAND Corporation, a political officer with the United Nations Assistance Mission to Afghanistan in Kabul, and a senior research associate at USIP's Center for Conflict Analysis and Prevention. Her research focuses on political and military affairs in South Asia (Afghanistan, Pakistan, India, Bangladesh, Sri Lanka). Her most recent book is *In Their Own Words: Understanding the Lashkar-e-Tayyaba* (Oxford University Press). Additionally, she has authored, coauthored, and co-edited several books, including *Fighting to the End: The Pakistan Army's Way of War* (Oxford University Press), *Pakistan's Enduring Challenges* (University of Pennsylvania Press, 2015), *Policing Insurgencies: Cops as Counterinsurgents* (Oxford University Press, 2014); *Political Islam and Governance in Bangladesh* (Routledge, 2010); *Treading on Hallowed Ground: Counterinsurgency Operations in Sacred Spaces* (Oxford University Press, 2008); *The Madrassah Challenge: Militancy and Religious Education in Pakistan* (USIP, 2008), *Fortifying Pakistan: The Role of U.S. Internal Security Assistance* (USIP, 2006); and

The Cuisines of the Axis of Evil and Other Irritating States (Globe Pequot, 2008). Dr Fair is a frequent commentator in print (*New York Times, Foreign Affairs, Foreign Policy, The National Review* among others) as well on television and radio programs (CBS, BBC, Al Jazeera, CNN, Voice of America, Fox, Reuters, BBC, NPR, among others). She is a member of the Council on Foreign Relations, Women in International Security, International Studies Association, American Political Science Association, and the American Institute of Pakistan Studies and serves on the editorial board of numerous scholarly and policy-analytic journals. She has a PhD from the University of Chicago, Department of South Asian Languages and Civilization, and an MA from the Harris School of Public Policy, also at the University of Chicago.

Daniel Fiott is Security and Defense Editor at the EU Institute for Security Studies. He is also a Visiting Professor at the Institute for European Studies at the Free University of Brussels (VUB) and a Visiting Lecturer at the Brussels School of International Studies at the University of Kent. From 2012 until 2016 he served as a researcher at the Free University of Brussels (VUB). From 2014 until 2016 Daniel was a fellow of the Research Foundation—Flanders (FWO). He specializes in defense and defense-industrial matters. He holds an MPhil from the University of Cambridge and a PhD from the Free University of Brussels (VUB).

Ghaidaa Hetou received her PhD in political science from Rutgers University, she also holds a BA and MA in Economics, and an MS in Global Affairs. Dr Hetou is fluent in Arabic, English, and German. Her recent book is titled: *The Syrian Conflict: The Role of Russia, Iran and the US in a Global Crisis* (Routledge 2018). Her research focuses on foreign policy, security, strategy, trade and political risk in the Middle East and North Africa. Dr Hetou founded i-Strategic LLC, a political risk consulting company specializing in Middle East and North Africa affairs. She also is an Adjunct Professor at Rutgers University, the United Nations and Global Policy Studies Masters program.

Robert Johnson is the Director of the Changing Character of War (CCW) research program at Oxford. The CCW Programme brings together academics, policymakers, and armed forces professionals in the study of armed conflict and its consequences, pursuing a variety of research themes including the future character of armed conflict, violent nonstate actors, civil-military relations, strategy and decision-making, technological developments, and the moral-legal dimensions of war. Rob Johnson's primary research interests are in the history of strategy and war, and how these are understood and utilized in contemporary applications. Rob acts as a specialist advisor to governments and international armed forces on security, stabilization, and strategy. He has run "Insight and Understanding" courses for a number of agencies on areas of security interest. He is author *The Afghan Way of War* (Oxford University Press, 2011), as well as several other works on conflicts in the Middle East, Asia, and Europe. He has examined the problems of strategy in a variety of contexts and publications, and draws attention to the local perspectives as well as the difficulties of forming judgements based on a selective reading of history or on the misuse of theories of international relations and politics. In an article in *Parameters*, on "predicting future war," Rob Johnson analyzed *how* we reach deductions about future operating environments. He has recently completed a monograph on the history of partnering irregular indigenous forces, and a strategic study of the First World War in the Middle East. In order to encourage the introduction of new thinking into British government policy on defense and security, he convened the UK strategy forum for the the Chief of the Defence Staff.

Céline Marangé is a research fellow at the Institute for Strategic Research (IRSEM), a research center affiliated with the French Ministry of Defense. Her current research interests include Russian foreign and defense policy, Russian political and military elites, Russian strategy of influence in Europe and the post-Soviet space, and the international consequences of Russian military interventions. Dr Marangé holds a PhD in political science from the Paris Institute of Political Studies (Sciences Po). Prior to her current position, she was a lecturer at Columbia University, a Fox International Fellow at Yale University, and a postdoctoral fellow in Cold War history at Panthéon-Sorbonne University. A graduate of the Institute of Oriental Languages and Civilizations (Paris), she is also a Russian translator. She recently edited and introduced two special issues devoted to Russia's new strategic posture: one deals with the reconfiguration of the European order in the aftermath of the conflict in Ukraine (*Champs de Mars*, Spring 2017); the other one explores Russian strategic strengths and weaknesses, and the security dilemma for Russia (*Revue de Défense nationale*, 2017).

Carlos R. S. Milani holds a *Doctorat* from the *Ecole de Hautes Etudes en Sciences Sociales* (France, 1997), and was in 2007 a Visiting Scholar at Berkeley's Center for Latin American Studies. He is Associate Professor at the Rio de Janeiro State University's Institute for Social and Political Studies (IESP-UERJ), and Senior Research Fellow with Brazil's National Research Council (CNPq) and Rio de Janeiro State Research Foundation (FAPERJ). He is also Associate Editor of the *Brazilian Political Science Review*. His research agenda focuses on Brazilian foreign policy, international development politics, and comparative foreign policy. His latest publications include: "Brazil's Foreign Policy and the Graduation Dilemma," *International Affairs* (2017), *Atlas of Brazilian Foreign Policy* (CLACSO/EDUERJ, 2015); "The Politics of Brazilian Foreign Policy and Its Analytical Challenges," *Foreign Policy Analysis* (2016). During his stay at Berkeley he started writing a book whose provisional title is *South-South Cooperation and Foreign Policy Agendas: Comparing the cases of Brazil, China, India, Mexico, South Africa and Turkey*.

Tiago Nery received his PhD in political science from the Institute for Social and Political Studies of the State University of Rio de Janeiro (IESP-UERJ). He is a a researcher at the World Political Analysis Laboratory/Labmundo (IESP-UERJ/IHAC-UFBA) and works as a civil servant at the Undersecretariat for International Relations, Executive Office of the State Government of Rio de Janeiro. His research agenda focuses on Brazilian foreign policy, international political economy and regional integration. His most recent publication is *Brazilian Foreign Policy: The Coalitions of Power and UNASUR: Rise and Deconstruction of South America as a Geopolitical Bloc* (Mural Internacional, 2018).

Wendy Ramadan-Alban is a PhD candidate in security studies at the University of Namur and at the EHESS (Ecole des Hautes Etudes en Sciences Sociales, in Paris), working on Iran's strategic thought. She holds a doctoral grant from the French government. She has published in the *European Review of International Studies*. She graduated in Persian language from the Dehkhoda institute based in Tehran.

Norrin M. Ripsman (PhD University of Pennsylvania, 1997) is Monroe J. Rathbone Distinguished Professor of International Relations at Lehigh University. His primary research interests include: democracy and national security, postwar peacemaking, constructing regional stability, the political economy of national security, neoclassical realism, and the impact of globalization on national security. He has published nine books, most recently *Peacemaking from Above, Peace from Below: Ending Conflict Between Regional Rivals* (Cornell University Press, 2016) and (with Jeffrey W. Taliaferro and Steven E. Lobell) *Neoclassical Realist Theory of International Politics* (Oxford University Press, 2016), and over twenty-five peer-reviewed articles in *International Security, International Studies Quarterly, Security Studies*, and other high-quality outlets.

Eitan Shamir is a Senior Lecturer at the Political Studies Department, Bar Ilan University and a Senior Research Fellow with the Begin Sadat Center for Strategic Studies (BESA Center). Prior to his academic position, he was in charge of the National Security Doctrine Department at the Ministry of Strategic Affairs, Prime Minister Office. He is the author of *Transforming Command: The Pursuit of Mission Command in the US, UK and Israeli Armies* (Stanford University Press, 2011). His most recent book (ed.) is *Insurgencies and Counterinsurgencies: National Styles and Strategic Cultures* (Cambridge University Press, 2017, with Beatrice Heuser). Shamir has published many articles in leading journals and various book chapters on the topics of military strategy and national security. He holds a PhD from the Department of War Studies, King's College London.

Luis Simón is Research Professor at the Institute for European Studies (Vrije Universiteit Brussel) and Director of the Brussels office of the Royal Elcano Institute. He is also Associate Fellow at the Royal United Services Institute (RUSI) and the Baltic Defense College (Estonia), and a member of the Editorial Board of *Parameters: The US Army War College Quarterly*. Luis is a frequent lecturer on geopolitical and strategic affairs at several universities and defense colleges, and his research has appeared in prestigious journals, such as *Security Studies, International Affairs, Journal of Strategic Studies, Geopolitics, Survival, Orbis*, the *RUSI Journal, Comparative Strategy, Parameters*, and *The International Spectator*. His current research interests include the evolution of US geostrategy and its impact upon the transatlantic relationship; European security; the future of NATO; and changing geostrategic dynamics in Asia and their implications for Europe. Luis has a PhD in international relations from the University of London (Royal Holloway College) and a Masters in European studies from Sciences-Po (Paris).

1 Introduction

Comparing Grand Strategies in the Modern World

THIERRY BALZACQ, PETER DOMBROWSKI, AND SIMON REICH

In this book, we outline a novel, comparative, and systematic approach to the study of grand strategy. Our contributors then use it to examine ten countries and the European Union. Our goal, as editors, is ambitious: to initiate a new research program in the field of grand strategy that links international relations theory to area studies. In the most general terms, we seek to address two lacunae. The first is a scholarly reliance on abstract theorizing that employs rationalist assumptions and thus presupposes what other countries value, and how they formulate and implement strategy. In essence, we seek to re-emphasize the importance of context in the study of grand strategy. The second, for policymakers, it is to describe those values, processes, and strategic goals in a way that may modestly help avoid some of the common mishaps that have characterized policymaking in the twenty-first century.

Within that broad rubric, we attempt to achieve four specific objectives. First, we propose a concrete basis on which to analyze contemporary grand strategy beyond the common rationalist approach adopted by Liberals and Realists—by emphasizing the significance of perceptual factors, such as historical memory and resulting national pathologies. Second, we imbue the study of grand strategy with the characteristics of a productive research program commonly found in other areas of international relations and foreign policy—including standards for theory-building and testing. Third, we develop a new framework that explains how a nation's grand strategy is constituted and implemented. Finally, we expand the empirical study of grand strategy beyond the well-trodden examples of a few great powers.

This volume therefore comparatively examines how a variety of states (both "great" and "small") devise and execute grand strategies. It also analyzes the consequences of those choices. States strategize in diverse ways: they vary in their objectives; in how they formulate strategy; in how they think about the geographic scope of their strategy; in the type and amount of resources that they have at their disposal; and in the ways in which they configure those resources in implementing a strategy. We attempt to reflect that diversity within a common framework that addresses the why, who, what, and how of grand strategy.

1.1 Prevailing assumptions and the questions they generate

American scholars dominate the growing literature on grand strategy. But their work raises a number of important unanswered, and problematic, questions. Succinctly stated, American debates (largely among and between Realists and Liberals) are predicated on five common assumptions. The first is that a single definition of what constitutes a grand strategy is essential to framing study in the field. Yet which definition should be used, the character of the national interest, and thus what form of strategy to adopt remain heavily contested. Definitions extend from a classical approach derived from historical research on major wars to an international relations one that stresses the importance of institution building. Second, only a superpower (in practice, solely the United States), or minimally a great power (extending the list to China and Russia), has the sufficient institutional and material resources to formulate and implement a grand strategy.[1] The universe of cases worthy of study is therefore nominal, thus justifying ignoring other potential cases despite a wealth of evidence that other countries comprehensively strategize. Third, grand strategizing is predominantly a rational, objective response to the exigencies of the external environment. Some historians and a few political scientists do examine the domestic determinants of grand strategy. But the vogue is to focus on systemic constraints or, minimally, foreign threats and opportunities as the drivers of grand strategy.

Fourth, in contrast to the impression created by the news cycle or the wishful thinking of some commentators, the external environment is actually quite stable and the fundamental characteristics of the global system has changed relatively little in the twenty-first century.[2] The threat remains primarily state-based for many scholars working in the field of grand strategy. The questions include whether there is a pressing need to maintain American preeminence, whether to address or subvert the claims of revisionist powers, whether there is a need to sustain the liberal international order in its current form, and, finally, how the United States should best—prescriptively—balance questions of strategy and national resources. Finally, the fifth assumption is that the purpose of grand strategy, and thus in practice American grand strategy, is more to shape the nature and characteristics of the global system than adapt to it. American policymakers can and should therefore design a preemptive and in practice enduring (and, as a result, reasonably inflexible) grand strategy—rather than a reactive, adaptive one—chosen from a variety of options prescribed by scholars that stretch from isolationism at one extreme to primacy at the other. Other states will simply have to adjust. Hubris is therefore endemic to this last assumption.

Critics of this characterization may justifiably point to greater nuance in scholarship and certainly to exceptions. We concur. But these five elements nonetheless predominate, especially in scholarship about US grand strategy but also in somewhat different forms in work on the grand strategies of other great powers. Our collective work therefore begins by questioning these foundational assumptions. In effect, we turn them into questions, justified by our focus on the varying domestic origins of the grand strategies that our contributing authors study.

1.2 Countervailing assumptions

First, we theorize that the very conception of what constitutes a grand strategy may itself be contested. Scholars often associate grand strategizing with a particular institutional structure (a centralized bureaucracy) or means of implementation (the military). But, as our cases suggest, some countries, for example, employ what amounts to a grand strategy while not being conscious that they are formally doing so or without using formal Western structures. They behave in a way consistent with the formulation of a grand strategy without labeling it as such, preferring to attribute comprehensive forms of behavior as simply adhering to national values or goals. Some lack the domestic bureaucratic structure for formulating strategy commonly assumed as a requisite. Others still may (and do) confound these conceptions of grand strategy by utilizing tools unrecognized by standard political science—such as proxy groups, network organizations, or even tribal affiliations rather than components of the state. Or they may employ elements of social power (such as religious fundamentalism directed through either formal education or online recruitment) often overlooked by scholars focusing on instruments of soft power such as markets or mass culture. A standardized definition of grand strategy clearly has its advantages. It delineates what to both include and exclude—and therefore what to analyze. But, as we subsequently discuss, a narrow formulation of grand strategy often ignores important elements based on national history, values, and institutions. Excluding them clashes with the intent of these cross-national studies where these elements matter and, our country studies suggest, are often critical in explaining behavior.

Second, we evaluate whether other states, beyond great powers, have the institutional and material resources to create and implement what amounts to a grand strategy. Certainly, this multi-country, cross-national study highlights the fact that there are distinct parameters to such initiatives. Grand strategizing inevitably varies in geographic scope. Some states have a regional focus while others have global aspirations. They also considerably differ in their resources, roughly understood as "military power, bureaucratic/administrative capacity, and the quality and coherence of political institutions,"[3] as well as the ability to muster social, private, and religious instruments for state ends. As our contributors demonstrate, policymakers both vary in terms of whether they think about their strategizing as "grand" and if they have the institutions dedicated to such a task—or use other facets neglected by most international relations (IR) scholars. Nonetheless, our focus on the breadth and capacity for such behavior reformulates an assumption into a question about the conditions under which states can and do create grand strategies—and their varying objectives in doing so.

Third, we question both the rationalist and systemic roots of strategizing. Over two decades ago, Richard Rosecrance and Arthur Stein published a seminal article in which they argued that domestic factors had been neglected as determinants of grand strategy.[4] Their observation, with a few commendable exceptions among historians and political economists, has largely been ignored by IR scholars in the grand strategy literature.[5] In this volume we return to their original insight, combining the fundamentals of IR theory with the knowledge of country specialists familiar with the history and historical memory, domestic politics, decision-making processes, strategic imperatives, and resource capacities of the countries that they study. We thus reject a preponderantly systemic and rationalist approach in favor of a heterogeneous one that focuses on the interaction between the external environment, subjective interpretations of that environment, and the key historical and domestic political factors that condition state responses.

The fourth assumption that we challenge concerns the character of the global system. The simplified, elegant assumptions embedded, for example, in structural realism proved lacking in predicting the decline of the Soviet Union, among other important developments.[6] An anarchic, if stable, system assumed a continuity in the bipolar system subsequently confounded by events. Yet, at the risk of overgeneralization, an obdurate propensity to rely on a common assumption that the characteristic features of that global system endure among many realists and liberals, even as they continually debate the issue of American decline, is challenged by the capacity of states that are not great powers to destabilize the system—as North Korea's behavior in 2017 acutely demonstrates. New elements of power—such as cyber warfare, for example—have created schisms in these formulations. We thus question a continued focus on the attributes of the global system, whether it is anarchic (Realists) or increasingly institutionalized (Liberals). Instead, as we subsequently discuss, we focus on its dynamic features that underpin its fluidity in the twenty-first century[7]—notably the proliferation of actors, threats, and forms of conflict—that influence the formulation and implementation of grand strategy, albeit on different states in different ways.

And finally, we question the assumption of the very purpose of a grand strategy. Stephen Krasner offers a representative view among American scholars when he states that

> A grand strategy is a conceptual framing that describes how the world is, envisions how it ought to be, and specifies a set of policies that can achieve that ordering. Grand strategies are designed to mold the international environment by regulating international regimes, influencing the foreign policy choices made by other states, and shaping or even determining the domestic regime characteristics of other countries.[8]

But if you begin with the assumption that the purpose of grand strategy primarily involves molding the global system, rather than responding to its exigencies, then the belief that few states can do so is self-affirming, perhaps even tautological: only the few can (grand strategize), so we shall study only the few who do. In contrast, asking the questions: "Who does strategize? How do they do it? And with what goals in mind?" releases us from that constraint. In the ensuing pages, we develop these criticisms. And in the case study chapters that follow, the contributors attempt to address them empirically, introducing a whole potential field of study. As with most generalizations, our contributors vary in the degree to which they share conventional assumptions or, conversely, the editors' counter-assumptions.

1.3 Defining and classifying grand strategy

The contemporary study of grand strategy is rife with debates about which definition to employ.[9] Scholars often talk past each other without agreement on a universal definition. Some see grand strategy as part of foreign policy.[10] Inverting this view, others believe it "encompass(es) foreign policy, military doctrine, and even tactics."[11] Still, others consider it largely a synonym of strategy.[12] For the purposes of the volume, we accept the conventional assumption that grand strategy links explicit values to "ways, means and ends."[13]

But a substantial spectrum exists within that broad parameter. Lukas Milevski has identified a lack of consensus in the meaning of grand strategy, which he attributes to its "popular and widespread use and misuse."[14] Aware of this limitation, we begin by identifying where authors disagree: Some authors focus exclusively on traditional military threats; others also incorporate economic and institutional dimensions; and policymakers and official strategy documents often extend the analysis to nontraditional threats such as climate change, pandemics, and economic security.[15] Among more recent, important works, Stephen Brooks and William Wohlforth in one book, and Barry Posen in another, illustrate the differing definitions of grand strategy. Posen, reflecting a classicist approach, for example, suggests that:

> A grand strategy is a nation-state's theory about how to produce security for itself. Grand strategy focuses on military threats, because these are the most dangerous, and military remedies because these are the most costly. Security has traditionally encompassed the preservation of sovereignty, safety, territorial integrity, and power position—the last being the necessary means to the first three.... A grand strategy contains explanations for why threats enjoy a certain priority, and why and how the remedies proposed could work. A grand strategy is not a rulebook; it is a set of concepts and arguments that need to be revised regularly.[16]

More economically, Brooks and Wohlforth suggest that "Grand strategy is a set of ideas for deploying a nation's resources to achieve its interests over the long run."[17] Nonetheless, their conception is effectively broader than Posen's because it evaluates economic opportunities as well as military threats.[18] It also addresses national interests more broadly conceived—military, diplomatic, legal, technological, and economic—than Posen's, which focuses most closely on security threats to "sovereignty, safety, territorial integrity, and power position." Hal Brands, while recognizing that grand strategy "defies any singular definition," offers yet another definition—"I define grand strategy as the intellectual architecture that gives form and structure to foreign policy."[19] As a result of these varied definitions, the field lacks an integrated conceptual apparatus. Milevski recognizes this abundance of definitions is a historical problem, and that the term is thus consistently used in promiscuous ways."[20]

This lack of convergence impedes communication among and between both scholars and policymakers. Work on grand strategy effectively coalesces around two contending formulations that run in parallel silos. These are the *Classicist* and the *International Relations* interpretations, which we now describe.

1.3.1 THE CLASSICIST APPROACH

Advocates of the Classicist tradition of grand strategy, in the words of Robert Art, "concentrate primarily on how the military instrument should be employed to achieve them [a nation's goals]."[21] Classicists employ a "periodized" nineteenth-century usage of the concept, preoccupied by military issues. Their understanding of grand strategy clearly specifies a logic—the preparation for and fighting of wars—and a substance—military capabilities and how they are employed in war. In practice, this approach therefore assimilates much of the rubric of the study of contemporary military strategy.

In the words of Barry Posen, efforts to explore the nonmilitary bases of grand strategy are problematic because they "dilute the most important purpose of grand strategy, which is to address the fact that the state exists in a world where war is possible." A grand strategy therefore "enumerates and prioritizes threats, and potential political and military remedies to threats." The purpose of the study of grand strategy is to subject "military power...to the discipline of political science."[22] In that spirit, the concept of grand strategy, according to Colin S. Gray (another adherent of this approach), should be reclaimed by strategic studies in order to deflect the menace of demilitarization that stems from security studies.[23] Proponents of this view therefore reject the securitization of various nontraditional, human security elements—from migration to climate change, job security, and democracy promotion.

1.3.2 THE INTERNATIONAL RELATIONS APPROACH

Others reject this narrow Classicist formulation. William Martel, for example, suggests that "Grand strategy is not and never has been simply about war or the conduct of war—in fact, war often represents a failure of grand strategy."[24] He favors broadening the concept—in the International Relations tradition of grand strategy.

Among notable recent contributions, Hal Brands argues that grand strategy mediates "between short-term actions and medium- and long-term goals."[25] According to this approach, strategy is submerged into grand strategy, inverting its nineteenth century Classicist usage.[26] Proponents of the International Relations approach thus recognize the role of military capabilities but assume that "grand strategy controls military strategy, which is one of its elements."[27] Others include diplomatic, economic, societal, and technological instruments.

The formulation of a grand strategy, the configuration of its instruments, and subsequent selection of policies and tactics, correspond to the nature of a state's interests and the threats they face. The pursuit of security is therefore explicitly subject to the effective marshaling of a variety of instruments that a grand strategy is meant to rank, balance, and coordinate. Brooks and Wohlforth vividly demonstrate this approach in developing a framework that interweaves security, economics, technological, and institutional elements.[28] Jeffrey W. Taliaferro, Norrin M. Ripsman, and Steven E. Lobell reflect a similar view when they suggest that "A grand strategy...is the organizing principle or conceptual blueprint that animates *all* [italics added] of the state's relations with the outside world, for the purpose of securing itself and maximizing its interests."[29]

Proponents of the International Relations tradition therefore generally believe that a state must employ various instruments, and permutations and combinations of policies, to realize its goals. Paul Kennedy cogently expresses this view when he states that

The crux of grand strategy...lies...in *policy*, that is, in the capacity of the nation's leaders to bring together all the elements, both military and non-military, for the preservation and enhancement of the nation's long-term (that is, in wartime and in peacetime) best interests.[30]

Material and social forms of power thus work in tandem. Peter Feaver concurs when suggesting that "grand strategy refers to the collection of plans and policies, that comprise the state's deliberate effort to harness political, military, diplomatic, and economic tools together to advance that state's national interest."[31]

This International Relations perspective has two implications for this volume. First, that different states, with different institutional arrangements, resources, and geopolitical circumstances, will use these tools for different purposes and in different proportions. Second, over time, they will adjust grand strategies according to the tools available, evolving interests, and the threats posed by and opportunities offered in their regional and global security environments. States, we reasonably conclude, will be influenced by domestic and international factors in different ways.[32]

1.4 The relevance of this debate in moving from a field to a research program

An important implication emerges from this debate when contemplating how and what to study when it comes to grand strategy. Scholars working in the field often study completely different activities.[33] To paraphrase Gray, "right enough" definitions when analyzing different aspects of the same phenomenon is one thing. But "right enough" definitions of different phenomenon—labeled grand strategy—is quite another.[34] Nina Silove, for example, has illustrated a pervasive tendency to employ the term "grand strategy" in incompatible ways. She identifies three uses of grand strategy which she labels "grand plans" (a deliberate, purposive blueprint for action), "grand principles" (conceptual coordinates), and "grand behaviors" (a consolidated pattern of behavior or a "practice").[35] Brands reinforces Silove's suggestion that these three categories become blurred in practice when he asserts that "grand strategy is as much a process as it is a single principle."[36] In illustrating this problem, the "deep engagement" grand strategy advocated by Brooks, G. John Ikenberry, and Wohlforth, and Posen's one of "restraint" have been extensively debated in the last half-dozen years.[37] Adopting Silove's categorical distinction, however, do either refer to a plan, a pattern of action, or a principle? The answer is unclear. As Kevin Narizny argues, "There is little analytical difference between a plan (e.g., NSC 68) and a pattern of behavior that reflects consistent values, goals, and trade-offs (e.g. Containment)."[38] Borders between them can therefore only be loosely drawn, reinforced by the fact that Silove acknowledges that the main criterion for drawing a distinction between grand plans and grand principles is the "level of detail" that separates them.[39]

From the perspective of conducting research into a state's grand strategy, however, Silove's formulation is significant for our purposes in highlighting the relationship between a state's articulated principles, its strategic planning, and its behavior in attempting to implement a grand strategy.[40] Scholars often overlook the issue of principles—and their source—in the formulation of grand strategy in favor of a focus on national security interests. This often leads them to presuppose why a grand strategy is implemented and to what ends. It is to this omission that we now turn.

1.5 From rationalist to interpretive formulations

Structural Realists would logically conclude that only a combination of the character of the global system and a state's material resources determine its grand strategy.[41] This leaves little room for agency. We reject that formulation. In contrast to either the Classicist or IR formulations, the contributors to this book treat grand strategy as an "empirical concept." The relevance of either approach is contingent, dependent on direct observations rather than employing either version a priori. States may therefore utilize one or the other for a variety of historical and contextual reasons. We adopt this pluralistic approach because we conceive of grand strategy as a polythetic concept. It combines elements which recur in political processes—through which a state articulates its ways, means, and ends. But the task and form, as the authors demonstrate, vary by country.

We accept, however, that a minimalist definition of grand strategy (ends, ways, and means) is likely to be regarded by many academics in the field as inadequate. Consistent with Giovanni Sartori's suggestion,[42] we propose to broaden the class of phenomena, the universe of cases, to which grand strategy applies by examining a series of countries hitherto largely ignored in the literature. But we control for that empirical extension by focusing on four attributes of a grand strategy. The first is the national pathologies that form the basis for a country's grand strategy, often characterized in unrelated literatures as "historical" or "collective" memory.[43] The second is the linkage between grand strategy and the prioritization of long-term objectives. While remaining agnostic on the content of these objectives, we retain a belief that they are intrinsically linked to ends, ways, and means, which they rank. The third is the adjustment by states of their limited resources to serve those ends. Grand strategies require a long-term perspective. But both policies and resources are often contextual and may be reconfigured in various ways. Finally, we focus on agency and process, not simply structure. Grand strategies require the identification of an intellectual framework, preferably an overarching concept, which anchors a nation's policies. That process is often indeterminate because it is reactive to, and thus interactive with, other states. It involves trade-offs and prioritization.[44]

The ends, ways, and means may therefore be indeterminate. But the framework is not, consistent with Gary Goertz's admonition that:

a concept involves a theoretical and empirical analysis of the object or phenomenon referred to by the word.... [A]ll those who focus on purely semantic issues are liable to end up seeing definitions as arbitrary. If the concept is not intimately related to the *empirical analysis* [emphasis added] of a phenomenon then there is nothing to which one can anchor the concept, and everything becomes a matter of who is in charge of the definition.[45]

The authors in this volume thus examine how countries strategically respond to a specific set of external challenges, given the combination of their domestic values, processes for decision-making, and resources. They comparatively examine the ways in which countries—some positioned differently, others similarly in the global system—conceive of and execute grand strategy.

Two strong arguments favor this approach. First, not all countries make sense of their external relations in grand strategic terms, nor do they all approach their external policies exclusively through the lens of material forms of power. Accordingly, analyzing their behavior using only a category which focuses on those forms could be misleading or even counterproductive for both scholars and policymakers. Second, there are practices which are, in most relevant aspects, similar to grand strategizing, but in which the military component is either trivial or absent. In such cases it would be misleading to categorize it as something else.

Avery Goldstein offers a radical response to these dilemmas. He suggests that grand strategy may simply not be the kind of phenomenon that is cut out "for a distinct theoretical literature."[46] Clearly, we reject that opinion in favor of a reformulation of the core concept. One possibly fruitful option embedded in Brands's remark is that the exercise of defining the substance and contours of the concept of grand strategy is "subjective."[47] Conceiving of grand strategy as interpretative, thus abandoning a rationalist approach, may be advantageous when comparing ten countries and the European Union. While a rationalist ontology lends itself to parsimony, consistency, and (possibly) an elegant research design, it may obscure key components of collective memory and domestic politics (such as institutional design and the internal distribution of power) that are essential building blocks in the formulation and implementation of a grand strategy. In contrast to a variant of rationalism

(Liberal or Realist), it may be useful to utilize an interpretative approach more consistent with a Constructivist formulation that relies on perception and a subjective definition of interest as the basis for understanding how policymakers understand the external environment, and the threats and opportunities it presents.

There is no rationalist formulation, for example, that can be reconciled with what Israelis themselves characterize as "the Massada Complex"—a foundational component of their collective memory that recalls the refusal of the Zealots to surrender to the Romans, and ended with the mass suicide of 960 people. The modern interpretation of those events, fundamental to the identity of Israelis and embedded in their collective memory, is the importance of uncompromising survival in a hostile world—and the belief that any future mass self-sacrifice must be accompanied by mutual sacrifice. So, while saving Israeli lives is sacrosanct, the counterpart to the annihilation of Israel will be a huge cost borne by others. Yet there is a specific Israeli twist to this conventional strategy: As an anonymous Israeli source suggested to their surprised European counterparts, it is a great thing that Iran has built a long-range missile—because it has now become their problem as well. The Massada Complex, in effect, is therefore part of the foundation for a doctrine of mutually assured destruction that, perhaps uniquely, extends beyond adversaries to allies—one embedded in Israel's collective memory.[48]

The contributors to this volume therefore embrace an inductive rather than deductive approach, in practice, by asking two questions: how is grand strategy defined in these countries? And what are the subjective factors that influence which elements legitimately define the objectives and contours of the "ways, means, and ends" of any given grand strategy? Together, the answers may define a comparative grand strategy research program in the twenty-first century.

1.6 Why compare?

Comparison is at a premium in the study of grand strategy. Williamson Murray, for example, with characteristic directness, asserts that "Grand Strategy is a matter involving great states and great states alone" and "no small states...possess the possibility of crafting a grand strategy."[49] Yet, this assertion is questionable.

If, as discussed earlier, both Classicist and IR versions of grand strategy are concerned with how a state defines and provides for its national security, why should not a state, of any size, formulate and implement a grand strategy? Beyond a group of extreme, failed states, the answer is theoretically unclear and repeatedly challenged empirically. We therefore reject a formulation that suggests that a country's ability to formulate and implement a grand strategy is determined by its position in the global system. Clearly, other countries do make choices about strategic engagement. And their choices are conditioned as much by a combination of external pressures, domestic debates, and effective leadership as are great powers. Indeed, arguably, smaller countries, with fewer resources, facing existential threats, who therefore have less latitude for failure, are more likely to develop such blueprints. They may need to be tactically more adept and efficient if they are to achieve their economic, diplomatic, and security goals. Their strategies might be more reactive than proactive. Their geographic scope may be smaller. But studying these kind of countries might help explain how each cope with the challenges posed by the global economy and regional security structure.[50] Regardless, the reliance on the single case, one that is not in the sense denoted by Harry Eckstein as "critical" for theory-building, is problematic: It is idiographic, and thus limits the capacity for generalizability or comparison.[51]

Yet most work does exactly that, by focusing almost exclusively on the United States. This hinders the development of a research program by essentially rejecting the idea of a cross-national, comparative study of grand strategy. Such a choice is mystifying if the goal is theory-building or developing diagnostics for policymakers. Grand strategy research seems tailor-made for comparative case study analysis, especially process-tracing which entails "the systematic examination of diagnostic evidence selected and analyzed in light of research questions and hypotheses posed by the investigator."[52] Yet relatively few scholars of grand strategy have done so.[53]

A minority do compare. Their work takes one of two forms. The first approach is historical, comparatively examining the grand strategies of several American presidents.[54] Hal Brands, for example, compares the strategies of the Truman, Reagan, and George W. Bush administrations.[55] The second are in fact cross-national studies. A recent example is William I. Hitchcock, Melvin P. Leffler, and Jeffrey W. Legro's *Shaper Nations*.[56] It is a notable contribution, but addresses a limited range of countries and employs no specific comparative framework that allows for generalization, theory-building, or expanded cross-national comparisons.

Our aspirational goal is to replace a loosely defined field of grand strategy, focused overwhelmingly on the United States, with a research program on comparative grand strategy, with all its inevitable pluralistic disagreements about theories, methods, and case selection. We are not wedded to one theory or approach. But in this volume we explicitly compare for three reasons: (1) to discover causal relationships between the domestic drivers and the implementation of grand strategies overlooked in the American-dominated literature; (2) to identify areas of convergence and divergence across cases; and (3) to highlight key empirical aspects of national strategies.

We divide the countries examined in this volume into two major groups for analytic purposes. The first is composed of the traditional great powers, the

United Nations' big five: China, France, Russia, the United Kingdom, and the United States. Their objectives, historically, have been preponderantly motivated by proactive efforts to mold the global system. Their institutional and material resources differ but they are traditionally regarded (currently or historically—in the case of France and the UK) as having sufficient quantities of both to formulate and implement a grand strategy.

The second group is composed of Brazil, India, Iran, Israel, and Saudi Arabia, important regional powers that we collectively label "pivotal states." They share a key characteristic in that their actions all influence the economic or security stability of the global system. Yet we recognize that this group does vary significantly in terms of their resources, forms of power, and global or regional influence. We therefore subdivide them into two groups, adding further nuance to our analysis.

Brazil and India are influential regional powers, but they combine that importance with global aspirations. They share key elements. Policymakers in both countries, as the authors demonstrate, are focused more on economic development than military conquest. Domestic poverty alleviation is a priority in each. Yet their contrasts are just as notable. First, policymakers in each have to respond to very different external environments. Interstate war is an anomaly in Latin America. Indian policymakers, however, have to address the threat of Chinese border and maritime incursions as well as the existential threat of war (conventional and nuclear) with Pakistan. Second, their degree and forms of domestic security concerns differ. The threat of terrorism is nominal in Brazil, but violent criminality is a grave national concern. Contrastingly, Indian policymakers have to routinely plan counterstrategies against terrorists, whether domestic or imported from Pakistan or Afghanistan, and insurgents from Kashmir. Examining their distinctive grand strategies as a paired comparison therefore potentially offers valuable insights: two countries with very different security challenges who nonetheless converge in terms of their strategic goals.

The group composed of Israel, Iran, and Saudi Arabia operate in another context that potentially enriches the texture of our comparison. Unlike Brazil and India, they operate in a similar external environment. Policymakers in these three countries, far more than any other examined in this volume, face realistic existential threats. They share two further features that justify their inclusion in this volume. First, unlike many other states in the global system, each has a magnified capacity for destabilizing that system relative to their size, either through warfare or (in the case of Saudi Arabia) their influence as a supplier of fossil fuels to the global system.[57] Second, they share a mutual hostility to each other as the primary source of threats, although the major focus of that hostility has dynamically shifted historically—with Saudi Arabia having moved its primary concern from Israel to Iran, and the Israeli focus having also shifted to Iran. Iran was Israel's close ally. Now it is Israel's sworn enemy. Yet, comparable to both the other great and regional powers that our authors examine, each country configures elements of material and social resources in vastly different ways. The Saudi reliance on fossil fuels and its export of a very specific variant of Sunni Islam, for example, is distinct from Israel's emphasis on technological innovation or Iran's reliance on asymmetric military force and nonstate proxies to implement its strategy.

Our study of this group of pivotal powers therefore incorporates two elements of a research design. Brazil and India represent a most different pairing where the grand strategies are comparable. Iran, Israel, and Saudi Arabia represent a most similar design (at least in terms of the external environment and a reciprocated focus) where the strategies differ markedly.

Finally, in a novel attempt to expand beyond the traditional strictures of state-based analysis, we examine the European Union. We justify this choice by the fact that its diplomatic, economic, and (potential) military resources are far greater than the overwhelming majority of states in the global system. And, importantly, its policymakers have periodically proclaimed that one of the organization's primary objectives is to formulate and implement a global strategy, albeit that such debates are in their relative infancy.[58] Evaluating this group collectively provides a common set of benchmarks about the processes of strategy formation, adjudication, and implementation against which to comparatively examine other actors less associated with grand strategizing.

Examining ten states and the EU presents both intellectual and organizational challenges. Their national pathologies, and economic and military security concerns, clearly differ. So do their resulting objectives, grand strategies, and the ways in which they combine material forms of power (employing military capabilities and economic resources) with social ones (diplomatic and societal tools like education policies) in attempting to implement those grand strategies. Moreover, politicians, policymakers, and military leaders in the various countries are more or, in many cases, less self-conscious about designing and implementing grand strategies in the ways understood by the academic community focusing on the US case or the other great powers. Our hope is that the systematic examination of how they deliberate and ultimately configure these forms of power will be a major contribution of this volume.

1.7 Framework for the volume (and beyond)

Comparing these countries requires a coherent framework that recognizes the universal contours within which each operates, one that generates a relevant set of questions applicable to each country. In developing one, our objective embraces the spirit of David Milne's comment in a book on diplomacy, where he suggests that successful diplomacy requires policymakers to "study dilemmas, contextualize threats, compare their magnitude to the resources available, weigh humanitarian and reputational imperatives, and offer appropriately calibrated responses."[59]

Developing a dynamic research program on grand strategy first requires that we examine how "ends, ways, and means" concretely operate within a "contrast of contexts."[60] Our proceeding in this manner is inspired by Theda Skockpol and Margaret Sommers, who argue that the goals of comparative analysis (causal analysis, parallel demonstrations of theory, and a contrast in contexts) often occur at different stages of research.[61] This book can be usefully read as an initial heuristic attempt to generate a research program because it is one of the first systematic attempts to compare grand strategies across such a wide assortment of countries. Ideally, scholars will identify value in our collective findings and subsequently test more complex hypotheses about causal relationships.

In employing a comparative approach in this volume, we note the importance of not falling prey to a trap that James Rosenau warned of five decades ago with regard to the then nascent subfield of comparative foreign policy. Scholars, he said, should not "settle for juxtaposition without comparison."[62] Rather we, and the chapter authors, acknowledge Rosenau's admonition and ask "What aspects of foreign policy [grand strategy] should be compared, [and] how should they be compared?"[63]

Valerie Hudson and Christopher S. Vore noted that Rosenau's objective in his early work on comparative foreign policy was to pre-theorize, which "encouraged scholars to tease out cross-nationally applicable generalizations about the foreign policy behavior of states in a systematic and scientific fashion."[64] Critics charged that such efforts offered an "unparsimonious laundry list of variables, not a single theory."[65] Indeed, as Juliet Kaarbo concluded, Rosenau's approach to comparative foreign policy fizzled out, in part because his approach, "eschewed deductive theorizing for 'pretheory' and a positivist, inductive, quantitative search for general patterns, causal laws, and a grand theory of foreign policy."[66] The contrast with the largely deductive and systemic approaches of IR's major paradigms was unattractive for many scholars. Foreign Policy Analysis, especially the variants focusing on comparative studies, either degenerated into limited case studies or failed to engage with IR variants that had little interest in opening up the "black box" of the state.[67]

Aware of this admonition, the contributors to this volume examine both the international and domestic dimensions of formulating and implementing their chosen nation's grand strategy—linking elements of IR theory to area studies. In the spirit of Rosenau, "we can no longer allow the domestic-foreign boundary to confound our understanding of world affairs."[68] We therefore asked contributors to view the external environment through the lens of three factors. The first is the kind of actors with whom domestic strategists contend—from nation-states to various nonstate actors ranging from terrorist groups and insurgents to nongovernmental organizations (NGOs), foundations, and even corporations. The second is the preponderant threats they face and opportunities they might seize, again ranging from the traditional military to economic, diplomatic, and nontraditional social dimensions. Finally, we asked them to consider what kinds of conflict states strategize against—conventional and nuclear, asymmetric or hybrid forms.[69]

Yet the contributors' work does eschew a focus on the "objective" external factors. They favor, instead, an approach in which each examines five sets of issues: the source and forms of national values that collectively define the contours of a grand strategy; how these values influence the ways in which policymakers identify, interpret, and define these actors, threats and opportunities, and potential forms of conflict—which Colin Gray characterized as the "national style";[70] how policymakers debate in a national context, both in terms of regional and international threats and opportunities; the institutional process by which strategy is formulated; and the combination of resources (material and social) that they can and do utilize as instruments in implementing a grand strategy.

The product is an interpretive view about how and why states strategize in an effort to provide security, for and against what they strategize, and the consequences of those choices. We recognize that each component may evolve over time, and thus domestic policymakers may choose to pursue different grand strategies. But these changes occur at the domestic level, distinct from—but related to—developments in the international environment. These questions, addressed collectively, firmly focus on describing and explaining grand strategies, rather than the optimistic venture of prescribing them common to much scholarship.[71]

1.8 Chapter summaries

In Chapter 2, Peter Dombrowski and Simon Reich begin with an analysis of the American case, located there as the traditional benchmark in the study of grand strategy. The novelty of the chapter may lie in their effort to systematically link antecedent cultural myths to contemporary strategizing, and describe how grand strategy is made and implemented. Céline Marangé, in her chapter on Russia, highlights the importance of recent events—the West's treatment of Russia at the end of the Cold War—in explaining the rudiments of Putin's regional and global policy. She characterizes it as defensive in orientation yet, paradoxically, aggressive in practice. Andrew Erickson's chapter on China, in contrast, seeks to link the disparate elements of state policy, recalling—and attempting to recapture—the significance of the country's imperial past to Xi Jinping's contemporary vision of China's grand strategy.

Both Thierry Balzacq's chapter on France and Robert Johnson's chapter on the UK examine the question of how former empires strategize as they cope with the shift from a central to a marginal position among the great powers. Notably, Balzacq argues that the shift in the French case in the last two decades has been from a unilateral one (which he labels "grandeur") to a more integrationist one (of "Liberal Engagement.") Johnson's chapter on the UK contrasts in highlighting the opposite shift, as the UK seeks to disengage from Europe and re-establish itself once again as an autonomous actor.

As mentioned, Brazil and India live in very different neighborhoods. But, as Carlos R. S. Milani and Tiago Nery point out in their chapter on Brazil, and Christine Fair does with regard to India, in both cases their elites do not consciously pursue a grand strategy, even if the product looks something like one in practice. What is perhaps more intriguing is that this lack of recognition—or admission—of the pursuit of a grand strategy by policy-makers in both countries may have more to do with historical factors (such as the innate distrust of the military) and a belief that a strategy focusing on economic development is distinct from one focusing on military dimensions (as in the Classicist view discussed earlier).

The three case chapters by Eitan Shamir on Israel, Ghaidaa Hetou on Saudi Arabia, and Thierry Balzacq and Wendy Ramadan-Alban on Iran demonstrate how continuing old pathologies afflict the new configurations of the Middle East. In Israel's case, Shamir points out, this stretches back into antiquity. In Saudi Arabia's case, it stems from imperial British rule and the need to balance conflicting demands within its narrow elite. And in Iran's case it entails combining the desire to recapture a glorious Persian past with a fear of effective American re-annexation invoked by the CIA-inspired coup against the Mossadegh government in 1953. The distinctiveness of the timeframes each explores is matched by the ways in which they describe each states' use of the instruments of grand strategy, ranging across vastly different combinations of diplomatic, economic, military, and social forms of power. Yet all these authors clearly characterize elites as acutely concerned about national survival and a country wrought with internal tensions—in contrast to the confident arrogance with which each is often depicted by allies and adversaries alike.

The final case study chapter by Daniel Fiott and Luis Simón on the European Union examines the question of whether a state is the only mechanism for formulating, consolidating, and implementing a grand strategy. The assortment of EU institutions, in collaboration with the member states, does present a unique array of problems in fulfilling this task. Nonetheless, the authors suggest that the EU's achievements pose a significant challenge for traditional IR approaches that rely on the state as an essential actor.

In the conclusion, Norrin Ripsman takes up these themes, evaluates the authors' individual and collective capacity to form the rubric of a comparative program on grand strategy, and considers the abiding questions such a program will face.

NOTES

1. For example Stephen Krasner, "An Orienting Principle for Foreign Policy: The Deficiencies of 'Grand Strategy'," *Policy Review*, no. 163 (October/November 2010), http://www.hoover.org/research/orienting-principle-foreign-policy
2. Stephen Brooks and William Wohlforth, *America Abroad: The United States' Global Role in the 21st Century* (London: Oxford University Press, 2016).
3. Cullen S. Hendrix, "Measuring state capacity: Theoretical and Empirical Implications for the Study of Civil Conflict," *Journal of Peace Research* 47, no. 3 (May 2010): 273.
4. Richard N. Rosecrance and Arthur A. Stein, "The Study of Grand Strategy," in *The Domestic Bases of Grand Strategy*, eds. Richard N. Rosecrance and Arthur A. Stein (Ithaca, NY: Cornell University Press, 1993), 11.
5. As examples see Hal Brands, *What Good Is Grand Strategy? Power and Purpose in American Statecraft from Harry S. Truman to George W. Bush* (Ithaca, NY: Cornell University Press, 2015); Kevin Narizny, *The Political Economy of Grand Strategy* (Ithaca, NY: Cornell University Press, 2007). For a notable exception to this generalization about IR scholarship see the work of Jeffrey W. Legro, for example, his "What China Will Want: The Future Intentions of a Rising Power," *Perspectives on Politics* 5, no. 3 (September 2007): 515–34, http://www.jstor.org/stable/20446501
6. Kenneth Waltz, *Theory of International Politics* (New York: Addison-Wellesley, 1979).
7. For studies that emphasize very contrasting perspectives on the fluid nature of the global system see, Amitav Acharya, *The End of the American World Order* (Cambridge: Polity, 2014); Charles Kupchan, *No One's World: The West, The Rising Rest, and the Coming Global Turn* (Oxford: Oxford University Press, 2012).
8. Krasner, "An Orienting Principle for Foreign Policy."
9. Most studies implicitly or explicitly subscribe to a specific definition of a grand strategy. For a mere sample of discussions of the term over the last four decades, see John M. Collins, *Grand Strategy: Principles and Practices* (Annapolis, MD: Naval Institute Press, 1973); Barry Posen, *The Sources of Military Doctrines: France, Britain, and Germany between the World Wars* (Ithaca, NY: Cornell University Press, 1984); Paul Kennedy, "Grand Strategy in War and Peace: Toward a Broader Definition," in *Grand Strategy in War and Peace*, ed. Paul Kennedy (New Haven, CT: Yale University Press, 1991), 1–7; Williamson Murray and Mark Grimsey, "Introduction: On Strategy," in *The Making of Strategy: Rulers, States, and War*, eds. Alvin H. Bernstein, MacGregor Knox, and Williamson Murray (New York: Cambridge University Press, 1994), 1–2; Robert Art, *A Grand Strategy for America* (Ithaca, NY: Cornell University Press, 2003); Avery Goldstein, *Rising to the Challenge: China's Grand Strategy and International Security* (Stanford, CA: Stanford University Press, 2005); Christopher Layne, *The Peace of Illusions: American Grand Strategy from 1940 to the Present* (Ithaca, NY: Cornell University Press, 2006); Colin Dueck, *Reluctant Crusaders: Power, Culture, and Change in American Grand Strategy* (Princeton, NJ: Princeton University Press, 2006); John Lewis Gaddis, "What Is Grand Strategy?" (keynote address, *American Grand Strategy After War*, sponsored by the Triangle Institute for Security Studies and the Duke University Program on American Grand Strategy, February 26, 2009); Edward Luttwak, *The Grand Strategy of the Byzantine Empire* (Cambridge:

Cambridge University Press, 2009); Colin Gray, *The Strategy Bridge: Theory for Practice* (Oxford: Oxford University Press, 2010); Krasner, "An Orienting Principle for Foreign Policy"; William C. Martel, *Grand Strategy in Theory and Practice: The Need for an Effective American Foreign Policy* (New York: Cambridge University Press, 2015).
10. Dueck, *Reluctant Crusaders*, 11.
11. Posen, *The Sources of Military Doctrines*, 220.
12. Gregory Foster, "Missing and Wanted: A U.S. Grand Strategy," *Strategic Review* 13, no. 4 (Fall 1985): 22.
13. Not all scholars are enamored with this classic formulation. Jeffrey W. Meiser, "Ends + Ways + Means = (Bad) Strategy," *Parameters* 46, no. 4 (Winter 2016–17): 81–91.
14. Lukas Milevski, *The Evolution of Modern Grand Strategic Thought* (London: Oxford University Press, 2016), 127.
15. For example, *National Security Strategy of the United States 2015* (Washington, DC: The White House, February 2015), https://obamawhitehouse.archives.gov/sites/default/files/docs/2015_national_security_strategy_2.pdf
16. Barry R. Posen, *Restraint: A New Foundation for U.S. Grand Strategy* (Ithaca, NY: Cornell University Press 2014), 1.
17. Brooks and Wohlforth, *America Abroad*, 75.
18. Posen, *Restraint*, 3.
19. Brands, *What Good Is Grand Strategy?*, 3.
20. Milevski, *The Evolution of Modern Grand Strategic Thought*, for example, 1, 25, 104, 127.
21. Art, *A Grand Strategy for America*, 2.
22. See Posen, *Restraint*, 2.
23. For a recent presentation of this debate, see Philippe Bourbeau, Thierry Balzacq, and Myriam Dunn Cavelty, "International Relations: Celebrating Eclectic Dynamism in Security Studies," in *Security: Dialogue Across Discipline*, ed. Philippe Bourbeau (Cambridge: Cambridge University Press, 2015), 111–36. Earlier contributions attempting to delineate the parameters of security studies and strategic studies include, most prominently, Stephen M. Walt, "The Renaissance of Security Studies," *International Studies Quarterly* 31, no. 2 (1991): 211–39; David A. Baldwin, "The Concept of Security," *Review of International Studies* 23, no. 1 (January 1997): 5–26; Richard K. Betts, "Should Strategic Studies Survive?," *World Politics* 50, no. 1 (October 1997): 7–33.
24. Martel, *Grand Strategy in Theory and Practice*, 4.
25. Brands, *What Good Is Grand Strategy?*, 4.
26. See Charles James, *A New and Enlarged Military Dictionary, or, Alphabetical Explanation of Technical Terms* (London: The Military Library, 1805).
27. Collins, *Grand Strategy*, 15.
28. Brooks and Wohlforth, *America Abroad*, 75.
29. Jeffrey W. Taliaferro, Norrin M. Ripsman, and Steven E. Lobell, "Introduction: Grand Strategy between the World Wars," in *The Challenge of Grand Strategy: The Great Powers and the Broken Balance between the Wars*, eds. Jeffrey W. Taliaferro, Norrin M. Ripsman, and Steven E. Lobell (Cambridge: Cambridge University Press, 2012), 15.

30. Kennedy, "Grand Strategy in War and Peace," 5.
31. Peter D. Feaver, "What Is Grand Strategy and Why Do We Need It?," *Foreign Policy*, April 8, 2009, http://foreignpolicy.com/2009/04/08/what-is-grand-strategy-and-why-do-we-need-it/
32. This resonates with work that emphasizes the emergent and/or pragmatic approach to grand strategy. But instead of pitching one against the other, we propose that any grand strategy involves an element of adaptive flexibility given that states operate with different degrees and forms of uncertainty: one relating to intentions, a second to capabilities, and another regarding the nature of both their domestic and the international environment. The scope and domain of such a pragmatic adaptation depends, inevitably, on the magnitude of new developments. On an emergent approach to grand strategy, see Ionut C. Popescu, "Emergent Strategy vs. Grand Strategy in the Conduct of Foreign Policy," *Journal of Strategic Studies* 41, no. 3 (March 2018): 438–60. Popescu draws heavily on Henry Mintzberg and James A. Waters's article "Of Strategies, Emergent and Deliberate," *Strategic Management Journal* 6, no. 3 (July–Sepember 1985): 257–72.
33. See Hew Strachan, *The Direction of War: Contemporary Strategy in Historical Perspective* (Cambridge: Cambridge University Press, 2013).
34. Gray, *The Strategy Bridge*, 17.
35. Nina Silove, "Beyond the Buzzword: The Three Meanings of 'Grand Strategy'," *Security Studies* 27, no. 1 (January 2018): 27–57, http://doi.org/10.1080/09636412.2017.1360073
36. Gaddis, "What Is Grand Strategy?," quoted in Brands, *What Good Is Grand Strategy?*, 4.
37. Stephen G. Brooks, H. John Ikenberry, and William C. Wohlforth, "Don't Come Home America: The Case against Retrenchment," *International Security* 37, no. 3 (Winter 2012/13): 7–51; Posen, *Restraint*.
38. Narizny, *The Political Economy of Grand Strategy*, 10.
39. Narizny, *The Political Economy of Grand Strategy*, 13.
40. The ability of states to carry out plans and/or pursue principles is largely a function of policy implementation, a process that has been relatively understudied. For an exception see Steve Smith and Michael Clarke, eds., *Foreign Policy Implementation* (London: Unwin & Allen, 1985).
41. Realists, of course, vary on this issue. Christopher Layne argues that domestic factors matter. For example, Layne, *The Peace of Illusions*, 8, 28–9. John Mearsheimer points to the importance of geography in John Mearsheimer, *The Tragedy of Great Power Politics* (New York: W.W. Norton & Company Inc., 2001), 138. But many Realists do rely on traditional notions of material power coupled with structural constraints. For example, Ronald L. Tammen et al., *Power Transitions: Strategies for the 21st Century* (New York: Chatham House Publishers, 2000), 16–18; Ronald L. Tammen and Jacek Kugler, "Power Transition and China-US Conflicts," *Chinese Journal of International Politics* 1, no. 1 (July 2006): 35–55.
42. See Giovanni Sartori, "Concept Misformation in Comparative Politics," *The American Political Science Review* 64, no. 4 (December 1970): 1033–53.
43. For example, Andrei S. Markovits and Simon Reich, *The German Predicament: Memory and Power in the New Europe* (Ithaca, NY: Cornell University Press,

1997); for an elaboration of this point see Katherine Hite, "Historical Memory," in *International Encyclopedia of Political Science*, eds. Bertrand Badie, Dirk Berg-Schlosser, and Leonardo Morlino (Thousand Oaks, CA: SAGE, 2011), http://dx.doi.org/10.4135/9781412959636.n251.
44. These issues are addressed at far greater length in Thierry Balzacq, Peter Dombrowski, and Simon Reich, "Is Grand Strategy a Research Program? A Review Essay," *Security Studies* (published online October 2018 at https://www.tandfonline.com/doi/full/10.1080/09636412.2018.1508631).
45. Gary Goertz, *Social Science Concepts: A User's Guide* (Princeton, NJ: Princeton University Press, 2005), 4.
46. Goldstein, *Rising to the Challenge*, 18.
47. Brands, *What Good Is Grand Strategy?*, 1, 3.
48. See Eitan Shamir's chapter on Israel (Chapter 10 of this volume).
49. Williamson Murray, "Thoughts on Grand Strategy," in *The Shaping of Grand Strategy: Policy, Diplomacy, and War*, eds. Williamson Murray, Richard Hart Sinnreich, and James Lacey (New York: Cambridge University Press, 2011), 1–2.
50. According to Milne, a number of American strategic thinkers, especially those trained in the social sciences (notably Wilson, Nitze, and Wolfowitz), view the international system as "makable [sic] following the identification and application of appropriate patterns and theories." David Milne, *Worldmaking: The Art and Science of American Diplomacy* (New York: Farrar, Straus and Giroux, 2015), 16.
51. Harry Eckstein, "Case Study and Theory in Political Science," in *Case Study Method*, reprint, eds. Roger Gromm, Martyn Hammersley, and Peter Foster (London: SAGE Publications, 2009), 118–64.
52. David Collier, "Understanding Process Tracing," *PS: Political Science and Politics* 44, no. 4 (October 2011): 823.
53. Christopher Layne serves as an exception. Layne, *The Peace of Illusions*, 11–12.
54. On comparing different administrations, a notable example is Martel, *Grand Strategy in Theory and Practice*.
55. Brands, *What Good Is Grand Strategy?*
56. William I. Hitchcock, Melvin P. Leffler, Jeffrey W. Legro, eds., *Shaper Nations: Strategies for a Changing World* (Cambridge, MA: Harvard University Press, 2016).
57. We could have examined North Korea, for example, according to that criteria, but for the dearth of data about its domestic politics and grand strategizing.
58. As examples see European Security Strategy, "A Secure Europe in a Better World," December 12, 2003, https://europa.eu/globalstrategy/en/european-security-strategy-secure-europe-better-world; European Union Global Strategy, "Shared Vision, Common Action: A Stronger Europe," June 2016, https://europa.eu/globalstrategy/sites/globalstrategy/files/eugs_review_web.pdf
59. Milne, *Worldmaking*, 526.
60. David Collier, "The Comparative Method," in *Political Science: The State of the Discipline II*, ed. Ada W. Finifter (Washington, DC: American Political Science Association, 1993), 108.
61. Theda Skockpol and Margaret Sommers, "The Uses of Comparative History in Macrosocial Inquiry," *Comparative Studies in Society and History* 22, no. 2 (April 1980): 174–97.

62. James N. Rosenau, "Comparative Foreign Policy: Fad, Fantasy, or Field," *International Studies Quarterly* 12, no. 3 (September 1968): 307.
63. Rosenau, "Comparative Foreign Policy."
64. Valerie M. Hudson and Christopher S. Vore, "Foreign Policy Analysis Yesterday, Today, and Tomorrow," *Mershon International Studies Review* 39, no. 2 (October 1995): 212.
65. Juliet Kaarbo, "A Foreign Policy Analysis Perspective on the Domestic Politics Turn in IR Theory," *International Studies Review* 17, no. 2 (June 2015): 189–216.
66. Kaarbo, "A Foreign Policy Analysis."
67. Although Caporaso sympathetically examines several efforts, including the literatures on two-level games, the second image reversed, and efforts to understand the emergence and significance of the European Union. See, James A. Caporaso, "Across the Great Divide: Integrating Comparative and International Politics," *International Studies Quarterly* 41, no. 4 (December 1997): 563–59.
68. James N. Rosenau, *Along the Domestic-Foreign Frontier: Exploring Governance in a Turbulent World* (Cambridge: Cambridge University Press, 1997), 4.
69. For an extended discussion of these issues see Simon Reich and Peter Dombrowski, *The End of Grand Strategy: US Maritime Operations in the Twenty-First Century* (Ithaca, NY: Cornell University Press, 2018), 18–27.
70. Colin S. Gray, "National Style in Strategy: The American Example," *International Security* 6, no 2 (Fall 1981): 21–47. In this spirit see also Jack L. Snyder, *The Soviet Strategic Culture: Implications for Limited Nuclear Operations* (Santa Monica, CA: RAND Corporation, September 1977), https://www.rand.org/content/dam/rand/pubs/reports/2005/R2154.pdf
71. Reich and Dombrowski, *The End of Grand Strategy*, 9–12.

Part I
Major Powers

2 The United States of America

PETER DOMBROWSKI AND SIMON REICH

In the context of a volume dedicated to comparative grand strategy, one that favors expanding the universe of cases, the United States provides a benchmark. It has been the preeminent global military, diplomatic, and economic power for seven decades. Currently, if increasingly questionably, it remains the dominant power, even if the unipolar moment has past.[1] Furthermore, as a hegemonic power for much of that period, America is predominantly responsible for the values, regimes, and institutions that structure the contemporary international system. It was American "worldmaking," in conjunction with its allies, that created the Bretton Woods system, buttressed the United Nations, and, eventually, formed its most critical formal military alliance—the North Atlantic Treaty Organization (NATO).[2] Unsurprisingly then, the US case and, indeed, American-based scholarship, dominates the contemporary literature on grand strategy.[3] However, as we argue elsewhere, most of this work is normative and prescriptive rather causative and descriptive.[4] It therefore provides an insufficient basis for comparing and contrasting the US approach to grand strategy with other countries.

In contrast, this chapter describes both historical and current US grand strategy, explains why the nation has adopted and adapted its grand strategies, and, outlines the basic processes that produce American grand strategies. We therefore first briefly revisit the underpinnings of its grand strategy—the traditions, culture, history and, ultimately, the myths that collectively form the foundational "Creed" that encapsulates how the United States views itself and the world—in essence, its historical or collective memory. Second, we connect national security strategy to the broader concept of grand strategy. Third, we examine the legal basis, institutions, and instruments of statecraft employed by the United States. Fourth, we describe the "outputs"—the formal documents—of the foreign and security policymaking process, and the extent to which they are implemented. Finally, we consider the question of continuity and change in the context of the first year of the Trump administration, given the widespread belief that its grand strategy substantially differs from its predecessors and may alter the long-term trajectory of America's role in the world.

2.1 Historical memory and the "American Creed"

The United States has a surprising number of foundational myths for a relatively young nation.[5] These influence how its contemporary policymakers understand grand strategy. Here we admittedly only briefly synthesize, and stylize, an overview of the three most influential components in its formulation—messianism, exceptionalism, and frontierism.[6] Their historical accuracy are understandably contestable. Nonetheless, we recognize that American strategists persistently return to them when rationalizing their choices—and employ narratives that legitimate them.[7] These themes recur in political and policy rhetoric as well as in official strategy documents.

2.1.1 THE SHINING CITY ON THE HILL

John Winthrop made a speech on his ship the *Arabella* in 1630 when establishing the Puritan Massachusetts Bay colony. He borrowed the phrase "A City upon a Hill" from Jesus' Sermon on the Mount: "You are the light of the world. A city that is set on a hill cannot be hidden."[8] Winthrop could not have anticipated its lasting significance. President Ronald Reagan was the first modern politician to invoke it. He added the adjective "shining" to Jesus's and Winthrop's words—and thus introduced a new mythological leg of the tripod upon which America's view of itself today stands.[9]

This metaphor's relevance is that many Americans, regardless of the criticism, believe that the United States is indeed an exemplar to others.[10] It also contributes to the national self-confidence necessary to justify the political, diplomatic, and financial commitment to twice propose remaking the international system. First, Woodrow Wilson advocated Fourteen Points (and thus helped create the League of Nations). Then Franklin Roosevelt proposed (during a global war) establishing both a new international political order at the San Francisco Conference and a global economic order at the Bretton Woods and Havana Conferences. Neither would be imaginable without the underlying belief that the United States had the right—and ideas—to build a new international order.[11] Finally, even as new challengers to American hegemony arose and the post–world war settlement has frayed, American leaders (including President Trump) continue to evoke America's role as a model, although the substance of that model changes over time.[12]

2.1.2 AMERICAN EXCEPTIONALISM

Related to this trope is the long-standing belief, common to both citizens and elites, that America and Americans are somehow exceptional.[13] From the outset, American political leaders rhetorically contrasted themselves with

Europe's great powers. Presidents, from Washington to Wilson, argued "that Americans deprecate power politics and old-fashioned diplomacy, mistrust powerful standing armies and entangling peacetime commitments, make moralistic judgments about other people's domestic systems, and believe that liberal values transfer readily to foreign affairs."[14] This view was epitomized by Rudyard Kipling's famous poem, "The White Man's Burden," first published in 1899. Proponents of exceptionalism widely misinterpreted it as a paean to American intervention in the Philippines. America was, rather, an exceptional power that brought enlightenment values through the "burden of empire" rather than imperialism and enslavement. Theodore Roosevelt, for example, commented that it was "rather poor poetry, but good sense from the expansionist point of view."[15]

Others have criticized this notion. Harold Koh, for example, wrote that "when the United States actually uses its exceptional power and wealth to promote a double standard … it proposes that different rules apply to itself than applies to the rest of the world."[16] "Ultimately," Koh added, "this can lead to American 'exemptionism',"[17] justifying exemptions from international law rules and agreements, even ones that it may have played a critical role in framing.[18] This pattern of behavior is evident in relation to the significant number of major international protocols that the US has refused to sign, stretching from conventions on children's rights, discrimination against women, and persons with disabilities to those with direct national security implications such as on the Law of the Sea and Anti-Personnel Mines.[19]

2.1.3 FRONTIERISM

The United States grew geographically from a disparate set of small communities to a nation with preeminent global reach. This evolution required both an explanation and a narrative justification that supported continued engagement with states, people and, eventually, issues far from American shores.

Scholars have sought to explain the causes and consequences of America's geographic expansion—first domestically, and subsequently globally.[20] Frederick Jackson Turner, a formative proponent of the idea, argued that the energy and drive of Americans was uncontainable and the westward frontier was "a gate of escape from the bondage of the past."[21] William Appleman Williams subsequently argued that Turner's analysis foreshadowed open-door diplomacy and full engagement with foreign (and now global) markets.[22] The "Frontier Thesis," as it became known, continues to have resonance among Americans. This logic was applied to space ("the final frontier") and even echoes in contemporary debates about cyberspace, where romanticists extolled the virtues of creating a new virtual frontier while many national security specialists view it as an exploitable domain or a "badlands" to be policed.[23]

Ultimately, the combination of these three myths generated a national security culture that is activist, engaged, robust, and, often muscular.[24] That culture is reinforced by values—life, liberty, and the pursuit of happiness—that its adherents believe are universal aspirations. It incorporates both political beliefs (such as democracy) and economic ideals (a liberal form of capitalism). Many Americans therefore regard globalization as synonymous with Americanization.[25] Correspondingly, it is the United States and the international financial institutions it devised (and helps sustain) that dictates the prescription of the "Washington Consensus"—of liberalization, deregulation, and privatization.[26]

Regardless of their veracity, these traditions, myths, and underlying values of the United States matter. Today, they are foundational to both an American "strategic culture" and its grand strategy.[27]

2.2 National security and grand strategy

American policymakers have commonly preached that the United States is a nation that believes in the rule of law based on the US Constitution. Yet Louis Henkin notes that "the constitutional blueprint for the governance of our foreign affairs has proved to be starkly incomplete, indeed skimpy."[28] Many of the challenges for US foreign and security policymaking—the separation of powers and system of checks and balances—are endemic to the American policy process.[29] Both domestic and foreign policymaking is commonly accused of being overly responsive to interest groups, slowed by conflicts among the three branches, and, hamstrung by Congress's budgetary powers.[30]

Indeed, American scholars have long lamented the stringency of democratic institutions on the conduct of foreign affairs.[31] The formulation of American strategy requires the authority, contribution, and participation of the President, the executive branch, Congress and, broadly speaking, the public. Responsibility for implementing strategies largely falls to the president, executive branch agencies, and the military services and intelligence agencies. This is especially true when it concerns national security issues and the military dimensions of war, where the Constitution grants the president, as commander-in-chief of the armed forces, the sole power to declare war. Yet, even these enumerated powers have generated an implicit "invitation to struggle"[32]—over war powers and the US military's overseas deployment—notably with the rise of what Arthur Schlesinger described in 1973 as the "Imperial Presidency."[33]

2.2.1 LEGISLATIVE PARAMETERS

Until World War II, the United States operated with a minimalist national security establishment. International affairs were handled by a War, a Navy, and a modest State Department. The vast modern intelligence community, economic agencies and departments, and the variegated military organizations, were considered unwarranted.[34] The size, professionalism, and capacity of the US government in domestic, foreign, and then security policy expanded in successive stages: during the Progressive era of the late 1800s, then World War I, the Great Depression, and the New Deal.[35]

The demands of World War II, however, led to a vast expansion of America's global responsibilities, and thus the bureaucratic and organizational complexity of those government departments responsible for foreign affairs.[36] The so-called six "Wise Men"—including Dean Acheson, John McCloy, and George Kennan—developed both the domestic and international legislative framework for pursuing a global security agenda.[37] Senior military leaders began the structuring of national security decision-making in the war's waning months, based on their wartime management experience, the idiosyncratic decision-making style of President Franklin Roosevelt, and the need to regularize institutional authorities and relationships in the postwar period.[38] The US invention and use of atomic weapons, the Soviet Union's subsequent development of comparable capabilities, and, perhaps most importantly, their poorly understood impact on American strategy, gave further impetus to institutional and strategic reforms that would take nearly a decade to implement.[39] The most significant legislation that emerged from this period was the National Security Act of 1947. It created a new national security structure that included the National Security Council (NSC), the Central Intelligence Agency (CIA), the Department of Defense (DOD), an independent Department of the Air Force, and the Joint Chiefs of Staff.[40] Congress intended that the Act would

> provide a comprehensive program for the future security of the United States; to provide for the establishment of integrated policies and procedures for the departments, agencies, and functions of the Government relating to the national security; to provide three military departments for the operation and administration of the Army, the Navy (including naval aviation and the United States Marine Corps), and the Air Force, with their assigned combat and service components; to provide for their authoritative coordination and unified direction under civilian control but not to merge them; to provide for the effective strategic direction of the armed forces and for their operation under unified control and for their integration into an efficient team of land, naval, and air forces.[41]

As we discuss shortly, the Act also required that the US have a National Security Strategy (NSS) document.

Over the next four decades relatively minor changes were made to the structures created by the National Security Act of 1947. The first reform only took place in the mid-1980s following the failure of Desert One, the disastrous effort to rescue fifty-two American staffers held captive at the US Embassy in Iran in April 1980. The intended purposes of the Goldwater–Nichols Defense

Reorganization Act of 1986 (Public Law 102-496, Stat. 3190, USC. 50) were, in brief, to:[42]

- Clarify the military chain of command;
- Give service chiefs responsibility for training and equipping forces;
- Make the chairman of the Joint Chiefs of Staff the principal military advisor to the president;
- Require senior military personnel to have experience working with the other services; and
- Establish the means for military services to collaborate when developing capability requirements and acquisition programs.[43]

In terms of grand strategy, the Goldwater–Nichols Act's most crucial element was the changes it made to the process by which presidents received military advice. It was centralized in the chair of the Joint Chiefs who was designated as the president's principal military adviser. Simultaneously, the Act gave the chair a greater capacity to both provide advice and direct overall strategy, and it awarded greater authority to "unified" and "specified" field commanders, notably in terms of military operations within their areas of operations and what types of weapons and military systems were required to fight wars.[44]

James Locher III, the primary congressional staffer responsible for the legislation, later gave it low grades in two important areas related to the formulation of grand strategy: "The Goldwater–Nichols objective of strengthening civilian authority has produced results of a 'B-minus,' middling quality; there are problems here." He further added that "Strategy making and contingency planning under Goldwater–Nichols collectively merits a grade of C—unimpressive."[45]

Congress and the wider national security community have since struggled to adapt existing structures to the needs of a dynamic security environment. Apart from reforms in homeland security and limited changes in the intelligence community,[46] the US foreign and security structure remains much the same as it was during the Cold War. Numerous initiatives have intended to revisit Goldwater–Nichols, including suggested acquisition reforms and efforts to stimulate greater technological, organizational, doctrinal, and strategic innovation, often with no or little effect. Consistent with that theme, the Trump administration has emphasized organization innovations and business reforms, although it is too early to tell if they will be implemented.[47] Evidence suggests—at most—the likelihood of incremental change.

2.3 Strategy-making institutions, processes, and instruments

Academics and policymakers may debate grand strategy as if the US as a nation is a unitary actor whose capacities for formulating and implementing grand strategy are cohesive and fluid. The reality differs. No single institution is charged with producing a grand strategy, despite America's abundant institutional and operational resources. Instead, there are a selection of national security institutions that employ a nominally coordinated, often ad-hoc process to produce a set of often loosely linked policies. These are occasionally implemented—based on the skills of civilian and military officials, the availability of specific resources, and the influence of inevitable, but unpredictable (and thus contingent), domestic and international events.

Rarely do presidents or other policymakers talk about grand strategy in terms that would sound familiar to academics, with the notable exception of President Eisenhower's Solarium project, which was designed to study "alternative policies to counter the Soviet objective of world domination."[48] Grand strategy is a term largely used by media commentators and academics who observe the strategy-making process and subsequent outputs, and seek to make sense of a chaotic and nontransparent system. Moreover, official statements, documents, and declaratory policies are written for varied audiences—foreign governments, nonstate actors, Congress, the less senior officials populating the military and government agencies, political (and party) elites, and the general public—for whom discussion of grand strategy is often not a suitable part of the lexicon.

2.3.1 THE INSTITUTIONS OF GRAND STRATEGY

Most of the executive branch institutions involved in developing national security strategies were created seven decades ago. As the United States was learning how to lead the world it was, effectively, simultaneously reorganizing administratively to facilitate its global leadership. Three critical organizations now play the greatest roles in crafting most of the public documents underpinning US grand strategy: the NSC, the DOD, and Department of State (DOS). Other departments and agencies play significant roles,[49] notably the CIA and the new Office of the Director Intelligence (ODNI) as part of the intelligence community. The Director of National Intelligence (DNI), for example, coordinates and oversees numerous agencies. And both may be part of the strategy development process—the production of "long-term strategic analysis" which, theoretically, should help drive grand strategy.[50] But neither directly formulates grand strategy.

2.3.1.1 National Security Council

The NSC has served a variety of purposes and played differing roles since 1947.[51] But experts see its current "intent" as being "to manage and direct this wide range of actors."[52] Theoretically, the process of devising strategic documents across the US government is hierarchical. An incoming administration develops the NSS, setting in motion a process of strategy development in specific issue-areas, departments, and agencies, the military services, and even (occasionally) regions.[53]

This process is far more complex in practice. First, as discussed below, not every presidential administration is able to generate an NSS within its first year in office, and they generally have chosen not to produce one annually. Meanwhile, strategy development occurs incrementally in the various subordinate departments and agencies because that is essential for establishing policy priorities, allocating resources, and developing future year budgets. Second, even the most prominent documents, such as the NSS or the National Defense Strategy (NDS), do not result in immediate strategic changes. Barack Obama's 2015 *National Military Strategy* (NMS), for example, remained in place long after Donald Trump's inauguration.[54]

2.3.1.2 Department of Defense

The DOD has played an increasingly important role in the development of a grand strategy since the late 1990s,[55] partially because each new presidential administration delivers the Quadrennial Defense Review (QDR) as its first major strategy document to the relevant Congressional committees. A yearlong process, staffed by the military services and other defense agencies, produced a detailed and comprehensive defense document "to determine the force structure, modernization plans, and infrastructure required to implement that strategy; and to craft an associated budget plan."[56]

The QDR provided the basis for a range of implementing documents internal to the DOD, including the Defense Planning Guidance, the Guidance for Employment of Force document, and the Joint Capabilities Integration and Development System.[57] This does not, however, guarantee that other non-DOD national security departments and agencies are consulted, agree with, or coordinate the range of defense activities undertaken by the Department and the Armed Services.

The FY2017 National Defense Authorization Act changed the name of the QDR to the NDS. The Secretary of Defense is directed to include "priority missions," assumptions about the "strategic environment," a "strategic framework" for prioritizing threats, an explanation of "roles and mission of the armed forces," the required "force size and structure" and the "major investments" needed over the next five years in the NDS.[58]

The impetus for this new title and enabling legislation was Congressional dissatisfaction with the state of US strategizing. Members concluded that such strategic documents provided insufficient insight for congressional authorizers and appropriators, despite the vast amounts of time and energy devoted to producing them. Part of the problem, they suspected, was that the unclassified status of most DOD strategic documents, by necessity, masked the real strategic challenges or the state of the nation's armed forces.[59] This critique resonated with the assessment of insiders familiar with DOD's strategy development process.⁶⁰ Yet, whether the creation of a classified NDS will produce better results remains unclear.

2.3.1.3 Department of State

The DOS lacks a planning process equivalent to the strategic documents produced by the DOD. The exception proves the rule: in 2009, then Secretary of State Hillary Clinton instructed Jack Lew, then Deputy Secretary of State for Management and Resources, to provide "a comprehensive assessment for organizational reform and improvements to our policy, strategy and planning processes."⁶¹ But as the Congressional Research Service observed about only the second ever *Quadrennial Diplomacy and Development Review* (QDDR), it "is not required or defined by statute or regulation and, as a result, could take whatever form the Secretary of State chooses to give it, including following (or ignoring) procedural precedents set by QDDR I."⁶²

The QDDR has not gained the bureaucratic, organizational, or political traction of the DOD's NDS for manifold reasons. These include the vastly greater bureaucratic planning capacity of the DOD and the military services, the enormous funds at their disposal and, perhaps, the DOD's grander ambitions. Moreover, in recent administrations, the NSC has played an increasingly important role both in devising, with the president, the general direction of foreign policy and in overseeing strategies.

The DOS does have an office, the Policy Planning Staff, charged "to take a longer term, strategic view of global trends and frame recommendations for the Secretary of State to advance US interests and American values."⁶³ Policy Planning was founded by George Kennan at then-Secretary of State George Marshall's behest. Paul Nitze followed him in the role of director. Subsequent successors have included Walt Rostow and Paul Wolfowitz. But none have managed to wield the broader political influence of the early directors.⁶⁴

The major institutions involved in the formal strategy development process—the NSC, the DOD, and the DOS—have therefore had varied roles and capabilities with regard to the formulation of grand strategy. While early discussions were dominated by DOS officials and career members of the foreign service, the DOD, and the NSC have gained greater influence over time. This is partially explained by budgetary and organizational changes. The DOD, because it directs the military services and defense agencies, has far greater human and material resources to address long-term strategic issues. The NSC works in close proximity to the commander-in-chief. The DOS, in contrast, is relatively constrained by its limited resources, daily global responsibilities, and, ultimately, the preferences of strong secretaries of state. Indeed, recent secretaries of state have preferred high-profile diplomacy vice strategy and bureaucratic infighting. Ultimately, Michael O'Hanlon's comments with regard to Obama's last secretary of state, John Kerry, applies to many: "He really is a diplomat, more than a strategist or a wartime officeholder."[65]

2.3.2 THE INSTRUMENTS OF GRAND STRATEGY

Over the course of a century, the United States has developed a variegated set of instruments to implement a strategy of global engagement. Employing the DOD's lexicon, the elements of power are characterized as Diplomatic, Information, Military, and Economic actions (DIME); and their effects are Political, Military, Economic, Social, Information, and Infrastructure (PMESII). Richard Kugler succinctly argues, however, that there are three principal instruments for pursuing US grand strategy: "Political diplomacy, military power, and economic strength [which] provide the United States with impressive assets for carrying out its strategic functions around the world."[66]

Most academics who study grand strategy prioritize America's military capacities. In the words of Richard Betts, many scholars believe in "The Enduring Priority of Military Instruments."[67] Betts is skeptical about the strategic use of military force.[68] But Barry Posen, Robert Art, and John Mearsheimer, all prominent scholars, focus their analysis and prescriptions on the military as a coercive instrument of grand strategy.[69] Nuclear weapons, however, occupy an anomalous position in US defense policies and grand strategy. Despite the truism that nuclear weapons are unusable, they play an outsized role in determining the American position in the world.[70] American nuclear weapons thus add a separate and distinct dimension of American hard power and security, in contrast to conventional military forces that are eminently usable in peace and war.

Critics, however, argue that US foreign policy has become overly militarized.[71] Few scholars who focus on grand strategy suggests that economic or diplomatic instruments play a crucial role,[72] although historical accounts—in contrast—often suggest that they play significant roles in resolving crises and pursing national policy objectives.[73]

America's diplomatic power may vary, depending on public perception of a president's legitimacy or their administration's policies.[74] Yet, its vast (if currently diminished) diplomatic service provides an unrivaled capacity for bilateral and multilateral communication. Advocates contend public diplomacy is augmented by a variety of other social forms of power, stretching from government programs such as the academic exchanges instituted by the Fulbright-Hays Act to Joseph Nye Jr's famous "soft" forms of power that reputedly generate sympathy for American values, culture, and foreign policy.[75]

American scholars of grand strategy, focusing on the military, often understate the significance of the power of the US economy in the global economic system. First, and foremost, the liberal international order built by the US after 1945, and sustained through a series of crises, has proven critical for Washington in pursuing a grand strategy. It effectively retains, for example, a veto power at the World Bank (even as the bank's importance has diminished).[76] It also remains a powerful actor at the International Monetary Fund and the World Trade Organization. Second, the role of the dollar as the foremost reserve currency generates benefits.[77] Third, while the US consumer market's global proportionate share may be diminishing, it remains the largest national one. Any threat to curtail access to it generates a significant economic and political reaction.[78] And finally, the American imposition of financial and trade sanctions can have an outsized influence on the fate of individuals, and sometimes entire economies—as the imposition of sanctions on Iran demonstrates.[79] In sum, the US retains an economic instrument that can be used to great effect, even if it remains a blunt one often wielded with unforeseen consequences.[80]

Yet, when it comes to defense spending, Gordon Adams and Cindy Williams provide evidence that "money is policy."[81] Even a cursory examination of the federal budget reveals that the US spends far more on the military than it does on diplomacy, foreign aid, or intelligence collection and analysis. In fiscal year 2017, for example, the US Congress appropriated $57.5 billion for foreign operations (including everything from foreign aid to fund for the DOS and US contributions to international organizations), while it appropriated $586.2 billion for defense spending.[82]

2.4 Grand strategic outputs

No single document elaborates American grand strategy. George Kennan's "Long Telegram" and "Mr. X" article in *Foreign Affairs* served as touchstones for the duration of the Cold War. They influenced generations of policymakers, although they were unofficial statements by a mid-level State Department employee and were nowhere codified in US government policy or official statements. Their underlying baseline logic was subsequently modified in numerous official documents, most notably the NSC's top secret policy paper NSC-68, authored by a team of DOS and DOS experts led by Paul Nitze.[83] NSC-68 remained classified until 1975.[84] It may, however, serve as the best, if controversial, single guide to Cold War American, anti-communist grand strategy. NSC-68 took a more expansive view of American interests vis-à-vis the Soviet threat than Kennan, proposed that the United States devote more material resources to geostrategic competition, and that it rely more heavily on military instruments.

Since 1991, however, the executive branch has tended to publicly articulate national objectives and the instruments that will be used to implement them. Nonetheless, public documents are more aspirational and declaratory—signaling the administration's goals to the national security bureaucracy, varied international actors (states, international organizations, and even transnational actors), and attentive publics. Indeed, since 1993, most American strategic documents have posited a relatively stable set of national objectives than laid out in the "Bottom Up Review" undertaken by then Secretary of Defense Les Aspin for President Clinton:[85]

1. Survival of the nation;
2. Prevention of catastrophic attack against US territory (expanded after 9/11);
3. Security of the global economic system;
4. Security, confidence, and reliability of our allies;
5. Protection of American citizens abroad; and
6. Preservation and extension of universal values.[86]

This list's impressive breadth has, arguably, created a series of insurmountably challenging tasks for any one strategy, an issue we discuss in the conclusion.

2.4.1 OVERVIEW OF POSTWAR GRAND STRATEGIES

America's first president, George Washington, famously warned against "entangling alliances"[87] while President John Quincy Adams in 1821 averred that the United States "goes not abroad in search of monsters to destroy."[88] Even the Monroe Doctrine was more an expression of a hope than a strategy, given America's reliance on the British navy to enforce noninterference in the Western Hemisphere.[89] Presidents focused on the westward expansion of the nation rather than overseas before the 1880s. The US generally relied on commerce and a series of purchases to expand territorially.[90] It only used military force abroad when specific circumstances dictated, such as the formation of a navy to deal with Barbary piracy.

America entered both world wars relatively late, and only fully committed to a "war economy" in the latter. The Cold War, in contrast, signaled a commitment to a global strategy, characterized by variations of, and modifications to, the containment principle first articulated by Kennan:[91]

[T]he main element of any United States policy toward the Soviet Union must be a long-term, patient but firm and vigilant containment of Russian expansive tendencies... Soviet pressure against the free institutions of the Western world is something that can be contained by the adroit and vigilant application of counterforce at a series of constantly shifting geographical and political points, corresponding to the shifts and maneuvers of Soviet policy, but which cannot be charmed or talked out of existence.[92]

Kennan's nuanced view of the Soviet threat was soon supplanted by Paul Nitze's NSC-68, in 1950. It "argued that the best course of action was to respond in kind with a massive build-up of the US military and its weaponry."[93] Containment's militarization then helped define strategy until the end of the Cold War. The US built an enormous military establishment of both conventional and nuclear forces. It employed force in the service of containment—evidently in Korea during the Truman administration, covertly (for example in Iran) during the Eisenhower administration,[94] and most overtly by Johnson and Nixon in Vietnam. The US established a network of alliances and partnerships, all entailing the creation of military bases. To support this global strategy, it built a formidable domestic military-industrial-university complex capable of generating trained manpower and innovative military capabilities.[95]

Yet containment's rationale disappeared with the Soviet collapse. Strategic drift followed and a competition ensued to formulate a suitable strategic approach in the absence of the unifying Soviet threat.[96] From the George H. W. Bush to the Obama administration, officials searched for an enduring set of principles capable of addressing a far more variegated set of economic, political, and military challenges. Transnational terrorism (al-Qaeda and the Islamic State) and so-called "rogue states" first dominated as security threats, only to be supplanted by the rise of China.

America's willingness to lead politically has been repeatedly questioned, both domestically and abroad.[97] Japan and then the European Union grew as potential economic challengers. Yet repeated predictions of American economic decline (and possible collapse) have proved premature, dating from at least the Oil Crisis of the 1970s to the 2008 Financial Crisis. Today, of course, China appears poised to surpass America's leadership of trade, investment, and, eventually perhaps, finance.[98] Its "Belt and Road" infrastructure initiative provides it with a significant potential instrument for expanding its economic and geostrategic influence.[99] Yet, gross alarmists aside, American commentators claim that it currently lacks the necessary balance of instruments to match America's global preeminence.[100]

American debates about the best grand strategy remain heavily contested.[101] As we discuss in the conclusion, Donald Trump's administration may currently be in the process of recasting American grand strategy. But the instruments available in the formulation and implementation of any particular strategy remain potent, with uniquely global implications for other actors in the system.

2.4.2 STRATEGIC DOCUMENTS AND GRAND STRATEGY

The "NSS is the only complete whole-of-government national security document that the US Government publishes."[102] According to the

Goldwater–Nichols Act of 1986, the NSS was to be annually submitted to Congress, and each new presidential administration was required to produce the document within 150 days of assuming office. But only seventeen NSS documents were published between 1986 and 2017.[103] Critics suggest that is because the international environment, and thus the evolving thinking of administration officials, changes insufficiently annually to justify the cost of developing a new NSS. Furthermore, the difficulty of getting a sufficient number of key DOD officials confirmed and familiar with the NSS drafting process often precludes publishing within the mandated period.[104] Only the Clinton administration (with seven reports) made an effort to publish one annually. But the Trump administration's NSS was clearly delayed by both phenomena.[105]

2.4.3 THEORY AND PRACTICE

Yet even clearly articulated and coherent strategic documents are insufficient. Grand strategies require implementation. Cabinet officials, a variety of government bodies, and the military itself must implement the ideas and policies articulated in strategy documents.

In Peter Feaver's words,

Grand Strategy begins with theory: leaders' theories about how the world works and what is or ought to be their states' roles in that world. Yet it is embodied in policy and practice: government action and reaction in response to real (or perceived) threats and opportunities. Grand strategy may be born in debates at the highest levels of national power, but it lives or dies in the collaborative action of myriad junior officials.[106]

William Martell is a rarity among scholars of grand strategy because he emphasized the important of implementation. He argued that implementation often fails because policymakers do not balance desired ends against available means. Betts echoes Martell's sentiment, noting the gap between the visions created by leaders and those charged with executing the strategy. As he notes,

Strategy in theory is whatever the government's political leaders believe it to be, which is usually something very general if not vague. This is often called grand strategy. Strategy in practice is what the government's professional diplomats, soldiers, and intelligence agents actually produce in specific programs, plans, and operations. As in most of life, the levels of theory and practice in strategy are not always aligned.[107]

Indeed, our own research has demonstrated that any specific grand strategy, regardless of its content, is often far less important than the operational choices made by military commanders in potential or operational conflict zones. Those choices, which we term "calibrated strategies," are dictated more by local environmental factors and the accruing specific challenges to American security objectives. They are conditioned by the character of the threats, the types of actors posing those threats, and the nature of the actual or potential conflict in a specific theater. All three have become more diverse in the twenty-first century than the more homogenous challenge posed during the Cold War, undermining efforts to implement any grand strategy. The product is often strategies that resemble one of the debated options, but defy any one-size-fits-all formulation. A multilateral liberal response, such as American leadership of NATO, may be appropriate for addressing the challenge posed by Russian aggression in the Baltics. But a more nuanced sponsorship strategy (what its critics characterize as "leading from behind") is required when coordinating with other countries in dealing with piracy off the coast of Africa. Likewise, a modified form of isolationism may be employed by American forces when interdicting drugs on the US border. Civilian and military leaders, however, concur that a unilateral primacist strategy is generally more effective in carrying out freedom of navigation operations against Chinese claims of sovereignty in the South China Sea, given the lack of appropriate resources of America's regional partners.[108]

We are not suggesting that strategy documents are irrelevant. But their importance risks being overstated. Military officials and civilian leaders, by necessity, must now engage in an ongoing dialogue about how the US should operate that often diminishes their significance. Military leaders offer their advice based on local conditions. Whether officials accept that advice when it strays from the principles embedded in those documents, is another matter.

2.5 Continuity or change in the twenty-first century?

Barack Obama gave a forthright interview in 2015 in which he decried what he termed "The Washington Playbook" on foreign policy. He instead called for "strategic patience."[109] Donald Trump has repeatedly decried his predecessor's strategy and vehemently insisted that he would pursue a different approach. Patience does not appear part of the process, evident in the repeated hiring and firing of senior officials and numerous policy reversals.

Like many scholars, we have grappled with the extent and nature of President Trump's grand strategy—and whether it signals change.[110] Actions such as the decision to withdraw from the Paris Accord, and grumbling about NATO contributions, would suggest it affirms change. Yet we concluded that, in the first year of his presidency, his tweets and public persona belie the fact that there was clear continuity in his administration's military operations, resembling his two predecessors'. Examples abound—notably in combatting the Islamic State in Syria and Iraq, in continuing the Afghan war, and even in addressing the growing North Korean nuclear threat.[111]

This is less true in the economic and diplomatic realm. Here, early indicators suggest substantive change, not just from his predecessors but from the entire post–World War II consensus. Both Trump's speeches and his actions in pursuing an "America First" foreign economic policy, such as on trade and tariffs, run counter to American-led efforts to promote a liberal international economic order by promoting free trade.[112] Certainly, there are historical precedents for the imposition of trade tariffs—for example in steel, aluminum, autos, and machine tools—during the Reagan and George W. Bush administrations. But these were then characterized as limited and temporary, unlike those imposed by the Trump administration.[113] Similarly, the US withdrew from the then embryonic free trade Trans-Pacific Partnership Agreement (TPPA) which Trump condemned as "another disaster done and pushed by special interests who want to rape our country, just a continuing rape of our country."[114]

In terms of diplomacy, the Trump administration's recognition of Jerusalem as Israel's capital and withdrawal from the United Nations Educational, Scientific and Cultural Organization (UNESCO) signaled a clear departure from traditional American postwar strategy. America First may not signal America alone, as the president declared in a Davos speech in January of 2018.[115] Yet falling US favorability ratings in global opinion poll surveys,[116] its inability to garner substantial UN General Assembly support for its recognition of Jerusalem as Israel's capital, and universal criticism of its withdrawal from the Paris Agreement, are just three examples of the Trump administration's weakening diplomatic influence.[117]

American forms of grand strategy have historically oscillated between extremes, from realist forms of global primacy or neoconservative nation-building, to liberal formulations entailing multilateral leadership and even aspects of isolationism before 1945. It is therefore not surprising to discover that Trump's departure from more popular recent formulations, encapsulated in his "Make America Great Again" mantra, has an historical precedent. Walter Russell Mead, for example, claims to have identified one, nineteenth-century Jacksonianism, which,

is less an intellectual or political movement than an expression of the social, cultural and religious values of a large portion of the American public. And it is doubly obscure because it happens to be rooted in one of the portions of the public least represented in the media and the professoriat.[118]

The mixed evidence of his first year suggests that even Trump's efforts to implement this type of grand strategy may be thwarted by the vicissitudes of politics. Nonetheless, it serves as a timely reminder that any effort to implement an American one remains uniquely consequential for both global stability and prosperity.

NOTES

1. For contrasting views on American unipolarity, see Charles Krauthammer, "The Unipolar Moment," *Foreign Affairs* 70, no. 1 (1990/1991): 23–33; Christopher Layne, "The Unipolar Illusion: Why New Great Powers Will Rise," *International Security* 17, no. 4 (Spring 1993): 5–51; and William C. Wohlforth, "The Stability of a Unipolar World," *International Security* 24, no. 1 (Summer 1999): 5–41.
2. David Milne borrows from analytic philosophy to define world making as "formulating strategies that sought to deploy the nation's vast military and economic power—or indeed it retraction through domestic orientation—to 'make' a world in which America is best positioned to thrive." Milne, *Worldmaking: the Art and Science of American Diplomacy* (New York: Farrah, Straus, and Giroux, 2015), 10.
3. For a few representative examples of differing schools of thought see Robert J. Art, "A Defensible Defense: America's Grand Strategy after the Cold War," *International Security* 15, no. 4 (Spring 1991): 5–53; Eugene Gholz, Daryl G. Press, and Harvey M. Sapolsky, "Come Home America: The Strategy of Restraint in the Face of Temptation," *International Security* 21, no. 4 (Spring 1997): 5–48; Christopher Layne, "From Preponderance to Offshore Balancing America's Future Grand Strategy," *International Security* 22, no. 1 (Summer 1997): 86–124; Barry Posen, "The Case for Restraint," *The American Interest* 3, no. 2 (November/December 2007): 7–32; and Stephen G. Brooks, G. John Ikenberry, and William C. Wohlforth, "Don't Come Home, America: The Case against Retrenchment," *International Security* 37, no. 3 (Winter 2012/13): 7–51.
4. Thierry Balzacq, Peter Dombrowski, and Simon Reich, "Is Grand Strategy a Research Program? A Review Essay," *Security Studies*, October 2018, doi.org/10.1080/09636412.2018.1508631.
5. "Gunnar Myrdal, who characterized the United States as the most 'moralistic' and 'moral conscious' branch of Western civilization," referred to *"the American Creed, where the American thinks, talks, and acts under the influence of high national and Christian precepts."* Myrdal, *An American Dilemma, Volume 1: the Negro Problem and Modern Democracy* (New York: Harper & Brothers, 1944; sixth printing, New Brunswick, NJ: Transaction, 2009), lxxviii, lxxix, emphasis in the original, citations refer to the Transaction edition, quoted in David Hughes, "Unmaking an Exception: A Critical Genealogy of US Exceptionalism," *Review of International Studies* 41, no. 3 (July 2015): 546. One more recent use of the term expands it to include "'liberty, egalitarianism, individualism, populism and laissez-faire', or 'liberty, equality, democracy, individualism, human rights, the rule of law and private property'." Robert R. Tomes, "American Exceptionalism in the Twenty-First Century," *Survival: Global Politics and Strategy* 56, no. 1 (January 2014): 28.
6. For accessible accounts of the ideas underpinning US foreign and security policies see, Walter McDougall, *Promised Land, Crusader State: The American Encounter with the World Since 1776* (New York: Houghton Mifflin,1997); and Walter Russel Mead, *Special Providence: American Foreign Policy and How It Changed the World* (London: Routledge, 2002).

7. Walter A. McDougall, "Back to Bedrock: The Eight Traditions of American Statecraft," *Foreign Affairs* 76, no. 2 (March–April 1997): 134–46.
8. Matthew 5:14.
9. James W. Ceaser, "The Origins and Character of American Exceptionalism," *American Political Thought* 1, no. 1 (Spring 2012): 7.
10. James Chace, "The Dilemmas of the City upon a Hill," *World Policy Journal* 14, no. 1 (Spring 1997): 105–7.
11. Jonathan Monten characterizes this as a combination of exemplarism and vindicationalism—Americans believe they are both a role model and a force for global change. Jonathan Monten, "The Roots of the Bush Doctrine: Power, Nationalism, and Democracy Promotion in U.S. Strategy," *International Security* 29, no. 4 (Spring 2005): 114.
12. Fact Sheet, The White House, "President Donald J. Trump's 'American Model' Economy," January 30, 2018, https://www.whitehouse.gov/briefings-statements/president-donald-j-trumps-american-model-economy/
13. Seymour Martin Lipset, *American Exceptionalism: A Double-Edged Sword* (New York: W. W. Norton & Company, 1997); and Hughes, "Unmaking an Exception," 529.
14. Joseph Lepgold and Timothy McKeown, "Is American Foreign Policy Exceptional? An Empirical Analysis," *Political Science Quarterly* 110, no. 3 (Autumn 1995): 369–84; and Stanley Hoffmann, "The American Style: Our Past and Our Principles," *Foreign Affairs* 46, no. 2 (January 1968): 362–76.
15. Howard Zinn, *A People's History of the United States, 1492-Present*, revised and updated (1980; repr., New York: Harper Perennial, 1995), 292–3.
16. Harold Hongju Koh, "On American Exceptionalism," *Stanford Law Review* 55, no. 5 (May 2003): 1485–986.
17. Michael Ignatieff, "Introduction: American Exceptionalism and Human Rights," in *American Exceptionalism and Human Rights*, ed. Michael Ignatieff (Princeton, NJ: Princeton University Press, 2005), 4–7.
18. Koh, "On American Exceptionalism," 1482–3.
19. For numerous examples see Simon Reich, "Congress' Walk of Shame on International Deals," *The New Republic*, March 12, 2015, https://newrepublic.com/article/121281/republicans-have-been-stalling-bills-years
20. William Appleman Williams, "The Frontier Thesis and American Foreign Policy," *Pacific Historical Review* 24, no. 4 (November 1955): 379–95; Louis Hartz, *The Liberal Tradition in America* (New York: Harcourt, Brace and World, 1955); and Alfred Thayer Mahan, *The Influence of Sea Power Upon History, 1660-1783* (New York: Dover Publications, 1987).
21. Fredrick Jackson Turner, *The Frontier in American History* (New York: Henry Holt and Company, 1928), 38.
22. Allan G. Bogue, "Frederick Jackson Turner Reconsidered," *The History Teacher* 27, no. 2 (February 1994): 198, 206.
23. Chris C. Demchak and Peter Dombrowski, "Rise of a Cybered Westphalian Age," *Strategic Studies Quarterly* 5, no. 1 (Spring 2011): 32–61.
24. Simon Reich and Richard Ned Lebow, *Good-Bye Hegemony! Power and Influence in the Global System* (Princeton, NJ: Princeton University Press, 2014): 139.

25. Richard Higgott and Simon Reich, "Globalisation and Sites of Conflict: Towards Definition and Taxonomy" (Working Paper Number 1, Centre for the Study of Globalisation and Regionalisation, Warwick University, Coventry, UK, June 1998), https://warwick.ac.uk/fac/soc/pais/research/researchcentres/csgr/papers/workingpapers/1998/wp0198.pdf
26. John Williamson, "A Short History of the Washington Consensus," *Law and Business Review of the Americas* 15, no. 1 (Winter 2009): 7–23.
27. Alastair Iain Johnston notes that proponents of strategic culture "argue, explicitly or implicitly, that different states have different predominant strategic preferences that are rooted in the early or formative experiences of the state, and are influenced to some degree by the philosophical, political, cultural, and cognitive characteristics of the state and its elites." Johnston, "Thinking about Strategic Culture," *International Security* 19, no. 4 (Spring 1995): 34.
28. Louis Henkin, "Foreign Affairs and the Constitution," *Foreign Affairs* 66, no. 2 (Winter 1987): 287.
29. Ibid., 284.
30. James M. Lindsay, *Congress and the Politics of U.S. Foreign Policy* (Baltimore, MD: Johns Hopkins University Press, 1994).
31. Miroslav Nincic, "The Terms of the Debate," in *Democracy and Foreign Policy: The Fallacy of Political Realism* (New York: Columbia University Press, 1992).
32. Cecil Van Meter Crabb, Jr. and Pat M. Holt, *Invitation to Struggle: Congress, the President, and Foreign Policy*, 4th ed. (Washington, DC: CQ Press, 1992).
33. Arthur M. Schlesinger Jr., *The Imperial Presidency* (New York: Houghton, Mifflin, Harcourt, 1973).
34. George F. Kennan's memoirs detailing his entrance into the Foreign Service (founded in 1924), his training, and the resources available in the late 1920s and early 1930s are instructive. State was a small club run by a network of professional amateurs. Kennan, *Memoirs 1925–1950* (New York: Pantheon, 1983).
35. Stephen Skowronek, *Building a New American State: The Expansion of National Administrative Capacities, 1877–1920* (Cambridge: Cambridge University Press, 1982). For a view of the relationship between American wartime mobilization and the growing capacities of the state see Marc Allen Eisner, *From Warfare State to Welfare State: World War I, Compensatory State-Building, and the Limits of the Modern Order* (State College, PA: Penn State University Press, 2000).
36. The last two volumes of Paul A. C. Koistinen's multivolume history of the Political Economy of American Warfare deal with this period. Koistinen, *Arsenal of World War II: The Political Economy of American Warfare, 1940–1945* (Lawrence: University Press of Kansas, 2004) and his *State of War: The Political Economy of American Warfare, 1945–2011* (Lawrence: University Press of Kansas, 2012).
37. Walter Isaacson and Evan Thomas, *The Wise Men: Six Friends and the World They Made* (New York: Simon and Shuster, 1986).
38. Charles A. Stevenson, "Underlying Assumptions of the National Security Act of 1947," *Joint Forces Quarterly*, no. 48. (First Quarter 2008): 129–30; and Charles A. Stevenson, "The Story Behind the National Security Act of 1947," *Military Review* 88, no. 3 (May/June 2008): 13–20.

39. H. W. Brands, "The Age of Vulnerability: Eisenhower and the National Insecurity State," *The American Historical Review* 94, no. 4 (October 1989): 963–89.
40. For the origins and evolution see, Amy B. Zegart, *Flawed by Design: The Evolution of the CIA, JCS, and NSC* (Stanford, CA: Stanford University Press, 1999).
41. National Security Act of 1947, Pub. L. No. 253, 61 Stat. 496 (1947).
42. James R. Locher III, *Victory on the Potomac: The Goldwater-Nichols Act Unifies the Pentagon*, rev. ed. (2002; repr., College Station, TX: Texas A&M University Press, 2004); and Richard B. Doyle, "The U.S. National Security Strategy: Policy, Process, Problems," *Public Administration Review* 67, no. 4 (July–August 2007): 625.
43. Kathleen J. McInnis, *Goldwater-Nichols at 30: Defense Reform and Issues for Congress*, CRS Report No. R44474 (Washington, DC: Congressional Research Service, June 16, 2016), 8.
44. Section 162(b) of the Act prescribes that "unless otherwise directed by the President, the chain of command to a unified or specified combatant command runs 'from the President to the Secretary of Defense,' and 'from the Secretary of Defense to the commander of the combatant command'."
45. James R. Locher, III, "Has it worked? The Goldwater-Nichols Reorganization Act," *Naval War College Review* 54, no. 4 (Autumn 2001): 95–115.
46. See for example, Paul Pillar, *Intelligence and U.S. Foreign Policy: Iraq, 9/11, and Misguided Reform* (New York: Columbia University Press, 2014).
47. "In 2014, for example, the Congressional Research Service counted 'more than 150 major studies on acquisition reform since the end of World War II' while, in the last three fiscal years, legislators have passed 247 Defense Authorization Act provisions for reregulating military acquisition." See, Simon Reich and Peter Dombrowski, "Has a Trumpian Grand Strategy Finally Stepped into the Light?," *War on the Rocks*, January 29, 2018, https://warontherocks.com/2018/01/trumpian-grand-strategy-finally-stepped-light/
48. Raymond Millen argues that "As remarkable as it may seem, the only time the United States has had a formal grand strategy was during the Dwight D. Eisenhower administration," in "Eisenhower and US Grand Strategy," *Parameters* 44, no. 2 (Summer 2014): 35–47.
49. Mark Cancian et al., *Formulating National Security Strategy: Past Experience and Future Choices* (Washington, DC: Center for Strategic and International Studies, 2017), 11, https://www.csis.org/analysis/formulating-national-security-strategy. Ciancian et al., also include the Department of Homeland Security, the Department of Energy, the Department of Commerce, the Department of Treasury and the Department of Health and Human Services as instrumental contributors to national security strategy.
50. ODNI relies in large part on the National Intelligence Council (NIC). See https://www.dni.gov/index.php/who-we-are
51. Karl F. Inderfurth and Loch K. Johnson, eds., *Fateful Decisions: Inside the National Security Council* (New York: Oxford University Press, 2004); David Rothkopf, *Running the World: The Inside Story of the National Security Council and the Architects of American Power* (New York: Public Affairs, 2006); and Ivo H. Daalder and I.M. Destler, *In the Shadow of the Oval Office: Profiles of the*

National Security Advisers and the Presidents They Served—From JFK to George W. Bush (New York: Simon & Schuster, 2009).
52. Cancian et al., *Formulating National Security Strategy*, 11.
53. Examples of issue areas include nuclear and cyber; service strategies would include maritime strategies which currently includes the US Navy, the Marine Corps, and Coast Guard; and regional strategies include the effort during the Clinton presidency to create whole-of-government interagency strategies on a geographic basis.
54. "Fact Sheet: The 2015 National Security Strategy," https://obamawhitehouse.arch ives.gov/the-press-office/2015/02/06/fact-sheet-2015-national-security-strategy
55. The National Defense Authorization Act (NDAA) for FY1997 established the original requirement for a one-time QDR based on the recommendations of the 1995 Commission on Roles and Missions. Subsequently, the QDR was routinized by the NDAA for FY2000, which amended Title 10 of US Code to that effect. Catherine Dale, *National Security Strategy: Legislative Mandates, Execution to Date, and Considerations for Congress*, CRS Report No. RL34505 (Washington, DC: Congressional Research Service, July 28, 2008), 5.
56. Catherine Dale, *National Security Strategy: Legislative Mandates, Execution to Date, and Considerations for Congress*, CRS Report No. R43174 (Washington, DC: Congressional Research Service, August 6, 2013), 5.
57. Cancian et al., *Formulating National Security Strategy*, 14.
58. 10 U.S.C. § 113 (2016).
59. Cancian et al., *Formulating National Security Strategy*, 20.
60. Barry Watts and Andrew F. Krepinevich, *Regaining Strategic Competence* (Washington, DC: Center for Strategic and Budgetary Assessments, September 1, 2009), http://csbaonline.org/research/publications/regaining-strategic-compe tence; and F. G. Hoffman, "Grand Strategy: The Fundamental Considerations," *Orbis* 58, no. 4 (Fall 2014): 472–85.
61. U.S. Department of State, "Town Hall on the Quadrennial Diplomacy and Development Review at the Department of State," July 10, 2009, https://2009-2017.state.gov/secretary/20092013clinton/rm/2009a/july/125949.htm
62. Susan B. Epstein and Alex Tiersky, *The Quadrennial Diplomacy and Development Review (QDDR)*, CRS Report No. IN10139 (Washington, DC: Congressional Research Service, August 27, 2014).
63. "Policy Planning Staff," US Department of State, accessed August 14, 2018, https://www.state.gov/s/p/
64. "Directors of Policy Planning," US Office of the Historian, accessed August 14, 2018, https://history.state.gov/departmenthistory/people/principalofficers/director-policy-planning
65. Michael E. O'Hanlon, "Making the Grade? Assessing John Kerry's Record as Secretary of State," *Order from Chaos* (blog), The Brookings Institution, January 20, 2016, https://www.brookings.edu/blog/order-from-chaos/2016/01/20/making-the-grade-assessing-john-kerrys-record-as-secretary-of-state/
66. Richard L. Kugler, *Policy Analysis in National Security Affairs: New Methods for a New Era* (Washington, DC: National Defense University Press, 2011), 94.
67. Richard K. Betts, *American Force: Dangers, Delusions, and Dilemmas in National Security* (New York: Columbia University Press, 2013), 7–11.

68. Betts, *American Force*.
69. Barry R. Posen, *Restraint: A New Foundation for Grand Strategy* (Ithaca, NY: Cornell University Press, 2014). On the logic of offensive realism as applied to the role of military force in future Sino-American relations see John J. Mearsheimer, "Can China Rise Peacefully?," *The National Interest*, October 25, 2014, https://nationalinterest.org/commentary/can-china-rise-peacefully-10204. Robert Art suggests, "This means that military power is useful for producing not only military but also nonmilitary results, and therefore that the United States can use its military forces to help shape the international environment so as to make it more congenial to America's political and economic interests." Robert K. Art, "Geopolitics Updated: The Strategy of Selective Engagement," *International Security* 23, no. 3 (Winter 1998/99): 80–1.
70. See, for example, Robert Jervis, *The Illogic of American Nuclear Strategy* (Ithaca, NY: Cornell University Press, 1985); and Francis J. Gavin, *Nuclear Statecraft: History and Strategy in America's Atomic Age* (Ithaca, NY: Cornell University Press, 2014).
71. Gordon Adams and Shoon Murray, eds., *Mission Creep: The Militarization of US Foreign Policy?* (Washington, DC: Georgetown University Press 2014).
72. For an exception see Jonathan Kirshner, *Currency and Coercion: The Political Economy of International Monetary Power* (Princeton, NJ: Princeton University Press, 1995); and more recently his "Dollar Diminution and New Macroeconomic Constraints on American Power," in *Sustainable Security: Rethinking American National Security Strategy*, eds., Jeremi Suri and Benjamin Valentino (New York: Oxford University Press, 2016).
73. Alexander L. George, *Forceful Persuasion: Coercive Diplomacy as an Alternative to War* (Washington, DC: United States Institute of Peace, 1992); and David Allen Baldwin, *Economic Statecraft* (Princeton, NJ: Princeton University Press, 1985).
74. Peter J. Katzenstein and Robert O. Keohane, *Anti-Americanisms in World Politics* (Ithaca, NY: Cornell University Press, 2007).
75. Joseph S. Nye, Jr., "Public Diplomacy and Soft Power," *The Annals of the American Academy of Political and Social Science* 616, no. 1 (March 2008): 94–109.
76. For a historical analysis on the role of the US at the World Bank see Catherine Gwin, *U.S. Relations with the World Bank, 1945–92* (Washington, DC: The Brookings Institution, 1994); and Robert Hunter Wade, "US Hegemony and the World Bank," *Review of International Political Economy* 9, no. 2 (May 2002): 201–29.
77. Jonathan Kirshner, "Dollar Primacy and American Power: What's at Stake?" *Review of International Political Economy* 15, no. 3 (August 2008): 418–38; and Carla Norrlof, *America's Global Advantage: US Hegemony and International Cooperation* (Cambridge: Cambridge University Press, 2010).
78. Nyshka Chandran, "Global retaliation to Trump tariffs: 'It could get pretty ugly pretty soon'," *CNBC*, March 2, 2018, https://www.cnbc.com/2018/03/01/trumps-steel-and-aluminum-tariffs-global-response-to-get-ugly.html
79. Akbar E. Torbat, "Impacts of the US Trade and Financial Sanctions on Iran," *The World Economy* 28, no. 3 (March 2005): 407–34.

80. For a more general discussion of the robustness and importance of the U.S. economy see Daniel W. Drezner, "The System Worked: Global Economic Governance during the Great Recession," *World Politics* 66, no. 1 (January 2014): 123–64.
81. Gordon Adams and Cindy Williams, *Buying National Security: How America Plans and Pays for Its Global Role and Safety at Home* (London: Routledge, 2009).
82. The figures for foreign operations and defense spending include enduring expenditures and temporary spending associated with overseas contingency operations. For details, see Pat Towell and Lynn M. Williams, *Defense: FY2017 Budget Request, Authorization, and Appropriations*, CRS Report No. R44454 (Washington, DC: Congressional Research Service, April 12, 2016); and Susan B. Epstein, Marian L. Lawson, and Cory R. Gill, *State, Foreign Operations and Related Programs: FY2017 Budget and Appropriations*, CRS Report No. R44391 (Washington, DC: Congressional Research Service, May 26, 2017).
83. For an examination of Kennan's view on the Soviet Union compared to Nitze's, see John Lewis Gaddis, *Strategies of Containment: A Critical Appraisal of Postwar American National Security Policy* (Oxford: Oxford University Press, 1982), especially chapter. 4.
84. "NSC-68, 1950," Milestones: 1945–1952, Office of the Historian, accessed August 14, 2018, https://history.state.gov/milestones/1945-1952/NSC68
85. Eric V. Larson, David T. Orletsky, and Kristin J. Leuschner, *Defense Planning in a Decade of Change: Lessons from the Base Force, Bottom-Up Review, and Quadrennial Defense Review*, MR-1387-AF (Santa Monica, CA: RAND, 2001).
86. Cancian et al. *Formulating National Security Strategy*, 3.
87. Washington's Farewell Address (1796), http://avalon.law.yale.edu/18th_century/washing.asp
88. John Quincy Adams, "'She Goes Not Abroad in Search of Monsters to Destroy,' July 4, 1821," *The Repository* (archive), *The American Conservative*, http://www.theamericancon servative.com/repository/she-goes-not-abroad-in-search-of-monsters-to-destroy/
89. Mark T. Gilderhus, "The Monroe Doctrine: Meanings and Implications," *Presidential Studies Quarterly* 36, no. 1 (March 2006): 8.
90. Bruce Cumings, *Dominion from Sea to Sea: Pacific Ascendancy and American Power* (New Haven, CT: Yale University Press, 2010).
91. Gaddis, *Strategies of Containment*.
92. "X," "The Sources of Soviet Conduct," *Foreign Affairs* 25, no. 4 (July 1947): 575–6.
93. "NSC-68, 1950."
94. Stephen Kinzer, *The Brothers: John Foster Dulles, Allen Dulles, and Their Secret World War* (New York: Times Books, 2013).
95. Aaron L. Friedberg, *In the Shadow of the Garrison State* (Princeton, NJ: Princeton University Press, 2000); and Linda Weiss, *America Inc.? Innovation and Enterprise in the National Security State* (Ithaca, NY: Cornell University Press, 2014).
96. Bruce Berkowitz, "Handicapping the George Kennan Sweepstakes," *Orbis* 42, no. 3 (Summer 1998): 465–74.
97. Samuel P. Huntington, "The U.S.—Decline or Renewal?" *Foreign Affairs* 67, no. 2 (Winter 1988/1989): 76–96.

98. For an assessment of China's and the US's role in the 2008 financial crisis see Carla Norrlof and Simon Reich, "American and Chinese Leadership during the Global Financial Crisis: Testing Kindleberger's Stabilization Functions," *International Area Studies Review* 18, no. 3 (March 2015): 1–23.
99. "What is China's belt and road initiative?," (blog) *The Economist*, May 15, 2017, https://www.economist.com/blogs/economist-explains/2017/05/economist-explains-11
100. This implication in Stephen G. Brooks and William C. Wohlforth, *America Abroad: Why the Sole Superpower Should Not Pull Back from the World* (Oxford: Oxford University Press, 2016).
101. For an overview the varied options see Simon Reich and Peter Dombrowski, *The End of Grand Strategy: Maritime Operations in the 21st Century* (Ithaca, NY: Cornell University Press, 2018), 28–46.
102. Alan G. Stolberg, *How Nation-States Craft National Security Strategy Documents*, enlarged ed. (Carlisle Barracks, PA: Strategic Studies Institute, U.S. Army War College, October 2012), xi.
103. Updated to include President Obama's second term and President Trump's administration from Stolberg, *How Nation-States Craft*, 70–1.
104. Ibid., 71.
105. See Peter Dombrowski and Simon Reich, "Beyond the Tweets: President Trump's Continuity in Military Operations," *Strategic Studies Quarterly* 12, no. 2 (Summer 2018).
106. Peter Feaver, "What is grand strategy and why do we need it?," *Foreign Policy*, April 8, 2009, http://foreignpolicy.com/2009/04/08/what-is-grand-strategy-and-why-do-we-need-it/
107. Richard K. Betts, "U.S. National Security Strategy: Lenses and Landmarks," presented for the launch conference of the Princeton Project "Toward a New National Security Strategy" (Woodrow Wilson School of Public and International Affairs, Princeton University, November 2004, originally presented May 2004), http://inbody.net/research/nss/NSS/betts.pdf
108. For further details on these and other cases, see Reich and Dombrowski, *The End of Grand Strategy*.
109. Barack Obama, quoted in Jeffrey Goldberg, "The Obama Doctrine," *The Atlantic*, April 2016, http://www.theatlantic.com/magazine/archive/2016/04/the-obama-doctrine/471525/
110. Peter Dombrowski and Simon Reich, "Does Donald Trump have a grand strategy?," *International Affairs* 93, no. 5 (September 2017).
111. Dombrowski and Reich, "Beyond the Tweets."
112. Jeremy Diamond, "Trump hits China with tariffs, heightening concerns of global trade war," *CNN.com*, March 22, 2018, https://www.cnn.com/2018/03/22/politics/donald-trump-china-tariffs-trade-war/index.html
113. Simon Reich, "Restraining Trade to Invoke Investment: MITI and the Japanese Auto Producers," Case Studies in International Negotiation (Philadelphia, PA: Pew Foundation, 1991); and Neil Irwin, "The Real Risks of Trump's Steel and Aluminum Tariffs," *New York Times*, March 1, 2018, https://www.nytimes.com/2018/03/01/upshot/trump-tariff-steel-aluminum-explain.html

114. Quoted in Jose A. Del Real and Sean Sullivan, "Trump: TPP trade deal 'pushed by special interests who want to rape our country," *Washington Post*, June 28, 2016, https://www.washingtonpost.com/news/post-politics/wp/2016/06/28/trump-tpp-trade-deal-pushed-by-special-interests-who-want-to-rape-our-country/?utm_term=.525d6a7a342a
115. "Trump Davos speech: 'America First policy is not America alone'," BBC News, January 26, 2018, http://www.bbc.com/news/world-us-canada-42835934
116. Global Attitudes and Trends, "Opinion of the United States," Global Indicator Database, Pew Research Center, http://www.pewglobal.org/database/indicator/1/survey/all/
117. Global Attitudes and Trends, "Opinion of the United States"; Rick Gladstone and Mark Lander, "Defying Trump, U.N. General Assembly Condemns U.S. Decree on Jerusalem," *New York Times*, December 21, 2017, https://www.nytimes.com/2017/12/21/world/middleeast/trump-jerusalem-united-nations.html; "President Trump pulls out of U.S. Paris Climate Accord, Sparking Global Criticism," *PBS*, June 1, 2017, https://www.pbs.org/newshour/nation/president-trump-pulls-u-s-paris-accord-sparking-global-criticism
118. Walter Russell Mead, "The Jacksonian Tradition: And American Foreign Policy," *The National Interest*, no. 58 (Winter 1999/2000): 5–29.

3 Russia

CÉLINE MARANGÉ

Prince Klemens von Metternich, the Austrian statesman who duped Napoleon into believing that Austria supported the French invasion of Russia in 1812, is known to have once said: "Russia is never as strong as it seems and is never as weak as it appears." Although the authorship of the quotation is disputed—some attributed it to the crafty and irremovable French diplomat Prince of Talleyrand—it expresses laconically two enduring characteristics of Russian power throughout the ages.[1] Its limits—but also its strength—often lie in the discrepancies between Russia's real power and its perceived power. Ideologically motivated overinvestment in military means also results from structural vulnerabilities, notably the weakness of the state, reflected in its poor economic development and performance.

If "strategy" is about balancing ends, ways, and means to achieve vision and objectives, a classicist "grand strategy" usually entails the search for order and consistency, and focuses on military threats. In Barry Posen's definition, it is "a nation-state's theory about how to produce security for itself. Grand strategy focuses on military threats, because these are the most dangerous, and military remedies because these are the most costly. Security has traditionally encompassed the preservation of sovereignty, safety, territorial integrity, and power position."[2] Russia's current leaders may not articulate an explicit grand strategy. Examining their doctrines and practices, though, it can be argued that they do, in fact, promote a grand strategy design—one that is fundamentally defensive in nature and offensive in practice.

The chapter explores contemporary Russian grand strategy through the intersection of domestic and international politics. It first examines how contemporary Russian leaders perceive the global system and the security threats surrounding their country. It then explores the foreign and security objectives that have been pursued since the mid-2000s and the systemic problems encountered in achieving them. Finally, it investigates the new ways and means developed to reach these goals, focusing on the time period that began after the annexation of Crimea in March 2014 and the subsequent deterioration of relations between Russia and most Western countries.

The study reveals the role of reputation and the prevalence of Soviet strategic culture. Imbued with assumptions about Russia's enduring interests and traditional opponents, Russian leaders tend to focus solely on some challenges, such as NATO, and underappreciate other risks, such as China's military buildup. They have deployed policies aimed at regaining global status and asserting regional dominance, implicitly taking, as a referent point, the position that Moscow used to enjoy during the Cold War. To achieve the desired outcomes, they first used the tools of public, economic, and multilateral diplomacy. Unable to preserve its interests using only these tools and alarmed by social protests first in Russia in 2011–12 and then in Ukraine in 2013–14, the Kremlin adopted an unwavering stance: from that moment on, military means and strategic intimidation were amply used to compensate for its lack of political attractiveness; propaganda instruments served to galvanize support within the Russian society and gain in popularity around the world.

3.1 Institutional settings and political premises

In Russia, institutional setting and political culture play a crucial role in the formulation of a security and foreign policy agenda. The Russian constitution, adopted in December 1993, two years after the dissolution of the Soviet Union, established a federal semi-presidential republic. Inspired by the 1958 French Constitution of the Fifth Republic, it promotes a strong presidency and gives extensive power to the president.

Since Vladimir Putin became president in 2000, a growing personalization of power has taken place and an authoritarian system of government has developed behind a semblance of a democratic process. Representatives of the higher and lower chambers of the Parliament, where the president's United Russia party holds an overwhelming majority, fully support the course taken by the president in international affairs, as do the three other "institutional" opposition parties (the Communist, the Nationalist "LDPR," and the moderate "A Just Russia"). Freedom of speech exists even though constraints have multiplied. But politicians and journalists known for their outright criticism of the regime are regularly pressured, vilified, and sometimes imprisoned or forced into silence.[3]

As far as the intricacies of the Russian regime are known, all important foreign and security decisions are made by President Putin himself, whereas his inner circle, high-ranking officials on the Security Council of the Russian Federation (Sovet bezopasnosti) whom he nominates, and to a lesser extent the minister of foreign affairs, can give an opinion when requested. As a former Kremlin insider vividly explained: "Putin does not consult them for strategic advice, preferring to discuss the particulars of special operations. At meetings he asks specific questions to his subordinates, and they supply answers; there is no larger discussion. His decision-making has become almost purely reactive."[4] Vladimir Putin's personality was described as a combination of six identities, predominantly conservative. A former case officer, he is seen as both statist and survivalist, and very much attached to history.[5]

In the booming 2000s, political legitimacy came from the government's capacity to ensure political and economic stability after years of uncertainty, war, and chaos in the 1990s. In the gloomy 2010s, the regime's political legitimacy has become highly personalized and interrelated with diplomatic and military achievements. It relies mostly on ideology and charismatic authority because other sources of legitimacy—be it legal authority or economic prosperity—are exhausted. The turning point can be traced to the street demonstrations that took place in Moscow in the winter 2011–12 in protest against the irregularities and fraud that stained the legislative elections. Vladimir Putin had just announced his decision to run for a third presidential term. Alarmed by the Arab revolutions and by the Libyan leader's brutal assassination in 2011, he saw a danger to his own power and safety.

Since his re-election in May 2012, and even more so after March 2014, the Russian political system has undergone important changes which have had a clear impact on Russian strategies abroad. The Russian security and intelligence community, commonly named *siloviki* (supporters of force) reinforced its positions to the detriment of the "liberal" wing of the government. In parallel, competition heightened between "power structures," which are subjected to large-scale forced reforms, with the creation of the National Guard, for instance.[6] Uncertainty is cultivated among political elites through continuous new nominations and occasional arrests, which tends to indicate mounting insecurity at the top of the system.[7] Meanwhile, Russian media ignited nationalist sentiments and spurred patriotic mobilization.

In more general terms, the socio-historical and cultural milieu in which most Russian high-ranking officials were socialized is of utmost significance to understand their relationship with the world. Until 2016, most of the regime's key figures came from the Soviet security and secret services. They were men who studied in KGB institutions and underwent extensive ideological conditioning at an early age. They began their careers in espionage or counter-espionage services, often abroad, where their main activities consisted in conducting subversive activities and recruiting agents. In addition to acquiring the Bolshevik culture of secrecy, conspiracy, and party discipline, they were taught to view the external world in a binary and hostile way. Belonging to one of the pillars of the Soviet regime, they were sure to enjoy a well-paid job with lifetime tenure and full benefits. Most of them experienced the collapse of the Soviet Union and the subsequent economic chaos as a national cataclysm, if not as a personal humiliation.

3.2 Perception of the strategic environment

Underlying premises and unwritten rules are likely to play a crucial role, owing to the structure of the political power, one characterized by its increasing concentration and an emphasis on charismatic authority. A comparative examination of doctrines, combined with the study of official discourses, highlights how Russian leaders perceive their strategic environment. However, their beliefs and backgrounds should also be taken into account, if only because any *worldview* is a perceptual representation of reality. The way the Russian president and his entourage understand Russia's security environment in terms of actors, threats, and potential forms of conflict highly depends upon subjective factors, such as long-standing mistrust and reputational challenges.

3.2.1 THE CHARACTER OF THE GLOBAL SYSTEM

The changing global balance of power is a permanent source of discontent in Russia. Nostalgic for the times when their country was a "superpower," Russian leaders express dissatisfaction with the rules of the post–Cold War order. In a famous speech at the Munich security conference in February 2007, Vladimir Putin examined the dysfunction of the international system. While referring, first implicitly and then directly, to the United States (US), he denounced what he considered their "disdain for the basic principles of international law." He noted that there was "an uncontained hyper use of force—of military force—in international relations, force that [was] plunging the world into an abyss of permanent conflicts" and that hampered the search for comprehensive solutions, particularly in the Middle East. He also challenged the North Atlantic alliance (NATO)'s right to substitute itself for the United Nations (UN) in deciding on the use of force against sovereign states, calling for "serious reflection on the global security architecture," which would "proceed by searching for a reasonable balance between the interests of all participants in the international dialogue."[8] Since then, the Russian president has lost no opportunity to denounce what he perceives as the dangers of a unipolar world and the destabilizing role played by the US.

Generally speaking, the Russian ruling elite and strategic community have drawn a dark picture of their external security environment. They often assert, with regret, that instability is the new normal and that the world is caught up in a growing chaos because of Western military interventions and support for "regime change." In October 2017, during his speech at the annual meeting of the Valdai discussion club, Vladimir Putin reiterated this observation:

The world becomes less secure. Instead of progress and democracy, free rein is given to radical elements and extremist groups that reject civilization itself and seek to plunge it into the ancient past, into chaos and barbarism. . . . It is enough to see what has happened in the Middle East, which some players have tried to reshape and reformat to their liking and to impose on it a foreign development model through externally orchestrated coups or simply by force of arms.[9]

Equipped with this mindset, Russian leaders oppose "regime changes" and favor a realist approach to international affairs. They believe in balance of power and zero-sum relations between major powers. They also presume "the primacy of hard power, the centrality of the great powers, and the abiding importance of geopolitics."[10] Consistent with this set of preconceptions, they believe that history and geography entitle Russia, a permanent member of the UN Security Council and the largest country in the world, to a great power status and to a regional hegemonic role.

3.2.2 THE CHANGING NATURE OF WARFARE

Besides, high-ranking military officials declare that the very rules of war have significantly evolved as a result of the digital revolution and technological advances. The current chief of the general staff Valery Gerasimov, who is also first vice-minister of defense, famously described the changing nature of warfare in a long article titled "The Value of Science is in the Foresight" and published in the *Military-Industrial Courier* in early 2013, only a few months after his appointment.

In what soon became known as the "Gerasimov doctrine on non-linear warfare," he examined how combat operations should be carried out in adapting to the identified new forms of warfare. In doing so, he singled out at least three major changes. First, "long-distance, contactless actions against the enemy are becoming the main means of achieving combat and operational goals," and "the role of non-military means of achieving political and strategic goals has grown," exceeding "in many cases the power of force of weapons in their effectiveness." Second, "weapons based on new physical principles and automated systems are being actively incorporated into military activity." Third, the use of indirect operations and the role of special operation forces have dramatically increased.[11]

Interestingly enough, General Gerasimov postulates that the very distinction between the states of war and peace has been deliberately blurred, and that "wars are no longer declared." These comments echo a widespread view among the *siloviki*, as well as in prime-time television debates: Russia is already at war with "the West," because "the West" has already launched an undeclared "war of information" against it globally; the attacks are carried out through economic sanctions, diplomatic pressure, and "information weapons," aimed at bringing about regime change in Moscow or leading to the country's new dismemberment. High-rankings officials, such as Alexander Bastrykin, the head of the Investigative Committee and Vladimir Putin's university classmate, or Serguey Ivanov, former defense minister (2001–7) and chief of the presidential administration (2011–16), endorsed such views in the past.

This understanding of information age warfare has led them to expand the Russian art of war, developing new warfare techniques and an all-embracing approach. To quote Dima Adamsky, this *non-linear* warfare "combines hard and soft power across military, diplomatic, and economic domains" and "capitalizes on indirect action, informational operations, paramilitaries, and special operation forces backed by sophisticated military capabilities."[12] It revives the Soviet "tool box" intended to "prepare and shape the battlefield," such as *agit-prop, maskirovka*, clandestine operations, and radio-electronic combat.[13] Conceptually, it builds on Russian strategic culture and Soviet military thought. The fear of a surprise attack runs deep in Russian history from the devastating Mongol invasion of Rus' in the thirteenth century to the Nazi Germany invasion of the Soviet Union in June 1941, also including Napoleon's Russian campaign and the burning of Moscow in 1812. Because of the landlocked nature of the country, Russian and Soviet strategists have always been concerned about the risks of encirclement and a massive attack throughout the depth of the territory, especially its Western part.[14]

3.2.3 THE CHALLENGES TO RUSSIA'S INTERESTS

Finally, Russian leaders consistently see the US and NATO as deliberately spoiling Russia's interests in Europe. In his Munich speech, Vladimir Putin stated that it had "turned out that NATO [had] put its frontline forces on [Russian] borders," and strongly criticized the plan to extend the missile defense system in Europe—a contentious issue that raised the most distrust.[15] In fact, the 2007 Munich speech expressed the exasperation of the Russian leadership in the face of the enlargements of the European Union (EU) and NATO in Eastern Europe, and their growing cooperation with post-Soviet states.

By then, all the former members of the Warsaw Pact, dissolved in July 1991, had already joined the Atlantic Alliance. NATO had enlarged to include Poland, Hungary, and the Czech Republic in 1999 and the three Baltic States (Estonia, Latvia, and Lithuania), Romania, Bulgaria, Slovenia, and Slovakia in 2004. Indeed, in 2004, ten new states, among which three were part of the Soviet Union and five belonged to the Warsaw Pact, had become EU members. Furthermore, in the mid-2000s, NATO successfully established Individual Partnership Action Plans (IPAP) with countries that had belonged to the Soviet Union and, for some of them, to the Russian Empire before the Bolshevik revolution: Georgia in 2004, Azerbaijan and Armenia in 2005, Moldova in 2006. NATO also set up a "reinforced dialogue" with Ukraine in 2005 and intensified its relations with Georgia in 2006 at the request of these countries' leaders.

These rapprochements had become possible after protest movements had arisen in opposition to pro-Russian governments in Georgia in 2003 (the rose revolution), in Ukraine in 2004 (the orange revolution) and in Kyrgyzstan in 2005 (the tulip revolution), bringing about a regime change that, according to Moscow, emerged thanks to "external intervention and manipulation." At its

Bucharest summit in April 2008, NATO endorsed the principle of integration, stating: "NATO welcomes Ukraine's and Georgia's Euro-Atlantic aspirations for membership in NATO" and its members "agreed today that these countries will become members of NATO."[16] As a result of German and French opposition, NATO did not, however, grant Membership Action Plans (MAP) to Ukraine and Georgia on this occasion as US President George W Bush had wanted. Only two month later, in June 2008, the EU announced that a specific Eastern dimension would be added to the Neighborhood Policy. From the Russian establishment's perspective, all final red lines had been crossed. In August 2008, a five-day war broke out in Georgia following skirmishes. The Russian army launched a full-scale invasion into the secessionist enclave of South Ossetia. In September, Russia unilaterally recognized South Ossetia and Abkhazia, two secessionist Georgian provinces, as independent countries.

As the chairman of the Committee for Foreign and Defense policy Fyodor Lukianov put it, many Russian officials experienced a "feeling of helplessness in the face of the remodeling of Europe managed by the West according to its own criteria."[17] Affected by a loss of power that followed the collapse of the Soviet Union, a majority of Russian politicians across the political spectrum continue to regard their country as a besieged fortress under NATO and the EU pressure. As proof of ill intent, they often refer to the thesis developed by Zbigniew Brzezinski in the late 1990s. As President Jimmy Carter's National Security Advisor from 1977 to 1981, Brzezinski contributed to bringing the Detente to an end. The resumption of the arms race in the early 1980s, combined with the war in Afghanistan (1979–89) and the fall in the price of oil, stifled the already sluggish Soviet economy, precipitating the collapse of the Soviet Union. In the *Grand Chessboard*, Brzezinski argued in favor of maintaining American hegemony as guarantee of stability. He believed that the US should focus on isolating Russia from its "near abroad" and, in particular, from Ukraine. Indeed, he explained, deprived of Ukraine, Russia would lose its historical legitimacy, its status as an imperial power, and its ability to exert the same level of control over the Black Sea, the gateway to the Mediterranean. Russia would thus be confined to the status of regional power.[18]

3.3 **Russia's characterization of threats**

In sum, Russian leaders, experts, and pundits regularly contend that what they name indistinctively the "West" (*zapad*)—as if it was a homogenous whole—has maintained a fundamentally hostile position towards Russia since the end of the Cold War. They suggest that the US and its allies have purposely undermined Russia's influence, security, and status in Europe and in the post-Soviet space. They further assert that their political regime and Russia's territorial integrity are under attack and that, consequently, they have to be on the defensive. These claims and grievances are evident in all official doctrinal documents that are descriptive rather than prescriptive.

3.3.1 NATO MILITARY POWER

A new doctrinal document has been published almost yearly since the war in Ukraine erupted. In December 2014, Putin enacted a new military doctrine in replacement of the 2010 one. In December 2015, he ratified the new National Security Strategy,[19] intended to identify Russia's strategic interests and determine the domestic and foreign policy measures to ensure its long-term security and development. In November 2016, he promulgated a new Foreign Policy Concept of the Russian Federation. A month later, he adopted the doctrine of information security.[20] Apparently, the doctrines are elaborated at ministerial level in concertation with the Security Council, and think tanks can be consulted. They are later submitted for approval to the presidential administration.

All above-mentioned documents contend that Western countries are hostile towards Russia. The 2014 military doctrine establishes a list of dangers and threats that overwhelmingly focus on the US and NATO. It distinguishes between Russia's external military dangers (*vnešnie voennye opasnosti*) and threats (*ugrozy*), the latter entailing more immediate consequences. The increased activity of NATO forces and their new proximity to Russian borders tops the list. Then come the destabilization of regions and states; the deployment of anti-missile systems near Russian borders; "territorial claims" towards Russia and its allies; interference in internal affairs; ... the use of armed forces and the emergence of armed conflicts on the territories of states bordering Russia without a UN mandate (no. 12).[21] Although it paints a slightly different picture, the 2015 National Security Strategy reflects a comparable hostility towards NATO. It states that "NATO military build-up ... constitutes a threat (*ugroza*) to national security" (no. 15), and that it remains "unacceptable for Russia that NATO intensifies its activities, brings its military structures closer to the Russian borders ... and assigns global functions to itself, thus replacing the UN" (no. 106).

3.3.2 WESTERN SUBVERSIVE CAPABILITIES

Doctrinal documents also assert that Russia's opponents intend to erode social order and political stability in Russia through a process of manipulation and disinformation. The 2014 military doctrine lists "external military dangers" that include political threats: "the use of communication and information technologies for political and military purposes, in order to undermine states' sovereignty, political independence and the territorial integrity of states," and "the subversive activities carried out by other states' intelligence agencies" (no. 12). Similarly, the National Security Strategy blames the US for supporting "unconstitutional regime changes" and even accuses it of "extending a network of military-biological laboratories on the territory of Russia's neighbors" (no. 19). Reflecting this sentiment, Vladimir Putin publicly stated in October 2017 that "biological material [were] collected all over the country for different ethnic groups," suggesting that biological weapons were specifically being developed against Russian citizens.[22]

Finally, the National Security Strategy also enumerates "threats to the security of the state," noting (1) the activity of foreign intelligence services "impeding national interests"; (2) the activity of extremist and terrorist organizations; (3) the activity of social groups determined to undermine the country's unity and territorial integrity, to destabilize the political situation by taking inspiration from color revolutions and "to destroy Russia's traditional moral and spiritual values"; and (4) the use of information and communication technologies to spread "the ideology of fascism, extremism, terrorism, and separatism." Far from rebutting these assertions, President Putin claimed in interviews with American filmmaker Oliver Stone released in 2017 that there was evidence that the "US special services" had supported "terrorists" in Chechnya, without specifying if he was referring to the first (1994–96) or second (1999–2009) Chechen war.

In response to these perceived risks of breaking up the country or bringing down the regime, the 2015 National Security Strategy proposed to strengthen the role of the state, police, and special services, and advocates taking measures to immunize citizens and society against the "destructive influence of information coming from extremist and terrorist organizations,foreign secret services and propaganda agencies." External threats are, therefore, connected to "enemies within" and serve as a justification for hardening the political regime and stepping up surveillance of civil society groups.

3.3.3 BLIND SPOTS AND RISKS OF INSTABILITY

The hierarchy of threats amplifies some political and military challenges, while neglecting others. Not all security threats are concentrated in the Western part of Russia. The Russian territory stretches more than 10,000 km from east to west, representing almost 11 percent of the world's landmass, spanning eleven time zones, and two continents. It consists of 20,700 km of borders with fourteen countries including 6,846 km with Kazakhstan, 4,250 km with China and 19 km with North Korea. Meanwhile, global warming opens new waterways in the Arctic.

China's military expansion and new global status is seen as a source of concern in Moscow, although the topic appears neither in doctrinal documents nor in public statements.[23] Russia has enjoyed a good relationship with China since the restoration of their diplomatic relations in 1989, after thirty years of animosity. The two countries enhanced their comprehensive strategic partnership in 2012. They have strong common interests both regionally and globally, and deepen their defense cooperation by engaging in annual military exercises. Nevertheless, Russia wants to retain parity in conventional capabilities, so it keeps a conventional deterrent in addition to nuclear deterrence. For this purpose, the Far East military district is given priority in rearmament programs, receiving new weapons first.[24]

One growing concern has been the problems that hotbeds of instability in Afghanistan, Iraq, and Syria generate for Russia's partner countries in Central Asia and the Caucasus, as well as in the Muslim-majority "subjects of the Russian Federation" (constituent entities of Russia). At the height of the Ukrainian crisis, Russian media attributed the emergence of the Islamic State (ISIS) to the intrigues of Western intelligence agencies. This interpretation had two corollaries. Internationally, it led to Russia's military support of Bashar al-Assad's regime in Syria.[25] Domestically, it led to efforts to minimize the effects of ISIS ideology in Russia. Surveys, nonetheless, indicated that it had spread from the North Caucasus to the Moscow area, in large cities, in the Muslim-majority republics of the Volga and even in the Far East.[26]

Russian authorities became more aware of the potential consequences of the Syrian conflict in Russia, as they simultaneously witnessed both threatening rhetoric and a resurgence of terrorism. In September 2014, ISIS addressed a menacing message to Putin, announcing that the organization intended to "free Chechnya and the entire Caucasus." Most North Caucasian Islamist leaders had then already pledged allegiance to ISIS. By the early fall of 2015, just before the Russian military intervention in Syria, between 5,000 and 7,000 Russian-speaking combatants were believed to be among the ranks of various Islamist groups in Iraq and Syria. This included hundreds of Chechens, some of whom held leadership positions. Maintaining stability in the North Caucasus remains a constant source of concern.

3.4 Security and foreign policy objectives

There is a consensus regarding the founding premises: the assumptions that Russia's status has been purposely diminished and that the strategic environment poses a direct threat to both national interests and the regime's survival. Consequently, when formulating strategies, its leadership has prioritized security and the quest for recognition. Although defensive and reactive in nature, Russian strategies have embraced bold, proactive, and transformational agendas that have extended beyond military actions. Their two main objectives have consisted in regaining global status both diplomatically and economically, and asserting regional leadership through political means and the use of energy resources.

3.4.1 THE RETURN TO GLOBAL STATUS

Since Vladimir Putin's rise to power, an enduring objective has been to win back a central role in world affairs. Regional leadership is considered a necessary stepping stone to attaining global power. Although this ultimate aim has remained unchanged over the years, the intermediate goals that it entails have evolved significantly: the main focus has progressively shifted from economic projects to diplomatic and, more recently, military means.

In the 2000s, various outward-looking strategies, such as diplomatic activism and energy policy, were implemented to increase the country's global influence. Russia battled for years to become a member of the World Trade Organization, finally succeeding in August 2012. It invested massive amounts in energy and transport infrastructures, such as ports, pipelines, and hinterland connections, to boost its exports and improve its economic integration into the world economy.[27] Large Russian companies, both private and state-owned, successfully positioned themselves in key sectors, notably in the oil, gas, and precious metals markets. High oil prices favored the development of ambitious projects, and Russia's economic growth significantly increased between 1999 and 2013, with the exception being the aftermath of the 2008 financial crisis, which hit Russia's economy hard. Nonetheless, even then, Russian companies were able to diversify their trade relationships while ensuring substantial revenues to the Russian state.

In parallel, Russia consolidated its security and military partnerships within the framework of the Shanghai Cooperation Organization (SCO), founded with China and four Central Asian countries in 2001, and in the Collective Security Treaty Organization (CSTO), a military alliance created with six post-Soviet states in 2002. The Kremlin also committed to maximizing Russia's leverage at the UN as a veto power, and promoting multilateral diplomacy by establishing parallel multilateral institutions. The first BRIC summit (Brazil, Russia, India, China), for example, was held in Yekaterinburg, Ural, in June 2009.

This Russian effort to hasten the onset of a multipolar system was also a way of undermining the preeminence of the US in international relations. According to Angela Stent, "a major reason for the chronic difficulties [between Moscow and Washington] is that the way in which Russia was reborn after 1991 created inequalities between [them] that Russia found hard to accept and that Putin is determined to reverse."[28] Russian opposition to American power has significantly intensified since 2014. While harboring resentment towards, and often confronting, the US, the Kremlin also pursues an active foreign policy: engaging China and other East Asian countries, and intervening in the Middle East. Its aim is to weaken American military power and decouple the US from its allies.[29] Meanwhile, it champions conservative values and embraces an anti-liberal agenda, offering a counter-model that could help build good relations with conservative regimes that are opposed to liberal values and Western-style democracy and suspicious of civil society and Western media.

3.4.2 THE PRESERVATION OF REGIONAL LEADERSHIP

Another core Russian interest has been to assert regional dominance in Europe and the post-Soviet space, by halting what is seen as "NATO expansion" and offering an alternative model to the EU. The primary goal is to form a diplomatic and military buffer zone consisting of countries that would be favorable to Russia in the case of military confrontation. Dissatisfied with Europe's new borders, the Kremlin resolutely opposes the remapping of the post-Soviet space, and forcefully rejects countries with common borders and strong historic ties, like Ukraine and Georgia, joining NATO. In doing so, it advocates the delimitation of spheres of influence, challenging the very idea of the sovereign equality of states which serves as a foundation to the international system, tacitly adhering to the theory of "limited sovereignty" proposed by Leonid Brezhnev after the Soviet invasion of Czechoslovakia in 1968 that presumes that an ally regime cannot embrace a different model of government.

After the war with Georgia, Russia increased its military pressure. Its intent was to heighten its security and deterrence. In response, the EU intensified negotiations on an Eastern Partnership. Promoted at the initiative of then Polish Foreign Minister Radosław Sikorski to revitalize its floundering neighborhood policy, the Eastern Partnership program was inaugurated in Prague in May 2009. It involved six former Soviet states: Armenia, Azerbaijan, and Georgia, in the Caucasus, and Belarus, Moldova, and Ukraine, in Eastern Europe. The EU relied on two levers of influence: the conditionality of aid and the socialization of political actors. It allowed the gradual opening of the European markets to these six countries, provided that they sign an "Association Agreement" and adopt European standards.

That same year, the EU decided to open up its gas and electricity markets and increase cross-border trade. The EU Third Energy Package entered into force in September 2009, legally separating transport, storage, and sale operations. This law impeded the prior policies that had facilitated Gazprom, the largest Russian gas company, securing a major position in Europe's markets thanks to long-term contracts. Since Gazprom then contributed 20 percent of federal budget revenue, Moscow reacted negatively to these two EU initiatives, perceived as a deliberate attempt to harm Russia's economic and geopolitical interests. Russian suspicion was sharpened by the fact that Sikorski led the New Atlantic Initiative in Washington from 2002 to 2005, a think tank with American neoconservative links.

The Kremlin subsequently announced its intention to accelerate the creation of two regional organizations designed to replace the EU proposals. The Customs Union between Russia, Kazakhstan, and Belarus entered into force in July 2010. The three capitals also signed an agreement founding the Eurasian Economic Union (EEU) in December 2010. Despite these ambitious projects, Russia nonetheless continued to lose momentum in its "near-abroad." On the one hand, the Russian projects were met with caution by post-Soviet regimes willing to preserve their sovereignty and limit Russian interference in their domestic affairs. On the other, competition intensified not only in Eastern Europe, but also in Central Asia.[30] In September 2013, Chinese President Xi Jinping launched in Kazakhstan the Belt and Road initiative, which consists of building new infrastructure along the ancient silk roads in Central Asia, while the EU was finalizing talks on Association Agreements.

The Kremlin used all its influence to deter the post-Soviet countries from signing this agreement with the EU. Armenia withdrew in September 2013 while Georgia and Moldova, two countries locked in frozen conflicts with Russia, resisted. Ukraine, the "cradle of Rus'," wavered. Without Ukraine's membership, a country of 45 million, the EEU lost its legitimacy. On November 9, 2013, Putin secretly met with his Ukrainian counterpart Yanukovych at the Vnukovo military airport near Moscow. He promised to grant Ukraine preferential tariffs for oil and gas for an annual budget of $12 billion if Yanukovych agreed to join the EEU.[31] The latter delayed for ten days before announcing that he abandoned the agreement with the EU. His decision and subsequent police abuse triggered a protest movement in Kiev that caused his government's fall in February 2014.

Given the cultural and historical proximity of the two countries, the outcome of the Maidan protest in Kiev could not but have a political resonance in Russia. Russia's annexation of Crimea in March 2014 allowed it to divert attention and resume control of the situation. Although the annexation was justified by irredentist and historical motives, strategic and political purposes are believed to have played a predominant role. Putin's aim was to signal deterrence to any further incursion in its sphere of influence. As a secret brief written in early February 2014 and leaked a year later suggests,[32] the Russian president and a few aids had planned to seize Crimea before Yanukovich lost power. They were apparently convinced that a regime change in Ukraine would eventually encourage NATO to deploy military bases in the peninsula and that the Russian army would lose access to its Sebastopol facilities.[33]

3.4.3 THE PERSISTENCE OF POWER IMBALANCES

In the 2000s, the high oil price environment was favorable to the development of ambitious projects and to Russia's economic growth, which significantly increased between 1999 and 2013, except in the year following the 2008 financial crisis. Russian companies were able to diversify their trade relationships while ensuring substantial revenues to the Russian State. In contrast, the deterioration of relations between Russia and Western countries that followed the war in Ukraine jeopardized Russian economic strategy. Russia was excluded from the G8, faced sanctions imposed by the EU and the US, while oil prices were sharply dropping. After a period of financial instability in 2014, the Russian economy nonetheless recovered. Inflation was contained, falling from 15 percent in 2015 to 7 percent in 2016 and 4.2 percent in 2018. Similarly, after a 2.8 percent GDP decline and sharp recession in 2015, economic growth experienced a small (0.2 percent) decline before returning to modest growth (1.5 percent) in 2017 and reaching 2.3 percent in 2018.

Economic indicators highlight the substantial power gaps between Russia and what it regards as its geostrategic competitors. According to World Bank estimates, Russia is ranked twelfth in GDP in 2016, the US and China ranking first and second. Its GDP amounted to about one-fifteenth of the US's and half of France's; its economy was of the same size as Spain's and slightly smaller than South Korea's. Its GDP fell from US$2.231 billion in 2013 to US$1.283 billion in 2016. Russia performs no better according to other indicators. Russian GDP per capita remains low and decreasing; it fell from US$9.329 in 2015 to US$8.769 in 2016. That is higher than in China's, but one-seventh that of the US.[34] In the twenty-first century, power relies on the capacity to generate innovation and attract investors. In 2016, Russia was the sixteenth largest export economy in the world and the thirty-seventh most complex economy according to the Economic Complexity Index which measures the knowledge accumulated and expressed in industrial composition.[35] The same year, flows of foreign direct investments (FDI) to the US reached an estimated US$385 billion; mainland China received US$139 billion in this time. In contrast, FDI flows to Russia amounted to US$19 billion in 2016, up from US$12 billion in 2015 largely due to the privatization and sale of state-owned assets (a 19.5 percent stake in the oil company Rosneft was sold to generate cash flow).[36]

Russia remains a rentier state with an economy based on resource extraction even if it is the second largest exporter of major weapons after the US. In the early 2010s, revenues from the oil and gas sector represented close to 50 percent of the federal budget revenues. By 2016, crude and refined petroleum still accounted for 42 percent of its exports (US$119 billion out of US$282 billion),[37] representing 36 percent of the overall federal budget revenues. The Kremlin has attempted to reorient its interests in Asia. Founded on "an axis of convenience" approach in the 2000s,[38] the Sino-Russian relationship took on a new dimension after 2014. Moscow made concessions to Beijing, selling an S-400 missile defense system.[39] Nonetheless, Chinese banks remain reluctant to invest in Russia. Many Russian economists express concerns about the lack of economic options and the absence of an economic strategy. Sanctions on cutting-edge technologies prevent Russia's oil and gas companies from expanding their activities on the shale gas and oil market. Furthermore, the development of an innovative economy is hampered by the lack of judicial independence and the outflow of qualified scientists and young entrepreneurs. Human capital flight is resurging because the prospects for political reform and economic prosperity appear limited.

In a nutshell, evidence regarding the size and the structure of its economy suggests that Russia is a middle power. Yet the country enjoys the military attributes of a great power. It therefore remains a major power only because of its status at the UN Security Council and its advanced nuclear and conventional capabilities. The disparity between the ranking of Russia's economy and the ranking of its military may well explain its strong investment in hard power. In 2016, military expenditures represented 5.4 percent of its GDP and amounted to $66.4 billion, which was only about 10 percent of the amount spent by the US.[40]

3.5 Ways and means

In sum, the annexation of Crimea coincided with the difficulties the Kremlin was experiencing in preserving what is perceived as Russia's strategic and economic interests, and in convincing post-Soviet states to be part of its geopolitical projects. In that regard, the annexation not only revealed a renewed confidence in military instruments and a radicalization of the regime, it was also the sign of great insecurity. By failing to maintain the status quo or to achieve its desired results in its environment, Russia became a revisionist power.

Indeed, arguably, the failure (or incomplete success) of economic and diplomatic initiatives, and persistent power imbalances, have engendered the growing militarization of Russian foreign and security policy. Thus, the Russian case confirms the main tenets of defensive neorealist theory: first, that states are primarily concerned with ensuring security and maintaining their position in the international system rather than with maximizing power;[41] second, that state aggression often derives from elite false perceptions about the intentions of other states.

Russia's leadership assumes that a show of force and the use of political influence are necessary tools to both restore its power and status and to protect the regime. They have developed an unspoken threefold strategy, based on limited military intervention, on deterrence and strategic intimidation, and on influence and political destabilization. Since 2014, they have increasingly resorted to military threats and political subversion, although other dimensions of power, such as economic incentives, energy policy, and diplomatic ambitions, continue to be of importance. Overall, there has been no change in approach, but an expansion of both offensive means and subversive capabilities.

3.5.1 MILITARY INTERVENTION AND HYBRID WARFARE

The war in Georgia revealed serious capability flaws, triggering large-scale military reforms. A full-range military buildup was instituted in order to modernize the Russian army and reinforce its conventional capabilities. It was composed of several components: a reorganization of the armed forces on the Russian territory and at the command level; changes in recruitment patterns, with the creation of professional contract-based service; the reinforcement of special forces units and the creation of private military companies; the multiplication of snap military exercises focusing on high-intensity conventional operations; and, notably, a large-scale and well-endowed rearmament program.

Russia's military has gained in efficiency. This is evident in its demonstrated tactical, logistic, and technical performances in external theaters, as well as its ability to use proxies and to link several fields of operation. Russia's greatest strength probably rests on its unabashed willingness to use force and coercion. The use of force is considered as an effective and legitimate means to achieve political ends and diplomatic goals. Military interventions are used as a tool for obtaining diplomatic concessions, empowering regional players, and transforming the international order. This offensive stance has allowed Russia to surprise opponents and gain some strategic victories.

Globally, the Kremlin wants to modify the balance of power at the expense of the US. It seeks to limit the opportunities of the American army on many theaters by exporting S-300 and S-400 air defense systems, to China, Iran, or Turkey. It also creates situations in which the country seems to be settling world affairs. As Russian academic Timofei Bordachev explains, the purpose of the Russian military involvement in Syria is not limited to attaining Russia's return as a global power; it aims to break up the post–Cold War order, so the rules of the game are no longer solely defined by the US. As a result, Russia and "non-Western actors," such as China, have now the responsibility, so goes the argument, to limit "Western excesses" and promote their own agendas in order to guarantee a more stable world.[42]

Regionally, Russia is engaged in a series of hostile and subversive actions to destabilize targets, both militarily and politically. The methods of hybrid warfare employed usually attempt to foster nationalism and fuel secessionism in bordering countries. Then, after a conflict has broken out, Russia claims to defend the interests of one minority and deploys troops on the ground. Meanwhile, Russia develops disinformation operations entailing a set of irregular methods that have become more sophisticated and coordinated over time.[43] But these activities draw on a traditional Russian art of war strategy originating in the 1930s, based on dissimulation and subversion, and on Soviet operational doctrine emphasizing "deep operations." The aim is to disorganize and destroy enemy forces not only at the line of contact, but "throughout the depth" of the theater. For the assailant, hybrid warfare has the advantage of inflicting significant damage at a low cost: it generates little risk and requires few means, whereas its effects are difficult to preempt.

3.5.2 STRATEGIC DETERRENCE AND INTIMIDATION

Furthermore, consistent efforts have been made to enable power projection and alter the power balance in areas considered of strategic importance: the Arctic, the Baltic Sea, Eastern Europe, the Black Sea, the Eastern Mediterranean, the Middle East and the North Atlantic. The Russian military has buttressed its denial capabilities by developing a combined approach on land, in the air, and at sea. Its objective is twofold: to deny opponents either access to or full control over entire zones, and to maintain escalation dominance at every level of conventional and nuclear conflict.

Accordingly, it uses anti-missile defense systems to establish large exclusion zones, commonly called anti-access/area-denial (A2AD) bubbles, over both its own territory, and possible theaters in Eastern Europe, the Middle East, and East Asia.[44] Cutting-edge S-400 anti-aircraft systems were deployed to various venues in Russia's Arctic region in 2015, to Syria in November 2015, Kaliningrad in early 2016, Crimea in August 2016, and near Vladivostok in 2017. These air defense bubbles hinder the US and NATO air forces, by preventing them from first entering an operational theater, and from accessing areas considered vital to Russian security. In addition, the Russian army seeks to reinforce both direct and indirect territorial control. It strengthens its military strongholds in Crimea and Kaliningrad, as well as the Latakia and Tartus facilities in Syria. It has urged its Belarussian ally to authorize the creation of a Russian airbase in Belarus, to date unsuccessfully. An ambitious maritime strategy is being implemented encompassing the Atlantic, the Pacific, and the Arctic Oceans, as well as the Mediterranean and the Black Seas. Naval forces have grown in both quantity and quality. Common to the Soviet era, submarines and long-range bombers are regularly deployed in the North Atlantic in order to be able to secure or cut sea lines.

Finally, Russia resorts to nuclear intimidation through a combination of rhetoric and actions. When tensions reached a new threshold during the

Ukrainian crisis, Russian political and military leaders, as well as high-profile Russian pundits, repeatedly referred to Russia's nuclear capacity and hinted at the possibility of nuclear conflict. In addition to these threatening statements, the Russian army has adopted a deliberately ambiguous attitude. It tests Russia's opponents by regularly sending nuclear bombers and submarines near the airspace and territorial waters of NATO or neutral countries, forcing them to remain on alert. Simultaneously, it increases its conventional deterrence capacity by deploying such armaments, as Kalibr multi-role missiles armed with precision-guided munitions that can be fired from submarines or surface ships or Iskander new-generation ballistic missiles that can be equipped with nuclear warheads.

As of 2016, Russia possesses the biggest nuclear arsenal in the world.[45] In 1993, it abandoned its "no-first-use" commitment. Subsequently, nuclear deterrence served to compensate for capacity gaps and conventional inferiority vis-à-vis other nuclear powers. Some Russian experts suggested in the late 1990s the possibility of "limited" nuclear strikes, whether to deter further escalation or to de-escalate and terminate a conventional conflict. Declassified documents identify neither this option nor the possible targets of a nuclear attack. The military doctrines of 2010 and 2014 only specify that Russia reserves the right to use nuclear weapons if it is subjected to nuclear strikes itself, or if a conventional conflict evolves in such a way that it puts at stake the "very existence of the state."[46] There seems to be, in fact, two strategies of nuclear deterrence: one refers to classical global nuclear deterrence; a second, aimed at preventing large-scale conventional wars, is known as regional nuclear deterrence (RND).[47] This does not mean that Russia has a "doctrine of escalate-to-de-escalate," as is often assumed in strategic literature despite weak evidence.[48]

3.5.3 COMPREHENSIVE INFLUENCE AND POLITICAL DESTABILIZATION

In parallel with this military assertiveness, Russia has put a comprehensive influence strategy in place. Its scope and sophistication have been constantly expanded to cover new functions. Russian leaders endorsed Joseph Nye's concept of *soft power* over a decade ago. Initially, Moscow regarded soft power as a new attribute of power and an instrument for developing public diplomacy. Its purpose was to restore Russia's damaged image among Western decision-makers and the general public. It was also a means to attain or maintain Russia's "great power" status. Now, information operations are considered not only as an instrument to gain the upper hands in the "global rivalry" between antagonistic systems of civilization, but are also supposed to engage in undeclared warfare in the same "information space."

The Kremlin has thus developed media outlets to spread its views to international audiences. Russia Today, better known as RT, is a government sponsored television channel created in 2005. It broadcasts in four languages: English, Arabic, Spanish, and French, and reaches vast audiences in the US and the Middle East, even if figures are contested.[49] Seen alternatively as a propaganda machine or an instrument for promoting Russian foreign policy, RT pointedly explains Russia's official viewpoint on major international issues and makes "available to the public information concealed by mainstream media," occasionally relaying on conspiracy theories.[50] In December 2013, in the midst of the Maidan mobilization in Kiev, the Russian authorities created a new official communication body bearing the same name in Russian as the RT television channel: *Rossiâ Segodnâ* (Russia Today). This media brings together the radio "Voice of Russia" and the news agency Ria Novosti, renamed "Sputnik" in autumn 2014. It is presented as an online newspaper available in more than thirty languages, including those from almost all post-Soviet countries and secessionist territories. This outlet's global reach is far from negligible, notably in Arab countries.[51]

Finally, a large array of tactics, such as political subversion and infiltration, trolling, fake news and cyber-attacks, and weaponization of elections, has increasingly been used against the US and EU countries to blur perceptions, exploit democratic disarray, and test both the solidity of alliances and the solidarity between allies. Originally developed in post-Soviet countries, these techniques have been successfully applied in Western countries in the 2010s. Russian special services allegedly finance far-right (and probably far-left) Eurosceptic political parties everywhere in Europe.[52] However, the full range of their subversion capabilities was probably best illustrated by their interference in the 2016 American presidential election.

3.6 Conclusion

Russia has consistently employed what the authors of the introductory chapter to this volume labeled a classicist grand strategy. Its focus and resource capability are mostly defined in military terms. And its leadership demonstrates, in a classical realist sense, both "skill and will" when it comes to the formulation and implementation of its grand strategy.[53] Indeed, the sum of capability and resolve is high. There has been a rearming and modernizing of the armed forces, a willingness to use military force and extend projection capabilities, and the extensive use of strategic intimidation, both conventional and nuclear. Russian leaders have cherished ambitions of grandeur and seem nostalgic for the "superpower" status and world influence that Moscow once enjoyed. Challenged on different fronts, they increasingly resort to military means to impose their views internationally, while using military rhetoric and victories to conceal their economic shortcomings domestically.

The confrontational strategy to heighten Russia's security began in Munich in 2007 and culminated with the annexation of Crimea in 2014. It has brought significant political and diplomatic dividends globally since the Russian intervention in Syria. These actions, however, come at a price. The militarization of Russia's foreign policy may prove unsustainable in the long run because it hampers economic growth and prevents the transformation of its economy. At a regional level, it also undermines the country's security and alienates former partners in the "near abroad." In that respect, Russia's situation reflects the security dilemma as articulated by Robert Jervis.[54] To avert perceived threats and to shore up its declining status, Russia increased and deployed its military power, which was in return perceived as a threat both regionally and globally. It thus contributed to increasing the level of insecurity and undermining its own security. In fact, the Ukrainian crisis raises concerns even among Russia's allies, such as Belarus and Kazakhstan, slowing down Russian projects of regional and military integration. Ukraine moved closer to the EU and NATO in 2017. NATO, for its part, has already strengthened its defense and deterrence, and enhanced its forward presence in Eastern Europe, which was exactly what Moscow wanted to avoid in the first place.

NOTES

1. Lawrence T. Caldwell, "Russian Concept of National Security," in *Russian Foreign Policy in the Twenty-First Century and the Shadow of the Past*, ed. Robert Levgold (New York: Columbia University Press, 2007), 279–343.
2. Barry Posen, *Restraint* (Ithaca, NY: Cornell University Press, 2014), 1.
3. Françoise Daucé, *Être opposant dans la Russie de Vladimir Poutine* (Paris: Le Bord de l'eau, 2016); Vladimir Gelman, *Authoritarian Russia: Analyzing Post-Soviet Regime Changes* (Pittsburgh, PA: Pittsburg University Press, 2015).
4. Gleb Pavlovsky, "Russian Politics Under Putin: The System Will Outlast the Master," *Foreign Affairs* 95, no. 3 (May–June 2016): 12.
5. Fiona Hill and Clifford G. Gaddy, *Mr. Putin: Operative in the Kremlin* (Washington, DC: Brookings Institution Press, 2013).
6. Mark Galeotti, "Putin's Hydra: Inside Russia's Intelligence Services," *European Council on Foreign Relations*, no. 169 (May 2016).
7. Nikolai Petrov and Kirill Rogov, "Ispolnitel'naâ vlast' i silovye korporacii" [The executive power and the corporations of force], in *Političeskoe razvitie Rossii. 2014–2016: Instituty i praktiki avtoritarnoj konsolidacii* [Russia's Political Development. 2014–2016: Institutions and Practices of authoritarian consolidation], eds. A. V. Kynev, A. G. Kačkaeva, and È. L. Paneâh (Moscow: Fond Liberal'naâ Missiâ, 2016), 133–53; Nikolai Petrov, "Postroenie silovikov," *Vedomosti* (July 25, 2016).

8. Vladimir Putin, "Munich speech of Vladimir Putin" [in Russian] (speech, Munich Security Conference, Munich, February 10, 2007), http://archive.kremlin.ru/eng/speeches/2007/02/10/0138_type82912type82914type82917type84779_118123.shtml
9. Vladimir Putin, "Final plenary session: The World of the Future: Moving Through Conflict to Cooperation" [in Russian] (speech, 14th Annual Meeting of the Valdai International Discussion Club, Sochi, October 19, 2017), http://en.kremlin.ru/events/president/news/55882
10. Bobo Lo, *Russia and the New World Disorder* (London: Chatham House, 2015), 40.
11. Valery Guerasimov, "Cennost' nauki v predvidenii" [The Value of Science is in the Foresight], *Voenno-promyšlennyj kur'er (VPK)* 476, no. 8 (February 27–March 5, 2013); Mark Galeotti, "The 'Gerasimov Doctrine' and Russian Non-Linear War," *In Moscow's Shadows. Analysis and Assessment of Russian Crime and Security* (blog), July 6, 2014, https://inmoscowsshadows.wordpress.com/2014/07/06/the-gerasimov-doctrine-and-russian-non-linear-war/
12. Dmitry Adamsky, "Putin's Syria Strategy: Russian Airstrikes and What Comes Next," *Foreign Affairs*, October 1, 2015, https://www.foreignaffairs.com/articles/syria/2015-10-01/putins-syria-strategy
13. Diego A. Ruiz Palmer, "Back to Future? Russia's Hybrid Warfare, Revolutions in Military Affairs, and Cold War Comparisons," in *NATO's Response to Hybrid Threats*, eds. Guillaume Lasconjarias and Jeffrey A. Larsen, NDC Forum Paper 24 (Rome: NATO Defense College, December 17, 2015): 65.
14. Jean-Christophe Romer, *La pensée stratégique russe au XXe siècle* [Russian strategic thinking in the Twentieth Century] (Paris: Economica, 1997), 8–9.
15. Robert H. Donaldson, Joseph L. Nogee, and Vidya Nadkarni, *The Foreign Policy of Russia: Changing Systems, Enduring Interests*, 5th ed. (New York: M. E. Sharpe, 2014), 391.
16. North Atlantic Treaty Organization, "Bucharest Summit Declaration" press release no. (2008) 049, April 3, 2008, no. 23, https://www.nato.int/cps/us/natohq/official_texts_8443.htm
17. Fiodor Loukianov, "La Russie, une puissance révisionniste?," *Politique étrangère*, no. 2 (Summer 2015): 18.
18. Zbigniew Brzezinski, *The Grand Chessboard: American Primacy and Its Geostrategic Imperatives*, 1st ed. (New York: Basic Books, 1997).
19. Vladimir Putin, *National Security Strategy* [in Russian] (Moscow: the Kremlin, 2015), http://rg.ru/2015/12/31/nac-bezopasnost-site-dok.html
20. Vladimir Putin, *Doctrine of Information Security* [in Russian] (Moscow: the Kremlin, 2016), http://www.mid.ru/en/foreign_policy/official_documents/-/asset_publisher/CptICkB6BZ29/content/id/2563163
21. Vladimir Putin, *The Military Doctrine of the Russian Federation* [in Russian] (Moscow: the Kremlin, 2014), rg.ru/2014/12/30/doktrina-dok.html; Polina Sinovets and Bettina Renz, "Russia's 2014 Military Doctrine and Beyond: Threat Perceptions, Capabilities, and Ambitions," *NATO Defense College Research*, Paper no. 117 (July 10, 2015).
22. "Putin: Nekie sily sobiraût bilogičeskij material rossiân" [Putin: Some forces collect the biological material of the Russian citizens], *Novaâ Gazeta*, October 30, 2017.

23. See Jeffrey Mankoff, *Russian Foreign Policy. The Return of Great Power Politics* (Lanham, MD: Rowman & Littlefield Publishers, 2012), 177, 180–1.
24. Interviews with two Russian experts on Sino-Russian relations and Chinese armaments, Moscow, January 2018.
25. Alexey Malashenko, "Divisions and Defiance Among Russia's Muslims," *Carnegie Moscow Center*, November 20, 2015.
26. Opinion polls indicated that in late 2015 half a million Muslims in Russia had sympathies for ISIS, whereas there were "thousands of Salafist cells belonging to the radical Hizb ut-Tahrir movement" (an Islamist organization born of a split with the Muslim Brotherhood) across the country. To give a point of comparison, Russia has a total population of 143 million inhabitants, among which 16.5 million are believed to be of Muslim faith or tradition. There are also an estimated 4 million Muslim immigrants from Central Asia and Azerbaijan living in Russia.
27. Jean Radvanyj, "Adapter les réseaux de transport eurasien: réussites et défis," *Revue de Défense nationale*, no. 802 (Summer 2017): 84–9.
28. Angela E. Stent, *The Limits of Partnership. US-Russian Relations in the Twenty-First Century* (Princeton, NJ: Princeton University Press, 2014), 255.
29. Natasha Kuhrt, "Russia and Asia Pacific: Diversification or Sinocentrism?," in *Russia's Foreign Policy. Ideas, Domestic Politics and External Relations*, eds. David Cadier and Margot Light (London: Palgrave Macmillan, 2015) 175–88.
30. Vladimir Fedorenko, "The New Silk Road Initiatives in Central Asia," *Rethink Paper*, no. 10 (August 2013).
31. See "Summit of failure: How the EU lost Ukraine," *Der Spiegel*, November 24, 2014.
32. "It seems right to initiate the incorporation of the Eastern regions of Ukraine into Russia." Publication of the plan established by Russia to seize a number of Ukrainian territories when Yanukovich was still in office, *Novaya Gazeta* [in Russian], February 24, 2015, http://www.novayagazeta.ru/politics/67389.html
33. Alexander Lukin, "What the Kremlin Is Thinking: Putin's Vision for Eurasia," *Foreign Affairs* 93, no. 4 (July–August 2014).
34. World Development Indicators collected by the World Bank.
35. "Russia," *The Observatory of Economic Complexity (OEC)*, MIT, accessed August 20, 2018, https://atlas.media.mit.edu/en/profile/country/rus/
36. "Global Investment Trends Monitor," *United Nations Conference on Trade and Development (UNCTAD)*, no. 25 (February 1, 2017), http://unctad.org/en/PublicationsLibrary/webdiaeia2017d1_en.pdf
37. "Russia," OEC.
38. Bobo Lo, *Axis of Convenience: Moscow, Beijing and the New Geopolitics* (London: Chatham House, 2008).
39. Céline Marangé, "Russia's Rapprochement with China: Does Strategy Triumph over Tactics?," Notes de Recherche Stratégiqueno, no. 19 (Paris: Institute for Strategic Research, 2015); Céline Marangé, "Poids et perception de la Russie en Asie du Nord-est," in Anne de Tinguy (ed), La Russie dans le monde, Paris, CNRS éditions, 2019, 193–221.
40. "Military expenditure by country as percentage of gross domestic product, 2003–2016," in "SIPRI Yearbook 2017: Armaments, Disarmament and International Security," *Stockholm International Peace Research Institute*, 2017.

41. Kenneth N. Waltz, *Theory of International Politics* (New York: McGraw Hill, 1979).
42. Timofej Bordachev, "Dlâ sebâ i dlâ mira" [For Ourselves and For the World], *Izvestiâ*, September 29, 2017.
43. Andras Racz, *Russia's Hybrid War in Ukraine. Breaking the Enemy Ability to Resist* (Helsinki: The Finnish Institute of International Affairs, June 2015).
44. Stephan Frühling, Guillaume Lasconjarias, "NATO, A2/AD and the Kaliningrad Challenge," *Survival. Global Politics and Strategy* 58, no. 2 (March 2016): 95–116; Kathleen Weinberger, "Russian Anti-Access and Area Denial (A2AD) Range," *Institute for the Study of War*, August 29, 2016, http://www.understandingwar.org/backgrounder/russian-anti-access-and-area-denial-a2ad-range
45. "SIPRI Yearbook 2016: Armaments, Disarmament and International Security," *Stockholm International Peace Research Institute*, 2016, https://www.sipri.org/yearbook/summaries
46. Céline Marangé, "Le nucléaire russe: un instrument de dissuasion et d'intimidation," *Revue de Défense nationale*, no. 802 (Summer 2017): 50–7.
47. Dmitry Adamsky, *Cross-Domain Coercion: The Current Russian Art of Strategy*, Proliferation Papers, no. 54 (Paris: Institut Français des Relations Internationales, November 2015), 13–14.
48. Bruno Tertrais, "Russia's Nuclear Weapons: Worrying for the Wrong Reasons," *Survival: Global Politics and Strategy* 50, no. 2 (April–May 2018): 33–44.
49. Katie Zavadski, "Putin's propaganda TV lies about its popularity," *The Daily Beast*, September 17, 2015.
50. Ilya Yablokov, "Conspiracy Theories as a Russian Public Diplomacy Tool: The Case of Russia Today (RT)," *Politics* 35, no. 3–4 (2015): 301–15.
51. Antonio Missiroli, Jan Joel Andersson, Florence Gaub, Nicu Popescu, John-Joseph Wilkins et al., *Strategic Communications: East and South*, no. 30 (Paris: European Union Institute for Security Studies, July 29, 2016), 9–10.
52. Anton Shekhovtsov, "The Kremlin's marriage of convenience with the European far right," openDemocracy, April 28, 2014, https://www.opendemocracy.net/od-russia/anton-shekhovtsov/kremlin%E2%80%99s-marriage-of-convenience-with-european-far-right; A. Shekhovtsov, *Russia and the Western Far Right: Tango Noir* (London: Routledge, 2018).
53. Hans Morgenthau, *Politics Among Nations: The Struggle for Power and Peace* (New York: Knopf, 1973).
54. Robert Jervis, "Cooperation under the Security Dilemma," *World Politics* 30, no. 2 (January 1978): 167–74; Robert Jervis, *Perception and Misperception in International Politics* (Princeton, NJ: Princeton University Press, 1978), 58–113.

4 China

ANDREW S. ERICKSON

The very concept of a Chinese grand strategy (大战略) remains surprisingly controversial, with extreme interpretations ranging in recent years from ad-hoc opportunism to century-long plans.[1] The truth is more complex than either extreme, but to the extent that any grand power today has a grand strategy today, China most certainly does.[2] Under the ambitious reign of Xi Jinping, the Chinese Communist Party (CCP)'s goal of achieving a twenty-first century version of the glory and successes of Qing dynasty China at its eighteenth century height at home and abroad has been packaged rhetorically as the "China Dream" of "national rejuvenation."[3] This quest to make China great again represents an all-encompassing thirty-five-year plan that is the most forthright and ambitious of any major power. The potential specifics, shaped in part by emerging opportunities, may be gleaned deductively from leadership and policy statements and inductively from capabilities and actions. Despite relative strategic clarity, however, gathering challenges suggest that there is no guarantee of ever-rapid outward expansion of China's geostrategic accomplishments to include Xi's most ambitious, distant targets. Indeed, both China's history and current context suggest that its leaders pursue a hierarchy of priorities akin to a Maslow's Hierarchy of Needs for a "re-rising" great power. Given favorable conditions allowing achievements closer to home, CCP leaders will pursue further progress in ever-distant geographic layers and strategic domains; but if they encounter significant difficulties they will likely retrench to protect "core" interests—most importantly, political continuity. A consequential leader, Xi is pursuing objectives towards the top of the "band" (range of possibilities, in ascending level of ambitiousness) in strength and speed that might be expected of a paramount CCP leader of his generation. But even he cannot ensure their realization and would almost certainly fall back on such top priorities as preserving the continuity of CCP rule if circumstances rendered broader ambitions unrealistic. To elucidate these critical dynamics and their implications for China's grand strategy, its development over time, its prospects for further evolution, and the implications, this chapter (1) survey's Xi's grand strategy, (2) discusses its historical continuities, (3) lists the modern factors that shape and complicate it, and then focuses on how it is operationalized (4) internationally through the Belt and Road Initiative (BRI) to bind Eurasia to China through infrastructure and commercial development, and (5) domestically by undergirding societal stability with a stronger surveillance state, the last as part of initiatives designed to mitigate the impact of demographic decline and an S-curved slowdown in the growth of China's economy and other elements of national power.

4.1 Xi's grand strategy for China

While some scholars still contest the very notion of a Chinese grand strategy, recent leadership and policy statements and their explicit linkage to historical patterns suggest that China may well have the most forthright grand strategy of any major power today. To the extent that any nation may be said to have a grand strategy, China certainly has one.

China's paramount leader, Xi Jinping, has a great decisional power and his vision matters greatly. A consequential leader, he has consolidated his power and clearly eclipsed his immediate predecessors Hu Jintao and Jiang Zemin in a way that might well have eluded alternative contenders. The recent overturning of the ten-year term limits on China's presidency instituted by its last leader of similar consequence—the more unassuming, domestically focused Deng Xiaoping, who reversed Maoist excesses and launched pragmatic reforms—gives Xi both a potentially long time horizon to implement his grand strategy and a staggering degree of ownership for its success or failure. Xi portrays his leadership as crucial for now, and his eighty-million-member party's leadership as crucial out to any foreseeable time horizon. Chinese grand strategy overall under Xi is not secret. His goal is to make China empowered and respected again, at home and abroad. To facilitate the internal and external implementation of his strategy, Xi is overseeing sweeping bureaucratic, Party, and military reforms.

Xi Jinping's speech at the 19th CCP National Congress on October 18, 2017 spans sixty-five dense pages in the official English translation, but is readily summarized.[4] A commentary in China's state media offered a pithy encapsulation of Xi's speech: "The Chinese nation...has stood up, grown rich, and become strong. It will move toward center stage and make greater contributions for mankind."[5] By this logic, China's success proves that its form of Leninist authoritarianism works: "It is time to understand China's path, because it appears it will continue to triumph."[6] In the new era, Xi emphasizes, China is embarked on a domestically popular, historically redolent mission to realize the dream of national rejuvenation championed by all would-be Chinese leaders since imperial disintegration in the early twentieth century following a "Century of Humiliation" at the hands of foreign powers.[7] Elaboration on these points is offered below.

4.2 Two centenary goals

To an extent that is rare for durable public documents, the Chinese grand strategy revealed by Xi has very precise time horizons. These correspond to specific anniversaries. By 2021 (the centenary of the CCP's establishment), the goal is to "Finish building a moderately prosperous society in all respects." Between its 19th and 20th National Congresses, China is envisioned to shift its focus from the first to the second centenary goal. By 2049 (the centenary of the founding of the People's Republic), China's state media explains, the aim is to "Build China into a modern socialist country that is prosperous, strong, democratic, culturally advanced, and harmonious."[8]

During the first half of the next several decades (2020–35), Beijing is to focus on increasing China's economic and technological strength significantly and "become a global leader in innovation." Soft power should be greatly increased, and China's laws, environment, and living standards also improved. During this time, Xi charges his nation with completing its defense modernization to meet related targets in 2020, 2035, and 2050: "Our military must regard combat capability as the criterion . . . and focus on how to win when it is called upon."

During the second half of the next several decades (2035–49), Xi envisions that China will achieve, domestically, "Common prosperity [and a harmonious society with good governance and a comprehensive welfare state] for [all Chinese citizens]." In the words of its state media, "China is set to become the world's largest economy . . . with an effective social welfare system, [and] a responsive . . . government."[9] Abroad, Xi intends for China to "Become a global leader in terms of [comprehensive] national strength and international influence." As a state media commentary elaborates, "By 2050 . . . China is set to regain its might and re-ascend to the top of the world."[10] Overall, as part of this re-emergence, China should "Become a proud and active member of the community of nations." To support more specific objectives, China should fully transform its armed forces into world-class forces. This is intended to further, and actually achieve, "China's complete reunification," most importantly by "resolving the Taiwan question." This is a point of crucial importance: Xi has given the CCP a deadline of 2049 to reincorporate Taiwan into the People's Republic of China (PRC) in some fashion.

Certainly, articulating and operationalizing Xi's broad policy guidance will require interpretation and translation—including by his speechwriter, strategist, and fellow Politburo Standing Committee Member Wang Huning, Director of the Central Policy Research Office[11]—as well as time and effort. However, it already contains kernels of meaning that must be taken seriously. Other nations' leaders articulate positive, somewhat nebulous goals, but few if any emphasize such transformative objectives as these. Almost none are backed by a powerful Leninist superstructure vested in the public promulgation of planning documents to direct national initiatives centrally. And perhaps no other leader today enjoys Xi's combination of national power and singlehanded ability to define and direct its allocation and employment. For all these reasons, Xi's grand strategy may well be the grandest and most strategic of any current national effort.

4.3 China's hierarchy of national security priorities

Xi's grand strategy is not simply a list of goals, but a prioritization of them as well. It is rooted not only in an (idealized) vision of the past, but also in historic and geographical patterns.[12]

4.3.1 HISTORICAL CONTINUITIES

Since its emergence more than a millennium ago as periodically reunified "civilizational state" with continually reestablished bureaucracy centred on a relatively fixed cultural homeland core,[13] China's hierarchy of national-security priorities has been grounded in consistently identifiable geographic layers and historical patterns. Particularly striking is the extent to which China's current heartland, geographic periphery, and hierarchy of national security priorities overlaps cartographically with those often manifested previously. At the core: a relatively self-sufficient, defensible heartland amenable to Han Chinese agriculture, contained by consistent geophysical and climatic boundaries as well as marauding nomads and smaller polities limited in potential to pose significant threats or to serve as allies against external threats.[14] To the extent that they first achieved internal order and prosperity, Chinese regimes have consistently striven to maximize their control of this historic homeland and their influence over its immediate surroundings.[15] Michael Swaine and Ashley Tellis identify long-term geographic and political constants in China's security environment that help inform such imperatives:

- A long and in many places geographically vulnerable border,
- The presence of many potential threats, both nearby and distant,
- A domestic political system marked by high levels of elite internecine conflict at the apex and weak institutions or processes for mediating and resolving such conflict, and
- A great power self-image.[16]

Imperial China's security prioritization was arguably informed in part by challenges of holding any massive, diverse polity together facing continental empires generally (e.g., Russia, the Ottomans, and Napoleonic France). Swaine and Tellis acknowledge variation in the operationalization of China's national security priorities over time, but document a notably robust hierarchy of interests in China's security calculus:

the maintenance of domestic order and well-being usually takes precedence over the preservation of geopolitical centrality and the establishment of influence over the Chinese periphery, for two reasons. First, the latter two goals cannot be reached without the prior attainment of the former objective. Second, historically, domestic order and well-being have often proved to be extremely difficult to achieve and preserve over time...and thus usually require enormous efforts by the state.[17]

As a successor state to the Qing dynasty, the PRC too is a multiethnic empire—albeit a Leninist one—and inherited the Qing's strategic challenges.[18]

But what distinguishes China from all other diverse continental empires in modern history is that it was neither fully protected, nor is now fully limited, by the "stopping power of water" that John Mearsheimer reifies.[19] Instead, across time and government system, Beijing's concentric continentalist rings of security prioritization and achievement have radiated progressively outward—up to and well beyond its claimed land frontiers. Qing era leaders debated whether external territorial threats in the maritime or continental direction should be prioritized, and were ultimately overwhelmed by both; as well as by internal upheaval. During the Cold War, as M. Taylor Fravel documents, Chinese leaders overcame these earlier limitations but still pursued more conciliatory approaches to border disputes when domestic factors (particularly ethnic rebellion) challenged their power from within and foreign cooperation might facilitate Beijing's influence over the people and territory under its control.[20] Strategic advancement has followed a logical geographic progression: "for most of the imperial era, China's strategic periphery consisted primarily of inland regions adjoining its continental borders. During the modern era (i.e., since the mid-nineteenth century), China's strategic periphery has expanded to fully encompass both continental and maritime regions."[21] That dual land–sea power identity informs Beijing's strategic calculus fundamentally today,[22] even as new strategic frontiers including outer space and cyber have also emerged. This long-term progression renders China an exceptional power with an exceptionally operationalizing grand strategy.

4.3.2 MODERN MANIFESTATIONS

Echoes of historical Chinese grand strategy reverberate in the contemporary Leninist-nationalist political context. Since its founding in 1921, the CCP has regarded its own leadership as the most important and fundamental priority, followed by (2) party-state-military administration, (3) governance of the Han-majority homeland, (4) stability in ethno-religious minority borderlands,

(5) integrity of land borders, (6) upholding and furthering disputed sovereignty claims in the Near Seas (Yellow, East, and South China Seas), and (7) addressing emerging interests in the Far Seas beyond.[23] In the latest iteration of a dynastic pattern, Swaine and Tellis relate, "The communist regime moved to reaffirm or consolidate Chinese control over virtually all the above periphery areas (including Taiwan,[24] but excluding Outer Mongolia) within the first decade of its establishment in 1949, through a combination of political and military means."[25] A Mongol innovation, the reorganization of Han-populated areas into provinces for better administrative control, was retained by subsequent dynasties. Similarly, the Qing designated Han-dominated areas of its empire as the "eighteen interior provinces."[26] As evidenced by everything from decades-long military developments optimized to increase Beijing's ability to coerce the island[27] to concerted efforts to isolate Taipei diplomatically,[28] Taiwan's reincorporation—thwarted by US intervention in the Korean War in 1950—remains a core CCP objective.

Since its emergence as the dominant force in the late 1940s, the CCP's survival in power has been reified and justified as essential to ensuring accomplishment of all other priorities. Following CCP capturing of China as a nation-state in 1949, the next priority has been domestic legitimacy and stability in the core Han-dominated heartland,[29] followed by firm control of Han-minority or -plurality border areas.[30] Since the end of the Cold War, success internally, together with the near-complete settlement of land border disputes, has allowed intensified focus on the next layer: advancing control over Taiwan and other unresolved maritime claims in Near Seas.[31] Xi's new diplomatic emphasis reflects this sharpened focus: "in recent years, the positive features of periphery diplomacy in advancing stability, harmony, and development have been augmented by a clearer and greater stress on the need to safeguard China's national interests and defend its rights in periphery regions, especially with regard to territorial sovereignty and maritime resources."[32]

This cartographic hierarchy aligns strikingly with the performance parameters of Chinese military platforms and weapons systems. Like the operating areas, range ring coverage, and potential kinetic fires of China's military systems, its intensity diminishes progressively with distance.[33] This is no coincidence: this hierarchy of diminishing returns likewise aligns with China's future military and geostrategic prospects (Figure 4.1).[34]

It may seem a truism that a state should prioritize its security interests and efforts to act on them. But China has done so, and continues to do so, in a way that is unique to its circumstances. In fact, China differs from many other states in important respects, including in key factors that inform its grand strategy. Some are strategically constraining, others strategically enabling. Beijing's approach is shaped by the following distinctive constraining factors, even as Xi seeks to alleviate them:

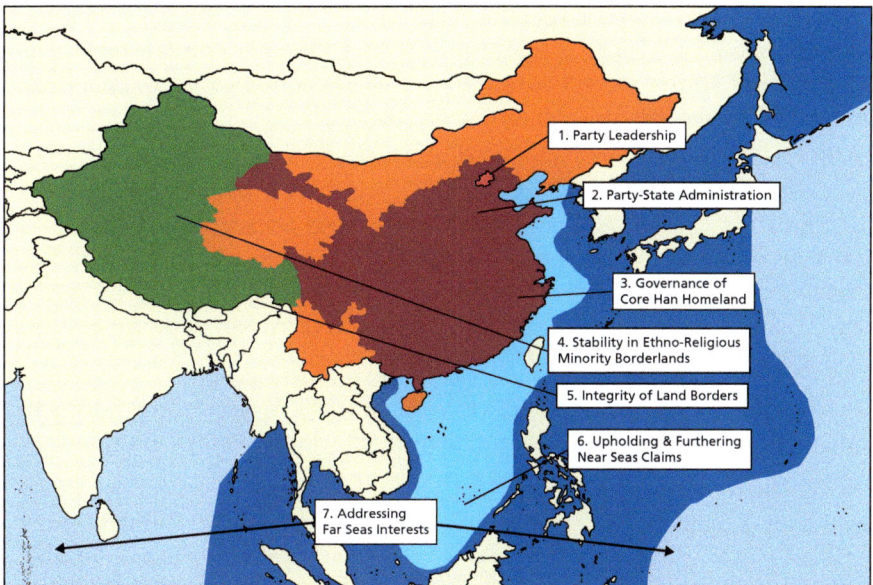

Figure 4.1. China's Hierarchy of National Security Priorities

Notes: The lighter blue/near seas is made from combining the 9 dash line with China's claimed EEZ Yuan hai—dark blue, more or less follows 2nd Island Chain and Andamans/Western Exit from Malacca.

Han core follows Wiki article in Chinese on the subject based on Qing definitions, though I did not include Yunnan because I'm unsure as to how formally incorporated it was in modern Chinese history.

Domestic-Political Precariousness: Unlike all but a handful of nations, China is ruled by a Leninist Party that has linked its legitimacy in retaining absolute power over society to the maintenance and validation of an ambitious if shape-shifting ideology—an ideology that it has stretched close to the limit in papering over logical contradictions. As the Party itself fears greatly, policy failure or opposition that hits close to home geographically or symbolically could rapidly undermine its rule. Xi's own highly-leveraged position atop cutthroat bureaucratic contention is the ultimate example of this. This motivates the dedication of tremendous resources to domestic surveillance, security, and propaganda.

Unfavorable Political Geography: Unlike the uniquely well-situated United States and advantageously insular maritime powers like Britain, Japan, and Australia, China lies in a geopolitically rough neighborhood with many contested borders and maritime claims. In the assessment of Andrew Nathan and Andrew Scobell, "China's immediate periphery has a good claim to be the most challenging geopolitical environment in the world for a major power."[35] The Middle Kingdom is surrounded by fourteen land neighbors, from atomically ambitious North Korea, to terrorism-plagued Afghanistan, to nuclear-armed

Pakistan. It retains land border disputes with India and Bhutan. Counting as-yet-un-reunified Taiwan, it has disputes with all eight of its maritime neighbors, coupled with a critical constraint on its resolution of them: America's entrenched presence in the region.

Restive Periphery: Unlike many other nations, including virtually all industrialized democracies, China faces significant danger of borderlands such as Tibet and Xinjiang slipping away from the central government's control—a risk that its leaders condemn as "separatism" and invest considerably to counter with local economic development, surveillance, and security measures. Chinese leaders seek to halt an historical cycle of imperial decline, dissipation, and disunity.

China also enjoys some distinctive enabling factors—some the products of contemporary Chinese strategies themselves, all which Xi seeks to exploit:

Continental and Maritime Power: Unlike many other land powers tied down by difficult neighbors and trapped by unfavorable geography, China is also a great sea power with major maritime interests and capabilities. It has arguably been the only continental power in modern history to achieve a successful, sustained maritime transformation into a hybrid land–sea power—however uneven and unfinished in some respects. Each of China's three sea forces is already the world's largest in numbers of ships.[36] Their numbers continue to grow, even as the vast majority of their foreign counterparts stagnate or shrink. As historian Paul Kennedy observes, there have recently emerged "massive differences in the assumptions of European nations and Asian nations about the significance of sea power, today and into the future."[37] China's navy and coast guard are among the most advanced in the world, while China's maritime militia is greatly superior to Vietnam's—the only known equivalent.

Strong Resource Base: Unlike virtually all other developing countries, with which it shares common problems of internal disparities and nationalistic expectations, China has a mammoth economy—the world's largest by purchasing power parity and second largest by market exchange rates. Despite its internal development goals and increasing limitations, it still has resources to devote to its grand strategic priorities virtually unmatched by any other government today.

Fiscal Flexibility: The CCP does not have to worry about mandatory spending because it can unilaterally readjust its budget without a vote, something that no democracy can do. For now, at least, individual Chinese citizens have established lesser claims to national resources than their voting counterparts in more per-capita-affluent democracies. This gives Beijing tremendous space to develop and implement grand strategy, rather than being constrained by immediate popular referenda, let alone the rising proportion of mandatory entitlement spending burdening Western welfare states.

Chinese Exceptionalism: Unlike those of all but a few nations, China's leaders and many citizens consider their nation to be a great power that merits significant respect and deference. This exceptionalism motivates a significant Chinese regional and global role even amid other pressing priorities. Moreover, while many nations have some remaining dispute(s) with their neighbor(s), virtually none shares China's combination of ideological motivation and hard power ability to press its claims over time.

No Overseas Imperialism: Finally, and perhaps most intriguingly, China thus far has never pursued overseas empire-building outside its immediate region, even though it has pursued continental empire-building all the way into Central and Southeast Asia many times[38] and some view Taiwan as a Han settler colony much as Australia and New Zealand may be considered British settler colonies.[39] CCP propaganda whitewashes the hard power dimensions of and local opposition within China's own imperial history, exaggerates the historical clarity of and continuity in Chinese authority over various polities, and dismisses resentment at Chinese bullying that is particularly pervasive among its neighbors. Nevertheless, no Chinese state ever had the far-flung geographically non-contiguous empires once common among European powers or even America's quasi-imperial appropriation of Spain's colonies. Unlike imperial or Nazi Germany, or Japan, no Chinese predecessor regime suffered catastrophic defeat in pursuing militaristic domination of neighbors against the opposition of intervening great powers. Since the Cold War's end, Beijing's leaders ostensibly pursued policies explicitly designed to eschew Soviet-style overstretch. The closest historical analogy may lie in American activities in the Caribbean and Latin America prior to Theodore Roosevelt's Corollary and Franklin Roosevelt's Good Neighbor policy—again, a home region phenomenon far from the outermost geographic layers. Looking forward, however, might the ambitious goals of Xi or his successor(s) play out imperially in the eyes of foreign subalterns and/or risk an unprecedented shift from "inside-out" to "outside-in" prioritization that generates a slippery slope toward overstretch? These possibilities will be explored in the following section.

4.3.3 UNCHARTED TERRITORY

Beyond this attempt to assert greater control over its periphery, China is radiating ripples of capability and activity to promote its expanding overseas interests. Here Chinese grand strategy encompasses diplomatic, economic, and military means in service of safeguarding such interests as energy supply security. In parallel, Chinese naval doctrine encompasses progressively-less-intense arcs of control, influence, and reach.[40] Here Xi's efforts represent the latest stage in a longer-term plan by further pursuing the four New Historic

Missions (新的历史使命) articulated by Hu Jintao in 2004[41] and adding as a fifth mission the realization of his own Centenary Goals.[42]

Even the next layer of ripples—throughout maritime Southeast Asia, across the Indian Ocean, into the Red Sea, and down Africa's east coast—overlaps geographically with the seven imperially sponsored voyages of eunuch Admiral Zheng He (conducted 1405–33) and enduring Chinese interests.[43] The Mongols and later the Ming intervened militarily in places like Java and Ceylon. The show of naval force to get Malacca to trade could also be seen today as a form of gunboat diplomacy.[44] "[T]oday's global and regional trading networks and China's gravitational pull on world trade are very much akin to the late Ming," Andrew Wilson notes,

> leading me to conclude that maritime China in the twenty-first century will look much more like China in the sixteenth century than China of the recent past... [T]here is ample historical precedent for China as a major sea power, an innovator in nautical technology, and a significant player in East and Southeast Asia as well as in the Indian Ocean.[45]

Progress still farther from China's shores is rapid from a low baseline, but its hard power elements diminish rapidly with distance. Already, however, China has achieved a status and confidence unseen symbolically in nearly two centuries and unprecedented in geographic scope and sophistication—going, literally and figuratively, where elements of Chinese state power have not gone before. Here, the predictive power of China's geostrategic history may finally be attenuating, but only in the positive direction: setbacks closer to home could readily redirect Beijing's focus inward. For further specifics, we must analyze Xi's own policy mapping.

4.4 Operationalizing grand strategy and managing its implementation

Mindful that designing and implementing a grand strategy requires an effective coordinating mechanism, Xi is reorganizing the Party, bureaucracy, and military to see through his strategic vision. The organizations, decision-making, and bureaucratic processes involved in operationalizing and managing Xi's grand strategy are already broadly clear; as well as the prioritization, strengths, and weaknesses embodied therein. As paramount leader, Xi holds three top positions: General Secretary of the CCP, Chairman of the Central Military Commission and Commander-in-Chief of the People's Liberation Army (PLA), and President of the PRC. In the first role, he leads the political organization in charge of Chinese politics and policy; in the second, he leads China's armed forces in implementing the military component of that policy, and in the third he represents China abroad as head of state in pursuing the diplomatic component of that policy. The Xi-led Party dominates all: in civil affairs, by supervising a civilian bureaucracy; and in military affairs, by supervising a chain of command and administrative apparatus. In foreign policy, Party hegemony is exemplified by the fact that China's most important and powerful diplomat is not the minister of foreign affairs, but rather the State Councilor under the Premier holding the foreign affairs portfolio. Here, the political power of the key figure responsible for foreign affairs (and limitations on that power) derives from his seat on the Politburo. In defense, the Party commands the Gun through a supervisory system of political commissars, forbids the PLA (a Party-army) from becoming a national army, condemns those who seek "nationalization" of the military, and thereby relegates the "Ministry of National Defense" to a shell organization confined to military diplomacy. This extraordinary concentration of power transmits Xi's grand strategy into Chinese action.

This system, broadly shared with only the few remaining communist nations—all far less capable than China—exhibits strengths and weaknesses diametrically different from those of leading industrialized democracies. China's vast Party-state structure, its work synchronized through countless Party Committee meetings, typically excels at planning, publicly communicating, and implementing a set of top national priorities over time. It suffers from corresponding limitations in real-time interagency information sharing and coordination, particularly in crisis. Xi is pursuing ambitious bureaucratic reforms to reduce such weaknesses, including by establishing a Central State Security Commission (CSSC, 中央国家安全委员会) in 2013, and implementing a new foreign policy management structure as part of a recent State Council reorganization that includes increasing the number and utilization of specialized leading groups and placing the Coast Guard directly under the Central Military Commission. These measures are needed to conceptualize and execute both legs of his strategy. In prioritizing Party survival above all else, however, Xi is unlikely to optimize the system across the board. Together with the Party's bureaucratic hegemony, for example, internal security concerns have thus far dominated the focus of the CSSC, leaving it substantially different from the more externally focused national security councils of the US, Japan, and other major powers.[46]

4.4.1 BRI AS AN EXTERNAL MANIFESTATION OF GRAND STRATEGY

In the foreign policy, geoeconomic, and geostrategic realm, operationalizing Xi's grand strategy of realizing a "China Dream" of national rejuvenation involves making China great again abroad while supporting its internal development. The vision for these ambitions is encapsulated by his signature

BRI, focused primarily on infrastructure development to encourage greater regional integration and connectivity in Eurasia; some of it building on prior initiatives, some of it not yet realized. In a sign that the international and domestic pieces of Xi's grand strategy are linked, many would argue that BRI is least as much (if not more) about supporting domestic growth and stabilizing border regions as it is about gaining influence in distant places. Nevertheless, Xi's foreign policy, centered on BRI, has strong geoeconomic and geopolitical implications for Asia and the world.

BRI encompasses most of the world, albeit in different layers of prioritization and functionality. In 2014, Xi gave a speech introducing his concept of "holistic security" (总体安全观) and emphasized that potential interdependence among traditional and nontraditional factors could potentially impact Beijing's hierarchy of security concerns.[47] Timothy Heath assesses that "Adoption of the holistic security concept now means anything Chinese authorities deem an impediment to the realization of any of the country's developmental objectives—regardless of whether it is economic, political or another category—may now be deemed a 'security threat'" and justify military action of some kind.[48]

On the soft power side of the equation, Xi's vision for an international "community of shared future [common destiny] for mankind" (人类命运共同体), itself based on a "new type of international relations" more favorable to Beijing, is designed to transform "the international environment to make it compatible with China's governance model and emergence as a global leader."[49] Cooperating under the rubric of such Chinese initiatives as BRI accords special priority to regional relations, as embodied in a White Paper on "China's Policies on Asia-Pacific Security Cooperation." Within that context, this document states, "Focusing on common development, China has put forward and actively promoted the Belt and Road Initiative and initiated the establishment of the Asian Infrastructure Investment Bank and the Silk Road Fund."[50]

Specifically, BRI consists of both a Silk Road Economic Belt from China through Eurasia to Europe; and a twenty-first-century Maritime Silk Road from Southeast Asia and the Indian Ocean to Africa, the Middle East, and beyond.[51] As will be discussed below, Xi has also announced a "Polar Silk Road" as part of BRI.[52] BRI leverages infrastructure and trade to integrate Eurasia and its periphery, perhaps ultimately within a Sinocentric geoeconomic and geopolitical order.[53] BRI's connection to grand strategy is suggested by both the prestige Xi has invested in it and the Party institutions involved in it; including, apparently, a dedicated Leading Small Group chaired by Xi himself.

Yuan Peng, Vice President of the influential Ministry of State Security–run think tank China Institutes of Contemporary International Relations, suggests a new foreign policy approach that builds on both the aforementioned Chinese security hierarchy and Xi's emphasis on periphery diplomacy. As such, it may offer a basis for prioritizing BRI efforts. "This 'great periphery' should be a 'concentric circle' structure with China at the core, specifically including 'three rings'," Yuan elaborates.

'The inside ring' consists of the fourteen countries contiguous to China on land; for particular geographical and historical reasons, these are irreplaceably important for China. The 'middle ring' consists of the maritime countries extending from the 'inner ring,' and also areas from the west Pacific to the Indian Ocean to the Middle East and then to parts of central Asia and Russia that are not directly contiguous on land with China. The 'outer ring' continues to extend out to the circle of Africa, Europe, and America, including the poles.[54]

Echoing the geographic basis for China's aforementioned national security priorities, Nathan and Scobell articulate a similar set of four "concentric circles."[55] Both overlap with Sinocentric cartographic conceptions from the imperial era.[56] Such images also sow discomfort among China's neighbors as they imply China's overlordship and a condescending view that they are somehow "less civilized."[57]

Presently, the poles merit particular mention. Beijing depicts its burgeoning polar activities selectively and ambiguously, heretofore attracting little notice outside specialized professional communities that interact minimally. Nevertheless, as a component of an ambitious maritime strategy as part of Xi's grand strategy that is now enshrined in a first-ever Arctic White Paper,[58] China's development as a polar great power will critically shape the emerging new geopolitical order and the way it is governed. China seeks to join the US as the only other nation capable of comprehensive presence, activities, and influence in both the Arctic and Antarctic. Beijing regards the polar regions as vital domains rich in fish, energy, and minerals, as well as a permissive zone for the expansion of Chinese influence and norm-creation—a view that Washington encourages through lack of focus and investment.[59] As they gradually open to seasonal shipping, Arctic sea lanes help China reduce reliance on such potential chokepoints as the Malacca Strait. In keeping with Xi's grand strategy, China has a timetable for polar development that corresponds to his Two Centenary rubric.

All told, however, Xi's BRI is an ambitious, expensive, time-consuming enterprise. Its nascent articulation and implementation leaves many questions, including how internal policy debates will play out. One of the great Chinese foreign policy questions at issue is to what extent Beijing will seek to shape the domestic politics of other countries. Some influential Chinese thinkers have argued for BRI approaches precisely to allow China to develop as much as possible with as little opposition as possible for the US and its allies. Perhaps most prominent is the work of Peking University professor Wang Jisi, formerly a top advisor to Hu Jintao, and today an influential thinker at the nexus of Beijing's academic and policy communities. In an October 2012 article, Wang advocated a "March West" (西进) of Chinese development into Eurasia just as the US was rebalancing toward East Asia.[60] A Chinese expert consulted by the author echoes what other sources have suggested:

> the 'Marching West' proposition is integrated into the BRI, and constitutes an organized part of the BRI. Professor Wang was entrusted to make such a proposition as a precursor to the unveiling of BRI in order to test the public reactions and responses to the BRI. This is following the common practice of the Chinese government.

In possible indicator of still greater ambitions, in a departure from post-Mao avoidance of political evangelism, the state media distillation of Xi's speech states, "China's success proves that socialism can prevail and be a path for other developing countries to emulate and achieve modernization." This is not simply an endorsement of the standard state-directed developmentalism of the sort that Japan used to practice: "The new world order cannot be just dominated by capitalism and the West, and the time will come for a change."[61] This potentially heralds an ambitious and potentially highly competitive geopolitical strategy. Several prominent Chinese scholars, including Tsinghua University professor Yan Xuetong[62] and PLA Sr. Col. Liu Mingfu,[63] argue that China can and should become a true peer competitor of the US, and perhaps even surpass and replace it in many respects.

Nevertheless, some influential scholars and officials question the current operationalization of China's current grand strategy, particularly regarding specific foreign policy applications. In the view of Renmin University's Shi Yinhong,

> if the focal points of Chinese diplomatic policies are too scattered, or if Beijing fails to calculate the possible risks in the One Belt and One Road initiative and the negative global response toward China's increasing military power, we might not be able to make use of the opportunities brought by the decline and disorganization in the West.[64]

Infrastructure development can be locally disruptive and Chinese entities may have a need to secure their investments, including through the hiring of private security firms. This has the potential to cause local instability that will draw in more resources and thereby undermine the profitability and sustainability of such projects. Another strategic risk relating to BRI is its cultivation of local political parties and strongmen in places where institutions are weak. This exposes China to potential blowback if these groups lose power, especially if they are repressive and China seems complicit in the repression. If the American and Soviet experiences during the Cold War and the recent US forays into Afghanistan and Iraq are any indication, working with local powers in unstable settings can prove highly risky. Qin Yaqing of China

Foreign Affairs University cautions that "a strident turn from one strategy to the other is inadvisable," while maintaining that Beijing's foreign policy to date displays "the existence of both continuity and change, although the former is its main theme with regards to strategic goals, designs, and policies as a whole."[65] Such moderating views are important, even in the Xi era.

In addition to domestic political debate, Xi's ambitious foreign policy may face external pushback, particularly from the US and its allies. For example, at a recent conference,

Li Ruogu, President of the China Export-Import Bank, expressed his views on China's external situation. He specifically mentioned that the U.S.'s judgment about China has undergone a fundamental change. Sino-U.S. trade friction is essentially a controversy on the direction of China's development. Li Ruogu said that Sino-U.S. relations will not continue along the path they have taken over the past 40 years. Specifically, in the United States, no matter what party or class, most of them advocate a tough attitude towards China. This allows the U.S. to move beyond partisan lines on its China strategy and operate quickly and effectively.[66]

Li's observation is significant: managing major power relations is as important, or even more important, than BRI's success or failure per se.

In any case, China's government and academic community have closely studied the experiences of previously rising great powers.[67] They continue to seek lessons and to avoid mistakes even as they debate the best way to apply them.[68] Whatever challenges Xi's grand strategy may face, considerable thought informs its development and implementation.

4.4.2 DOMESTIC REFORMS AS INTERNAL MANIFESTATIONS OF GRAND STRATEGY

As with foreign and military policy, Xi seeks to implement the domestic components of his grand strategy successfully through manifold reforms. He embraces the Maoist mantle of Party discipline coupled with bureaucratic reforms, including the reorganization of state-owned enterprises and other efforts to broaden prosperity. Constraints endemic to China's Leninist system (stove piping, corruption, etc.) persist, however: even in its ambitious encapsulation of Xi's speech, China's state media acknowledges that realizing his goals "will take immense work." Specifically, "China needs to tackle the new contradiction between unbalanced and inadequate development and the people's ever-growing needs for a better life. China will need to prove it can survive the middle income trap."[69]

Domestic instability is a long-term concern of China, which is becoming an ever-greater surveillance state that monitors its people and shapes their activities and communications using both physical and electronic means.[70] Neither can one ignore the possibility of external tensions, which could divert

China from fully developing economically. The attainment of a plateau in the growth is also a possibility and could drive China into a potential decline after its golden era of rapid catch-up growth following Maoist malpractice.

Even if Xi and his fellow leaders navigate China's many domestic challenges reasonably well, they may still be constrained in the implementation of their grand strategy by a slowdown in the growth rate of China's economy, and its overall national power. Here, China is almost certainly subject to the same slowing that has bedeviled other great powers,[71] but—for reasons specific to its own conditions—may suffer from such an S-curved slowdown even more rapidly and disruptively than those that have gone before it.[72]

The S-curve concept comes from a mathematical model later applied to other fields—including physics, biology, and economics—to show how entities' growth patterns typically change over time. Robert Gilpin argues that a state must inevitably decline because of an historical tendency for national efficiency to decrease as society ages, thereby creating a downward spiral of increasing consumption and decreasing investment that undermines the economic, military, and political underpinnings of a state's international position.[73] A society or country experiences slow growth at its inception, then enjoys more rapid growth as it consolidates, develops, and more resources flow into the treasury.

The process continues until the state reaches its maximum growth rate, an inflection point at which various countervailing forces begin to constrain expansion and set the economy onto a slower growth path or even stagnation. Domestically, social spending and rent seeking behavior may threaten productive investment and economic growth. Internationally, a hegemon tends to "overpay" for influence in the international system because of the tendency for allies to "free-ride." The inherent propensity toward technological diffusion may threaten to undermine a hegemon's economic and technological leadership.

While it is not overextended internationally thus far, China is encountering the domestic aspect of these headwinds at a much earlier stage in its development than did the US and other great powers, thanks in part to its late start in modernization and post-Mao pent-up debt-fueled growth, its dramatic internal disparities, its extraordinary pollution and resource depletion, and its draconian one-child policy and corresponding gender imbalance and aging. Debates over national priorities in the form of gun vs butter, or even guns vs canes,[74] may constrain the operationalization of China's grand strategy sooner, and to an even greater extent, than many currently anticipate.[75]

Aware of these challenges, Xi is taking action in an attempt to counter it and thereby operationalize his grand strategy effectively over time. To this end, the CCP is trying to incentivize childbearing to shore up demographics. It has invested in the world's most sophisticated facial recognition (which can track someone down in minutes). Chinese technology companies are now required to store all their data with the Ministry of Public Security. For some time to come, increased state penetration and control of society may strengthen existing power structures rather than signify regime weakness. For all these efforts, however, Xi's China appears to be shifting from an era of upside potential to one of downside risks. The Party is not paranoid for nothing.

4.5 Conclusion

Provided that he can continue to dominate, China is poised to be led for years to come by Xi, an ambitious leader with a grand strategy to match. Xi's vision faces great challenges and he himself faces fissiparous bureaucratic politics and accumulating resentment at his heavy-handed political maneuvering. But he stands astride a powerful state with great determination, and will receive the ultimate credit (good or bad) for whatever it achieves. This chapter's key findings are as follows: Xi has a grand strategy for China that he has announced; this strategy has a hierarchy of aims rooted in history; this strategy is shaped by unique modern factors; China is operationalizing its strategy abroad through BRI; and China faces an S-curved slowdown and at the domestic level is operationalizing its grand strategy through initiatives designed to prepare it for this challenge of ebbing national power growth. With China having already arrived as the world's second-most-powerful nation,[76] the question remaining is how much more powerful China will become by when; and with what implications, for what particular realization, of Xi's "China Dream."

China has already made a remarkable achievement: the world's first successful transformation from a land power to a land–sea power in more than a millennium. Accompanying this sea change is arguably the closing of an era begun six centuries ago, when China turned inward and Western nations spread power and influence around the world by sea, ultimately helping to create the liberal international order that since World War II has underwritten a rich network of international institutions, rules, and norms. One key question of our age is to what extent China will continue to rise and develop within this existing framework, and to what extent it will seek to modify it.[77] The nature and scope of Xi's grand strategy suggests that China under his leadership will pursue a strong continued rise, in some ways well within the postwar international system, and in some ways pushing hard at its edges.

In some ways, those edges are already eroding. And, as other chapters in this volume explain, China is not the only power seeking to fray those edges—Russia is pursuing its own irredentism, particularly through hybrid warfare somewhat more intense than China's maritime gray zone operations. In combination, as Peter Dutton argues, these rivalrous great power efforts have the potential to produce something even more significant than China's emergence as a sea power: the retreat of the liberal international maritime order developed over the past half-millennium in the face of a rising illiberal continental order.[78] With Russia's climatic, demographic, and economic limitations, the rise of such an illiberal order will largely hinge on China, and the operationalization of its grand strategy. These dynamics are encapsulated in the recently issued US National Security Strategy,[79] which itself offers a reasonable basis for an American grand strategy. Will this document's contents ultimately offer some semblance of a twenty-first century grand strategy for Washington, with buy-in from its allies and partners? While the present author would argue in favor of such an approach, this admittedly remains very much an open question.

What is certain is that Xi has a clear grand strategy for China, as well as a clear sense of urgency: "The wheels of history roll on; the tides of the times are vast and mighty. History looks kindly on those with resolve, with drive and ambition, and with plenty of guts; it won't wait for the hesitant, the apathetic, or those shy of a challenge."[80]

NOTES

1. Angela Stanzel, Nadège Rolland, Jabin Jacob, and Melanie Hart, *Grand Designs: Does China Have a "Grand Strategy"?* (European Council on Foreign Relations, October 18, 2017), http://www.ecfr.eu/publications/summary/grands_designs_does_china_have_a_grand_strategy; Sun Xuefeng, M. Taylor Fravel, and Liu Feng, eds., *Understanding China's Foreign Policy Transformation: A Chinese Journal of International Politics (CJIP) Reader*, https://academic.oup.com/cjip/pages/understanding_china_foreign_policy_transformation_reader; Lukas K. Danner, "The Debate on China's Grand Strategy," *China Policy Institute*, University of Nottingham, May 4, 2015, https://cpianalysis.org/2015/05/04/the-debate-on-the-direction-of-chinas-grand-strategy/; Lukas K. Danner, *China's Grand Strategy: Contradictory Foreign Policy?* (New York: Palgrave Macmillan, 2018); Elizabeth C. Economy, *The Third Revolution: Xi Jinping and the New Chinese State* (Oxford: Oxford University Press, 2018).
2. The approach to grand strategy employed here concerns both international and domestic factors, as seen in Aaron L. Friedberg, *The Weary Titan: Britain and the Experience of Relative Decline, 1895–1905* (Princeton, NJ: Princeton University Press, 2010).
3. "Achieving Rejuvenation is the Dream of the Chinese People," November 29, 2012, in Xi Jinping, *The Governance of China* (Beijing: Foreign Languages Press, 2014), 37–9.
4. Xi Jinping, "Secure a Decisive Victory in Building a Moderately Prosperous Society in All Respects and Strive for the Great Success of Socialism with Chinese Characteristics for a New Era," Delivered at the 19th National Congress of the Communist

Party of China, October 18, 2017, http://english.qstheory.cn/2018-02/11/c_1122395333.htm. Unless otherwise specified, quotes in this and succeeding paragraphs are from this speech. Chinese-language text: 习近平, "决胜全面建成小康社会 夺取新时代中国特色社会主义伟大胜利——在中国共产党第十九次全国代表大会上的报告," 2017 年10月18日, http://politics.people.com.cn/n1/2017/1028/c1001-29613514.html

5. "Milestone Congress Points to New Era for China, The World," *Xinhua*, October 24, 2017, http://news.xinhuanet.com/english/2017-10/24/c_136702090.htm
6. Ibid.
7. See Orville Schell and John Delury, *Wealth and Power: China's Long March to the Twenty-first Century* (New York: Random House, 2013). Arguably, the concept of rejuvenation came primarily in the twentieth century as a response to the "Century of Humiliation" narrative. It was first discussed by the KMT, including Sun Yet-sen, but especially by Chiang Kai-shek in his book *China's Destiny*. The idea of rejuvenation was taken up by Mao ("the Chinese people have stood up!"), which Xi tends to reiterate. Deng likewise exhibited this line of thinking in his Four Modernizations concept. Chinese emperors, by contrast, tended not to have this focus on rejuvenation because those regimes took for granted the view that whichever dynasty ruled was and would be the center of all under heaven (天下) and the celestial empire. Even the Southern Song Dynasty liked to invoke its cultural and moral superiority despite being weaker militarily than its neighbors. See Ja Ian Chong, "Popular Narratives Versus Chinese History: Implications for Understanding An Emergent China," *European Journal of International Relations* 20, no. 4 (2014): 939–64, http://journals.sagepub.com/doi/pdf/10.1177/1354066113503480
8. "Milestone Congress," *Xinhua*.
9. Ibid.
10. Ibid.
11. Nectar Gan, "Who's on China's New Team Handling U.S. Relations? Meet the Most Influential Negotiators," *South China Morning Post*, May 29, 2018, http://www.scmp.com/news/china/diplomacy-defence/article/2148296/whos-chinas-new-team-handling-us-relations-meet-most
12. Andrew S. Erickson and Joel Wuthnow, "Barriers, Springboards and Benchmarks: China Conceptualizes the Pacific 'Island Chains'," *The China Quarterly* 225 (March 2016): 1–22; Andrew S. Erickson and Joel Wuthnow, "Why Islands Still Matter in Asia: The Enduring Significance of the Pacific 'Island Chains'," *The National Interest*, February 5, 2016, http://www.andrewerickson.com/wp-content/uploads/2016/02/Island-Chains_Why-Islands-Still-Matter-in-Asia_Erickson-Wuthnow_TNI_20160105.pdf; Andrew S. Erickson, "Doctrinal Sea Change, Making Real Waves: Examining the Naval Dimension of Strategy," in *China's Evolving Military Strategy*, ed. Joe McReynolds (Washington, DC: Jamestown Foundation, 2016), 99–132; Andrew S. Erickson, "China's Naval Modernisation, Strategies, and Capabilities," in *International Order at Sea: How it is challenged. How it is maintained*, eds. Jo Inge Bekkevold and Geoffrey Till (New York: Palgrave Macmillan, 2016), 63–92; Andrew S. Erickson, "Chinese Statesmen and the Use of Air Power," in *The Influence of Airpower upon History:*

Statesmanship, Diplomacy, and Foreign Policy since 1903, eds. Robin Higham and Mark Parillo (Lexington: University Press of Kentucky, 2013), 237–71; Andrew S. Erickson and Gabriel B. Collins, "China's Oil Security Pipe Dream: The Reality, and Strategic Consequences, of Seaborne Imports," *Naval War College Review* 63, no. 2 (Spring 2010): 88–111, http://www.andrewerickson.com/wp-content/uploads/2010/03/China-Pipeline-Sealane_NWCR_2010-Spring.pdf

13. Peter J. Katzenstein, "China's Rise: East Asia and Beyond," *East Asia Institute Working Paper* 12 (April 2008), https://www.files.ethz.ch/isn/137725/2009052018244858.pdf. The mainstream view of ruling imperial houses, the KMT, and the CCP reifies a continuous notion of Chinese regimes, in part to create an impression of legitimacy. As with much history, much remains debated. For examination of China's historical internal diversity, particularly along its periphery, see Pamela Kyle Crossley, Helen F. Siu, and Donald S. Sutton, eds., *Empire at the Margins: Culture, Ethnicity, and Frontier in Early Modern China* (Berkeley: University of California Press, 2006); Christine Moll-Murata and Ulrich Theobald, "Military Employment in Qing Dynasty China," in *Fighting for a Living: A Comparative Study of Military Labour 1500–2000* ed. Erik-Jan Zürcher (Amsterdam: Amsterdam University Press, 2013), 353–92.
14. Michael D. Swaine and Ashley J. Tellis, *Interpreting China's Grand Strategy: Past, Present, and Future* (Santa Monica, CA: RAND, 2000), 74–6; maps, 87–92, https://www.rand.org/pubs/monograph_reports/MR1121.html. See also Su Hao 苏浩, "缘重心与世界政治的支" [Geogravitational Centers and World Political Fulcrums], 现代国际关系 [Contemporary International Relations], no. 4 (2004): 54–61.
15. Su Hao, 79. Many scholars agree that there is a recognizable homeland core; some contend that it is more cultural and less political. It is a later claim that reinterprets this core as political as well as cultural. The 5,000 years of history narrative in particular, which is of late nineteenth century vintage—as anti-Manchu revolutionaries were trying to find reason to overthrow the Qing.
16. Su Hao, 45.
17. Swaine and Tellis, *Interpreting China's Grand Strategy*, 53.
18. For an argument that the Qing should be understood as a multiethnic empire, see the work of scholars of the New Qing History school, particularly Peter Perdue and Mark Elliot, as discussed by Guo Wu, "New Qing History: Dispute, Dialog, and Influence," *The Chinese Historical Review* 23, no. 1 (2016): 147–69.
19. John J. Mearsheimer, *The Tragedy of Great Power Politics* (New York: W. W. Norton, 2014), 113–27.
20. M. Taylor Fravel, *Strong Borders, Secure Nation: Cooperation and Conflict in China's Territorial Disputes* (Princeton, NJ: Princeton University Press, 2008).
21. Swaine and Tellis, *Interpreting China's Grand Strategy*, 72.
22. Andrew Erickson, Lyle Goldstein, and Carnes Lord, "When Land Powers Look Seaward," *U.S. Naval Institute Proceedings* 137, no. 4 (April 2011): 18–23; Andrew Erickson, Lyle Goldstein, and Carnes Lord, "China Sets Sail," *The American Interest* 5, no. 5 (May/June 2010): 27–34; Andrew S. Erickson, "Can China Become a Maritime Power?" in *Asia Looks Seaward: Power and Maritime Strategy*, eds. Toshi Yoshihara and James Holmes (Westport, CT: Praeger Security International, 2008), 70–110.

23. Andrew S. Erickson, "Through the Lens of Distance: Understanding and Responding to China's 'Ripples of Capability'," *Changing Military Dynamics In East Asia Policy Brief* 3, no. 9 (January 2012), https://escholarship.org/uc/item/9t8894kv; Andrew S. Erickson, "China's Modernization of Its Naval and Air Power Capabilities," in *Strategic Asia 2012–13: China's Military Challenge*, eds. Ashley J. Tellis and Travis Tanner (Seattle, WA: National Bureau of Asian Research, 2012), 60–125.
24. Alan M. Wachman, *Why Taiwan? Geostrategic Rationales for China's Territorial Integrity* (Stanford, CA: Stanford University Press, 2007).
25. Swaine and Tellis, *Interpreting China's Grand Strategy*, 82.
26. See Mark Elliott, "Frontier Stories: Periphery as Center in Qing History," *Frontiers of History in China*, 9, no. 3 (2014): 336–360, https://scholar.harvard.edu/files/elliott/files/elliott_frontier_stories_frontiers_of_history_in_china_2014.pdf; Tianyang Xi, "All the Emperor's Men? Conflicts and Power-Sharing in Imperial China," *Comparative Political Studies*, published online October 29, 2018, https://doi.org/10.1177/0010414018806538.
27. William S. Murray, "Revisiting Taiwan's Defense Strategy," *Naval War College Review* 61, no. 3 (Summer 2008): 13–38.
28. Joel Wuthnow, *Chinese Diplomacy and the UN Security Council: Beyond the Veto* (New York: Routledge, 2013), 20, 22–3.
29. Swaine and Tellis define the Han homeland as follows: "a Chinese cultural, geographic, and sociopolitical heartland ... over 90 percent of the occupants ... are ethnic Han Chinese or descendants of mixed Han-nomadic or Han-Southeast Asian peoples." Swaine and Tellis, *Interpreting China's Grand Strategy*, 69. Heartland Han arguably represent "a highly homogeneous culture and civilization." Swaine and Tellis, 86.
30. These areas were not assimilated until relatively recently. Swaine and Tellis, 74.
31. Andrew S. Erickson, "China's Maritime Ambitions," in *Routledge Handbook of Asian Security Studies*, 2nd ed., eds. Sumit Ganguly, Andrew Scobell, and Joseph Liow (New York: Routledge, 2017), 100–14; Andrew S. Erickson, "China's Near-Seas Challenges," *The National Interest*, no. 129 (January–February 2014): 60–6.
32. Michael D. Swaine, "Chinese Views and Commentary on Periphery Diplomacy," *China Leadership Monitor* 44, no. 3, https://www.hoover.org/sites/default/files/research/docs/clm44ms.pdf
33. Andrew S. Erickson, Evan Braden Montgomery, Craig Neuman, Stephen Biddle, and Ivan Oelrich, "Correspondence: How Good Are China's Antiaccess/Area-Denial Capabilities?," *International Security* 41, no. 4 (Spring 2017): 202–13; Andrew S. Erickson, "How Strong Are China's Armed Forces?" in *The China Questions: Critical Insights into a Rising Power*, eds. Jennifer Rudolph and Michael Szonyi (Cambridge, MA: Harvard University Press, 2017), 73–80; Andrew S. Erickson, "China's Military Modernization: Many Improvements, Three Challenges, and One Opportunity," in *China's Challenges*, eds. Jacques deLisle and Avery Goldstein (Philadelphia: University of Pennsylvania Press, 2014), 178–203; Andrew S. Erickson, "Rising Tide, Dispersing Waves: Opportunities and Challenges for Chinese Seapower Development," *Journal of Strategic Studies* 37, no. 3 (Summer

2014): 1–31; Andrew S. Erickson, "Beijing's Aerospace Revolution: Short-Range Opportunities, Long-Range Challenges," in *Chinese Aerospace Power: Evolving Maritime Roles*, eds. Andrew S. Erickson and Lyle J. Goldstein (Annapolis, MD: Naval Institute Press, 2011), 3–18.

34. Ely Ratner, Elbridge Colby, Andrew Erickson, Zachary Hosford, and Alexander Sullivan, *More Willing and Able: Charting China's International Security Activism* (Washington, DC: Center for a New American Security, May 2015), https://s3.amazonaws.com/files.cnas.org/documents/CNAS_ChinaMoreWillingAndAble_Final.pdf; Andrew S. Erickson, "China's Strategic Objectives at Sea," in *Asia-Pacific Regional Security Assessment 2017: Key Developments and Trends*, eds. Tim Huxley and William Choong (London: IISS, 2017), 37–50.

35. Andrew J. Nathan and Andrew Scobell, *China's Search for Security* (New York: Columbia University Press, 2014), 5. For related concerns, see Li Yihu 李义虎, "从海陆二分到海陆统筹—对中国海陆关系的在审视" [Sea and Land Power: From Dichotomy to overall Planning—A Review of the Relationship Between Sea and Land Power], 现代国际关系 [Contemporary International Relations] (August 2007): 1–7, esp. 4.

36. Andrew S. Erickson, "Numbers Matter: China's Three 'Navies' Each Have the World's Most Ships," *The National Interest*, February 26, 2018, http://nationalinterest.org/feature/numbers-matter-chinas-three-navies-each-have-the-worlds-most-24653.

37. Paul Kennedy, "The Rise and Fall of Navies," *New York Times*, April 5, 2007, https://www.nytimes.com/2007/04/05/opinion/05iht-edkennedy.1.5158064.html

38. The closest arguable approximation was the efforts during the Yuan Dynasty to control the Korean peninsula, India, Japan, Burma, and Java, but this was brief and occurred under the Mongols as part of their temporary domination of much of Eurasia.

39. See works by Bruce Jacobs and Tonio Andrade, as well as Ruiping Ye, "Colonisation without Exploitation: The Qing Policies in Taiwan during the High Qing Period (1684–1795)," *Journal of the Australasian Law Teachers Association*, no 8 (2013), http://classic.austlii.edu.au/au/journals/JlALawTA/2013/8.pdf.

40. Peter A. Dutton, "Three Disputes and Three Objectives: China and the South China Sea," *Naval War College Review* 64, no. 4 (Autumn 2011): 42–67.

41. At an expanded Central Military Commission conference on December 24, 2004, Hu introduced new military policy that defined four "new historic missions" for the PLA: first, to serve as an "important source of strength" for the Chinese Communist Party (CCP) to "consolidate its ruling position"; second, to "provide a solid security guarantee for sustaining the important period of strategic opportunity for national development"; third, to "provide a strong strategic support for safeguarding national interests"; and fourth, to "play an important role in maintaining world peace and promoting common development." The latter two were unprecedented. "Earnestly Step Up Ability Building within CPC Organizations of Armed Forces," 解放军报 [Liberation Army Daily], December 13, 2004, available at http://www.chinamil.com.cn/; "三个提供，一个发挥" [Three Provides and One Bring into Play], 新浪 [Sina], September 29, 2005, http://news.sina.com.cn/c/2005-09-29/08517064683s.shtml

42. This was enshrined in China's latest Defense White Paper as "strive to provide a strong guarantee for completing the building of a moderately prosperous society in all respects and achieving the great rejuvenation of the Chinese nation." *China's Military Strategy* (Beijing: Information Office of the State Council, May 2015), http://www.xinhuanet.com/english/china/2015-05/26/c_134271001.htm
43. Edward L. Dreyer, *Zheng He: China and the Oceans in the Early Ming Dynasty, 1405–1433* (London: Pearson, 2006).
44. Yuan-kang Wang, *Harmony and War: Confucian Culture and Chinese Power Politics* (New York: Columbia University Press, 2011); Geoffrey Wade, ed., *China and Southeast Asia* (New York: Routledge, 2009), vols. 1–6; Geoffrey Wade, "The Zheng He Voyages: A Reassessment," *Journal of the Malaysian Branch of the Royal Asiatic Society* 78, no. 1 (288) (2005): 37–58.
45. Andrew R. Wilson, "The Maritime Transformation of Ming China," in *China Goes to Sea: Maritime Transformation in Comparative Historical Perspective*, eds. Andrew S. Erickson, Lyle J. Goldstein, and Carnes Lord (Annapolis, MD: Naval Institute Press, 2009), 242.
46. Samantha Hoffman and Peter Mattis, "Managing the Power Within: China's State Security Commission," *War on the Rocks*, July 18, 2016, https://warontherocks.com/2016/07/managing-the-power-within-chinas-state-security-commission/
47. "习近平: 坚持总体国家安全观 走中国特色国家安全道路" [Xi Jinping: Adhering to an Overall National Security Concept and Taking the National Security Road with Chinese Characteristics], *Xinhua*, April 15, 2014, http://www.xinhuanet.com/politics/2014-04/15/c_1110253910.htm
48. Timothy R. Heath, "The 'Holistic Security Concept': The Securitization of Policy and Increasing Risk of Militarized Crisis," Jamestown *China Brief* 15, no. 12 (June 19, 2015): 8, https://jamestown.org/wp-content/uploads/2015/06/China_Brief_Vol_15_Issue_12_v2_5.pdf.
49. Liza Tobin, "Xi's Vision for Transforming Global Governance: A Strategic Challenge for Washington and Its Allies," *Texas National Security Review* 2.1 (December 2018): https://tnsr.org/2018/12/xis-vision-for-transforming-global-governance-a-strategic-challenge-for-washington-and-its-allies/; "Xinhua Insight: Xi's World Vision: A Community of Common Destiny, A Shared Home for Humanity," *Xinhua*, January 15, 2017, http://www.xinhuanet.com/english/2017-01/15/c_135983586.htm
50. *China's Policies on Asia-Pacific Security Cooperation*, 1st ed. (Beijing: State Council Information Office of the People's Republic of China, January 2017), http://www.scio.gov.cn/32618/Document/1539667/1539667.htm
51. Joel Wuthnow, *Chinese Perspectives on the Belt and Road Initiative: Strategic Rationales, Risks, and Implications*, China Strategic Perspectives 12 (Washington, DC: National Defense University, September 27, 2017), http://inss.ndu.edu/Media/News/Article/1326963/chinese-perspectives-on-the-belt-and-road-initiative-strategic-rationales-risks
52. Zhang Yunbi and Zhang Yue, "Xi Backs Building of Polar Silk Road," *China Daily*, November 2, 2017, http://www.chinadaily.com.cn/world/cn_eu/2017-11/02/content_34007511.htm
53. Nadège Rolland, *China's Eurasian Century? Political and Strategic Implications of the Belt and Road Initiative* (Seattle, WA: National Bureau of Asian Research, May 2017), http://www.nbr.org/publications/issue.aspx?id=346

54. Yuan Peng 袁鹏, "关于新时期中国大周边战略的思考" [Thoughts on China's Great Periphery Strategy in the New Period], 现代国际关系 [Contemporary International Relations] 10 (October 2013): 31.
55. Nathan and Scobell, *China's Search for Security*, 3–7.
56. "天下圖 Cheonhado (Map of all under Heaven)," http://digitalatlas.asdc.sinica.edu.tw/map_detail.jsp?id=A103000040; Stein Tønnesson and Hans Antlöv, eds., *Asian Forms of the Nation* (New York: Routledge, 1996).
57. Tim Oakes, "Looking Out to Look In: The Use of the Periphery in China's Geopolitical Narratives," *Eurasian Geography and Economics* 53, no. 3 (2012): 315–26.
58. *China's Arctic Policy* (Beijing: State Council Information Office of the People's Republic of China, January 2018), https://www.chinadailyasia.com/articles/188/159/234/1516941033919.html
59. Anne-Marie Brady, *China as a Polar Great Power* (Cambridge: Cambridge University Press, 2017).
60. Wang Jisi, "Marching Westwards: The Rebalancing of China's Geostrategy," *International and Strategic Studies*, no. 73 (2012). See also Wang Jisi, "China's Search for a Grand Strategy: A Rising Great Power Finds Its Way," *Foreign Affairs* 90, no. 2 (March/April 2011): 68–79, https://www.foreignaffairs.com/articles/china/2011-02-20/chinas-search-grand-strategy. For related analysis, see Wu Zhengyu, "Toward 'Land' or Toward 'Sea'? The High-Speed Railway and China's Grand Strategy," *Naval War College Review* 66, no. 3 (Summer 2013): 53–66.
61. "Milestone Congress," *Xinhua*.
62. Yan Xuetong and Sun Xuefeng, eds. 阎学通、孙学峰等著, 中国崛起及其战略 [The Rise of China and its Strategy], (北京 [Beijing]: 北京大学出版社 [Beijing University Press], 2005); Yan Xuetong, "How China Can Defeat America," *New York Times*, November 20, 2011, http://www.nytimes.com/2011/11/21/opinion/how-china-can-defeat-america.html
63. Liu Mingfu, *The China Dream: Great Power Thinking and Strategic Posture in the Post-American Era* (New York: CN Times Books Inc., 2015).
64. Shi Yinhong, "Amid Western Uncertainties, China Mustn't Spread Too Thin," *Global Times*, October 26, 2016, http://www.globaltimes.cn/content/1013884.shtml
65. Yaqing Qin, "Continuity through Change: Background Knowledge and China's International Strategy," *The Chinese Journal of International Politics* 7, no. 3 (September 2014): 285–314, https://doi.org/10.1093/cjip/pou034
66. "中国崛起恐进入瓶颈期 两高官披露'内忧外患'" [China's Rise May Be Entering a Bottleneck Period; Two High-Level Officials Disclosed "Internal and External Problems"], 多维新闻 [Duowei News], May 22, 2018, http://news.dwnews.com/china/news/2018-05-22/60059651.html
67. Andrew S. Erickson and Lyle J. Goldstein, "Studying History to Guide China's Rise as a Maritime Great Power," *Harvard Asia Quarterly* 12, no. 3–4 (Winter 2010): 31–8, http://www.andrewerickson.com/wp-content/uploads/2011/01/Studying-History-to-Guide-Chinas-Rise-as-a-Maritime-Great-Power_Erickson-Goldstein_HAQ_2010-Winter.pdf; Andrew S. Erickson and Lyle J. Goldstein, "China Studies the Rise of the Great Powers," in *China Goes to Sea*, eds. Erickson, Goldstein, and Lord (Annapolis, MD: Naval Institute Press, July 2009).

68. See, for example, Wang Jisi 王辑思, "苏美争霸的历史教训和美中国的崛起新道路" [The Historic Lesson of the U.S.-Soviet Contest for Hegemony and China's Peaceful Rise], essay in 中国和平崛起新道路 [China's Peaceful Rise: A New Path] (Beijing: 中共中央党校国际战略研究所 [International Strategy Research Institute, Central Party School], April 2004).
69. "Milestone Congress," *Xinhua*.
70. See Samantha Hoffman, "Programming China: The Communist Party's Autonomic Approach to Managing State Security," *MERICS China Monitor*, December 12, 2017, https://www.merics.org/en/microsite/china-monitor/programming-china; Peter Mattis, "China Adaptive Approach to the Information Counter-Revolution," Jamestown *China Brief*, June 3, 2011, https://jamestown.org/program/chinas-adaptive-approach-to-the-information-counter-revolution/; Bethany Allen-Ebrahimian, "Chinese Police Are Demanding Personal Information From Uighurs in France," *Foreign Policy*, March 2, 2018, http://foreignpolicy.com/2018/03/02/chinese-police-are-secretly-demanding-personal-information-from-french-citizens-uighurs-xinjiang/. To coerce those living beyond its physical control, the Party-state may detain their family members. Simon Denyer, "China Detains Relatives of U.S. Reporters in Apparent Punishment for Xinjiang Coverage," *Washington Post*, February 28, 2018, https://www.washingtonpost.com/world/china-detains-relatives-of-us-reporters-in-apparent-punishment-for-xinjiang-coverage/2018/02/27/4e8d84ae-1b8c-11e8-8a2c-1a6665f59e95_story.html
71. Paul Kennedy, *The Rise and Fall of the Great Powers: Economic Change and Military Conflict from 1500 to 2000* (New York: Vintage Books, 1989).
72. Gabriel B. Collins and Andrew S. Erickson, "China's S-Curve Trajectory: Structural Factors Will Likely Slow the Growth of China's Economy and Comprehensive National Power," *China SignPost* (洞察中国), no. 44 (August 15, 2011), http://www.chinasignpost.com/wp-content/uploads/2011/08/China-SignPost_44_S-Curves_Slowing-Chinese-Econ-Natl-Power-Growth_20110815.pdf; Erickson and Collins, "China's S-Shaped Threat," *The Diplomat*, September 6, 2011, https://thediplomat.com/2011/09/chinas-s-shaped-threat/
73. Robert Gilpin, *War and Change in World Politics* (Cambridge: Cambridge University Press, 1983), 78, 107.
74. Howard French, "China's Twilight Years," *The Atlantic* (June 2016), https://www.theatlantic.com/magazine/archive/2016/06/chinas-twilight-years/480768/
75. Michael Beckley, "China's Century? Why America's Edge Will Endure," *International Security* 36, no. 3 (Winter 2011/12): 41–78, https://www.mitpressjournals.org/doi/pdfplus/10.1162/ISEC_a_00066
76. Andrew S. Erickson, "Evaluating China's Conventional Military Power: The Naval and Air Dimensions," in *Assessing China's Power*, ed. Jae Ho Chung (New York: Palgrave Macmillan, 2015), 65–90.
77. See, for example, Thomas J. Christensen, *The China Challenge: Shaping the Choices of a Rising Power* (New York: W. W. Norton & Company, 2015); Thomas J. Christensen, "China's Military Might: The Good News," *Japan Times*, June 8, 2015, https://www.japantimes.co.jp/opinion/2015/06/08/commentary/world-commentary/chinas-military-might-the-good-news/#; Thomas J. Christensen,

"Managing Disputes with China," *Japan Times*, June 9, 2015, https://www.japantimes.co.jp/opinion/2015/06/09/commentary/japan-commentary/managing-disputes-china/#; Aaron L. Friedberg, *A Contest for Supremacy: China, America, and the Struggle for Mastery in Asia* (New York: W. W. Norton & Company, 2011); Evan A. Feigenbaum, "Reluctant Stakeholder: Why China's Highly Strategic Brand of Revisionism is More Challenging Than Washington Thinks," *Macro Polo*, April 27, 2018, https://macropolo.org/reluctant-stakeholder-chinas-highly-strategic-brand-revisionism-challenging-washington-thinks/.
78. Peter A. Dutton, "A Maritime or Continental Order for Southeast Asia and the South China Sea?" (address, Chatham House, London, UK, February 16, 2016); reprinted in *Naval War College Review* 69, no. 3 (Summer 2016): 5–13.
79. *National Security Strategy of the United States of America 2017* (Washington, DC: The White House, December 2017), https://www.whitehouse.gov/wp-content/uploads/2017/12/NSS-Final-12-18-2017-0905.pdf
80. The views expressed in this chapter are those of the author alone. He acknowledges with appreciation valuable insights from the volume editors and other contributors, as well as from Dingding Chen, Ian Chong, Rush Doshi, Peter Mattis, Joel Wuthnow, and an anonymous Chinese expert; as well as fellow participants at two conferences: the "Princeton-Harvard China and the World Program Workshop," University of Maryland, College Park, February 28–March 2, 2018; and the "Rising Power Grand Strategies Workshop," Paul Tsai China Center, Yale Law School, March 9, 2018.

5 France

THIERRY BALZACQ

France pursued a unique grand strategy, initially crafted and promoted by Charles de Gaulle, characterized best as "grandeur," unaltered for three decades from the late 1950s onwards.[1] The key elements of grandeur were a search for status and rank, the need for autonomy in decision-making epitomized by *force de frappe*, a reticence toward American hegemony, the prioritization of national defense, and the centrality of the French nation-state.[2] Successive presidents, both from the right and left, did not question these strategic principles. Indeed, they each carefully proclaimed their loyalty to them.[3] In a country wherein defense and foreign policy fall within the *domaine réservé* (exclusive domain) of the president, the enduring adherence to grandeur by the left and right is rather puzzling, as each president could be tempted to leave its marks on France's relation with the outside world.

Since the end of the Cold War, however, a number of shifts in the international system have forced France to move away from some of the basic tenets of grandeur. These include, most pointedly, the collapse of the Soviet Union, the reunification of Germany, the gradual reduction of the American presence and role in Europe, and the emergence of the European Union coupled, tellingly, with increasing domestic financial constraints.

These changes generated the belief that grandeur was no longer able to serve France interests in the twenty-first century.[4] In policy terms, France's return to NATO's military command structure stands out as the main indicator of its new attitude toward the world. This is often explained through a purely instrumental lens (i.e., a shrinking defense budget would be compensated by membership in the Alliance).[5] Others, however, interpret this reintegration into NATO's military command structure as a product of an ideological victory of those in France who construe world politics as a field of battle between the West and the rest. This network of like-minded people is either called "French neoconservatism" or "Occidentalism."[6]

I argue, however, that these characterizations—"French neoconservatism" and "Occidentalism"—belie a more profound rupture undergone by France's grand strategy, since the beginning of the 1990s. In my view, contemporary French grand strategy is more accurately denoted by the label "Liberal Engagement." The latter has fundamentally changed the strategic means, ways and ends of France's global commitment. Consistent with the approach of this volume, I eschew normatively prescribing this strategy. My goal is to describe and explain the adoption of this new grand strategy, although I will return if briefly to the question of its long-term sustainability in the conclusion.

Liberal engagement combines both neoconservative and liberal internationalism ideas, albeit in unequal parts. It shares the internationalism of neoconservatism but not the primacy it accords to the role of military action. For proponents of liberal engagement, in contrast, France should primarily focus on entrenching powerful states within the constraining structure of world politics rather than pursuing unilateral options. Military power should only be employed prudently when the utility of other instruments have been exhausted. Furthermore, liberal engagement substitutes multilateral Western leadership for American primacy, enhancing the prospect of stability and peace among states. Finally, while grandeur lauded French exceptionalism, liberal engagement aims to present France as a power whose strength derives from its ability to muster two main levers. The first is France's commitment to Western values. France's interest extends beyond its capacity to defend itself to enhancing the security of its allies, either within multilateral alliances (such as NATO) or through specific bilateral security agreements (such as with sub-Saharan states). These are as instruments for extending Western ideals. The second is the capacity of France to "soft balance" contenders for influence within the framework of international organizations.[7] This preference explains the frequent advocacy by successive French presidents, at least since Chirac, of opening the permanent seats of the United Nations Security Council to new members, in particular to those that might enable it to balance its current membership (e.g., Germany). The adoption of the strategy of liberal engagement has a significant bearing on the prioritization of threats, the implementation of strategy and, accordingly, both the balance and ways that diplomatic, military, and economic instruments have been employed.

I structure this chapter in four parts in substantiating these claims. First, I describe the premises of grandeur, which engrossed the political imagination of seven successive presidents, and provided them with strategic guidance. Second, I discuss France's "grand strategic system."[8] Third, I identify both the international and domestic factors that sustain the strategy of liberal engagement. Finally, I examine the main elements of liberal engagement itself, along three axes: theoretical bases, causal logic, and policy components.

5.1 Grandeur and the historical foundations of France's grand strategy

Grandeur stood as France's only grand strategy for approximately three decades. It notably originated from different philosophies: romanticism (which celebrated nationalism, mysticism, war, and heroes) and classicism (de Gaulle admired Louis XIV, who personified the classical leader whose political system and policies ideally were shaped by balance, restraint, and order). Grandeur thus reflects the continuing aspiration of France to fashion a vibrant domestic national identity and, as a consequence, to outperform other states internationally. The strategy of grandeur sought to maintain France's privileged position vis-à-vis both the West and the East in order to maximize its prestige, to increase its influence, and to husband the resources necessary for its independence.[9]

Originally, the most elementary task of grandeur was therapeutic—intended to heal the societal scars left by Word War II, which had torn French society and weakened the state. The strategy of grandeur was a means to rebuild a national consensus, and to revive and strengthen national consciousness. The strategy of grandeur therefore compensated for domestic pathologies and divisions. As Maurice Vaïsse noted, "pursuing grandeur harnesses the energies of Frenchmen, distracting them from petty personal concerns and mutual animosities."[10] Foreign policy thus served domestic purposes. "France is not really herself unless she is in the first rank; that only vast enterprises are capable of counterbalancing the ferments of disintegration inherent in her people... France cannot be France without grandeur," claimed De Gaulle.[11] Philip Gordon, further argued in 1993 that "French grandeur... is still important; the French feel they are destined to play leading global and European roles and are loathe to renounce them."[12]

The strategy of grandeur is embedded in a realist theory of international politics. Specifically, grandeur subscribes to the tenets of offensive realism because it emphasizes the centrality of war in resolving conflicts of interests and privileges temporary alliances over long-term institutionalized cooperation. For grandeur, the analytical unit is the French state. Offensive realism does not rule out the possibility of cooperation between sovereign units. Rather, it argues that cooperation does not guarantee that a state's survival will not be threatened or attacked by another. The centrality of grandeur for the French at this time, in the aftermath of World War II, is explained in part by the pressure war exerts on nations, and the benefits it brings: "victory in war is the ultimate expression of grandeur, as war inspired the best in each nation."[13] A nation achieves a sense of grandeur by defeating its enemies. Indeed, war explicitly enables a domestic population to accept the importance of a nation's identity by consciously acting together. The sources of this belief run deep in French history. Central to the Gaullist myth, for example, is the notion that the Gauls achieved a sense of shared destiny through their resistance to the Roman Empire.

The strategy of grandeur places a great value on France's "exceptional" heritage and a sustained commitment to common identity. In this respect, grandeur is nationalistic. Indeed, according to Gordon, "it should not be forgotten" that it is "the nationalist tradition that played a prominent role in the intellectual life of France in the early twentieth century" which prompted de Gaulle's defense of France's grandeur place in the world.[14] However, it is seldom recognized that de Gaulle employed nationalism as an alternative ideology to both Marxism, championed by the Soviet Union, or liberalism, promoted by the United States.

From de Gaulle's perspective, grandeur's concern with the nation was intrinsically associated with the need to build and preserve a strong state, because the state is the effective political institution through which a nation accumulates and exercises power. Only the nation-state is therefore capable of pursuing a "higher synthesis of unity-in-diversity which is the goal of all political action."[15] In contrast, a political community such as the EU, even if it were to achieve a cultural reality and legitimacy, would be unable to undertake the tasks that accrue to a nation-state. Ultimately, Philip Cerny notes, "the success or failure of the nation-state depends upon the collective consciousness of the social base."[16] The state, to be effective, therefore requires "a social base, an ability to reflect psychological identity as well as goals."[17] In Gaullist doctrine, the nation-state is the instrument for the specific articulation of needs and constraints. In this context, institutions such as the EU cannot evolve into an entity that replaces the nation-state's political function because it lacks two fundamentals attributes: a firmly rooted and established state and a common consciousness.

"Independence," says Stanley Hoffman, "is the condition of grandeur."[18] Grandeur and independence are not substitutable, but "integrally related to one another."[19] Gaullists believed that independence was crucial because France had to be autonomous from any other power (or perceived to be so), in particular the United States, in order to rise to a prominent status within the international system and thus able to contribute a degree of direction to the international order. Further, independence was thought to enable France to determine its security commitments in core areas without any external interference. France withdrew from NATO military structure in 1966 in implementing this version of independence.[20]

For de Gaulle, a primary lesson drawn from World War II was that military dependency undermines political autonomy. The strategy of grandeur attempted to solve this problem by developing an independent nuclear capacity. Nuclear weapons were a measure of status and a guarantor of security. Nuclear deterrence would protect France, strengthen its military credibility, and complement its diplomatic initiatives. Grandeur as strategy, according to Edward Kolodziej, thus signaled,

a big-power role for France, much like that understood and acted upon by those responsible for French foreign policy under the Third and Fourth Republics. Along with a small number of other chosen states, France has the responsibility to define the hierarchical structure of international relations and the role to be played by lesser units, to determine and assure basic security arrangements, and to regulate the economic and diplomatic processes by which relations are to be conducted. As a great power, France's actions are an example and its policies a guide for other states, both large and small.[21]

The presidents who followed exhibited a remarkable continuity with the nuclear policy's coordinates set by de Gaulle. However, this does not mean that domestic critics have not raised concerns about French nuclear policy.[22] But the path-dependency created by the premises of independence made it difficult for any president to challenge its relevance. To illustrate this point, consider the evolution of Mitterrand's attitude toward nuclear capacities. At first, Mitterrand ran for president in 1965 and 1974 on a program that denounced France's nuclear posture. But assuming office, he finally supported and eventually bolstered the Gaullist initiative of a France's nuclear force, even as the Cold War ended. In fact, as William Nester points out, "France's largest expansion of nuclear power occurred during Mitterrand's presidency as the number of nuclear weapons rose from 80 in 1983 to 592 in 1994."[23] Here, too, Mitterrand's policy was based on de Gaulle's main foreign policy principles. Indeed, Mitterrand asserted on various occasions that he aspired to uphold France's independence and rank as the world's "third military power" and to "preserve our strategy, and therefore the instrument of this strategy . . . nuclear deterrence."[24]

A multipolar balance of power was regarded as the best mechanism against the encroachment of other powers according to grandeur's advocates, in contrast to the principle of collective security. During the Cold War, France perceived the bipolar preponderance enjoyed by the Soviet Union and the United States as an obstacle to its existence as an independent actor in world politics and thus the pursuit of its own vital interests. In this context, nuclear power allowed France to ensure that it would not be subservient to either superpower. The strategy of grandeur rested on the core belief that "it is only in equilibrium that the world will find peace."[25] Balancing, however, was a condition for peace, not a goal in itself, "the vehicle by which nation-states begin to cooperate and to realize their common ideals."[26] As president, de Gaulle's understanding of the balance of power was therefore "based upon those universal values (peace, independence, etc.) which [he] believed to be the culmination of the evolution of civilization."[27] As such, although de Gaulle was primarily a realist, his philosophy of international relations was sensitive to elements of liberalism: effectively, liberalism is contingent upon balance of power. As long as no nation attempts to achieve hegemony, the mutual pursuit of the national interest could bring together states of various sizes and cultures.

5.2 France's grand strategic system

France's grand strategic system vests authority in the president. Indeed, among European democracies, the French president holds unparalleled powers in defense and foreign affairs.[28] In the French system, these policies belong to the so-called *domaine réservé* (exclusive domain) of the president. He or she dominates the decision-making process, sets policy priorities, and aligns means to ends in these domains, assisted by the prime minister and ministers of foreign affairs and defense. Although several reforms have introduced some nuance in the ways the *domaine réservé* is actually practiced, this has not affected the president's overall status in France's grand strategic system. The *domaine réservé* remains a regulative institution of both French strategy making and implementation. Textually speaking, however, the *domaine réservé* does not appear in the French Constitution. The concept is primarily meant to metaphorically reflect the way the president (as part of the executive, along with the prime minister) interacts with both the government and the parliament and with the military forces.

Yet, the French Constitution does formally organize the relationship between different members of the Fifth Republic's grand strategic system. It is characterized by three principles: First, a strict hierarchy of subordination between the executive and the Armies (the general term for all of France's military forces) in which the president serves as Commander-in-Chief. Second, a co-rulership of the executive, in legal terms, but a prevalence of the president over the prime minister in practice. Third, the parliament has little leverage in defense and foreign affairs.[29] Its oversight is exerted indirectly, that is, by its right to question the government's policy. Notably, the president's actions in the field of defense cannot therefore be subject to the parliament's direct control. Although the executive must inform the parliament three days after the beginning of a foreign intervention,[30] and seek its authorization to prolong the intervention should it exceeds four months,[31] for example, the parliament often has to deal with a fait accompli, which makes it difficult to reverse the president's decision.

The parliament and the president are commonly affiliated to the same political party (except under the rare instances of "cohabitation"). This drastically impairs either the will or ability of the parliament to publicly denounce the president's political choices. In rare periods of "cohabitation," the parliament can also control government's actions *ex post*. Then, the prime minister may demonstrate some autonomy, albeit at the risk of causing a domestic political crisis.

According to the Constitution, the prime minister is in fact "responsible for national defense" (article 21). In reality, however, the prime minister's main function is to implement the presidential policy. Nonetheless, there are two circumstances during which the prime minister's role becomes more salient. First, the prime minister enjoys a cardinal place when the budget of the army is under discussion before the parliament. That is, during debates over the *Loi de programmation militaire* (Military Planning Law), which normally authorizes the government's investment in defense for a defined period of time. Second, the prime minister also plays a central role when a policy involves a relative degree of interministerial coordination, as many issues pertaining to grand strategy (in any whole-of-government approach) often do. The requirement for intergovernmental coordination is reinforced by France's conception of global security, which distributes security responsibilities across different ministries according to their expertise. Article 18, for example, explicitly stipulates that, for defense purposes, the Economics Ministry, "orient the action of ministries tasked with the production, gathering and utilization of diverse range of resources and industrial organization of the territory."

The Defense Minister (or Minister of Armies, as it is sometimes called in France) plays a central role in the routine management of the Armies. But the minister is constrained in three ways. First, the president can arbitrarily intervene in the conduct of military affairs, both directly or indirectly through his or her private Chief of Staff. Second, in practice, the Minister of Defense's operational autonomy depends less on her/his expertise than on the quality of their personal relationship with both the president and the prime minister. Third, the Minister of Defense has to assert her/himself against the Chief of the General Staff, who enjoys extensive operational management powers and on some important budgetary issues, which affect all the Chief of Staffs of the different armed forces. In sum, the Minister of Defense's authority is challenged both internally by the Chief of the General Staff and externally by the prime minister and the president.[32]

Nonetheless, if these are the legal and practical distributions of authority, where are the major decisions made when it comes to the formulation and implementation of French grand strategy? While the Council of Ministers deliberates on general defense policies, most decisions on major strategic orientations are crafted within the *Conseil de défense et de sécurité nationale* (Council of Defense and National Security). The meetings of the Defense Council are either plenary or restricted, but they are all chaired by the president and seconded by the prime minister (cf. articles 15 and 20 of the Constitution). Additional members of the plenary defense council include the ministers of defense, foreign affairs, economics and finance, Chief of Staffs, and any other minister as the agenda demands. High-ranking civil servants can also be invited to the plenary defense council in order to share their knowledge of a specific topic under consideration.

Restricted councils of defense deal with decisions concerning the use of force. Decisions adopted therein have immediate effect. The composition of the restricted council is smaller, composed of the president, the prime minister, and the ministers of foreign affairs and defense. Other ministers can be invited on an ad hoc basis. Furthermore, the restricted council includes the Chiefs of Staff of different armies, the Chief of the General Staff, the President's private Chief of Staff, and the Secretary General of Elysée who drafts the minutes. The General Secretariat of Defense and National Security (SGDSN) is the main body that prepares the meetings, providing background material and reports, writing syntheses, and ensuring the follow-up of the Council of Defense and National Security's meetings.[33] The SGDSN also ensures the oversight of the agency responsible for France's cybersecurity (*ANSSI: Agence nationale de la sécurité des systèmes de l'information*).

Members of the council also draw upon their own in-house expertise, in order to prepare the meetings most effectively. The Minister of Defense relies on the work carried out by the Directorate General for International Relations and Strategy (DGRIS), whereas the Minister of Foreign Affairs receives policy notes from different directorates of that ministry and the *Centre d'analyse, de prévision et de stratégie* (CAPS), which constitutes the French Policy Planning Staff. The DGRIS and CAPS are not legally equivalent and have dissimilar structures, both in terms of their constitutive membership and with regard to their position within the architecture of their respective ministry. But their primary functions are relatively similar: they assist their ministers in taking informed decisions. While formal relations between the CAPS and the DGRIS are nominal, it is not uncommon to have a civil servant moving from the ministry of foreign affairs to the ministry of defense (although the reverse is less frequent), which to some extent facilitates the circulation of ideas and strengthens the coherence of French grand strategy.

To summarize, France's grand strategy is formulated by a large variety of actors situated within different institutional environments, but all the trends converge toward the Elysée. France's grand strategic system is characterized by the centrality of the executive and a soft parliamentary role. The president heads the decision-making apparatus, assisted by the prime minister, the Minister of Defense, the Minister of Foreign Affairs, the Chief of the General Staff and the president's private Chief of Staff. The organizational system is reliant on interministerial coordination because so many ministries are involved in defense and national security matters. France's grand strategic system, the source of it strategic ideas and policies, is a constellation of semi-autonomous bodies which all fall under the authority of the president. Such a strong hierarchical structure lends coherence to the grand strategy selected. Finally, notably, in this arrangement, one of the weakest figures of France's grand strategic system is the Minister of Defense, whose influence is constrained by various figures: the Chief of the General Staff, the president's private Chief of Staff, and by the prime minister and the president. Furthermore, in advocating any strategy or policy, the Minister of Defense has to surmount the thick layers of expertise offered by a large number of institutions that are involved in defense and security matters.

5.3 From grandeur to liberal engagement

Having presented France's grand strategic system, this section discusses France's contemporary grand strategy, emphasizing its new characteristics, which differentiate it from grandeur's main tenets.

By the end of the 1980s, the global environment started to change dramatically. Yet, the broad consensus around grandeur created strong incentives for strategic inertia. The historical force associated with its progenitor, de Gaulle, might explain why the move from grandeur took almost three decades. No French president was bold enough to proclaim that grandeur was outdated nor had the temerity to assert that France had lost its global role and status. Changes was therefore incremental. Three White Papers (hereafter: WP), published over considerable intervals in 1994, 2008, and 2013, heralded this transformation. The *Strategic Review of Defence and National Security*, issued by Emmanuel Macron in 2017, mostly confirmed both the threat environment and the strategic options defined in these prior WPs.

The product is a grand strategy of liberal engagement. It is predominantly concerned with consolidating France's ties with a liberal international order. This promotion of international order explains France's advocacy of international law. In fact, France now considers legal regulation—not nuclear power—as the main instrument of security. For example, the 2013 WP emphasizes the role of international legitimacy in the implementation of a defense and national security strategy, which is a necessary complement to national legitimacy: "France believes that an international order based on the rule of law rather than on the use of force is an essential condition for international security. It therefore considers the legal regulation of relationship between States as a cornerstone of its security."[34] Furthermore, unlike grandeur, France new strategy does not aim to maximize power but rather to enhance its security through multilateral arrangements. Finally, although all official documents reiterate that France seeks autonomy, there are clear signs that France's liberal engagement strategy has tilted toward integration. France's grand strategy has therefore veered into a new direction.

Liberal engagement is based on seven assumptions that can be succinctly stated. First, in a multipolar world, independence is a burden for nations like France, not an asset. Second, to advance its interests and buttress its credibility, France needs to work with the US, not against it. Third, grandeur and prestige should be deemphasized in strategic planning. Fourth, obtaining effective alliance commitments offers France a powerful leverage that surpasses what it can achieve unilaterally. Fifth, multilateralism favors states that obey normative principles rather than ignoring or contravening them. Sixth, preserving and promoting democratic values is a prerequisite for systemic stability, consistent with a liberal peace argument. Finally, emerging powers such as China can only be effectively engaged through multilateral institutions. Liberal engagement therefore fundamentally challenges the precepts of grandeur.

A strategy of liberal engagement aims to address global forces that no state can handle unilaterally: principally globalization, transnational terrorism, fissile material proliferation, and global warming. It assumes that a lack of political leadership has disrupted international rules, moral coordinates, and conventional references to identity. This diagnosis leads proponents of liberal engagement to argue that "a politics of civilization" can counteract these global forces.[35] As Sergei Fedorov states, "the politics of civilization at the present state should prioritize such values as solidarity, the sense of identity, and friendliness, as opposed to isolation and separatism, the lack of identity, degradation of the quality of life, and irresponsibility."[36] The politics of civilization is one vector of global influence but encapsulates ambivalent elements. It does reinforce the Gaullist belief in the universalist importance of French values.[37] According to Bruno Tertrais, for example, "France continues to believe that it has global responsibilities due to its permanent status at the UN Security Council, and also that it can be a force for good by defending universal values."[38] In this sense, when encroached, solidarity with Western powers should be put at the service of human rights. Yet simultaneously, the politics of civilization implicitly recognizes that these values are primarily Western, not exclusively French.[39] Liberal engagement is thus underpinned by a form of Occidentalism. The referent vocabulary, however, has varied between presidents: Nicolas Sarkozy theorized about Western civilization, François Hollande employed the idea of "Occidental solidarity,"[40] and Macron now speaks of the preservation of an "international order" imbued with Western values.

Liberal engagement converges with defensive realism's assumption that security is not a scarce commodity in international politics: states seek to maximize their security, not their power.[41] Those who act otherwise make other states suspicious of their intentions, and generate conditions that are conducive to war. As Fareed Zakaria notes, defense realism "assumes that the international system provides incentives only for moderate, reasonable behavior."[42] Aggression, from this perspective, results from unit-level pathologies, such as domestic failures, or the misperception of other states intentions.[43] The pursuit of democracy, a commitment to economic interdependence, and compliance with rules of international institutions, produce greater national security. The strategy of liberal engagement therefore assumes that France can do little to prevent the emergence of new contenders that may generate security dilemmas. The accumulation of power is an inadequate response to the threats France faces. Liberal engagement thus prescribes that France pursues deeper forms of cooperation to alleviate potential threats. This implies two notable changes to France's strategy: First, it must accept the constraints imposed by others, which it did by fully reintegrating NATO military structure; Second, France must support multilateral schemes of security cooperation, such as the UN, the Organization for Security and Co-operation in Europe (OSCE), or the EU. This does not mean that institutions necessarily change France's policy goals but that multilateral security cooperation is likely to reinforce France's strategic preferences.

5.3.1 REORIENTING INSTRUMENTS

In this section, I address the question of how France's grand strategic instruments—military, economic, diplomatic (and other social forms of power)—are pursued in light of liberal engagement's assumptions.

5.3.1.1 Military power and alliances

For grandeur, states are "the only entities that have the right to order and authority to act."[44] Liberal engagement accords a greater significance to alliances and international institutions in France's approach to military power. It bestows international institutions with a cardinal responsibility for ensuring international security. As the 1994 WP suggests,

> The *interdependence* of our interests with that of our main partners is continuously growing. Our relative weight within the concert of states incites us to seek the best alliances and the best instruments that would enable us to multiply our power. That is why the action of France is increasingly embedded within a multilateral framework—... European Union, OSCE, Transatlantic Alliance, UN.[45]

Further, in the section titled "Collective Security in the 21st Century," the 2008 WP confirms this orientation, arguing that the new threats confronting the world—war, proliferation, terrorism, pandemic disease, organized crime, wide-ranging natural catastrophes—have taken on a global dimension and therefore cannot be fought (exclusively) at either the national or the regional level.[46] The WP suggests that these threats must be addressed by mobilizing an effective and legitimate international security system.

A strategy of liberal engagement thus seeks to utilize the capacity of international institutions to augment French power on the world stage. Moreover, its "operational language"[47] is mostly that of values rather than interests. Indeed, it asserts that one of the most effective ways to mobilize alliances and international institutions is to invoke common values rather than interests. Yet, values and interests are complementary, not in conflict, in the contemporary French strategic lexicon.[48] Justifying France's return to NATO military structures, for example, Sarkozy argued that, "Grounded upon a community of values and interests, (NATO) is a democratic alliance within which each state is free to make its voice heard. The Transatlantic Alliance plays a central role for the security of Europe. It is *essential* to the security of France."[49]

This indispensable status granted to NATO is extended to the EU in the 2013 WP: "the European framework is set to *become the reference framework* in situations requiring the mobilization of the whole range of civil and military instruments required to implement a global approach to crises."[50] Regarding NATO, the WP argues that France "intends to make an active contribution to the vitality and the future of the organization, which is an essential collective defense alliance and, as such, a major part of its defense and security."[51] Thus, the 2017 Strategic Review renews France's commitment to raise its defense budget to the level set by NATO (i.e., 2 percent of the GDP) by 2025.

In sum, although France maintains the fifth largest military,[52] liberal engagement acknowledges the changing international environment with the intent of adjusting France's diplomatic and military instruments to novel threats and challenges, yet uses international institutions as a force multiplier to avoid unaffordable strategic and budgetary overstretch.[53]

This growth in the strategic importance of international institutions in France's strategy, and the types of concerns it raises, is illustrated by France's reintegration into NATO's military command structure (IMCS) following the Strasbourg-Kehl Summit in 2009. One of the reasons used to explain France reintegration is that it remains outside IMCS, which has created a significant imbalance between France's overall contribution to NATO and its ability to exert influence on the Alliance.[54] With a budgetary contribution of roughly 10.5 percent to NATO's overall budget, France is the third largest contributor after the United States and Germany, whose respective average budgetary contributions amount to 22 and 14.5 percent. Furthermore, throughout the 1990s, France regularly deployed forces under NATO command in Bosnia (IFOR and SFOR) and Kosovo (KFOR). In 2001, France joined NATO combat forces in Afghanistan, and remained there as one of the top five contributors to NATO troops for thirteen years.

Collectively, these initiatives reflect France's continuing commitment to transatlantic security. But it could not be characterized as a full partner because it could not take part in the decisions regarding the operations in which it participated, nor contribute to shaping doctrinal discussions within NATO in some of the most important forums, such as the Defense Planning Committee. As such, France's uncoupling from the IMCS appeared increasingly ineffectual. In this context, a return to NATO's integrated military structures, regardless of its accompanying restrictions,[55] was meant to enhance its interactions with other NATO members along strategic, doctrinal, and operational lines, allowing France a higher degree of influence within

NATO. A key lever of influence has been the appointment of French nationals (generals) to major Strategic Commands, such as the ACT in Norfolk (Virginia) and the Joint Command Lisbon.

This integration however, has entailed a cost: France has had to change its position on some historically divisive issues. One example is the evolution of French policy toward the Anti-missile Defense Project.[56] France's main opposition to the project was that the missile shield would compromise its ability to select the most appropriate nuclear strategy for its security. Although the then (more Gaullist) Minister of Defense, Hervé Morin, appeared reluctant, Sarkozy conceded that, "missile defense capabilities against limited attack could be a useful complement to nuclear deterrence, without of course substituting it."[57] Missile defense was no longer interpreted a threat to France's "freedom of action." The return to NATO has therefore led to a deepening of the interdependence between France and NATO.

5.3.1.2 Economic leverage

France lacks a specific ministry dedicated to external trade. The Undersecretary who performs this function reports directly to the Minister of Foreign Affairs. Policies related to external trade belong to the domain of "economic diplomacy." While this reinforces France's strategic cohesion, it also means that trade and commercial relations do not enjoy a specific autonomous domain.

Within this context, France has an export profile that concentrates on high-tech goods. Largest commodity exports include "machinery and transport equipments" (e.g., aeroplanes, helicopters, etc.), "medicaments" (or medicines) and "motor-car and other motor-vehicles."[58] The United States is France's second trade partner. But the top ten biggest trade flows are with other European countries, including Germany, Spain, Italy, and Belgium, United Kingdom, Holland, Switzerland, and Poland. They account for almost 60 percent of France's external trade relations. France, however, incurs a structural balance of trade deficit that now amounts to an average €70 billion per annum. That deficit is the highest (€30 billion) between France and China. In fact, France imports from China twice what it exports to the same country.

France reluctantly embraced economic liberalization. It was regarded as disruptive to the social fabric through job loss. The uncertainty about economic liberalization was internally debated during the Sarkozy presidency. He ordered four major government reports on the relationship between France and "globalization."[59] They reflected a clear concern that globalization had created unlawful and unfair practices that had corrupted the competition between international firms, sometimes with state support.[60]

In response, inherent within liberal engagement is French promotion of a stronger regulation of the economic sphere and commercial relations. For

France, without tighter rules, it is difficult either to draw earned benefits from economic liberalization or to convince the French public of its value. France therefore acts within the World Trade Organization, the G20 or the EU, for the development of common rules that ensure that states share equal rights and duties in the trade domain. France, for example, has proved instrumental in the fight against states and territories that fail to comply with international standards about exchanges of tax information. Further, France aims to level the playing field by advocating more stringent rules against *Base Erosion and Profit Shifting* (BEPS), that is, "tax avoidance strategies that exploit gaps and mismatches in tax rules to artificially shift profits to low or no-tax locations."[61] Finally, there are simmering concerns that the American hegemony, or that of its legal system, threatens the global performance of French companies. Arnauld Montebourg,[62] a former French Minister of Economics, argued that the United States was waging a "war of law" or "lawfare"[63] on French companies (e.g. Alcatel, Alstom, BNP Paribas, etc.) under the so-called principle of legal "extraterritoriality" established by the 1977 Foreign and Corrupt Practices Act, thus skewing the rules of fair competition in favor of American firms.[64]

Here, too, France strives to multilateralize the issue. For example, the EU is regarded as an actor that could naturally potentially collaborate with French efforts. In France's view, submitting the activities of French companies in a third country to the jurisdiction of the US legal system is tantamount to renouncing the capacity of French firms to compete on equal grounds.[65] In response, French laws endorsing a similar principle—i.e., extraterritoriality—have been ratified by its legislature, thus making it theoretically possible for France to retaliate. While these measures may have an essentially deterrence function, many voices are demanding tougher policies were the United States tempted to attack another French company in the future. France demonstrates that this endeavor is important and that it can be strengthened within a multilateral context by calling upon the Francophonie and the EU. But in the present situation, France operates alone, with the resort to the EU standing as, primarily, attempts to widen the scope of its ideas, improve the effectiveness of its policies, and to contain any international pressure, through joint action.

5.3.1.3 Diplomacy, Francophonie, and French social power

Cultural diplomacy has been a perennial feature of French relations with the rest of the world, at least since the Third Republic coined the concept.[66] While the word "Francophone" was adopted in the nineteenth century, it was not until 1967 that an institution—the Parliamentary Assembly of the Francophonie, tasked with creating bonds between French speaking peoples—was set up. In 2006, that agency was transformed into the International Organization of the Francophonie (OIF).

In general terms, there is a tight linkage—generally neglected by many scholars studying France strategy—between liberal engagement and the new impetus gained by the Francophonie. The strategy of liberal engagement assumes that social power can enable France to derive influence from cultural policies. But it incorporates seemingly contradictory assumptions about how best to employ social power. On the one hand, France wants to maintain a distinct voice in the international arena, drawing upon its cultural heritage. On the other hand, France is committed to the multilateral promotion of French culture and language, which the Francophonie embodies. As will be shown below, however, the legacy of France individual exceptionalism casts a shadow over the normal operation of Francophonie and influences its strategic effectiveness.

The Francophonie is enshrined in the French Constitution (article 87). It states that, "The Republic contributes to the development of solidarity and cooperation between the states and the peoples having the French language in common." The Francophonie pursues four main objectives: to promote the French language, and cultural and linguistic diversity; to support peace, democracy, and human rights; to advocate education, training, higher education, and research; and to encourage cooperation at the service of sustainable development. Much of the importance of Francophonie lies not in the sheer number of people who speak French globally (274 million) but in the political significance of the language's use. Thus, the aims of the Francophonie are closely interconnected and, in reality, inseparable: the promotion of linguistic diversity enables French to remain one of the more widely spoken languages in most international organizations; the support of democracy and human rights reinforces France's own idea of its special mission in the world; the steps Francophonie takes to develop education, training, higher education, and research contribute to the amplification of France's understanding of the world, in particular its idea of a "humanist globalization."[67] That is a globalization that puts human emancipation and well-being at its center. Often, however, it seems tricky to differentiate France's diplomatic initiatives from Francophonie's policies, as France sees itself as acting on behalf of or amplifying Francophonie's projects.

Nonetheless, there are distinct identifiable operational spheres. In fact, the Francophonie is deployed within and through specific international diplomatic, military, economic, and cultural fields.[68] It is probably in the diplomatic domain that Francophonie has claimed one of its most symbolic victories, namely, UNESCO's recognition of the principle of "cultural diversity" which paved the way for the 2001 Universal Declaration on Cultural Diversity.[69] Certainly, the legal regime of languages within International Organizations (IOs) provides France with a distinct standing. For example, 2016 data show that there are over 18,900 French working in IOs, constituting 9 percent of their staff. According to Dominique Hoppe, France's personnel contribution to IOs almost matches that of the United States, the largest.⁷⁰ Thus, one of the biggest challenges for France is to ensure that the French language maintains its status within IOs and multilateral negotiations. To do so, France vets new appointees' knowledge of French, checks the availability of translation services, and monitors the use of French in official documents, communiqués, and websites.

Be that as it may, many international civil servants have an insufficient—if any—knowledge of French. To remedy this situation, France and the Francophonie offer language training. In fact, since 2003, France and the Francophonie have trained over 60,000 European civil servants.⁷¹ However, despite these efforts, France has still struggled to secure mid- or senior management positions for its citizens within EU institutions, which limits its overall influence, mainly during the preparatory stage of policies when major options are crystallized.⁷² In 2018, for example, there was a heated debate in France about the appointment of a German as the General Secretary of the European Commission. Some pundits interpret this appointment, with no visible negotiated reciprocal benefits for France, as a clear indication of its declining influence in Brussels.⁷³

France also relies on Francophonie to extend the multilateralization of its strategic and security initiatives. Indeed, in keeping with the Francophonie's mandate on peace and security, France advocates a greater involvement of Francophonie in the governance of various international security issues, including conflict resolution, peacemaking and peacekeeping missions.⁷⁴ But the scope of France's interventions abroad does not calibrate with the Francophonie's geographical scope, reflecting a schism between its commitments to traditional alliances such as NATO and its leadership within the Francophonie sphere. At the height of France presence in Afghanistan, for example, there were 4,000 French troops training Afghan security forces. This compares unfavorably to those sent to Haiti (126 soldiers) under UN auspices, a full member of the Francophonie, to deliver basic security.⁷⁵

This multilateralization of French military action coincides with the dwindling number of French soldiers deployed overseas.⁷⁶ As France retreats, other powers fill the gap. China and the US have installed military bases in Djibouti when France was reducing, although not completely withdrawing its military presence in the country. Finally, arguably, France's interventions in Central Africa and Mali in 2013 contradict the idea of a multilateralization of its policy. Yet, in both cases France insisted that other countries joined its operations, or that the EU or the UN assume responsibilities for these operations. Barkhane, a regional operation, thus replaced Serval in Mali, and the UN peacekeeping force MINUSCA became the main authority in 2014 in Central Africa. Indeed, both operations enforced United Nations Council resolutions. They illustrate the extent to which liberal engagement's assumptions, including compliance with international law, have transformed the way France deals with its foreign interventions; reflect the departure from independence that underlies grandeur; and demonstrate France's reliance on international organizations as essential actors for the preservation of international order.

Economic diplomacy is the second important if underdeveloped area of cooperation between members of the Francophonie. Indeed, the Francophonie provides France with a large network of potential trade partners. Consider the following figures: The Francophonie accounts for 16 percent of the global gross product, 14 percent of world natural resources, and for approximately 4 percent of the global population. In Africa, for example, most French entrepreneurs establish their businesses in countries that have French as one of their main working languages. BearingPoint, a consulting firm, stresses that linguistic affinity often trumps the economic vitality of the country, when French entrepreneurs chose where to settle abroad.[77]

Two main policy instruments are employed by France in an attempt to widen the scope and economic reach of the Francophonie. The first is to support the integration of new members into the Francophonie, mainly as observers (e.g., Mexico, South Korea, etc.). A related mechanism employed is to negotiate a special status with foreign countries for the French language. A leading example is Nigeria's recognition of French as its official second foreign language in 2008 after English. The second instrument utilized by France to sway how social and economic intercourse between states is framed is to support the use of French in business transactions, in particular by proposing language courses geared toward economic elites; by creating institutional circumstances conducive to attracting more foreign students or in setting up French university campuses abroad; and by promoting a Francophone legal environment as a counterweight to the American legal system.

The fourth sphere of activity of the Francophonie is cultural. Here, too, France's efforts are combined with that of the Francophonie to maximize its strategic effects. Cultural advisors (often called *"conseiller de coopération et d'action culturelle"*), posted to French embassies, work closely with ambassadors in order to harness all the necessary resources that contribute to promoting French culture abroad. French cultural diplomacy pursues three objectives: supporting the use of the French language and development of French-language teaching programs abroad; promoting international student exchanges; and supporting the development of French as an international medium of communication including on the Internet, and in international media, such as TV5, *Radio France Internationale*, and France 24. The fact that France 24 broadcasts in other languages (e.g., Arabic, English) ensures that a diversity of views is promoted. In this context, France 24 is a tool at the service of the diplomacy of diversity advocated by France.

France supports a wide network of 494 schools (primary, secondary, and high school) established in 136 countries. The *Agence pour l'enseignement du français à l'étranger* (French Agency for French Education Abroad) assists these schools in accomplishing their objectives. The teaching of French is primary carried out by *Alliance française*, first set up in 1883. However, the 835 *Alliances françaises* now also aim to promote "cultural diversity," in particular Francophone cultures in the broadest sense, thus situating French culture in relation to its interactions with other cultural systems. Furthermore, the promotion of the French culture is also entrusted to the *Institut français*, whose activities cover, *inter alia*, the dissemination of French book and films, the promotion of French thought and knowledge, and the development of artistic exchanges. By linking these efforts to the Francophonie, France aspires to project its cultural power beyond what it could possibly attain unilaterally. Yet the significance of defending French language, culture, and ideas is not accurately reflected in the government budget allocated to "cultural diplomacy and influence." In the last ten years, the maximum allocated to this item in the French budget has been approximately €768 million, roughly 0.18 percent of its annual spending. Notably, French schools abroad suffered a 10 percent reduction in their budget in 2018.[78] In contrast, the French contribution to the EU budget rose from €18.7 billion in 2017 to €20.2 billion in 2018.

5.4 Conclusion

The strategy of grandeur set the parameters of France's grand strategy in a specific context, that of the immediate post–World War II period. It combined an internal (national pride and cohesion) with an international dimension (reclaiming a crucial status for France among major powers). The privileged way to attain grandeur was independence and its ultimate end was autonomy. Nuclear power served as a key instrument in the service of grandeur. However, this chapter has shown that grandeur as an orienting strategy has decisively been eroded, primarily (although not exclusively) by shifts in the international system.

France has therefore had to redefine its strategy. Domestic actors undoubtedly played a role in political transformation that resulted in France's embrace of the grand strategy of liberal engagement. But I address that in other forthcoming work.[79] Yet, this description of France's system of grand strategy provides clues as to how this happened. In the French grand strategic system, ideas have to percolate through the Council of Defense and National Security apparatus. In other words, presidential leadership, coalition between members of the Council of Defense and National Security, and strategic subcultures all intersect in various ways with the international circumstances in producing the contents of France's grand strategy.

On balance, however, traces of grandeur remain within the strategy of liberal engagement. Liberal engagement, for example, requires France to entrench its values and interests in broader institutional structures that are adroit at wielding the necessary quantum of power to simultaneously promote and preserve *both* France's status and the international order. If grandeur sometimes drew its appeal if not its efficacy from rhetorical theater, the success of liberal engagement hinges upon the ability of France to convert its multilateral commitments into a multifaceted leverage (diplomatic, military, economic, and cultural) over other nations.

Whether liberal engagement will enable France to maintain or consolidate its international influence will depend on how well several challenges are met. First, while grandeur was understood approvingly by the majority of the population, the assumptions guiding liberal engagement remain contested. They require a greater political effort to win popular support in favor of France's changing role involving complex, large-scale commitments. Second, and relatedly, France has always had a complicated relationship with "liberalism" in general, which is identified as American. Thus, a strategy inspired by any brand of liberalism might prove ideologically ill-fitting with French political culture, fermenting resistance within national institutions that contribute either to the definition or the implementation of France's grand strategy. Third, an inherent risk of liberal engagement is that, in the absence of an intellectual anchor, it could veer into a technocratic strategy, with no guiding principle or "spirit" that provides its policies with the required legitimacy, and motivate sacrifices in its name. Thus, Jean-Pierre Raffarin, former French prime minister, writes that "diplomacy is a strength if it knows where it goes," while Hervé Gaymard, a former Minister of Economics, paraphrases Ernest Renan to call for a "moral and intellectual reform" of France if it is to leave up to its "grammar."[80] Finally, while grandeur could survive under shrinking resources, thanks in part to its appealing connotation,[81] liberal engagement is more dependent on how well France marshals all the instruments of grand strategy and fulfills its international commitments. In this context, rather than making it simpler for France, liberal engagement has perhaps set the bar higher than grandeur actually did.[82]

NOTES

1. See William R. Nester, *De Gaulle's Legacy: The Art of Power in France's Fifth Republic* (New-York: Palgrave Macmillan, 2014).
2. See Maurice Vaïsse, *La Grandeur: Politique étrangère du général de Gaulle* (Paris: Fayard, 1998), 24–5; Maurice Vaïsse, *La puissance ou l'influence: la France dans le monde depuis 1958* (Paris: Fayard, 2008).
3. Edward A. Kolodziej, *French International Policy Under de Gaulle and Pompidou* (Ithaca, NY: Cornell University Press, 1974), 19.

4. On the burden created by the politics of grandeur and prestige, see Albrecht Sonntag, "The Burdensome Heritage of Prestige Politics," in *France on the World Stage: Nation State in the Global Era*, eds. Mairi Maclean and Joseph Szarka (Basingstoke: Palgrave Macmillan, 2008), 77–90.
5. See, for instance, Bruno Tertrais, "Leading on the Cheap? French Security Policy in Austerity," *The Washington Quarterly* 36, no. 3 (Summer 2013): 47–61.
6. On neoconservatism in France, see Hadrien Desuin, *La France atlantiste ou le naufrage de la diplomatie française* (Paris: Les Editions du Cerf, 2017). On the notion of "Occidentalism" as it permeates France foreign relations, see Christian Lequesne, *Ethnographie du Quay d'Orsay* (Paris, CNRS Editions, 2016).
7. On "soft balancing," see T. V. Paul, "Soft Balancing in the Age of U.S. Primacy," *International Security* 30, no. 1 (Summer 2005): 46–71; Stephen G. Brooks and William C. Wohlforth, "Hard Times for Soft Balancing," *International Security* 30, no. 1 (Summer 2005): 72–108.
8. I use "grand strategic system" in the simplest and most general sense of the term to designate the different actors, institutions, and interactions—formal or informal—between them, which account for the values, ways, means and ends of grand strategy in any given country.
9. See Pernille Rieker, *French Foreign Policy in a Changing World* (London: Palgrave Macmillan, 2017), 2–3.
10. Vaïsse, *La Grandeur*, 28.
11. Charles de Gaulle, *Mémoires*, vol. 1: *Le renouveau*, 1958–1962 (Paris: Plon, 1970), 5.
12. Philip H. Gordon, *A Certain Idea of France: French Security Policy and Gaullist Legacy* (Princeton, NJ: Princeton University Press, 1993), 17.
13. Ibid., 12.
14. Ibid., 16.
15. Philip G. Cerny, *The Politics of Grandeur: Ideological Aspects of De Gaulle's Foreign Policy* (Cambridge: Cambridge University Press, 1993), 45.
16. Ibid., 46.
17. Ibid., 45.
18. Stenley Hoffman, "De Gaulle, Europe, and the Atlantic Alliance," *International Organization* 17, no. 3 (Winter 1964): 2.
19. Gordon, *A Certain Idea of France*, 18.
20. See Frédéric Bozo, *Deux stratégies pour l'Europe: De Gaulle, les Etats-Unis et l'Alliance Atlantique, 1958–1969* (Paris: Plon, 1996).
21. Kolodziej, *French International Policy*, 28.
22. See Bruno Tertrais, *L'arme nucléaire* (Paris: PUF, 2008).
23. Nester, *De Gaulle's Legacy*, 131.
24. Ibid., 151.
25. Cerny, *The Politics of Grandeur*, 49.
26. Ibid., 51.
27. Ibid., 51.
28. See Pascal Vennesson, *Politique de défense: institutions, innovations, européanisation* (Paris: L'Harmattan, 2001); Sten Rynning, *The Changing Military Doctrine: Presidents and Military Power in Fifth Republic France, 1985–2000* (Westport, CT: Praeger, 2001); Shaun Gregory, *French Defense Policy into the Twenty-First Century*

(London: Macmillan, 2000); Pierre Barral, *Pouvoir civil et commandement militaire: du roi connétable aux leaders du XXe siècle* (Paris: Presses de Sciences Po, 2005).
29. François Lamy, *Le contrôle parlementaire des opérations extérieures*, Assemblée Nationale—Commission de la défense nationale et des forces armées, Rapport d'information, n° 2237, 2000.
30. French Constitution, Article 35 (2008).
31. French Constitution, Article 35 § 3 (2008).
32. Louis Gautier, *La défense de la France après la guerre froide* (Paris: PUF, 2009), 247–93.
33. "Assurer le Secrétariat du Conseil de Défense et de Sécurité Nationale," *Secrétariat Général de la Défense et de la Sécurité Nationale (SGDSN)*, accessed August 21, 2018, http://www.sgdsn.gouv.fr/missions/assurer-le-secretariat-du-conseil-de-defense-et-de-securite-nationale/
34. Livre Blanc sur la Défense et la Sécurité Nationale, 2013, p. 23, https://www.defense.gouv.fr/actualites/operations/livre-blanc-2013
35. The "politics of civilization" was spelled out by Edgar Morin, *Pour une politique de civilisation* (Paris: Arléa, 2002).
36. Sergei Fedorov, "Nicholas Sarkozy's European Policy," *International Affairs* 54, no. 5 (2008): 72.
37. Daniel Collard, "Le président Sarkozy et l'aggiornamento de la politique étrangère de la France acte 1: 2007–2008," *Arès* 23, no. 3 (2010–2): 79.
38. Tertrais, "Leading on the Cheap?," 54.
39. Frédéric Charillon, "Hollande and Sarkozy's Foreign Policy Legacy," in *France after 2012*, eds. Gabriel Goodliffe and Riccardo Brizzi (New York: Berghahn Books, 2015), 172.
40. Christian Lequesne, "La politique extérieure de François Hollande: entre interventionnisme libéral et nécessité européenne" accessed August 20, 2017, https://halshs.archives-ouvertes.fr/halshs-01063241/document
41. Charles L. Glaser, "What Is the Offense-Defense Balance and Can We Measure It?," *International Security* 22, no. 4 (1998): 44–82.
42. Fareed Zakaria, "Realism and Domestic Politics," *International Security* 17, no. 1 (Summer 1992): 190.
43. Most analysis on defensive realism have been applied to the American Case. In addition to Fareed Zakaria's "Realism and Domestic Politics," see, for instance, Jack Snyder, *Myths of Empire: Domestic Politics and International Ambition* (Ithaca, NY: Cornell University Press, 1991); Anthony Lake, *Laying the Foundation for a New American Century* (Washington, DC: The White House, Office of the Press Secretary, April 25, 1996); Joseph S. Nye, *Bound to Lead: The Changing Nature of American Power* (New York: Basic Books, 1990).
44. Charles De Gaulle, *Discours et messages* (Paris: Plon, 1975), vol. 3: *1958–1962*, p. 245.
45. Livre Blanc sur la Défense, 1994, p. 23, http://www.livreblancdefenseetsecurite.gouv.fr/pdf/le-livre-blanc-sur-la-defense-1994.pdf (emphasis and translation are mine).
46. Livre Blanc sur la Défense et la Sécurité Nationale, 2008, p. 113, http://www.ladocumentationfrancaise.fr/var/storage/rapports-publics/084000341.pdf

47. On this concept, see Odile Rudelle, *Mai 1958: La République* (Paris: Institut Charles de Gaulle, 1988).
48. See Frédéric Charillon, "Valeurs et intérêts national: le faux dilemme de la politique étrangère française," in *Notre interêt national: Quelle politique étrangère pour la France?*, eds. Thierry de Montbrial and Thomas Gomart (Paris: Odile Jacob, 2017), 185–98.
49. The translation and emphasis are mine. Livre Blanc, 2008, p. 99.
50. Emphasis added. Livre Blanc, 2013, p. 62.
51. Livre Blanc, 2013, p. 16.
52. See "2017 France Military Strength"—https://www.globalfirepower.com/country-military-strength-detail.asp?country_id=france
53. See de Montbrial and Gomart, eds., *Notre interêt national*, in particular chapters I, III, IV, and X.
54. Jolyon Howorth, "Prodigal Son or Trojan Horse: What's in It for France?," *European Security* 19, no. 1 (October 2010): 11–28.
55. The three main limitations were: (1) Exclusive authority of France on its nuclear weapons; (2) France maintains control of the deployment of its troops in military operations; (3) During peacetime, France troops would not be put under NATO command. Jeremy Ghez and Stephen F. Larrabee, "France and NATO," *Survival* 51, no. 2 (March 2009): 81.
56. Hollande accepted the ongoing development of the allied missile-defense system on five conditions, which, according to Tertrais, were rather classic from the French standpoint: it should complement, not substitute, nuclear deterrence; political control should oversee its use; French industry should have freedom to participate in the project; costs should be acceptable; and dialogue with Moscow should continue. Tertrais, "Leading on the Cheap?," 54.
57. Quoted in Julia Zamecnick, "Obama's European Missile Defense Strategy: Will France Play Nice?," *The Monitor: Journal of International Studies* 16, no. 1 (Winter 2010): 33.
58. Department of Economic and Social Affairs, *International Trade Statistics Yearbook*, vol. I: *Trade by Country*, 2016, p. 172. See: https://comtrade.un.org/ITSY2016VolI.pdf
59. See Hubert Védrine, *Rapport pour le Président de la République sur la France et la mondialisation* (Paris: Fayard, 2007); Laurent Cohen-Tanugi, *Euromonde 2015— Une stratégie européenne pour la mondialisation* (Paris: La Documentation française, 2008); Zinsou Lionel, *France 2025—Europe et mondialisation* (Paris: La Documentation française, 2008); Christine Boutin, *De la mondialisation à l'universalisation. Une ambition sociale* (Paris: La Documentation française, 2010).
60. Sophie Meunier, "La France face à la mondialisation: se protéger ou se projeter?," Institut de l'entreprise, *Working Paper*, September 2012, https://scholar.princeton.edu/sites/default/files/france_face_mondialisation_web_0.pdf
61. OECD, "Base Erosion and Profit Shfiting," http://www.oecd.org/tax/beps/
62. See Proceedings of a Conference on the topic ("L'extraterritorialité du droit Américain"): https://www.fondation-res-publica.org/L-extraterritorialite-du-droit-americain_r129.html

63. See Charles J. Dunlap, Jr., "Lawfare Today...and Tomorrow," *US Naval War College International Law Studies*, no. 87 (2011): 315–25, Https://scholarship.law.duke.edu/cgi/viewcontent.cgi?article=3090&context=faculty_scholarship
64. See also Revue Stratégique de Défense et de Sécurité Nationale, p. 20. https://www.defense.gouv.fr/dgris/politique-de-defense/revue-strategique/revue-strategique
65. Since the US pulled out of the Iran nuclear deal on May 12, 2018, many French politicians, including the Minister of Economics, have been calling for EU countries to develop legal instruments that would enable EU member states' companies to trade with Iran without having to incur US sanctions. See, for example, "Iran: Bruno Le Maire appelle les Européens à contrer les décisions US," Reuters, May 11, 2018, https://fr.reuters.com/article/topNews/idFRKBN1IC1FE-OFRTP
66. For a book that maps the evolution of France cultural diplomacy, see Philippe Lane, *French Scientific and Cultural Diplomacy* (Liverpool: Liverpool University Press, 2013).
67. Anne Gazeau-Secret, "Francophonie et Diplomatie d'Influence," *Géoéconomie* 4, no. 55 (2016): 40.
68. See Niagalé Bagayoko and Frédéric Ramel, eds., "Francophonie et profondeur stratégique," *Etudes de l'Irsem*, no. 26 (2013).
69. Sébastien Palissier and Alexandra Crépy, "La France dans les Organisations internationales: quelles influences pour quels projets?," *Association AEGE*, April 10, 2010, http://bdc.aege.fr/public/La_France_dans_les_organisations_inter nationales_Quelles_influences_pour_quels_projets.pdf
70. Dominique Hoppe, "La langue française dans les organisations internationales: le dernier contre-pouvoir?," *HuffingtonPost*, January 4, 2013, https://www.huffingtonpost.fr/dominique-hoppe/langue-francaise-_b_2979045.html
71. France Diplomatie, "Promouvoir la langue française dans le monde," accessed January 1, 2018, https://www.diplomatie.gouv.fr/fr/photos-videos-publications-infographies/publications/enjeux-planetaires-cooperation-internationale/documents-de-strategie-sectorielle/article/promouvoir-la-langue-francaise-114859
72. This trend is slightly different from the one identified by Simon Reich and Richard Ned Lebow, who noted that a series of appointments of French bureaucrats to key international positions, including the EU, had a decisive effect on the character of the EU. See Simon Reich and Richard Ned Lebow, *Goodbye Hegemony! Power and Influence in the Global System* (Princeton, NJ: Princeton University Press), 64.
73. Le Monde and AFP, "Commission européenne: la nomination de Martin Selmayr était 'politique', reconnaît un commissaire," accessed March 29, 2018, http://www.lemonde.fr/europe/article/2018/03/27/commission-europeenne-la-nomination-de-martin-selmayr-etait-politique-reconnait-un-commissaire_5277242_3214.html
74. On Francophonie and peacekeeping missions, see Justin Massie and David Morin, "Francophonie et opérations de paix. Vers une appropriation géoculturelle," *Etudes internationales* 42, no. 3 (2011): 313–36.
75. Ibid., 315.
76. France's overseas forces are divided in four groups: Temporary forces, forces under an international mandate, forces of presence, and forces of sovereignty (that is, forces in French territories beyond the "Métropole"). These forces have gone from 40,000 in 2003 to 19,000 in 2018, on average.

77. "La nouvelle équipe Afrique de BearingPoint voit le jour," September 28, 2017, accessed December 28, 2017, https://www.bearingpoint.com/fr-fr/qui-sommes-nous/actualites/presse/communiques-de-presse/la-nouvelle-equipe-afrique-de-bearingpoint-voit-le-jour/
78. Adrien de Tricornot, "Forte mobilization contre la baisse du budget des lycées français de l'étranger," accessed November 29, 2017, http://www.lemonde.fr/campus/article/2017/11/28/forte-mobilisation-contre-la-baisse-du-budget-des-lycees-francais-de-l-etranger_5221641_4401467.html
79. Thierry Balzacq and Simon Reich, "Reinventing Grand Strategy" (working title), book manuscript.
80. See Jean-Pierre Raffarin, "Une diplomatie est une force si elle sait où elle va," in *Notre intérêt national*, eds. de Montbrial and Gomart, 105–20; Hervé Gaymard, "La ligne de force," in *Notre intérêt national*, 128.
81. For de Gaulle, grandeur activated positive emotional feelings such as national self-esteem, respect, and recognition as a major international power.
82. I thank Benjamin Puybareau, Eric Sangar, and Benoît Siberdt for their research assistance. I am grateful to Peter Dombrowski and Norrin Ripsman for comments and suggestions on the chapter's various iterations. I am grateful to Barry Posen and the MIT Security Studies Program for inviting me to give a talk, which allowed me to clarify some of the assumptions supporting this chapter. Simon Reich contributed enormously to the overall quality of this chapter by offering generous comments on different drafts. Research was made possible in part by the financial support from the Francqui Foundation and the Namur Advanced Research College (NARC). The Asia-Pacific College of Diplomacy at the Australian National University provided me with a wonderful working environment.

6 United Kingdom

ROBERT JOHNSON

Every generation reinterprets the past for its own purposes, often to contrast the distinctions between its contemporary values and those that it has inherited or jettisoned. British politicians have been reluctant to speak of a grand strategy because, for the past century, Britain's policy has been the management of its relative decline with respect to other, larger powers. In recent decades, politicians have been eager to distance themselves from Britain's history, the agonies of decolonization and the wars on the European continent in the mid-twentieth century. Yet this deliberate effort ignores enduring strategic realities for Britain, not least the imperative to encourage the global free flow of trade on which its logistical lifeline depends, and the desire to avoid isolation, or major war. History has a strong influence on Britain's grand strategy, but so have more recent events, particularly 9/11, the Iraq War and Brexit, all of which involved its relationship with the United States, Europe, and the world.

Consistent with the structure of this volume, this chapter examines the values, ends, ways, and means of British grand strategy. It does so, seeking to answer the question as to whether the balance of instruments and processes set out to *shape* the global and regional strategic environment or *adapt* to them. It acknowledges the role of perception in this assessment, with prominent historical influences. It also illustrates the gap between the British aspiration to shape events and their ability to do so. In the early 2000s, for example, the British tried to influence American and continental European policies and act as a strategic bridge between them, but with limited results. Likewise, the chapter also addresses the question of which domestic institutions and decision makers formulated Britain's grand strategy, and how far political changes impacted upon them. Finally, it analyses the interaction of the external and domestic elements, and institutions and instruments, which invariably constrained particular leaders and policies.

One of the most striking features of British grand strategy is the prominence of history as an influence on its formulation, perception, and reception. Equally, despite denials that Britain pursues a grand strategy, British political and military elites have debated the subject with some intensity, and British thinkers have been prominent in defining and shaping the subject.[1] What is clear, however, is that the British have adapted their grand strategy to match their changing relative power position over the last half-century and in response to a series of significant events, both domestic and foreign.

In theory, British governments have been clear about their enduring interests, namely the protection of sovereign territory and the people, their political economy, culture and way of life, and their economic survival. British ways of fulfilling their grand strategy incorporated their geographical island setting, offering both opportunities and corresponding constraints, such as the need to focus on maritime security and an expeditionary military posture. Britain's relatively small size, compared with other Continental powers, has tended to produce a preference for multilateral coalitions, and, where it did not curtail freedom of action, more lasting alliance partnerships. Britain has also made use of its wealth, influence, and patronage, usually under the encompassing heading of "influence," to exercise a form of "soft power." Yet, in terms of ways, Britain has been prepared to demonstrate its hard power, through air, sea, and land operations and its continuous, at sea, nuclear deterrent.

In practice, British grand strategy has been subject to the contestation of domestic politics, and perceptions of their world role: where some have favored a proactive international posture, this has been tempered by a strong moral agenda. Leading liberal politicians questioned more assertive and imperial foreign policies in the nineteenth century, but there was considerable ideological unity over the defense of democracy and liberties that carried Britain through global campaigns in two world wars. In the Cold War, there were deep divisions about the moral responsibility to project power, and to protect the public and Britain's allies, but also to avoid nuclear war in favor of spending on a "welfare state." British self-perception has long been expressed in historical metaphors, but, in more recent decades, a new generation has favored diversity, multiculturalism, and technological innovation, with a preference for international cooperation.[2] Yet, these remain peacetime interpretations, since challenges to British interests, including global terrorism or state threats, have generated a more traditional willingness to defy, fight, and deploy a range of instruments of national power.

There are elements of Britain's national interests which exist, but which are rarely expressed. The less often stated, but self-evident priority concerning foreign affairs and defense, is to remain close to, and protected by, the United States. The scale of America's forces, and its nuclear umbrella, compensate for the diminished defense capabilities of the British. A second unstated, but characteristic, element of Britain's national interests is a pragmatic recognition of the need to adapt to changing geopolitical and economic circumstances. This sort of gradualism has been the long-term hallmark of the British in domestic affairs too, but that does not mean they are not prepared to act on principle. Indeed, the third element of their national strategy is their desire to uphold the international rules-based order, since history indicates to policy-makers that the alternatives are far more detrimental to British interests.[3]

Historically, the British government has utilized four grand strategic instruments.[4] The first was to use diplomacy to negotiate on any dispute with its antagonists to avoid war. The second was to seek new alliance partnerships to share defense burdens. Third, they could increase defense spending as a form of conventional "deterrence." Fourth, they could reconfigure their defense policy to meet future challenges.

The first, diplomacy, was successful to a point. International institutions can only function if there is sufficient will by the leading powers to compromise on their immediate national interests. It is precisely at times of crisis, however, that these powers will assert their own national interests and priorities. Britain's solution was to continue to work on pragmatic, bilateral agreements and focus only on areas of common concern. In recent decades, the apparent weakening of international institutions has once again raised the importance of bilateralism in British grand strategy.

The second option, joining alliances, was not a favored option for British governments until the Cold War, because of concerns about a loss of freedom of action, articulated by Prime Minister Lord Palmerston's famous injunction: "We have no eternal allies, and we have no perpetual enemies. Our interests are eternal and perpetual, and those interests it is our duty to follow."[5] Today, Britain is part of an alliance network, and it seems to have overcome, by necessity, its preference for avoiding obligations.

The third and fourth options, defense spending, and changes to defense policies, have been interdependent. As a share of British GDP, defense spending has fallen steadily since the 1940s and more starkly since the Cold War, reaching its current level of 2.2 percent. The cost of small-scale arms and equipment programs is nevertheless higher, and the UK defense industry has been unable to offset these higher costs with increased overseas sales.

In this chapter, there are six sections which successively explain: the influence of the world wars on Britain's grand strategy and the close alignment to the United States; domestic political debates that were concerned with Britain's grand strategy; the various bodies that formulate and shape Britain's grand strategy; changes from the Suez crisis to the Gulf Wars; the impact of the Global War on Terror and the Iraq War; and, finally, the continuing challenges and constraints of a shifting geo-strategic environment.

6.1 The influence of the world wars on Britain's grand strategy and the US alignment

Britain's grand strategy should be understood as the product of historical experience, its geographical setting and through combined levers of power, and it had long predicated its grand strategy on the idea of limited war to preserve its wealth and influence. For an island power like the United Kingdom, limited war was an option. That possibility was effectively denied to Continental powers, because the vulnerability of their interests, lying adjacent to neighboring states, would lead to the need to escalate war and mobilize their entire national resources. Yet, there was a paradox. At sea, rather than being limited to confined areas of operations, as the land environment was, maritime warfare was potentially always global. Britain could therefore not avoid a global grand strategy, despite its limited resources. Its worldwide colonial and commercial commitments further increased both its strengths and its vulnerabilities. The challenges reached their most acute, and existential, in the two world wars.

Britain possessed several objective strategic advantages as a result of its geography. As an island, it was relatively well protected from Continental invasions, which, in turn meant it could afford to maintain a small army. It had a strong industrial base, even if it was weakening compared with its rivals. It possessed large financial reserves, which could be converted into military and naval means if required. It dominated global communications, held numerous bases, and world telegraph systems. It could call on the manpower reserves of the British Empire and some allies, and it still had the world's largest navy. Diplomatically, Britain's maritime and commercial power gave it significant influence around the world, and Royal Navy warships provided a reassuring or intimidatory "presence."

The constraints were nevertheless significant. The scattered nature of the British Empire meant vulnerabilities in every quarter, especially where there were land frontiers to garrison with a relatively small army, such as India. Unlike Russia or the United States, it did not have a large land mass as a core. It was therefore dependent on the network of imported resources, commercial exchange, and manpower movements, which put it firmly in favor of the policy of free trade. The absence of any single geographical threat location meant that its strategy of imperial defense had to be global. But since the most significant threats would arise from Europe, it favored a "balance of power" between the rival European states, with cooperation through diplomacy. A breakdown in diplomacy would mean some form of commitment to defend Britain's national interests, but it was still hoped that this lay primarily in the navy and avoidance of too strong a Continental commitment. Britain's grand strategy could be summed up as an attempt to avoid antagonizing other powers, including the United States, and to accommodate them as long as its vital interests were not directly threatened.

Militarily, British grand strategy was successful. Britain fought a successful war between 1914 and 1918 as part of an alliance and restored a European power equilibrium in 1919. Had it not been for the unexpected fall of France in 1940, the British desire for a balance in Europe would have been maintained in

World War II. Throughout the world wars, the minimization of Britain's global commitments was sustained. The most vulnerable strategic locations for Britain in the wars, after the European theater, were the Middle East, which was successfully defended, and Southeast Asia (including routes to Australia), which was entirely lost. The Atlantic and Mediterranean were severely contested, but were recovered. Nevertheless, the number of commitments in Africa and the Middle East actually increased, forcing a readjustment through the necessity of cost, and the situation became so severe in Ireland (1919–21), Iraq (1920–32), Egypt (1919–22), India (1946–47) and Palestine (1947–48) that Britain could not resist decolonization after the war. Moreover, the American condemnation of colonialism influenced Britain's global grand strategy, first in 1919, but more obviously so after 1945.[6]

The apparent British preference for an indirect strategy, rather than a direct confrontation with its enemies on the European continent, had been the chief source of dispute with the other Big Three powers in the world war, but after 1945, the growing awareness of the new threat posed by the Soviets to Eastern and Central Europe led to a dramatic shift in policy.

While Britain emerged as one of the victorious Allies in 1945, Winston Churchill and his successors were anxious that the United States would abandon Europe and the Continent would fall to Communism, which explains Britain's eagerness to see France resurrected as a major security provider in 1945. There were sufficient numbers of Communist partisans and parties across Europe to make this concern credible. In Britain itself, pro-Soviet rhetoric was common. British leaders hoped that Britain might retain its global influence after the war, but, despite their efforts and membership of NATO, World War II marked the decisive eclipse of Britain as a preeminent world power. Churchill could still mobilize opinion with his Iron Curtain speech at Fulton, Missouri, but Britain had been bankrupted by the war, its relative power was permanently damaged, its share of global commerce had been diminished, and imperial cohesion was in serious jeopardy.

6.2 Who makes British grand strategy and where is it made?

The primary organization for the creation of Britain's grand strategy is the United Kingdom government, but this institution is, in fact, an amalgam of individuals, groups, units, and directorates. The Secretary of State for Defence is the minister responsible for the Ministry of Defence, but the role is constrained by the prime minister, the cabinet, the Foreign and Commonwealth Office (FCO), and the Treasury in the first instance. In major decisions on defence, the minister will often find themselves compelled to consult these and other colleagues. Budgetary constraints are especially keenly felt, as large departments, such as Health, Trade and Education, compete for the available resources. The minister is nevertheless supported by a Permanent Undersecretary (PUS), who is a senior civil servant charged with supervision of budgets, reforms, ministry efficiency, personnel performance, organization, and departmental strategy. The "Permanent Secretary," as they are known, is supported by a group of specialist directors, drawn from the civil service, in areas such as nuclear capability, security, procurement, and finance. The management of this organization is led by the Defence Board (and, on legal matters, the Defence Council), but, as a body they do not decide on Britain's grand strategy. Instead, grand strategy is a policy that emerges from several strands and organizations.

The first source is the prime minister, who, in consultation with the cabinet and advisors in the Ministry of Defence, will initiate the creation of a National Security Strategy. Advice will also be sought from the body that oversees the implementation of Britain's grand strategy, namely the National Security Council (NSC). This grouping, consisting of the prime minister, selected cabinet members, the intelligence service chiefs, the head of GCHQ (the Global Communications Headquarters), the military Chief of the Defence Staff, and the National Security Advisor, is responsible for the coordination of intelligence, foreign engagement, cybersecurity, energy and resource security, and national resilience (including the protection of "critical national infrastructure"). The NSC emulates the American model, but was only established in 2010 in an attempt to create a more efficient architecture against terrorism, growing numbers of cyberattacks, and other anticipated, emerging threats. Periodically, the government, on the prime minister's initiative, will consider a defense and security review, which will coincide with the development or renewal of a national security strategy. The concurrency of the approach ensures that the ends, ways, and means of Britain's strategy are aligned, and programmed procurement is in place in good time. The delivery of the strategy is also supervised by Parliament, and subjected to intense scrutiny in a parliamentary defense select committee. Despite the apparent pluralistic nature of its formulation, Britain has had long experience of creating an appropriate grand strategy, and the elasticity of its approach is one of its strengths. The parliamentary system meant that policy was interrogated frequently, and subcommittees were able to scrutinize the detail.[7] A sudden change of policy was therefore unlikely without a thorough examination of the likely consequences.

The consultative and advisory approach of British strategy formulation continues with the participation of the rest of the civilian staff of the Ministry of Defence and the individual service chiefs. Despite a long-standing tendency for "tribal" loyalties towards their own service, to maximize the budgetary support they might receive, the creation of a joint warfighting capability and the emphasis on a "comprehensive," interagency approach in recent operations, have led to more unity of effort and closer cooperation. Civilian staff from the Stabilisation Unit, for example, work closely with their military counterparts.

Outside of the government, there are further sources of advice, scrutiny, and debate. The media have a strong presence, and many leading outlets in the UK have specialist defense correspondents eager to analyze every aspect of the government's strategy and its spending.[8] In addition, in reflecting public concerns, the media can influence the strategic agenda, which would explain why a nonexistential threat, such as terrorism, can occupy a central position in government strategic documents. This should not be exaggerated, however. Grand strategy is characterized by enduring policies and behaviors in international affairs, while public concerns tend to be short-term. A more sustained influence would instead come from the British and international think tanks, including The Royal United Services Institution (RUSI), the International Institute for Strategy Studies (IISS), and Chatham House, which scrutinize and advise, as well as offering platforms for leading defense spokesmen and women to amplify defense policy. Academic institutions also have a part to play, and many defense staff, civilian and military, have attended leading British universities with a strong background in strategic studies, including Oxford, Cambridge, and King's College London.

The execution of grand strategy, and the return loop of influence, falls not only to the Ministry of Defence but also to the Foreign and Commonwealth Office. The FCO's pragmatic approach to diplomacy has traditionally worked well.[9] Its commitment to a multilateral system means that Britain tends to consult and then act with the consensus of its allies, not least in the UN Security Council. It has subscribed to a number of international efforts on conflict prevention, for example, such as the UN Secretary General Bhoutros-Gahli's 1994 initiative, the Responsibility to Protect, and the R2P Pillar II agreements. British grand strategy spells out its support for the North Atlantic Treaty Organization (NATO) in defense; the European Union, in economic security and mutual support; the G8 and G20 in global financial leadership; and the Commonwealth in shared commitments to democracy and human rights. Britain is the third largest financial contributor to UN peacekeeping operations and uses its wealth to honor its pledge to eradicate poverty.

Britain's grand strategy is not implemented therefore solely by "hard" means, but also through so-called "soft power." The British Council, founded in 1934, was established with a Royal Warrant in 1940 to promote cultural understanding of Britain and to encourage the use of the English language worldwide. Today it describes itself as a language and cultural organization, but its roots indicate that its purpose is to promote a friendly appreciation of the British. The British Council's work is closely related to another organ of soft power, that of education. Each year, thousands of foreign scholars study at British schools, colleges, and universities, to equip them with both a set of skills and a positive view of the United Kingdom. The Chevening Fund, for example, assists East Asian students, emulating the success of the American Rhodes and Fulbright schemes. More direct aid, for education and relief, is orchestrated by the Department of International Development (DfID), totaling £13 billion per annum (or 0.7 percent of annual GDP) but a number of nongovernmental organizations have their own education and aid programmed. These tend to be popular among the British public, and the tradition of charitable giving connects citizens with particular international causes, many of which coincide with the government's defined national interests. In 2016, the public donated £9.7 billion to charities.[10] Relief in South Sudan, for example, came from Britain as charitable donations, £200 million in government "UK Aid" funding, and further government contributions to international aid organizations, and these complemented efforts in conflict prevention.[11]

The sources of "soft power" can also be found in the financial services of the City of London and in business or property investments. Insurance services, for example, provide important support to foreign governments and organizations, and create a favorable impression of Britain.[12] Critics argue that the government lost control of financial services in the capital which precipitated the 2008 global financial crash, an event which required billions in bailout packages to prevent the collapse of certain banks. There are further criticisms of the globalized nature of financial services, and the impact on London has not always been positive, with exorbitant property prices and an inflow of investment of illicit origins.[13]

6.3 Managing change: Domestic debates

There was considerable debate about Britain's best strategic course after each world war, and, despite the apparent stability of the Cold War, the United Kingdom's grand strategy and its place in the world have been much contested after 1991. These debates were concerned with the central themes of this volume: the degree to which the country was shaped by its new external and regional environment; its self-perception and domestic political situation; and the relative power of its strategic instruments, and especially where it should direct its power.

Captain Basil Liddell Hart's exposition on a "British Way of War," first delivered at the Royal United Services Institute in 1931 and subsequently reiterated while he was defense correspondent for *The Times* newspaper, reinforced the anxiety of the interwar years: that Britain could no longer shape the strategic environment in such a way as to preserve the balance of power in Europe while, simultaneously, ensuring the security of the British Empire.[14] The dilemma expressed itself in the rearmament priorities of 1938, but it occurred at a time when, according to contemporary Mass Observation polling data, there was no public appetite for engaging in another conflict. The emphasis, the public believed, should be on the multilateral approach of the League of Nations and diplomatic resolution. Like many of his generation, Liddell Hart was appalled by the scale of the casualties in World War I but also by the loss of Britain's strategic advantages that the war had precipitated. He attributed this to a misunderstanding about Britain's grand strategy and a deviation from the policies which, hitherto, had served the country so well. Liddell Hart believed that where the phenomenon of war bounded strategy, grand strategy was not so confined, for it included a range of issues, such as diplomatic influence, the performance of the economy, and, other factors that concerned war *and* peace. It was for this reason that Liddell Hart felt Britain, despite military victories in 1918 and 1945, had failed in its grand strategy: its position in 1919, and in 1950, was far weaker than it had been in 1900. Historian Paul Kennedy noted that there was a significant division in perception and objectivity about Britain's relative strength compared to Germany in this period. So appeasement, as a government policy to buy time, was ultimately, he believed, a strategic failure.[15]

Liddell Hart claimed that there was a British tradition in this "indirect approach," which had favored historically peripheral operations, that is, naval and expeditionary missions, against major powers rather than Continental alliances and commitments. This concluded, at the time, with a partiality for deploying armor, air, and other maneuvrist technologies in geographically peripheral regions against the Axis powers. Liddell Hart was reacting to what he termed the "Clausewitzian fallacy"—the erroneous belief that waging absolute war against the main enemy forces—would produce victory, because he had witnessed costly attacks against German entrenchments of the Western Front in World War I. Yet this claim in favor of a consistent way of war, while appealing, can be challenged by a slew of evidence: of Britain's military commitments to continental fighting from the Seven Years War, if not earlier, to the end of World War I; by the nature of its commitment to the intense fighting in the Middle East, North Africa, and Southeast Asia between 1941 and 1945; and by the subsequent deployment of forces to Europe during the Cold War. These cases were neither aberrations, given their frequency and scale, nor were they exceptions to the fulfillment of Britain's grand strategy.

After World War II, the grand strategic environment was graver than it had been in 1918. While British institutions and values had survived, with an even stronger commitment to social welfare and parliamentary democracy, the country was in a dire economic situation, Europe was in ruins and therefore dependent on Allied security, and Britain's colonial possessions across the globe were seething with unrest. The overriding concerns, however, later expressed by Lord Ismay as Secretary General of NATO, were closer to home in Europe, namely to "keep the Germans down, the Americans in and the Russians out."

The grand strategic priority of the United Kingdom from 1945 was to remain closely linked to the United States. This was not, of course, automatic, despite wartime cooperation in intelligence and military affairs. The Truman administration viewed Clement Attlee's socialist government with deep suspicion and Jewish lobbyists were angry at British restrictions on migration to Palestine. Yet, despite these initial concerns, American financial generosity and the loan of 1945 made a significant difference. The quid pro quo, at least from a moral perspective, was Britain's abandonment of Palestine, withdrawal from India, and the initiation of a long process of decolonization. Britain's commitments to Turkey and Greece were also terminated within a generation; it would also give up it possessions in the Gulf. Britain's global position was evidently being diminished, and superpower influences were increasing. In Europe, however, there was no question of withdrawal, because of the Soviet threat: it was in Britain's interests to fight the Soviets, should that occur, on the Continent and not on its own shores. The Americans too recognized the menace, responding with the Truman Doctrine and the Marshall Aid package. The bond between Britain and the United States grew closer as Soviet assertiveness increased. In 1949, the partnership was enshrined in NATO and has remained strong, as a "special relationship," ever since.

Yet, economically, Britain was in a long-term relative decline compared with the superpowers. Britain's industrial base was too small to compete with that of the United States and the Soviets, once these powers had begun to industrialize at scale, unless it could retain a lead in technological innovation and productivity rates. The relative decline of the British economy reduced its strategic options. In the 1930s, Britain's international credit was less secure, it held less gold and fewer dollars, domestic manufacturing was relatively weak, Britain was still emerging from the financial crash, and there was a shortage of skilled workers. In World War II, as in World War I, there were state takeovers and intensive planning, but these short-term measures were unable to arrest the overall decline of Britain's global position.[16] The idea of a Sterling Bloc, preserving its currency with fixed exchange rates in the regions where it had enjoyed considerable influence, was eroded by the dominance of the dollar and was effectively abandoned by the Bank of England in 1972. Nevertheless, the continued success of Britain's financial services tended to offset the decline in manufacturing and heavy industry, and its commercial strength was sustained by improving trade with Western Europe from the 1950s onwards. Domestically, in economic terms Britain may have lost ground to other powers, but it was far more self-assured than its critics would claim.

6.4 Grand strategy from the Suez crisis to the Iraq War

British defense cooperation with Western Europe, its independent atomic arsenal from 1952, and its close relationship with the United States seemed to have placed Britain in a stronger strategic situation in the 1950s than in 1945. Although there was some discussion of economic cooperation with Europe, and eventually membership of a European Economic Community, British politicians viewed European integration with suspicion. Instead, Britain developed global connections through SEATO (The Southeast Asia Treaty Organization) and CENTO (Central Treaty Organization), the latter with Turkey, Iraq, Iran, and Pakistan. The 1952 Global Strategy Paper reclaimed Britain's historic worldwide role, and placed some emphasis on the nuclear-armed V-Bomber as the weapon system that, along with the Royal Navy, gave it global influence. There was also a focus on global bases, including important stations in Cyprus and Aden, although it was the controversy over the control of the Suez Canal Zone that caused the greatest rupture in Britain's grand strategy.

The Egyptian declaration of the nationalization of the Suez Canal provoked a strong British government reaction. The administration of Anthony Eden was convinced that the expanding Communist influence was manifest in the apparently Hitlerian figure of President Gamal abd' al Nasser. Eden was personally haunted by the failure of appeasement and eager to acquire the mantle of Churchill. Yet, despite the successful Anglo-French military operation into the Canal Zone in 1956, the decision to intervene divided British politics and angered the United States. The Soviets capitalized on the dispute within the West, with their operations into Hungary, but the damage to British prestige and the basis of its grand strategy was far-reaching. Secretary Dulles refused to back the pound and Eden was forced to announce a withdrawal, which appalled the French. The Commonwealth, with the exception of Australia, condemned Britain's actions. The trauma ran deep and Harold Macmillan, Eden's successor, tried to refocus the country on domestic policies.

Analogies have been drawn with the British intervention in Iraq in 2003, although the most important difference was Britain's alignment to American policy there, in contrast to Suez. The connection is primarily domestic, where in both cases a popular prime minister (Eden and then Tony Blair, the British prime minister between 1997 and 2007) foundered on a foreign policy "adventure" of questionable legality or ethics. In grand strategic terms, both believed their actions were aligned with Britain's interests; that they faced an imminent and unprecedented threat; and that acting within a coalition would be sufficient justification to exonerate their actions. The instruments of grand strategy were limited—military tools with diplomatic preparation—but there would be no question of the full deployment of national resources. The perverse outcome of the Iraq War was a significant amount of damage to the special relationship. Having spent years telling the Americans that they knew better how to conduct counterinsurgency, the British lost control of Basra, which they had been allocated as an area of responsibility. Then, the Labour government withdrew British forces precisely at the moment the Americans were trying to surge forces into Iraq in order to quell popular resistance. It was an ignominious ending to a period devoid of government strategy.[17]

Common to both the later 1950s and the aftermath of the Iraq War were continued cuts in UK defense spending and capability with a greater emphasis on nuclear or alliance strength. In the 1957 Defence Review, the government announced reductions, and a steady fall in the share of defense spending as a share of GDP. Further attempts to reduce the size and deployments of the British armed forces followed, sometimes accelerated by financial crises, such as Wilson's devaluation of the pound in 1967. The imperative to pay for a burgeoning health service bill added further pressure to cancel defense procurement programmed (such as the F-111 fighter) or to withdraw from the Gulf, Malaya, and Singapore. By the 1970s, both leading political parties started to embrace the idea that Britain could redefine itself as a European power, integrated into a cheaper collective defense and an economic system. Blair subsequently shared this aspiration in the 1990s. This seemed appropriate when the emphasis was on the dual Cold War conventional and nuclear defense posture, and Europe was the main theater of operations.[18] However, once the Soviet Union collapsed as a major threat in the 1990s, and the predominant modality of war shifted to combatting international terrorism or multi-theater insurgency by non-state actors, then Britain could consider once again a global strategy—an aspiration Blair shared by 2003.

The enduring importance of Britain's relationship with America, rather than Europe, the need to retain a global naval expeditionary role, and the value of a military counterterrorism specialism while holding on to a "balanced force" for collective, conventional defense, were all justified in 1982 during the Falklands conflict. Britain demonstrated that it possessed the capability and will to conduct a limited war of liberation against the Argentine Junta which had seized territory, in contravention of the UN Charter. It also provided an opportunity to shape Britain's external situation. Despite its orientation towards European defense, the British government quickly assembled a naval task force. And its American alliance ensured the neutrality of other South American powers and the Soviets. Its amphibious operation, despite some losses in ships and personnel, proved rapidly successful and the Falkland Islands were recovered before the arrival of winter. Critics, not least the Argentines, portrayed the British as unreconstructed imperialists, reckless in their pursuit of an outdated colonial prestige. London, however, adroitly avoided any such association, arguing clearly for the self-determination of peoples (for the Falklands islanders) and the upholding of international law (through an unambiguous UN Security Council Resolution).

In Defence Review documents, the British emphasized their adherence to international law and norms. In 1980, it had captured international attention by refusing to accept the takeover of the Iranian embassy in London, and its dramatic storming by 22 SAS, its elite Special Forces, marked the United Kingdom out as a state unlikely to allow its policies to be determined by terrorism. In fact, it endured three decades of terrorism in Northern Ireland and on the mainland, against Irish Republicans, using its military and policing instruments to contain and counter violence while searching for a political resolution. There were controversies in its approach, particularly in the episode where British paratroopers opened fire on a hostile demonstration in 1972 and when the SAS unit caught and killed an IRA (Irish Republican Army) unit preparing a bomb attack in Gibraltar in 1988. Nevertheless, against a background of improving economic conditions, the British government successfully brokered a final peace settlement a decade later, the so-called Good Friday Agreement, which involved diplomatic engagement with Eire. It continued this theme of upholding the international order in its participation in the Gulf War against Saddam in 1990–91 to liberate Kuwait, and then in its deployment of peacekeeping forces into Bosnia. Britain demonstrated its preparedness to accept international agreements that might not necessarily be in its own national interests by the peaceful transfer of power of Hong Kong in 1997, and also diplomatically protested against the Chinese repression of pro-democracy demonstrators at Tiananmen Square in 1989, and against Burmese military actions during that decade.

A consistent theme for the United Kingdom was also its "prosperity agenda" and generosity in providing international aid. Successive British governments have seen the rising GDP of the country as a key policy imperative, but equally there has been an altruistic pride in the UK's willingness to support both Commonwealth and poorer countries. There are evident benefits for Britain in its aid packages, in terms of influence and access, but the drivers are as much to do with a sense of obligation, after its colonial history, rather than a Machiavellian foreign policy.

The divisions in the United Kingdom's grand strategy were most evident in its approach to Europe. On the one hand, its membership of NATO made it an integrated power and few questioned the benefits of free trade after joining the European Common Market in 1973. The problem instead lay in the European Commission's desire for an ever-closer political union. Pro-Europeanists argued that the special relationship with the US was not one of parity and that American interests diverged from Europe, a charge made more emotive by Britain's participation in the Iraq and Afghanistan wars. They claimed that Britain could no longer think of itself as an independent global power. There had instead been the promise of an industrial boom, an increase in British invisible earnings, and the benefits of cheaper consumer products caused by an economy of scale in Europe.

In fact, none of these materialized. European cooperation in defense procurement projects proved more expensive than its American commercial links. Cheaper consumer products were available from East Asia and, less significantly, from Europe. The industrial boom failed to materialize, and instead British heavy industry declined, with all its associated social and political unrest. The service sector also thrived less on European markets than on global ones. In purely defense terms, NATO allies in Europe spent a lot less on their armed forces or equipment, with the consequence that military interoperability declined. Worse, European powers asserted "national caveats" and restrictions on operations outside of Europe. Furthermore, with the recovery of Russia in the early 2000s, newly joined Eastern European members argued that they needed to focus on the conventional threat posed by Moscow, not global interventionism under the so-called "Responsibility to Protect." It is striking that Britain is regarded as one of the leading defenders of Eastern Europe with its enhanced forward presence deterrent deployments in Poland and the Baltic States. Additionally, NATO allies only inconsistently committed to operations in Afghanistan. The British, with the largest European contingent, took on the troublesome province of Helmand, and fought there in brigade strength alongside the Americans. Other European countries, however, made only token deployments. If, as some critics claimed, Britain was only a European power, it was at the very least the most dedicated one from a defense perspective.

The 9/11 terrorist attacks in the United States in 2001, and subsequent jihadist terrorism in Britain and Europe; an increasing number of cyberattacks emanating from Russia, China, and their proxies; the violent aftermath of the Middle Eastern uprisings known as the Arab Spring, which produced Daesh (the so-called Islamic State movement) and its wave of barbarous attacks, all seemed to indicate a period of instability. Indeed, the UK's 2010 *National Security Strategy* described it as "an age of uncertainty."[19] Given these events, it was logical to expect some enhancement to Britain's defenses and the articulation of a grand strategy. There was certainly a strong expression of values and aspirations in the report, with references to global reach, a continuous sea-based nuclear deterrence, new aircraft carriers to project power, an expeditionary army of two divisions and an air arm possessing the latest strike, surveillance, and lift capabilities. Its armed forces work continuously in a joint posture, and the Combined Joint Expeditionary Force deployed to Eastern Europe consists of an all-arms British force within a NATO structure.

In support, Britain established a national cybersecurity center to augment the work of GCHQ, a government communications center, and continued to develop its whole-of-government approach to a range of nonconventional threats. The government adheres to three principles: budgetary investment in new technologies; strategic capabilities for 2040, including a new class of nuclear submarine, new F-35 fighters and cyber projection; and stronger international partnerships and coalitions, under the umbrella phrase of "international by design."[20] Committed to learning from the Iraq Enquiry and the conflict in Afghanistan, the government also placed its decision-making processes under review, and set itself the objective of regularly updating its strategy.

In a more hostile world, however, there are evident limits to the techniques of grand strategy that have worked historically. Like their predecessors in 1914 and 1938–39, government officials find that diplomacy has its limits. In the 2010s, North Korea, Iran, China, and Russia have been unwilling to adhere to the injunctions of the Western powers. Critics stated that the cost of the conventional maritime forces of the carrier groups was prohibitive and appeared at odds with the investment in new technologies and counterterrorism, which seemed more pressing. Yet, there were also doubts about the entire resilience of the United Kingdom to address combined forms of attack, from a DDOS (Deliberate Denial of Service) cyber offensive on critical financial infrastructure to the conventional destruction of forward-deployed forces and the ability of the public to stomach resulting heavy casualties. There was further confusion in 2017 when British Prime Minister Theresa May tried to reassure the British public that there would be no further expeditionary operations comparable to Iraq or Libya, while her government's defense policy and the armed forces seemed postured entirely for that eventuality.

In 2016, the majority of voters in the UK referendum on EU membership voted for Brexit, the departure from the European Union. The national turnout for European elections had been low for years and European officialdom in Brussels was considered too remote from the issues that mattered to the public. Despite the irritation of the "Remain" lobbyists, who blamed a "Little Englander" mentality, British sentiments had always been far more expansive and global. There was an inherent dislike of a large European bureaucratic bloc, which the public associated with entities like the Soviet Union, while the inherently protectionist (and agrarian) cartel within the EU sat uneasily with a country that was wedded to free market economics and consumerism. In contrast to the Commonwealth, the EU seemed less of a "free association" of nations than a system that would apply punishments for noncompliance, as Ireland and Greece experienced over two decades. Moreover, the British still identified more closely with Americans, despite the unpopular wars, because of economic systems, language, and culture. Above all, the majority of the British public in favoring Brexit were establishing a claim to their identity, based on a sense of history, and rejected a series of integrationist, multicultural neoliberal mantras. Yet the public was divided. The minority of voters felt strongly that Britain's future lay in Europe. The left, which had long struggled to accept an EU it associated with big business, concluded that European courts might provide a mechanism to defeat British laws that curbed the power of trades unions. Others saw kindred spirits in Europe that prioritized rights over economic performance. But, in essence, both sides were projecting onto Europe much older British political and ideological divisions: between free markets or socialism; rights or responsibilities; and freedom or regulation. British grand strategy cannot remain immune from these debates, although it is striking that NATO, including collective defense in Europe, has remained central to British strategic thinking.

6.5 The United Kingdom's grand strategy during the War on Terror and the era of confrontation

The Iraq War of 2003–9 had an undeniably negative impact on British policymaking. The Iraq Enquiry, the 2.6 million-word report published in 2017, revealed, among its many findings, an absence of strategic education in the UK's decision makers. One former Defence Minister admitted that there was too much optimism, and mistakes were made, some willfully, by members of the government of the day. The conclusion, he confessed, was that "we should have asked more questions."[21] Cross government cooperation had been lacking and civil–military relations had been marred by misunderstandings. The report focused on the lack of preparedness for the reconstruction phase of the conflict. But the most egregious error was the premature withdrawal from the campaign in 2009, at the precise moment when the Americans were calling for a surge of forces. The British contribution had been to support the United States, so the decision to pull out appeared to be particularly inconsistent.

The seed of these problems had emerged earlier. The end of the Cold War, the multinational efforts to liberate Kuwait (1991) and those to resolve the Balkans conflicts (1994, 1999) produced over-optimism in successive governments. But the defense cuts they orchestrated as part of the post–Cold War "peace dividend" meant they could not fulfill the expectations they set out for themselves in their defense reviews. In the early 2000s, the Labour government of Tony Blair emphasized its desire to align Britain's foreign policy, and thus its strategic influence, with the "millennium goals" of eradicating poverty in the Global South, but, despite its generous aid budget, the scale of the problem and international trade restrictions made this unlikely. The Labour Foreign Secretary, Robin Cook, had claimed that Britain would pursue an "ethical foreign policy," and immediately ran into a diplomatic storm with Israel when he argued in favor of a Palestinian state and border revisions.[22] Britain's aspiration to sustain the international rules-based system to preserve the status quo seemed increasingly unlikely, given Russia and China's efforts to assert themselves as global powers with revisionist intent. Above all, the decision in 2003 to invade Iraq in order to eradicate a Weapons of Mass Destruction (WMD) program and democratize the Middle East turned out to be ill-considered. The WMD program was practically nonexistent, the intelligence was deliberately manipulated to justify intervention, and the invasion created chaotic destabilization. Curiously, when democratizing movements emerged in 2011, during the so-called "Arab Spring," Britain only reluctantly intervened in Libya as part of a coalition. The subsequent empowerment of local militias and the collapse of authority led to protracted violence there and a flood of refugees into Europe.

Prime Minister David Cameron's claim to be "international by design" in defense policy raised more questions than it answered. The phrase implied that small nations might look to internationalize any dispute in order to obtain Britain's, and, by extension, America's backing. This was certainly the view in Scandinavia and the Baltic states, because they felt that, militarily, they could not survive without Allied intervention.[23] The key question was about Britain's capability: how could it possibly manage all its global commitments if more than one was challenged at the same time? Naval personnel questioned the ability of Britain to "do another Falklands" given years of defense cuts.[24]

6.6 Continuing challenges and constraints

A number of challenges continue to affect the United Kingdom's grand strategy.[25] The most pressing and visible is the means with which to protect the public from acts of terrorism, not least because it is not possible to offer a complete guarantee of safety. The homegrown nature of the terrorist threat also makes domestic surveillance and privacy a contested issue, while sustaining public vigilance, a vital part of the country's defense, is difficult. Yet, the broad-based effects of terrorist attacks tend to be short-lived. Unlike France and Belgium, the British have not committed their army to the streets of major cities. Transport systems recover quickly, financial losses are addressed, and the British public, who are familiar with such attacks since the 1970s by the IRA, exhibit a phlegmatic defiance. The widespread popularity of the pre–World War II slogan "Keep Calm and Carry On" in the 2000s is an indicator of the public mood and emulates the expression from that era that "Britain Can Take It." That is not to diminish the existence of panic and fear during incidents, or defeatism among elements of the population, but it is remarkable that the British public tend to reach for icons of defiance and resistance, like Winston Churchill's rhetoric, when they are confronted by such challenges.

A second challenge is global interconnectedness, particularly when it comes to the supply chain of sensitive information and technologies. The private sector plays a key role in the development of defense and security technologies, from the software of detection and cyber penetration to the aerial development of platforms of surveillance. Private security contractors and military companies are considered a necessary element in state stabilization and logistical support to Western forces. The burden on government resources, particularly after the economic crisis of 2008, has added to this pressure to engage with and subcontract to the private sector for a range of defense needs, from real estate to research. Maintaining the operational security of future developments will certainly be more challenging for Britain. Like many Western countries, it expects that it will possess a leading technological edge for only a short period, although new breakthroughs will occur thick and fast.

A third challenge is the development of Britain's new nuclear capability. The Dreadnaught class of submarine will be equipped with the new generation of nuclear weapons, but the costs will be prohibitive unless the UK can spread them and set aside approximately £1 billion a year for their introduction. Here the European Union's insistence on continued payments by Britain through Brexit reveals its rather short-term view: their demanding bills paid for European integration projects, rather than strategically enabling Britain to commit to future nuclear defense costs for collective defense. Europeanists would argue that Britain needs to pay for pledges already made, but there is no doubt that the EU wanted the UK to pay for forthcoming projects too, including infrastructural development. The British argument was that, as one of the largest contributors to European defense, in contrast to many EU member states, it already had paid its share.

The next challenge relating to expenditure and defense concerns the UK's reserve forces. To reduce costs, the Ministry of Defence had announced that part-time volunteer forces would be more closely integrated into the regulars, and, in the event of conflict, these reserves would augment the deployed formations. A Reserve Forces Act in 1996 had provided for reserves that were in a state of "high-readiness" and who could be brought onto the operational tours of Iraq and Afghanistan. Reservists did so from all three services. The problem was that the Reserves were unable to maintain the high levels of training efficiency of the regulars, and the high turnover of personnel tended to reinforce the requirement for basic proficiency levels, although some had gained valuable operational experience. Moreover, in the future, a major conflict would require most of the Reserves to be maintained in the United Kingdom in home defense and internal security roles, leaving the regulars with their anticipated shortfall.

The fifth challenge is the constant uncertainty of the type of war they will be expected to fight. While the tactical experiences of sailors, airmen, marines, and soldiers are invariably similar, their operational and strategic requirements over the last three decades have radically differed. Technological innovations can only provide part of the solution. The British forces undoubtedly enjoyed a technological superiority over the Taliban of Afghanistan and Jaish al Mahdi of Iraq, for example, but this did not make it any easier for the British to conclude the conflicts in Helmand and Basra satisfactorily. The British, in common with their NATO allies, have struggled to determine their military posture towards cyberattacks, hybrid warfare, and proxy wars. Herein lays another issue—the extent to which the European defense systems are integrated, from the legislation required in the event of conflict, to decision-making about the hybrid threats and what constitutes grounds for an allied military response. To this one might also add the questionable track record of conventional deterrence, although, admittedly the methodology for measuring what has been deterred remains unclear.

The sixth challenge is the geostrategic balance of power, which has undoubtedly shifted since 2000. The United States remains the preeminent global superpower, but China's rapid economic development has created a significant challenge for the Americans, generally in terms of Chinese aspirations to participate in global affairs and specifically in the Chinese view of their exclusive sovereignty in the South and East China Seas. The first test of Chinese power politics in this new era is likely to be over the handling of North Korea, a close ally of Beijing, but also in its ability to manage diplomacy with its regional neighbors, all of whom view the Chinese claims to world power status with suspicion. The United Kingdom is not immune from American–Chinese rivalry, seeing commercial opportunities with the latter but clearly unwilling to forego its strategic relationship with the former. It finds itself in a better position than Australia, which has commercial dependencies on China but which remains an American ally. The same is true of the British view of the Central and Eastern European states, which are dependent on Russian hydrocarbons and consequently reluctant to criticize Moscow. Given this European temptation to accommodate Russia, it is not hard to see why the British would be reluctant to remain beholden to the EU's foreign policy.

There are significant opportunities for the United Kingdom among the emerging states of the world. Alongside its close relationship with the Commonwealth countries, Britain may well be an important partner of a new Atlantic regionalism, which would include numerous countries including the United States, Canada, Brazil and Nigeria. Moreover e-commerce, which Britain champions, may well address many of historical and geographical restrictions, and gradually force open the authoritarian states of Russia and China regardless of their attempts to prevent it. The economic liberalism which the United Kingdom has championed could again prove to be a much more successful model of global influence.

The British will certainly face ongoing disputes with Europe post-Brexit, with the most likely issues being the status of Gibraltar, access to fishing zones, agricultural products, the Northern Irish border, financial sector rivalries, and the juridical authority of the European Court of Justice. It is likely these will be resolved through the normal course of political dialogue and diplomacy, much as they have been in the last forty years.

As an island nation, the UK recognized the need for persistent foreign engagement long before the phrase entered the defense lexicon. Keeping enemies at arm's length was the role of the navy and the air force, but the UK's global interests mean that it cannot afford to look only to the protection of its immediate borders. Fighting at home is damaging and unattractive to policymakers. Defence is therefore projected forward, across the continent of Europe, and through its regional allies in the Middle East, Africa, the Caribbean, South Asia, Southeast Asia, and the Pacific. This means that Britain's partners can anticipate a continued forward posture minimally over the next ten years, but probably far longer, as it constitutes an integral part of its strategic culture.

6.7 Conclusion

An assessment of the United Kingdom's values, ends, ways, and means indicates that the British have been compelled to make significant adjustments over time to preserve their interests. They have moved from a situation where they could shape the strategic environment to one where they have had to adapt to it, working more closely with coalitions and allies to preserve Britain's influence. They have transformed its grand strategy and global role, and the values which were once used to justify its strategic posture had been adjusted or jettisoned accordingly. Several inflexion points have marked the transformation of Britain's grand strategy, the most prominent of which have been discussed in this chapter: the world wars, the Suez crisis, decolonization and the Cold War, and, in the more recent decades, the changing relationship with Europe and responses to global terrorism.

There have been several causes of the setbacks in the United Kingdom's grand strategy. These include the ignoring of strategic principles; a relative decline in economic power; periodic lack of coordination of the armed forces, and episodic weaknesses in coalition strength. Yet British strategy has long recognized the limits to national power and adjusted to avoid catastrophic failure. Part of this is the institutional setting. Decision-making has been scrutinized by committees and cabinets. The Chiefs of Staff have accepted committee decision-making, and civil primacy in strategic design, and have not tried to assert their autonomy. British decision makers have also recognized the importance of building coalitions to augment strength, especially in land-based conflicts where they have been at disadvantaged compared to other large powers. They have often recognized the need to open new "fronts," to absorb the strength of the enemy and play what the Duke of Wellington once described as the "sure game" of a long, attritional conflict.

The test for the success of the United Kingdom's grand strategy is whether, in the long term and globally, it has secured a national advantage.[26] Britain failed to obtain a better position after 1945 for its economy or its people.[27] Britain did less well after World War II in a number of areas than in World War I, and, after 1945, Britain was evidently dependent on the United States. It proved impossible for Britain to reshape the postwar world, evident in the severe blow it suffered in the Suez crisis of 1956.

History and time have had a significant effect on UK grand strategy. History has weighed heavily on Britain's perception of itself, but this has not prevented it from adjusting to ensure its survival or to improve its situation. Britain has often abandoned those aspects which might impair its diplomatic influence, especially in its crucial relationship with the United States. Successful grand strategy has often depended on this good timing. In political and diplomatic terms, it has meant timely adjustments to new realities. In technological terms, it has meant not just generating innovation and the right budget, but having the equipment in place, tested, integrated, and prepared—or minimally the surge capacity to have it in readiness for a crisis or threat. In economic terms, it has meant having the installations, factories, capital, trained workforce, education, and training to underpin the developments required.[28] Taken together, it reveals a country that has a strong thread of pragmatism—and thus a willingness to adapt—in its grand strategy.[29]

▧ NOTES

1. Paul Kennedy, *The Realities Behind Diplomacy: Background Influences on British External Policy, 1865–1980* (London: Fontana, 1981).
2. John Charmley, *Splendid Isolation? Britain and the Balance of Power* (London: Hodder and Stoughton, 1999), 397ff.
3. *A Strong Britain in an Age of Uncertainty: The National Security Strategy* (London: Crown Copyright, 2010), 5.
4. David French, *The British Way of Warfare, 1688–2000* (London: Unwin Hymen, 1990), 148.
5. Lord Palmerston, speech in the House of Commons, March 1, 1848, *Hansard*, vol. 97 cc. 66–123.
6. French, *The British Way of Warfare*, 206–7, 216; D. Reynolds, *The Creation of the Anglo-American Alliance, 1937–41: A Study of Competitive Cooperation* (London: Europa, 1981); Henry Kissinger, *Diplomacy* (New York: Simon and Schuster, 1994), 532; John Lewis Gaddis, *The Cold War* (London: Allen Lane, 2005), 127; Hugh Thomas, *The Suez Affair* (London: Weidenfeld and Nicolson, 1957).

7. Max Beloff, *Imperial Sunset*, I, (London: Alfred A. Knopf, 1969); Kennedy, *The Realities Behind Diplomacy*, 254; Paul Kennedy, "Grand Strategies and Less-than-grand Strategies: A Twentieth Century Critique," in *War, Strategy and International Politics*, eds. Lawrence Freedman, Paul Hayes, and Robert O'Neill (Oxford: Clarendon Press, 1992), 233.
8. See, for example, the bulletins of Robert Fox, Defence Correspondent of the *London Evening Standard*, and his "The MoD's theatre of the absurd," *The Guardian*, July 20, 2010, https://www.theguardian.com/commentisfree/2010/jul/20/defence-cuts-liam-fox-trident-treasury
9. Kennedy, *The Realities Behind Diplomacy*, 253–7; Kennedy, "Grand Strategies and Less-than-grand Strategies," 234.
10. Charity Aid Foundation data, accessed March 2018, https://www.cafonline.org/about-us/publications/2017-publications/uk-giving-report-2017
11. Chris Morris, "Reality Check: How much does the UK spend on overseas aid?," BBC, April 20, 2017, http://www.bbc.co.uk/news/uk-politics-39658907; government data is available at: https://www.gov.uk/government/organisations/department-for-international-development, accessed March 2018.
12. Tony Barber, "London's place in the world," *The Financial Times*, December 4, 2014, https://www.ft.com/content/f370ff24-51f0-11e3-8c42-00144feabdc0
13. Janan Ganesh, "London: the capital of globalisation," *The Financial Times*, September 29, 2014, https://www.ft.com/content/40e307c2-3aa1-11e4-bd08-00144feabdc0
14. Basil H. Liddell Hart, *Strategy* (London: Faber and Faber, 1954), 322 and *The British Way in Warfare* (London: Faber and Faber, 1932); Kennedy, "Grand Strategies and Less-than-grand Strategies," 232.
15. Kennedy, *The Realities Behind Diplomacy*, 293.
16. Beloff, *Imperial Sunset*, I, 180.
17. Christopher L. Elliott, *High Command: British Military Leadership in the Iraq and Afghanistan Wars* (London: Hurst & Co.: 2015), 116ff.
18. Kennedy, *The Realities Behind Diplomacy*, 376.
19. *A Strong Britain in an Age of Uncertainty*; see also the *National Security Strategy and Strategic Defence and Security Review* (London: Crown Copyright, 2015).
20. *National Security Strategy and Strategic Defence and Security Review* (2015), 49.
21. Desmond Browne, "The Political-Military Relationship on Operations," in *British Generals and Blair's Wars*, eds. Jonathan Bailey, Hew Strachan, and Richard Iron (London: Routledge, 2014), 273.
22. "Netanyahu Angrily Cancels Dinner With Visiting Briton," *The New York Times*, March 18, 1998, http://www.nytimes.com/1998/03/18/world/netanyahu-angrily-cancels-dinner-with-visiting-briton.html
23. Author's interviews in Sweden (July 2017), Finland (November 2017), Norway (November 2017) and with the Baltic representatives in Poland (November 2017).
24. "Royal Navy could lose 'beach-landing' ships in next round of defence cuts," *The Telegraph*, October 6, 2017, http://www.telegraph.co.uk/news/2017/10/06/royalnavy-could-lose-beach-landing-ships-next-round-defence/
25. Julian Lindley-French, "Could Britain respond strategically to Russian aggression," in *Ukraine and Beyond: Russia's Strategic Security Challenge to Europe*, eds. Janne Haaland Matlary and Tormod Heier (Basingstoke: Palgrave Macmillan), 112.

26. Kennedy, "Grand Strategies and less-than-Grand Strategies," 238.
27. Liddell Hart, *Strategy*, 357.
28. G.C. Peden, *British Rearmament and the Treasury, 1932–39* (Edinburgh: Scottish Academic Press, 1979).
29. I am very grateful to the editors of this volume for their patient advice on the shaping of this chapter, particularly its shift towards the post-1945 period, and for the interviewees who assisted in its formulation.

Part II
Pivotal Powers

7 Brazil

CARLOS R. S. MILANI AND TIAGO NERY

In general, the analysis of a country's grand strategy suffers from two main shortcomings: first, a one-dimensional approach to national and global security, exclusively focused on military strength, relations, and threats; second, a conception of strategy that tells foreign and defense policies apart, and does not fully embrace diplomatic, economic, social, and cultural matters. In the particular case of Brazil, the republican history of relationships between foreign policy and defense policy, starting in 1889, ended up producing not only a separation between the two policy tracks, thus building a mutual defiance between the two oldest state bureaucracies, the military and the diplomats (first divorce); moreover, it has also resulted in a conception of military matters as though they were not of civilians' interest (second divorce). As we shall see throughout this chapter, it was only in the aftermath of the 1988 Constitution that the Brazilian federal government started to construct a bridge between these two public policies, their bureaucracies, and constituencies.

In the 1990s Fernando Henrique Cardoso's government started to implement a strategy that aimed to keep the armed forces under civilian control, resulting in the creation of the Ministry of Defense (MD) in 1999. Cardoso's foreign policy was rooted in a diplomacy of prestige and international credentials, and during his two presidential mandates (1995–2002) Brazil set up an alliance with Western powers and championed human rights, global environment, and trade multilateralism. However, we argue in this chapter that it was only under Lula da Silva's two mandates (2003–10) and Dilma Rousseff's first mandate (2011–14) that Brazil laid out what we herein call "a sketch of a grand strategy," which was interrupted by Rousseff's controversial impeachment at the beginning of her second term in 2016. Based on this argument, this chapter intends to analyze the main challenges concerning the conception (values and goals) and the implementation (ways and means) of a Brazilian grand strategy during the governments of the Workers' Party (*Partido dos Trabalhadores*—PT) particularly between 2003 and 2014, thus demonstrating how Brazil's development model and its domestic politics both played a key role in this process. The chapter is structured around five sections, aside from this introduction and the concluding remarks: (1) Brazil's geopolitical thought and its *aggiornamento*; (2) who and where; (3) ways, means, and ends; (4) values and goals; (5) implementing the grand strategy: domestic politics and development strategies.

7.1 Brazil's geopolitical thought and its *aggiornamento*

Brazil is a second-tier country and a non-nuclear regional power. Its foreign and defense policies are not only instrumental as boundary-producing practices that frame the state and constitute its political order; moreover, they are fundamental tools for the projection of international power, also drawing on a national and endogenous geopolitical thought. In Brazil, the intellectual framing of geopolitical debates all along its republican history (after 1889) bore influence on norms, values, conception, and implementation of its grand strategy between 2003 and 2014. Until recently, studies on geopolitics have been a quasi-monopoly of the military, especially those linked to the Higher School of War (ESG, *Escola Superior de Guerra*), as well as researchers connected with national security institutions. As in other national traditions, the Brazilian geopolitics was born as a science at the service of the state, and the territory was then exclusively thought of as a resource of state power.[1]

Studies on geopolitics began in the aftermath of the World War I. In 1925, Everardo Backheuser pioneered geopolitical studies in Brazil, having been responsible for the first efforts to systematize information about the nation's space, territory, and unity. A few years later, in 1931, army officer Mario Travassos published *Aspectos geográficos sul-americanos* (South American geographical aspects), considered of fundamental importance for the understanding of Brazilian geopolitical thinking. Travassos revised and republished it a few years later with the title of "The Continental Projection of Brazil."[2] During World War II, Brazil was the first South American country to join the Allies in 1942. Brazil and Mexico were the only countries in Latin America that had sent troops to war, and in the Brazilian case, the mobilization of combatants was significant. With the victory of the Allies and the end of World War II, Brazil was invited to join the postwar Conferences, but its greater expectation, obtaining a permanent seat in the UN Security Council, was not fulfilled.[3]

Nevertheless, the most important impact of Brazil's participation in World War II was the creation in August 1949 of the *Escola Superior de Guerra* (the Brazilian War College, known as ESG), which marked a new stage in the field of geopolitical studies nationwide. Because of the Cold War and its consequences in the United States' foreign policy towards Latin America, ESG gave geopolitics a doctrinal twist, thus transforming it into a typical state science until very recent times. During this period, there was a clear increase in the production of geopolitical studies in Brazil, with a whole new generation of scholars, such as Therezinha de Castro, Delgado de Carvalho, General Meira Mattos, General Golbery do Couto e Silva, General Lyra Tavares, among others. ESG quickly became the military laboratory of ideas also contributing with intellectual input to the post-1964 *coup d'état*.[4]

In the late seventies and early eighties, within the framework of the negotiated transition from the military rule to democracy, scholars who were not affiliated with the armed forces scrutinized geopolitics as a field of expertise. Moniz Bandeira was working on the Brazilian presence in the La Plata Basin, Gerson Guimarães on General Golbery's contribution to the concept of national security, Sônia de Camargo on the geopolitics of generals Meira Mattos and Golbery do Couto e Silva, Shiguenoli Miyamoto on the overall assessment of the field, and Bertha Becker on the geopolitics of Amazonia. According to Costa,[5] Bertha Becker singularly advocated for a new geopolitical vision that should be theoretically rooted, autonomous from the state, and interdisciplinary. Her work has later influenced new generations, such as Lia Osório Machado and Paulo César da Costa Gomes.[6]

At the same time, the French geopolitical school had a major impact on this movement of epistemological renewal: building on older university linkages between France and Brazil, authors such as Yves Lacoste, Claude Raffestin, Béatrice Giblin, and the journal *Hérodote* heavily influenced the minds of the new generations of researchers. Moreover, there was a boom of Political Science and International Relations undergraduate and graduate programs, which also contributed to the development of conceptual, historical, and empirical research related to North–South relations, Center–Periphery relations, South America and its regional strategic resources, the Amazonian region, as well as the relationship between autonomy and foreign policy.[7] This rejuvenated scholarship led to an intellectual shift from more classical conceptions of geopolitics and strategy towards a more pluralistic set of visions on Brazil's international relations, thus preparing the field for institutional changes in the second half of the nineties.

7.2 Who and where

Brazil's re-democratization coincided with an inherited double divorce in its international strategies: first, between the country's foreign and defense policies, and second, between the military and civil society. According to the 1988 Constitution, the president chairs the Defense Council, whose members are consulted on matters of war, peace, and national security.[8] Nevertheless, due to the nature of the Brazilian transition from military rule to democracy, the first National Defense Policy (NDP) was only published in 1996, before the actual creation of the Ministry of Defense in 1999. Two among the ten ministers since 1999 have been diplomats: José Viegas Filho (between January 2003 and November 2004) and Celso Amorim (from August 2011 to December 2014). It was mainly after 2003 that political bridges were built to improve the policy dialogue between defense and foreign affairs, but also between civilians and the military. The ministries of foreign affairs and defense were primarily responsible for the drafting and implementation of a grand strategy between 2003 and 2014.

During PT's governments, Brazil tried to combine soft and hard power through an active and autonomous foreign policy, alongside an increase in its dissuasive capacity. The second NDP was published in 2005, which resulted in the first National Defense Strategy (NDS) in 2008 and the first White Paper on National Defense (WP) in 2012. The NDS established medium- and long-term strategic goals and actions to modernize the country's defense structure. It also addressed political-institutional issues that should ensure the means for Brazil's government and society to engage in the nation's building of a grand strategy.[9] The NDP and the NDS can be seen as evolutionary stages in the formulation of Brazilian defense policy and both represent an important agreement between diplomacy and defense to steer Brazil's international relations. Moreover, the ministries of foreign affairs and defense have worked together to consolidate a defense-industrial base both at the national and regional levels.[10]

After the 2008 NDS, the ministries of defense and foreign affairs began to strengthen their mutual ties in the field of technical cooperation with South American and African countries. According to the 2012 WP, foreign and defense policies should join their efforts to maintain regional stability and build a more cooperative international environment. Since 2010, the Brazilian Cooperation Agency has maintained a partnership with defense's international affairs division, and both have sought to enable the participation of military personnel from various South American and African countries in courses offered by the armed forces, intensifying bilateral and regional relations through policy transfer and capacity-building.

Moreover, as an attempt to bridge the gap between defense policy and civil society, graduate programs and scholars obtained significant support from the ministry of defense to establish the Brazilian Association of Defense Studies (ABED) in 2005. Since its inception, ABED has held annual meetings, counting on the participation of military and civil, senior and younger researchers from all regions of the country. In 2013, the ministry of defense founded the Pandiá Calogeras Institute aiming to fund networks in which both military and university researchers should participate and develop joint projects. In the aftermath of the 2016 institutional crisis, the institute continued its activities, albeit its budget was decreased, and its political focus was diluted.

7.3 Ways, means, and ends

Brazil's sketch of a grand strategy had two main dimensions: regional and global. Regionally, in the field of defense, Brazil has the largest number of tanks, artillery pieces, combat ships, as well as submarines and tactical aircraft. This does not mean, however, that the country has an absolute material superiority in case of a military coalition in the region. Also in terms of military spending, the comparison between Brazil and its neighbors (especially Argentina, Chile, Colombia, and Peru) expresses a strong asymmetry when each of these countries is taken individually, but the Brazilian weakness is revealed in the disaggregated analysis of its military budget. Between 2007 and 2016, on average, the army was responsible for 43.1 percent of global expenditures, the navy for 25.6 percent, and the air force for 22.6 percent. In addition, due to the very high participation of personnel expenses and charges in the overall budget (on average, 88.2 percent in the army, 76.9 percent in the navy, and 75.3 percent in the air force), the investment rate for the same period was very low (3.7 percent for the army, 11.4 percent for the air force, and 12.4 percent in the navy). Such a low investment rate in the defense sector denotes structural limitations in Brazil's capacity to project power regionally and globally.[11]

It is true that in 2008 Brazil signed an agreement with France for the development of the nuclear fast-track submarine and that in 2015 Brazil and Sweden signed a contract for building and transferring technology of Saab fighter jets. Nevertheless, even though Brazil is the largest holder of traditional military capabilities when compared to countries in its immediate and extended strategic environment, it is much less clear whether it has the military capacity to protect and to project itself over the area that it defines as its own strategic environment, which encompasses South America, the South Atlantic, the African western coast, and Antarctica, as well as strategic resources situated in the Green and Blue Amazonia as mentioned in the NDS.[12]

During the PT's governments, Brazilian foreign policy reaffirmed the fact that South America does not represent a threat to the country, even though the 2012 WP stressed the need to protect strategic resources in the Brazilian Amazonia and to fight against cyberthreats, drug trafficking, weapons trafficking, and maritime piracy. PT's governments also stressed the centrality of MERCOSUR (Common Market of the South) and pushed its expansion in terms of institutions and membership, as in the case of Venezuela's adhesion to the bloc in 2012. MERCOSUR has a strategic importance to Brazil because it absorbs more than 60 percent of the country's foreign direct investment in South America and approximately 90 percent of Brazilian manufactured exports to this region.[13]

After Mexico joined the North American Free Trade Zone (NAFTA) in 1994, Brazil pursued a policy of engagement, both economic and political, with its immediate neighbors in South America.[14] After Lula's inauguration, Brazil tried to transform South America into a cohesive region in world politics, thus projecting it as a global pole under Brazil's leadership, even if this leadership was not always acknowledged or even contested by neighbors.[15] In 2008, the creation of the Union of South American Nations (UNASUR) represented the political dimension of the subcontinental integration. Under Brazil's grand strategy, UNASUR should work as a forum and allow its twelve members—all South American countries—to coordinate shared political stances and to deal with eventual contexts of institutional instability and uncertainty.

Globally, between 2003 and 2014 Brazil's foreign policy was based on a singular framing of international politics and the country's assets to deploy its national strategy: a multipolar world where globalization and diffusion of power would have promoted a fundamental structural shift in the world economy, which would have resulted in a redistribution of power from the West to the East and from the North to the South. Such a world vision implied opportunities and challenges to Brazil's grand strategy: in a scenario of relative fragmentation of global governance and a mismatch between norms and power, Brazil tried to combine the use of classical soft power attributes with the expansion of its aspirations to move beyond the previous boundaries of its diplomatic performance.[16] When compared to other developing countries, Brazil has clearly differentiated itself in terms of its material capabilities, diplomacy, and relative international recognition. The country has never sought international primacy; however, between 2003 and 2014 it has shown a clear ambition to rise in, and redefine, international hierarchies. Brazilian foreign policy was very active in world economic forums, championing the internationalization of the country's transnational firms' interests and supporting an autonomous and more equitable regional integration project.[17]

Moreover, as part of Brazil's grand strategy, the federal government promoted development cooperation in Latin America, the Caribbean, and Africa. Brazil's global governmental expenses including educational, scientific, financial, humanitarian, and technical cooperation increased from $158 million in 2005 to approximately $923 million in 2010.[18] Between 2003 and 2014, Brazil also took an active position affirming its leadership at the UN and in the South Atlantic. Brazil decided to accept the role of force commander of the United Nations Stabilization Mission in Haiti (MINUSTAH) in 2004, although this step went directly against the Brazilian traditional position related to UN peacekeeping operations. In the aftermath of the mission sent by Brazil's Defense Ministry for tying contacts with Multinational Interim Force commanders and surveying the necessary logistics to proceed with the operation, more than 1,200 Brazilian soldiers representing the armed forces plus the military police arrived in Haiti in May 2004.[19] Brazil also aimed to consolidate the South Atlantic as a zone of peace and prosperity. The country devoted special attention, along with its neighbors in West Africa, to the construction of a cooperative environment free of nuclear weapons in this area, under the aegis of the Zone of Peace and Cooperation of the South Atlantic—ZOPACAS, an initiative launched by the Brazilian diplomacy in 1986 and firmly retaken by Amorim when he was defense minister.[20]

Nevertheless, Brazil's international power projection was not consensual, neither externally nor domestically. As we shall see in the coming sections, the attempt to conciliate a global focus on the geopolitical South with the prioritization of regional integration, especially in South America, was domestically criticized by opposition parties and mainstream media outlets.

7.4 Values and goals

As part of Brazil's grand strategy, the emphasis on multipolarity became a powerful normative principle considered morally superior to any other global power distribution model. The goal of multipolarity was sought in different fronts, such as the priority given to South American integration and Latin American solidarity through new institutions (UNASUR, CELAC, and FOCEM within MERCOSUR), the democratization of international organizations, the struggle for fairness in global trade negotiations, and the articulation of new coalitions among developing countries. Multilaterally accepted norms seemed to offer the most permissive conditions for Brazil to define its interests with autonomy and to carry out a grand strategy that included the goal of being not only a peaceful country, but one that provides peace and participate in the construction of development norms.[21]

Brazilian foreign policy was then characterized by a soft brand revisionism, which contrasts with India's consistent revisionism as well as China's recent turn towards overt revisionism. Due to the absence of nuclear weapons and its geopolitical situation, inside the United States' geopolitical area of direct influence, Brazil seems to have less room for maneuver than the two Asian countries. Moreover, Brazil is not a pushover by any means: the country's diplomacy is a historical mix of 'acceptance of' versus 'resistance to' international norms, regional versus global ambitions, middle power diplomacy versus greater power aspirations. Lula's and Rousseff's activist foreign policy did not imply direct confrontation, but rather a more assertive policy pursued through engagement and negotiation. Brazil did not unconditionally embrace the status quo, nor did it adopt a deeply revisionist position.[22]

For Brazil, this process of reconfiguration of the global governance was intertwined with an expanded use of its soft power assets that aim to transform the political pillars of world affairs based upon innovative and more inclusive forms of representation and rule-making in multilateral settings. Among Brazilian foreign policy aspirations, two should be emphasized: a greater influence in the design of a reformed multilateral global architecture and an amplified South–South cooperation. Since 2003, Brazilian foreign policy has contributed to the institutionalization of some relevant South–South coalitions, such as the IBSA Forum (India, Brazil, and South Africa),[23] the G20 under the World Trade Organization (WTO) and the BRICS (Brazil, Russia, India, China, and South Africa) group,[24] but also summits between South American and African countries or between South American and Arab countries.[25]

7.5 Implementing the grand strategy: Domestic politics and development strategies

In this section, we analyze the importance of the domestic support coalitions and the development model in the implementation of the Brazilian grand strategy during the PT governments. Under Lula and Dilma, Brazil associated an assertive foreign policy with a development strategy that has increased the role of state in the economy. In addition, the country carried out modernization projects in the defense realm while maintaining the guiding principle of prioritizing social welfare. In those years, the federal government tried to effectively coordinate foreign policy, national defense, economic, and social policies. According to the country's NDS, a national defense strategy is inseparable from a national strategy of development. However, the combined effects of a political and economic crisis affected the foreign policy, the development model, and the defense policy, with impacts on Brazil's grand strategy.

Since re-democratization, it has been observed that the increasing influence of political coalitions in foreign policy decision-making and the linkages between Brazil's foreign policy and its development model has done away with the classic realist idea that foreign policy begins where domestic policy ends. The interplay between international relations and domestic politics shapes not only the country's foreign policy but also its general development. Therefore, to explain why a governmental decision was made, or why a specific pattern of governmental behavior emerged, it is necessary to identify the games and the players, as well as to display the coalitions, bargains, and compromises. Thus, by conceiving foreign policy as a public policy, we emphasize contingency and remove foreign policy from an inertial condition associated with a supposedly self-evident and permanent national interest.[26]

Until recently, Brazilian foreign policy used to be perceived as a state policy relatively immune to changes and to the interference of governmental agencies, businesses, unions, media outlets, political parties, and civil society actors. This was partly due to the Ministry of External Relations' (Itamaraty's) unique historical role. However, in the last twenty years, Brazilian foreign policy has been characterized by the pluralization of actors, presidential diplomacy, and politicization. This pluralization involves not only new state actors, but also nonstate actors, social movements, interest groups, and political parties.[27] In a presidential system, the president has a central role in setting the political agenda and guiding the strategic direction, in addition to his/her power to choose and dismiss the minister according to the 1988 Constitution.[28] Lastly, we must consider the internal distributive effects of foreign policy decisions, increasing the influence of domestic politics in foreign policymaking; it also implies the intensification of the public debate around ideas, interests, and values related to policy choices.[29] Based on the assumption that foreign policy changes according to the incumbent government, we argue that there is no consensus within Brazil's strategic elite members about the country's pattern of international relations, which is one of the conditions for a successful confrontation of what has been called "the graduation dilemma."[30]

In this connection, Peter Gourevitch[31] classified as a critical juncture the simultaneous combination of systemic and domestic transformations. Critical junctures are moments in which the dominant patterns of domestic development and international integration are exhausted, thus making room for the emergence of a new sociopolitical coalition, with repercussions on economic policy and foreign policy. In analyzing critical junctures that affected Brazil, Maria Regina Soares de Lima and Monica Hirst[32] identified two of them throughout the twentieth century: the first in the 1930s, with the crisis of the agro-exporting economy and the subsequent adoption of the import-substitution industrialization model (ISI); the second in the 1990s, with the depletion of ISI and the advent of a logic of competitive integration to the global economy. Both critical junctures brought about re-articulations involving the domestic and international dimensions. Nowadays, a new critical juncture may be underway in Brazil.

Historically, since the transition that occurred between 1930 and 1940, foreign policy has established a close and virtuous link between the objectives of the ISI model and the emphasis on autonomy. There has been a perception that foreign policy should supplement the internal effort of development, displaying a new historical functionality. However, the transition from an agro-export model to an industrial one proved to be politically contentious, as entrenched and emerging factions fought for influence in the new configuration. It was not until the mid-1950s that a political consensus in support of a national industrialization process began to emerge. This agenda required a new domestic support coalition (developmentalist and nationalist) formed by industrial entrepreneurs, bureaucrats, progressive intellectuals, and urban workers. To boost this development effort, President Vargas created the Brazilian National Development Bank (BNDES) in 1952, which became one of the most visible and influential tools of state-managed industrialization.[33]

Nevertheless, the old developmentalism left behind a contradictory legacy. On the one hand, industrialization projected Brazil beyond the classical agro-exporting model. Between 1947 and 1980, the Brazilian economy had an average economic growth of 7.5 percent a year. The Brazilian economy was the only one in Latin America that completed the inter-industrial matrix corresponding to the technological paradigm of the second industrial revolution. In spite of its contradictions and limits, the industrialization process created industries, such as automobiles and aircraft, which are still today responsible for the few high-value-added goods that Brazil mass-produces and exports. On the other hand, Brazil amplified its external vulnerability by becoming more dependent on foreign direct investment and foreign technology for industrial production. In addition, economic development did not improve social conditions, as social inequality and regional disparities deepened.[34]

In this section, we argue that an autonomous foreign policy presupposes an ambition for international prominence, the claim of a rule-maker role in the international order, a geopolitical vision of the South that emphasizes a long-term grand strategy and a commitment to regional integration.[35] These features were present during the independent foreign policy (1961–64), the responsible pragmatism (1974–79), as well as PT's "assertive and active" foreign policy. More strictly speaking, however, only the first and third of these two policies could be entirely accurately classified as autonomous foreign policies, because both tried to combine democracy and social inclusion at the domestic level with a moderately revisionist foreign policy, and both were interrupted by institutional ruptures backed by national and transnational conservative social forces.[36]

In our argument, we also draw a parallel between different political conceptions of autonomy in foreign policy and debates on the country's development model. Since the 1990s, the political-ideological cleavages that have affected Brazilian foreign policy reflect the absence of a national consensus on a new development model. In fact, there are clear differences between Fernando Henrique Cardoso's foreign policy of prestige and the ambition for international prominence under Lula and Rousseff. In order to understand the differences between Brazilian foreign policy under PSDB and PT, two major issues must be taken into consideration: first, the linkages between global contexts and the country's domestic developments; second, the different political-ideological preferences of governments, and the degree of cohesion of the partisan coalitions of support. At the international level and for dissimilar reasons, Cardoso and Rousseff had to deal with slow-growth economic contexts, whereas Lula benefited from a boom of commodities that helped Brazil to achieve high rates of economic growth.[37] Table 7.1 shows the average growth rates of the gross domestic product between 1995 and 2014.

From the domestic political standpoint, Cardoso's government, supported by a relatively homogeneous center-right coalition, faced easier governability

Table 7.1 Brazil: average rates of GDP growth (1995–2014)

Government	Period	Average
Fernando Henrique	1995–2002	3.2
	1995–98	3.4
	1999–2002	3.1
Lula	2003–10	4.8
	2003–6	3.6
	2007–10	6.0
Dilma	2011–14	2.7

Source: IMF, *World economic outlook: a survey by the staff of the International Monetary Fund*. Washington, DC: International Monetary Fund, 2015.

conditions. Cardoso led a broad and solid parliamentary coalition, which provided him the most stable government of the two Brazilian democratic periods, between 1946 and 1964, and from 1985 until the 2016 controversial impeachment.[38] Lula and Rousseff were elected by a center-left coalition, based on a much more fragmented and heterogeneous coalition of political parties. However, the combination between successful social policies and the improvement of economic conditions, on one hand, with a favorable international context, on the other, provided Lula's government a wide popular support and the means to link domestic change with a moderately revisionist foreign policy. Although the Rousseff administration followed the same path, her government had to face a combination of three crises: the worsening of the international economic crisis that started in 2008, the decline of commodities' prices, and increasing economic, political, and social problems at home.[39]

Cardoso took office in 1995 believing that a unipolar world was not a fleeting moment but a new feature of the international order that was likely to endure. During his presidency, foreign policy was oriented toward monetary stabilization and the search for credentials within the international community. He resumed the prestige foreign policy of previous governments and reinforced Brazil's activism in multilateral forums. According to this view, Brazil had limited ability to shape the international system, and the best foreign policy was one that avoided conflict with the major centers of power and sought to adapt to the dominant regimes and institutions. For this reason, Brazil adopted a compromising attitude toward the West, and deployed a strategy that involved strengthening ties with the United States and Europe. In addition, the country adhered to international regimes and ratified international protocols in different areas, such as environmental protection, human rights, and nuclear nonproliferation.[40]

Lula da Silva held a very different view of the international system when he took office in 2003. Lula and his main foreign policy advisors—ambassador Celso Amorim (Itamaraty's minister), ambassador Samuel Pinheiro Guimarães

(Itamaraty's secretary-general) and Marco Aurélio Garcia (presidential advisor)—believed that a significant world power transition was under way, and that it could benefit Brazil. Thus, Brazilian foreign policy tried to combine a soft revisionism of multilateral institutions, an activist policy of development cooperation, and public policy transfer programs in the field of poverty reduction and the fight against hunger. A presidential diplomacy was concerned simultaneously with deepening ties with the geopolitical South and with regional partners, without underestimating the importance of developed countries. Brazil reshaped its relations with the United States and Europe, and deepened its ties with China, Russia, India, and South Africa. Moreover, the country has expanded its presence in South America, either through strengthening and creating mechanisms of regional integration or through the expansion of its transnational corporations.[41]

During the PT's administrations, many analysts considered that Brazil adopted a neo-developmentalism model. Differently from the old developmentalism, the new version has a considerably less ambitious program. Neo-developmentalism is conceptualized as a development strategy for middle-income countries based on a moderate state intervention in the economy, the maintenance of a competitive exchange rate and dynamic social policies.[42] In this regard, it is worth making a brief comment on the persistence of "developmentalism" as a concept, and its subtypes (national developmentalism and associated-dependent developmentalism), in Brazilian and Latin American economic thinking. Both subtype strategies were a result of the incapacity of private entrepreneurs to lead an industrialization process, due either to the nonexistence of technological knowledge or low capital levels. In the national-developmentalism model, the state should play a central role, being responsible for strategic investments. Under the associated-dependent model, foreign investment should assume a central place. Despite the retreat of development debates at the end of the twentieth century, neo-developmentalism policy proposals introduced by some center-leftist governments at the beginning of the twenty-first century suggest that it represents a deep-rooted phenomenon in Latin American societies. Historical conditions that were responsible for its appearance, usually referred to by different terms such as "underdevelopment," "structural heterogeneity," or "dependence," have not yet been overcome.[43]

Under Lula and Rousseff, the association of economic, foreign, and social policies contributed to displace the hegemony of the financial international capital within the power bloc. The reorientation of state policies sought to comply with the yearnings of the Brazilian internal *grande bourgeoisie*, which is distributed throughout many sectors of the economy: commodity-processing industries, construction, mining, shipbuilding, and segments of agribusiness. What brings together these different sectors is their demand for favorable treatment and acceptance of state intervention in their competition with international capital. This fraction of the capitalist class maintained its own basis for capital accumulation and vied with the international financial capital to construct an alliance with the PT's government.[44] Both Lula and Rousseff strengthened the connections between the internal neo-developmentalism model and Brazilian foreign policy. After 2007, the Lula administration intensified the use of BNDES capital to promote an active industrial policy aimed at creating the so-called "national champions" (i.e. large transnational companies capable to compete and struggle for international markets). In such effort, BNDES supported their internationalization strategy, mainly in Latin America and Africa.[45]

Therefore, to understand the political crisis that affected the PT's governments and the attempt to sketch a grand strategy, it is necessary to briefly analyze the two opposing coalitions that had been structured in those years: the "rentist" *versus* the "productivist" or "neo-developmentalist." On the one hand, the rentist coalition is oriented toward neoliberal orthodoxy, and is mainly represented by the PSDB. The orthodox neoliberal field encompasses national and international financial capital, some of the large landowners, and the upper middle class of the private and public sectors. On the other hand, the neo-developmentalist front is characterized by heterogeneity and plagued by contradictions, and is mainly represented by the PT. This front is made up by the internal *grande bourgeoisie*, some organized factions of the working class, the lower middle class, and impoverished rural workers.[46]

The rentist coalition program intended to keep Brazil aligned with neoliberal policies, as well as in the orbit of the great international capital and under the United States' geopolitical leadership. Otherwise, the productivist coalition program aimed to accelerate economic growth through state intervention and reindustrialization. This program was for some time compatible with the foreign policy emphasis in South–South relations and the prioritization of South American integration. It is worth remembering that in 2005 some industrial sectors helped to block the American proposal to create a Free Trade Agreement of the Americas.[47] In addition, the internal *grande bourgeoisie*'s commercial goals were met by initiatives such as BRICS, G20, and IBSA.[48]

Dilma Rousseff succeeded Lula in 2011 in a completely different global and domestic context, which severely affected her government's "developmental rehearsal" in support of the country's reindustrialization effort. Between 2011 and 2013, Rousseff implemented several policies demanded by the most important industrial federations: the reduction of interest rates and bank spreads, tax exemptions, the requirement of national content by the industrial policy, the increase of BNDES's subsidized credit lines, an infrastructure plan, and the devaluation of the exchange rate. However, the combined effects of the international crisis and the growing domestic distributive conflict led to the collapse of the neo-developmentalist front.[49] After 2013, the gap between industrialists and workers deepened, ending the "win-win" game and preparing the conditions that provoked Rousseff's controversial impeachment.

This turbulent environment gave Rousseff far less leeway to conduct an activist foreign policy. Her opportunity to implement such a foreign policy further diminished as the internal *grande bourgeoisie* moved toward the rentist coalition. The main industrial federations started to defend the signature of free trade agreements with the United States and the European Union, leaving MERCOSUR in a second plan.[50] These industrial demands coincided with the foreign policy orientation that had been implemented by President Michel Temer, who seized power after Rousseff's controversial impeachment.

In the defense realm, for the first time in eighteen years, Temer's administration (2016–2018) nominated a military as head of the MD, which affected civil-military relations within the MD system. Besides, his government has resorted to budgetary cuts that heavily impacted the MD. For instance, in 2016 the MD's planned budget represented half of its nominal value compared to 2014. These reductions affected modernization programs such as the Submarine Development Program (PROSUB) and the F-X Project involving the partnership between Brazilian Embraer and Swedish Saab for the acquisition of new jet fighters, which included technology transfer.[51] Recently, Temer announced the willingness to transfer Embraer's capital control to Boeing, a measure that will probably be implemented by his successor elected in the 2018 elections, the far right-wing extremist Jair Bolsonaro However, as a high-tech company, whose capital is primarily Brazilian, Embraer is the most important element of the country's military complex. All these measures have the potential to negatively affect the consolidation of a defense-industrial base.

Both Temer and Bolsonaro's administrations have placed Brazil in the geopolitical orbit of the United States. In March 2017, Brazil and the US signed a military agreement that paves the way for the joint development and sale of defense products. Other military deals and joint exercise in the Amazonia are being discussed, which could pave the way for an American use of Brazil's rocket launch site, the Alcantara base. In addition, the recent use of the armed forces against drug trafficking and in the occupation of Rio de Janeiro's poor urban areas seems to follow the US Drug Enforcement Administration (DEA) recommendations, reproducing the same strategy already used in Colombia and Mexico. Thus, the combined effect of these policies breaks with UNASUR's attempt to coordinate the foreign and defense policies of South American countries.

In sum, the cycle of PT's governments sketched a grand strategy characterized by a soft revisionism in foreign policy, an emphasis in South–South relations, and the prioritization of regional integration. Moreover, Lula's and Rousseff's administrations sought to link this foreign policy to a neo-developmentalist model and inclusive and innovative social policies. However, the confluence of systemic transformations with domestic ruptures has contributed to interrupt the sketch of a grand strategy based on an autonomous foreign policy, an expansion of regional defense programs, and a political ambition for international prominence. The recent events that affected the Brazilian democracy showed that foreign policy not only is a public policy, but also that the implementation of a grand strategy is contingent on the political and ideological variations of successive governments, their support coalitions and social forces, as well as their internal contradictions and shortcomings in establishing a set of development strategies.

7.6 Conclusion

At the turn of the twenty-first century, Brazil was acclaimed as a "rising economic power" and a dynamic democracy with a government that implemented progressive public policies in one of the world's most unequal societies. Brazilian "best practices" were high on the international agenda. Developing countries sent envoys to Brasília to learn from the gradual results of the social policies that were being implemented. In the aftermath of the controversial impeachment of president Rousseff, Brazil's diplomatic dynamism and the sketch of a grand strategy were left behind, and the country plunged into a profound institutional, political, economic, and societal crisis.

In broader terms, the transition from the presidency of Fernando Henrique Cardoso to Lula da Silva and subsequently to Dilma Rousseff represented the continuity of the 1988 Constitution political pact, consensus on macroeconomic stability, and respect for the rule of law, as well as the implementation of creative and inclusive social policies, particularly in the field of poverty reduction. It goes without saying that each president had his/her own idiosyncrasies in terms of building coalitions, dealing with business and social movements, or relating to the mass media. Moreover, they were noticeably quite distinct from one another in the way they projected Brazil's political ambitions and roles internationally.

Nevertheless, the distinction between the two historical periods becomes clearer when we look at the changes in Brazil's foreign policy agenda. Under Lula, Brazil's grand strategy focused on regional integration in South America and South–South cooperation; the formation of the IBSA Dialogue Forum; the creation of the BRICS group; and an increased dialogue between foreign policy and defense, explicitly demonstrating an ambition for international prominence. These were important features of Brazil's international projection of power between 2003 and 2010, which together with the pre-salt oil discovery announced in 2007, boosted the country's diplomatic efforts to question asymmetric global governance structures and call for political reforms in global institutions. Under Lula, Brazil also revealed its ambition for graduation and an increased role in international rule-making; both in the WTO's meeting in Cancun in 2003 and through the Turkish–Brazilian mediation proposal for the Iranian nuclear program in 2010, Brazil's government demonstrated that it also wanted to "act globally" and to contribute to the construction of international norms. Benefiting from the commodities boom cycle and impressive Chinese economic growth rates, Brazil increased its accumulation of gross international reserves from approximately $37.8 billion in 2002 to $288.5 billion in 2010, according to the International Monetary Fund (IMF) historical series.[52] When Lula was preparing to step down in December 2010, opinion polls showed that his personal approval rating had reached a dizzying high of approximately 87 percent.

Being the successor of such a popular president was no easy task for Dilma Rousseff. She did not enjoy the same charismatic leadership profile, nor did she benefit from a favorable global economic context for Brazil's development. The effects of the 2008 global economic crisis on the Brazilian economy were clear during her first mandate, and despite her attempts to reduce the banking system's interest rates and excessive gains, her government failed to stimulate growth through public and private investments, diversify the industrial infrastructure, and thereby, reorient the Brazilian macroeconomic development model. Moreover, Rousseff's political coalition was ideologically too broad, and party leaders did not agree on all the policies she was trying to implement. Once the commodity boom was over, growth rates declined significantly, and it was impossible to maintain Lula's previous development pact of "gains for the poor and for the wealthy" at the same time. Despite this change in the political game, Rousseff still insisted on increasing the minimum wage, expanding social policies to fight against poverty, as well as fostering nationwide technical and professional capacity-building programs.

The "grand strategy" sketched under Lula and Rousseff also counted on the important leadership of Ambassador Celso Amorim, who had been Lula's Minister of Foreign Affairs for eight years, then Rousseff's Minister of Defense for more than three years. Irrespective of the high quality of this leadership, the sketch of Brazil's grand strategy required a strong social coalition to support the implementation of decisions in the legislative branch, the judiciary, the mass media, and civil society. It also required a national entrepreneurship capacity and a productive sector associated with the nation's future. The failure in the implementation of Brazil's grand strategy suggests that it suffered from inconsistencies in its conception, which generated a "capability-expectations" gap, mainly after the systemic financial crisis and the end of the commodities "boom." Moreover, it also suggests that the Brazilian productive sector's interests shifted over time, and were increasingly linked to the financial sector, more oriented towards global markets, and much less prone to accepting the implementation of a neo-developmentalist socioeconomic model. Paraphrasing Steven E. Lobell, Jeffrey W. Taliaferro, and Norrin M. Ripsman,[53] the sketch of Brazil's grand strategy, even though it was intentional, did not entail "a calculated relationship between strategic ends and available means," and did not anticipate "likely reactions of one or more potential opponents."

After Rousseff's impeachment, Brazil's government launched in July 2017 a document about the country's grand strategy and foreign policy. The paper criticizes the Brazilian foreign policy during the PT's administrations. It states that in the last years Brazil did not accomplish any of its major foreign policy goals, such as the South American integration, the South–South cooperation, and the global role of the BRICS.[54] However, we argue that there is also an international dimension to Brazil's institutional and political crisis that prevented the country's grand strategy from flourishing, which must not be neglected. As Hal Brands[55] stated, under Lula, Brazil's grand strategy had successfully raised the country's profile and increased its diplomatic flexibility, but had also exposed it to economic, social, regional leadership, and global dilemmas that could undermine its ascent, as well as one dilemma related to its relationship with the United States:

while Lula has maintained good relations with Washington, his grand strategy unavoidably entails a growing risk of conflict over issues like Iran, trade policy, and the USA diplomatic and military role in Latin America. Looking ahead, the efficacy of Brazilian grand strategy and its consequences for American interests will be contingent on how Lula's successors address these dilemmas.[56]

It seems clear that the debate on Brazil–USA bilateral relations is of great relevance in view of the country's aim to implement a more autonomous foreign policy in the West, but also to sketch a grand strategy and therefore to show through practices and behavior its clear political ambition for graduation. As we have demonstrated in this chapter, the graduation dilemma is associated with a cleavage within Brazil's strategic elite members (cosmopolitan/globalists versus sovereign-based nationalists) from both public and private sectors. In 2003, Brazil's foreign policy moved away from its previous trajectory that had been almost automatically aligned with the Western world. Although Lula and Rousseff had differences, their approaches to foreign policy were based on a shared interpretation of the world order (less hegemonic and more multipolar) and the defense of values associated with Brazil's self-esteem, political autonomy, and national development. After August 2016, these foreign policy frames and grand strategy values, ways, and means have been set aside. The interruption of the PT governments' cycle meant the dismantling of an autonomist foreign policy and the interruption of a grand strategy rooted in regional cooperation, South–South relations, and institutional building.

For future analyses of Brazil's grand strategy, we select some important issues that should be addressed by scholars and practitioners. First, Brazilian elites should arrive at a minimum consensus over a national development project, which must have interconnections with both foreign and defense policies, but also with modalities of social policies to overcome inequality and extreme poverty. Second, Brazil must improve civil-military relations within MD's decision-making structure, which is necessary to consolidate democratic values. Third, it is important to improve strategic planning and to develop a proper interface between the armed forces, the private sector, and universities in order to build a defense-industrial base. Finally, a deeper integration of foreign and defense policies should become part of Brazil's strategic guidelines to address regional and global challenges, fostering a double external–internal movement to harden the country's soft power, and to connect a peaceful foreign policy to a robust defense policy, but also to encourage bureaucracies from both ministries to expand policy dialogues with all segments of Brazil's society, thus institutionalizing practices of transparency and accountability.

NOTES

1. Wanderley Messias da Costa, *Geografia Política e Geopolítica: discursos sobre o território e o poder* (São Paulo: Editora HUCITEC; Editora da Universidade de São Paulo, 1992); Shiguenoli Miyamoto, "Os Estudos Geopolíticos no Brasil: uma contribuição para sua avaliação," *Perspectivas São Paulo* 4 (1981): 75–92.
2. Miyamoto, "Os Estudos Geopolíticos no Brasil"; Mário Travassos, *Projeção Internacional do Brasil* (São Paulo: Companhia Editora Nacional, 1931).
3. Costa, *Geografia Política e Geopolítica*; Maria Regina Soares de Lima et al., *Atlas of Brazilian Defence Policy* (Buenos Aires: CLACSO, 2018); Miyamoto, "Os Estudos Geopolíticos no Brasil."
4. Therezinha de Castro and Carlos Delgado de Carvalho, "A questão da Antártida," *Boletim Geográfico* 14, no. 135 (1956): 502–6; Therezinha de Castro, "Antártica, o assunto do momento," *Boletim Geográfico* 17, no. 150 (1959): 238–45; Golbery Couto e Silva, *Geopolítica do Brasil* (Rio de Janeiro: José Olympio, 1967); Carlos de Meira Mattos, *Brasil, geopolítica e destino* (Rio de Janeiro: José Olympio, 1975); Carlos de Meira Mattos, "Uma geopolítica pan-amazônica," *A Defesa Nacional* 677 (1978): 5–13.
5. Costa, *Geografia Política e Geopolítica*.
6. Paulo Cesar da Costa Gomes, *Geografia e modernidade* (Rio de Janeiro: Bertrand, 2010); Lia Osório Machado, "A Estratégia Nacional de Defesa, a geografia do tráfico de drogas ilícitas e a Bacia Amazônica Sul-americana," in *Seminário de Defesa e Desenvolvimento Sustentável da Amazônia*, eds. Escola de Comando and Estado Maior do Exército; Secretaria Assuntos Estratégicos (Rio de Janeiro: Sá Ribeiro Multimidia, 2011), 99–106.
7. Bertha K. Becker, *Geopolítica da Amazônia* (Rio de Janeiro: Zahar, 1982); Costa, *Geografia Política e Geopolítica*; Maria Regina Soares de Lima and Carlos R. S. Milani, "Política Externa Brasileira: Campo de Estudos e Principais Avanços," in *A ciência política no Brasil: 1960-2015*, eds. Leonardo Avritzer, Carlos R. S. Milani, and Maria do Socorro Braga (Rio de Janeiro: FGV, 2016), 393–422.

8. Articles 84 and 91 of the Constitution foresee that the members of the Defense Council are the vice president, the president of the federal chamber of deputies, the president of the senate, the heads of the three armed forces, as well as the Ministers of Defense, Foreign Affairs, Justice, and Planning.
9. Celso Amorim, *A grande estratégia do Brasil: discursos, artigos e entrevistas da gestão no Ministério da Defesa (2011–2014)* (Brasília: Fundação Alexandre de Gusmão; Editora UNESP, 2016); Nelson A. Jobim, Sergio W. Etchegoyen, and João Paulo Soares Alsina Júnior, eds., *Segurança internacional: perspectivas brasileiras* (Rio de Janeiro: FGV Editora, 2010).
10. Marco Cepik and Frederico Licks Bertol, "Defense policy in Brazil: bridging the gap between ends and means?," *Defence Studies* 16, no. 3 (July 2016): 229–47.
11. Lima et al., *Atlas of Brazilian Defence Policy*.
12. Alsina Júnior and João Paulo Soares, *Política externa e poder militar no Brasil: universos paralelos* (Rio de Janeiro: FGV Editora, 2009); Hal Brands, *Dilemmas of Brazilian Grand Strategy* (Carlisle, PA: US Army War College, Strategic Studies Institute Monograph, 2012).
13. Monica Hirst and Maria Regina Soares Lima, "Rethinking Global and Domestic Challenges in Brazilian Foreign Policy," in *Routledge Handbook of Latin America in the World*, eds. Jorge I. Domínguez and Ana Covarrubias (New York: Routledge, 2015), 139–52.
14. Leslie Bethell, "Brazil and Latin America," *Journal of Latin American Studies* 42, no. 03 (August 2010): 457–85; Maria Regina Soares de Lima and Monica Hirst, "Brasil como poder intermediário e poder regional," in *Os Brics e a ordem global*, ed. Andrew Hurrell (Rio de Janeiro: FGV Editora, 2009), 43–73.
15. Sean W. Burges, "Consensual Hegemony: Theorizing Brazilian Foreign Policy after the Cold War," *International Relations* 22, no. 1 (March 2008): 65–84; Andrés Malamud, "A Leader Without Followers? The Growing Divergence Between the Regional and Global Performance of Brazilian Foreign Policy," *Latin American Politics and Society* 53, no. 3 (2011): 1–24.
16. Amorim, *A grande estratégia do Brasil*; Hirst and Lima, "Rethinking Global and Domestic Challenges"; Robert J. Lieber, "The Rise of the BRICS and American primacy," *International Politics* 51, no. 2 (March 2014): 137–54; James Parisot, "American Power, East Asian Regionalism and Emerging Powers: *in* or *against* empire?," *Third World Quarterly* 34, no. 7 (August 2013): 1159–74.
17. Carlos R. S. Milani, Leticia Pinheiro, and Maria Regina Soares de Lima, "Brazil's foreign policy and the 'graduation dilemma'," *International Affairs* 93, no. 3 (May 2017): 585–605.
18. For more details on this, see IPEA and ABC, *Brazilian Cooperation for International Development 2005–2009* (Brasília: Instituto de Pesquisa Econômica Aplicada and Agência Brasileira de Cooperação, 2010). Two subsequent reports were published in 2013 (covering data from 2010) and 2016 (covering years 2011, 2012, and 2013). IPEA & ABC, *Cooperação Brasileira para o Desenvolvimento Internacional 2010* (Brasília: IPEA & ABC, 2013); IPEA & ABC, *Cooperação Brasileira para o Desenvolvimento Internacional 2011–2013* (Brasília: IPEA & ABC, 2016).
19. Ricardo Seitenfus, *Haiti: dilemas e fracassos internacionais* (Ijuí, Bra.: Editora da Unijuí, 2014).

20. Amorim, *A grande estratégia do Brasil*; José Luís Fiori, *História, estratégia e desenvolvimento: para uma geopolítica do capitalismo* (São Paulo: Boitempo Editorial, 2014). ZOPACAS was created in 1986 by the Resolution 41/11 of the United Nations General Assembly. Nowadays, it has twenty-four members: South Africa, Angola, Argentina, Benin, Brazil, Cape Verde, Cameroon, Congo, Côte d'Ivoire, Gabon, Gambia, Ghana, Guinea, Guinea Bissau, Equatorial Guinea, Liberia, Namibia, Nigeria, Democratic Republic of the Congo, Sao Tome and Principe, Senegal, Sierra Leone, Togo, and Uruguay.
21. Amorim, *A grande estratégia do Brasil*; Hirst and Lima, "Rethinking Global and Domestic Challenges."
22. Maria Regina Soares de Lima, "Brasil e Polos Emergentes do Poder Mundial: Rússia, Índia, China e África do Sul," in *O Brasil e os demais BRICS—comércio e política*, ed. Renato Baumann (Brasília: CEPAL/IPEA, 2010), 155–76; Amrita Narlikar, *New Powers: How to Become One and How to Manage Them* (Hurst: London, 2010).
23. The IBSA Forum works both as a coalition and a cooperative arrangement, thus involving the exchange of material and ideational goods among its members. In multilateral forums, India, Brazil, and South Africa usually stand together in the defense of the principles of sovereignty and nonintervention, in addition to support human rights causes. The IBSA has engaged itself in some initiatives related to South–South cooperation, to the benefit of poorer or vulnerable nations such as Haiti, Guinea Bissau, and Palestine. Moreover, cooperation between IBSA countries has been progressively extended to the defense area, including naval exercises, known as *Ibsamar* (Amorim, *A grande estratégia do Brasil*; Lima, "Brasil e Polos Emergentes do Poder Mundial").
24. Since the group's first summit in 2009, the BRICS group has expanded its profile in world economics, politics, and security issues to promote the idea that such a coalition ought to generate alternative interpretations and procedures vis-à-vis dominating Western-oriented worldviews. In the sixth summit in 2014, the BRICS approved an agreement to create two multilateral financial institutions, the New Development Bank (NDB) and the Contingency Reserve Arrangement (CRA), now being implemented (Lieber, "The Rise of the BRICS"; Parisot, "American Power").
25. Amorim, *A grande estratégia do Brasil*; Hirst and Lima, "Rethinking Global and Domestic Challenges"; Narlikar, *New Powers*; Tullo Vigevani and Gabriel Cepaluni, *Brazilian Foreign Policy in Changing Times: The Quest for Autonomy from Sarney to Lula* (Lanham, MD: Lexington Books, 2012).
26. Graham T. Allison and Philip Zelikow, *Essence of Decision: Explaining the Cuban Missile Crisis* (New York: Longman, 1999); Armando Boito and Tatiana Berringer, "Social Classes, Neodevelopmentalism, and Brazilian Foreign Policy under Presidents Lula and Dilma," *Latin American Perspectives* 41, no. 5 (September 2014): 94–109; Peter Gourevitch, "The Second Image Reversed: The International Sources of Domestic Politics," *International Organization* 32, no. 4 (September 1978): 881; Christopher Hill, *The Changing Politics of Foreign Policy*, (Hampshire, UK: Palgrave MacMillan, 2003); Carlos R. S. Milani and Leticia Pinheiro, "The Politics of Brazilian Foreign Policy and Its Analytical Challenges," *Foreign Policy Analysis* 13, no. 2 (April 2016): 278–96.

27. The two main political parties which have included foreign policy issues in their platforms are PT (the Workers' Party) and PSDB (the Brazilian Social Democratic Party). Both have also been the two most influential parties in Brazil's re-democratization process, having fought the last six presidential elections in the past twenty years (1994 to 2014). PT was founded in 1980, and began as an independent socialist party with strong ties to anti-imperialist movements worldwide; within a decade it had become the most important leftist party in Latin America. PSDB was founded in 1988, and presented itself after its Western European namesakes, with strong preferences for the parliamentary system and market-oriented reforms Jeffrey W. Cason and Timothy J. Power, "Presidentialization, Pluralization, and the Rollback of Itamaraty: Explaining Change in Brazilian Foreign Policy Making in the Cardoso-Lula Era," *International Political Science Review* 30, no. 2 (March 2009): 117–40.
28. Cason and Power; Maria Regina Soares de Lima and Rubens Duarte, "Diplomacia Presidencial e Politização da Política Externa: Uma Comparação dos Governos FHC e Lula," *Observador On-Line* 8, no. 9 (2013): 1–24.
29. Maria Izabel V. de Carvalho, "Estruturas domésticas e grupos de interesse: a formação da posição Brasileira para Seattle," *Contexto Internacional* 25, no. 2 (December 2003): 363–401; Maria Regina Soares de Lima, "Instituições Democráticas e Política Exterior," *Contexto Internacional* 22, no. 2 (2000): 265–303; Milani and Pinheiro, "The Politics of Brazilian Foreign Policy."
30. Carlos R. S. Milani, Leticia Pinheiro, and Maria Regina Soares de Lima, "Brazil's foreign policy and the 'graduation dilemma'."
31. Peter Gourevitch, *Políticas estratégicas en tiempos difíciles: respuestas comparativas a las crisis económicas internacionales* (Mexico City: Fondo de Cultura Económica, 1993).
32. Lima and Hirst, "Brasil como poder intermediário e poder regional."
33. Luiz Carlos Bresser-Pereira, *A construção política do Brasil sociedade, economia e estado desde a independência* (São Paulo: Editora 34, 2016); Ian R. Carrillo, "The New Developmentalism and the Challenges to Long-Term Stability in Brazil," *Latin American Perspectives* 41, no. 5 (September 2014): 59–74; Amado L. Cervo, "Political Regimes and Brazil's Foreign Policy," in *Foreign Policy and Political Regime*, ed. José Flávio Sombra Saraiva (Brasília: IBRI, 2003), 341–61; Lima and Hirst, "Brasil como poder intermediário e poder regional."
34. Fernando Henrique Cardoso, *Xadrez internacional e social-democracia* (São Paulo: Paz e Terra, 2010); Carrillo, "The New Developmentalism."
35. Milani, Pinheiro, and Lima, "Brazil's foreign policy and the 'graduation dilemma'."
36. Maria Regina Soares de Lima, "A agência da política externa brasileira (2008–2015): Uma análise preliminar," in *Crise sistêmica e inserção internacional: A política externa brasileira de 2008 a 2015*, eds. W. Desiderá and H. Ramanzini Jr (Brasília: IPEA, FUNAG, 2017).
37. Hirst and Lima, "Rethinking Global and Domestic Challenges."
38. Octavio Amorim Neto, *De Dutra a Lula: a condução e os determinantes da política externa brasileira*, (Rio de Janeiro: Campus, Konrad Adenauer Stiftung, 2011).
39. Hirst and Lima, "Rethinking Global and Domestic Challenges."

40. Boito and Berringer, "Social Classes, Neodevelopmentalism, and Brazilian Foreign Policy"; Hirst and Lima, "Rethinking Global and Domestic Challenges"; Lima, "A agência da política externa brasileira (2008–2015)"; Matias Spektor, "Brazil: Shadows of the Past and Contested Ambitions," in *Shaper Nations: Strategies for a Changing World*, eds. William I. Hitchcock, Melvyn P. Leffler, and Jeffrey Legro (Cambridge, MA: Harvard University Press, 2016), 17–35.
41. Hirst and Lima, "Rethinking Global and Domestic Challenges"; Spektor, "Brazil."
42. Bresser-Pereira, *A construção política do Brasil*; Carrillo, "The New Developmentalism."
43. Pedro Cezar Dutra Fonseca, *Desenvolvimentismo: a construção do conceito* (Brasília: IPEA, 2015).
44. Boito and Berringer, "Social Classes, Neodevelopmentalism, and Brazilian Foreign Policy"; Tatiana Berringer, *A burguesia brasileira e a política externa nos governos FHC e Lula* (Curitiba: Editora Appris, 2015).
45. Boito and Berringer, "Social Classes, Neodevelopmentalism, and Brazilian Foreign Policy"; Carrillo, "The New Developmentalism."
46. Boito and Berringer, "Social Classes, Neodevelopmentalism, and Brazilian Foreign Policy"; Berringer, *A burguesia brasileira*; Andre Singer, "Cutucando Onças com Vara Curta: O Ensaio Desenvolvimentista no Primeiro Mandato de Dilma Rousseff (2011–2014)," *Novos Estudos* 102 (2015): 42–71.
47. Carvalho, "Estruturas domésticas e grupos de interesse."
48. Boito and Berringer, "Social Classes, Neodevelopmentalism, and Brazilian Foreign Policy"; Berringer, *A burguesia*; André Singer, "A (Falta de) Base Política para o Ensaio Desenvolvimentista," in *As contradições do Lulismo: a que ponto chegamos?*, eds. André Singer and Isabel Loureiro (São Paulo: Boitempo, 2016).
49. Singer, "A (Falta de) Base Política."
50. Singer, "A (Falta de) Base Política."
51. Cepik and Bertol, "Defense policy in Brazil."
52. http://www.imf.org/external/country/BRA/index.htm
53. Steven E. Lobell, Jeffrey W. Taliaferro and Norrin M. Ripsman, "Introduction," in *The Challenge of Grand Strategy: The Great Powers and the Broken Balance between the World Wars*, eds. Jeffrey W. Taliaferro, Norrin M. Ripsman and Steven E, Lobell (Cambridge: Cambridge University Press, 2012).
54. Document available at http://www.secretariageral.gov.br/noticias/copy_of_titulo-da-noticia-entre-35-e-90-caracteres-com-espaco/BrasilUmPasemBuscadeumaGrande Estratgia.pdf
55. Brands, *Dilemmas of Brazilian Grand Strategy*.
56. Brands, *Dilemmas of Brazilian Grand Strategy*, v.

8 India

C. CHRISTINE FAIR

Prior to 1947, the Raj was the most important imperial subsystem in the British Empire. Situated strategically in the middle of the Indian Ocean, the British deployed civil servants, police, military forces as well as bonded and other forms of labor to Africa, Southeast, and Northeast Asia and even the British West Indies from British India. From its sinecure in the South Asian subcontinent, imperial Britain built an elaborate security architecture which it used to protect its treasured colony while also contesting and thwarting Russia and various Chinese dynasties as it continued to expand. The Indian Army, whose rank and file were largely native, fought wars throughout the British Empire. The British enlisted millions of Indians (mostly voluntarily) to fight and die on all fronts in World Wars I and II and extracted food resources to feed its globally deployed army, even though this policy caused deadly food shortages in the very areas that sent their sons to fight for the interests of their imperial masters. Without this abundant wealth of usurped South Asian manpower, it is quite possible that Britain would have been unable to hoist the Union Jack from the Caribbean to Cape Town to Canton.[1] In fact, writing at the apex of British imperial power in South Asia, Lord Curzon, a Viceroy of India and British Foreign Secretary, observed that

the master of India, must, under modern conditions, be the greater power in the Asiatic Continent, and therefore, it must be added, in the world. The central position of India, its magnificent resources, its teeming multitude of men, its great trading harbours, its reserve of military strength ... are assets of precious value.[2]

When India became independent in 1947, with Britain in a postwar retrenchment and divesting of its colonial assets, India could have been the inheritor of this massive ability to project power throughout the Indian Ocean and beyond. However, unlike Pakistan, which retained much of the British grand strategy it inherited from the departing British with a paltry fraction of the resources, India charted a different course. Under the leadership of Jawaharlal Nehru, a prominent leader of the Indian National Congress and independence movement who became India's first prime minister, India forewent its extraordinary influence throughout the South Asian subcontinent and abutting areas. Nehru forged a grand strategy that comprised three elements: adoption of federal democracy as a means to preserve India's political unity; an economic strategy that privileged so-called "self-reliance" which was overseen by a statist system of central planning as the most expedient path to technological modernization and poverty alleviation; and a foreign policy of nonalignment as the preferred route to construct a favorable international environment which would enable India to avoid military entanglements and focus upon mitigating the various privations of the public.[3]

Nehru governed India until he died in 1964. During his long tenure, he fortified bureaucratic arrangements to secure these objectives and oversaw the absolute subordination of the armed services to the civilians. Nehru's grand strategy perdured until the dawn of the 1990s, after which developments in the South Asian environment, ruptures in the international system, and shifting visions of key Indian political leaders prompted a re-examination of this grand strategy. Since then, numerous Indian strategists have risen to prominence who have offered their vision of what India's grand strategy should be. But, as I argue here, despite the passage of several decades and the various ink that has been spilled on this topic, India remains in search of a grand strategy. This is not due to a paucity of strategic thinking as some have posited; rather, it is due in considerable measure to the momentum of the vast infrastructure built by Nehru and his successors, which political leadership has been unable to reform due to the complex domestic politics of modern India.

In this chapter, I map out India's quest for a new grand strategy and the obstacles that have precluded a new grand strategy from fructifying. I first describe the lineaments of Nehru's grand strategy and the systems and procedures that India adopted in to pursue them. Second, I exposit the factors that have galvanized a debate about discarding these Nehruvian commitments. Third, I describe the various schools of thought about what India's grand strategy should be. Fourth, I detail the various bureaucratic and political hindrances that impeded this transition. Finally, in the concluding section, I submit that what has resulted is a form of incrementalism that has precipitated important changes in India's behavior politically, diplomatically, and militarily away from these past Nehruvian commitments. While many are optimistic that India's current prime minister, Narendra Modi, will be able to muster the requisite political will to overcome the significant ambivalence about these changes that exists across India's varied political classes and public alike, I am less persuaded that Modi will be able to do so given the nature of India's vociferous democracy and its various centers within each state and at the center absent a serious exogenous event that catalyzes more agreement across these stakeholders and requisite political will to effectuate change more rapidly.

8.1 Nehru's enduring legacy

In 1992, an American scholar at the RAND Corporation named George K. Tanham alleged that "Indian elites show little evidence of having thought coherently and systematically about national strategy"[4] and moreover Indians' "acceptance of life as a mystery and the inability to manipulate events impedes preparation for the future in all areas of life, including the strategic. The Indian belief in life cycles and repetitions, in particular, limits planning in the Western sense."[5] While some Indians agreed with Tanham at the time, more recently, several scholars have repudiated his assertion, often in language that would be dismissed as Orientalist today, that India lacks a grand strategy.

For example, Ashley Tellis, a doyen of South Asian strategic studies, concedes that India lacks a document that articulates India's grand strategic objectives and the means by which to achieve them; this is a ludicrous measure by which to assess the question. After all, the United States is an exception in that it does have such a document, which is available to the American public to consider and debate. Most democracies do not. Tellis argues that despite the absence of such a document India's grand strategy can be inferred from the country's actions over the course of its history. To make this claim, Tellis mobilizes Paul Kennedy's useful definition of grand strategy as comprising a set of policies that reflect "the capacity of [a] nation's leaders to bring together all of the elements, both military and nonmilitary, for the preservation and enhancement of [a] nation's long-term (that is, in wartime and peacetime) best interests"[6] to assert that "independent India has always possessed a grand strategy."[7]

While it is true that India may not have been successful in prosecuting its most ambitious goals and that it selected suboptimal instruments to pursue them; these shortcomings are an artifact of India's grand strategy rather than evidence of its absence. In fact, "from the moment it gained liberty from the Raj, India pursued a grand strategy focused on preserving political unity amid its bewildering diversities and potential rifts, protecting the nation's territory from internal and external threats, and realizing the economic development that would transform the country into a genuinely great power."[8] K. Subrahmanyam, India's first grand strategist, agrees and furthers that

> India is unusual in having had a grand strategy at Independence to meet the external and internal challenges to its growth in order to become a major international actor. The Constituent Assembly's oath in 1947 implied that India would promote world peace for the welfare of mankind, including its own population, and it would assume its rightful global position by developing itself to the standards of the industrialised world. This was the strategic goal. It had to be achieved in a world recovering from a war-ravaged economy and entering the Cold War. At Independence, India was a downtrodden former colony with 80 per cent poverty, a life expectancy of 31, food

shortages and low literacy. India's grand strategy during the second half of the 20th century, therefore, involved a policy of non-alignment to deal with external security problems, the adoption of the Indian Constitution to address governance challenges, and a partly centrally planned development strategy to accelerate growth.[9]

There are several aspects of Indian strategic thought that are encapsulated by the rubric of "Nehruvian" approaches to grand strategy.

First, India's early leadership led by Nehru adopted democracy as the system of self-rule. Prior to independence, the Indian National Congress (INC) was able to establish itself as a genuinely grass-roots party throughout the expanse of British India. It stood in notable contradistinction to its primary rival, the Muslim League, which could never overcome its elitist roots centered in the north of India.[10] The adoption of a federal democracy that incorporated separation of powers at the center as well as reserved powers for the states and state neutrality towards established religions was both a natural extension of the INC's pre-partition positions and it was instrumentally the best way of managing a massive population across a large landmass riven with economic disparities, differing levels of education as well as bewildering diversity based upon caste, ethnolinguistic, as well as religious differences.[11]

Second, India embraced an autarkic economic strategy of "self-reliance" and a statist system of centralized planning. Nehru believed that the experiences of the Soviet Union offered the "quickest path to technological modernization, rapid economic growth, and the defeat of immiseration."[12]

Third, Nehru believed that it could best achieve its domestic goals of consolidating democracy and economic uplift of its massive population by steering clear of external conflicts. For this reason, he avoided aligning with either of the two blocs during the Cold War in a policy that came to be known as "nonalignment." When it suited India's purposes, it reached out to the United States or the Soviet Union for various forms of political, diplomatic, military, or economic assistance, and the two hegemons either acquiesced or rebuffed these entreaties per their own interests. Nehru believed that it was imperative to avoid needless arms-racing which diverts resources that would be better deployed in the service of bolstering India's economy, mitigating poverty, and tempering other forms of socioeconomic differences across India's complex polity.[13]

An additional feature of this grand strategy espoused by Nehru pertained to nuclear weapons. India inherited a civilian nuclear program from the British. While Nehru did not necessarily feel comfortable with nuclear weapons specifically or military force more generally, Homi Bhaba—one of the early architects of India's nuclear program—argued successfully for keeping the option of nuclear weapons alive even while India campaigned, perhaps disingenuously, for a nuclear-free world.[14]

In retrospect, this grand strategy generally served India's interests well into the latter half of the twentieth century. By 1990 when the Cold War ended,

India managed to remain intact despite various insurgencies and institutional stresses while Pakistan, which was also cleaved from the Raj, had broken into two in 1971. Moreover, India generally remained a democracy (with the notable exception of Prime Minister Indira Gandhi's Emergency[15]) and committed to its peculiar form of secularism, while its neighbors failed to do so. Nonalignment generally allowed India to reap the benefits of exploiting superpower rivalry on its own terms without the costs of entanglement. Economically, the autarkic strategy proved less fruitful: India, unable to increase its growth rates or otherwise modernize its economy, failed in significant measure to mitigate poverty much less become a significant economic or military power.

Many of the institutions that Nehru and his successors built have proven extremely difficult to reform despite the burgeoning interest from various quarters in the Indian security elite to adopt a post-Nehruvian grand strategy. This is likely due to the nature of India's domestic politics as much—if not more—than the suitability of those institutions for a modern state that aspires to be a rising power. Nehru's aversion to military force and the institutional arrangements he promulgated to circumscribe the power of the armed forces have proven particularly obdurate. Nehru was chary of the Indian military because the British used it to enforce their enslavement during British rule. It took the 1947–48 war in which the Indian Army protected India against Pakistan for Nehru to relax his distrust of the armed forces he inherited from the British.[16]

While Congress' secular and democratic moorings buttressed its popular legitimacy, Nehru was so concerned about the potential for a coup that he deliberately studied the factors that contributed to coup-making in postcolonial states. Nehru initiated several steps with the explicit goal of coup-proofing the Indian army, some of which were undertaken prior to independence. For example, he altered the "symbolic structure of power... by altering the status of the army in the warrant of precedence and in public life, by limiting the wearing of uniforms in public, and by personally taking over the commander in chief's house in New Delhi as his new prime ministerial residence."[17] His new government also took steps to restrain the army's ability to coordinate against the state. Given the immediate security threat posed by Pakistan, Nehru was unable to simply disband the "martial class" army that India inherited or to undertake steps to significantly widen the recruitment base. Instead he took steps to balance within the army by "continuing the British system of having the majority of the army's infantry battalions structured in 'fixed class' units, in which each of the four companies was ethnically cohesive, but the battalion as a whole contained at least two different ethnic groups."[18] Wilkinson details Nehru's thwarting innovations that would facilitate mobilization along ethnic or provincial lines while decreasing army cohesion by maximizing ethnic diversity among the senior officers to ensure that the command was more diverse than it would have been otherwise and to exploit ethnic differences between the officers and the enlisted ranks.[19] This was particularly evident with regards to Punjabis, who were overrepresented in the ranks in the officer corps. To prevent Punjabis generally or Sikhs specifically from wielding too much influence, there was a "de facto policy of ensuring that they were less successful than they would have been otherwise been in getting appointed to the top corps commands, and in particular to the top job of"[20] chief of army staff. In addition to increasing the number of recruitment streams in an effort to diversify the officer corps and increase training opportunities to develop their professionalism, Nehru—working through his Defense Ministers—ensured that the Intelligence Bureau surveilled the generals as well as some retired generals.[21]

While Nehru took many of these steps within the first decade of independence, China's shocking defeat of India in the 1962 war (see section 8.2) forced India to reverse the retrenchment that had taken place since independence: it nearly doubled the army, raised a fighting air force (as opposed to the previous transport fleet) and eschewed its previous opposition to forging relationships with outside powers like the United States and the Soviet Union.[22] With the military forces effectively more than doubled, Congress Party leadership feared that extant coup-proofing efforts would be inadequate. In response, the state bolstered intelligence capabilities and redoubled monitoring of senior army leadership and army movements. Nehru even brought in a close ally to "coup proof" the capital and prepared a variety of contingency plans to remove political leadership at the first sign of trouble.[23]

Perhaps one of the most enduring legacies of Nehru's reforms was restructuring the system of higher defense organization, which Lord Ismay—a staff member of the last Viceroy Mountbatten—developed. Nehru, working with his Ministry of Defense, restructured the military command to render it less cohesive and less able to mobilize against civilian leadership. In 1947, Nehru's government removed the Commander in Chief from the cabinet and subordinated him to the Defense Minister, which along with the Ministry of Finance retained expenditure decisions. This decision subordinated the army chief both to elected representatives of the people and to Ministry of Defense bureaucrats. In the structure that India inherited, the Chief of the Indian Army held the position of the Chief of Staff of the armed forces. This position was abolished, which rendered the chiefs of the three services coequals with the title of Commander in Chief. In 1955, the title "of Commander in Chief" was replaced with "Chief of Staff." Downgrading the position of the army Commander in Chief and making all service chiefs coequals had the desired effect of intensifying interservice rivalries.[24] Moreover, Nehru promulgated a three-tiered system that extended from the cabinet level to that of the three service chiefs. At the apex was the Defense Committee of the Cabinet (DCC) under which was the Defense Minister's Committee (DMC). (In 1978, the DCC became the Political Affairs Committee of the cabinet.) At the third level was the Chiefs of Staff Committee (CSC), in which the three service chiefs have formal equality despite enormous differences in the sizes of the forces and their respective share in the budget. This structure, which excludes the service chiefs from apex decision-making structures, has remained intact over the decades even though many Indian security elites believe that this structure is no longer appropriate for contemporary India. Specifically, some defense professionals and commentators alike believe that an overall commander would better coordinate the services, afford greater jointness, and bring more coherence to strategy, defense planning, and procurement.[25]

During Nehru's time and for decades after his death, the Indian leadership generally avoided confrontation in what analysts have dubbed "strategic restraint." Nehru understood that sometimes force was necessary; however, it was not the preferred means. As Raghavan scrupulously details, Nehru preferred "measures the demonstrated resolve without recklessness, for coupling military moves to pressure the adversary with diplomatic ones to explore opportunities for a settlement."[26] This approach best suited Nehru's chariness about the exercise of power and his belief that this approach could avoid war without sacrificing India's core interests. By most metrics this policy of "strategic restraint" persists to date, with notable exceptions when the Indian leadership episodically and briefly engaged in brief periods of what Cohen and Gupta call "strategic assertion." An example of such strategic assertion is afforded by India's test of a nuclear device in 1974, which was precipitated by the American decision to dispatch US Navy Task Force 71 of the Seventh Fleet to the Bay of Bengali during the 1971 war. Prime Minister Gandhi was convinced that the United States would not have dispatched the world's first nuclear-powered aircraft carrier if India had nuclear weapons. But India did not conduct further tests until 1998, even though the scientists understood the 1974 test was inadequate to confer upon India a thermonuclear capability.[27] Other episodes of "strategic assertion" include: the 1984 occupation of Siachen Glacier before Pakistan could do so, the 1986 massive military exercise called Operation Brasstacks during which Prime Minister Rajiv Gandhi sought to punish Pakistan for its significant support to the Sikh insurgency in the northern Indian state of Punjab,[28] and Prime Minister Rajiv Gandhi's 1987 decision to dispatch the Indian Army to enforce a defunct peace deal between the government of Sri Lanka and the Tamil Tigers. Because of the latter, a Tamil Tiger suicide bomber killed him in 1991. The gambit ended in a chastising fiasco which convinced India to never leave India unless it did so under a United Nations mandate or if required to respond to a belligerent neighbor.[29]

8.2 The Cold War and beyond: Caught between the past and an uncertain future

Several events in the South Asian region as well as the international system have caused some Indian security elites to reflect upon the salience of this Nehruvian grand strategy for contemporary India. Perhaps one of the first strains to Nehru's beliefs about the world and the need for the exercise of force came as early as 1962 when India went to war with China. Nehru welcomed the revolution in China and saw India and China as potential collaborators in Asian security. Nehru seriously misread the potential for conflict, and the defense structure that he carefully built to ensure civilian domination proved to be inadequate to protect India's interests.[30] The conventional narrative of the 1962 war suggests that India lost due to excessive intrusion of the civilians into military affairs. With this lesson duly learned, when Pakistan instigated war with India in 1965, civilians stood back, providing political guidance but avoided micro-managing the conflict of war. Pakistan's failure to defeat India and inability to significantly change the territorial status quo was taken as evidence that this lesson was well learned.[31] Relying upon archival material, Raghavan counters that while the civilians indeed had little to offer in the conduct of the 1962 war and indeed were responsible for the conflict in the first instance, the military's policy of defense of depth, by which Indian defensive lines were well within Indian territory, offered no protection against Chinese incursions. Moreover, civilians' absence in the conduct of the 1965 war resulted in India prematurely seeking a ceasefire in part because the army chief mistakenly reported that the army had run out of ammunition. More generally, he argues that had there been greater civilian oversite and management of the 1965 war, India was in a position to deliver a decisive defeat to Pakistan which could have altered the course of Pakistan's relentless security competition with India.[32]

Despite the 1962 fiasco, Nehru's legacy endured without domestic challenge throughout the Cold War. However, several events took place in short succession that prompted many observers within and without India to question whether or not India needed a new grand strategy and if so, what would that strategy look like? First, the so-called anti-Soviet jihad in Afghanistan ended with the 1988 Geneva Accords. On February 15, 1989 the last Soviet soldier crossed the Friendship Bridge spanning the Amu Darya river leaving Afghanistan. The Geneva Accords emplaced the pro-Soviet Dr Najibullah as president to the unending ire of Pakistan's General Zia, who wanted an Islamist in power. On December 25, 1991 the Soviet Union collapsed. Najibullah was able to hang onto power until April 1992, when Russia, the successor to the Soviet Union, could no longer continue financially supporting him.

After Najibullah fell, Afghanistan was beset by warring so-called Mujahideen factions. Pakistan continued manipulating events in the country by backing Gulbuddin Hekmatyar (a Pashtun, Islamist leader of a so-called mujahideen faction during the anti-Soviet jihad) until he proved unable to do Islamabad's bidding efficaciously. By 1994, Pakistan threw its weight behind the Taliban. With Pakistani assistance, the Taliban were able to take control of Kabul by 1996 and consolidate much of their hold upon power. Pakistan used Taliban-controlled Afghanistan to co-locate and train anti-India terrorist groups which it had nurtured for operations in Indian-administered Kashmir and beyond. Iran, for its part, was disquieted by the rise of militant Sunni Islam in Afghanistan and the Central Asian republics. Motivated by this convergence of interests, India and Iran began an important diplomatic opening that culminated in a series of agreements that allowed India to use Iran as a base from which it could project influence into Afghanistan and Central Asia. With the collapse of the Soviet Union and the recrudescence of Islamism in the successor states, India—allied with Iranians and the Russians—and Pakistan—allied with Saudi Arabia—began competing for influence.[33]

The collapse of the Soviet Union not only created regional concerns for India, it also elucidated the fatal flaws of statist economic planning, which had been preferred by Nehru. In the same period, in 1990, India was wracked by a severe balance of payments crises. With the financially strained USSR unable to help and nowhere else to turn, India embarked upon a serious project of economic reforms in 1991 which paved the way for India's subsequent economic growth. During the 1990s, India's economic growth rates averaged around 6 percent, which exceeded that of its western nemesis, Pakistan, and arrested its decline relative to China. These economic resources allowed India to establish its primacy in South Asia and facilitated the aforenoted competition in India's extended neighborhood beyond South Asia.[34] Additionally, the 1991 American defeat of Iraq, which relied upon Russian weapon systems, persuaded India that its stock of Russian military systems may be inadequate in a war with Pakistan, which had many American systems in its arsenal. This realization, coupled with India's newfound economic heft, motivated India to launch a massive conventional military modernization even though the efficiency and efficacy of this effort has drawn considerable criticism.[35] Increasingly, Western countries and Israel found themselves competing for Indian business. (Below, in 8.4, I discuss the problems with India's defense acquisitions process.)

The 1990s also brought about further changes in the international system which forced India to re-evaluate its strategic options. Critically, in 1995, the Nuclear Nonproliferation Treaty, which India denounced as nuclear apartheid, was indefinitely extended. At that time, India also (inaccurately) assessed that the Fissile Material Cutoff treaty and the Comprehensive Test Ban Treaty would come into force. India's weapons developers knew that the 1974 "peaceful nuclear explosion" was inadequate to confer upon India a nuclear weapons capability. With the global nonproliferation regime tightening and the need to test, Indian leadership assessed that delays in testing would be costlier than testing before these treaties came into force. When the Hindu-nationalist party, the Bharitiya Janata Party (BJP) campaigned in the general elections in 1998, it promised to exercise the nuclear option. In addition to these structural concerns and the willingness of the BJP leadership to test again sooner than later, the immediate precipitant of India's 1998 nuclear test came from Pakistan. In May of 1998, Pakistan tested its Ghauri missile which could target all of India. This was a significant development for India's security managers: many Indians did not believe that Pakistan was so capable and many more were deeply vexed by the ongoing nuclear and missile cooperation between China and Pakistan and between North Korea and Pakistan. Delhi was further disquieted about seeming American insouciance about these exchanges despite Washington's ostensible interests during President Bill Clinton's tenure in a so-called US–India strategic dialogue. India concluded both that its long-standing commitment to a nuclear-free world (advanced while India continued to sustain its own nuclear option) had failed and, worse, Pakistan now had a missile which could target every major Indian city. Soon thereafter, the BJP honored its promise and conducted a series of nuclear tests in the Rajasthan desert. Within days, Pakistan followed suit. With these reciprocal tests, the subcontinent was not overtly nuclearized.[36] Even though Washington initially sanctioned India as well as Pakistan for these tests, ironically, India's tests precipitated a sustained strategic dialogue which culminated not only in Washington accepting India's nuclear status but, by 2005, actually dedicating its own resources to bolstering India's nuclear weapons capabilities and the means to deliver then as a part of an overall strategy of managing China's rise.[37]

Despite these important exogenous and endogenous shocks to India's system, India's rise in the international system owing to its economy and military size, and the emergence of Indian analysts who want a different grand strategy for India, India has not entirely jettisoned the Nehruvianism of the past. While India could most certainly exercise power—and many analysts outside of India have expected it do so—"India continues to be ambivalent about power ... [and has] failed to develop a strategic agenda commensurate with its growing economic and military capabilities."[38] Pant identifies a curious conundrum: India's "political elites desperately want global recognition as a major power and all the prestige and authority associated with it. Yet, they continue to be reticent about the acquisition and use of power in foreign affairs."[39] This discomfort with exercising power *outside of* India is doubly perplexing, Pant observes, because India's political elites have never been reticent about maximizing domestic power even when doing so has "corrod[ed] the institutional fabric of liberal democracy in the country."[40]

8.3 Strategic thinking abounds: But a new grand strategy remains elusive

Despite Tanham's Orientalist assertion that India is inherently unable to engage in grand strategic thought, India has a surfeit of grand strategists: "grand strategy" is a cottage industry within India as many writers compete for dominance in a political space in which policymakers seem to evidence little will to embrace a new grand strategy and formally shrug off the vestiges of Nehruvianism, and their copious publications vie for purchases and downloads. Some of these contenders have even proffered up a new version of Nehruvianism (Nonalignment 2.0) that retains most of its lineaments pertaining to the use of power but embracing a capitalist economic strategy.[41] India has also seen the arrival of think tanks that seek to influence the government. However, think tanks in India have struggled to be relevant sources of independent guidance to the government, which privileges inside thinking.

Kanti Bajpai does yeoman's service in summarizing the three leading schools of thought on Indian grand strategy: Nehruvianism, neoliberalism, and hyperrealism. He argues that the Cold War's demise has brought these schools into sharp relief and their adherents can be found within the civil services, armed forces, political parties, academia, think tanks, and media alike even if the terms themselves are not necessarily in use and even if proponents of these schools would demure from describing themselves in such terms.[42]

With respect to the international system, all three fundamentally accept the anarchic nature of international relations, and in this anarchic system, all states will seek to protect their territory and autonomy. They all recognize the staples of international relation—interests, power, and violence—and all concede that power is derived from both economic and military capabilities, at a minimum. However, beyond these core areas of agreement, these schools diverge. For example, proponents of Nehruvianism assert that states and their people can better understand one another and thus avoid conflict. For them, violence is a regrettable last resort. Nehruvians also believe that the inherent state of anarchy can be mitigated if not outright supervened by international laws and institutions, military restraint, compromise and negotiations, and so forth. For them, preparing for war and the balance of power create the conditions to sustained conflict and misdirect precious resources that should be used to mitigate poverty. Neoliberals accept the general state of the international system is a state of war, but they contend that pursuit of economic power is just as important as the pursuit of military power if for no other reason than the simple fact that economic might permits the accumulation of military power. They hold that economic power may be more effective than military power and pursuing military power may result in a nonproductive diversion of finance and capital, which will further degrade India's domestic and global economic prowess. (Given India's inability to engage in strategic planning, translate strategic aims into military requirementsl and equally problematic procurement system, this concern merits significant reflection.) Neoliberals also believe that economic security is important for national security in a broader sense: economically dissatisfied citizens cannot be secure. Hyperrealists are the most pessimistic about the international system. Whereas both Nehruvians and neoliberals believe that international relations can be transformed in some measure, hyperrealists see only threat and counter-threat.[43]

Bajpai explains that the three schools differ in their views about the use of force. Nehruvians believe that communication, contact, and interdependence are more useful in securing India's interests than is force. Moreover, the adversary will surely reciprocate forcefully, leaving the fundamental nature of the dispute unresolved. For neoliberals, force is simply a blunt, antiquated instrument that is not suitable for the modern world order. While states should be capable of defending themselves, it is "economic power and capacity to innovate in a global economy that eventually makes society secure."[44] For hyperrealists, force is the only means through which a state can secure its interests whether deployed defensively or offensively. In their view, no responsible leadership—whether civilian or military—can avoid planning to use coercive force. "Only 'idealists' of various stripes—Nehruvians or Neoliberals—could fool themselves into thinking that a more aggressive posture is always bad."[45]

For reasons noted below, among others, India's leadership and the political parties they represent have not embraced any of these schools of thought as its grand strategy. Perhaps oddly, in differing measures, all three coexist or have shown the potential to emerge depending upon the prime minister in power and the circumstances that prevail. Thus, it is useful to find what Bajpai calls the "lowest common denominator" among them, which appears to be an embrace of "defensive realism." This seems to correspond with a greater affinity for Nehruvianism infused with neoliberal economic commitment, inclusive of expanding global economic engagement, even if specific prime ministers at specific points in time seem to evidence a greater personal predilection for alternative grand strategies. Why, despite decades of growth and expanding acceptance of India as a major regional and even global power by others and successful confrontation and ultimate defeat of the global nonproliferation regime in 1998, remain defensive in orientation and fundamentally uncomfortable with power projection? Given the centrality of the prime minister in Indian decision-making, what prevents any given prime minister with defensive predilections from effectuating his or her preferences? I explore these issues below.

8.4 Impediments to change?

India's strategic establishment remains, in the words of Mohan, "overly cautious and slow in responding to new geopolitical opportunities" as well as the wellspring of India's economic, political, diplomatic, and even military import.[46] What explains India's persistent gravitation to Nehruvianism infused with liberal economic policies? Why does India remain reactive instead of working proactively to shape its near and far neighborhood more consistently and aggressively, consonant with India's rising stature in the international system? Mohan describes this search for a new grand strategy as India's need to rediscover Lord Curzon, who described in his 1909 essay *The Place of India in the Empire* India's pivotal role:

On the West, India must exercise a predominant influence over the destinies of Persia and Afghanistan; on the north, it can veto any rival in Tibet; on the north-east and east it can exert great pressure upon China, and it is one of the guardians of the autonomous existence of Siam [Thailand]. ON the high seas it commands the routes to Australia and to the China Seas.[47]

After the passage of well over one hundred years and after becoming one of the world's eight nuclear powers and having the world's fourth most powerful military,[48] and ranked fifth in military expenditure,[49] today's India's strategic elites have generally failed to embrace a less defensive posture commensurate with India's widely recognized potential for becoming a great power.[50] There are several potential explanations, many of which operate in an adverse synergy that ensures that India remains mired in some variant of Nehruvian discomfort with power despite having the trappings of actual power.

First, as described in the beginning of this chapter, India's military remains excluded from the apex of national decision-making. Instead, all significant defense matters reside in India's bureaucracy by design, subjugated to the Ministries of Defense and Finance. In India, the ministers rarely have the expertise of the ministries they lead because ministerial positions are usually awarded to stalwarts of the party in power and its coalition members. This state of affairs is exacerbated by the fact that India's administrative service deliberately precludes bureaucrats from developing any particular expertise. This has devastating impacts upon strategic planning, translating strategic goals into military capabilities, generating defense requirements and procuring the same.

By design, there is a serious imbalance among the services, with significant interservice rivalry, little strategic planning, let alone operational coordination. For example, India's notion of Cold Start is essentially an army-led strategy to punish Pakistan for using nonstate actors in India and to coerce Pakistan to cease and desist from using them in the future.[51] Such a doctrine is predicated—or should be—upon a supporting role of India's Air Force;

however, India's Air Force refuses to see itself in such a role and instead envisions that it—not the army—will be the lead service in confronting Pakistan in the future. A former Indian naval chief summarized the services' predicament, "India has services' doctrines, but these lack credibility and weight because they do not represent a comprehensive view of national priority."[52] Along the same lines, while India's security elites understand the need for greater interoperability *in principle*, "the Navy and the Army still want to be self-sufficient in light air power... [and] do not want to rely on the Air Force to provide support, and the Air Force does not to be an appendage to the Army and Navy."[53]

As Perkovich and Dalton perspicaciously observe, none of these issues are likely to be resolved in the policy-relevant future in large measure due to the lack of civilian expertise in defense and security matters, despite emergence of various research centers purporting to focus upon defense and security affairs.[54] Worse yet, they correctly argue that addressing these critical shortcomings "require much greater expertise and attention on the part of top political leaders, and improved integration of military leaders into policy-making deliberations."[55] Even if the military *did* have greater input, it is uncertain how useful their inputs would be given their moorings in "mid-twentieth century industrial warfare."[56] In any event, this is a moot point because if there is little sustained civilian interest in forging a new grand strategy for a contemporary—much less future—India, there is even less interest in integrating the military into apex decision-making structures.

Not only are India's security elites generally unable to undertake strategic assessments of its future needs from which it generates joint defense requirements, the inadequacies of its defense procurement process are notorious within and without India.[57] Even though India is one of the world's largest arms importers, India's armed forces "lack the quantity and quality of weapons, supplies, and enabling technologies that they, in principle, are supposed to have acquired."[58] Part of the problem is India's fetishization of "indigenous production." In its origins, India did not want to be dependent upon outside suppliers and it also wanted to develop indigenous technologies. In effect, this policy has allowed India's Defense Research and Development Organization (DRDO) to forge a monopoly on defense development even though it consistently fails to deliver while, at the same time, the Ministry of Defense often fails to make important acquisition deals in part because it lacks a specialized cadre of defense professionals. India generally persists upon this pathway, largely due to domestic political constraints, even though advanced militaries routinely rely upon proven defense producers which need not be entirely indigenous. Moreover, accustomed to the relationship that India enjoyed with the Soviet Union, India expects foreign defense suppliers to license and/or share technology with India, which many are reluctant to do for a variety of reasons. This has resulted in a nonproductive tension between "aspirations for indigenous design and production" on the one hand and the clear "superiority of foreign-supplied capabilities" on the other, which is further exacerbated by the "inefficiencies of India's procurement processes."[59] India's challenges can be summarized thusly: India must overhaul virtually every aspect of its civilian–military relations and higher defense organization, reconfigure its defense procurement process, vigorously pursue defense modernization and service-specific visions of the future battlefield, among other initiatives.[60] However, there is simply little political will to redress these sundry hindrances.

India's political system mitigates the likelihood of India's leaders anachronizing strategic commitments that are now ill-suited for an emerging great power and adopting new ones that are. Since the 1990s, India's polity has experienced a steady federalization which has occurred along with the decline of the Congress Party system that more or less dominated Indian politics for the first thirty years after independence. Until recently, with the rise of the BJP, the decline of the Congress Party had not been replaced with a similar dominance of another party. However, even the BJP with current dominance at the center, state-based politics remain important. The BJP must not only maintain its base at the center, it must also continually aim for a seemingly endless lineup of state elections. While this this federalization of the Indian system and the collapse of the Congress Party, until the recent consolidation of the BJP, generally prevented the overconcentration of power in the hands of one person and required more consultation at federal and state levels in decision-making, the same developments have also imposed a "democratic constraint" on forging economic, foreign, and national-security policies.[61]

Examples of this dynamic abound. In 2008, the government of then Prime Minister Manmohan narrowly survived a no-confidence vote when his Marxist coalition partners withdrew over Singh's pursuit of the so-called US–India Civilian Nuclear Deal. The deal and his government survived because Singh, in an uncharacteristically bold move, sought support from India's smaller, regional parties as well as independent lawmakers. His government also encouraged abstentions in the vote and sought to secure defectors from other parties. In fact, the parties even arranged for the temporary release of jailed legislators such that they could vote. In some cases, parliamentarians were even pushed into the assembly in their wheelchairs, despite their hospital treatments and illnesses.[62] In other cases, political leaders in India's various states have influenced the country's foreign policy by asserting their polity's preferences in adjacent countries with ethnic ties or historical and cultural links. India's Punjab has pressured the center to expand greater cross-border— especially commercial—contacts with Pakistan's Punjab,[63] and Indian Sikhs, concentrated in the Punjab, have also sought greater access to historical Sikh shrines in Pakistan.[64] Similarly, Bengal's powerful powerbroker, Chief Minister Mamata Banerjee, is able to exert enormous influence over the country's policies with respect to Bangladesh whether one focuses upon trade policies, water disputes, border concerns, or the ongoing Rohingya crisis.[65] During the 1980s, India's Congress Party even provided military and other assistance to Sri Lanka's ethnonationalist insurgency group the Tamil Tigers in effort to woo Tamils in Tamil Nadu as state politicians engaged in competitive outbidding over who could support the insurgents more. At the same time, the turnabout of the same voters and politicians after a Tamil Tiger suicide bomber killed Rajiv Gandhi was equally critical in the government's ability to turn against the group.[66] Both the BJP and Congress, at various points in time, also shaped their party's policies towards the Sri Lankan civil war with the explicit aim of not alienating their coalition partners in Tamil Nadu.[67]

Similar "democratic constraints" render further economic reforms extremely difficult in large measure because politicians are wary of generating resentment among India's voters should they do so. Politicians instead have focused upon relatively easier reforms that do not directly affect the general population or have pursued "reform by stealth...which has involved manipulating the presentation of economic reforms by suggesting that the reforms were not significant departures from the status quo, dress the reforms as pro-poor and shifting the responsibility for implementation of the reforms to other levels" such as the states.[68] A third approach has been to focus upon gradual moves rather than decisive shifts.[69]

These same democratic constraints also preclude India from being able to reorient is civil–military balance, its bureaucratic inadequacies, inability to conduct strategic assessments and translate them into defense policies, and effective acquisition of requisite capabilities inclusive of a functional procurement system that produces value for the Indian taxpayer. These economic constraints also preclude India from making a decisive shift from its traditional defensive strategic culture and grand strategy which remains imbricated with Nehruvian commitments but updated with neoliberal economic policies. As a consequence, we should expect India to generally persist upon this path of incremental or even ad hoc innovation. An example of the former is afforded by India's acquisition of its first nuclear-armed submarine, the *INS Arihant,* which emerged from "an ad hoc and secret development process" that spanned decades but was never informed by an understanding of its role in India's overall maritime or other strategy. In fact, as the submarine neared completion and as more technical information came available about its capabilities, roles and missions were discussed *ex post facto.*[70]

8.5 What future for India: Taking bold steps or inching forward?

India's various political leaders have evinced a distinct willingness and ability to make important changes in reaction to global, regional, and domestic events as exemplified by, *inter alia,* India's decision to test a nuclear device in 1974 and to conduct more comprehensive tests in 1998. Equally important, key leaders have been able to muster the requisite political will and necessary political capital to overcome resistance to new initiatives when they are convinced of the urgency to do so (e.g. Manmohan Singh and the US–India Nuclear Deal). The current government under Prime Minister Modi frequently speaks about taking a harder line towards Pakistan; progress has been less apparent with two exceptions: in 2016, it undertook shallow punitive cross-border raids in response to a terrorist attack at Uru (in Kashmir) and in 2019, when it attacked a terrorist training facility in Balakot (in Pakitsan's Khyber Pakhtunkhwa Province) in relation for a sanguinary suicide bombing of a convoy of Central Reserve Police Forces. In both cases, the government likely exaggerated what it did with little accountability.[71] However, one should not confuse these responses with more significant changes in Indian strategy absent more information. Modi's government has been more aggressive in pursuing defense ties with other countries and appears more interested in effectuating controversial policies such as India's Cold Start Doctrine[72] and a more confrontational posture with respect to China.[73] Thus, one can never rule out the possibility of significant changes in response to new opportunity structures.

Notwithstanding these important instances of punctuated equilibrium, for the foreseeable future, India is mostly likely to follow the past approach of incremental and even ad hoc evolution which will inch it, over time, towards a newer grand strategy that looks increasingly less like its current updated version of Nehruvian orientation. Over time, it is reasonable to assume that India will become more assertive in shaping regional and extraregional events and ever more comfortable in the exercise of power, inclusive of military force if its extraregional interests are threatened. India's civilian and military security establishment will most likely be cajoled towards this direction owing to India's expanding commercial and energy interests far beyond South Asia. India's large bureaucracy, institutional commitments to civilian dominance over the military and resistance to modifying civil–military relations, domestic stakeholders who can slow reforms in the procurement process, and other democratic and political constraints will dampen the pace of this transformation.[74]

NOTES

1. Thomas R. Metcalf, *Imperial Connections: India in the Indian Ocean Arena, 1860–1920* (Berkeley: University of California Press, 2007).
2. Cited in C. Raja Mohan, *Crossing the Rubicon: The Shaping of India's New Foreign Policy* (New Delhi: Penguin/Viking, 2003), 204.
3. Ashley J. Tellis, *Nonalignment Redux: The Perils of Old Wine in New Skins* (Washington, DC: Carnegie Endowment for International Peace, 2012), http://carnegieendowment.org/2012/07/10/nonalignment-redux-perils-of-old-wine-in-new-skins-pub-48675
4. George K. Tanham, *Indian Strategic Thought: An Interpretative Essay*, R-4207-USDP (Santa Monica, CA: RAND Corporation 1992), v, https://www.rand.org/pubs/reports/R4207.html
5. Tanham, *Indian Strategic Thought*, 17.
6. Cited in Tellis, *Nonalignment Redux*, 3.
7. Ibid., 3.
8. Ibid., 3.
9. K. Subrahmanyam, "India's Grand Strategy," *Indian Express*, February 3, 2012, http://indianexpress.com/article/opinion/columns/indias-grand-strategy/
10. Sumit Ganguly, "From the Defense of the Nation to Aid to the Civil: The Army in Contemporary India," *Journal of Asian and African Studies* 24, no. 1–2 (1991): 11–26.
11. Tellis, *Nonalignment Redux*; and K. Subrahmanyam, "India's Grand Strategy."
12. Tellis, *Nonalignment Redux*, 5; and K. Subrahmanyam, "India's Grand Strategy."
13. Tellis, *Nonalignment Redux*, 5; and K. Subrahmanyam, "India's Grand Strategy."
14. K. Subrahmanyam, "India's Grand Strategy"; George Perkovich, *India's Nuclear Bomb: The Impact on Global Proliferation* (Berkeley: University of California Press, 1999); Ashley J. Tellis, *India's Emerging Nuclear Posture: Between Recessed Deterrent and Ready Arsenal* (Santa Monica, CA: RAND Corporation, 2001); Itty Ibrahim, *South Asian Cultures of the Bomb: Atomic Publics and the State in India and Pakistan* (Bloomington: Indiana University Press 2009).
15. Sumit Ganguly, "The Crisis of Indian Secularism," *Journal of Democracy* 14, no. 4 (October 2003), 11–25.
16. Ganguly, "From the Defense of The Nation To Aid To The Civil."
17. Steven I. Wilkinson, *Army and Nation: The Military and Indian Democracy Since Independence* (Cambridge, MA: Harvard University Press, 2015), 21.
18. Ibid., 21.
19. Ibid.
20. Ibid., 22.
21. Ibid.
22. Stephen P. Cohen and Sunil Dasgupta, *Arming without Aiming: India's Military Modernization* (Washington, DC: Brookings Institution, 2010).
23. Neville Maxwell, *India's China War* (London: Jonathan Cape, 1970); Wilkinson, *Army and Nation*.
24. Wilkinson, *Army and Nation*; Ganguly, "From the Defense of the Nation to Aid to the Civil."

25. Ganguly, "From the Defense of the Nation to Aid to the Civil."
26. Srinath Raghavan, *War and Peace in Modern India* (Bangalore: Orient Black Swan, 2010), 18.
27. See *inter alia*, C. Christine Fair, "Learning to Think the Unthinkable: Lessons from India's Nuclear Test," *India Review* 4, no. 1 (2005): 23–58; Sumit Ganguly, "India's Pathway to Pokhran II: The Prospects and Sources of New Delhi's Nuclear Weapons Program," *International Security* 23, no. 4 (1999): 148–77; Tellis, *India's Emerging Nuclear Posture*.
28. C. Christine Fair, "Lessons from India's Experience in the Punjab, 1978–1993," in *India and Counterinsurgency: Lessons Learned*, eds. Sumit Ganguly and David P. Fidler (London: Routledge, 2009); Ian Talbott, "Pakistan and Sikh Nationalism: State Policy and Private Perceptions," *Sikh Formations* 6, no. 1 (2010): 63–76.
29. Cohen and Dasgupta, *Arming without Aiming*; C. Christine Fair, "US-Indian Army-to-Army Relations: Prospects for Future Coalition Operations?," *Asian Security* 1, no. 2 (2005): 157–73.
30. For a more careful exposition of Nehru's reading of Chinese intent and the role of Russian influence upon China, see Raghavan, *War and Peace in Modern India*.
31. See for example, Ganguly, "From the Defense of the Nation to Aid to the Civil."
32. Srinath Raghavan, "Civil–Military Relations in India: The China Crisis and After," *The Journal of Strategic Studies* 32, no. 1 (February 2009): 149–75.
33. C. Christine Fair, "Indo-Iranian Relations-What Prospects for Transformation?" in *India's Foreign Policy: Retrospect and Prospect*, ed. Sumit Ganguly (New Delhi: Oxford University Press, 2010), 132–54.
34. C. Raja Mohan, "Poised for Power: The domestic roots of India's slow rise," in *Strategic Asia 2007–08: Domestic Political Change and Grand Strategy*, eds. Ashley J. Tellis and Michael Wills (Seattle: National Bureau of Research, 2007), 177–207.
35. Cohen and Dasgupta, *Arming without Aiming*; George Perkovich and Toby Dalton, *Not War. Not Peace?* (New Delhi: Oxford University Press, 2016).
36. See *inter alia*, Fair, "Learning to Think"; Ganguly, "India's Pathway to Pokhran II."
37. Strobe Talbott, Deputy Secretary of State, led this engagement from the American side. He authored his account of being persuaded by Indian arguments; Strobe Talbot, *Engaging India: Diplomacy, Democracy, and the Bomb* (Washington, DC: The Brookings Institution, 2010). Jaswant Singh, Minister of External Affairs, led the Indian side. He has written several accounts, one of which is Jaswant Singh, *In Service of Emergent India: A Call to Honor* (Bloomington: Indiana University Press, 2007). Also see Ashley J. Tellis, *India as a New Global Power: An Action Agenda for the United States* (Washington, DC: Carnegie Endowment for International Peace, 2005), http://carnegieendowment.org/files/Tellis.India.Global.Power.FINAL.pdf; Ashley J. Tellis, "The Merits of Dehyphenation: Explaining U.S. Success in Engaging India and Pakistan," *The Washington Quarterly* 31, no. 4 (2008): 21–42.
38. Harsh V. Pant, "A Rising India's Search for a Foreign Policy," *Orbis* 53, no. 2 (Spring 2009): 255.
39. Ibid., 255.
40. Ibid., 256.

41. Sunil Khilnani et al., "Nonalignment 2.0: A Foreign and Strategic Policy for India in the Twenty First Century," *Centre for Policy Research*, February 29, 2012, http://www.cprindia.org/research/reports/nonalignment-20-foreign-and-strategic-policy-india-twenty-first-century
42. He also suggests that one could conceive of three minor schools of grand strategy based upon Marxism, Hindutva (political Hinduism), and Gandhianism. However, because—as he concedes—"none of the three has been articulated very clearly and in any great depth or specificity in relations to what we are calling grand strategy," I omit them from further consideration. Kanti Bajpai, "Indian Grand Strategy: Six Schools of Thought," in *India's Grand Strategy: History, Theory, Cases*, eds. Kanti Bajpai, Saira Basit, and V. Krishnappa (London: Routledge, 2014), 114.
43. Ibid.
44. Ibid., 124.
45. Ibid., 124–5.
46. Mohan, "Poised for Power," 195.
47. Cited in Mohan, *Crossing the Rubicon*, 205.
48. Global Fire Power, "2017 Military Strength Ranking," 2017, https://www.globalfirepower.com/countries-listing.asp
49. In 2016, India outlaid the fifth largest military expenditures globally with nearly $56 billion, which was on par with France and higher than of the UK. In contrast China spent $215 billion (est) and the United States $611 billion. SIPRI, "Trends in World Military Expenditures 2016," April 2017, https://www.sipri.org/sites/default/files/Trends-world-military-expenditure-2016.pdf
50. Mohan, "Poised for Power," 195.
51. Walter C. Ladwig, "A Cold Start for Hot Wars? The Indian Army's New Limited War Doctrine," *International Security* 32, no. 3 (2008): 158–90.
52. Perkovich and Dalton, *Not War. Not Peace?*, 31.
53. Ibid., 54.
54. Quoted in ibid., 53.
55. Ibid., 31.
56. Ibid., 31.
57. Cohen and Gupta, *Arming without Aiming*.
58. Perkovich and Dalton, *Not War. Not Peace?*, 57. See also Cohen and Gupta, *Arming without Aiming*.
59. Perkovich and Dalton, *Not War. Not Peace?*, 59. See also the discussion in C. Christine Fair and Dan Shalmon, "India's Strategic Win: The Upsides of the Lockheed Martin Deal to Produce F-16s In Indian," *Foreign Affairs* (Online), November 3, 2016, https://www.foreignaffairs.com/articles/india/2016-11-01/indias-strategic-win
60. Cohen and Gupta, *Arming without Aiming*; and Perkovich and Dalton, *Not War. Not Peace?*
61. Mohan, "Poised for Power."
62. Rama Lakshmi and Emily Wax, "India's Government Wins Parliament Confidence Vote," *The Washington Post*, July 23, 2008, http://www.washingtonpost.com/wp-dyn/content/article/2008/07/22/AR2008072200161.html

63. Tridivesh Singh Maini, "India-Pakistan Tensions: Why Indian Punjab Is Watching," *The Diplomat*, August 24, 2016, https://thediplomat.com/2016/08/india-pakistan-tensions-why-indian-punjab-is-watching/
64. G. S. Paul, "Centre lets pilgrims visit Pak Sikh shrines," *The Tribune*, October 28, 2017, http://www.tribuneindia.com/news/punjab/centre-lets-pilgrims-visit-pak-sikh-shrines/488393.html
65. Madhuparna Das, "Central agencies accuse Bengal of rule breach in Rohingya shelter," *Economic Times*, January 16, 2018, https://economictimes.indiatimes.com/news/politics-and-nation/central-agencies-accuse-bengal-of-rule-breach-in-rohingya-shelter/articleshow/62520123.cms; Shikha Mukerjee, "Is Mamata Banerjee Willing to Do What It Takes to Keep BJP Out of Bengal?," *The Wire*, January 27, 2018, https://thewire.in/218146/mamata-banerjee-tmc-west-bengal-bjp-cpim/; Arkamoy Dutta Majumdar, "Why Mamata Banerjee is opposed to sharing Teesta waters," *Live Mint*, April 11, 2017, http://www.livemint.com/Politics/dtlGtxiSUVDJgo7eoBxxDL/Why-Mamata-Banerjee-is-opposed-to-sharing-Teesta-waters.html
66. See discussion in Devin T. Hagerty, "India's Regional Security Doctrine," *Asian Survey* 31, no. 4 (April 1991): 351–63.
67. Sandra Destradi, "India and Sri Lanka's civil war: The failure of regional conflict management in South Asia," *Asian Survey* 52, no. 3 (2012): 595–616.
68. Mohan, "Poised for Power," 190.
69. Mohan, "Poised for Power."
70. Frank O'Donnell and Yogesh Joshi, "Lost at Sea: The Arihant in India's Quest for a Grand Strategy," *Comparative Strategy* 33, no. 5 (2014): 466.
71. Shashan Josh, "Everything that we know about India's cross-LoC strikes before Uri," *Scroll.in*, October 5, 2016, https://scroll.in/article/818324/everything-that-we-know-about-indias-cross-loc-strikes-before-uri and Nathan Ruser, "Did Balakot Airstrikes Hit Their Target? Satellite Imagery Raises Doubts," *The Wire*, March 1, 2019, https://thewire.in/security/balakot-airstrikes-india-pakistan-satellite-images.
72. Ankit Panda, "A Slip of the Tongue on India's Once-Hyped 'Cold Start' Doctrine?" *The Diplomat*, January 07, 2017, https://thediplomat.com/2017/01/a-slip-of-the-tongue-on-indias-once-hyped-cold-start-doctrine/; Walter C. Ladwig III, "Indian Military Modernization and Conventional Deterrence in South Asia," *Journal of Strategic Studies* 38, no. 5 (2015): 729–72.
73. Rajeev Chandrasekhar, "Doklam Heralds the Arrival of a Confident and Assertive India," *The Diplomat*, August 30, 2017, https://thediplomat.com/2017/08/doklam-heralds-the-arrival-of-a-confident-and-assertive-india/
74. The author acknowledges, in alphabetical order, Chris Clary, Sumit Ganguly, and Walter Ladwig III for perusing earlier drafts of this chapter. All errors of fact and interpretation are mine alone.

9 Iran

THIERRY BALZACQ AND WENDY RAMADAN-ALBAN

Although they hardly—if ever—use the term, leaders of the Islamic Republic of Iran (IRI) have long shared a sense of grand strategy. In fact, since the establishment of the IRI, foreign policy goals have increasingly been incorporated into the framework of a long-term strategy.[1] An analyst for the Center for Strategic Research (CSR),[2] one of the most influential official Iranian think tanks, writes "priorities of foreign policy in every country are formulated and articulated in the framework of long-term strategies."[3] Therefore, this chapter examines the content and principal orientations of Iran's contemporary grand strategy, specifying its historical lineage and exploring the changes brought by the Islamic Revolution of 1979.

The study of Iran's grand strategy is carried out within two main "schools." Put simply, one school emphasizes cultural elements. However, by only linking the cause of Iran's behavior to ideological or religious characteristics, cultural approaches tend to reify Iran's identity.[4] Further, most of these studies neglect the importance of nonideological and nonreligious factors as well as overlook how external factors interplay with domestic ones to shape identities. The second school, inspired by neorealism, focuses on structural factors.[5] These approaches emphasize international conditions as explanatory forces behind Iran's interest in a nuclear capacity and its competition with Saudi Arabia.[6] However, by black-boxing the debates within the Iranian state, they fail to explain the competing discourses between elites as well as their impact on both the definition of national interests and the development of the policies that guide Iran's relations with the rest of the world (i.e., its grand strategy).

This chapter argues that Iran's grand strategy is the result of continuous interactions and mutual influences within domestic politics—factional struggles—on the one hand and the geopolitical environment on the other. In many ways, factions diverge over Iran's priorities and understand the external context in dissimilar terms. Thus, Iran's decisions reflect, more often than not, shifting power terrains within domestic politics. However, factional divisions sometimes lead to inconsistencies, and sometimes contradictions become public. Take the Holocaust controversy: Mahmoud Ahmadinejad denies the Holocaust while Mohammed Javad Zarif, the Foreign Minister of Hassan Rouhani, acknowledges it. Taken seriously, such disagreements express a running divide that separates those who privilege an offensive, ideological, and antagonizing strategy and those who want to promote a more defensive, economically orientated approach to domestic and international politics.

While the ideological optic may vary in intensity, the guiding principle behind Iran's relations with the rest of the world has remained almost unaltered since the mid-nineteenth century. Introduced by the then prime minister, Amir Kabir, the principle of "equilibrium" (*tavāzon*) is the center of gravity of Iran's external relations. It has taken different names and been mobilized on various occasions to curb different kinds of threats. For instance, the principle of equilibrium was used by Amir Kabir to fend off British and Russian imperialism. The idea of equilibrium at that time was somewhat synonymous with "impartiality" or nonalignment. It drifted under Mossadegh to become "negative equilibrium." Be that as it may, Mehdi Bazargan invoked the principle of equilibrium to terminate Iran's dependency on the United States. In sum, the ultimate aim of equilibrium is to preserve Iran's independence against the encroachment of foreign powers.

The principle of equilibrium derives its importance from Iran's pivotal character. A pivot state sits both politically and geographically at the seam of major power rivalries. It is a pivot in at least two ways. First, a pivot state constitutes a nodal point around which the activities of great powers revolve due to its overall geostrategic salience. Second, a state is pivotal in the sense that its fate determines the strategic environment in decisive ways; literally, it can drive the system to oscillate in a different direction.[7] In this light, Iran's pivotal nature is mainly the product of its geographic location, first acknowledged during the Anglo-Russian rivalry. Further, in the mid-twentieth century, Iran was regarded as a country of central and vital strategic importance by the United States, Great Britain, and France, which led to the Baghdad Pact security organization (1955–79).[8] However, Iran became known as a "pivot-challenger state" after the revolution; as noted, "shifting pivot states can dramatically upstage the regional balance of power and upset regional peace and stability."[9] Finally, Iran's enormous natural resources (oil and gas) provide additional leverage for its pivotal role (see section 9.4.2).

This chapter is concerned with the grand strategy of a pivotal state torn between ideological survival and economic imperatives. We proceed as follows. First, we argue that Iran's strategy is shaped by the different meanings of sovereignty and independence found in its political history. However, we hasten to add that concerns with sovereignty and independence have been appropriated by different factions with mixed results. Second, we examine Iran's "grand strategic system," showing how each actor stands vis-à-vis the others.[10] This section enables us to untangle the complexity of domestic decision-making. Third, we argue that while the Supreme Leader of Iran is the final arbiter, Iran's grand strategy system is captive to competing factions, in particular, "those who believe in the service of Iran by means of Islam" and those who "believe in the service of Islam by means of Iran."[11] Fourth, we examine the ways and means supporting contemporary Iran's grand strategy, including alliances and ideological exports. The conclusion argues that the amount of power Iran wields depends primarily on its ability to reconcile the conflicting orienting principles promoted by domestic factions.

9.1 Historical foundations of Iran's grand strategy

Iran grand strategy is essentially defined by its quest for sovereignty.[12] Since the beginning of the nineteenth century, Iran has had to navigate major power competitions, which has contributed to defining its pivotal nature. Both its geographical location and natural resources are assets that many major powers want to access if not control. In 1925, safeguarding Iranian sovereignty became a cardinal state policy when Reza Shah Pahlavi founded a new dynasty, ending the Qajar Empire.

In general, sovereignty is considered to be the first type of status to promote in international relations.[13] Indeed, "once sovereignty is conferred via recognition by others, a State may eventually seek membership in a status group within the overall system of states, most notably great power status."[14] However, sovereignty can assume different meanings. For instance, in international public law, sovereignty refers to the independence of one state against others.

In this sense, sovereignty belongs to the state. By contrast, national and popular sovereignty means that independence is owned by the people, not the state.[15] In Iran, there is a clear tension between these two forms of sovereignty. Both Reza Shah and Mohammad Reza Shah promoted the policy of state independence.[16] Such a policy has been challenged twice, resulting in a more popular understanding of sovereignty: first, during the Mohammad Mossadegh Premiership (1951–53) and second, during the revolutionary events that culminated in the establishment of IRI

The discourse on popular sovereignty is employed as a tool against two types of oppressors: the global (i.e., Russia/the Soviet Union, the UK, and the US) and the domestic (i.e., the elite). Such views were echoed at the time in the pro-Mossadegh daily paper *Bākhtar-e Emrouz*. In this context, the nationalization of Iran's oil by Mossadegh—passed by the *Majles* on March 15, 1951—was a clear attempt to reassert Iran's national sovereignty. For the first time since the Constitutionalist movement that led to the creation of the Parliament (1905–11), the prime minister was said to be "building a political community" against imperialism and its domestic "stooge," i.e., Mohammad Reza-Shah.[17] In contrast, members of the pro-Shah faction were perceived as British "stooges" trying to "sell the Nation."[18] The 1953 CIA- and MI6-sponsored coup that toppled Mossadegh crystallized anger against the British and laid the ground for resentment against the regime that came to power. The 1979 revolution drew on these emotions to galvanize popular support.

What did sovereignty mean to Rouhollah M. Khomeini? The Supreme Leader of Iran went a step further, adding and prioritizing Iran's cultural integrity over economic and political factors. For him, the fight against *Westernization* through a political and revolutionary Islam became a core policy goal subsuming all others.[19] Khomeini was thus one of the first Iranian leaders to explicitly contest "Western culture."[20] Because the revolution had mass support, Khomeini's early leadership embodied *popular sovereignty*, similar to Mossadegh's. However, unlike Mossadegh, Khomeini challenged nationalist ideas, which he construed as imported, that is, as corrupted Western ideology.[21] In this respect, the Islamic community (*Ommat-e Eslāmi*), including Shiites and Sunnis,[22] was set to replace the "Iranian community" (*Ommat-e Irāni*).[23] In this light, Khomeini's strategy was a revisionist approach to the regional and international order; it not only challenged the Western-dominated system, similar to Mossadegh's nationalism, but proposed an alternative transnational order that consisted of shaping regional identities through Islam to fight Western imperialism. In sum, Mossadegh's democratic nationalism, the trauma of its removal with the support of foreign powers, and Khomeini's anti-Western culture are deeply connected elements of Iran's grand strategy.

9.2 Iran's grand strategic system

In the grand strategic system of Iran, informal networks tend to trump formal roles. Indeed, examining Mohammad Reza Shah's reign, Marvin Zonis has shown that any decision-making analyses of Iran's strategy that solely rest upon Iran's formal institutions are shortsighted, as the personal linkages at work are often stronger than the institutional ones.[24] In fact, Wilfried Buchta and Eva Patricia Rakel argue that informality is a long-standing feature of Iran grand strategic system.[25] However, there is a substantial difference between the pre- and post-1979 regimes. The IRI is characterized by a certain degree of diversity,[26] whereas the two Pahlavi monarchies stood out as strong and vertical regimes, making the Shahs the first and final decision makers.

However, the diversity that characterizes the contemporary Iranian regime is not necessarily conducive to effective decision-making. Rather, it tends to engender the formation of factions that vigorously vie for power. Factions can be cross-institutional, and they generally coalesce around thematic issues. That is, factions are not similar to parties in the classical sense but look like a "loose coalition" that connects different kinds of organizations and networks.[27] In this light, the different institutions examined below exert their influence not only through individual agency but also as part of a faction. Further, members of an institution can disunite into estranged factions from one issue to another, making it difficult to trace the effect of a formal agency over time. As such, factions more often than not disrupt the normal, meaning formal, interactions between institutions.

At the formal level, the 1989 constitution allocates responsibilities in the field of defense and foreign affairs. According to Article 177, the Supreme National Security Council (SNSC) "determine(s) the national defense-security policies within the framework of general policies laid down by the (Supreme Leader)."[28] In addition to the Supreme Leader and the SNSC, a third important actor in Iran's grand strategic system is the Islamic Revolutionary Guard Corps (IRGC). We discuss each in turn.

9.2.1 THE SUPREME LEADER OF IRAN (RAHBAR)

The Supreme Leader of Iran is the Chief of the State and is commonly perceived as the overarching institution. Put otherwise, no one can act without the Guide's approval. Constitutionally, indeed, the Supreme Leader has the final word in all decisions, even regarding direct universal suffrage in the Assembly of the Experts, the Parliament, and the presidency, through his indirect filtering control via the Guardian Council. However, in practice, his role has more to do with smoothing the interactions between power circles and factions. That was, to some extent, already the case with Ayatollah Khomeini, who practiced *"dual containment"* between the then two opposing factions, the radical-leftists and the conservatives, criticizing either when it suited him.[29] Likewise, Khamenei first sided with the neoconservative president Ahmadinejad (2005–9) and then rejected his views during his second term (2009–13). By the same token, he backed Rouhani in the nuclear deal in 2013, though the two leaders had some disagreements under Khatami's presidencies (1997–2005).

9.2.2 THE SUPREME NATIONAL SECURITY COUNCIL (SNSC)

Chaired by the president, the SCNSC comprises all Iran's high-ranking political officials, including members of the executive power, the Speaker of the Parliament, the Chief of the Supreme Command Council of the Armed Forces (SCCAF), IRGC and regular Army commanders, and the representatives of the Supreme Leader. The politicization of security debates, often beyond their potential strategic value as such, places a constraining pressure on the work of the SNSC. Indeed, some experts downplay the decisive power of the SNSC, which they perceive as a purely consultative body. However, studies reveal that the SNSC is one of the institutions most subject to factional assaults.[30]

9.2.3 THE ISLAMIC REVOLUTIONARY GUARD CORPS (IRGC)

Because of its revolutionary function, the IRGC has drawn international attention at the expense of other security agencies, such as the MOIS (Ministry of Intelligence and Security), LEF (Law Enforcement Forces, which is subordinated to the Ministry of the Interior),[31] and more importantly, the regular army—*Artesh*. While raising no attention from international media and scholars, the mid-1920s institution has avoided UN sanctions, insofar as it is recognized as a defensive force.[32] In addition, ballistic and nuclear programs are said to be under the IRGC's control.

It is routinely observed that the IRGC's power extends beyond the military sector. Indeed, its economic and political activities have gradually developed since the end of the war with Iraq.[33] Ironically, this expansion was an indirect consequence of Hashemi Rafsanjani's "de-revolutionization plan,"[34] which actually aimed at containing the IRGC and merging it with Artesh.[35] However, following the US-led intervention in Iraq (2003), scholars have been divided over its precise role, power, and intentions. In the aftermath of the collapse of the Ba'athist regime in Iraq and Ahmadinejad's presidencies, under which the IRGC's members obtained strong political positions, some authors have stressed the IRGC's growing regional influence.[36] The main concern here is to see the IRGC controlling the state and eventually substituting a theocracy with a "military dictatorship."[37] By contrast, the IRGC omnipotence thesis is under pressure. First, like all IRI institutions, the IRGC is beset by factionalism.[38] For example, many of the rank-and-file members supported Khatami's reformist agenda and his candidacy for presidency, while the IRGC's senior commanders uncompromisingly aligned with Khamenei and his conservative constituency.[39] On the face of it, it would be misleading to assume that the IRGC acts as a homogenous body. Moreover, the Iranian system is characterized by a fierce domestic competition over the economy, the military, and politics, involving various actors beyond the IRGC. Indeed, according to Thierry Coville, "it is in the basic nature of a rent-seeking economy...to be the locus of an internal economic competition between different sociopolitical groups, each trying to use its political leverage to reach its economic objectives."[40] Militarily, the MOIS "liaises with several foreign Shi'a militant groups and insurgent organizations", while the LEF's responsibilities include "counternarcotic, riot control, border protection, morals enforcement, and anticorruption",[41] more importantly, the regular army has not eventually been dismantled following the revolution, despite pressure from the Tudeh Communist Party, Mojahedin-e Khalq (MEK), and leading clerics such as Ayatollah Mohammad Hosseini Beheshti,[42] and its post-1979 functions partly overlap those of IRGC against the backdrop of a long-term rivalry.[43] Finally, politically, even the Supreme Leader Khamenei has tried to contain the IRGC by insisting that they should not engage in politics.[44]

However, this evidence is nuanced. A spate of studies on Iran's intervention in Syria has shown how the IRGC has imposed its agenda within the domestic establishment against Rouhani's approach. Indeed, Rouhani, who benefits from the support of the Iranian Sunni minority, had to walk a fine line. Hence, he condemned the chemical attack on Ghouta on August 21, 2013 without blaming the Syrian opposition. Overall, however, Rouhani's voice on Syria has been ignored by the international community, leading to the "humiliation" of the Geneva II peace talks (January 2014), where Iran was suddenly withdrawn from the planning by the UN Secretary General. According to the authors, this event, combined with the rapid rise of ISIS and pressure from "hardliners," left no room for Rouhani's agenda. To some extent, therefore, the Syrian case appears to show limitations to Rouhani's leadership on Middle East affairs.[45]

9.3 The goals of Iran's grand strategy

The objectives of Iran's grand strategy are encapsulated in distinct, opposite political "factions," which transcend the formal institutions discussed in the previous section. In other words, to understand the goals of Iran's grand strategy and the choices it makes in the use of specific instruments, one needs to have a clear sense of the evolving balance of power between political lines. This section therefore examines the main political factions that shape Iran's grand strategy and presents the objectives each faction prioritizes. While some of the objectives pursued by these different factions overlap (e.g., the pursuit of sovereignty), there are nonetheless fundamental chasms between them, in terms of both their understanding of threats to Iran and the best way to achieve Iran's ends.

Since Anoushiravan Ehteshami's pioneering 1995 work, *After Khomeini: The Second Iranian Republic*, the division between "pragmatists" and "hardliners" has become the main lens through which Iran's policy outcomes, especially Iran's foreign policies, are examined and assessed.[46] However, we believe these terms inadequately capture the intellectual landscape of Iran's strategy. In our view, "pragmatist" is a misnomer.[47] The "pragmatist" rhetoric belongs to political discourses and was used for a limited period of time. Indeed, as a motto, "pragmatism" was employed mainly by Rafsanjani's coalition, "the Servant of the Reconstructions" (*Kārgozārān-e Sāzāndegi*), during the 1989 presidential campaign. We therefore suggest a different way of accounting for the ideas that organize foreign policy goals in Iran: the Progressive line (*Pishraft-e-Mahvar*) and the Conservative line (*Hefz-e Mahvar*).[48] The first conditions Iran's strategy for economic development, whereas the Conservative line, also known as the "Imam's line," places state ideology at the center of Iran's relations with the rest of the world.

9.3.1 THE PROGRESSIVE LINE

The Progressive line brings together leading political figures including Rafsanjani, Mohammad Khatami, and Rouhani.[49] The Progressives can largely be grouped into two main factions:[50] reformists and conservatives.[51]

The reformists comprise the post-Islamist generation, that is, religious intellectuals. They are mostly former radical-leftists, who in the 1990s rejected all kinds of totalitarian ideologies (e.g., Marxism) that they had previously embraced during the revolution under Ali Shariati's intellectual guidance and Khomeini's leadership.[52] Reformists support political liberalism, democracy (with a strong focus on civil society and human rights), and religious pluralism. Finally, they regard Western civilization as a model of freedom of thought.[53]

The second faction, the conservative politicians, includes Rouhani and Ali Akbar Velayati, the former Minister of Foreign Affairs (1981–97). To them, Iran should pursue three main objectives, the first of which is to restore Iran's status in the international system. This is reflected in the political language they use, which emphasizes words such as "prestige" (*Prestij*) or "Iran's restoration" (*Ehiā-ye Irān*).[54] For example, Rouhani does not just want to consolidate social justice and welfare. Rather, his project is to make Iran the China of the Middle East, thus echoing the Shah's ambition to transform Iran into the "Japan of the Middle East."[55]

Second, conservatives are worried by the growing gap between the population and the regime. This explains why the idea of "popular sovereignty" has gained traction in the political thought of some leaders, such as Rouhani. Popular sovereignty serves three main purposes, the first of which being social cohesion, which is regarded as a shield against external interference. The second, related, objective is to mobilize the population against external enemies of the regime. Third, popular sovereignty enables leaders to preserve the status quo and prevent regime change. In this light, Rouhani has put great care into gaining the support of public opinion, which he regards as a key factor in national security.[56] Thus, bridging the gap between the regime and the people is a matter of national security because without the support of public opinion, external actors are likely to exploit this weakness to their advantage and prompt regime change.[57] "National Union" (*vahdat-e melli*) is therefore an integral component of Iran's strategy.[58] Indeed, the weight of public opinion in the strategic debate has taken on new significance since the 2009 Green movement (*jombesh-e sabz*) and the set of sanctions starting in 2006 (UN, EU, bilateral ones) that plunged Iran into a deep economic crisis, especially after the EU oil embargo was enacted in July 2012. In other words, the regime faces resistance from public opinion due to poor economic performance and corruption. In fact, corruption is the main driver behind the "Eggs Revolution" that erupted on December 28, 2017 in Mashhad.[59] In sum, the concern with regime stability and national security has meant that the Progressive line, notwithstanding its heterogeneous components, has had to focus on economic development as the main objective that Iran should pursue. Whether justified or not, the argument of economic development has been utilized by the regime to make the case for civil nuclear technologies as a vital component of its economic well-being and sovereignty.[60]

The third objective of the Progressive approach to strategy is to preserve Iran's security against external threats. In fact, the Progressives no longer consider the United States and Israel to be the only threats to Iran's security. Weak states such as Iraq and Afghanistan are major security concerns. The main threats are Sunni terrorism, drug and arms trafficking, interethnic tensions, and organized crime. Because these threats are regional, the Progressive line proposes cobuilding a regional security order with Saudi Arabia.[61] This needs to be put in context, however, as these two countries entertain very difficult relations. For instance, on January 3, 2016, for the second time since 1979, the two regional rivals broke their diplomatic ties after a series of escalating events ending with the execution of the Shiite Cheikh al-Nimr in Saudi Arabia and the attacks on two Saudi diplomatic representations in Iran. The Saudi regime has called Washington to "cut the head of the snake." It fears that Iran will create a Hezbollah branch in Yemen, while Iran is regularly accused by the international community of militarily supporting the Houthis. Be that as it may, reconciling with Saudi Arabia was considered a top priority when Rouhani came to office in August 2013.[62]

9.3.2 THE IMAM'S LINE

This group includes sections of the IRGC, and especially their senior commanders, the *bassiji*, some conservative figures, the entire neoconservative faction, and the Supreme Leader Khamenei himself until 2013. Neoconservatives particularly opposed the notion of development (*towse'e*), initially promoted by Rafsanjani during his first term. They perceive it as the "Trojan Horse" that will entail the opening to the West and thus cause the collapse of the revolution.[63] Worth noting is the recent threat issued by the Secretary of the Expediency Discernment Council and former IRGC commander-in-chief Mohsen Rezaee to close the CSR in the aftermath of the death of Rafsanjani (January 8, 2017).[64] The CSR is criticized for what is perceived as a pro-Western leaning. Ironically, however, during electoral campaigns, holders of the Imam's line usually first and foremost emphasize economic well-being to counter the Progressive arguments. For example, Ahmadinejad was elected on an economic and social justice agenda, but his term in office was marked by frequent conflicts with the United States and Israel, especially through his aggressive rhetoric denying the Holocaust and his defense of a noncomplying posture during the nuclear negotiations. In fact, Ahmadinejad refused the EU3's negotiated uranium suspension, the P5+1 package of June 2006, and the UN demand to stop uranium enrichment, leading to the three Security Council resolutions in 2006–7 setting multilateral sanctions.[65]

In sum, Iran's grand strategy is torn between Progressives and the Iman's lines. While the former privileges economic development and social cohesion through the promotion of popular sovereignty, the latter is concerned with ideological orthodoxy and the integrity of the principles of the revolution. At root then, one could argue, the debate pitches those who want to preserve the revolutionary character of the state against those who believe Iran would be stronger by being perceived and dealt with as an ordinary, normal state that is nonrevisionist, with its own preferences and strategic priorities.[66]

9.4 Ways and means

The revolutionary discourse on foreign policy supported by Khomeini during the first years of the IRI had two complementary priorities: on the one hand, export the Islamic revolution, and on the other, promote a policy of neutrality during the Cold War—i.e., a "Neither East, nor West policy."[67] However, foreign policy was not a pressing objective. In addition, for some time, debates occurred mainly within the terms set by the revolutionary ideology. The Progressive line, from Rafsanjani's presidency to Rouhani's, contributed to the emergence of a new understanding of foreign policy. For the Progressive line, Iran's foreign policy should be dealt with outside of the IRI's ideology. According to Rafsanjani, even Khomeini himself supported dropping the slogan "Death to America!" (Marg bar Amricā!) as early as 1984.[68]

In 2006, the CSR initiated a discussion about Iran's foreign policy. Taking into account the post–Cold War environment, a recommendation of the CSR was that Iran had to forsake the politics of neutrality and forge new strategic partnerships. In particular, considering the growing economies of India and China, "look to the East" stood out as the main potential guiding principle. In practice, however, the Progressive group supported a West-directed policy. This occurred gradually. Initially, Rafsanjani started to connect economic development to foreign policy through the "critical dialogue" launched in 1992 between Iran and the European Union. Further, Khatami undermined the taboo of the "West Policy" by pleading for the inclusion of talks with the United States. Finally, Rouhani's team subscribed to the Joint Comprehensive

Plan of Action—JCPOA (*BARJAM*)[69]—on July 14, 2015, ending a conflicted negotiation process that started in 2002 after the MEK opponent Alireza Jafarzadeh disclosed the existence of the Natanz and Arak nuclear sites.

It is worth recalling that the Supreme Leader initially opposed Khatami's West policy when he proposed opening a dialogue with European countries.[70] However, he later changed his mind when Rouhani's team embarked on talks about Iran's nuclear program with Western countries, including the United States. In contrast, the Imam's line has exclusively focused on the look to the East. This policy was partially conducted by Ahmadinejad, when Iran faced a set of sanctions. Referring to Iran's lack of engagement with China's Silk Road project, which aims to connect China and Europe, some pundits within CSR have criticized the "Middle East centrism" of IRI's identity. This, they claim, is one of the main impediments—along with bureaucracy—preventing Iran from achieving either regional or international status.[71]

In the remainder of this section, we present and discuss the different instruments used to pursue Iran's grand strategy. We argue that military capabilities are the primary way through which Iran pursues its grand strategy. Along the way, we show that other instruments, such as social and economic power, have been subject to ebbs and flows, due in part to competition between internal factions and changes in the international environment.

9.4.1 MILITARY CAPABILITIES

Iran's grand strategy is tilted toward military capabilities. After a steady contraction of 7.3 percent between 2007 and 2016, Iran's military expenditures increased by 17 percent in 2015 and 2016, reaching a peak of 12 billion dollars, that is, 1.6 percent of its GDP.[72] It is worth noting, however, that Iran's defense budget does not include resources allocated to paramilitary forces such as the IRGC nor does it always factor in spending on Iran's foreign operations and proxies. However, Iran has invested in military technologies and equipment to bolster its military capacities, including investments in "ballistic missiles, cruise missiles, armed small boats, unmanned aerial vehicles, submarines, and other capabilities that could put U.S. and allied air and naval forces in the region—and the Strait of Hormuz at increasing risk."[73] However, Iran lacks an integrated defense system, and its network of radars appears to be substandard.[74]

Two principal forces occupy the center of Iran's military strategy. The first is called the Artesh. This is a remnant (though an extremely transformed version) of the pre-revolutionary regular army era. The second cluster of forces goes under the name of the Sepah-e Pasdaran-e Enghelāb-e Eslami (IRGC) and became dominant after the Iran–Iraq war (1980–88). Roughly, the Artesh is credited with 350,000 soldiers (among them, 220,000 conscripts), while there are 125,000 Pasdarans. In principle, both corps fall under the authority of the SCCAF.[75] However, the identity and functions of the Artesh and the Pasdarans remain distinct to such an extent that these two groups are better described as contending corps than as a single army. As a result, competition between the two often undermines the SCCAF's attempts to effectively coordinate their activities.[76]

On the operational terrain, the IRGC are the main actors, both in material and symbolic terms.[77] Materially, they are better trained and endowed with more advanced equipment. In addition to the government's annual allotment, the IRGC can tap into resources generated by its internal economic activities, in particular in real estate.[78] Further, they tend to exert an exclusive right to foreign military operations through their *niru-ye Qods* units (known as the Quds brigade or Jerusalem Forces). On the domestic front, the Basij Resistance Forces (*niru-ye basij-e moqavemat*) are tasked with defending the integrity of the revolution's values.[79] Finally, the Pasdarans are the cardinal forces supporting Iran's strategy of deterrence, which emphasizes asymmetric forms of military engagement. Second, at the symbolic level, the Pasdarans have managed to confiscate the prestige emanating from the battle against Iraq, thus further stripping the Artesh of any appeal.[80]

However, recent events suggest that the Artesh has begun to reclaim its operational clout. Thus, the Artesh has been leading the defense of the Iranian border with Iraq in the fight against ISIS. One might interpret the operational role granted to the Artesh as yet another index of the changing equilibrium in the power struggle between military bodies within Iran, each aligning with a specific political aisle. On this count, because Artesh exhibits a more reformist line, its voice tends to draw the attention of Iranian leaders who share its political view. In other words, each army component's responsibilities and related leverage depend on the political line that dominates in Teheran.

A cardinal pillar of Iran's strategy is asymmetric deterrence.[81] For Iran, asymmetric deterrence has two main components: one is the ability to offset potential threats posed by challengers in the region (e.g., Saudi Arabia, Israel, and the US). This is its defensive aspect. The second, offensive component is the capacity to develop counterthreats that neutralize the willingness of any challenger to attack Iran. Specifically, Iran's asymmetric deterrence rests upon three interconnected levers, including naval forces, its ballistic program, and the so-called Resistance Network. First, naval leverage depends, essentially, upon small armed boats produced by Iran since 2010.[82] In operational terms, responsibilities are split between the Islamic Republic of Iran Navy, which operates beyond Iran's coastal lines, in particular in the Gulf of Oman, and the IRGC Navy (IRGCN), which has exclusive power to patrol the Persian Gulf. Second, Iran strives to bolster its ballistic capabilities. In a 2017 bill proposal, the Iranian Parliament sought to allocate 260 million dollars to its ballistic missile program.[83] For Iran, the ballistic missile program, one aim of which is to compensate for aging military aircraft, is considered to be a part of its defensive strategy, but it is perceived as an offensive program by its challengers. The third element of Iran's asymmetric deterrence is the Resistance Network, which brings together eclectic actors including state (e.g., Syria) and nonstate actors (also referred to as "proxies") some of which are Shiites (e.g., Lebanese Hezbollah, the Badr Corps, the Supreme Council for Islamic Revolution in Iraq, the Dawa Political Party) while others are Sunnis (e.g., Hamas, and the Islamic Jihad). Finally, and more recently, the IRGC has been extending its influence in Latin America, including in Bolivia and Venezuela, thus widening its network of resistance.[84]

The role of Syria in Iran's strategy is crucial. The geographic location of Syria offers Iran a strategic depth that enables it to deploy its deterrence instruments beyond its borders while inhibiting or limiting the effectiveness of any military counter-reactions. On the face of it, Iran's intervention in Syria is not as much motivated by ideological factors—exporting a type of Islam—as it is induced by strategic calculations. Syria is "IRGC's primary forward-operating base in the Middle East and forms the political and logistical backbone for Iran's activities in Lebanon and the Palestinian territories. Iran calculated that the loss of Syria could fatally damage the Resistance Network."[85] However, the intervention, some authors argue,[86] was not the result of a consensus within Iran's grand strategic system. In fact, it was mainly promoted by the IRGC, which confined Rouhani's line to the marches. By collaborating with Hezbollah, IRGC Quds forces built a network of transnational fighters extending up to Afghanistan. Ultimately, the objective is to raise the costs (real or perceived) of any attack against Iran, thus consolidating its deterrence strategy.

9.4.2 ECONOMIC INSTRUMENTS

The main components of Iran's economic power lie in its natural resources. According to BP Statistical Review 2017, Iran possesses the world's greatest reserve of natural gas (18 percent) just ahead of the Russian Federation (17 percent). A founding member of the Organization of the Petroleum Exporting Countries (OPEC), Iran harbors the fourth largest reserve of oil in the world (9.3 percent) after Venezuela (17.6 percent), Saudi Arabia (15.6 percent), and Canada (10 percent).[87] However, this wealth remains mostly dormant, given that the regime has had to weather a series of international sanctions.[88] Before the European sanctions (2012), oil revenues accounted for 55 percent of Iran's budgetary resources and represented 80 percent of its exports.[89] If sanctions were considerably eased or lifted, Iran would probably emerge as one of the leading regional powers. For example, in a 2017 Report, Goldman Sachs included Iran in its list of "next 11," that is, countries that could in the long run compete with the G7.[90]

Since 1979, Iran's economy stands as an illustration of Islamic socialism, meaning that the whole economy, including the financial sector, is nationalized. In terms of its overall architecture, the economy is organized around three sectors: public, private, and cooperative. An important change brought by the 1979 Constitution is the development of Revolutionary Foundations chaired by former IRGC leaders. For instance, the IRGC real estate company (*Khatam al-Anbia*) employs more than 135,000 people and involves a network of over 5,000 subcontractors. In the financial sector, the IRGC owns two Islamic banks, namely, Ansar and Mehr.[91] This further increases its financial and strategic leverage.

The weight of the IRGC in the Iranian economy raises two challenges, however. On the one hand, many small businesses are wary about growing further as they fear being crushed or absorbed by the IRGC. On the other hand, as the IRGC strengthens its hold on the economy, it extends its control over larger portions of society. This means that any economic or political reform is difficult to undertake without the support of the IRGC.[92] In sum, the balance of power between the government and the IRGC seems to be skewed in favor of the latter. In this light, economic sanctions tend to weaken the government at the expense of the IRGC, which is able to generate international reserve currency through its various activities abroad.[93] Therefore, Rouhani's push toward the Joint Comprehensive Plan of Action (i.e., nuclear agreement) was meant not only to relax the pressure of sanctions on Iran's economy but also to provide a means to undercut the IRGC's grip on Iranian strategy and society. In addition, the new Five-Year Development Plan (2016–21) aims to improve the business environment, reform companies that belong to the public sector (e.g., bring banks back to the private realm), bolster the efficiency of the labor market, and consolidate the nonoil sector.[94] Taken together, these policies serve three main objectives: diversify the sources of Iran's wealth and its commercial partners, ameliorate the growth rate of Iran's economy, and, more importantly, enable the government to control the business environment and generate additional resources that it can employ in both domestic (e.g., strengthen social cohesion through the distribution of wealth) and international projects (e.g., support its proxies and finance its education network—see section 9.4.3).[95]

China is the main trade partner of Iran, and their commercial relationships cut across different areas, including oil and nonoil commodities. In the fiscal year 2016–17, for instance, commercial exchange with China accounted for over 20 percent of Iran's total trade relations with any other country.[96] In 2017, the total amount of transactions between the two countries was 37 billion dollars, and the trade balance benefited Iran by 200 million dollars. China's imports from Iran are mainly natural resources, in particular, crude oil, and in return, Iran provides China with a large market for various consumer goods and investment.[97] While the trade relationship with China does not enable Iran to accumulate sufficient capital to fulfill its domestic commitments and international strategy, it nonetheless allows Iran, on the one hand, to balance Russia in the energy market with China and, on the other hand, to somewhat loosen US pressure on the regime.

9.4.3 SOCIAL POWER

Iran has striven to develop a social power component, but with mixed outcomes. Specifically, the social power of Iran has two interrelated pillars. One, and the earliest component, is to promote Islamic revolution externally. The second pillar, in simple terms, is to fight imperialism. This aspect has a strong anti-Zionist wing to it, which veered into international anti-Semitism under Ahmadinejad. True, after the revolution, Khomeini contemplated the idea of exporting the Islamic revolution around the world, starting with Muslim countries. To that end, the Supreme Leader of Iran called for popular uprisings to topple governments in order to establish new regimes.[98]

However, Iranian-specific pan-Islamism ran out of steam by the mid-80s; as critics argued, attempts to export the Islamic revolution were undermining Iran's foreign policy effectiveness.[99] The rise of Hezbollah during the same period did not stem the decline of the ambition to export the government of the Islamic Jurist. In fact, although Hezbollah supports the idea of the government of the Islamic Jurist, it has progressively become an essential actor in Iran's deterrence strategy.

In Iraq, the very idea of the Islamic revolution has been cast aside. Thus, in 2007, even the Supreme Council of the Islamic Revolution of Iraq changed its name to the Islamic Supreme Council of Iraq, thus clearly distancing itself from the project of an Islamic revolution, as understood by the Iranian *Velāyat-e faqīh*. To some extent, this testifies to the waning of Iran's religious influence in the Middle East and beyond after Khomeini's death. For instance, most Iraqi Shiites do not recognize Ali Khamenei as a *marja'*. In the same vein, Hezbollah's members have a divided loyalty. While the majority consider Khamenei to be a *marja'*, others follow Mohammad Hussein Fadlallah. The upshot of this analysis is that Iran's religious influence is anything but widely accepted. In a detailed study, Bayram Balci shows that with the notable exception of Azerbaijan, Iran was unable to shape the contours of Islamic movements in Central Asia and South Caucasia.[100]

Iran's social power must accommodate Saudi Arabia's interests. In many ways, Iran's social power competes with the Sunni soft-power strategy, which sometimes crystalizes around the oversight of religious sites. In addition, Iran promotes Shia education by establishing branches of al-Mustafa International University in foreign countries (e.g., India, Indonesia, Malaysia, Nigeria, Ghana, Senegal, etc.).[101] Be that as it may, in Iran, religious sects often overlap with ethnic allegiances: the Sunnis, being mostly non-Persians, represent approximately 10 percent of the population and have been subject to discrimination for decades.[102] In a very perceptive study, Stéphane Dudoignon shows, however, that Iran has managed to maintain a relative balance between S*unnis* and *Shiites*, avoiding sectarian armed conflict within the country. This strategy has relied upon the transnational Sunni nexus (e.g., the Deoband School), which has developed an Iranian branch and helped Iranian authorities and the local population to interact.[103]

In contrast to Iran's Shiite religious influence and to the failure to export the Islamic revolution, the very anti-imperialist pillar of Iran's social power has been embraced by some state and nonstate actors. For instance, the romance between Ahmadinejad and Hugo Chavez was mainly fed by anti-imperialist and anti-capitalist beliefs.[104] Iran's social power in Latin America is conveyed through a combination of different types of instruments, including its observer status within the Bolivarian Alliance for People of our America (ALBA), the opening of new—formal and informal—embassies in the region, and the broadcasting of Hispanic TV programs in the region.[105] However, the death of Chavez and the marginalization of Ahmadinejad in Iran has meant that the Latin American connection has become less salient to Iran's foreign policy. Further, since 2011, Brazil has also been more critical of Iran's Latin America's push, questioning the values underlying Iran's policy in the region. Finally, the fact that this policy was mainly overseen by the IRGC has also raised concerns as regards the legality of some of their economic activities.[106] In Yemen, too, it is the anti-imperialist content of Iran's social power that is emulated. Indeed, some social-political movements that are Zaidist, and thus thought to be close to Iran, explicitly reject the government of Jurist. However, its leader, Sheikh Hussein Badreddin al-Houthi, champions Iran's anti-imperialism and anti-Zionism and considers this a model worth mimicking.[107]

In sum, the demise of the export of the Islamic revolution and the uncertain curve of its anti-imperialist policy mean that Iran's social power remains the weakest plank of its grand strategy. In part, this is due to the negative images such policies raise around the world. In fact, a 2017 BBC global survey revealed that Iran receives the highest level of negative views in terms of its influence in the world (61 percent), followed by North Korea (59 percent), Pakistan (58 percent), Israel (50 percent), and Russia (49 percent). By contrast, the aggregate positive opinion of its influence is very low (15 percent).[108] Thus, there have been increasing calls to reorient Iran's social power to improve its global approval and fight against so-called Iranophobia (Iranhorasi). Such a policy relies primarily on developing tourism in Iran. As a consequence, the budget allotted to Iran's Cultural Heritage, Handicrafts and Tourism Organization has risen by 17 percent in 2017, reaching a total sum of 200 million dollars. The long-term goal is to quadruple the number of foreigners visiting Iran by 2025, thus superseding the current average of 5 million visitors generated mainly by religious pilgrims. Be that as it may, a difficult issue for Iran to arbitrate is the extent to which a different kind of social power, that is, one that emphasizes cultural heritage and neither religious exceptionalism nor its Islamic revolutionary feature, would enable it to alter global perceptions without having to explicitly settle on either of the alternative identities, namely, being a "revolutionary state" or an "ordinary state."[109]

9.5 Conclusion: Indicators of continuity and change

Iran's grand strategy is characterized by a high degree of continuity, both in its objectives[110]—e.g., the preservation of Iran's sovereignty, the achievement of national development, the recognition of its international stature—and its preferred way to achieve them—asymmetric deterrence. However, while it tends toward military instruments, Iran's grand strategy has seen its other instruments, such as its social power and economic instruments, fluctuating in strength and relevance.

As we argued in the introduction, the distinctive content and orientation of Iran's grand strategy derive from its pivotal character. The pivotal character of the country has been used by Iran since the beginning of the twentieth century to respond to the economic, political, and, to some extent, military threats posed by great powers. For instance, Reza Shah's "Third Policy" aimed precisely at deflecting the pressure applied by the then two competing powers, Great Britain and Russia, by calling upon a third state, i.e., Germany.[111] In *Pivotal States*, Robert Chase, Emily Hill, and Paul Kennedy define specific strategic behavior that differentiates pivotal states from others.[112] What, in short, characterizes a pivot state?

Instead of being satellite states or "shadow states" (i.e., those states that "remain frozen in the shadow of a single power"), pivot states are able to "take advantage of opportunities to form one-on-one relations with multiple other governments, playing one off [against] another to secure the most profitable terms of engagement."[113]

The reliance on its pivotal status has also led to some misperceptions of the changing international environment by Iran. Consider Iran's behavior during the nuclear negotiations in 2006. Many have overplayed the factional element, highlighting the 2005 elections resulting in the neoconservative presidency of Ahmadinejad.[114] However, one must recall that beyond the appearances, on some occasions Khatami's administration threatened to resume nuclear suspension of enriched uranium. This begs the question: why did its pivotal status not provide Iran with the leverage it thought it would?

The CSR provides an interesting explanation. Before the dossier was transferred to the UN under EU pressure (4 February 2006), a large majority of

Iranian politicians emphasized the energy competition between Europe and the United States, thinking that Europe would support Iran against Washington on the nuclear dossier. They recalled the charisma of General De Gaulle advocating national autonomy. Taken together, these beliefs prevented the Iranian political elite from appreciating the rise of a new grand strategy in France—"liberal engagement,"[115] combining neoconservative and liberal internationalist elements.[116] There is a precedent to such a misinterpretation. During his time in office, Mossadegh went on to nationalize Iran's oil, thinking the United States would support Iran against the British. However, the cohesion of the Atlantic Alliance appeared stronger than he had thought. In addition, he overestimated Iran's position in the oil market.[117]

However, following the worsening of the nuclear talks, the CSR analyst Nasser Saghafi-Ameri admitted that Iranian politicians had completely misjudged the strong partnership between the US and European countries. Above all, they had to understand that Europeans truly fear the Iranian nuclear threat.[118] This new understanding of the situation was followed by a redefinition of the means and ways, under Rouhani's first term, that brought a change in Iran's negotiating posture.[119] Indeed, since "Iranophobia" (*Iranhorasi*) has been analyzed as the main barrier to Iran achieving its ends,[120] Rouhani relied on strategic recognition as a mean to advance Iran's position.[121] Through active diplomacy, Rouhani's team wanted to show that Iran could comply, Iran wanted to normalize its behavior, and that it was a "moderate" (*E'tedal*) state.[122] While complying with conditions set by the JCPOA, Iran has increasingly invested more resources in other pillars to support its deterrence architecture. Proxies and the development of ballistic missiles have come to fulfill that role. The question therefore becomes, how will Iran adjust its grand strategy after the US scraps the nuclear deal? Of course, the answer depends in part on whether the other signatories maintain the integrity of the deal, whether they attempt to bring the US back in by substantially altering the terms of the previous compact, and ultimately, if Iran accepts and trusts such a new deal. The answer would also depend on the power balance between factions in Iran.

While the pivotal character of Iran could account for both continuity and change, this chapter has also found that discontinuities or lags in Iran's grand strategy usually depend on three factors: changes in the international environment with a greater sensitivity to its regional context, the power balance between internal factions, and economic imperatives. Of these three factors, economic imperatives have gained enormous importance recently, as they condition domestic stability and support Iran's international strategy. On the one hand, Iran needs resources to sustain its network of resistance. On the other hand, Iran relies on economic assets to consolidate its welfare system, improve its employment rate, and increase allegiance to the regime. These are the two planks of its asymmetric deterrence strategy. In this respect, the struggle between the Imam's line and the Progressive line takes on new meaning. It is less about Islamic identity versus prosperity than about whether one takes precedence over the other, and whether they can effectively be articulated through the formation of long-term strategic choices without undercutting what Iran wants to represent, achieve, or be.[123]

NOTES

1. Ali Ansari, "Iranian Foreign Policy under Khatami: Reform and Reintegration," in *Politics of Modern Iran*, ed. Ali Ansari (London: Routledge, 2001), 13–31.
2. Created in 1989, the CSR (Markaz-e Tahqiqat-e Estratejiki) is an important official think tank addressing strategic issues. It reports directly to the Expediency Discernment Council. Before being elected, Hassan Rouhani was the president of CSR.
3. Nasser Saghafi-Ameri, "Iran and look to the East policy," *CSR*, May 25, 2008, http://www.isrjournals.com/en/experts/295-iran-and-look-to-the-east-policy.html
4. Alex Grinberg, "The Concept of Deterrence in Arab and Muslim Thought—Iran," in *The 13th Herzliya conference* (Herzliya 2013); Shmuel Bar, *Can Cold War Deterrence Apply to a Nuclear Iran?* (Jerusalem: Center for Public Affairs, 2011); Vali Nasr, "When the Shiites Rise," *Foreign Affairs* 85, no. 4 (July/August 2006): 58–74.
5. Shmuel Bar, "Can Cold War Deterrence apply to a Nuclear Iran?," *Strategic Perspectives*, Jerusalem Center for Public Affairs, no. 7 (2011); Shahram Chubin, "Extended Deterrence and Iran," *Strategic Insights* 8, no. 5 (December 2009), https://calhoun.nps.edu/bitstream/handle/10945/11140/chubinDec09.pdf?sequence=1; Grinberg, "The Concept of Deterrence"; Matthew Moran and Christopher Hobbs, "The Iranian Nuclear Dilemma: Light at the End of the Tunnel?," *Defense & Security Analysis* 28, no. 3 (June 2012): 202–12; Peter Jones, "Learning to Live with a Nuclear Iran," *The Nonproliferation Review* 19, no. 2 (July 2012): 197–217.
6. James M. Lindsay and Ray Takeyh, "After Iran Gets the Bomb: Containment and Its Complications," *Foreign Affairs* 89, no. 2 (March/April 2010): 33–49; Robert Baer, *L'iran, L'irrésistible Ascension* (Paris: Gallimard, 2009); Kenneth N. Waltz, "Why Iran Should Get the Bomb: Nuclear Balancing Would Mean Stability," *Foreign Affairs* 91, no. 4 (July/August 2012): 2–5.
7. See Tim Sweijs et al., *Why are Pivot States So Pivotal? The Role of Pivot States in Regional and Global Security* (The Hague: The Center for Strategic Studies, 2014), https://hcss.nl/sites/default/files/files/reports/Why_are_Pivot_States_so_Pivotal__The_Role_of_Pivot_States_in_Regional_and_Global_Security_C.pdf
8. See Rouhollah K. Ramazani, *The Foreign Policy of Iran: A Developing Nation in World Affairs, 1500–1941* (Charlottesville: University Press of Virginia, 1966), 89–92, 141; Freidoune Sahebjam, *L'iran Des Pahlavis* (Boulogne-Billancourt, Fra.: Berger-Levrault, 1966), 280.
9. Sweijs et al., *Why are Pivot States So Pivotal?*, 2.

10. In this book, Thierry Balzacq has defined a "grand strategic system" as "different actors, and interactions—formal and informal—between them, which account for the shape of grand strategy in any given country."
11. Mehdi Bazargan, *Enqelāb-e Irān dar Do Harekat* (Tehran: Chap-e Sevom, 1983/1984), 110–11.
12. J. Matthew McInnis, "Iran's Strategic Thinking: Origins and Evolution," *American Enterprise Institute*, May 12, 2015, http://www.aei.org/wp-content/uploads/2015/05/Irans-Strategic-Thinking.pdf; Shmuel Bar, "Iranian Defense Doctrine and Decision Making," in *The 5th Herzliya Conference* (Herzliya 2004).
13. Based on Max Weber and Emile Durkheim's understanding, status is defined as "a collective belief about a given State's ranking on valued attributes (wealth, coercive capabilities, culture, demographic position, socio-political organization and diplomatic clout)." Deborah Welch Larson, T. V. Paul, and William C. Wohlforth, "Status and World Order," in *Status in World Politics*, eds. T. V. Paul, Deborah Welch Larson, and William C. Wohlforth (Cambridge: Cambridge University Press, 2014), 7.
14. Larson, Paul, and Wohlforth, "Status and World Order," 7.
15. *Lider Bal, Le Mythe De La Souveraineté En Droit International, La Souveraineté Des Etats À L'épreuve Des Mutations De L'ordre Juridique International* (Strasbourg: Université de Strasbourg, 2012), 20–3.
16. Yann Richard, Bernard Hourcade, and Jean-Pierre Digard, *L'iran Au Xxe Siècle* (Paris: Fayard, 1996), 115.
17. Majid Sharifi, *Imagining Iran: The Tragedy of Subaltern Nationalism* (Lanham, MD: Lexington Books, 2013).
18. Ibid., 97–8.
19. Ref: FBIS-MEA 79–242,1, supp.040, December 14, 1979; Marvin Zonis and Daniel Brumberg, *Khomeini, the Islamic Republic of Iran, and the Arab World* (Cambridge, MA: Center for Middle Eastern Studies, Harvard University, 1987), 18.
20. Sharifi, *Imagining Iran*, 99.
21. Mohammad-Reza Djalili, *Diplomatie Islamique: Stratégie Internationale Du Khomeynisme* (Paris: PUF, 1989), 54.
22. Ibid., 65.
23. Mostafa Vaziri, *Iran as Imagined Nation: The Construction of National Identity* (New York: Paragon House, 1993), 199.
24. Marvin Zonis, *The Political Elite of Iran* (Princeton, NJ: Princeton University Press, 1971); James A. Bill, *The Politics of Iran: Groups, Classes and Modernization* (Columbus, OH: Merrill, 1972).
25. Wilfried Buchta, *Who Rules Iran?: The Structure of Power in the Islamic Republic* (Washington, DC: Washington Institute for Near East Policy, 2000); Eva Patricia Rakel, "The Iranian Political Elite, State and Society Relations, and Foreign Relations since the Islamic Revolution" (thesis, University of Amsterdam, 2008), https://pure.uva.nl/ws/files/1110757/54677_thesis.pdf; Mehdi Moslem, *Factional Politics in Post-Khomeini Iran* (Syracuse, NY: Syracuse University Press, 2002).
26. Rakel, "The Iranian Political Elite," 2–6.
27. Moslem, *Factional Politics in Post-Khomeini Iran*, 90–6; Buchta, *Who Rules Iran?*, 13.

28. http://www.iranonline.com/iran/iran-info/government/Supreme-National-Security-Council.html, accessed May 1, 2018.
29. Moslem, *Factional Politics*, 74.
30. Robert Baer, *L'iran: l'irresistible ascension* (Paris: Gallimard, 2009), 32.
31. Frederic Wehrey, *The Rise of the Pasdaran: Assessing the Domestic Roles of Iran's Islamic Revolutionary Guards Corps* (Santa Monica, CA: RAND Corporation, 2009).
32. Laura Grossman, "Sanctioning Iran's Military-Industrial Complex," *The Artesh: Iran's Marginalized Regular Army* 2011, 13; Katzman, "The Politics of Iran's Regular Military," 10, https://www.mei.edu/sites/default/files/publications/2011.11.The%20Artesh%20Full%20PDF.pdf
33. See, for example, Afshon P. Ostovar, *Guardians of the Islamic Revolution: Ideology, Politics, and the Development of Military Power in Iran (1979–2009)* (Ann Arbor: University of Michigan, 2009).
34. Ibid., 135.
35. Anthony H. Cordesman, *Iran's Military Forces in Transition, Conventional Threats and Weapons of Mass Destruction* (Westport, CT: Praeger, 1999), 31–54.
36. Ostovar, *Guardians of the Islamic Revolution*, 15.
37. See Ali Alfoneh, *Iran Unveiled: How the Revolutionary Guards is Transforming Iran from Theocracy into Military Dictatorship* (Washington, DC: AEI Press, 2013).
38. On the militarization tendencies of the Iranian political structure, see Youhanni Najdi and Mohd Azhari Bin Abdul Karim, "The Role of the Islamic Revolutionary Guards Corps (IRGC) and the Future of Democracy in Iran: Will Oil Income Influence the Process?," *Democracy and Security* 8, no. 1 (2012): 72–89; Elliot Hen-Tov and Nathan Gonzales, "The Militarization of Post-Khomeini Iran: Praetorianism 2.0," *The Washington Quarterly* 34, no. 1 (December 2010): 45–59; Kazem Alandari, "The Power Structure of the Islamic Republic of Iran: Transition from Populism to Clientelism, and Militarization of the Government," *Third World Quarterly* 26, no. 8 (2005): 1285–301; Kenneth Katzman, *The Warriors of Islam: Iran's Revolutionary Guard* (Boulder, CO: Westview, 1993).
39. Ostovar, *Guardians of the Islamic Revolution*, 131.
40. Thierry Coville, "The Economic Activities of the Pasdaran," *Revue internationale des études du développement*, no. 1 (2017): 91.
41. Wehrey, *The Rise of the Pasdaran*, 10–11.
42. Alfoneh, *Iran Unveiled*, 32.
43. Alfoneh, *Iran Unveiled*, 32.
44. See Shahram Akbarzadeh and Dara Conduit, eds., *Iran in the World: President Rouhani's Foreign Policy* (Berlin: Springer, 2016).
45. Shahram Akbarzadeh and Dara Conduit, "Charting a New Course? Testing Rouhani's Foreign Policy Agency in the Iran-Syria Relationship," in *Iran in the World*, eds. Shahram, and Conduit, pp. 133–54.
46. Anoushiravan Ehteshami, *After Khomeini: The Second Iranian Republic* (London: Routledge, 1995).
47. Ali Akbar Rezaei, "Foreign Policy Theories: Implications for the Foreign Policy Analysis of Iran," in *Iran's Foreign Policy: From Khatami to Ahmadinejad*, eds. Anoushiravan Ehteshami and Mahjoob Zweiri (Reading, UK: Ithaca Press, 2008), 17–36.

48. Rouhani subscribes to this understanding; see Hassan Rouhani, *Andishehā-Ye Siāsi-Ye Eslāmi; Jelv-E Dovvom: Siāsat-E Xareji* (Tehran: Center for Strategic Research, 2009), 19.
49. A caveat is in order. Rouhani was not part of the Reformist movement in the 1990s, but his views converged with the Reformist agenda during the first term of Ahmadinejad. See Yadullah Shahibzadeh, *Islamism and Post-Islamism in Iran: An Intellectual History* (Berlin: Springer, 2016), 215–16.
50. For a valuable account of factions in post-1979 Iran and their categorization, see the work of Mehdi Moslem, *Factional Politics in Post-Khomeini Iran*, who based his classification on Behzad Nabavi's one. Basically, the three original factions in the 1980s—the radical-leftists, the conservatives, and the pro-Rafsanjani—were rebuilt in the 1990s.
51. It is worth mentioning that there are other fractures within each of these groups.
52. Yadullah Shahibzadeh, *Islamism and Post-Islamism in Iran*, 99–109.
53. Ibid., 185.
54. Rouhani, *Andishehā-Ye Siāsi-Ye Eslāmi*, 20.
55. Hassan Rouhani, "Servat-E Melli Yā Qodrat-E Melli, Avaliat Bā Kodām Ast?," *Rahbord* 1385, no. 39 (Spring 2006): 10.
56. Hassan Rouhani, "Enfedjārhā-Ye Amrikā Va Manāfé-Ye Melli-Ye Jomhuri-Ye Eslāmi," *Rahbord*, no. 21 (Autumn 2001): 49.
57. "Estrāteji-Ye Jomhuri-Ye Eslāmi-Ye Irān Dar Barobar-E Tahdidat-E Āxir-E Āmrikā," *Rahbord*, no. 24 (Summer 2002): 23–4.
58. "Estrāteji-Ye Jomhuri-Ye," 27.
59. In July 2012, demonstrations burst out in Nishapur against high chicken prices due to a high inflation rate. The "eggs revolution" was triggered on December 28, 2017, driven by economic grievances first and foremost, and diffused across the country. This event has been considered to be the most challenging mobilization since the 2009 Green movement. "Des Iraniens manifestent contre la hausse marquée du prix du poulet," *Huffington Post*, July 23, 2012, https://quebec.huffingtonpost.ca/2012/07/23/des-iraniens-manifestent-_n_1696069.html
60. Hassan Rohani, *Amniat-E Melli Va Diplomāsi-Ye Hastéi—Introduction* (Tehran: Center for Srategic Research, 2011).
61. For more details, see Bérénice Alma, "The Iranian Strategic Thought and Its Recent Evolution," *ERIS–European Review of International Studies* 2, no. 1 (2015): 62–71.
62. See Baer, *L'iran: l'irresistible ascension*.
63. Mehdi Moslem, *Factional Politics in Post-Khomeini Iran*, 134.
64. (1396 مرداد 31–2017 اوت), منحل می‌شود, accessed May 1, 2018, http://www.bbc.com/persian/iran-41010485
65. Robert Litwak, "Iran's Nuclear Chess: After the Deal," *Woodrow Wilson International Center for Scholars* (2015), 26–7.
66. Litwak, "Iran's Nuclear Chess," 43–57.
67. The "Neither East, nor West Policy" formulation echoes a revolutionary claim through the motto: "Neither East, nor West: Islamic Republic" (*Na sharq, na gharb, jomhuri-ye eslāmi*). Accessed January 31, 2017, http://www.lexpress.fr/actualite/monde/proche-moyen-orient/iran-mort-a-l-amerique-le-slogan-dont-rohani-voudrait-se-debarrasser_1296360.html

68. Rakel, *The Iranian Political Elite*, 155–7.
69. Persian acronym of JCPOA.
70. Rakel, *The Iranian Political Elite*, 211–12.
71. Mohsen Shari'tiniâ, "Iran Va Tarh-E Abrisham, Bâzgasht Be Pol-E Sharq Va Qarb," (2016), http://www.csr.ir/fa/news/530/ایران-و-طرح-ابریشم-بازگشت-به-پل-شرق-و-غرب
72. Nan Tian, Aude Fleurant, Pieter D. Wezeman, and Siemon T. Wezeman, "Trends in World's Military Expenditure, 2016," *SIPRI Fact Sheet*, April 2017, p. 7. See also SIPRI, "Military Expenditure by Country as Percentage of Gross Domestic Product," accessed April 25, 2017, https://www.sipri.org/sites/default/files/Milex-share-of-GDP.pdf
73. McInnis, "Iran's Strategic Thinking," 17.
74. Hossein Aryan, "The Artesh: Iran's Marginalized and under-Armed Conventional Military," *The Middle Institute Viewpoints, The Artesh: Iran's Marginalized Regular Military*, no. 15 (November 2011).
75. The International Institute for Strategic Studies, *The Military Balance 2018* (London: Routledge, 2018), 334.
76. Ostovar, *Guardians of the Islamic Revolution*, 135.
77. Anthony H. Cordesman, *Iran's Military Forces in Transition*, 40.
78. On the economic role of the IRGC, see M. Mahtab Alam Rizvi, "Evaluating the Political and Economic Role of the IRGC," *Strategic Analysis* 36, no. 4 (June 2012): 584–96.
79. Ostovar, *Guardians of the Islamic Revolution*, 150.
80. Gawdat Bahgat, "Iran's Regular Army: Its History and Capacities," *The Middle Institute Viewpoints, The Artesh: Iran's Marginalized Regular Military*, no. 15 (November 2011): 18–19.
81. On asymmetric deterrence, see Frank C. Zagare and D. Marc Kilgour, "Asymmetric Deterrence," *International Studies Quarterly* 37, no. 1 (March 1993): 1–27.
82. Baer, *L'iran: l'irresistible ascension*, 171–5.
83. Thomas Erdbrink, "Iranian Parliament, Facing U.S. Sanctions, Votes to Raise Military Spending," *The New York Times*, August 13, 2017, https://www.nytimes.com/2017/08/13/world/middleeast/iranian-parliament-facing-us-sanctions-vote-to-raise-defense-spending.html
84. See Álvaro Uribe Vélez et al., *Iran's Strategic Penetration of Latin America* (Lanham, MD: Lexington Books, 2014).
85. McInnis, "Iran's Strategic Thinking," 17.
86. Akbarzadeh and Conduit, "Charting a New Course?"
87. BP Statistical Review of World Energy June 2017, accessed May 8, 2018, https://www.bp.com/content/dam/bp/en/corporate/pdf/energy-economics/statistical-review-2017/bp statistical-review-of-world-energy-2017-full-report.pdf
88. See, for example, Suzanne Maloney, *Iran's Political Economy since the Revolution* (Cambridge: Cambridge University Press, 2015).
89. Mehrdad Vahabi and Thierry Coville, "L'économie Politique De La République Islamique D'iran," *Revue internationale des études du développement*, no. 1 (2017): 18.
90. Goldman Sachs, "Beyond the BRICs: A Look at the 'Next 11'," accessed April 27, 2018, http://www.goldmansachs.com/our-thinking/archive/archive-pdfs/brics-book/brics-chap-13.pdf

91. Coville, "The Economic Activities of the Pasdaran," 93–6.
92. Mehrdad Vahabi, "A Positive Theory of the Predatory State," *Public Choice* 168, no. 3–4 (June 2016): 153–75.
93. Álvaro Uribe Vélez et al., *Iran's Strategic Penetration of Latin America*.
94. "La Banque Mondiale En Iran," *Banque mondiale*, April 1, 2018, http://www.banquemondiale.org/fr/country/iran/overview
95. The World Bank, "The World Bank in Islamic Republic of Iran," http://www.worldbank.org/en/country/iran/overview, accessed April 15, 2018.
96. "Iran-China H1 Trade Up to 31% to $18 Billion," *Financial Tribune*, July 30, 2017, https://financialtribune.com/articles/economy-domestic-economy/69312/iran-china-h1-trade-up-31-to-18-billion, accessed April 28, 2018.
97. Chen Aizhu, "China's Iran Oil Imports to Hit Record on New Production: Sources," *Reuters*, January 5, 2017, https://www.reuters.com/article/us-china-iran-oil/chinas-iran-oil-imports-to-hit-record-on-new-production-sources-idUSKBN14P15W, accessed April 28, 2018.
98. Zonis and Brumberg, *Khomeini*, 17–18.
99. See Laurence Louër, *Chiisme et Politique au Moyen-Orient: Iran, Irak, Liban, Monarchies Du Golfe* (Paris: Autrement, 2008).
100. See Bayram Balci, *Renouveau de l'Islam en Asia Centrale et dans le Caucase* (Paris: Editions du CNRS, 2017).
101. See Masooda Bano, Keiko Sakuri, eds., *Shaping Global Islamic Discourse: The Role of Al-Azhar, Al-Medina, and Al-Mustafa* (Edinburgh: Edinburgh University Press, 2015).See also Alexander Thurston, "Islamic Universities and their Global Outreach," *Oxford Islamic Studies Online*, http://www.oxfordislamicstudies.com/Public/focus/essay1009_Islamic_Universities.html, accessed February 10, 2017.
102. There is no official confessional statistics that separate Sunnis from Shiites in Iran. The Sunnis are estimated through ethnic groups mainly: the Arabs, Baluch, and Kurds.
103. Stéphane Dudoignon, *The Baluch, Sunnism and the State in Iran* (London: Hurst, 2017).
104. See Ilan Berman, "What Iran Wants in the Americas?," in *Iran's Strategic Penetration of Latin America*, 3.
105. Jon B. Purdue, "A Marriage of Radical Ideologies," in *Iran's Strategic Penetration of Latin America*, 15–17.
106. Leonardo Coutinho, "Iran and Islamic Extremism in Brazil," in *Iran's Strategic Penetration of Latin America*, 41–50.
107. Louër, *Chiisme et Politique Au Moyen-Orient*, 251–67.
108. See "Sharp Drop in World Views of US, UK: Global Poll," *BBC*, July 4, 2017, https://globescan.com/images/images/pressreleases/bbc2017_country_ratings/BBC2017_Country_Ratings_Poll.pdf
109. See Litwak, "Iran Nuclear Chess," 43–57.
110. Mohammad Javad Zarif, "What Iran Really Wants: Iranian Foreign Policy in the Rouhani Era," *Foreign Affairs* 93, no. 3 (May/June 2014): 49.
111. Ramazani, *The Foreign Policy of Iran*, 203.
112. See Robert S. Chase, Emily Hill, and Paul M. Kennedy, eds., *Pivotal States: A New Framework for U.S. Policy in the Developing World* (New York: W. W. Norton & Co, 2000).

113. Sweijs et al., *Why are Pivot States So Pivotal?*, 8.
114. This point has been highlighted by Ariane Tabatabai, "Presidential Elections and Nuclear Policy in Iran," *Arms Control Today* 43, no. 5 (2013), https://www.armscontrol.org/act/2013_06/Presidential-Elections-and-Nuclear-Policy-In-Iran
115. See Thierry Balzacq, "France," Chapter 5 of this volume.
116. On the evolution of France's policy towards proliferation in general and Iran in particular, see Florent Pouponneau, "Diplomatic Practices, Domestic Fields, and International System: Explaining France's Shift on Nuclear Nonproliferation," *International Studies Quarterly* 61, no. 1 (March 2017): 123–35. See also Nasser Saghafi-Ameri, "New Trends in the EU-US Security Relationship: Implications for the Middle East, Persian Gulf and Iran- Introduction," *CSR*, July 29, 2004, http://www.isrjournals.com/en/monograph/291-new-trends-in-the-eu-us-security-relationship-implications-for-the-middle-east-persian-gulf-and-iran.html
117. Sahebjam, *L'iran Des Pahlavis*, 263–64, 70.
118. Nasser Saghafi-Ameri, "The Strategic Interaction between Iran and Europe," Abstract, *CSR*, May 24, 2006, http://www.isrjournals.com/fa/iran-foreign-policy/848-the-strategic-interaction-between-iran-and-europe.html.
119. For more details on the subject, see Alma, "The Iranian Strategic Thought," 68–9.
120. Hassan Rouhani, "Introduction" of *National Security and Nuclear Diplomacy (Amniat-e melli vā diplomāsi-ye hastéi)*, Centre for Strategic Research, November 2011, http://www.csr.ir/Pdf/Books241/Nuclear%20Diplomacy.pdf.
121. Strategic recognition is defined by Thomas Lindemann in the following: "A good reputation is essential to obtaining advantages in terms of material resources." Thomas Lindemann, *Causes of War: The Struggle for Recognition* (Colchester, UK: Essex, 2010), 2.
122. See Rouhani's speech at the 72nd United Nations General Assembly, September 19–25, 2017, https://gadebate.un.org/en/72/iran-islamic-republic.
123. We would like to thank Peter Dombrowski, Stéphane Dudoignon, Simon Reich, and Eitan Shamir for their very useful comments and suggestions on previous drafts of this chapter.

10 Israel

EITAN SHAMIR

10.1 Historical experiences that have affected Israel's grand strategy

The state of Israel is the birth child of the Zionist movement formed towards the end of the nineteenth century with the sole purpose of creating a Jewish homeland in the historic land of Israel. From the outset, the Zionist goal to establish a Jewish state in the ancient Jewish homeland seems like an impossible dream. The most famous quote of Theodor Herzl,[1] founder of the Zionist movement, was "If you will it, it is no dream;[2]... and if you do not will it, a dream it is and a dream it will stay,[3] conveying what seemed at the time impossible.

Against odds, the Zionists persisted in their pursuit and the twist and turns of history was on their side: from the collapse of the Ottoman Empire and British Empire following two world wars, to the rare moment in the history of the Cold War when both belligerents, the US and USSR, voted together (each for its interests) for a partition and the establishment of a tiny Jewish state next to an Arab state.[4] In the immediate Jewish–Arab conflict that ensued, objective observers gave little chance for the Jewish community of 650,000 to survive the struggle against 1,250,000 Palestinian Arabs, let alone the planned invasion of the surrounding Arab State armies. However, not only did the Jewish state emerge from the war victorious, but it has also increased its territory, even more importantly, the Jews became the majority, thus, in essence, fulfilling the Zionist goal of a Jewish state.

The Zionist movement has therefore secured its primary objective against overwhelming odds. Not surprisingly, David Ben Gurion, Israel's first prime minister and founding father, said that in Israel he who does not believe in miracles is not a realist, Chaim Herzog, Israel's sixth president, quipped that "Israelis might not believe in miracles, but they do plan on them."[5] But Israel's founders were *not* waiting for miracles to happen, but followed a few strategic imperatives: building *capacities* and *capabilities*, *strategic patience*—waiting for the opportunity history will present—and *seizing the moment*—when such an opportunity finally presents itself.

Two traumatic historical experiences are fundamental if one is seeking to understand Israel's strategic view of the world. The first is the Jewish loss of their homeland and subsequently 2,000 years of exile and persecutions—following the Jewish revolt against the Roman Empire (70–73 AD). The second, culminating from the first and more recent, the Jewish Holocaust during the World War II.[6]

The link to these historical memories is being reinforced in various events, such as the basic training graduation ceremony of the Israel Defense Forces (IDF) which takes place on *Masada*, the last Jewish stronghold of the Jewish revolt; the young draftees make their oath and promise: "Masada will not fall again." Another example is the organized annual trips of IDF soldiers and high school students to visit the Nazi death camp in Poland design to create a clear link between past and present.

From an early stage of the Jewish immigration to Palestine, conflict with the local Arab community seemed almost inevitable. Therefore, early on questions of security and survival became paramount and shaped the development of the small "*Yishuv*"[7] to statehood. One of the most prominent Zionist activists and ideologists, Vladimir Ze'ev Jabotinsky, published a seminal article in November 1923 following an Arab assault on the Jewish community in Palestine in the years 1920–21. Analyzing the unavoidable and tragic clash of interests between the two sides, Jabotinsky concluded that in the future coexistence between the two communities is possible, but only if the Jews create and sustain what he termed as an "Iron Wall."[8] Indeed some pundits argue that the idea of the "Iron Wall" served ever since as the ideational pillar of Israel's national security concept despite the many changes since Jabotinsky's era.[9]

The first stage of Israel's Independence War 1948 was essentially a violent struggle between the two ethnic-religious communities: Jews and Arabs. The second stage (May 1948) involved a coalition of Arab states versus the Jewish state. From that point onwards, most of Israel's strategic focus was given to the threat posed by an invasion of an Arab state, or a coalition of states.

The 1949 Armistice Agreements were followed by the onset of low-intensity warfare, (constant attacks from across the border by armed Palestinians gangs), it was clear that another high-intensity round would occur.[10] At the same time, the newly established country was confronted with enormous short- and long-term challenges in numerous areas, such as the economy and the absorption of the many recently arrived immigrants.

Against this background, in 1953 Prime Minister David Ben Gurion produced his "18 Points Document." First Ben Gurion laid out a list of assumptions:[11]

- Arab hostility toward the State of Israel will likely continue for decades.
- Israel suffers from chronic inferiority in both territory and demographics.
- The major threat: a potential invasion of Israel by strong conventional forces ending the life of the young Jewish state.
- Israel borders are long and lack natural barriers. However, Israel enjoys the advantage of "interior lines."

- Also, the continuous terror attacks against border-settlements might slowly erode the population's confidence in the young state and endanger its existence in the long run.
- Given the physical asymmetry between Israel and the hostile Arab nations, Israel cannot achieve a decisive military victory to compel the Arabs to give up.

Israelis can only hope that by repeatedly achieving partial victories, they will cause Arab resolve against Israel to dissipate gradually. Those partial victories would, meanwhile, bring temporary respite between rounds of violence.

Ben Gurion concluded that only a series of decisive defeats on the battlefield might convince Arab regimes to accommodate the notion of Israel's permanence. Following his analysis, Israel's strategic tenets as prescribed by Ben Gurion were the following:[12]

- Defend ourselves by ourselves and exhibiting conventional superiority and self-reliance on the battlefield.
- Develop and maintain a "special relationship" with a superpower for the sake of diplomatic and material support—Israel sought an alliance with the French and later on with the United States.
- Obtain technological superiority based on superior education and academic achievements to nurture a thriving industry and economy, the only way to compensate for resource inferiority.
- Possess moral and ideological certainty that Israel's struggle is inherently just, which is critical for mobilizing a society that has to endure a long struggle.
- Nuclear capability—Israel will not get a second chance to correct its initial failures and therefore seeks the ultimate insurance.[13]

The asymmetry in resources also means that Israel cannot maintain a standing army large enough to face all level of threats. Therefore, the major portion of Israel's military has to be a part-time force intended to be mobilized only when fighting intensifies to a level beyond the capability of the standing force. This, in turn, means that the army has to receive advance warning of the need to mobilize extra forces. Furthermore, in order not to cripple the national economy, operations involving such a mobilization must be brief enough to return mobilized soldiers to their civilian lives as soon as possible. The resulting security concept was summed up in three catchwords: Deterrence, Early-Warning, Decision.[14]

Since 1949, Israel's military objectives is to temporarily reduce enemy military capabilities and create deterrence by impressing on that enemy the cost of attacking Israel and the absence of substantive returns for that aggression.[15]

10.2 Who makes Israel's grand strategy?

The Israeli system of government is a parliamentary democracy. The prime minister of Israel is the head of government and leader of a multiparty system, in essence, the most powerful and influential position. The government exercises executive power. Legislative power is vested in the Israeli Parliament, the Knesset, with its 120 members. The leader of the party that receives the largest number of seats in the Knesset and/or has the best chance of forming a coalition is selected by Israel's president to form a coalition and lead it as the country prime minister. Because there is no single party that holds a decisive majority, there are constant disagreements between the parties of the coalition. This method empowers small parties, because if they leave the coalition, the government will fall and the country will have to go to an election.

This state of affairs also allows small and radical parties to pressure and extort the government by threats to leave the coalition and thus to cause its downfall.[16]

Israel's government consists of twenty ministers, too many for sensitive discussion and deliberations of key strategic decisions. These decisions are taken at the Security Cabinet (*HaKabinet HaMedini-Bithoni*), or Ministerial Committee on National Security Affairs (*Va'adat HaSarim Le'Inyanei Bitahon*). This is a smaller forum of ministers chaired by the prime minister, who is in charge of the most critical foreign and defense policy decisions, especially those decisions related to war. The cabinet includes five permanent members and up to five additional members[17] appointed by the prime minister, often according to the coalition makeup.[18]

The political echelon is supported by professional echelon, which includes the attorney general and the national security advisor, and is often joined by the IDF chief of staff and the heads of Israel's Security Agencies: *Mossad* and *Shabak*.

In addition to a formal cabinet, some prime ministers have established a smaller and less formal group that would meet and consult. These forums were called the "The Kitchen Cabinet" (*HaMitbah*).[19]

The professional and state bureaucracy have a substantial influence on matters of security and foreign policy. First and foremost, there is the Defense Ministry who receives the lion's share from Israel's state budget.[20] In addition to overseeing the IDF, the ministry is in charge of major security projects and Israel's military industries. The role of the minister of defense is second only to the prime minister, in fact so important is it that in the past some prime ministers preferred to keep the defense portfolio for themselves and act as both prime minister and defense minister.

Due to the centrality of defense, the IDF and its head, the chief of staff, enjoy a special status in Israel. The IDF chief is the de facto commander of the entire military: Army, Navy, and Airforce and hence substantial power is entrusted to one person. The authority vested in the role combined with the prestige the IDF enjoys in Israeli society explains his enormous influence.[21]

Another military position that enjoys special status is the major-general who heads the Directorate of Military Intelligence (*Agaf HaModi'in*, or Aman). Aman is a separate service like the Air Force, Army, and Navy. Historically its special status stemmed from the importance of "early warning" in the scenario of an Arab invasion order to allow the military to mobilize its reserve to repulse the attackers. For that purpose, heads of Aman were summoned for direct consultations with the prime minister and his cabinet and were given special status. Following the failure of Aman in the Yom Kippur war, a decision was made to diversify Israel's intelligence assessment by establishing assessments departments in a number of other security agencies. Nevertheless, given Aman's vast superiority in quantity and resources, it still dominates the intelligence discourse.[22]

All the heads of the main intelligence agencies report directly to the prime minister and meet him on a regular basis in a forum that consists of the heads of the intelligence agencies (Hebrew initials VERA *Vaadat Rashy Heshrotim*); this forum meets regularly with the prime minister for coordination, deliberation, and synergy. Chaired by the head of *Mossad* it also includes the heads of Aman, Shabak (Israel's internal security service equivalent to MI5 or FBI), the national security advisor and the major-general who is filling the position of military secretary to the prime minister. The heads of these intelligence agencies with the addition of the Ministry of Foreign Affairs will periodically brief the cabinet and provide their annual assessment.

The National Security Staff (*Hamatah leBitachon Leumi*) is a more recent organ that has emerged and gained more influence and importance in recent years. The National Security Staff (NSS) is part of the Prime Minister's Office and reports to him directly about issues related to national security.[23] It was established by Benjamin Netanyahu during his first term as prime minister in 1999 but became influential only after the Second Lebanon War in 2006 as part of the lessons drawn from that war. In 2008 a law establishing its responsibilities was formed and further institutionalized its role and influence.[24]

Much of its influence, however, still depends on who is filling the NSS director's position. Figures like Uzi Arad, retired senior executive in the *Mossad*, or Major-General Yaakov Amidror, former head of IDF Aman Research Division, enjoyed a personal prestige and were close to the ear of the prime minister.[25] Another important agency that has input on unconventional matters is the Israeli Atomic Energy Commission (IAEC). The Commission reports directly to the prime minister and among its official duties are to advise the government of Israel in areas of nuclear policy and in setting priorities in nuclear research and development. One can assume that given its expertise it advises the government in matters related to nuclear deterrence and proliferation of weapons of mass destruction in the region.

We will complete the institutional survey with a few words on Israel's Ministry of Foreign Affairs. Unlike in some Western countries whose foreign offices are relatively highly influential in shaping foreign policy, this has not been the case in Israel. The main reason is the dominant role of the defense establishment. This state of affairs has even become acuter since Prime Minister Netanyahu seems to have little trust in his Foreign Office diplomats and is under the impression they do not represent his policy the way he wishes them to do.[26]

As a free democracy, Israel's security and foreign policy is influnced by several civil society actors including the media, think tanks, academia, NGOs, etc. Some lobbies are very powerful and have a dramatic impact on Israel's politics and policy, one example being the well-organized settlers' movement and their main organization: the Yesha Council (*Mo'etzet Yesha*).[27]

For various reasons, Israel does not have a formal document that states its long-term strategy similar to the US or UK's National Security Strategy (NSS). The lack of a written document is mainly explained by Israel's strategic culture that is prone to improvisation and constant adaptation.[28] In the unending turmoil of the Middle East, even five-year plans are soon overtaken by events, so that many if not most multi-year programs require many changes and adaptations. a favorite IDF slogan has it that "plans are merely a basis for changes." Scholars describe Israel's culture as prone to an improvisational style over a more structured long-term planning.[29] Israel's national strategy could therefore be described as one that embraces emergence over more concrete planning.[30] Other explanations for the lack of such a document suggest that Israeli politicians are trying to keep their freedom of maneuver vis-à-vis critical issues such as settlement with the Palestinians and the need to safe-guard Israel's moves against tough opponents.[31]

Over the years a few attempts to formalize a national doctrine were made, the most notable attempt being that which took place under former Minister of Intelligence and Atomic Energy Dan Meridor, known as the Meridor commission.[32] After two years of intensive work, the commission issued a report in 2006 containing suggestions to update Israel's security doctrine. While the report has never been formally adopted by the government, it did, however, influence Israel's decisions makers at various levels.[33] In 2015, IDF Chief of Staff Gadi Eisenkot published the first IDF strategy document; the document relies on national objectives defined by the Meridor commission.[34]

10.3 Grand strategy goals and values

The Zionist movement's objective was to build a nation and gain Jewish independence. Since this objective was achieved, various belligerents, who seek to destroy it, have challenged the country, therefore, safeguarding its physical existence from an almost unparalleled array of threats has subsequently been its number one priority.

At the same time, Israel's objectives are beyond mere physical survival. Israel aspires to become a leading center for the Jewish people. It is also committed to maintaining democracy, freedom, and equal rights for all of its inhabitants, as stated in its founding document, Israel's Declaration of Independence.[35]

Some critics have pointed to the contradiction between its Jewish character and democratic values. Indeed, unable to separate "church and state" as in other Western democracies, issues of state and religion and settling the tension between the two have always been high on Israel's agenda and have significant daily political ramifications.[36]

Unlike some other powerful countries in the region which, either as leaders of the faith or in the name of a glorious past, are seeking dominance and regional harmony, such as Turkey, Egypt, Iran, or Saudi Arabia, Israel does not have such ambitions. It wants to be left alone outside the regional struggles. However, it does aspire for legitimacy and acceptance by its regional neighbors, as with the larger international community. While some countries, such as Iran, are utterly hostile to Israel, others condition normalizing relations upon Israel's progress in the peace process with the Palestinians. Essentially, a cold peace exists, for example, between some Arab countries and Israel.

Israel's foreign policy objectives are to gain international legitimacy and support without having to pay the currency to the Palestinians or change its policies. The recent world and regional development such as the War on Terror in Europe and the Sunni–Shia divide in the Middle East have helped Israel to advance its agenda, especially its relations with the Arab Sunni states, notably Saudi Arabia, which, like Israel, regards Iran as their main threat in the region.

10.4 Israel's main threats

Decades after Israel's founding fathers formulated the country's main strategic principles, historical developments have made their mark, profoundly changing the country and its surroundings, as new threats have emerged while others diminished (but not disappeared).

The most imminent threat in the first four decades of the country's life was an invasion of one or more Arab armies into Israel. However, since Egypt, the most powerful state on Israel's border, signed a peace deal with Israel (1977), the chances for such a scenario have diminished substantially.

Theoretically, at least, there is indeed no current high-intensity threat by a state army against Israel. Instead, a new threat has emerged, presented by strong nonstate organizations—mainly Hamas and Hezbollah. These organizations control territories next to the Israeli border, which they have used to develop militarily and are capable of launching thousands of missiles and rockets into Israel's civilian rear with strategic consequences.

Until a decade ago, Hamas and Hezbollah were incapable of escalating beyond low-intensity operations, but now that they are supported and supplied by Iran they have reached a capability to launch an attack against Israel's home front. According to intelligence estimates, Hezbollah has about 130,000 missiles and rockets deployed in Lebanon.[37] In addition, as a result of the Syrian civil war, Israel is facing growing Iranian and Hezbollah forces on its Syrian border.[38]

Nevertheless, the strength of these organizations compared to Israel's is limited and none of them are able to pose an existential threat even with Iranian support and sponsorship—although the potential damage they can cause is substantial. Currently, despite not sharing a border with Israel, Iran poses the gravest threat to Israel. Its revolutionary zeal and aspiration of dominance combined with a rich civilization, glorious past, and vast resources qualifies the country as a regional power. Using its revolutionary guard and various proxies, Iran is pushing for dominance throughout the region: in Iraq, Yemen, Lebanon, and Syria; and it is trying to create what seems to be an Iranian sphere all the way from Tehran to the shores of the Mediterranean.

Iran's nuclear program poses a challenge on a different level. Iranian leaders threaten to "wipe [Israel] off the map,"[39] specifying a date[40] and stating that "Israel is a one [nuclear] bomb country."[41] Such threats are taken particularly seriously by Israel.

Iran's geographical distance from Israel and its sheer size have made a possible strike by the Israeli Air Force, similar to the one conducted in Iraq and Syria, very difficult. Moreover, the Iranians have learned the lessons and have taken protective measures including redundancy, concealment, and protection. Not only do they have many installations; they are dispersed all over the country, concealed and buried under deep underground concrete shelters. In 1970, Iran ratified the Non-Proliferation Treaty (NPT), making its nuclear program subject to the IAEA's verification. Since 2011, the IAEA voiced growing concern over possible military dimensions to Iran's nuclear program and released some reports chastising Iran's nuclear program to that effect.[42] Although Iran has signed the Joint Comprehensive Plan of Action

(JCPOA) in 2015, designed to stop its nuclear program, Israel's government does not believe the agreement is enough to curb Iran's ambitions.

Another threat is the unresolved Palestinian issue that has been haunting the Zionist movement and the state of Israel since their foundation. To the uninformed observer there is a natural, rational solution: divide the land as the UN had proposed in 1947.[43] However the reality is more complicated, there are six core issues of dispute: borders, security arrangements, water allocation, Jerusalem, the right of return for refugees, and the Jewish settlements.

So far, both sides have failed to reach an agreement; it seems as if the maximum that an Israeli leader could afford to offer the Palestinians on the core issues is not even approaching the minimum a Palestinian leader could accept.[44]

The reality on the ground imposes its *modus vivendi*. Since the 2005 Israeli withdrawal from Gaza and the Hamas take over, there are three political entities west of the Jordan River: Hamas in Gaza, the Fatah-controlled Palestinian Authority (PA) in the West Bank, and Israel. While Hamas is calling for the complete destruction of Israel and maintains a continuous state of warfare with it, the Palestinian authority speaks of a two-state solution but on Palestinian terms. One can speak of a "division of labor" between Hamas and the PA: Israel is caught in a pincer between the two: while Hamas is using military means, the PA employs diplomatic and pressure.

The PA is challenged by its main opposition Hamas and fearful that the brutal "clean up" by Hamas of the PA in Gaza (2006–7) will reoccur in the West Bank, as Hamas is also popular there.[45] The PA is very much dependent on Israeli support to maintain its rule and therefore maintains good security coordination with Israel's security forces as both sides have an interest to ensure Hamas will not get stronger in the West Bank—the PA territory. Although the PA has officially given up armed struggle, it is engaged in a diplomatic campaign to brand Israel as the new South Africa, calling for Israel to be boycotted. Together with the international Boycott Divestment and Sanction (BDS) movement, it is promoting an agenda to isolate Israel in any possible sphere: economically, politically, culturally, academically, etc.

The PA is also capitalizing on the automatic voting of more than fifty Muslim states in various international organizations to gain status and international recognition, often at Israel's expense. Their most significant achievement was in 2012 when 136 out of 193 states recognized the state of Palestine. The PA's latest international achievement is an admission as a member state to Interpol, despite strong opposition from the US and Israel.[46]

To prevail in an ongoing attritional conflict such as the one Israel has to endure, the cohesiveness and unity of society plays a crucial factor. However, it seems that Israel is becoming more and more a divided society between what Israel's president, Reuven Rivlin, called Israel's "four tribes."

Israel used to be quite a monolithic society,[47] dominated by secular Jews with various degrees of affinity to Jewish tradition and observance. The country transformed in recent decades due to demographic trends into four main sectors, each committed to its own set of values, agenda, and national vision.[48] Israel's wealth distribution, education level, and workforce participation is by and large an outcome of the makeup of this social composition. These groups are the national religious (about 20 percent) whose political tendencies are right wing; they are devout Zionists committed to the building of settlements in the West Bank, a territory they see as part of historical Israel.[49] The ultra-orthodox (about 15 percent), devoted to Jewish Talmudic studies and life, are closed in their communities and are exempt from army service; most of them live on state subsidies and donations from abroad.[50] The third group is the secular and traditional Jews, (about 40 percent) committed to the state and its institutions, they form Israel's middle class and lead Israel's global economy. Lastly the Israeli Arab population (about 20 percent), who are part of the Palestinian people.[51] The Arab minority situation regarding identity and integration is a complex one, in practical terms, they have to overcome a century of animosity and suspicion between Arabs and Jews. These social forces were addressed in a speech delivered by Israel's President Reuven Rivlin in 2015, where he warned of the consequences:

The 'new Israeli order' is not an apocalyptic prophecy. It is the reality... A reality in which Israeli society is comprised of four population sectors, or, if you will, four principal 'tribes', essentially different from each other, and growing closer in size.

We must ask ourselves honestly, what is common to all these population sectors? Whoever is not willing to ask these questions today... is ignoring the most significant challenge put before the Zionist enterprise today.[52]

Rivlin offered a stable partnership between the groups based on a sense of identity and security for each sector with shared responsibility, equity, and equality that will lead to the creation "of a shared Israeli character—a shared 'Israeliness'."

Not everyone shares the same alarmist view as Rivlin vis-à-vis the demographic data.[53] "The tension between forging a unified nation and preserving the riches of multicultural variety should be seen as a fortunate advantage," they say.[54] Some also point to the positive changes in the Arab sector, which consistently shows basic loyalty to the state and its institutions and increasingly adopts middle-class life. The same is true for the ultra-orthodox who out of necessity join in growing numbers the workforce and more enter military service. Whether the pessimist view or the optimist view, these trends in Israeli society present a challenge at least as significant as the security challenges.

10.5 Israel's instruments of grand strategy

To counter the emerging array of threats, Israel has had to adjust its strategy to accommodate the new developments, with a growing emphasis on developing an integrated approach that combines a new and an old set of capabilities. Israeli policymakers and defense planners understand the need for a combination of diplomatic, military, economic, and media means as well as mastering new domains such as cyber.

Israel instruments of hard power include a powerful conventional military highly trained and modernly equipped.[55] Also, Israel's intelligence service such as the *Mossad* and *Shin Beit* are considered top of their kind, with a global reach to pursue various operations that advance Israel's objectives.[56] Its alleged nuclear power adds to its deterrence posture and the perception of power.[57]

Its "special relationship" with the world leading superpower, the US, provides Israel annual security aid of more the $3.5 billion, but more importantly, access to some of the US state of the art military technology, such as the F-35 fighters.[58] Maybe even more important, the US provides Israel with a diplomatic "umbrella" in international forums. Especially crucial is the US veto power that shields Israel from binding anti-Israeli UN Security Council resolutions—mostly related to the Palestinian issue and the occupied territories—and thus provides Israel with a diplomatic "defensive shield."[59]

Regarding "soft power," Israel offers its expertise in many areas such as hi-tech, cybersecurity, water management, agricultural technology, space, and medicine. The recent gas discoveries will further boost its economy and reduce energy dependency, always a point of vulnerability for the country.

Lastly, Israel is involved in various alliances. While not a full member in NATO, Israel has been a member of NATO's Mediterranean Dialogue since December 1994 and more recently opened offices at the North Atlantic Treaty Organization's Brussels headquarters.[60] Besides, Israel conducts various joint military exercises, such as the Blue Flag, a biennial aviation exercise held by the Israeli Air Force aimed at improving international air forces cooperation.[61]

Although Israel is not geographically located in Europe, it is a member of many European transnational federations and frameworks.[62] Israel, for example, enjoys free trade arrangements for industrial goods and was the first non-European country to be associated to the European Union's Framework Program for Research and Technical Development (RTD). Ever since Turkey's policies, under President Recep Tayyip Erdoğan, became hostile to Israel, an Eastern Mediterranean Sea alliance between Greece, Cyprus, and Israel has emerged, which includes energy and security cooporation.[63]

Israel has had to adjust its security doctrine as a result of the new threats it is facing: following decades of conducting limited operations, the IDF is preparing itself for larger and more decisive operations that will involve heavy armored formations maneuvering deep into enemy territory seeking decisive results.[64] In contrast to the past, there is also a new emphasis on defensive measures in the form of substantial investment in systems that can intercept incoming missiles and rockets, most notably the Iron Dome, David Sling, and Arrow system. The IDF has also formed its Homefront command with authority to guide civilians in time of crises, and invested in training first responders that have the expertise to intervene in disaster areas.

The magnitude of the missile threat had also led to increasing US–Israeli military cooperation (and a deviation from the complete self-reliance principle). Once every two years since 2001 the IDF and the United States European Command (US EUCOM) train together to improve cooperation and coordination between the armies. An essential part of the exercise is integrating US Navy warships equipped with the Aegis Ballistic Missile Defense System (Aegis BMD) designed against short- to intermediate-range ballistic missiles, with Israel's missile defense systems further enhancing Israel's missile defense capability.

Another new dimension to Israel's military doctrine is what the IDF calls "MABAM," the Hebrew acronym for the "operations between the wars." A constant string of covert operations designed to gather intelligence while hitting and destroying key assets of Israel's opponents such as Hamas in Gaza but increasingly Hezbollah and Iranian high-value assets in Syria.[65] The cumulative effect of these operations is to weaken the enemy's capabilities and postpone the next war.[66] The powerful presence of Russia in Syria has complicated things, but so far, it seems that Russia, which has good coordination with Israel, has been ignoring Israel's activities.

True to its policy that it cannot shape the political landscape around it but only deter, Israel did not intervene in the Syrian civil war (other than to offer some humanitarian assistance on the border and conduct strikes against weapon transfer to Hezbollah deemed as destined to be used against Israel at some point). However, now that the Assad regime with Iranian backing is securing its victory, the threat of a military Iranian presence on Israel's Syrian border is imminent.

While Israel is using some military means to curb Iranian expansionism in the region, Israel understands that it should not confront alone the Iranian threat and seek alliances.[67] The most pressing issue for Israel and the greatest future threat is the Iranian nuclear program.

In past cases when countries in the region embarked on developing a nuclear program, Israel was determined to stop them either by diplomatic or by military means under what is known as the "Begin Doctrine." It was under Prime Minister Menachem Begin that Israel launched "Operation Opera" in 1981. The Israeli Air Force destroyed Iraq's nuclear power plant Osirak. Following the strike Israel's government issued the following statement: "On no account shall we permit an enemy to develop weapons of mass destruction against the people of Israel. We shall defend the citizens of Israel in good time and with all the means at our disposal."[68] Israel's Prime Minister Menachem Begin said: "This attack will be a precedent for every future government in Israel.... Every future Israeli prime minister will act, in similar circumstances, in the same way."[69]

Proving its serious intentions, Israel's Air Force struck again on September 6, 2007, destroying Syria's nuclear reactor at Deir Ez-Zor, an area later captured by ISIS during the Syrian civil war. The strike, known as "Operation Orchard," was a covert operation and Israel neither confirmed nor denied it. The fact that both countries had an interest in denying the event prevented further escalation.[70] Israel is also determined to stop Iran's nuclear program and is using everything in its arsenal. While, as previously mentioned, a military strike is more complicated and risky in this case, the option is still on the table, although some critics believe it was only meant to pressure the US and the other P5+1 countries signatories of the JCPOA agreement to put more pressure on Iran.[71]

Israel was against the JCPOA—"Iran nuclear deal framework"—that the P5+1 signed with Iran.[72] The main Israeli points of discontent are that the agreement leaves the Iranians a free hand to continue with their subversive actions in the region as well as with their ballistic missiles program. The agreement does not stop the development of nuclear weapons, but merely delays it, while giving the Iranian regime economic support to maintain their hold on Iran and use other means to further their power-projection policies. Israel fears that when the agreement terminates, ten years from the date of signing, the Iranians will be in a better strategic position.

In another historical twist, in contrast to all predictions in November 2016, Donald J. Trump became America's 45th elected president. Trump was against the Iran agreement and true to his position, he withdraw from the deal on May 8, 2018[73] and renewed the economic sanctions on Iran.

The American retrenchment from the area is also worrying Israel, but it is not alone in that worry. However, the US vacuum led its former enemies, the moderate Sunni states such as Saudi Arabia, the United Arab Emirates, and other Gulf states closer to Israel, allowing covert relations to develop following the ancient axiom "the enemy of my enemy is my friend."[74]

Israel on its part, according to various sources, continues to build and prepare its second-strike option to ensure a state of MAD (mutually assured destruction) the day Iran will have a functioning nuclear arsenal.[75] Israel's official nuclear policy is that "Israel will not be the first country to introduce nuclear weapons into the Middle East." The actual policy is known as "*Amimut*"—"Ambiguity" in Hebrew. The policy served Israel well in many ways. First, by implying but denying that it has the capability, Israel has sought to deter by equipping itself with the ultimate "insurance policy." At the same time, other countries in the region are not provoked to develop a similar capacity. Thus, Israel enjoys a nuclear monopoly in the region. Also, by not declaring itself as a nuclear power, Israel is avoiding the scrutiny and occasional criticism directed by the rest of world on acknowledged nuclear powers.

It is believed that Israel had nuclear capability some time towards the end of the 1960s. As of present, Israel has not signed the NPT although, on June 12, 1968, Israel voted in favor of the treaty in the UN General Assembly. Historian Avner Cohen has written that US silent adherence to Israel's nuclear capability is under the condition that Israel would not test its nuclear weapons or announce that it possessed them.[76] According to various sources, Israel's nuclear arsenal consists of two to three hundred bombs.[77] Like more significant nuclear powers, Israel is believed to possess the "triad" means of delivery: aircraft, submarines, and missiles.[78]

Israel has always sought to maintain a conventional superiority, thus signaling that a nuclear option will be considered only as a last result in the most extreme case. In the future, a nuclear standoff between Israel and Iran is not unlikely; however, in such a scenario there is a high probability that other countries such as Saudi Arabia, Egypt, and Turkey will seek to join the nuclear club and the Middle East will enter a nuclear race. Israel hopes for another historical turn: the fall of the theocratic regime in Iran and the rise of a more liberal and peaceful regime that will focus on Iranian internal problems.

On another front, the Palestinian question means that Israel is facing a growing legitimacy problem. Israel's first response was to ignore the BDS movement as a strategic nuisance, since its economic damage is negligible.[79] However, with vocal demonstrations on campuses, growing pressures on artists and performers not to perform in Israel, and the continuous delegitimization of the country, Israel began to fight back, in order to contain such sentiments before they can become a real threat. Funds were allocated, and a new ministry has been established (the Ministry for Strategic Affairs) which works jointly with Israel's Ministry of Foreign Affairs to monitor the BDS and mobilize support groups with which to foil BDS activities.

However, while some groups are promoting a boycott, another development has occurred that has an immense impact on Israel's world position: the country's staggering development of its high-tech industry. Israel has become one the world leading centers for technology and R&D. According to one report, in 2015 the total number of new startups rose to 1,400, of which about 373 companies raised around $3.58 billion.[80] In the twenty-first century, Israel is a leader in several technological areas: information management, biotechnology, nanotechnology, cybersecurity, water desalination, agritech, artificial intelligence, and finally military technology. Israel is therefore in a position to leverage its technological expertise and know-how to gain a better standing in the international diplomatic arena.

Israel's Prime Minister Benjamin Netanyahu explicitly expressed this approach in his 2016 and 2017 UN speeches:

Governments are changing their attitudes towards Israel because they know that Israel can help them protect their peoples, can help them feed them, can help them better their lives.[81]

[S]o many countries around the world have finally woken up to what Israel can do for them.... I am confident that the revolution in Israel's ties with individual nations will ultimately be reflected here in this hall of nations.[82]

This is the prevailing attitude Netanyahu and his government are espousing in the decade since the formation of the second Netanyahu government in 2009. The idea is that Israel will not be a hostage of the Palestinian question, whether or not it will be possible to reach some compromise with the Palestinians, the issue should not and will not hold back Israel's improving international standing. Israel can leverage its economic achievements diplomatically despite differences of opinions with world leaders on issues of Palestine. Of course, not everyone in Israel agrees. Israeli opposition leaders argue that economic interests alone are not sufficient and that the only way Israel can have a fully legitimate standing in the world is if it breaks the current deadlock with the Palestinians.

Nevertheless, the main danger of the unresolved Palestinian situation emanates from splitting Israel's society into two opposing camps: the right and left. The Israeli right believes that there is no hope for a viable compromise with the Palestinians and therefore Israel should annex the territories and never relinquish its security control. The left believes that the effort to find a compromise must persist, and if not, then Israel should unilaterally withdraw, the same way it did in Gaza. Otherwise, it will cease either to be Jewish (in the case of annexation and the provision of full citizens' rights to all Palestinian in the West Bank) or will cease being democratic (in the case that no such rights are granted). In any case, it will not be the Israel that was founded in 1948.[83]

Each side holds an almost unshaken belief that the other side is leading the country to an existential catastrophe, which in turn, can lead to extreme actions such as the assassination of Prime Minister Yitzhak Rabin in 1995. Today there is a shared realization among the Israeli public that while the Palestinian issue will not be brushed away, a compromise cannot be reached in the foreseeable future and until conditions are right, Israelis should stand firm together.[84] In this way, Palestinian rejectionism and defiance is serving to unify Israeli society.

10.6 Conclusion: Is Israel's grand strategy a success?

"Bad newspaper headlines aside, it's been a pretty good century for the Zionists," wrote strategist Edward Luttwak.[85] Israel's grand strategy seems to have served it well. Behind the shield of their "Iron Wall," Israel not only survived but also prospered. In seven decades Israel transformed itself into a powerful state with more than 8.8 million citizens (more than ten times its population in 1948), and with a GDP per capita of close to $38,000 it is ranked among the leading world economies.[86] Relative to other developed economies, it enjoys an outstanding demographic growth and as a result a young, dynamic workforce. Israel maintains one of the strongest militaries in its region; it is allegedly a nuclear power, it is one of only twelve countries which manufactures and launches satellites into space. It enjoys a strong alliance with the US, dubbed as the "special relation," and has good relations with rising powers which are seeking access to its technological and military expertise such as India, Russia, and China. There is no doubt that Israel today is in a much better position of strength than ever before. One well-established news outlet has even ranked Israel as number eight in its most powerful countries list.[87]

One testimony to the success of the Zionist project is Israel's Jewish demographic growth. Although tracking Jewish demographics is elusive and a somewhat tricky business, there is a consensus among the experts that in recent years Israel has become the world-leading Jewish center, both regarding its demography and as a center for Jewish cultural and spiritual life, thus fulfilling the vision of the Zionist founders.[88] According to the *Economist*, 81 percent of the Jews in the world live either in Israel or the US. However, while in Israel they are constantly under potential physical threat from terror and war, their numbers are consistently rising. In contrast, the Jewish community in the US, maybe a victim of their success, is shrinking, mainly because of mixed marriages.[89] The prospect of a declining American Jewish community could have dire consequences for Israel, as the Jewish community plays a significant role in securing American support to Israel.

In essence, Israel's grand strategy has been characterized more by continuity than change, its main pillars of deterrence, nuclear ambiguity, special relations with a great power, and the conventional superiority which enabled her to deflect an attack not having changed since the time of David Ben Gurion.

At this time Israel is facing three major types of threats: a potential nuclear Iran and Iranian (and its proxies) aggression and expansion across the region; the unresolved Palestinian issue that undermines Israel's legitimacy and domestic unity; and the segmentation of its society into four distinct groups each with a different, even opposite, set of values and vision for the state. These are serious threats that have even led some pundits to question whether Israel will continue to exist.[90]

Future studies should look at how a nuclear Iran and regional nuclear proliferation could affect Israel's grand strategy. Another area of research is the relative decline of the US influence in the region versus the growing influence of Russia and China and the long-term effect on Israel's standing in the region.

Lastly, Israel's historical experience has proved that it has the capacity and the resolve to overcome the first two challenges. It is this author's opinion that in the long term it is the third threat, the fragmentation of Israel's society, that poses the greatest danger to Israel. Paradoxically, as long as the external pressures persist, Israel's society will close ranks to face them.

NOTES

1. Herzl (1860–1911) founded the Zionist movement after witnessing anti-Semitism in the Dreyfus affair of 1894. He envisioned a Jewish state fifty years ahead at the first Zionist Congress in 1897. The state of Israel was founded in 1948.
2. Theodor Herzl, *Altneuland*, trans. Shmuel Schnitzer (Israel: Haifa publishing company, 1961), I; Kalmar Zoltán, "Theodor Herzl's National Answer to the Misery of the Jewish People," *European and Regional Studies* vol. 1 (2010): 199, http://www.acta.sapientia.ro/acta-euro/C1-2/eur12-4.pdf
3. Theodor Herzl, *Altneuland*, trans. Dov Kimchi (Israel: Mitzpe publishing, 1939), 295.
4. Alon Silpin, "UN Resolution 181," *The Virtual Library of Center for Educational Technology* [Hebrew], http://lib.cet.ac.il/pages/item.asp?item=10126, accessed December 24, 2017.
5. Michael Ordman, "In Israel, In Order to be a Realist, You Must Believe in Miracles," *Jerusalem Post*, January 26, 2012, http://www.jpost.com/Blogs/Just-Look-At-Us-Now/In-Israel-in-order-to-be-a-realist-you-must-believe-in-miracles-366168
6. Survival is a main theme in Jewish tradition; a famous joke suggests that all Jewish holidays are similar in essence: "They tried to kill us, we won, let's eat!" Read more at https://www.brainyquote.com/quotes/alan_king_533079, accessed December 24, 2017.
7. Name used for the Jewish community during the British Mandate 1917–48.
8. Ze'ev Jabotinsky, "The Iron wall," *Razsviet*, November 4, 1923. The Iron wall is of course a metaphoric idea.
9. Issac Ben Israel, *Israel Defense Doctrine* [Hebrew] (Israel: Modan Publishing, 2013), 13.
10. Main editorial, "On the Second round" [Hebrew] *Davar*, October 27, 1949, http://jpress.org.il/Olive/APA/NLI_Heb/SharedView.Article.aspx?parm=CzRg1ZXxmns NeV487qhwrgvvKCi%2Fwr9kC9bBVU0V4n1bXq0r5rLKrX1yAl0I67MMYw% 3D%3D&mode=image&href=DAV%2f1949%2f10%2f27&page=1&rtl=true
11. David Ben-Gurion, *Uniqueness and Purpose* [Hebrew] (Tel Aviv: Ma'arachot, 1971), 219.
12. This summary is based on Isaac Ben Israel, *Israel Defense Doctrine* [Hebrew] (Ben Shemen, Isr.: Modan Publishing, 2013), 27–84.
13. Although this last point came years later in the 1960s, there is evidence that Ben Gurion was seeking such a capability very early on, see: Binyamin Pinkus, "Atomic Power to Israel's Rescue: French-Israeli Nuclear Cooperation, 1949–1957," *Israel Studies*, vol. 7 (Spring 2002): 110.

14. Yitzchak Ben-Israel, *Israel Defense Doctrine* [Hebrew] (Tel Aviv: Modan & Misrad Habitachon, 2013), 59–67.
15. Efraim Inbar and Eitan Shamir, "'Mowing the Grass': Israel's Strategy for Protracted Intractable Conflict," *Journal of Strategic Studies* 37, no 1 (February 2014): 65–90.
16. Main editorial, "The Process of Assembling a Government" [Hebrew], *Parliament* 40 (March 2003) https://www.idi.org.il/parliaments/11266/11274; Moran Azuly "The Ultra-Orthodox are Threatening: Work in Sabbath? The Government Will Fall" [Hebrew], *YNET*, November 22, 2017, http://www.ynet.co.il/articles/0,7340, L-5046700,00.html
17. The five permanent are: the prime minister, defense minister, treasury minister, foreign minister, minister of justice, minister of public security.
18. "Ministerial Committee on National Security Affairs (Security Cabinet)" [Hebrew], *Israel Prime Minster office web site*, http://www.pmo.gov.il/Secretary/ministersCommissions/Pages/cabinetleumi.aspx, accessed December 24, 2017.
19. The name is originated from Prime Minister's Golda Meir habit to hold such meetings in her private kitchen on Friday evenings in preparations for a full cabinet meeting on Sunday.
20. About 17 percent out of the entire budget. Moti Bassok, "The state's budget for 2017: about 447 billion shekels" [Hebrew], *The Marker*, November 11, 2016, https://www.themarker.com/news/macro/1.3109846
21. Yochai Ofer, "Survey: IDF Receive Public Trust—More Than the Supreme Court" [Hebrew], *NRG*, August 5, 2015, http://www.nrg.co.il/online/1/ART2/714/928.html
22. Moshe Ya'alon, "Intelligence from the Standpoint of the Decision-Maker" [Hebrew], in *the Challenges of the Israeli Intelligence Community*, ed. David Siman-Tov and Shmuel Even (Tel-Aviv: INSS, 2017), 15.
23. *The National Security Staff Law* [Hebrew], 2008 (Israel), law number 2178, https://www.nevo.co.il/Law_word/law14/law-2178.pdf; Uzi Arad and Limor Ben-Har, Hmall, *The Struggle to Establish the "National Security Council" and to Place it on Top* [Hebrew] (Israel: Zmora-Bitan, 2016), 5–6. [Hebrew].
24. *The National Security Staff Law*.
25. Yaakov Amidror served as the head of the NSS 2011–13, and Uzi Arad 2009–11. See "Heads of the NSS in the Past" [Hebrew], *The NSS website*, http://www.nsc.gov.il/he/About-the-Staff/Pages/FormerManagers.aspx, accessed December 27, 2017; Arad and Ben-Har, *The Struggle to Establish the "National Security Council"*, 1.
26. Herb Keinon, "Is Netanyahu Out to Destroy Israel's Foreign Ministry?," *The Jerusalem Post*, September 16, 2016, http://www.jpost.com/Israel-News/The-Netanyahu-led-Foreign-office-is-a-ministry-adrift-467848
27. Mordechai Shapira, "Lobby is Not a Dirty Word" [Hebrew], *The Marker*, November 5, 2017, https://www.themarker.com/opinion/1.4568821
28. Dima Adamsky, *The Culture of Military Innovation: The Impact of Cultural Factors on the Revolution in Military Affairs in Russia, the US, and Israel* (Stanford, CA: Stanford Press, 2010), 117.
29. Charles D. Freilich, *Zion's Dilemmas: How Israel Makes National Security Policy* (Ithaca, NY: Cornell University Press, 2012), 234, 244.

30. Ionut C. Popescu, "Grand Strategy vs. Emergent Strategy in the Conduct of Foreign Policy," *Journal of Strategic Studies* 41, no. 3 (2018): 438–60.
31. Arad and Ben-Har, *The Struggle to Establish the "National Security Council"*, 309.
32. The commission is classified. Some former senior security officials decided to fill this void with their own initiatives, such as Charles D. Freilich, *Israeli National Security: A New Strategy for an Era of Change* (Oxford: Oxford University Press, 2018); or Uzi Arad, *Grand Strategy for Israel: Deliberations and Directions* [Hebrew] (Haifa, Isr.: Samuel Neaman Institute and The Technicon, 2017). Both represents prescriptive views rather than descriptions and analysis of what the strategy is, as this chapter does.
33. Arad and Ben-Har, *The Struggle to Establish the "National Security Council"*, 307–8.
34. "IDF Strategy," August 2015.
35. "Proclamation of Independence," https://www.knesset.gov.il/docs/eng/megilat_eng.htm, accessed April 20, 2018.
36. Yehezkel Dror, *Israeli statecraft: National Security Challenges and Responses* (Abingdon, UK: Routledge, 2011), 13.
37. Eado Hecht and Eitan Shamir, "The Case for Israeli Ground Forces," *Survival* 58, no. 5 (October–November 2016): 123–48.
38. Shaul Shay, "Simulation—the Third Lebanon War (Prevention, Warning, Home Front and Subservience)" [Hebrew], *IDC*, Special Publication for the Herzlya Conference of 2015, last modified June 7, 2015, http://www.herzliyaconference.org/_Uploads/dbsAttachedFiles/SimulasionShaulShay2015.pdf
39. Nazila Fathi, "Wipe Israel 'Off the Map' Iranian Says," *The New York Times*, October 27, 2005, http://www.nytimes.com/2005/10/27/world/africa/wipe-israel-off-the-map-iranian-says.html
40. Toi Staff, "Khamenei: Israel won't Survive Next 25 Years," *The Times of Israel*, September 9, 2015, https://www.timesofisrael.com/khamenei-israel-wont-survive-next-25-years/
41. Saira Khan, *Iran and Nuclear Weapons: Protracted Conflict and Proliferation* (Abingdon, UK: Routledge, 2009), 86.
42. *Reuters*, "UN Nuclear Watchdog Sets Up 'Iran Task Force'," *The Jerusalem Post*, August 29, 2012, http://www.jpost.com/Breaking-News/UN-nuclear-watchdog-sets-up-Iran-Task-Force
43. Elad Ben-Dror, "How the United Nations Intended to Implement the Partition Plan: The Handbook Drawn up by the Secretariat for the Members of the United Nations Palestine Commission," *Middle Eastern Studies* 43, no. 6 (November): 997–1008.
44. Various attempts to reach an agreement ended with no results: Oslo negotiations (1993), Clinton's Framework (2000), Taba (2001), PM E. Olmert and President M. Abbas talks (2006–8).
45. Ohad Hemo and Munis Zahalka, "Hamas is Getting Stronger in the West Bank" [Hebrew], *MAKO*, September 15, 2014, http://www.mako.co.il/news-channel2/Channel-2-Newscast-q3_2014/Article-aa80615d2ca7841004.htm
46. "General Assembly Votes Overwhelmingly to Accord Palestine 'Non-Member Observer State' Status in United Nations," UN.org, November 29, 2012, https://

www.un.org/press/en/2012/ga11317.doc.htm; Peter Beaumont, "Interpol Votes to Admit Palestine as Full Member," *The Guardian*, September 27, 2017, https://www.theguardian.com/world/2017/sep/27/interpol-votes-to-admit-palestine-as-full-member

47. In terms of its Jewish population, Arabs historically made about 20 percent of the entire population.
48. There are other division lines in Israeli society such as between Ashkenazi and Sephardi Jews. However, if one examines cross-group marriages as a measure of the divide, while between the above marriage rates are almost 50 percent, between the four groups they are much less than 10 percent.
49. Tamar Hermann, *Religious? Nationalist!—The National Religious Camp in Israel* [Hebrew] (Israel: The Israel Democracy Institute, 2014), https://www.idi.org.il/media/6197/the_national_religious_sector_book.pdf
50. Michal Margalit, Omri Efraim, and Yaron Druckman, "In 50 Years every Third Israeli—Ultra Orthodox" [Hebrew], *YNET*, December 29, 2016, https://www.ynet.co.il/articles/0,7340,L-4900257,00.html
51. "Press Release of the Central Bureau of Statistics in Honor of the 69th Israeli Independence Day" CBS.gov, May 1, 2017, http://www.cbs.gov.il/reader/newhodaot/hodaa_template.html?hodaa=201711113
52. "President Reuven Rivlin Address to the 15th Annual Herzliya Conference," http://www.president.gov.il/English/ThePresident/Speeches/Pages/news_070615_01.aspx
53. Dror, *Israeli Statecraft*, 13.
54. Gershon Hacohen, "Israeli Identity: What Has Changed This Year?," *BESA Center Perspectives*, no. 599 (September 2017), https://besacenter.org/perspectives-papers/israeli-identity/
55. Jeremy Bender, "Ranked: The World's 20 Strongest Militaries," *Business Insider*, March 3, 2015, http://www.businessinsider.com/these-are-the-worlds-20-strongest-militaries-ranked-2015-9/#20-canada-1
56. Yossi Melman, "Global Warming: Israeli Intelligence Changes the Order of Priorities" [Hebrew], *Forbes Israel*, November 25, 2015, http://www.forbes.co.il/news/new.aspx?Pn6VQ=EG&0r9VQ=EGJLK
57. Judah Ari Gross, "In Leaked Emails, Colin Powell Says Israel Has 200 Nukes," *The Times of Israel*, September 15, 2016, https://www.timesofisrael.com/in-leaked-emails-colin-powell-says-israel-has-200-nukes/
58. Yaniv Kubovich, "Israel Air Force Declares First F-35 Squadron Operational," *Haaretz*, December 7, 2017, https://www.haaretz.com/israel-news/.premium-1.827177
59. Alex Lockie, "Here's Why the US and Israel are Such Close Allies," *Business Insider*, February 18, 2017, http://www.businessinsider.com/us-israel-allies-2017-2
60. "Israel's Status at NATO Headquarters Gets an Upgrade," *YNET*, May 7, 2016, https://www.ynetnews.com/articles/0,7340,L-4800276,00.html.
61. Judah Ari Gross, "IDF's Largest-Ever Aerial Exercise Takes Off, With India on Board," *The Times of Israel*, November 5, 2017, https://www.timesofisrael.com/idf-kicks-off-its-largest-ever-international-aerial-exercise/
62. Barak Ravid and Haaretz Correspondent, "EU Unanimously Upgrades Israel Ties, Turning Aside PA Objection," *Haaretz*, June 17, 2008, https://www.haaretz.com/news/eu-unanimously-upgrades-israel-ties-turning-aside-pa-objections-1.247988

63. Zenonas Tziarras, "Israel-Cyprus-Greece: a 'Comfortable' QuasiAlliance," *Mediterranean Politics* 21, no. 3 (February 2016): 1–2.
64. IDF Chief of the General Staff, "IDF Strategy" [English], July 2016, 36–37, 20–21, https://www.idfblog.com/s/Desktop/IDF%20Strategy.pdf
65. Yasser Okbi, "Reports: Israeli Aircraft Struck An Iranian Base Outside Damascus," *Jerusalem Post*, December 2, 2017, https://www.jpost.com/Arab-Israeli-Conflict/Reports-Israeli-aircraft-struck-an-Iranian-base-outside-Damascus-515789
66. "IDF Strategy," 2016, 28–31.
67. Major-General Yair Golan, "Fundamentals of IDF Operational Doctrine and Force Structure" [Hebrew] (Lecture, The Jerusalem Institute for Strategic Studies (JISS), Jerusalem, December 27, 2017), http://jiss.org.il/en/jiss-conference-idf-ready-next-war/
68. "Israeli and Iraqi Statements on Raid on Nuclear Plant," *The New York Times*, June 9, 1981, https://www.nytimes.com/1981/06/09/world/israeli-and-iraqi-statements-on-raid-on-nuclear-plant.html
69. Leonard S. Spector and Avner Cohen, "Israel's Airstrike on Syria's Reactor: Implications for the Nonproliferation Regime," *Arms Control Today*, vol. 38 (July–August 2008): 15–21.
70. On March 2018 Israel admitted it carried the attack. Stephen Farrell, "Israel Admits Bombing Suspected Syrian Nuclear Reactor in 2007, Warns Iran," *Reuters*, March 20, 2018, https://www.reuters.com/article/us-israel-syria-nuclear/israel-admits-bombing-suspected-syrian-nuclear-reactor-in-2007-warns-iran-idUSKBN1GX09K
71. Tamar Ish-Shalom, "Senior CNN Commentator: 'Israel Does Not Really Want to Attack Iran'" [Hebrew], *Channel 10*, July 30, 2012, http://10tv.nana10.co.il/Article/?ArticleID=914985
72. Dan Margalit, "The Iranian Threat: How to Fight the Dangerous Compromise" [Hebrew], *Israel Today*, February 12, 2015, http://www.israelhayom.co.il/article/258281
73. Mark Landler, "Trump Abandons Iran Nuclear Deal As he Long Scorned", *New York Times*, May 08, 2018, https://www.nytimes.com/2018/05/08/world/middleeast/trump-iran-nuclear-deal.html
74. See chapter on Saudi Grand Strategy; Oren Liebermann, "How a Mutual Enemy is Changing Israel-Saudi Relations," *CNN*, November 26, 2017, http://edition.cnn.com/2017/11/25/middleeast/israel-saudi-relations/index.html
75. Gross, "In Leaked Emails."
76. Douglas Birch and R. Jeffrey Smith, "Israel's Worst-Kept Secret," *The Atlantic*, September 16, 2014, https://www.theatlantic.com/international/archive/2014/09/israel-nuclear-weapons-secret-united-states/380237/
77. Gross, "In Leaked Emails."
78. P. K. Ghosh, "Emerging Trends in the Nuclear Triad," *Strategic Analysis* 25, no. 2 (July 2008): 264.
79. Ariel Kahane, "Israel is Convinced: That the Boycott Efforts Against Israel Have Failed" [Hebrew], *NRG*, March 6, 2014, http://www.nrg.co.il/online/1/ART2/563/922.html
80. Geek time and Zirra, "Annual Report 2015: Startups and Venture Capital in Israel," *Geek Time*, January 11, 2016, https://www.geektime.com/2016/01/11/annual-report-2015-startups-and-venture-capital-in-israel/

81. "Full text of Netanyahu's speech at 2016 UN General Assembly," *The Times of Israel*, September 22, 2016, https://www.timesofisrael.com/netanyahus-full-remarks-at-un-general-assembly/
82. "Full Text: Netanyahu's Address to UN General Assembly," *Haaretz*, September 19, 2017, https://www.haaretz.com/israel-news/1.813336
83. See: Micah Goodman, *Catch 67* [Hebrew] (Israel: Kinneret Zmora-Bitan Dvir, 2017).
84. Israelis therefore speak about "conflict management" versus "conflict resolution."
85. Edward N. Luttwak, "Why Obama, Kerry, Abbas, Hamas, BDS, AND Hezbollah Will All Go Poof!," *Tablet*, July 10, 2014, http://www.tabletmag.com/jewish-news-and-politics/178540/luttwak-zionism-history
86. "OECD's Selected Data indicators for Israel," Oecd.org, https://data.oecd.org/israel.htm
87. "Power Rankings," *US News*, accessed December 29, 2017, https://www.usnews.com/news/best-countries/power-full-list
88. "Alive and Well," *The Economist*, July 28, 2012, https://www.economist.com/node/21559464
89. Over half of U.S Jews married outside the Jewish religion in 2013. See Itzchak Tessler, "In the Next Generation, US Jews Will Disappear," *YNET*, February 15, 2014, https://www.ynetnews.com/articles/0,7340,L-4488219,00.html. Israel had become the home of the largest Jewish community, transcending the US Jewish community, in the early 2000s. See Sergio DellaPergola, *World Jewish Population: 2016* (New York: the Berman Jewish DataBank, 2017), 30.
90. For example, Victor Davis Hanson, "Can Israel Survive?," *The National Review*, January 29, 2015, http://www.nationalreview.com/article/412951/can-israel-survive-victor-davis-hanson ; Gregg Carlstrom, *How Long Will Israel Survive? The Threat from Within* (Oxford: Oxford University Press, 2017).

11 Saudi Arabia

GHAIDAA HETOU

The Kingdom of Saudi Arabia signed an historic arms deal with the United States in May of 2017 during President Donald Trump's first presidential state visit after his inauguration. The US–Saudi arms package has the potential of surpassing $470 billion over a decade in boosting the Kingdom's military and defense capabilities. Since 1945, such bilateral defense agreements between the United States and the Kingdom of Saudi Arabia were a defining hallmark of what scholars termed the "oil for security" alliance.[1] Implied in this characterization is that Saudi Arabia's foreign policy disposition is orientated towards accommodating US interests in the Middle East and North Africa (MENA).

Considering the contemporary landscape of regional threats, however, and the possible onset of a multipolar order, it is crucial to recognize that the US–Saudi alliance is entering a new era. Recent developments prompting this shift include greater US self-sufficiency in oil and gas production, lower oil prices, Iran's accelerated regional influence, transnational terrorism, and the increasing assertiveness of Russia and China in the Gulf Cooperation Council (GCC) states defense market. As a result, there is a recognizable Saudi agency crafting a purposeful regional foreign policy in the shadow of the United States' security umbrella. Yet, such strategic intent in Saudi foreign policy–making, I argue, is not an ad hoc reaction to current changing regional security threats, but rather a purposeful response to a sequence of aggregated domestic and regional factors dating from 1979, shaping a Saudi grand strategy in pursuit of security. In this chapter I therefore address the following questions: How did the evolving nature of regional threat and alliance formations since 1979 shape Saudi Arabia's regional strategic interests? What are the main domestic factors shaping Saudi Arabia's grand strategy? How is grand strategy formulated in the Saudi Kingdom? And what are Saudi Arabia's strategic objectives post-2011?

Grand strategy is a geopolitical quest to achieve a state's national interests. A grand strategy combines the tools of statecraft to devise a purposeful foreign policy by balancing military, economic and diplomatic means, and desired strategic ends. As discussed extensively in the introductory chapter, the International Relations' holistic approach to grand strategy explains strategic statecraft in its varies manifestations: military, diplomatic, social, and economic. Edward Luttwak conceptualized grand strategy as an interaction between military and economic strengths with the state's intelligence apparatuses and diplomacy to achieve certain outcomes or objectives. Luttwak's definition implies a relational foundation for this conception, not with a specified enemy however, but with other states with their own grand strategies.[2] I argue that Luttwak's grand strategy definition is most suitable for middle power states like Saudi Arabia, which have the economic and military capabilities to shape their environment, yet face competition, if not direct challenges, from other regional powers. While all developing states, as Walt[3] notes, have the autonomous capacity for foreign policy–making, Hussein contends that periodic asymmetric codependency confines the foreign policy of developing nations to a state of semi-autonomy.[4] Within this framework, middle power states such as Saudi Arabia, according to Bronson, have a better chance at autonomous foreign policy–making due to their economic leverage.[5] In this chapter I illustrate that Saudi Arabia is attempting to transition from patron–client relation with the United States, to a *threat-balancing*[6] strategy in what resembles a *deterrence network* with regional and international powers.

It is important to differentiate between how desired strategic ends are shaped in the MENA context, and how middle power states' behavior in MENA consistently aims at achieving security. Telhami and Barnett contend that, initially, material interests do not exclusively define the national interests of MENA states, and that ideational, symbolic, and legitimacy-driven concerns also influence national interests, and hence the strategic dimensions of foreign policy–making.[7] As such, I argue that a multicausal and contextual approach is required in order to understand what shapes and influences Saudi Arabia's grand strategy.

In the following section, I detail the conceptual framework guiding this multilevel approach, from strategic culture and Saudi institutions and regional threat perception, to alliance formation, and strategic hedging. Then, in the following section I offer an overview of Saudi "means and ends" including military, economic and social instruments, and its strategic objectives in the aftermath of the so-called Arab Spring. Then I discuss the factors shaping Saudi grand strategy: threat perception and threat assessment; who makes decisions and how; alliance formations; interests and ideology; building consensus; and the mobilization of economic, military, and social power. I then illustrate the dynamics of these factors in a case study on the fractured GCC, using elite interviews with Saudi officials, academics, and journalists combined with primary and secondary sources in English and Arabic.

11.1 A conceptual framework

State-level variables shaping foreign policy narratives within the evolutionary context of nascent MENA statehood are necessarily culturally bound. In the absence of influential public policy institutions in MENA in general and in Saudi Arabia specifically,[8] national culture forms the rationale for security policy and strategic thinking. Strategic culture is composed of cumulative historical memory,[9] enduring nation-specific narratives and modes of thinking, and accumulated beliefs about security, geographic, and material limitations. Collectively, this strategic culture is articulated through a specific security and military vision.[10]

Jack Snyder coined the concept of strategic culture. He defined it as the "sum total of ideals, conditional emotional responses, and patterns of habitual behavior that the members of the nation's strategic community have acquired through instructions or imitation and share with each other with regards to strategy."[11] Snyder then analyzed Soviet nuclear strategic thought, but the relevance of this concept endures. Snyder stressed the socialization aspect of decision makers to embrace and embody a specific optic of foreign policy orientation. His definition of the term accounts for the elasticity inherent in strategic culture, as deep-rooted beliefs might evolve and adjust to technical or environmental changes.

Saudi Arabia's foreign policy and strategic importance has been researched and analyzed predominantly through the prism of oil and Islam.[12] Robert Mason added to this pair the role of substate identities such as tribal, ethnic, and class groups in Saudi foreign policy–making.[13] Strategic culture, along with Saudi tribal institutions, together capture the intricacies of domestic factors shaping Saudi grand strategy, within which oil and Islam gained conventional preeminence.

11.2 The Saudi historical memory and strategic culture

The historical evolution of the three Saudi states, over two and a half centuries, carries significant historical memory, imprinting Saudi national identity with a sense of exceptionalism and exclusiveness. The Emirate of Dariyah began in 1744, ending with the Saud–Ottoman war in 1818. The second Saudi state Emirate of Najd lasted from 1882 to 1891. A vast military campaign started in 1902 to capture and unify the four regions in the Arabian Peninsula: Hijaz, Najd, al-Ahsa, and Asir, and establish the third Saudi state in 1932. The explicitly consistent *raison d'état* of Saudi policy, as far as the execution of strategy, has been evident since the founding days of the third kingdom. Saudi Arabia's first army, established in 1902, was called "Ikhwan" (Brethren). It was composed of chosen nomadic tribesmen, and entrusted with converting nomadic tribes on the Arabian Peninsula to the literal interpretation of

Islam of Ibn Saud/Shaikh Mohammad bin Abdul al-Wahhab's Salafism. The loyalist tribes among the Ikhwan later became the foundation for Saudi Arabia's National Guard.[14]

An enduring national characteristic stemming from this historical evolution of the Saudi state is the sense of exceptionalism: a declaration that traditional Salafism is the purist version of Sunni Islam for the Muslim Ummah, and that the descendants of Al Saud stand at the apex of a tribal coalition hierarchy on the Arabian Peninsula. Salafism and Al Saud's legacy have shaped an exclusive national character, with suprastate implications. The legitimacy of the Saudi state has been historically derived from its custodianship of the two holy mosques, and being the standard barrier of Sunni Islam. Furthermore, Saudi exceptionalism enriched Saudi strategic culture with a sense of mission and direction, which became part of a deliberate religiously infused Saudi regional strategy of social power projection; a classic intersection of religion and realpolitik. The absolute monarchy of Saudi Arabia does have an increasingly proactive consultative body, the "Majlis al-Shura." But it is devoid of a functioning Parliament or constitution. This political configuration allows for complete control by a small inner circle of Saudi royals over major domestic and foreign policy. This particular political system personified state security in the royal personnel's own security and survival as the main decision-making circle. Loyalty that engenders trust is therefore the main currency for gaining access and influence.

The promotion of traditional Salafism, which purposefully only allows the king or ruler to announce Jihad, was a reactive policy in the Saudi Kingdom after the success of the Iranian Islamic revolution in February 1979, and the subsequent Jihadist attack on Mecca in November 1979. The direction of causal linkages between some domestic and external factors are more obscure than others, as some traits in Saudi strategic culture like the Saudi policy of promoting Salafism (era of al-Sahwa), was a second-order effect stemming from the overthrow of Iran's shah and the successful Islamic revolution in 1979. While Iran began promoting its revolutionary anti-imperial Shia Islam as a political agenda, the Saudi authorities needed to showcase an Islamized national profile to counter Iran's anti-monarchy propaganda. Current Saudi authority still concurs that allowing for the social practice of Salafism as an extreme form of religiosity is a requisite for domestic stability, but will not be officially promoted as it was in the past. Saudi officials point to how Egypt under President Abdel Fattah al-Sisi tamed Islamists communities by tolerating religious and political freedoms for traditional Salafists, such as the Nour Party, within a hyper-securitized environment. Despite permission being granted to traditional Salafists to practice their variant of Islam, both Saudi Arabia and Egypt's current leadership, along with the UAE, are working to eradicate the influence of the Muslim Brotherhood and Salafi Jihadist thought in the region.

Rapid urban development in Saudi Arabia after the oil discoveries in the 1940s and 1950s linked national identity to the expanding oil wealth. It included the development of modern infrastructure, Western commercial centers, housing, in addition to educational institutions and the growth of international commerce. National projects—becoming the number one international wheat exporter in the 1980s, or building the highest skyscrapers, which were mostly trophy projects—are now transitioning into national sustainable investments such as advancing petrochemical industries and renewable energy resources. King Salman bin Abdul Aziz and his son the Crown Prince Mohammad bin Salman, the new line of Saudi leadership since 2015, are propelling a post-oil economy modernization agenda (Vision 2030), in addition to an extensive and accelerated social liberalization initiative. The accelerated liberalization has the potential to unify the altra conservative and exasperate domestic unrest. Saudi officials however contend that this new Saudi leadership is the necessary catalyst to opening the Kingdom's domestic realm to more religious and social freedoms, in essence rolling back the post-1979 pro al-Sahwa national policy, in addition to opening Saudi Arabia's foreign policy orientation to diverse economic and security partnerships.

11.3 The new threat environment

For the Saudi leadership, this domestic context coincides with a series of external factors—notably, the dominant regional alliance formations, their threat perception and the existent and potential forms of conflict. Stephen Walt points out that Middle Eastern states are prone to balance against a threat, hence threat perception and ideological solidarity play a role in these states' alignment choices.[15] Iran, for example, after the Islamic revolution in 1979, represented a consistent ideological and physical threat to the Kingdom. Iran's Islamic revolution in 1978–79 was a significant historical turning point infusing Saudi Arabia's regional threat perception with a lasting legacy. More important than simply losing an ally in Shah Mohamed Riza Pahlavi, the Islamic revolution in Iran challenged Saudi Islamic authority by pointing out Saudi Arabia's alleged irreconcilable position: of purporting to be a monarchy leading the Muslim Ummah while simultaneously being a Western "puppet." Iran aggressively expounded on this alleged Saudi hypocrisy, and Saudi Arabia has remained defensive on this issue ever since.

Yet Saudi Arabia seized an opportunity to regain legitimacy, Islamic authority—and regional leadership—by reviving social ultra-conservatism and utilizing Salafism during the Soviet invasion of Afghanistan 1980–88, while Iran was engaged in a war with Iraq. According to the Saudi leadership, since 1979 Iran has continued to employ traditional and nonconventional asymmetric methods in exporting its Islamic revolution regionally in a revisionist anti-West strategy. Iran continued to employ state capabilities with direct assistance from nonstate actors, duplicating the experience with Hezbollah in Iraq, Yemen, and Syria. After the events of 9/11, reinforced by the transnational threat of Radical Islamist organizations, the Kingdom could not afford to confront Iran with an Islamized counter-message. That is because the international community has willingly associated Saudi Arabia with terrorist funding and the "spread of Wahhabism." Its leadership now believes that "we need to open our communities and spread a message of moderate Islam and coexistence to corner the Islamists message of Iran," as explained by a Saudi official in an interview in 2017.

The regional threat environment is not confined with the threat posed by Iran. Ideological solidarities are shifting across MENA, even among the Gulf monarchies, which seem well-suited to forming a powerful regional alliance given their shared geopolitical challenges, shared cultural legacies and comparable resource riches. The Gulf States are the focus of American, Russian, and Chinese competition over territory, defense markets, and resources, while also contending with regional aspirations of Turkey and Iran. Yet there are intra-GCC disagreements on democratization, political Islam, investment strategies, and regional threat priorities that undermine a sense of solidarity among an otherwise homogenous group of states. The Saudi leadership currently considers Bahrain and UAE as the functioning core of the GCC and part of its overall deterrence network strategy in the region. It remains committed to the possibility of reviving a united front with Qatar, Kuwait, and Oman in the future. But none currently exists.

What once resembled a Cold War demarcation line between the pro-Soviet and pro-Western blocks in MENA during the Cold War era, is now a fractured and shifting environment of evolving, sometimes situational, alignment formations. The politically destabilizing uprisings of the Arab Spring, coupled with a perceived US retrenchment from the region, prompted Saudi Arabia's leadership to transition from the old "oil for security" relationship to one of balancing against threats through the formation of a regional deterrence network aimed primarily against Iran. Saudi Arabia's war in Yemen constitutes a forward projection of Saudi military power in part to exert influence on both sides of Bab al-Mandeb in the southeast, including Djibouti and Northern Somalia (Somaliland and Puntland). Furthermore, the joint mitliary and defense agreements with Sudan is an extension of the Saudi defense strategy of projecting influence over both Red Sea shore lines and the horn of Africa.

Egypt and Iraq are crucial gateways for Saudi leadership in the region and strengthening relations with Mr Haidar al-Abadi and General al-Sisi is of strategic importance to the Kingdom. When interviewed, an anonymous Saudi official was asked about Pakistan's close economic relations with China and military collaboration with Russia since 2015. He smiled and said "we don't blame them because we are doing the same, we are also diversifying our relations." Saudi Arabia has indeed been strategically hedging since 2015 by diversifying its relations with competing great powers. It signed $65 billion worth of contracts with China in 2017 and is in negotiation to join China's largest Eurasia economic integration project, the One Belt, One Road Initiative (BRI). Saudi Arabia also signed landmark defense and investment deals with Russia in October 2017. These included agreements to purchase anti-aircraft missiles, Kornet anti-tank guided missile systems, and multiple rocket launchers. An observation common to Saudis interviewed on their reaction to King Salman's visit to Russia was: "Unlike the US, the Russians do not put conditions on use with regards to military and defense contracts." Another was that "The more great powers invest in Saudi Arabia, the more secure we will be."

Saudi Arabia is indeed entering a new security era. It is meticulously constructing a deterrence network intended to counter and contain the Iranian axis. The Saudis believe that gaining leverage with Russia and China is as important as keeping pace with US policy and preferences in the region in an emerging global order and dynamic balance of threat environment. Nonetheless, Saudi Arabia is proving yet again to be a valued partner in a larger US containment and deterrence strategy for the current Trump administration that includes Iran, China, and Russia. Nothing has invigorated the new Saudi leadership and bolstered its strategic outlook in recent years more than President Donald Trump's determination to confront Iran, breaking with President Barack Obama's policy, and reconfirming the United States resolve to strengthen its alliances with traditional allies in the MENA region. As the following sections will demonstrate, however, there is an inherent risk in the Saudi grand strategy of overtaxing its means and underdelivering on its stated objectives.

11.4 The making of grand strategy

Saudi Arabia's grand strategy is not an explicit document, but rather is reflected in a consistent foreign policy trajectory that has operated in support of US foreign policy in the region since the success of the Islamic revolution in Iran in 1979. Saudi Arabia worked in tandem with the United States to stem the danger of Iran's Islamic revolution and its proxies in the region throughout the Iran–Iraq war (1980–88), Afghan–Soviet war (1979–88), and the economic sanctions on Iran's nuclear program (2003–11). Saudi Arabia's active foreign policy after 2011 demonstrated agency and an ability to sustain an Iran deterrence strategy despite the fundamental shift in US foreign policy during the Obama administration.

The decision-making hierarchy in the Saudi Kingdom has been rather well defined since 2015. The older generation of sons of King Abdul Aziz Al Saud, the founder of the third Saudi state, many of whom were at an advanced age at the time of their ascendance to the throne, have maintained a close circle of advisors who were the de facto decision makers. King Salman, the last of King Abdul Aziz's sons to assume the throne in 2015, has deliberately broken this mold and consolidated power with his son Crown Prince Mohammad bin Salman. The young Saudi leadership is at the helm of decision-making, with a concentrated executive power that has direct jurisdiction over the legislative and judicial branches of government, as well as foreign policy–making. Crown Prince Mohammad bin Salman, despite numerous challenges, is determined to single-handedly reform Saudi Arabia's social and economic policy and enhance the Kingdom's regional standing. He has brought the advice and consultation of Mohammad bin Zaid Al Nahayan, the Crown Prince of Abu Dhabi and Deputy Supreme Commander of the UAE Armed Forces, into the inner decision-making circle. The Saudi–UAE strategic partnership extends beyond war coalition in Yemen, to coordination with regards to Libya, Sudan, and Syria, despite UAE close business ties with Iran.

11.5 Saudi grand strategy: The means and ends

Saudi Arabia's grand strategy is intended to secure its position as a regional middle power and enhance its security and influence in MENA through its economic, military, and social instruments. This grand strategy has four objectives: First, containing Iran and its proxies by balancing these threats through a regional deterrence network, utilizing Saudi Arabia's vast economic, social, and military means; second, expanding Saudi Arabia's religious leverage and reformed Sunni authority in the Islamic world, by undermining competing legitimacy-seeking groups such as Iran, the Muslim Brotherhood, and Salafi Jihadists groups; third, maintaining high returns on investment in the oil and petrochemical sector; and fourth, gaining leverage and diversifying its oil/security/defense nexus with China and Russia, while maintaining strategic relations with the United States and Europe.[16] The following is a detailed account of Saudi Arabia's economic, military, and social forms of power, highlighting the interesting balance of Saudi resources, by virtue of its relatively small, high-tech military, and extensive economic and diplomatic influence.

11.5.1 SAUDI ECONOMIC POWER

Saudi Arabia controls 18 percent of the world's proven petroleum reserves and is the largest exporter of petroleum, which accounts for 92.5 percent of Saudi government revenues.[17] It had a population of 32.4 million and GDP growth of 1.6 percent. Its GDP per capita stood at $20,028 in 2016, and the official unemployment rate was between 10 and 15 percent, with inflation (CPI) at 3.5 percent, and foreign direct investment (FDI) inflow of $7.45 billion (2016).[18] Saudi Arabia is the largest economy in the Arab world and the only G20 member in the region. Saudi Arabia's trade balance steadily declined between 2013 and 2015 but has gradually rebounded after the spring of 2016, according to Saudi Arabia's Monetary Agency (SAMA).

Grand strategy and national security scholars have emphasized the crucial role of economic instruments in statecraft. Anticipating the primacy of economic power in grand strategy, Luttwark coined the term "geoeconomics" stating that "Geoeconomics...the best term I can think of to describe the admixture of the logic of conflict with the method of commerce—or as Clausewitz would have written, the logic of war in the grammar of commerce."[19] Economic instruments such as national oil and gas corporations and state-owned enterprises (SOEs), sovereign wealth funds (SWFs) and state-controlled banks are particularly powerful instruments of grand strategy in nondemocratic states because of the consolidated executive power and the absence of legislative checks and balances.[20]

Integrating Saudi economic power within the deterrence network in the service of the Kingdom's grand strategy pulled its economic and financial capabilities in numerous directions. The Kingdom is offering for the first time to roll out in 2020 an IPO for ARAMCO; the national Saudi oil conglomerate, and has confirmed the role of a third party audit to verify reserves. Although the percentage share offered is only 5 percent (2018), the United States NYC stock exchange, and China are competing to be the primary contenders for these shares. While economic relations and access to the Saudi market have been historically used by the Saudis as an incentive to improve relations, Saudi economic power has also been used to coerce regional states and reign them back into the Saudi sphere of influence. Egypt felt the economic wrath of Saudi displeasure numerous times in the last several years, including when it stopped the crucial monthly shipment of petroleum in October of 2016 after Egypt opposed a Saudi-supported proposal regarding Syria and voted for Russia's resolution at the UN. On the international front, Saudi Arabia allegedly tried initially to pressure US oil shell producers out of their potential market share by increasing output, thereby lowering oil prices in order to render shell oil extraction unprofitable. This Saudi strategy succeeded only partially because the fluctuation of the oil market post-2015 and the return of Iran's oil share in 2016 challenged Saudi Arabia's own financial return on its oil market share.

In fact the Saudi capacity to maneuver global oil production levels through OPEC is partially constrained by Russian interests, US oil production capacity, and general lower oil prices. Meanwhile, the $2 trillion dollars 2030 Vision and the $500 billion price tag for Neom—a proposed transnational city and economic zone—have yet to generate precise return on investment benchmarks for investors to generate sustained interest.[21]

Crown Prince Mohammad bin Salman's 2030 Vision[22] promised to diversify the Saudi economy by expanding the non-oil and Saudi private sectors. Numerous non-oil sectors have seen gradual growth in recent years, particularly the petrochemical sectors. However, the oil price crash in 2015 and the subsequent budgetary constraints made any accelerated progress based on the 2030 Vision a challenging objective, despite the concurrent privatization, taxation, and Saudification efforts to reduce some of Saudi Arabia's budgetary commitments. Consecutive budget deficits have increased the burden on Saudi foreign exchange funds, with a drop from $732 billion in 2014 to $623 billion in less than twelve months. Saudi reserves continued to decline, reaching $488.9 in January 2018. Based on current levels of spending and deficits, and assuming spending priorities and other conditions *ceteris paribus*, Saudi Arabia's sovereign reserves give Saudi Arabia an estimated fiscal buffer of around five years, according to a Brookings report.[23] This report represents indeed a worst case scenario, however, questions about the rate of spending from the Saudi SWF remain a concern for observers. Nevertheless, Saudi Arabia remains a resource-rich economy, with untapped resources including natural gas. The Kingdom consistently utilizes its economic bargaining leverage to increase non-oil revenue, foreign direct investment, and manage its dyadic relations.

11.5.2 SAUDI MILITARY CAPABILITIES

Military power was classically considered the central theme of grand strategies, as discussed in the introductory chapter. Scholars have argued that linking political intent with the threat of use of violence has to be grounded in an understanding of the complex nature of the environment.[24] There is a debate about Saudi Arabia's readiness to employ its military capabilities in dealing with external threats, but both Riedel and Cordesman concur on Saudi Arabia's fascination with owning the latest military technologies and the Kingdom's perpetual quest for security.[25]

The largest single allocation in the Saudi budget is for military and security services. In the recent SIPRI May 2018 report, Saudi Arabia ranked third globally in military expenditure after the United States and China.[26] Military and security services comprised, for example, more than 25 percent of the total budget in 2016. The Kingdom has a well-equipped military defense system, with a capable air force, but a coast guard rather than a navy. Saudi Arabia hosts multiple NATO-level air bases across the country, and a number of 200 personal (lily pads) US military bases. Saudi Arabia has a fleet of F-15s, Eurofighter Typhoons, and Panavia Tornados, in addition to AWACS planes, intelligence systems, and command and control facilities. It has more than 400 M1A1 tanks and another approximately 400 M2 Bradley IFV ones.[27] The Kingdom has a state-owned Military Industries Corporations (MIC) based in Riyadh, which specializes in munition, firearms, and armored vehicles. Saudi Arabia has approximately 680,000 active military personnel, including an army of 300,000 soldiers. Saudi security forces are highly trained and often supervised and trained by the United States and European countries. The Saudi Arabian National Guard (SANG) was originally the private army of the late King Abdulla in the 1960s but transitioned to a professional military force. SANG has remained independent from the Ministry of Defense, and it continues to serve as a counterbalance to the Sudairi faction within the royal family. King Salman and his powerful son, Crown Prince Mohammad bin Salman belong to the Sudairi group.[28] In November 2017, Crown Prince Mohammad bin Salman arrested Prince Mut'ib bin Abdullah, the head of SANG, who was later released. SANG is now under the leadership of Prince Abdullah bin Bandar; who is loyal to Crown Prince Mohammad bin Salman. These transpiring power consolidations in 2018 demonstrate and confirm the changing realities of the new hierarchy within the royal family.

Peculiarly, scholars have pointed to *efficiency gaps* existing at the operational level within the Saudi Armed Forces. While researchers have lauded the Saudi armed and security forces' professionalism and control over domestic security and counterterrorism,[29] critics have pointed out the lack of preparedness of the Saudi Armed Forces in fighting conventional wars. They note the persistent need to augment Saudi forces with foreign professional manpower, citing Saudi military performance in the ongoing Yemen war as an example.[30] There are numerous historical precedents for this reliance on foreign forces. During the November 1979 Mecca siege crisis led by Juhayman al-Otaybi, for example, the Kingdom received decisive military assistance from French commandos, and from Pakistan. Saudi Arabia provided Pakistan $1 billion in economic aid in return.[31] More recently, during the 2011 Bahrain uprising, the Bahrain government quelled the demonstrations by calling on the Saudi-led Peninsula Shield troops. To complete the mission, the Peninsula Shield troops needed Pakistani military and logistical support.[32] In both Saudi–Yemen wars, in 1962 and again in 2015, Saudi Armed Forces planned to rely on Pakistan army units to provide personnel, training, and military advice. When Pakistan's Parliament famously voted against engaging in the 2015 Yemen war,[33] Saudi Arabia turned to Egypt, and then Sudan personnel support. The relatively limited capabilities of the Saudi Armed Forces, when added to Saudi Arabia's limited naval capacity, constrains its aspirations as a regional middle power in competition with Turkey and Iran, each with larger and more capable armed forces and naval power. The ongoing talks with Israel, and the 2017 public discussion of the shared security interests of the two states, point to the possibility of Israel playing a greater role as a security and intelligence partner to the Saudi Kingdom.[34] Both states feel similarly threatened by Iran's nuclear capabilities and its support of Hezbollah.

As in Djibouti and Ethiopia, Saudi Arabia's efforts at securing an economic and military footprint in the Maldives provides an example of the Kingdom's efforts to form a deterrence network and strategic hedging in service of its grand strategy. The Republic of Maldives is a South Asian island country located in the Arabian Sea, a tributary itself to the Indian Ocean. During the Maldives' recent political crisis between pro-democracy presidential hopeful Mohammad Nasheed and current pro-Chinese President Abdullah Yameen, Saudi Arabian money and support backed the latter. Yameen employs Islamic rhetoric and constrains political freedoms, and is keen to accommodate both Saudi Arabian and Chinese interests in providing access to his country's strategically located archipelago.[35] Saudi Arabia's vocal support of pro-Islamic activism in the Maldives, coupled with its economic assistance, facilitated negotiations on possibly establishing a Saudi military outpost there. Such a step would provide Saudi Arabia with a forward posture in one of the busiest oil routes to China, one proximate to Iran. Balancing the perceived nuclear threat from Iran, however, requires more than traditional military maneuvers. Saudi Arabia is currently in the process of proposing a civil nuclear cooperation agreement with the United States that would allow the Kingdom to enrich uranium and reprocess spent reactor fuel, and thereby be on par with Iranian nuclear capabilities.[36]

11.5.3 SAUDI SOCIAL POWER

Social power entails a state's capacity to persuade, and thereby enhance its legitimacy.[37] Saudi Arabia's social power, derived from its custodianship of the two holy mosques, Mecca and Madinah, has been a core component of its grand strategy since 1979. Historically, the Kingdom's legitimacy was founded on a religious–military nexus. It was initially keen to preserve and enhance its religious authority, in the state's early history, through military means. But subsequently it has become reliant on social and economic incentives to advance its interests, trading off between diplomatic relations, economic funding, and coercive diplomacy.[38] While balancing and advocating a delicate line between Western commercial modernization and Islamic conservatism domestically, the Kingdom had to fulfill its missionary obligations to the Muslim Ummah. This took the form of religious welfare, along with providing Saudi preachers and funding for mosques and Qur'an schools, better known as madrassas. It was all part of an anti-Iran and anti-communism regional policy commencing after 1979.

Saudi Arabia's religious authority called for Islamic jihad against the "godless Soviets" in Afghanistan between 1979 and 1989. Saudi territory, in addition to being a preachers' haven for Salafism, also became a logistical transit area for Salafi Jihadists and a sanctuary for expelled Muslim Brotherhood (MB) exiles from Egypt and Syria during the anti-MB crackdown in both states. Their enhanced religious authority between 1980 and 2015 facilitated Saudi Arabia's famous large-scale donation drives, estimated to be hundreds of millions of dollars, for what was deemed Islamic causes in areas, ranging from Bosnia, Chechnya, and Dagestan, to the Palestinian Territory, Kashmir, and later Iraq and Syria.

These donations ended up being awarded to some Saudi and Islamic humanitarian agencies later accused of funding and aiding, either directly or indirectly, various terrorist-linked groups. Several other factors have undermined Saudi Arabia's credibility abroad: that fifteen Saudi nationals were among the nineteen perpetrators of 9/11; alleged Saudi funding of extremist elements in Europe and Asia; and direct challenges from rival regional contenders for Islamic authority, post-2011. These include, most pointedly, the Muslim Brotherhood (MB), al-Qaeda/ISIS, and Iran. In this sense, Iranian tacit logistical support for the MB (President Morsi and Hamas) and alleged logistical support for al-Qaeda is viewed by the Saudi leadership as a deliberate attempt by Iran to undermine Saudi Sunni authority. As such, Iran and its Revolutionary Guard-Quds Force devision (IRGC-QF) activism in the region, including the duplication of Hezbollah-like militia in Iraq, Yemen (Houthis) and Syria, remains the primary strategic factor influencing Saudi grand strategy.

Rehabilitating the Saudi Salafi brand will be a difficult, if not an impossible battle for the Kingdom, hence Crown Prince Mohamad bin Salman's insistence on breaking with the past (i.e. al-Sahwa) and launching an accelerated yet risky social liberalization. One impediment is the legal ramifications of the 2016 American congressional Justice Against Sponsors of Terrorism Act (JASTA), which allowed civil litigants to seek relief against persons, entities, or foreign countries who provided material support, directly or indirectly, to terrorist organizations.[39] Even close regional allies, such as Pakistan, now openly criticize the long-term adverse effects of Saudi-funded madrassas in Pakistan and Afghanistan, despite the Kingdom's continued economic aid.[40] The new Saudi leadership, headed by King Salman and his son the Crown Prince, have made significant efforts since 2015 to restrict Salafi promotion and MB influence in the Kingdom, especially in the public sphere and educational system. Saudi authorities now constrain the reach of religious policing, allowing public entertainment venues including theaters, and easing guardianship requirements on women and allowing them to drive. The Kingdom's leadership is signalling a break with the historical burden of radical Islamism, as the social reforms appear to be strategically used in counterinsurgency efforts across MENA, and to enhance the country's appeal internationally.

The following section examines the fractured Gulf Cooperation Council (GCC) in 2017–18. My intent is to illustrate Saudi grand strategy processes in action. The case study demonstrates several key points: how Saudi Arabia's grand strategy integrates threat perception and threat assessment; how its leadership consolidated domestic support; how they confronted domestic and regional security threats in attempting to shape a more favorable environment; the Kingdom's process and flexibility in forming regional alliances and deterrence networks; and, ultimately, how it protects its regional interests through the mobilization of economic, military, and social power.

11.6 **The fractured GCC**

The Cooperation Council of the Arab States of the Gulf (GCC) is a regional intergovernmental alliance composed of six states: Saudi Arabia, Bahrain, Kuwait, Qatar, Oman, and the United Arab Emirates. The founding Charter was signed in Abu Dhabi on May 25, 1981, announcing the GCC as a homogenous political structure bound by shared history, geography, borders, and common interests. The GCC formation was an institutional attempt to consolidate the Gulf States' political, economic, and defense capabilities in reaction to a series of regional developments: First, Shah Pahlavi's overthrow and Ayatollah Khomeini's ideological campaign to overthrow the Gulf monarchies due to their support of the "imperial West." Second, the Soviet invasion of Afghanistan and the threat it posed to oil export routes, especially after the USSR improved relations with Iraq and Kuwait. Third, the destabilizing effects of the Iran–Iraq war that began in 1981; and fourth, the incapacity of the twenty-two-member Arab League to cope with the adverse implications of the Egyptian–Israeli Peace Agreement of 1979.

These events convinced the Gulf States that they needed an alliance arrangement tailored to their security concerns, one that could also influence the direction of the Arab League through the use of their collective political and economic power. In practice, political integration and establishing joint defense and security agencies remained on the GCC agenda. Economic cooperation (especially on oil), in addition to streamlining trade relations and joint economic infrastructure was prioritized over more controversial political integration options.[41] External threats and opportunities were the main catalyst for the converging interests of the Gulf States.

The formation of the GCC served Saudi Arabia's long-term interests by facilitating its political leadership, beyond the service of Islam's two holy sites and being the region's top oil producer. By 2017, the GCC had a combined population of 54 million, of which 32.4 million reside in Saudi Arabia; a total GDP of $1.8 trillion (nominal) with an average of $40,500 GDP per capita; and a territory covering 1,032,093 square miles. It has been Saudi Arabia's reliable conduit for influencing regional affairs since 1981. While promoting a

"Gulf Policy," Saudi leadership maintained a paternal view of the smaller GCC counterparts, at the risk of exasperated resentment. The Kingdom's "Gulf Policy" translated into wider political and economic influence within regional organizations such as the Arab League, and global oil pricing and market share influence within OPEC. The coordination among the Gulf States, especially after the Iraqi invasion of Kuwait in 1990, was a direct product of the cooperative culture facilitated by the GCC, and an example of how this Council attempted to serve all its members.

The evolving nature of regional threats and opportunities, however, incrementally introduced fissures among the GCC members. Turkey, Israel, and Iran have gained influence in the region since 2003, and the renewed great power interests (US, China, and Russia) magnified diverging interests among GCC states. The first GCC state that broke out of the mold and chartered an autonomous and independent approach to regional affairs was Oman. While Saudi Arabia viewed Iran's activities in Iraq (and later in Syria and Yemen) with suspicion and rallied GCC states against Iran, Oman hosted mediation talks between the United States and Iran between 2009 and 2015. It was also the first GCC state to object to monetary union and a unified GCC currency in 2009, resolving to protect its sovereignty, while maintaining constructive relations with Iran, and recently hosting the Israeli prime minister. Oman's reticence towards the GCC has been echoed across the Gulf since 2011. During my interviews with Gulf State residents, the fear of a "Saudi takeover" as a result of a GCC-proposed political and economic integration was voiced, while residents from Bahrain for example saw in a unification with Saudi Arabia the best plan for survival.

Qatar, unlike Oman, maintained cordial relations with Saudi Arabia. It deferred to Saudi leadership, despite the turbulent relations between the two states since Qatar's independence in 1971, and the infamous Saudi-UAE-Egypt led 1996 coup against the Qatari leadership.[42] Qatar's activist foreign policy, however, has gradually expanded since. It began with attempts at mediation with the Taliban, Hamas, Hezbollah, and Sudan after 2003. By 2011, those efforts began threatening the political status quo in the Gulf region. Qatar, through Al Jazeera, its media arm, voiced support for protesters and uprisings across the MENA region, "giving a voice to the oppressed" against authoritarian governments.[43] This policy allegedly manifested itself later, according to Saudi Arabia, in funding and facilitating arms transfers to rebel fighters in Syria, Iraq, and Libya in alleged support of the Muslim Brotherhood. Qatar, like Turkey, viewed the Arab Spring upheaval in 2011 as a logical consequence of the suppressed political participation and denied economic opportunities. Both, Qatar and Turkey, viewed the Muslim Brotherhood organization as an integral part of the region's political history in its chronic search for agency and independence from Western dominance.

Qatar's activist foreign policy, through its diplomatic cadre and international media platform, was accused of becoming a propaganda tool for political exiles from Egypt, Syria, Libya, and Yemen, as it consistently provided a media outlet for Islamists opposition leaders and human rights activists in the region. Saudi Arabia traditionally resorted to discreet communications and mediation efforts to mitigate differences within the GCC states. The ideological differences with Qatar, however, were aired out in 2014 and again in 2017, when Saudi Arabia took an unprecedented firm stance against Qatar in 2017 by introducing measured designed to economically isolate it, and restrict its access to airspace, ground, and maritime routes. This fracture cannot be analyzed in isolation from the wider threat environment in MENA dating from the Arab Spring, coupled with the polarizing effects of Iran's assertive and revisionist outlook in the region.

From the Saudi perspective, there were several key elements to that changing threat environment. The first was a general sense of American strategic withdrawal under then President Barack Obama, one that created a vacuum filled by hostile state and nonstate actors. This was exacerbated by a second US policy engagement with Iran (commencing in March 2013) that resulted in the adoption of the Joint Comprehensive Plan of Action (JCPOA) by the UNSC resolution 2231 in July 2015. This shift in US policy, the Saudis concluded, signalled an attempt at the normalization of US–Iran relations. Furthermore, the 2011 Arab states uprisings have unleashed dormant political Islamist and anti-authority sentiments propagated by the Muslim Brotherhood and transnational Salafi Jihadism, both of which constitute existential threats to the Kingdom.

Saudi Arabia's warnings to Qatar in 2014 remained unheeded. From the Saudi perspective, the Qatari leadership persisted in defying Saudi Arabia on regional issues by siding with Iran, opposing president al-Sisi of Egypt, and supporting Libyan Islamists combatants against General Khalifa Haftar. They paid over $1 billion dollars in ransom to Shia militia in Iraq to free Qatari hostages, funded and supported Egyptian and Syrian Muslim Brotherhood opposition members, and collaborated with Turkey's President Erdogan on regional issues pertaining to Iraq, Syria, and Iran. Qatar signed an agreement with Turkey, Saudi Arabia's rival for Sunni leadership in MENA, establishing a Turkish military base in Qatar. Iran increased its intervention in Syria, Iraq, Yemen, and expanded its military and navy exercises with China and Russia, especially in the Gulf/Straight of Hurmuz.

Against this political backdrop, economic factors also heightened Saudi Arabia's concerns. A precipitous decline in oil prices (from over $100/barrel in 2011 to under $30/barrel in 2016) sharply decreased domestic spending and prompted Saudi authority to cover a budget deficit by liquidating assets. Between 2014 and 2017, Saudi foreign reserves shrank from a record high of $737 billion to below $500 billion. In this context, in 2016, the Saudis announced the comprehensive economic and social reform agenda, the 2030 Vision. Its goal is to reduce the Kingdom's dependence on oil revenue, and to challenge and modernize the traditional fundamentals of Saudi society since 1979. This vision partially depends on privatization and attracting FDI. Succession protocols to guarantee continued stability in the Kingdom after King Abdullah passed away in 2015 were organized in consultation with the thirty-four-member allegiance council. By most accounts, power is firmly consolidated in the young leadership of Crown Prince Mohamad bin Salman, who is determined to move ahead with modernization and reform in the Kingdom, curbing both the influence of Muslim Brotherhood and the radical elements of Salafism. Qatar, in this sense, is seen as countering and interfering in Saudi-accelerated reform efforts.

The Saudi emerging political discourse is therefore strongly opposed to the political Islam promoted by Iran, Qatar, and Turkey. In 2017, journalists, Imams, and broadcasters were banned from writing in national newspapers and appearing on TV because of their affiliation with the Muslim Brotherhood or their expressed admiration of Qatar or Turkey. Numerous Saudi human rights activists have been jailed and accused of treason. I interviewed the late journalist Jamal Khashogji for this chapter in December 2017, in Washington DC. His gruesome death at the Saudi consulate in Istanbul in October 2018 was a stark reminder that war on the Muslim Brotherhood, even those lightly affiliated with it, is in full force. Saudi authorities also embarked on an expansive anticorruption campaign, detaining numerous Saudi royals and wealthy businessmen. While the expressed intent of the campaign was to stem business corruption (which reached an average rate of 10 percent of GDP), international observers nonetheless increasingly question the guarantees offered by Saudi Arabia's legal system, independence of the judiciary and access to due process.[44]

11.7 **Adjusting the alliance formation**

The Saudi Kingdom interpreted Qatar's contrarian stance since 2011, emboldened by Turkey and Iran's support, as a direct challenge to Saudi leadership. Qatar criticized Saudi Arabia's internal reforms and social liberalization, magnified internal Saudi succession disagreements, and focused on the humanitarian crisis in the Yemen war. While Kuwait and Oman have taken a neutral stance in the Saudi–Qatar dispute, they both transitioned to a nonconfrontational policy towards Iran in part due to Kuwait's Shia population. The GCC, polarized by the Saudi–Qatari dispute, has clustered Oman, Kuwait, and Qatar on one side, and Saudi Arabia, Bahrain, and UAE on the other. The UAE is particularly important to Saudi Arabia with regards to defense, survailance and security matters. Saudi Arabia has also attempted a rapprochement with Iraq since 2015, and to strengthen defense and security agreements with Sudan and Egypt, with relative success.

For Saudi Arabia, the GCC crisis continued to be viewed through the lens of the threat posed by Iran. The GCC fracture fundamentally began when Qatar advocated engagement with Iran, Turkey and the Muslim Brotherhood as a regional necessity. Saudi Arabia perceived Qatar's maneuver as a departure from the foundational tenets of the GCC, and a challenge to Saudi leadership. Compromise with the defiant Qatari position was impossible, and the Saudi leadership demanded that Qatar unconditionally withdraw its support for and communication with the Muslim Brotherhood and Iran. Crown Prince Mohammad bin Salman is further emboldened by the Trump administration and the renewed US resolve to curb Iran's and the IRGC's regional influence to prevent the establishment of the Hezbollah model in Syria, Iraq, and Yemen.

The announcement of US troop withdrawal from Syria and Afghanistan however by the Trump administration in late 2018 only confirmed Saudi assessment for the need to craft an autonomous foreign-policy.The Saudi leadership's quest to establish a network of deterrence as a counterweight to Iran's regional military capabilities, and expanding Turkey assertiveness, had to include a considerable counterweight to Iran's power projection in the region. Saudi Arabia's consultations with Israel on regional matters, in addition to its involvement in possible Arab–Israel peace negotiations, has been an essential aspect of the Saudi grand strategy. Furthermore, to counter Iran's influence in Yemen, Saudi Arabia is intensifying its presence in nearby Djibouti (at the crucial Bab al-Mandeb straight to the Arabian Sea). Having long deployed Saudi assets in Djibouti, the strategic country home to the US Camp Lemonnier as part of AFRICOM, the Saudis have discussed establishing a military base there in the near future. Like Sudan, Djibouti severed its ties with Iran in 2017.

11.8 Mobilizing state power

The Saudis have demonstrated a capacity to deploy their diplomatic cadre effectively in complex environments since 2015, particularly in Iraq, Sudan, and Egypt. Saudi authorities were able to mitigate instances of incongruency in their bilateral relations with ease, especially during the disagreements with Pakistan on its participation in the Yemen war, which the Pakistani Parliament voted against. When I asked Prince Turki al-Faisal during an interview about Pakistan's parliamentary vote, he stated that "old historic relations between Pakistan and Saudi Arabia can overcome small disagreements for the benefit of long-term Saudi objectives." At times however, Saudi diplomacy got temporarily off its track record, most notably in 2017 with the Lebanese prime minister Saad Harriri's forced announcement of his resignation from office while visiting Riyadh. The international and regional response to the Harriri debacle detracted from Saudi historic influence in Lebanon for a short while, but relations have since resumed.

In response to the Qatari crisis, Saudi diplomacy launched a series of talks with the US, EU, and other regional states. It accused Qatar of supporting terrorism and interfering in the internal affairs of states, offering in 2017 a joint Saudi Arabia–Bahrain–UAE "terror list" identifying fifty-nine individuals and entities with Qatari ties.[45] Qatar disputed Saudi allegations and signed strategic dialogue agreements with the United States on trade, investment, and to combat terrorism in the Middle East.[46]

In addition to Saudi diplomacy, its economic power had a direct short term negative effect on Qatar. It introduced an economic boycott, to which Qatar countered by establishing a direct supply line with both Iran and Turkey, and domestic indusrial and agricultural projects to satisfy domestic demands. Qatar's oil production suffered however due to Saudi Arabia's Asian oil market strategy. Qatar's oil exports to Japan, for example, fell by more than 23 percent, to levels not seen since 1990, while Saudi oil supplies to Japan increased by 8.1 percent in 2017. As Saudi Arabia led production cuts in OPEC to reduce a global oil glut, curbing supplies to the US and Europe, it maintained sales in Asia, its most profitable region. Qatar however, suffered from both lower oil prices and reduced market share.[47] Limiting oil production, mainly maintained by Saudi Arabia, is anticipated to produce higher oil prices in 2019. Talks about using military power, or the aid of a *coup d'état*, was also unofficially discussed among academics and media personnel in both Saudi Arabia and UAE, although the reality of Qatar hosting the largest US military base in the MENA region, in addition to hosting a Turkish military base, curbed such discussions.[48] The GCC remains as an organization, yet its role and effectiveness is further limited by the Saudi-Qatari dispute.

11.9 Conclusion

Saudi Arabia's grand strategy embodies the nation's historical evolution, strategic culture, and geopolitical constraints. Eschewing the oil-for-security bilateral arrangement with the United States has allowed the Saudi Kingdom to employ a consistent strategic outlook in projecting its diplomatic, economic, social, and military power regionally. Networking deterrence against Iran and its close allies has become a core component of Saudi grand strategy. The return of great power rivalry in the region has resulted in the Kingdom of Saudi Arabia diversifying its relations and extending partnership dialogues in a process of strategic hedging. However, networking deterrence and strategic hedging—the two defining characteristics of Saudi grand strategy—are both in the service of balancing the perceived threat of Iran and its proxies as it expands and exerts influence in the region.

The main tenants of Saudi Arabia's grand strategy continues to meet realist expectations of balancing regional threats. Networking deterrence and strategic hedging—through military, economic, and social power—seem destined to continue as long as Saudi Arabia remains able to support and fund its regional military and economic posture. Strategic hedging with China and Russia might diversify security dependence away from the US but might eventually weaken expectations of support from historical allies. The GCC fracture highlights the fact that national interests are shaped by geopolitical constraints and that small states do acquire statues in a contested region among middle powers. Small states like Qatar increased their leverage as MENA middle powers: Turkey, Israel, Iran, and Saudi Arabia compete for influence in a contested region. Future research should re-evaluate Saudi Arabia's bargaining with great powers, and investigate the sustainability of Crown Prince, and future King, Mohammad bin Salman's decision-making abilities in the light of expansive political challenges, constrained investment flows and economic capabilities, possible domestic unrest, and limited institutional outlets for political discussions on national priorities. Future research questions could investigate how a possible nuclear race in the MENA region affects the need for strategic hedging, the role and implications of Israel as a security guarantor for Saudi Arabia on Saudi–US relations, and if and how Saudi Arabia can craft a secular, and national interest-guided foreign policy to mirror its domestic religious reforms.

NOTES

1. Aaron David Miller, *Search for Security: Saudi Arabian Oil and American Foreign Policy* (Chapel Hill: The University of North Carolina Press, 2017).
2. Edward Luttwak, *The Grand Strategy of the Byzantine Empire* (Cambridge, MA: Harvard University Press, 2009), 400.
3. Stephen M. Walt, *The Origin of Alliances* (Ithaca, NY: Cornell University Press, 1987).
4. Abdulrahman Assad Hussein, "The Foreign Policy of the Kingdom of Saudi Arabia, 1979–1991" (PhD diss., George Washington University, 1995; ProQuest, order no. 9522068).
5. Rachel Bronson, *Thicker than Oil: America's Uneasy Partnership with Saudi Arabia* (Oxford: Oxford University Press, 2006).
6. Balance of Threat Theory (Neorealism) was proposed by Stephen M. Walt in his book *The Origins of Alliances*. In balance of threat theory, four criteria are used to

evaluate a threat posed by a state: its aggregate size, population, economic, and military capabilities; geographic proximity; offensive capabilities; and offensive intentions.
7. Shibley Z. Telhami and Michael Barnett, *Identity and Foreign Policy in the Middle East* (Ithaca, NY: Cornell University Press, 2002).
8. It should be noted however that the King Faisal Center for Research and Islamic Studies مركز الملك فيصل للدراسات و البحوث الإسلامية is an established research center since 1983 and has made notable strides in research output. It retains an exclusive audience and has limited influence in society. SMT Studies Center مركز سمت للدراسات for example is a nascent yet interesting development and is closer to the beginnings of a think tank.
9. Eric Davis, *Memories of State: Politics, History and Collective Identity in Modern Iraq* (Berkeley: University of California Press, 2005).
10. Nayef al-Rodhan, "Strategic Culture and Pragmatic National Interests," *Global Policy Journal* (July 22, 2015).
11. Jack Snyder, *The Soviet Strategic Culture: Implications for Limited Nuclear Operations* (Santa Monica, CA: RAND Corp 1977). Also valuable contribution by Alastair Ian Johnston, "Thinking about Strategic Culture," *Journal of International Security* 19, no. 4 (Spring 1995): 32–64; and Colin Dueck, *Reluctant Crusaders: Power, Culture, and Change in American Grand Strategy* (Princeton, NJ: Princeton University Press, 2008).
12. Anthony H. Cordesman, *Saudi Arabia: National Security in a Troubled Region* (Santa Barbara, CA: Praeger Security International, an imprint of ABC-CLIO, LLC, 2009; published in cooperation with the Center for Strategic and International Studies); Anthony H. Cordesman, *Saudi Arabia, Guarding the Desert Kingdom* (Boulder, CO: Westview Press, 1997; published in cooperation with the Center for Strategic and International Studies).
13. Robert Mason, *Foreign Policy in Iran and Saudi Arabia: Economics and Diplomacy in the Middle East* (London: I.B.Tauris, 2015).
14. David Commins, *The Mission of the Kingdom: Wahhabi Power Behind the Saudi Throne* (London: I.B.Tauris, 2016).
15. Walt, *The Origins of Alliances*.
16. This assessment of Saudi Arabia's main grand strategy objectives is a result of Saudi news media analysis, Saudi Foreign Ministry statements, and interviews conducted by the author in 2017 with Saudi academics, journalists, and Saudi officials.
17. Saudi Arabian Monetary Authority, SAMA, http://www.sama.gov.sa/en-us/Pages/default.aspx (last accessed July 2018).
18. "Economic Freedom Index 2017," *The Heritage Foundation*, http://www.heritage.org/index/country/saudiarabia; *The World Bank FDI*, 2016, (last accessed September 2018) https://data.worldbank.org/indicator/BX.KLT.DINV.WD.GD.ZS (last accessed July 2018).
19. Edward N. Luttwark, "From Geopolitics to Geo-Economics: Logic of Conflict, Grammar of Commerce," *The National Interest*, no. 20 (Summer 1990): 17–23.
20. Ghaidaa Hetou, *The Syrian Conflict: The Role of Russia, Iran and US in a Global Crisis* (Abingdon, UK: Routledge, 2019).

21. Peter Waldman, "The $2 Trillion Project to Get Saudi Arabia's Economy Off Oil," *Bloomberg*, April 21, 2016, https://www.bloomberg.com/news/features/2016-04-21/the-2-trillion-project-to-get-saudi-arabia-s-economy-off-oil (last accessed February 2017).
22. The complete text of Saudi Arabia's 2030 Vision can be found at http://vision2030.gov.sa/en
23. Luay al-Khatteeb, "Saudi Arabia's Economic Time Bomb," *Brookings*, December 30, 2015, https://www.brookings.edu/opinions/saudi-arabias-economic-time-bomb (last accessed June 2017).
24. Richard Baily, James W. Jr. Forsyth, and Mark O. Yeisley, *Strategy: Context and Adaptation from Archidamus to Airpower* (Annapolis, MD: Naval Institute Press, 2016).
25. Cordesman, *Saudi Arabia: National Security*; and Bruce Riedel, *Kings and Presidents: Saudi Arabia and the United States since FDR* (Washington, DC: Brookings Institution Press, 2017).
26. Trends in World Military Expenditure, 2017, SIPRI Fact Sheet, https://www.sipri.org/sites/default/files/2018-05/sipri_fs_1805_milex_2017.pdf (last accessed June 2018).
27. *Trends in International Arms Transfer*, Stockholm International Peace Research Institute, 2014. Also, Ferran Izquierdo Brichs, ed., *Political Regimes in the Arab World: Society and the Exercise of Power* (London: Routledge, 2012). Further details are available at the webpage for Saudi Arabia's Defense Ministry: https://www.moda.gov.sa/Pages/Ministry.aspx (laset accessed June 2018).
28. Bernard Haykel and Thomas Hegghammer, *Saudi Arabia in Transition: Insights on Social, Political, Economic and Religious Change* (Cambridge: Cambridge University Press, 2015).
29. Cordesman, *Saudi Arabia: National Security*.
30. Ginny Hill, *Yemen Endures: Civil War, Saudi Adventurism and the Future of Arabia* (Oxford: Oxford University Press, 2017).
31. Richard Burt, "Pakistan Said to Offer to Base Troops on Saudi Soil," *The New York Times*, August 20, 1980, A.5.
32. Mujib Mashal, "Pakistani Troops Aid Bahrain's Crackdown," *Al Jazeera*, July 30, 2011, http://www.aljazeera.com/indepth/features/2011/07/2011725145048574888.html
33. Asad Hashim, "Pakistan Parliament Backs Neutrality in Yemen Conflict," *Al Jazeera*, April 10, 2015, http://www.aljazeera.com/news/2015/04/pakistan-rules-military-operations-yemen-150410074921586.html
34. Vivian Salama, "'An Open Secret': Saudi Arabia and Israel get Cozy," *NBC News*, November 15, 2017, https://www.nbcnews.com/news/mideast/open-secret-saudi-arabia-israel-get-cozy-n821136 (last accessed June 2018).
35. James M. Dorsey, "Crisis in the Maldives: A Geopolitical Chess Game," *Maldives Times*, February 7, 2018, https://maldivestimes.com/crisis-in-the-maldives-a-geopolitical-chess-game/
36. Henry Sokolski and William Tobey, "A Poorly Negotiated Saudi Nuclear Dear Could Damage Future Regional Relationship," *The National Interest*, February 5, 2018, http://nationalinterest.org/feature/poorly-negotiated-saudi-nuclear-deal-could-

damage-future-24367. There are other possible providers of nuclear reactors, such as South Korea, China, and France. Saudi Arabia owns 5 percent of the global reserve of uranium.

37. Simon Reich and Richard Ned Lebow, *Good-Bye Hegemony! Power and Influence in the Global System* (Princeton, NJ: Princeton University Press, 2014).
38. Saudi Arabia's diplomatic coercion may include reducing, restricting, or cancelling Haj and Omra visas to citizens from the target country if they are deemed a threat to national security.
39. Justice Against Sponsors of Terrorism Act, Pub. L. 114–222 (2016), https://www.congress.gov/bill/114th-congress/senate-bill/2040
40. Gleaned from author's interviews with Pakistani officials in 2017 who requested to remain anonymous.
41. For a detailed account of intertrade regulations, private ownerships, and equal treatment of Gulf citizens among GCC states, see Gulf States Common Market: http://www.gcc-sg.org/ar-sa/CognitiveSources/DigitalLibrary/Lists/DigitalLibrary/الإحصاءات/common%20market.pdf (last accessed June 2018).
42. مفيد الزيدي، ٢٠١٠. تاريخ قطر المعاصر ١٩١٣- ٢٠٠٨. دار المناهج للنشر و التوزيع., Modern History of Qatar, Mufid al-Zaidi, 2010.
43. Tal Saumel-Azran, *Intercultural Communication as a Clash of Civilizations: Al-Jazeera and Qatar's Soft Power*, Critical Intercultural Communications Studies (Bern, Switzerland: Peter Lang Inc., 2016).
44. Dominic Dudley, "Saudi Anti-Corruption Drive Hits Its $100B Target, But At What Cost?," *Forbes*, January 30, 2018, https://www.forbes.com/sites/dominicdudley/2018/01/30/saudi-anti-corruption-drive-hits-its-100b-target-but-at-what-cost/#1d8b2ae46af7 (last accessed June 2018).
45. "59 people, 12 groups with Qatar links on 'terror list'," *Al Jazeera*, June 8, 2017, https://www.aljazeera.com/news/2017/06/saudi-led-bloc-issues-terror-list-170608221049889.html
46. "Joint Statement of the Inaugural United States-Qatar Strategic Dialogue," *U.S. Department of State*, January 30 2018, https://www.state.gov/r/pa/prs/ps/2018/01/277776.htm
47. Tsuyoshi Inajima, "Saudi deal blow to small rival in top market," *World Oil*, January 31, 2018, http://www.worldoil.com/news/2018/1/31/saudis-deal-blow-to-small-rival-in-top-market
48. "Qatar: Saudi Arabia is 'promoting regime change'," *The New Arab*, October 18, 2017, https://www.alaraby.co.uk/english/news/2017/10/18/qatar-saudi-arabia-is-promoting-regime-change

12 The European Union

DANIEL FIOTT AND LUIS SIMÓN

It may come as some surprise to learn that an international organization such as the European Union (EU) has the capacity to form and articulate its own grand strategy. Indeed, many of the EU's strategic objectives are referred to in the treaties that form the legal basis of the EU. More specifically, the European Security Strategy (ESS) of 2003 and the EU Global Strategy (EUGS) of 2016 spell out, in a granular way, the EU's strategic objectives in foreign and security policy terms. There can be no doubt that the EU is an important and intriguing international actor, for institutions such as the Council of the EU, the European Commission, and the European External Action Service (EEAS) have competences that span policy areas as diverse as monetary policy, trade, energy, diplomacy, and security. Thus, EU grand strategy is shared between intergovernmental and supranational institutions. Although perhaps not as coherent a strategic actor when compared to the likes of the United States, China, and Russia (which are unitary states governed by central institutions), European countries do place a lot of stock in achieving their individual strategic objectives through the EU and its institutions. As a marketplace of close to 500 million consumers, the sheer weight of the EU in economic terms makes it vital to understand what type of strategic actor the EU actually is.

The EU's overall *raison d'être* and its strategic perspective borrow significantly from Europe's historical experiences. It is worth recalling that the EU's foundational historical experience was World War II, and this particular episode provided the "founding fathers" of European unity with the basic building blocks of what type of strategic actor Europe should or could become. These building blocks principally included a renunciation of the use of force as a way to manage political contestation, and a belief in and adherence to the principles of rule of law, democracy, and human rights. Furthermore, the EU's strategic assumptions about the world were also colored by the experiences of the Cold War. Under the conventional force and nuclear umbrella provided by NATO, and the unifying pressure emanating from the Soviet Union, the members of the then Western European Union (WEU) and European Economic Community (EEC) focused on their postwar economic recovery. Owing to the Marshall Plan and the establishment of NATO, WEU/EEC countries transformed into prosperous economies during the Cold War following the gradual reduction of trade barriers between WEU/EEC members. The economic and legal principles underlying this economic recovery were swiftly translated into a more general support for global trade and an outward looking foreign policy under European Political Cooperation (EPC) during the 1970s—EPC was an informal way for European foreign ministers to meet and discuss foreign policy issues.

It was during the Cold War that the members of the WEU/EEC sought to support European unity by nurturing liberal capitalism and democracy (within Europe and globally) through the formation of an economic community and later common market where membership was dependent on adherence to the principles of democracy, human rights, and rule of law. Yet, with the end of the Cold War, and the seeming victory of liberal capitalism and democracy, the EU emerged as one of the largest markets in the world. The reunification of Germany and the eventual accession of former Warsaw Pact countries into the EU did not just herald an expansion of the EU (and NATO), but it also presaged an increased role for the EU in international affairs. This was cemented following the 1992 Maastricht Treaty, and the formalization of the EU's Common Foreign and Security Policy (CFSP) which for the first time not only established foreign-policy-making institutions at the EU level but it also stressed the values on which EU foreign policy should be based. What is more, the CFSP set the foundations for the creation of the EU's own security and defense policy at the turn of the millennium. Through the Common Security and Defence Policy (CSDP) the EU seeks to intervene in crises that would have a direct impact on its own security and liberty. With a unique brand of diplomatic, humanitarian, developmental, and civil–military missions, the EU's strategic objective was and is to expand and solidify the liberal order (based on open markets, human rights, rule of law, and democracy) that it so successfully gave life to within the EU's borders.

However, identifying who makes EU grand strategy is not an easy endeavor. It should first be acknowledged that a range of institutions and actors play a role in the formulation and execution of the EU's grand strategy. Accordingly, various institutions not only define "grand strategy" in different ways, but some actors are more aware than others that they are engaged in "grand strategy"-making. What can be observed is that different strategic issues will require certain institutions to take the lead. The EU therefore represents a flexible institutional order when it comes to the formulation and execution of strategy. The aim of this chapter is not only to identify the leading actors in EU grand strategy but to also say something about how these actors pursue grand strategy goals. The chapter also pays special attention to the capabilities used by the EU in pursuit of its strategic objectives, as this will allow us to isolate and explain the ways in which the EU (thinks it) acts strategically. To this end, the chapter is divided into three main parts. Section 12.1 concentrates on the key actors and institutions involved in the forging of the EU's grand strategy.

Section 12.2 comments on the ends, values, and objectives of EU grand strategy. Finally, section 12.3 concludes with a critical engagement about the ways in which the EU operationalizes its grand strategy.

12.1 Locating the EU's strategy makers

The EU's strategy-making is divided between a range of intergovernmental and supranational institutions. Given the broad array of policy areas that are associated with grand strategy (i.e., trade, development, diplomacy, security, energy, etc.), it should be of little surprise to learn that strategy-making at the EU level is a complex business. As Table 12.1 makes clear, the principal institutions involved include the European Council, the Council of the EU, the European Commission, the EEAS, and the European Parliament.

The intergovernmental side of strategy-making is dominated by the European Council, which is composed of the heads of state and government of the EU member states. The European Council is responsible for setting the EU's overall strategic objectives related to foreign, economic, and justice and home affairs policies.[1] These objectives are formulated during the regular meetings of the European Council in Brussels (or, if deemed necessary, in other capital cities in the EU). In this sense, the strategic objectives emanating from the European Council are arrived at by unanimity, but these objectives set the tone for the direction of the EU overall. Interestingly, given the number of pressing issues facing the EU, the European Council is also the primary institution where some degree of prioritization between policy areas and policy issues takes place.[2] Reaching unanimity is not always simple in the European Council, especially where member state resources are to be used for a particular strategic objective. In this regard, the president of the European Council plays a pivotal role in ensuring consensus among member states and representing the EU in major international fora such as the G8 summits.

Supporting the European Council is another intergovernmental institution called the Council of the EU. The Council serves as the major preparatory body that debates and crafts most aspects of strategy in more detail than can be achieved by occasional meetings of the European Council. The Council of the EU is home to various ministerial configurations that comprise the individual ministers in EU member states (i.e. every foreign minister meets through the Foreign Affairs Council (FAC) and agricultural and economic ministers meet in other configurations). The day-to-day functioning of the Council is overseen by over 150 working groups and bodies comprising member state officials from various national ministries (and therefore not just from the national foreign ministries[3]).[4] Primarily, the Committee of

Table 12.1 The EU's principal strategy makers

Institution	Strategic direction	Foreign & security policy guidance	Trade policy	Development aid	Humanitarian assistance	Border management	Energy policy	Sanctions Policy	Military Operations	Civilian Missions
European Council	x									
Council of the EU		x				x	x	x	x	x
Foreign Affairs Council		x	x			x	x	x	x	x
COREPER		x		x	x	x			x	x
Political and Security Committee		x		x	x	x		x	x	x
EU Military Committee						x			x	
CIVCOM										x
European Commission	x	x	x	x	x	x	x	x		
Foreign Policy Instruments Service				x				x		
European External Action Service	x	x				x			x	x
EU Military Staff									x	
Military Planning and Conduct Capability									x	
Crisis Management Planning Division									x	x
Civilian Planning and Conduct Capability										x
European Parliament	x	x								
European Border and Coast Guard						x				

Source: Authors' own.

Permanent Representatives of the Member States to the EU (COREPER) is responsible for all aspects of the EU's international role, plus it serves as a direct interface between national capitals and Brussels. It is a preparatory body that lays out potential avenues of strategic action rather than a decision-making body, and it is comprises ambassadors from each member state that meet in Brussels on a weekly basis.[5] Finally, a Political and Security Committee (PSC) supports COREPER and is responsible for the day-to-day formulation and articulation of EU responses to international crises. The PSC is composed of ambassador-level representatives from each EU member state, and it meets weekly to plan approaches to crises and to prepare the groundwork for COREPER deliberations and, eventually, any decisions taken by the FAC.[6]

The role of the Council of the EU and its supporting bodies in the EU grand strategy should be examined with caution. As the Council of the EU is an intergovernmental body, one should expect the dominant logic to be one of the advancement and reconciling of national interests rather than "EU interests" per se.[7] The extent to which the Council of the EU and its supporting bodies are aware that they are conducting EU grand strategy can also be called into question. Indeed, while much of the fine detail of policy is debated in the Council of the EU, it is an institution dominated by coalition-building, negotiating and bargaining, and, perhaps most importantly, the Council of the EU opens up a multilevel governance structure whereby various ministries in the national capitals link up with Brussels.[8] Such a system not only gives life to a complex web of governance for a variety of potentially strategic decisions, but it also represents a diffuse decision-making structure where interests can converge and diverge in sometimes quite stark ways.

Supporting the work of Council, the EEAS plays an important role in forging and guiding EU grand strategy. The EEAS has been designed as a hybrid institution with both supranational and intergovernmental features.[9] For example, certain EEAS services such as the EU Military Staff (EUMS), Crisis Management Planning Division (CMPD), and the Civilian Planning and Conduct Capability (CPCC) provide the PSC with specific strategic advice and input. These EEAS services are staffed by a mix of permanent and temporary contract staff and seconded national experts. Headed by the Union's high representative for foreign and security policy and vice president of the European Commission (HRVP), the Service acts as the EU's diplomatic corps and it houses a range of departments focusing on different geographic regions.[10] These departments not only tackle particular regions with a certain degree of autonomy from the Council of the EU, but also cross-cutting themes such as nonproliferation, economic development, multilateralism, and human rights.[11] The individual EEAS departments in Brussels are supported by an extensive diplomatic capacity afforded by the 140 or so EU Delegations stationed across the globe. The EEAS also, however, plays an increasingly vital role in crisis management. To this end, the Service has its own in-house military and intelligence expertise, and it has started to tackle hybrid threats such as disinformation and "fake news."

While the EEAS is responsible for the day-to-day management of diplomatic relations with the world at the EU level, it is also an institution that takes the lead on a number of important strategic dossiers. The most obvious diplomatic portfolio taken on by the EEAS in recent years has been the Iran nuclear conflict.[12] While it is true that diplomacy with Iran involved the United States, the United Kingdom, Russia, France, Germany, and China, the EU played a key role in forging a deal with Tehran on limiting the Islamic Republic's nuclear program by assuming the role of an honest broker given the historic tensions between the US and Iran.[13] As a strategic issue for the EU, this dossier should not be underestimated: it touches upon a number of sensitive strategic issues of importance to the Union including Middle East security, nonproliferation, trade, and energy security.[14] Interestingly, however, the EEAS and the HRVP have taken on the burden of the EU's response to the nuclear deal, even though the UK, France, and Germany—as the most prominent members of the European Council—could have decided to direct EU efforts through the various Council bodies.

As the EU's principal supranational institution, the European Commission also plays an important role in the formulation of EU grand strategy. Not only does the Commission manage the EU budget, but it claims exclusive policy competence in a range of strategically important areas such as the common commercial policy, competition, common fisheries policy, and monetary policy for Eurozone countries. Individual European Commissioners and their respective directorates-general play a vital role in strategy-making. In particular, the Commissioners for neighborhood policy, international cooperation and development, humanitarian aid and civil protection, trade policy, security and defense, and enlargement meet under the so-called "RELEX" formation to discuss combined efforts in response to diplomatic issues and international crises. The European Commission's role in EU grand strategy-making has special characteristics. One needs to consider that the Commission approaches strategy from a specific angle and this in many respects differs to other EU institutions. Indeed, whereas the Council bodies are primarily focused on the resolution of different national interests, the Commission largely conceives of strategy as policy decisions that not only secure the competences of the EU institutional system but that advance EU integration more broadly. The European Commission views closer EU integration as a strategic objective in its own right.[15]

In general, the Commission is only really acutely involved in EU foreign policy when it comes to the implementation of CFSP policy decisions. This is demonstrated most clearly with regard to sanctions policy when the Foreign Policy Instruments Service coordinates the member states' national sanctions lists.[16] It is also true to recall that the European Commission saw a number of the RELEX issues it dealt with (and some of the associated staff) before the Lisbon Treaty transferred RELEX to the EEAS in 2010. However, policy issues such as development aid and trade are enacted in the context of the broader geopolitical climate facing the EU. Therefore, Commission decisions do not occur in a strategic vacuum, especially when one considers that the HRVP—since the Lisbon Treaty—has taken her seat as a vice president of the Commission. As well as the head of the EEAS and chair of the monthly FAC, the Lisbon changes were designed to increase strategic coherence. Yet even these institutional linkages pose questions about *who* leads on EU grand strategy. Different strategic issues will necessitate different institutions to take the lead and the institutional system as a whole adapts accordingly. For example, while the presidents of the European Council and the Commission have traditionally led the EU's relations with states such as the US and China,[17] on the issue of foreign policy dossiers such as security in Kosovo, the president of the European Council and the HRVP have taken the lead.[18]

Finally, a range of other strategy-relevant EU bodies are relevant to the process. The European Parliament, for example, plays less of a role in direct foreign policy decision-making. But it does have significant powers related to the EU budget and in holding the European Commissioners to account. For example, the HRVP reports to the Parliament at each plenary session. The European Parliament is home to a range of committees and subcommittees that play a role in the legislative process and also inform the broader policy debate. The differences in relevance of these committees should not be underestimated. For example, the committee for international trade (INTA) has significant sway over many of the trade deals the EU signs with third countries by scrutinizing the economic benefits of these deals and assessing the human rights and development aspects of their content. Yet committees such as that on foreign affairs (AFET) and security and defense (SEDE) have less influence on the overall direction of EU foreign policy. Additionally, a range of agencies support the work of the European Commission and Council of the EU. Indeed, the European Defence Agency (EDA), European Border and Coast Guard Agency (Frontex), European Union Agency for Network and Information Security (ENISA), and the European Policy Office (EUROPOL) are among the specific EU entities that work on strategy-relevant issues. Each of these institutions has an important role in feeding expertise into the decision-making process, although they do not have much in the way of decision-making powers by virtue of their particular governance statutes.[19]

With the above mapping exercise in mind, it is worth considering to what extent the EU system lends itself to effective strategic action. On the one hand, the Council of the EU, the EEAS, and the European Commission work in relative harmony (e.g. sanctions policy and trade policy) on a range of policy issues. However, on other policy areas there is less clarity over the strategic harmony of decisions. For example, since the Lisbon Treaty, the European

Commission has increased involvement in formulating and negotiating energy deals with third countries, but the geopolitics of energy ensures that member state governments, through the European Council and the Council of the EU, retain a large stake in energy policy.[20] Migration is another policy area where the intergovernmental and supranational institutions of the EU do not always share a common strategic vision. Therefore, locating the EU's strategy makers is relatively simple if the exercise is to simply map out key actors and institutions. What is less clear, however, is how far the various institutions involved can work coherently together and what is the balance between initiatives being driven by the member state governments through the Council(s) and those initiatives driven mainly by the EU institutions in Brussels.

12.2 The EU and its strategic purpose

Having now provided an overview of the key actors involved in EU grand strategy-making, it is worth considering the goals, ends, and values that the EU works towards. If one is to understand the overarching logic of the EU's grand strategy, the first place to begin is the constitutive treaties of the EU. The preamble of the Treaty on European Union, for example, outlines at least two major overarching strategic objectives: (1) to support the principles of liberty and democracy, respect for human rights and fundamental freedoms, and the rule of law; and, tangibly, (2) to avoid any future war or conflict on the European continent by creating a firm basis for European prosperity and security. More specifically, Article 3.1 of the Treaty states that the "Union's aim is to promote peace, its values and the well-being of its peoples."[21] To this end, the EU not only establishes an internal market where citizens can exercise their fundamental freedoms, but in its international relations it seeks to strictly observe and development international law and multilateral institutions such as the UN. This last point should not be a surprise, given that the EU is itself a multilateral institution with a vested interest as a key contributor to the liberal international order.

Yet this liberal constitutive basis has given rise to a number of competing interpretations of what type of strategic actor the EU actually is. One prominent conceptual approach sees the EU as a normative power. Owing to what appears to be the EU's essentially civilian nature,[22] many scholars believe that the strategic purpose of the EU is to essentially rewrite the traditional rules of international relations that are based on the balance of power and anarchy.[23] Such interpretations give greater prominence to the EU as a trade and diplomatic actor, rather than a military power. Furthermore, normative power proponents claim that the EU is able to change the rules on international relations by acting in its own right and upholding its values and norms. In this regard, the EU's strategic presence in the world is not merely defined by policy tools such as trade and diplomacy, but rather its ability to influence the actions of other actors by way of a sort of "leadership by example" or "power of attraction."[24] Nye has referred to this phenomenon as "soft power."[25] For example, when the EU attempts to spread human rights norms it does so primarily based on its ability to live up to the norms it values.[26] Ultimately, normative power approaches (Normative Power Europe, or NPE) see the EU as a *sui generis* actor that cannot be understood by traditional IR theories such as realism.[27]

These normative power claims have fomented much debate in IR and European integration studies.[28] In particular, it should be acknowledged that NPE has given rise to a much broader scholarly debate about the nature of the EU's "power" as an international actor. On the back of normative power concepts, scholars have gone on to label the EU as a "market power"[29] or a "liberal power."[30] Both of these particular approaches are designed to highlight the exact nature of the interests, identities, and institutions the EU seeks to export around the world. Yet other scholars are unsatisfied with basing explanations of the EU's grand strategy solely on what the treaties of EU officials say. Here, counterarguments include: first, the fact that the rest of the world clearly does not follow the EU's values and norms (i.e. normative power Europe is empirically falsifiable);[31] second, the EU does not exactly live up to its own purported values and norms;[32] and finally, normative arguments cannot be disassociated with the official rhetoric of EU officials, making it hard to sustain an objective view of EU strategy.[33]

Realist explanations of EU grand strategy have also emerged to counter these normative power arguments. Here, the key task has been to broaden the debate beyond a mere focus on norms and values to also include material interests. In essence, the argument is that if the EU is a trade or market power it will most certainly have interests to protect, especially in an international order that is still inherently anarchical.[34] In this vein, some neorealists have conceded that the concept of NPE may have made strategic sense in an era of Western unipolarity, whereby US hard power underpinned a stable global and regional order that allowed Europeans (and the EU more specifically) to focus on economic prosperity and value promotion.[35] Europeans have indeed had to grapple with two sets of structural challenges over the last few decades. The first relates to the ongoing process of US strategic retrenchment from Europe, punctuated by developments as varied as the end of the Cold War and the collapse of the Soviet Union but also, more recently, by the so-called "US rebalance to Asia" or President Trump's references to "America First."[36] The second has to do with repeated signs of US condescendence vis-à-vis European interests and opinions, with two prominent examples being Washington's disdain for Europe's perspectives on how to conduct operations in the Western Balkans[37] and the transatlantic rift over the 2003 Iraq War.[38] For structural realists, these developments have repeatedly forced Europeans to question the wisdom of delegating their security and, ultimately, the use of military force to the United States.

Notwithstanding these scholarly debates, it is clear that the strategic objectives set down by the EU (while still valid) do have to address international and regional developments. While the EU's recently signed free trade agreements with Canada and Japan highlight the EU's trade prowess and commitment to a liberal global order, geopolitical shifts make it incumbent upon any scholar to ask how the EU's grand strategy and objectives may need to be reappraised. Indeed, while the objectives set down in the treaties are in a sense timeless, more specific objectives and goals may need to be developed to deal with regional and global challenges. For example, the so-called "Arab Spring" in 2010 and its fallout (e.g., the implosion of the Libyan and Syrian states and migratory pressures) and Russia's seizure of Crimea in 2014 and resulting insecurity on Europe's eastern flank raise serious strategic questions for the EU. Additionally, the UK's departure from the EU points to concerns about the nature (and ability) of the EU to play a meaningful international role, given London's status as one of the most globally minded member states and Europe's foremost military power (alongside France).

Although the objectives set in the EU treaties remain the overarching objectives of the EU, there is some difficulty in operationalizing them for the purposes of strategic action. Policy responses to international crises and challenges cannot rely merely on words or ideal types. This is where more tailored strategic reflections and documents, such as the EU Global Strategy, are required. Although the EU had released a European Security Strategy in 2003, the 2016 EU Global Strategy sought to make sense of and lay down strategic objectives for a more fragile geopolitical landscape in and around Europe. Taking "Brexit," the continued threat from Daesh, and Russia's resurgence in the East, the EU Global Strategy reflected a more pessimistic understanding of the geopolitical threats facing the EU. Despite some critical remarks related to whether the strategy was indeed a strategy,[39] back in 2003 it was possible for the EU to boldly proclaim that Europe had never been "so prosperous, so secure nor so free."[40] By 2016, however, the opening line of the foreword produced by the HRVP bleakly asserted that the "purpose, even existence, of our Union is being questioned." If all strategies are responses to broader geopolitical challenges, then the EU not only ably described the major international challenges facing the EU (including its own unity) but it set the tone by which the EU would then implement a Global Strategy.[41]

Although the EU Global Strategy continued to speak about external crises and the importance of multilateralism, it also refocused attention on the promotion of citizens' interests. In the 2003 report, the mantra was "effective multilateralism." But in 2016 the new guiding message was that of "principled pragmatism." As the Global Strategy stated, Europe's principles "stem as much from a realistic assessment of the current strategic environment as from an idealistic aspiration to advance a better world."[42] While the EU Global Strategy still promoted the value of international cooperation, a rules-based order and values, it explicitly stated that threats such as terrorism, hybrid threats, and energy insecurity are endangering Europeans and their territory. Tackling these threats are important elements of an overall EU grand strategy.

To this end, the Global Strategy offered a sophisticated framework and terminology for the EU's international engagement. First, it recognized that state and societal resilience in the East and South of Europe are critical to Europe's own internal security. This means that the EU aims to support fragile states with their security and economic development, even in those cases where a repressive regime exists. Second, the EU needs to develop an "integrated approach" to conflicts and crises. As the Global Strategy stated, the EU needs to employ a multidimensional, multiphased, multilevel and multilateral approach to international crises. In essence, the EU wants to be able to respond to such crises by engaging at all levels (local, national, regional, and global) with the full range of the EU's foreign policy toolbox.[43] Such approaches are clearly still within the liberal understanding of international affairs—i.e. a correction of developmental problems, diplomatic engagement with international organizations and civil society groups as well as states, and finding long-term solutions to international crises.

Where perhaps the Global Strategy departed from a purely liberal interpretation is in its emphasis on security and defense. The drafters of the 2003 European Security Strategy did not devote much attention to security or defense, but the 2016 strategy argued that "Europeans must be able to protect Europe, respond to external crises, and assist in developing our partners' security and defence capacities."[44] In fact, one of the most important elements of the EU Global Strategy is that it has led to a specific implementation plan for security and defense that outlines in specific detail how the EU will implement the security and defense elements of its overarching strategy. Most controversially, the EU Global Strategy's specific plan on security and defense stated that the EU must take up more responsibility for the security of European citizens.[45] This is understandable, given that challenges such as migration, terrorism, and hybrid threats do not respect borders. Yet, what is perhaps intriguing is how the 2016 security and defense plan called for the EU to be able to undertake military tasks such as close air support and maritime security (including on the high seas).[46] What is perhaps even more intriguing about these revised set of military tasks is that there is no geographical delimitation to the tasks. Read at face value, one could be forgiven for thinking that the EU had given itself the task of undertaking operations anywhere in the world.

12.3 Implementing grand strategy in the EU

As section 12.2 outlines, the EU has a clearly defined set of strategic objectives that it seeks to reassert on a regular basis through its diplomatic, economic, and security activities. However, the way in which the EU implements its grand strategy is also relevant to our debate. To this end, in this section we look at specific policy areas such as trade, sanctions, and security and defense to illustrate the ways in which EU grand strategy functions. As far as trade policy is concerned, it should first be recalled that the European Commission has a right of initiative for trade via the Common Commercial Policy—although government preferences still play a key role during any EU trade policy formation and international negotiations.[47] As the EU has historically evolved from a customs union to a single market, trade policy has been central to the prosperity of European citizens—both in promoting trade and ensuring that anti-dumping measures and safeguards are put in place to protect European consumers and industry.[48] The Commission takes a lead role in promoting free trade with key external strategic partners. A vital precondition for the EU's trade policy is that the EU's own single market functions in a coherent way, in the belief that the more energy the Commission puts into liberalizing the European market, the more leverage and attractiveness it will have in international negotiations.

The EU has consistently attempted to promote free trade, albeit in a specific way. For example, when the then EEC signed the Lomé Convention with seventy African, Caribbean, and Pacific countries in 1975, it did so not only to promote the liberalization of agricultural products but also to stimulate economic growth in partner countries. Thus, development is an inherent aspect of EU trade policy—amplified by the adoption of the 2015 EU trade strategy, which sees the need for socially responsible trade. Nevertheless, the sheer size and importance of the EU's economy gives the Union an unprecedented leverage in political terms. This can be seen most clearly in the way that the strength of EU trade policy is used to ensure a more robust application of sanctions policy. Finally, as a way to extend the liberal international order and to capitalize on its relative economic strength, the EU—much like other major economies—has resolved to promote global free trade through bilateral rather than multilateral trade agreements. Indeed, the EU and South Korea signed a free trade deal in 2010 and it has also signed deals with Canada and Japan. Of course, the choice of these partner countries indicates an emboldening of the current liberal order rather than an extension of it beyond liberal democratic states. Current trade policy also does not necessarily address the rise of powers such as Brazil, China, and India.[49]

Sanctions also represent a key way in which the EU attempts to secure its strategic objectives. The trend of EU sanctions has evolved over time, with an initial focus on "blanket" sanctions for entire sectors of an offending country (e.g. oil production) to more specific or "smart" sanctions that pinpoint individuals by freezing assets or banning travel to the EU. Of course, the impact and dynamics of EU sanctions will depend to a large degree on the level of economic interdependence between the EU and the third-state or persons in question. The EU's ability to impose sanctions and to persuade third-countries to alter their behavior is directly related to the EU's market power. Without its economic prowess, sanctions by the EU would not carry much political weight. Notwithstanding occasional resistance to EU sanctions,[50] the EU displays remarkable unity when imposing sanctions on third-states and actors. But questions remain about how national policies within the EU can undermine overall sanctions efforts. For example, while the EU has been consistent in its sanctions policy towards Russia following Crimea, it has not entirely been able to prevent Russian influence in the form of "Trojan horses" (e.g. energy dependency, financial flows, military access, disinformation) in particular EU member states.[51] Thus, sanctions policy may be considered a significant tool in EU grand strategy, but it has its limits.

Finally, CSDP also plays an important part in EU grand strategy. As far as security and defense in the EU is concerned, the Union adopts a hybrid approach to missions and operations by utilizing both civilian and military capabilities. Civilian capabilities consist of police and judicial experts, customs and border officials, and administrative experts based in the EU which are then sent to a third-country to assist with security sector reform.[52] Military capabilities consist of a broad range of equipment and systems including personnel as well as land, naval, air, sea, and space assets.[53] CSDP missions and operations are deployed largely to buttress liberal values by supporting social and economic development in third-countries (usually in former colonies in continents such as Africa). Yet, as some scholars have pointed out, "CSDP operations have partly served the purpose of making Europe feel good about itself rather than responding to local needs" and good intentions behind deployment are not always backed up with the necessary material support, such as troops and capabilities.[54] Here, it is vitally important to recall that both civilian and military capabilities are not EU-owned. Instead, capabilities for CSDP missions and operations have to be routinely sourced from national expert and force pools. For example, for the EU's naval operation in the Mediterranean (EUNAVFOR MED Operation Sophia) countries such as Belgium, France, Germany, Greece, Ireland, Italy, Netherlands, Poland, Portugal, Slovenia, Spain, and the UK have contributed assets such as frigates, light aircraft carriers, patrol vessels, and anti-submarine and maritime surveillance aircraft from national force pools.[55]

The way in which the EU deploys missions and operations under the CSDP is, on the face of it, unique because it follows a "comprehensive" or "integrated" approach to international crises. In essence, this means that while the

EU will deploy a civilian and/or military mission to a given country or region in response to the symptoms of an underlying issues (e.g. piracy, human trafficking, protection of civilians), it also tries to use its diplomatic channels and development/humanitarian aid to respond to the root causes of crises. Critics of this approach are clear that there are two issues that hinder the EU's CSDP. First, there are significant difficulties in deploying EU CSDP missions because of a lack of political will and little strategic consensus between member states, incoherent financing options for missions and operations, and a lack of essential strategic enablers and civilian/military capabilities.[56] Second, other critics have pointed to the fact that coherence in crisis management planning is hindered not only because of strategic differences between member states but also because there are "separate command chains for civilian missions and military operations" and because each structure is financed differently (either from EU member state common costs for military operations, or the EU budget for civilian missions).[57]

One way of showing how various aspects of the EU's grand strategy operate is through the EU's response to the Crimea crisis and the conflict in Ukraine. Russia's seizure of Crimea not only raised serious questions about the values that the EU was pursuing in international affairs (respect for international law and borders), but it dragged the EU into a geopolitical situation that required (and still requires) the full use of the EU's foreign and security policy capabilities. The EU's relationship with Ukraine had for many years been characterized solely in economic terms, with the EU negotiating a Deep and Comprehensive Free Trade Agreement (DCFTA) with Kiev with a view to enhancing the EU–Ukraine economic relationship. Energy policy had also been a feature of EU–Ukraine relations before Russia's actions in Ukraine. The Union's response to the crisis was multifaceted, but initially it was Germany that took an early leadership position rather than the EU institutions, even though the then HRVP, Catherine Ashton, was one of the first European officials to visit Maidan Square. Indeed, Berlin was largely responsible for forging the Minsk II agreement and supporting talks between Russia and Ukraine.[58]

However, when EU action was taken on Ukraine it took on diplomatic, financial, and operational characteristics. For example, while negotiations for an EU–Ukraine economic association agreement and a DCFTA began in 2007 it was only on 1 September 2017 that the agreement and free trade agreement came into force. Despite Russia's activities in Crimea and in eastern Ukraine, the European Commission pursued these agreements in order to help Kiev modernize its economy and to ensure that Ukraine would adhere to human rights, democracy, and rule of law norms strongly espoused by the EU. The Commission also mobilized a range of financial instruments to assist Ukraine deal with its fragility since the Crimea crisis, including: EU macro-financial loans worth over €3 billion; infrastructure loans worth €3 billion; economic development investments to the tune of €2.7 billion; grants for state-building and civil society and energy security totaling close to €1 billion; and humanitarian assistance of approximately €222 million.[59] This financial response has sought to show that the EU is supporting Ukraine (short of a military response) and that it wants a stake in the future development of the country with a view to ensuring that as an EU neighbor Kiev respects the values favored by the Union—especially in a context where Russian, illiberal influence is present in the country.

With these economic measures in place, the HRVP and relevant EEAS services have attempted to keep up diplomatic pressure on Russia with a host of bilateral meetings between the HRVP and Russian Foreign Minister Sergei Lavrov. Such meetings have been a way to keep up the pressure on Russia over Crimea and its activities in Syria. Yet, these bilateral meetings only take on meaning because of the EU's financial measures in Ukraine and its sanctions against Russian individuals and government/economic entities responsible for the crisis in Ukraine. For example, in 2017 alone the EU and its member states prolonged sanctions against Moscow on six different occasions in relation to Russia's non-adherence to the ceasefire agreed to under the Minsk Agreements.[60] In one specific case in July 2017, the Russian Deputy Prime Minister Dmitri Rogozin was barred entry into Romania and Hungary during a flight into the EU. Furthermore, while conventional deterrence and reassurance measures were taken by NATO in the East of Europe, the EU nonetheless deployed a civilian operation (EU Advisory Mission) to Ukraine in 2014 to assist with law enforcement, security service reform, border and customs capacity building, justice reform, and anticorruption.

It is clear from this range of resources that the EU is seeking to extend its own values into Ukraine by focusing squarely on reform of the country in line with its own values, norms, and interests. It is also evident that no single EU institution has taken the lead and there is a pragmatic link between various actors with a stake in Ukraine. Of course, the EU's approach to Ukraine sits in stark contrast to Russia's strategy in Ukraine and the wider region because whereas the EU uses relatively soft[61]—perhaps more mercantilist—capabilities, in the absence of an effective economic presence in the country Moscow uses a combination of hybrid tactics (e.g. disinformation and cyberattacks) and conventional force to achieve its strategic objectives.[62] Furthermore, while various EU institutions are involved in crafting the EU's strategy towards Ukraine, it was a member state (Germany in this case) that initiated the response. It is also the collective interests of the member states working through the European Council and the Council of the EU that will largely shape the Union's political response to Russia and Ukraine in the future. In this respect, much depends on unity between EU member states and coherence among the EU's institutions.[63]

12.4 Conclusion

This chapter has shown how there are strong elements of continuity to the way in which the EU formulates strategy, the objectives it seeks to achieve, and the capabilities it employs to secure them. We have shown how despite some rhetorical rebranding since the establishment of the EEAS in 2011, the EU is still geared towards: (a) underpinning and extending the liberal international order through its support of multilateral institutions and trade; (b) securing peace and stability in its immediate and wider neighborhood; and (c) resolving conflicts through diplomatic, developmental, and largely nonmilitary means. In sum, the EU's overarching strategic objective is to secure its brand of liberal international order by focusing on the root causes of conflict and international instability. To be sure, the EU seeks to promote trade to ensure that the benefits of economic globalization are extended on a global basis, and to address the malcontents of globalization by investing in development and providing humanitarian aid both in its surrounding regions and far afield. It also seeks to respond to conflict principally through diplomatic means and, in so far as it does respond militarily to conflict, it does so in the fashion of peacekeeping or in combination with civilian missions that address security sector reform (e.g. border management, policing, judicial and customs reform, etc.). Collectively, these approaches have been a consistent hallmark of the EU's broader grand strategy.

Change has been evident in an institutional and rhetorical sense. The EU has buttressed its institutional foreign and security policy architecture with the creation of a more powerful HR/VP and a diplomatic service called the EEAS. In this respect, this chapter has demonstrated how the EU has largely sought to improve its strategic coherence and effectiveness through a process of inter-institutional coordination. While there is clear evidence to support the idea that the EU has taken steps towards creating a more unified strategic sense of purpose, questions remain over the coherence between and unity of the EU's constituent member states. In reality, the member states have provided the HR/VP and the EEAS with insufficient financial and political support to take a true lead on strategy. There exists a power differential on strategic questions at the EU level. Powerful member states pull EU grand strategy in a direction that better suits their own national interests, whereas institutions such as the Commission and EEAS pull strategy in other—occasionally incoherent—directions towards a more European approach.

While there is plenty of evidence to suggest that the EU is a strategic actor, there are a number of strategic challenges that it faces. First, the EU is dealing with the fact that its most effective strategic means—that of EU enlargement—has serious limitations. With the exception of the Balkan states, there appears to be little appetite to expand the EU, especially into geopolitically sensitive areas such as the Middle East (via Turkish accession) or the Caucasus (with

Georgian accession). If enlargement today is constrained as a powerful strategic device, then the EU must devise new and effective ways of attracting neighbors short of full membership. Indeed, one of the substitutes for enlargement has been to constantly revise the European Neighbourhood Policy (ENP) in order to respond to geopolitical and socioeconomic challenges in the EU's surrounding states and regions. The challenge facing the EU in this regard is to tailor the ENP to the particular needs of individual countries and regions, while also retaining a strong incentive and capacity to be able to change the behavior of neighboring states over the longer-term. Additionally, the ENP clearly has limits when faced with major geopolitical crises—e.g. the ENP could not prevent the "Arab Spring" or Russia's invasion of Ukraine.

Second, and perhaps most seriously, questions about the EU's internal political cohesion play a dual role in the formulation of EU grand strategy. The UK's decision to leave the EU by referendum may be the most obvious case of political disintegration in the EU, but perhaps of equal importance is the current stance of the respective governments in Hungary and Poland. Not only did the Hungarian Prime Minister use a July 2014 speech to call for a revision to the liberal democratic principles on which the EU is based, but in December 2017 the European Commission concluded that Poland was in serious breach of the rule of law following Warsaw's decision to reform its judiciary. What such examples highlight is that the traditional assumptions embedded in the EU's history and framework related to human rights, rule of law, and democracy are in fact open to question by member states. Accordingly, the EU's dual strategic challenge in the future will be to protect its foundational liberal basis with the shifting needs of individual member states. This is especially crucial, given the flourishing of populist movements and parties within many EU member states.

Third, the nature of the transatlantic relationship will profoundly affect the EU's ability to behave as a strategic actor. The longer-term position of the US has been to underwrite European security with both political support and conventional and nuclear forces. This security umbrella currently remains, but this does not address the issue of burden-sharing between European allies and Washington. Calls for Europe to play (and pay) a larger contribution for European security are unlikely to disappear after President Trump has left office. The most immediate impact of such calls from the US will obviously relate to issues such as defense spending, but it may equally open up a difference of opinion between the EU and the US as to what really should count as security investments. It is already clear that many European allies within NATO do not regard the much-vaunted "2% of GDP" investment pledge as the only way in which Europe can contribute to international security.[64] Indeed, many European states consider their investments in development and humanitarian aid, counterterrorism and homeland security as equally important symbols of a commitment to European security and the transatlantic bond. The evolution of this debate on burden-sharing is likely to increase in the future as resource and political pressures hit the US, especially in a context where Washington wants to maintain its strategic centers of gravity in Europe, the Middle East, and (increasingly) the Indo-Pacific.

Last, this chapter has shown how the EU appears to have a fixation with a discussion about strategic ways and means (which manifests itself most clearly in discussions about institutional coherence) and that it has largely taken for granted the permanence of its strategic objectives. While it is true that "Brexit" and the current US administration has given the EU much pause for thought about the nature and resilience of the Union and global order, much broader and no less significant questions about the state of the liberal international order are likely to increase in the future. Russia's resurgence in the European strategic theater and China's global rise to power may not only call into question the EU's strategic assumptions that it has carried into the post–Cold War era, but it may require the EU to focus less on discussions about institutional coherence and more on enhancing its capacity to secure its strategic objectives. The future is one in which the EU may find it more challenging to reconcile its strategic ways, means, and ends.

NOTES

1. For a comprehensive account of the European Council's role in the EU system see: Uwe Puetter, *The European Council and the Council: New Intergovernmentalism and Institutional Change* (Oxford: Oxford University Press, 2014).
2. Petya Alexandrova, Marcello Carammia and Arco Timmermans, "Policy Punctuations and Issue Diversity on the European Council Agenda," *Policy Studies Journal* 40, no. 1 (2012): 69–88.
3. David Spence, "The Evolving Role of Foreign Ministries in the Conduct of European Union Affairs," in *Foreign Ministries in the European Union: Integrating Diplomats*, eds. Brian Hocking and David Spence (London: Palgrave Macmillan, 2005), 23.
4. These groups include the Politico-Military Group (PMG), the EU Military Committee (EUMC), and the Committee for Civilian Aspects of Crisis Management (CIVCOM).
5. Stephan Keukeleire and Tom Delreux, "The EU's Foreign Policy System: Actors," in *The Foreign Policy of the European Union* (London: Palgrave Macmillan, 2014), 69.
6. For more on these structures see Chiara Steindler, "Mapping Out the Institutional Geography of External Security in the EU," *European Security* 24, no. 3 (2015): 402–19.
7. Desmond Dinan, "The Council of the European Union and the European Council," in *Routledge Handbook of European Politics*, ed. José M. Magone (London: Routledge, 2015), 219–47.

8. Wolfgang Wessels, Peter Valant, and Tobias Kunstein, "The EU Council(s) System and Administrative Fusion," in *The Palgrave Handbook of the European Administrative System*, eds. Michael W. Bauer and Jarle Trondal (London: Palgrave Macmillan, 2015), 265–80.
9. Thomas E. Henökl, "How Do EU Foreign Policy-Makers Decide? Institutional Orientations Within the European External Action Service," *West European Politics* 38, no. 3 (2015): 679–708.
10. Antonio Missiroli, ed., "The EEAS," in *The EU and the World: Players and Policies Post-Lisbon: A Handbook* (Paris: European Union Institute for Security Studies, 2017), 27–44.
11. Thomas E. Henökl and Jarle Trondal, "Unveiling the Anatomy of Autonomy: Dissecting Actor-Level Independence in the European External Action Service," *Journal of European Public Policy* 22, no. 10 (2015): 1426–47.
12. Mark Fitzpatrick, "Iran: A Good Deal," *Survival: Global Politics and Strategy* 57, no. 5 (2015): 47–52.
13. Steven Blockmans and Astrid Viaud, "EU Diplomacy and the Iran Nuclear Deal: Staying Power?," *CEPS Policy Insights*, no. 2017-28 (2017).
14. Ellie Geranmayeh, "Towards and Beyond a Final Nuclear Deal with Iran," *The International Spectator: Italian Journal of International Affairs* 50, no. 2 (2015): 1–7.
15. Ingeborg Tömmel, "The Presidents of the European Commission: Transactional or Transforming Leaders?," *Journal of Common Market Studies* 51, no. 4 (2013): 789–805.
16. Op. cit., note 4, p. 77.
17. Michael Smith, "EU Diplomacy and the EU-China Strategic Relationship: Framing, Negotiation and Management," *Cambridge Review of International Affairs* 29, no. 1 (2016): 78–98.
18. Maria Giulia Amadio Viceré, "The Roles of the President of the European Council and the High Representative in Leading EU Foreign Policy on Kosovo," *Journal of European Integration* 38, no. 5 (2016): 557–70.
19. Morten Egeberg and Jarle Trondal, "EU-level Agencies: New Executive Centre Formation or Vehicles for National Control?," *Journal of European Public Policy* 18, no. 6 (2011): 868–87.
20. Pami Aalto and Dicle Korkmaz Temel, "European Energy Security: Natural Gas and the Integration Process," *Journal of Common Market Studies* 52, no. 4 (2014): 758–74.
21. European Union, *Consolidated Versions of the Treaty on European Union and the Treaty on the Functioning of the European Union* (2016), 17.
22. Francois Duchêne, "Europe's Role in World Peace," in *Europe Tomorrow: 16 Europeans Look Ahead*, ed. Richard Mayne (London: Fontana, 1973).
23. Lisbeth Aggestam, "Introduction: Ethical Power Europe?," *International Affairs* 84, no. 1 (2008): 1; and Christopher Bickerton, "Legitimacy Through Norms: The Political Limits to Europe's Normative Power," in *Normative Power Europe: Empirical and Theoretical Perspectives*, ed. Richard G. Whitman (London: Palgrave Macmillan, 2011), 25–42.
24. Ian Manners, "The Normative Ethics of the European Union," *International Affairs* 84, no. 1 (2008): 45–60; and Ian Manners, "Normative Power Europe: A Contradiction in Terms?," *Journal of Common Market Studies* 40, no. 2 (2002): 235–58.

25. Joseph S. Nye, *Soft Power: The Means to Success in World Politics* (New York: Public Affairs, 2004).
26. Karen E. Smith, "The EU, human rights and relations with third countries: 'foreign policy' with an ethical dimension?," in *Ethics and Foreign Policy*, eds. Karen E. Smith and Margot Light (Cambridge: Cambridge University Press, 2001), 188.
27. Richard G. Whitman, "Norms, Power and Europe: A New Agenda for Study of the EU and International Relations," in *Normative Power Europe*, 1–22.
28. Whitman, "Norms, Power and Europe," 1.
29. Chad Damro, "Market Power Europe," *Journal of European Public Policy* 19, no. 5 (2012): 682–99.
30. Wolfgang Wagner, "Liberal Power Europe," *Journal of Common Market Studies* 55, no. 6 (2017): 1398–414.
31. Thomas Diez, "Constructing the Self and Changing Others: Reconsidering 'Normative Power Europe'," *Millennium: Journal of International Studies* 33, no. 3 (2005): 616.
32. Sonia Cardenas, "Norm Collision: Explaining the Effects of International Human Rights Pressure on State Behavior," *International Studies Review* 6, no. 2 (2004): 213–32; and Jennifer L. Erickson, "Market Imperative Meets Normative Power: Human Rights and European Arms Transfer Policy," *European Journal of International Relations* 19, no. 2 (2011): 209–34.
33. Helene Sjursen, "The EU as a 'Normative' Power: How can this be?," *Journal of European Public Policy* 13, no. 2 (2006): 235.
34. Adrian Hyde-Price, "A 'Tragic Actor'? A Realist Perspective on 'Ethical Power Europe'," *International Affairs* 84, no. 1 (2008): 29–44.
35. Adrian Hyde-Price, "'Normative' Power Europe: A Realist Critique," *Journal of European Public Policy* 13, no. 2 (2006): 217–34.
36. Luis Simón, "Understanding US Retrenchment in Europe," *Survival: Global Politics and Strategy* 57, no. 2 (2015): 157–72.
37. Alistair, J. K. Shepherd, "'A Milestone in the History of the EU': Kosovo and the EU's International Role," *International Affairs* 85, no. 3 (2009) 513–30.
38. Barry Posen, "European Union Security and Defense Policy: Response to Unipolarity," *Security Studies* 15, no. 2 (2006) 149–86.
39. Council of the EU, *European Security Strategy: A Secure Europe in a Better World* (2003).
40. François Heisbourg, "The 'European Security Strategy' is not a Security Strategy," in *A European Way of War*, eds. Steven Everts et al. (London: Centre for European Reform, 2004), 27–39. See also Asle Toje, "The 2003 European Union Security Strategy: A Critical Appraisal," *European Foreign Affairs Review* 10, no. 1 (2005): 117–33.
41. Nathalie Tocci, "The Making of the EU Global Strategy," *Contemporary Security Policy* 37, no. 3 (2016): 461–72.
42. High Representative/Vice-President, *Shared Vision, Common Action: A Stronger Europe—A Global Strategy for the EU's Foreign and Security Policy* (2016), 8.
43. Mai'a K. Davis Cross, "The EU Global Strategy and Diplomacy," *Contemporary Security Policy* 37, no. 3 (2016): 402–13.
44. High Representative/Vice-President, *A Global Strategy for the EU's Foreign and Security Policy*, p. 19.

45. Daniel Fiott, "European Defence: The Year Ahead," *Policy Brief*, no. 1 (Paris: EU Institute for Security Studies, 2017).
46. Council of the EU, "Council conclusions on implementing the EU Global Strategy in the area of Security and Defence," *14149/16*, Brussels, November 14, 2016.
47. Sophie Meunier, "Managing Globalization? The EU in International Trade Negotiations," *Journal of Common Market Studies* 45, no. 4 (2007): 905–26.
48. Stephen Woolcock, *European Union Economic Diplomacy: The Role of the EU in External Economic Relations* (Farnham, UK: Ashgate, 2012), 51.
49. Patricia Garcia-Duran, Montserrat Millet, and Jan Orbie, "EU Trade Policy Reaction to the BIC: From Accommodation to Entrenchment," in *EU Policy Responses to a Shifting Multilateral System*, eds. Esther Barbé, Oriol Costa, and Robert Kissack (London: Palgrave Macmillan, 2016), 93–114.
50. Clara Portela, "Member States Resistance to EU Foreign Policy Sanctions," *European Foreign Affairs Review* 20, no. 2 (2015): 39–61.
51. Mitchell A. Orenstein and R. Daniel Keleman, "Trojan Horses in EU Foreign Policy," *Journal of Common Market Studies* 55, no. 1 (2016): 87–102.
52. Catriona Gourlay, "Civilian CSDP: A Tool for State-Building?," in *The Routledge Handbook of European Security*, eds. Sven Biscop and Richard G. Whitman (New York: Routledge, 2013), 91–104.
53. Sven Biscop and Jo Coelmont, "Military CSDP: The Quest for Capability," in *The Routledge Handbook of European Security*, 78–90.
54. See for example, Benjamin Pohl, *EU Foreign Policy and Crisis Management Operations: Power, Purpose and Domestic Politics* (London: Routledge, 2014), 173.
55. European External Action Service, "EUNAVFOR MED Operation Sophia—Assets," 2016, https://eeas.europa.eu/csdp-missions-operations/eunavfor-med-operation-sophia/12215/assets_en
56. Tim Haesebrouck and Melanie Van Meirvenne, "EUFOR RCA and CSDP Crisis Management Operations: Back on Track?," *European Foreign Affairs Review* 20, no. 2 (2015): 267–85.
57. Alexander Mattelaer, "The Empty Promise of Comprehensive Planning in EU Crisis Management," *European Foreign Affairs Review*, vol. 18 (2013): 135.
58. Marco Siddi, "German Foreign Policy Towards Russia in the Aftermath of the Ukraine Crisis: A New *Ostpolitik*?," *Europe-Asia Studies* 68, no. 4 (2016): 665–77; and Ulrich Krotz and Richard Maher, "Europe's Crises and the EU's 'Big Three'," *West European Politics* 39, no. 5 (2016): 1053–72.
59. European External Action Service, "Ukraine and the EU," https://eeas.europa.eu/headquarters/headquarters-homepage/1937/ukraine-and-eu_en
60. European External Action Service, "EU extends sanctions in support of Ukraine's territorial integrity," https://eeas.europa.eu/headquarters/headQuarters-homepage_en/28967/EU%20extends%20sanctions%20in%20support%20of%20Ukraine%27s%20territorial%20integrity
61. Thomas Gehring, Kevin Urbanski, and Sebastian Oberthür, "The European Union as an Inadvertent Great Power: EU Actorness and the Ukraine Crisis," *Journal of Common Market Studies* 55, no. 4 (2017): 727–43.

62. Kristi Raik, "The Ukraine Crisis as a Conflict over Europe's Political, Economic and Security Order," *Geopolitics* (early view), DOI:10.1080/14650045.2017.1414046.
63. Portela, "Member States Resistance."
64. Sebastian Sprenger, "Germany and 2 percent for defense—it's complicated," *DefenseNews*, February 17, 2017, https://www.defensenews.com/smr/munich-security-forum/2018/02/17/germany-and-two-percent-for-defense-its-complicated/

13 Conclusion

The Emerging Sub-field of Comparative Grand Strategy

NORRIN M. RIPSMAN

"Grand strategy" is an imprecisely used term in international relations. Scholars who use it mean anything from a state's overall strategy in a war to a long-term blueprint for the state's foreign relations. Some view grand strategy (GS) as solely encompassing military considerations and means, whereas others incorporate economic and ideological considerations as elements of GS.[1] Furthermore, GS has typically been studied in a strictly national context, with scholars focusing on the GSs of great powers.[2] The few attempts to study states' strategic behavior in a comparative context have been useful, but may have suffered from a lack of in-depth contextual knowledge of all of the cases.[3]

To redress these problems, Balzacq, Dombrowski, and Reich make several important contributions in this volume. First, they articulate a rather flexible understanding of GS, encompassing the ways and means that states employ to pursue their strategic ends, however they define them. Avoiding a rigid definition enables them to assess the utility of the concept of GS across a range of states and strategic contexts, with states themselves determining the aims and content of their GS. Second, they bring together country specialists to focus on the unique domestic and international contexts of their country's quest for security. This allows for meaningful cross-case comparisons and guards against superficial overgeneralizations. Third, they explore the utility of the concept of GS as a means of understanding the behavior of a range of states, from great powers to smaller states. While global geopolitics may remain the privilege of great powers, smaller states may also engage in long-term strategic planning and, indeed, may be compelled to do so if they wish to survive a world inhabited by greater powers, as the editors argue. Finally, the editors seek to move our understanding of GS beyond a structural realist conception driven by traditional great power threats, prompting rather automatic, rational national responses. To begin with, embracing the insights of neoclassical realism, they acknowledge that, within the constraints of interstate imperatives, domestic politics, strategic culture, and the influence of individual leaders can exert an important influence in shaping a state's grand strategic choices.[4] Furthermore, they update the nature of global threats that states employ GS to counteract to include twenty-first century threats, such as nuclear proliferation, rogue states, and violent nonstate actors. These innovations make this a unique and important volume.

This concluding chapter is divided into five sections. In the first section, I consider several methodological challenges that complicate the mission of comparative GS analysis and, consequently, probe the limits of this exercise. The next three sections examine the aggregate conclusions and insights of the volume. In the second section, I discuss the sources of GS in the states examined in this book, principally who are its architects, and the role of history, geography, and strategic culture in defining it. The third section explores the range of goals that states pursue with their GSs, with a consideration of how a state's strategic environment and relative power can explain variation. The fourth section concentrates on the tools that states use to promote their geostrategic goals, including the varying degrees to which they employ economic and ideational means in addition to military and technological ones. In the final section, I evaluate additional insights suggested by this comparative exercise and explore avenues for inquiry.

13.1 Can we study comparative grand strategy?

While Balzacq, Dombrowski, and Reich make a strong case for the desirability of studying grand strategy outside the great power context and comparatively, such an effort must overcome several daunting obstacles. To begin with, for several reasons, it is difficult to determine what a state thinks about GS. After all, not all states think self-consciously about grand strategy, and not all that do document their efforts. In effect, researchers will encounter three types of states: (1) states that embrace the concept of GS and leave a paper trail in publicly accessible documents; (2) states that embrace the concept of GS, but do not leave a paper trail; and (3) states that do not even think in terms of GS. The first category includes states such as the US, with its tradition of publishing documents such as the National Security Strategy of the United States of America to inform the public about its strategic concepts.[5] Based on Celine Marangé's and Ghaidaa Hetou's chapters, the second category would include states like Russia and Saudi Arabia, which are more opaque and do not allow public scrutiny of documents of strategic importance. Since, according to Robert Johnson's chapter, British leaders have been reluctant to speak in terms of grand strategy, but nonetheless do plan strategy, Great Britain would also fit in the second category. Finally, the third category includes China—where Andrew Erickson says many Chinese leaders deny that they have a grand strategy and one must look to various sources to piece together the logic that underlies Chinese security behavior—and Brazil, where the Worker's

Party does not use the term grand strategy. For latter two categories of states, researchers are forced to read the tea leaves to determine what GS is and what its primary influences are, a task that is fraught with the risk of misinterpretation. Notably, it might lead to a functionalist/rationalist bias, where researchers seek to explain a state's strategic behavior and fit it into a rational framework when it may in fact have been the result of a nonrational bureaucratic process or even irrational decision-making, precisely the kind of error that the editors indicate in their introduction they wish to avoid.

A related problem is the gap between rhetoric and reality that sometimes exists, which complicates our analysis of even the first category of states. For a variety of reasons, states might make claims about their strategic logic that diverge from their true intentions.[6] States which have expansionist GSs might wish to have a more moderate declaratory policy to set neighboring states at ease and forestall the development of a balancing coalition. States with inadequate capabilities might wish to bluff their adversaries and reassure domestic opinion with a more vigorous GS declaration than they have the resources or national will to enact. How, then, can we trust the publicly released national security doctrines and official statements that are available?

To some extent, this problem can be dealt with by breaking inside the black box of the state, accessing government decision-making documents not intended for public release.[7] Nonetheless, this strategy presents additional problems. To begin with, while democratic states routinely declassify many older documents, nondemocratic states allow much more restricted access to government archives, if they allow any access at all. Even states that do allow regular access to national archives follow a thirty- or fifty-year rule, whereby scholars can only access files pertaining to historical cases, rather than more recent events. Moreover, especially in the national security area, even older files may be redacted or removed on the grounds that they are still sensitive. Thus—especially for more recent cases and the analysis of closed states, but even for historical cases—it might be impossible to gain sufficient access to a government's actual thinking to cut through misleading statements and rhetoric.

Another approach to dealing with this problem would be to impute the state's true goals from their actual behavior.[8] Yet this approach is fraught with its own risks. Notably, it may impute rationality and motives that do not exist. In other words, a researcher could mistakenly assume that behavior resulting from bureaucratic procedures, inter-organizational bargaining, or some other dysfunctional process is actually the product of a grand national design.[9] Thus, while the mission of studying GS comparatively is a worthy one, it may be a quixotic task.

A second concern relates to whether GS could be studied comparatively, even if we had perfect access to state records. All comparative analyses necessarily must confront the issue of generalizability, which requires concept equivalence across cases.[10] If "security" and GS mean different things in different contexts, can we truly generalize across cases? In a volume of this sort, can we have anything more than idiosyncratic cases that permit little or no generalization? I believe that there is merit in an effort to study GS comparatively, provided we do so cautiously and do not overreach. Subject to this caveat, this volume thus generates some interesting insights, which I discuss in the next three sections, that would benefit from more systematic investigation.

13.2 Where does grand strategy come from?

As the editors observe, the literature on GS has a rationalist bias, which places a heavy emphasis on the external environments states face as the principal determinant of their GS. States are presumed to pursue a particular GS because they are compelled to do so. The essays in this volume do not dispute the importance of the external environment, but they make a case for a broader understanding of the sources of GS, including the influence of particular actors and institutions, strategic culture, and historical memory in mediating the national strategic response to external threats and opportunities. In this regard, they justify a movement away from the paradigmatic rigidity of neorealism and liberalism toward more eclectic, multiparadigmatic approaches to international security.[11]

13.2.1 TRADITIONAL INPUTS: GEOGRAPHY, TECHNOLOGY, AND THE BALANCE OF POWER

Not surprisingly, the authors in this volume all anchor their analyses in the geostrategic realities that the states in question face. Thus, in the post–Cold War era, unipolarity is of particular importance in shaping the strategic choices of states. The unipole, facing no peer competitors, can seek to reshape the world in its image, pursue strategic objectives on a global scale, and prevent potential competitors from rising. Other states must frame their GS vis-à-vis that of the unipole, whether it is to counter US objectives in key regions (as Russia and Iran are doing within the Middle East), to avoid a major confrontation with the US while expanding its own power (as China has done), to work with an American ally to achieve global or regional objectives (as the Western European states, Australia and Brazil do), or to rely on the US to secure themselves in a hostile region (which has been the bedrock principle of Saudi and Israeli GS for decades).

Beyond the global distribution of power, states need to craft their GSs to navigate the particular regional security complex they face.[12] States in unstable environments, characterized by extreme power imbalances, enduring rivalries, and/or intense short-term threats, must have a shorter time horizon for the GS and tend to focus heavily on military means and traditional military alliances to achieve their objectives.[13] In this volume, this is illustrated by the cases of Israel and Saudi Arabia, which inhabit the perpetually unstable Middle East region with an intensifying Iranian threat. In contrast, states in more stable regions, without extreme power imbalances, militarized rivalries, and intense short-term threats can pursue a longer-range GS, using a wider degree of economic, political, and institutional tools. The prototypical case of this in this volume is Brazil, which lacks any serious near-term national security threats, but also the US and, to a lesser extent, France and the United Kingdom.

Two key inputs into relative power and regional stability—geography, technology, and the interaction between them—are of special relevance.[14] Geography affects not only the resources that states have at their disposal and thus their aggregate power, but also the timeframe and intensity of threats that they face. Consequently, it affects the freedom of action that states have to construct GS and their timeframes. States, such as the US and Brazil, which are geographically remote from other great powers and protected by ocean barriers, can pursue more proactive, open-ended, longer-term GSs that advance ideational objectives and seek to reshape their strategic environments. In contrast, Middle Eastern states, with little distance between themselves and a host of threats, or India, sandwiched between Pakistan and China, must be more reactive and focused on the shorter term.

Technological change, however, imbues geography with meaning and can reshape or reduce its impact in much the same way that the development of the aircraft carrier and rocketry reduced the importance of the US ocean buffers after World War II.[15] In the contemporary era, the advent of modern transportation and communication has eased power projection across national boundaries and the globe. Moreover, as I will elaborate below, states with fewer economic and military resources can attempt to develop nuclear weapons capability, as Iran and North Korea have, or cyber warfare capability, as have Russia, China, Iran, and North Korea, as a means of offsetting their power disadvantages.

These material inputs into GS remain merely the setting within which states construct GS. The chapters in this volume also consider the actors who respond to them and ideational context within which they do so.

13.2.2 THE PROCESS OF GRAND STRATEGY: WHO MAKES GRAND STRATEGY?

Different actors and institutions author GS. In some more authoritarian states, GS is the province of a single powerful leader or a leadership group. Marangé, for example, discusses Russian President Vladimir Putin's dominance of the Russian GS process. As Erickson indicates, Xi Jinping has similarly seized control over the Chinese GS process, giving himself far more influence over GS than his immediate predecessors. In other authoritarian states, however, participation in the making of GS expands slightly, with key groups, such as Iran's Islamic Revolutionary Guards Corp (IRGC), playing an important role together with the Supreme Leader. In contrast, liberal states expand participation in the formulation of grand strategy, involving government bureaucracies and the military establishment, together with the political leadership. In this context, Dombrowski and Reich's chapter notes not only the complications arising from the constitutional division of powers between the executive and the legislature—which Edward Corwin described as "an invitation to struggle for the privilege of directing American foreign policy"[16]—but also from the proliferation of loosely connected institutions and bureaucracies that contributed to US strategic policy. The British and French models described respectively by Johnson and Balzacq are somewhat less chaotic, as the institutional struggle is dominated by the prime minister and the president, for whom foreign policy is a *domaine réservé*. Nonetheless, GS in these democracies also have many authors, who try to shape policy. This may affect the longevity of the GS, as strategic blueprints adopted by individual leaders might change when a new leader comes to power, whereas doctrines with broad authorship and the input of multiple stakeholders might be more enduring until underlying strategic conditions change. Indeed, Christine Fair's chapter argues that, despite changing conditions, the bureaucratic structure of Indian foreign policy has been an impediment to jettisoning the Nehruvian approach to GS.

Of course, a focus on process and authorship presupposes that GS is not simply a product of the external environment, as structural realists assume. After all, if GS were merely a rational response to objective geostrategic conditions, then a state's GS should be essentially the same whether it was authored by a dictator or a ruling elite, or the result of a complex process involving a mix of organizations and bureaucracies.[17] The chapters herein do not explicitly demonstrate that agency or the procedure whereby GS is constructed has any causal weight over its content. Therefore, it remains an important avenue of future research to investigate whether the actors, processes, and procedures that produce GS actually affect its content or not.

13.2.3 ROLE OF STRATEGIC CULTURE AND HISTORICAL MEMORY

While it is tempting to think of GS as a rational response to a given set of external threats and opportunities, in practice, a state's unique strategic culture has an important impact on GS by influencing the threats and opportunities the leadership prioritizes and the means that it uses to advance national interests.[18] Thus, as Alastair Ian Johnston argues, although Ming

Dynasty China pursued a realist GS, it did so because of the package of ideas that comprised China's domestic strategic culture.[19] Moreover, the unique historical narratives that states use to make sense of their past and their present also have an important role in shaping GS.

This point is driven home in almost every chapter of this book. For example, Dombrowski and Reich highlight the importance of founding myths of messianism, exceptionalism, and frontierism in American foreign policy. Marangé's chapter stresses that Russian GS is a product of an ingrained Russian fear of the outside, growing out of the experience of the Soviet regime. Ramadan-Alban notes the persistence of narratives of independence and status in shaping Iranian GS. Balzacq's chapter underscores the significance of the Gaullist concept of *grandeur* for French GS until very recently. Shamir discusses the impact of the "Masada Complex" and the Holocaust on Israeli strategic thinking. Clearly, GS reflects more than simply strategic conditions, but also the heart and soul of the nation, which makes it more difficult to generalize across countries.

In this regard, the objective strategic environment can tell us only the parameters of the situation that states find themselves in. Subjective perceptions—influenced by strategic culture, historical memory, formative national narratives, or leader biases—may be even more consequential than objective conditions. Indeed, Marangé claims that the pervasive Russian sense of insecurity, rather than any objective threat, has led Moscow to pursue belligerent policies toward the West in the wake of the Cold War. The implication is that the research program of comparative GS that the editors seek to carve out should not simply focus on the differing strategic conditions of the states (e.g., their size, wealth, position, relative power, technological sophistication, etc.), but also upon *who* (i.e., the individuals, nations, parties, etc.) is responding to these conditions and with what perceptual, historical, cultural, and emotional baggage.

At the same time, going down this rabbit hole presents its own dilemmas for researchers. On one hand, too much emphasis on the unique contextual circumstances might sacrifice the social scientific generalizations inherent in a focus on comparative GS to the mission of thick description of idiosyncratic events. On the other, too much of an effort to achieve generalizable comparative theories of GS can obscure important contextual elements that undermine the utility of the enterprise.

13.3 Goals of grand strategy

More fundamentally, the chapters herein suggest that it would be a mistake to assume that GS is solely about external security. States pursue a variety of different goals with their GS, including traditional security maximization, the pursuit of status, economic growth, and even the advancement of important ideational and ideological goals that are central to the national mission.

At the core of GS lies the hard security goals that states were established to pursue.[20] These include avoiding wars, winning wars, balancing against threats, forestalling the development of hostile coalitions, and building/preserving the state's long-term power position. To these ends, states utilize deterrence, defensive strategies, arms buildups, alliances, and other traditional security measures. As Shamir indicates in his chapter, therefore, for embattled Israel, which faces a multiplicity of threats, survival is the central goal of GS and the Israeli Defense Forces remain its principal instrument. Ramadan-Alban emphasizes the importance of security against an activist American hegemon as an important goal of Iranian GS. As Marangé demonstrates, Russian GS is preoccupied by the threats posed by NATO military forces in Eastern Europe.

Yet other national goals appear to animate the GSs discussed in this book. Some states are clearly motivated by status competition. As William Wohlforth and others have observed, states are often motivated principally by status and prestige even in the security issue area.[21] Thus, grand strategy is often about seeking international privileges, membership in core groups, such as the UN Security Council, diplomatic recognition, and respect. Marange's chapter emphasizes that for Russian security planners, status matters an awful lot, especially after its humiliating defeat in the Cold War. Similarly, the Gaullist strategy of *grandeur* discussed by Balzacq was a means of preserving France's international status after French decline during the world wars. Shamir indicates that recognition by regional states was an important goal of Israeli GS since the country's independence. And the imperative of reversing the "century of national humiliation" is the dominant principle underlying China's approach to the outside world.[22]

Ideational/ideological goals also feature prominently in the security blueprints of states. States often view spreading their political, economic, or religious worldviews as essential to securing themselves. In this regard, ideational goals are not necessarily divorced from traditional security considerations, but may be designed to reinforce them. After all, if likeminded states or co-religionists are less likely to view us as threatening or are more likely to align with us, it makes sense to try to convert others to our beliefs.[23] If, as democratic peace theorists argue, spreading liberalism and democracy can foster a more stable environment or promote peace, it behooves security planners to take that seriously.[24] Consequently, the Balzacq chapter notes that French leaders view building a stable liberal order as a core component of their GS, and, at least before Trump's "America First" GS, it has been the foundation of US GS since the end of the Cold War, if not since World War II.[25] Hetou's chapter on Saudi Arabia acknowledges the kingdom's efforts to shape at least the Islamic world by exporting Salafism abroad, which can help counter the ideological threat posed by Iran. Iran, itself, has made its efforts at seeking to export its Shia revolution throughout the region a means of achieving its security interests.

Beyond attempts to shape the regional or global environment, the central values the state wishes to safeguard can also be informed by ideology and the state's identity.[26] As Arnold Wolfers observed, national security is not an end in itself, but a means to an end.[27] Consequently, the ends that states pursue will affect their understandings of "security" and the strategies they employ to obtain it. In this regard, Erickson notes that China seeks to preserve the dominance of the Party leadership above all, rather than merely the traditional national security concept. Shamir observes that Israel seeks survival in a hostile region above all, but does so in order for the country to function as a center for Jewish life and a beacon of democracy in the Middle East. France initially prioritized not merely survival, but *grandeur*, whereas it now seeks to entrench liberalism within Europe and beyond.

13.3.1 THREATS VS OPPORTUNITIES

Is GS merely an exercise in identifying and countering threats the state is likely to face, or is it also about opportunities for expansion and accumulating power? Certainly, as already mentioned, states in troubled regions must be preoccupied by existential threats, as the chapters on Israel and Saudi Arabia demonstrate. Yet states facing more permissive security environments, such as Brazil and the US, have more leeway to pursue different kinds of opportunities. But this choice between countering threats or pursuing opportunities may also relate to the ideational makeup of the state, particularly whether revisionist or status quo interests control the state.[28]

13.3.2 ECONOMIC GOALS

States also vary in the degree to which they make economic goals central foci of GS. As Robert Gilpin and other realists point out, differential economic growth rates are the driving force of world politics.[29] Consequently, wealth is the very foundation of military power and security, which enables military spending and R&D.[30] Therefore, it is not unreasonable for GS, which is about maintaining and growing power into the future, to concern itself with economic growth rather than strictly military matters. The quintessential example of this is China, which made promoting national wealth the key component of GS under Deng Xiaoping.[31] Fair's chapter emphasizes the importance of economic self-reliance in Indian GS. As Erickson observes, the Chinese government's current emphasis on achieving a "moderately prosperous society" and building China's ability to be "a global leader in innovation" is an important component of Chinese GS.

This volume, therefore, by addressing a range of states of varying sizes and in different regional contexts, has effectively illustrated the variety and complexity of grand strategic goals that states pursue better than idiosyncratic studies of individual states' GS could.

13.4 Tools of grand strategy

Beyond the different goals that states seek to achieve with their GSs, they also vary in the instruments they earmark to achieve those objectives. In general, states employ diplomatic, economic, military, and technological instruments to secure themselves. Nonetheless, these are combined in different ways with different emphases across the states in this study.

Military instruments remain at the core of GS. All of the states in this study maintained armed forces in the air, sea, and land and premise their national security planning on their use and readiness. Many also participate in military alliances, such as NATO, in an effort to cumulate power and deter rivals. The US, Russia, China, France, the United Kingdom, India, and, most likely, Israel, possess nuclear capabilities to deter rivals.

Yet states utilize other instruments, as well. In particular, economic tools remain a staple of the national security arsenal. Indeed, as Erickson demonstrates, a core aim of contemporary Chinese GS is to tie Eurasia to Chinese leadership through the Belt and Road Initiative.[32] Brazil has used the regional economic grouping Mercosur as a central component of its GS. As Simón notes, the European Union's principle security strategy is to spread the economic benefits of integration to states on the periphery. And, prior to Donald Trump's election victory, the US has made the expansion of the Western liberal order a strategic priority.

Technology and technological change loom large in the GSs of many of the states. In particular, some nongreat power states have sought to redress their insecurity and/or inferior status with the pursuit of nuclear weapons. This may explain the Iranian quest for nuclear weapons over the last few decades, as a way of cementing its dominance of the region and preventing the US from interfering with its regional interests. The centrality of Dimona in Israeli GS as a means of neutralizing the numeric superiority of the surrounding Arab and Islamic states and the importance of nuclear weapons for India also fit this pattern. Cyber warfare technology also has the potential to enable poorer and weaker states to level the playing field by interfering with other states' ability to utilize their national security apparatus or, potentially, by paralyzing a rival's civilian economy. States such as Russia, China, Iran, and North

Korea have invested heavily in cyber technology in recent years, with tests against civilian and military targets in variety of countries.[33] Going forward, therefore, technological change may change the emphasis and content of the GSs of all states.

States are increasingly relying on multilateral institutions to contribute to their security goals. Those in relatively secure neighborhoods rely especially heavily on institutional pillars.[34] Milani and Nery thus note that Mercosur and UNASUR feature prominently in Brazilian doctrine. Johnson points out that, even in the era of Euroskepticism and Brexit, NATO still retains its strategic importance to the UK. Balzacq notes that France utilizes not only the EU, but also La Francophonie, as a means of projecting French influence throughout the globe. As Dombrowski and Reich indicate, until Donald Trump's election even the world's greatest power, the US, was counting on the institutions of the liberal word order to help stabilize the global environment and, consequently, manage American security challenges.

In addition, although this is touched upon less in this volume, some states utilize nonstate actors, especially private military institutions (PMIs) and militant organizations in the service of their strategic aims.[35] These private entities can act as force multipliers, allowing states to do more with less.[36] In this regard, as Ramadan-Alban discusses, Iran utilizes militant organizations, such as Hezbollah and Hamas, which it funds and equips to project its power throughout the region. China has advanced its strategic interests through the use of its state-owned enterprises, which allow it to increase its wealth, procure needed resources, and extend its interests abroad.[37] For its part, the US has slowly started utilizing PMIs, at least in a supporting role, to help it achieve its strategic missions more efficiently and with less domestic resistance.[38]

Some states even use public relations as an instrument of GS. The chapters by Erickson and Balzacq demonstrate that both China and France are extremely concerned with how they present themselves to the world. Erickson points out that Xi Jinping's GS relies on political evangelism, focused on presenting Chinese socialism as a successful model for political development and a credible alternative to Western capitalism. Balzacq emphasizes the historical importance of presenting France to the world as a great power that underpinned the *grandeur* strategy, which has given way to a public relations campaign within the Francophonie to expand the use of the French language worldwide and maintain France's importance as the leader of the French-speaking world. Israeli strategic planners also are increasingly concerned about countering the influence of the boycott, divestment, and sanctions movement through public relations, as Shamir observes.

At first blush, the wide menu of instruments that states use to advance their GSs may appear at odds with a hard realist understanding of international politics and might suggest a change in the nature of security competition in the contemporary era. A more nuanced treatment of realism, however, will note that Hans Morgenthau's classic exposition of the elements of national power includes both the tangible—including a country's armed forces, population, and industrial capacity—but also less tangible elements, such as the quality of a state's leadership and diplomats.[39] The essays in this volume, therefore, encourage a return to the broader conception of national power that classical realists depicted, rather than the hardcore neorealist-inspired view that focuses almost exclusively on harder aspects of state power.[40]

13.5 Additional insights/issues

In light of the above, the essays in this volume suggest several other ways to differentiate between the GS of different states. They also raise important questions for future research.

13.5.1 TYPES OF STATES AND VARYING GRAND STRATEGY

Consistently with realist theory, we might be able to generalize about the content of state's GS based on its relative power and position in the international system. Great powers, such as the US, Russia, and China pursue the most independent GSs and aim to shape international conditions in their regions or globally. They typically employ a variety of means to pursue their geostrategic ends, including soft power and institutional arrangements, but have the greatest capacity to employ military means. In this regard, they pursue the most traditional, prototypical GSs.

Nonetheless, other states do engage in meaningful strategic planning, as well, particularly those the editors refer to as "pivotal states," either regionally or globally. These may be divided into middle powers and smaller pivotal states. Middle powers—states with more power resources than most, but far fewer than the greatest powers of the system—do not have the independence that great powers possess and tend to tether their strategic concepts to great power benefactors or alliances/institutions dominated by friendly great powers.[41] Lacking the resources that great powers possess, they try to shape their security environments collectively in multilateral fora and endorse international legal principles to help ensure that the great powers—even their allies—do not trample upon them. States in this category might include Brazil, India, the UK, and France.

Smaller pivotal states, which are at least important players in their regional security complexes, also engage in GS planning, although they have the least independence or military means to shape their environments. Indeed, especially if they face existential threats—as Israel and Saudi Arabia do—smaller states may be compelled to think more about GS than the great powers, as their survival depends on their ability to muster the strategic resources over the long-term to counter regional rivals. Their strategies focus almost exclusively on their region and typically rely on national military means, but they also must involve reliance on a friendly great power if they are to endure a long-term threat.

13.5.2 THE STABILITY OF THE STATE'S SECURITY ENVIRONMENT

The nature of a state's security environment also has important implications for a state's GS.[42] Countries in stable environments without enduring threats or rivals of greater or equal strength—such as Brazil and the US—have greater scope to carve out a positive, proactive GS. These states aim to advance their preferred ideational agendas and seek to reshape their regional and global environments consistently with their interests. Moreover, as they are largely liberated from short-term exigencies, they have a far longer time horizon for strategic planning than other states. In contrast, states in restrictive and unstable environments (e.g., South Asia, the Middle East, and, with greater Russian activism, increasingly Europe) remain more heavily focused on traditional military security, with shorter time horizons and less emphasis on ideational strategies or reshaping their environments.[43]

13.5.3 COOPERATIVE VS INDEPENDENT GRAND STRATEGY

The contributions to this book also highlight a divide between states that pursue largely independent GSs and those whose strategic blueprint are tethered to a great power. In general, the greatest powers—the US, China, and Russia—all outline highly independent strategies, which highlight the roles of their own military establishments and alliances/organizations that they lead. Iran, though not a great power, also pursues a rather independent GS, with no great power to rely on.

In contrast, the weaker states tend to premise their national security blueprints upon assistance from a great power benefactor, especially if they inhabit unstable regions and face noteworthy threats. In this project, for example, the role of the United States looms large for both Saudi Arabia and Israel. Robert Johnson's chapter details the importance of alignment with the United States within British GS during World War II and afterwards. No doubt Russia plays an important role in Syrian grand strategic calculations and China is of importance to North Korean GS. States in more stable situations, such as Brazil and the European states, can take a middle ground approach, relying less on great power benefactors and more on international institutions, such as MERCOSUR, the EU, or La Francophonie.[44]

Beyond these considerations of state size and relative power, Western states appear to be more likely to place cooperative regional or international military, economic, and political institutions at the heart of their strategic planning. As Milani and Neri observe, Brazil is the foremost example of this, making MERCOSUR and UNASUR key components of its strategic doctrine. Britain and France GSs are similarly situated in the context of NATO and the EU, as well as cooperation with the American unipole. It remains an open question to what degree the twin shocks of Donald Trump's America First doctrine and the British withdrawal from the EU will affect the Western predilection for cooperative GS, but for now at least that tendency has persisted.

In contrast, states such as Russia, China, India, and Iran pursue rather independent GSs, eschewing heavy reliance on other states or international institutions. To be sure, as Marangé indicates, Russian planners do value cooperation with China and the Shanghai Cooperation Organization against the US. But this is not as central to Russian strategic doctrine as NATO is to British, French, or even US GS.

13.5.4 UNIQUENESS OF EU CASE—INTERNATIONAL ORGANIZATIONS, NONMILITARY GRAND STRATEGY

By including Fiott and Simón's chapter on the European Union in this volume, the editors have raised an interesting question about whether international institutions can have a GS. These organizations are not states themselves and typically do not have control over armed forces independently of their member states. Moreover, they are agglomerations of states, each with their own distinct national interests, which renders the concept of a coherent GS rather problematic. Does their inclusion in this volume stretch the concept of GS beyond credulity? Yet, as Fiott and Simón demonstrate, the EU does engage in trying to alter the security environment in a manner to advance a certain package of common interests, particularly by maintaining and expanding the liberal order of which it is an integral part. If such chaotic, multilateral organizations can be considered to have GSs, what about more focused and coherent violent nonstate actors (VNSAs), particularly those such as Hezbollah, Hamas, or IS, with their own armed forces and aspirations for statehood or quasi-state status? It would be less of a stretch to imagine that these groups engage in long-range planning activities somewhat akin to states.[45]

*

In this volume, Balzacq, Dombrowski, and Reich have staked an ambitious claim to a research agenda on comparative GS. By addressing the strategic planning of multiple states with a common set of questions, they have shown that the concept of GS, at least in principle, is portable across different types of states and regions, making it a far more powerful concept than initially assumed. This book, however, reflects the starting point of the journey, rather than the end point of this analysis. Careful attention to the limits of comparative GS, whether the differences between strategic blueprints and planning processes are strategically significant, and the value-added yielded by stretching the concept of GS will ultimately be necessary to demonstrate that the endeavor is worth the effort. I expect it will be.

NOTES

1. For noteworthy attempts to define GS, see Barry Posen, *The Sources of Military Doctrines: France, Britain, and Germany between the World Wars* (Ithaca, NY: Cornell University Press, 1984); Paul Kennedy, "Grand Strategy in War and Peace: Toward a Broader Definition," in *Grand Strategy in War and Peace*, ed. Paul Kennedy (New Haven, CT: Yale University Press, 1991), 1–7; Williamson Murray and Mark Grimsey, "Introduction: On Strategy," in *The Making of Strategy: Rulers, States, and War*, eds. Alvin H. Bernstein, MacGregor Knox, and Williamson Murray (New York: Cambridge University Press, 1994), 1–2; Robert Art, *A Grand Strategy for America* (Ithaca, NY: Cornell University Press, 2003); Colin Dueck, *Reluctant Crusaders: Power, Culture, and Change in American Grand Strategy* (Princeton, NJ: Princeton University Press, 2006); Colin Gray, *The Strategy Bridge: Theory for Practice* (Oxford: Oxford University Press, 2010); and Steven E. Lobell, Jeffrey W. Taliaferro, and Norrin M. Ripsman, "Introduction: Grand Strategy between the World Wars," in *The Challenge of Grand Strategy: The Great Powers and the Broken Balance between the Wars*, eds. Jeffrey W. Taliaferro, Norrin M. Ripsman, and Steven E. Lobell (Cambridge: Cambridge University Press, 2012), 15.
2. Paul Kennedy, for example, argues, "No doubt it is theoretically possible for a small nation to develop a grand strategy, but the latter term is generally understood to imply the endeavors of a power with extensive (i.e. not just local) interests and obligations, to reconcile its means and its ends." Kennedy, *Grand Strategies in War and Peace*, 186 n18.
3. See, for example, Norrin M. Ripsman and T. V. Paul, "Assessing the Uneven Impact of Global Social Forces on the National Security State: A Framework for Analysis," *International Studies Review* 7, no. 2 (June 2005): 199–227; and Norrin M. Ripsman and T. V. Paul, *Globalization and the National Security State* (Oxford: Oxford University Press, 2010).
4. On neoclassical realism, see Gideon Rose, "Neoclassical Realism and Theories of Foreign Policy," *World Politics* 51, no. 1 (October 1998): 144–72; and Norrin M. Ripsman, Jeffrey W. Taliaferro, and Steven E. Lobell, *Neoclassical Realist Theory of International Politics* (Oxford: Oxford University Press, 2016).
5. "The National Security Strategy of the United States of America," December 2017, https://www.whitehouse.gov/wp-content/uploads/2017/12/NSS-Final-12-18-2017-0905.pdf

6. For a systematic discussion of the reasons states engage in deception, see Robert Jervis, *The Logic of Images in International Relations* (Princeton, NJ: Princeton University Press, 1970).
7. See Ripsman, Taliaferro, and Lobell, *Neoclassical Realist Theory*, 131–7; and Marc Trachtenberg, *The Craft of International History: A Guide to Method* (Princeton, NJ: Princeton University Press, 2006).
8. This is the approach taken by Ripsman and Paul, *Globalization and the National Security State*. As Christine Fair's indicates in Chapter 8 of this volume, scholars who try to discern Indian GS also use this approach.
9. The classic discussion of organizational and bureaucratic alternatives to the rational decision-making paradigm remains Graham T. Allison and Philip Zelikow, *Essence of Decision: Explaining the Cuban Missile Crisis* (New York: Longmans, 1999).
10. See, for example, Melinda Mills, Gerhard G. van de Bunt, and Jeanne de Bruijn, "Comparative Research: Persistent Problems and Promising Solutions," *International Sociology* 21, no. 5 (September 2006): 622–3.
11. On eclectic theory, see John A. Hall and T. V. Paul, "Preconditions for Prudence: A Sociological Synthesis of Realism and Liberalism," in *International Order and the Future of World Politics*, eds., T. V. Paul and John A. Hall (Cambridge: Cambridge University Press, 1999), 67–77; and Rudra Sil and Peter J. Katzenstein, *Beyond Paradigms: Analytic Eclecticism in the Study of World Politics* (London: Palgrave Macmillan, 2010). Neoclassical realism, a multi-paradigmatic approach that privileges the external environment but accounts for other unit- and sub-unit influences on strategy, is a particularly good fit with the essays in this volume. See Ripsman, Taliaferro, and Lobell, *Neoclassical Realist Theory*.
12. On regional security complexes, see Barry Buzan and Ole Waever, *Regions and Powers: The Structure of International Security* (Cambridge: Cambridge University Press, 2003); Douglas Lemke, *Regions of War and Peace* (Cambridge: Cambridge University Press, 2002); Benjamin Miller, "Explaining Variations in Regional Peace: Three Strategies for Peace-making," *Cooperation and Conflict* 35, no. 2 (June 200): 155–92; David A. Lake and Patrick M. Morgan, "The New Regionalism in Security Affairs," in *Regional Orders: Building Security in a New World*, eds. David A. Lake and Patrick M. Morgan (University Park, PA: Penn State University Press, 1997), 3–19; and T. V. Paul, "Regional Transformation in International Relations," in *International Relations Theory and Regional Transformation*, ed. T. V. Paul (Cambridge: Cambridge University Press, 2012), 4–6.
13. Ripsman, Taliaferro, and Lobell refer to this as a restrictive security environment, which compares unfavorably to a permissive security environment discussed below. *Neoclassical Realist Theory*, 52–6. See also Lobell, Taliaferro, and Ripsman, "Introduction: Grand Strategy between the World Wars," 23–4; and Ripsman and Paul, *Globalization and the National Security State*, 14–15.
14. Robert Jervis, "Cooperation under the Security Dilemma," *World Politics* 30, no. 2 (1978): 167–214.
15. Norrin M. Ripsmam, *Peacemaking by Democracies: The Effect of State Autonomy on the Post-World-War Settlements* (University Park, PA: Penn State University Press, 2002), 84.

16. E. S. Corwin, *The President: Office and Powers, 1787–1957* (New York: University Press, 1957), 171.
17. In this regard, Kenneth Waltz argues that despite their institutional and procedural differences, the postwar democracies conducted national security policy no differently from other states. Kenneth N. Waltz, *Foreign Policy and Democratic Politics, the American and British Experience* (Boston: Little, Brown, 1967).
18. In this regard, see Peter J. Katzenstein, *The Culture of National Security: Norms and Identity in World Politics* (New York: Columbia University Press, 1996); Asle Toje, *America, the EU, and Strategic Culture: Renegotiating the Transatlantic Bargain* (New York: Routledge, 2008); and Ripsman, Taliaferro, and Lobell, *Neoclassical Realist Theory*, 66–70.
19. Alastair Ian Johnston, *Cultural Realism: Strategic Culture and Grand Strategy in Chinese History* (Princeton, NJ: Princeton University Press, 1995). For a critical perspective, see Michael C. Desch, "Culture Clash: Assessing the Importance of Ideas in Security Studies," *International Security* 23, no. 1 (Summer 1998): 141–170, esp. 161.
20. Charles Tilly, *Coercion, Currency, and the European States, AD 990–1990* (Cambridge, MA: Blackwell, 1990).
21. William C. Wohlforth, "Unipolarity, Status Competition, and Great Power War," *World Politics* 61, no. 1 (January 2009): 28–57; Deborah Welch Larson, T. V. Paul, and William C. Wohlforth, "Status and World Order," in *Status in World Politics*, eds. T. V. Paul, Deborah Welch Larson, and William C. Wohlforth (Cambridge: Cambridge University Press, 2014), 33–57; and Tudor Onea, "Between Dominance and Decline; Status Anxiety and Great Power Rivalry," *Review of International Studies* 40, no. 1 (January 2014): 125–52.
22. Zheng Wang, "National Humiliation, History Education, and the Politics of Historical Memory: Patriotic Education Campaign in China," *International Studies Quarterly* 52, no. 4 (December 2008): 783–806.
23. See, for example, Mark L. Haas, *The Ideological Origins of Great Power Politics, 1789–1989* (Ithaca, NY: Cornell University Press, 2005); Mark L. Haas, *The Clash of Ideologies: Middle Eastern Politics and American Security* (New York: Oxford University Press, 2012); and Lawrence Rubin, *Islam in the Balance: Ideational Threats in Arab Politics* (Stanford, CA: Stanford University Press, 2014).
24. See, for example, Bruce M. Russett, *Grasping the Democratic Peace* (Princeton, NJ: Princeton University Press, 1993); and John M. Owen, "How Liberalism Produces the Democratic Peace," *International Security* 19, no. 2 (Fall 1994): 87–125.
25. See, for example, Stephen Brooks, G. John Ikenberry, and William C. Wohlforth, "Don't Come Home, America: The Case against Retrenchment," *International Security* 37, no. 3 (Winter 2012/13): 11–12.
26. In this regard, see Katzenstein, *The Culture of National Security*.
27. Arnold Wolfers, "National Security as an Ambiguous Symbol," in *Discord and Collaboration: Essays on International Politics* (Baltimore, MD: Johns Hopkins University Press, 1962), 147–65.
28. See, for example, Etel Solingen, *Regional Orders at Century's Dawn: Global and Domestic Influences on Grand Strategy* (Princeton, NJ: Princeton University Press, 1998).

29. Robert Gilpin, *War and Change in World Politics* (Cambridge: Cambridge University Press, 1981); and Klaus Knorr, *The Power of Nations: The Political Economy of International Relations* (New York: Basic Books, 1974).
30. David A. Baldwin, *Economic Statecraft* (Princeton, NJ: Princeton University Press, 1985), 72–7; Edward Mead Earle, "Adam Smith, Alexander Hamilton, Friedrich List: The Economic Foundations of Military Power," in *Makers of Modern Strategy*, ed. Peter Paret (Oxford: Clarendon Press, 1986), 217–61; Ethan Barnaby Kapstein, *The Political Economy of National Security* (New York: McGraw-Hill, 1992); and Norrin M. Ripsman, "False Dichotomy: Why Economics Has Always Been High Politics," in *Guns and Butter: The Political Economy of International Security*, ed. Peter Dombrowski (Boulder, CO: Lynne Reinner, 2005), 15–31.
31. Zheng Bijian, "China's 'Peaceful Rise' to Great Power Status," *Foreign Affairs* 84, no. 5 (September/October 2005): 18–24.
32. This strategy has elements in common with the German interwar strategy of binding the Central and East European economies to its own and the Japanese efforts to establish an economic Co-Prosperity Sphere in East Asia. See William Carr, *Arms, Autarky and Aggression* (New York: Norton, 1973); and Michael A. Barnhart, *Japan Prepares for Total War: The Search for Economic Security, 1919–1941* (Ithaca, NY: Cornell University Press, 1987).
33. Brandon Valeriano and Ryan C. Maness, *Cyber War Versus Cyber Realities: Cyber Conflict in the International System* (New York: Oxford University Press, 2015), 20–77. Valeriano and Maness, as well as Erik Gartzke, remain sceptical, however, that cyber competition will revolutionize international security. Erik Gartzke, "The Myth of Cyber War: Bringing War in Cyberspace Down to Earth," *International Security* 38, no. 2 (Fall 2013): 41–73.
34. Ripsman and Paul, *Globalization and the National Security State*, Chapter 4.
35. On PMIs, see Deborah D. Avant, *The Market for Force: The Consequences of Privatizing Security* (Cambridge: Cambridge University Press, 2005); and P. W. Singer, *Corporate Warriors: The Rise of the Privatized Military Industry*, updated ed., (Ithaca, NY: Cornell University Press, 2008).
36. Eugenio Cusumano, "Bridging the Gap: Mobilisation Constraints and Contractor Support to US and UK Military Operations," *Journal of Strategic Studies* 38, no. 5 (2015): 1–29.
37. William J. Norris, *Chinese Economic Statecraft: Commercial Actors, Grand Strategy, and State Control* (Ithaca, NY: Cornell University Press, 2016).
38. David Isenberg, *Private Military Contractors and U.S. Grand Strategy*, PRIO Report (Oslo: International Peace Research Institute, January 2009).
39. Hans J. Morgenthau and Kenneth W. Thompson, *Politics Among Nations: The Struggle for Power and Peace, Brief Edition* (New York: McGraw Hill, 1993), 124–65.
40. On the latter, see for example Randall Schweller, *Deadly Imbalances: Tripolarity and Hitler's Strategy of World Conquest* (Princeton, NJ: Princeton University Press, 1998), Chapter 1.
41. On middle powers, see Carsten Holbraad, *Middle Powers in International Politics* (London: Macmillan Press, 1984); Andrew F. Cooper, Richard A. Higgott, and Kim Richard Nossal, eds., *Relocating Middle Powers: Australia and Canada in a*

Changing World Order (Vancouver: UBC Press, 1993); and Eduard Jordaan, "The Concept of a Middle Power in International Relations: Distinguishing between Emerging and Traditional Middle Powers," *Politikon: South African Journal of Political Studies* 30, no. 1 (2003): 165–81.

42. On permissive versus restrictive security environments and their impact on a state's freedom of action, see Ripsman, Taliaferro, and Lobell, *Neoclassical Realist Theory of International Politics*, Chapter 2.
43. See Ripsman and Paul, *Globalization and the National Security State*.
44. See, for example, Ripsman and Paul, *Globalization and the National Security State*.
45. For a recent work that addresses the strategies and tactics of VNSAs, see Natasha Ezrow, *Global Politics and Violent Non-State Actors* (London: Sage, 2017).

BIBLIOGRAPHY

Aalto, Pami and Dicle Korkmaz Temel. "European Energy Security: Natural Gas and the Integration Process." *Journal of Common Market Studies* 52, no. 4 (2014): 758–74.

Acharya, Amitav. *The End of the American World Order*. Cambridge: Polity, 2014.

"Achieving Rejuvenation is the Dream of the Chinese People." November 29, 2012, in *Xi Jinping, The Governance of China* (Beijing: Foreign Languages Press, 2014), 37–9.

Adams, Gordan and Cindy Williams. *Buying National Security: How America Plans and Pays for Its Global Role and Safety at Home*. London: Routledge, 2009.

Adams, Gordon and Shoon Murray, eds. *Mission Creep: The Militarization of US Foreign Policy?* Washington, DC: Georgetown University Press 2014.

Adamsky, Dima. *The Culture of Military Innovation: The Impact of Cultural Factors on the Revolution in Military Affairs in Russia, the US, and Israel*. Stanford, CA: Stanford Press, 2010.

Adamsky, Dimitry. "Putin's Syria Strategy: Russian Airstrikes and What Comes Next." *Foreign Affairs*, October 1, 2015, https://www.foreignaffairs.com/articles/syria/2015-10-01/putins-syria-strategy.

Adamsky, Dimitry. *Cross-Domain Coercion: The Current Russian Art of Strategy*, Proliferation Papers, no. 54. Paris: Institut Français des Relations Internationales, November 2015.

Adams, John Quincy. "'She Goes Not Abroad in Search of Monsters to Destroy,' July 4, 1821." The Repository (archive), *The American Conservative*, http://www.theamericanconservative.com/repository/she-goes-not-abroad-in-search-of-monsters-to-destroy/.

Aggestam, Lisbeth. "Introduction: Ethical Power Europe?." *International Affairs* 84, no. 1 (2008): 1–11.

Akbarzadeh, Shahram and Dara Conduit, eds. *Iran in the World: President Rouhani's Foreign Policy*. Berlin: Springer, 2016.

Akbarzadeh, Shahram and Dara Conduit. "Charting a New Course? Testing Rouhani's Foreign Policy Agency in the Iran-Syria Relationship." In *Iran in the World*, edited by Shahram Akbarzadeh and Dara Conduit Shahram, 133–54. Berlin: Springer, 2016.

Alandari, Kazem. "The Power Structure of the Islamic Republic of Iran: Transition from Populism to Clientelism, and Militarization of the Government." *Third World Quarterly* 26, no. 8 (2005): 1285–1301.

Alexandrova, Petya, Marcello Carammia, and Arco Timmermans. "Policy Punctuations and Issue Diversity on the European Council Agenda." *Policy Studies Journal* 40, no. 1 (2012): 69–88.

Alfoneh, Ali. *Iran Unveiled: How the Revolutionary Guards Is Transforming Iran from Theocracy into Military Dictatorship*. Washington, DC: AEI Press, 2013.

al-Khatteeb, Luay. "Saudi Arabia's Economic Time Bomb." *Brookings*, December 30, 2015, https://www.brookings.edu/opinions/saudi-arabias economic-time-bomb.

Allen-Ebrahimian, Bethany. "Chinese Police Are Demanding Personal Information From Uighurs in France." *Foreign Policy*, March 2, 2018, http://foreignpolicy.com/2018/03/02/chinese-police-are-secretly-demanding-personal-information-from-french-citizens-uighurs-xinjiang/.

Allison, Graham T. and Philip Zelikow. *Essence of Decision: Explaining the Cuban Missile Crisis.* New York: Longmans, 1999.

Alma, Bérénice. "The Iranian Strategic Thought and Its Recent Evolution." *ERIS–European Review of International Studies* 2, no. 1 (2015): 62–71.

Amadio Viceré, Maria Giulia. "The Roles of the President of the European Council and the High Representative in Leading EU Foreign Policy on Kosovo." *Journal of European Integration* 38, no. 5 (2016): 557–70.

Amorim, Celso. *A grande estratégia do Brasil: discursos, artigos e entrevistas da gestão no Ministério da Defesa (2011–2014)*. Brasília: Fundação Alexandre de Gusmão; Editora UNESP, 2016.

Ansari, Ali. "Iranian Foreign Policy under Khatami: Reform and Reintegration." In *Politics of Modern Iran*, edited by Ali Ansari, 13–31. London: Routledge, 2001.

al-Rodhan, Nayef. "Strategic Culture and Pragmatic National Interests." *Global Policy Journal* (July 22, 2015).

Arad, Uzi. *Grand Strategy for Israel: Deliberations and Directions* [Hebrew]. Haifa, Israel: Samuel Neaman Institute and The Technicon, 2017.

Arad, Uzi and Limor Ben-Har, Hmall. *The Struggle to Establish the "National Security Council" and to Place it on Top* [Hebrew]. Israel: Zmora-Bitan, 2016.

Art, Robert J. "A Defensible Defense: America's Grand Strategy after the Cold War." *International Security* 15, no. 4 (Spring 1991): 5–53.

Art, Robert J. "Geopolitics Updated: The Strategy of Selective Engagement." *International Security* 23, no. 3 (Winter 1998/99): 80–1.

Art, Robert J. *A Grand Strategy for America.* Ithaca, NY: Cornell University Press, 2003.

Aryan, Hossein. "The Artesh: Iran's Marginalized and under-Armed Conventional Military." The Middle Institute Viewpoints, *The Artesh: Iran's Marginalized Regular Military*, no. 15 (November 2011).

Avant, Deborah D. *The Market for Force: The Consequences of Privatizing Security.* Cambridge: Cambridge University Press, 2005.

Baer, Robert. *L'iran, L'irrésistible Ascension.* Paris: Gallimard, 2009.

Bagayoko, Niagalé and Frédéric Ramel, eds. "Francophonie et profondeur stratégique." *Etudes de l'Irsem*, no. 26 (2013).

Bahgat, Gawdat. "Iran's Regular Army: Its History and Capacities." *The Middle Institute Viewpoints, The Artesh: Iran's Marginalized Regular Military*, no. 15 (November 2011).

Baily, Richard, James W. Jr. Forsyth, and Mark O. Yeisley. *Strategy: Context and Adaptation from Archidamus to Airpower.* Annapolis, MD: Naval Institute Press, 2016.

Bajpai, Kanti. "Indian Grand Strategy: Six Schools of Thought." In *India's Grand Strategy: History, Theory, Cases*, edited by Kanti Bajpai, Saira Basit, and V. Krishnappa. London: Routledge, 2014.

Bal, Lider. *Le Mythe De La Souveraineté En Droit International, La Souveraineté Des Etats À L'épreuve Des Mutations De L'ordre Juridique International.* Strasbourg: Université de Strasbourg, 2012).

Balci, Bayram. *Renouveau de l'Islam en Asia Centrale et dans le Caucase.* Paris: Editions du CNRS, 2017.

Baldwin, David Allen. *Economic Statecraft.* Princeton, NJ: Princeton University Press, 1985.

Baldwin, David Allen. *Review of International Studies* 23, no. 1 (January 1997): 5–26.

Balzacq, Thierry, Peter Dombrowski, and Simon Reich. "Is Grand Strategy a Research Program? A Review Essay." *Security Studies* 28, no. 1 (2019).

Bano, Masooda and Keiko Sakuri, eds. *Shaping Global Islamic Discourse: The Role of Al-Azhar, Al-Medina, and Al-Mustafa*. Edinburgh: Edinburgh University Press, 2015.

Bar, Shmuel. "Iranian Defense Doctrine and Decision Making." In The 5th Herzliya Conference, Herzliya Institute for Policy and Strategy (IPS), Lauder School of Government, Diplomacy and Strategy at the Interdisciplinary Center Herzliya, 2004.

Bar, Shmuel. "Can Cold War Deterrence apply to a Nuclear Iran?" *Strategic Perspectives*, Jerusalem Center for Public Affairs, no. 7 (2011).

Bar, Shmuel. *Can Cold War Deterrence Apply to a Nuclear Iran?* Jerusalem: Center for Public Affairs, 2011.

Barnhart, Michael A. *Japan Prepares for Total War: The Search for Economic Security, 1919–1941*. Ithaca, NY: Cornell University Press, 1987.

Barral, Pierre. *Pouvoir civil et commandement militaire: du roi connétable aux leaders du XXe siècle*. Paris: Presses de Sciences Po, 2005.

Bazargan, Mehdi. *Enqelā b-e Irān dar Do Harekat*. Tehran: Chap-e Sevom, 1983/1984.

Becker, Bertha K. *Geopolítica da Amazônia*. Rio de Janeiro: Zahar, 1982.

Beckley, Michael. "China's Century? Why America's Edge Will Endure." *International Security* 36, no. 3 (Winter 2011/12): 41–78.

Beloff, Max. *Imperial Sunset*, vol. I. London: Alfred A. Knopf, 1969.

Ben-Dror, Elad. "How the United Nations Intended to Implement the Partition Plan: The Handbook Drawn up by the Secretariat for the Members of the United Nations Palestine Commission." *Middle Eastern Studies* 43, no. 6 (November 2007): 997–1008.

Ben-Gurion, David. *Uniqueness and Purpose* [Hebrew]. Tel Aviv: Ma'arachot, 1971.

Ben Israel, Yitzchak. *Israel Defense Doctrine* [Hebrew]. Israel: Modan Publishing, 2013.

Berkowitz, Bruce. "Handicapping the George Kennan Sweepstakes." *Orbis* 42, no. 3 (Summer 1998): 465–74.

Berringer, Tatiana. *A burguesia brasileira e a política externa nos governos FHC e Lula*. Curitiba: Editora Appris, 2015.

Bethell, Leslie. "Brazil and Latin America." *Journal of Latin American Studies* 42, no. 3 (August 2010): 457–85.

Betts, Richard K. "Should Strategic Studies Survive?" *World Politics* 50, no. 1 (October 1997): 7–33.

Betts, Richard K. "U.S. National Security Strategy: Lenses and Landmarks." Presented for the launch conference of the Princeton Project "Toward a New National Security Strategy" (Woodrow Wilson School of Public and International Affairs, Princeton University, November 2004, originally presented May 2004), http://inbody.net/research/nss/NSS/betts.pdf.

Betts, Richard K. *American Force: Dangers, Delusions, and Dilemmas in National Security*. New York: Columbia University Press, 2013.

Bickerton, Christopher. "Legitimacy Through Norms: The Political Limits to Europe's Normative Power." In *Normative Power Europe: Empirical and Theoretical Perspectives*, edited by Richard G. Whitman, 25–42. London: Palgrave Macmillan, 2011.

Bijian, Zheng. "China's 'Peaceful Rise' to Great Power Status." *Foreign Affairs* 84, no. 5 (September/October 2005): 18–24.

Bill, James A. *The Politics of Iran: Groups, Classes and Modernization.* Columbus, OH: Merrill, 1972.

Birch, Douglas and R. Jeffrey Smith. "Israel's Worst-Kept Secret." *The Atlantic*, September 16, 2014, https://www.theatlantic.com/international/archive/2014/09/israel-nuclear-weapons-secret-united-states/380237/.

Blockmans, Steven and Astrid Viaud. "EU Diplomacy and the Iran Nuclear Deal: Staying Power?" *CEPS Policy Insights*, no. 2017-28 (2017).

Bogue, Allan G. "Frederick Jackson Turner Reconsidered." *The History Teacher* 27, no. 2 (February 1994).

Boito, Armando and Tatiana Berringer. "Social Classes, Neodevelopmentalism, and Brazilian Foreign Policy under Presidents Lula and Dilma." *Latin American Perspectives* 41, no. 5 (September 2014): 94–109.

Bourbeau, Philip, Thierry Balzacq, and Myriam Dunn Cavelty. "International Relations: Celebrating Eclectic Dynamism in Security Studies." In *Security: Dialogue Across Discipline* edited by Philippe Bourbeau, 111–36. Cambridge: Cambridge University Press, 2015.

Boutin, Christine. *De la mondialisation à l'universalisation. Une ambition sociale.* Paris: La Documentation française, 2010.

Bowen, Desmond. "The Political-Military Relationship on Operations." In *British Generals and Blair's Wars* edited by Jonathan Bailey, Hew Strachan, and Richard Iron, 273–80. London: Routledge, 2014.

Bozo, Frédéric. *Deux stratégies pour l'Europe: De Gaulle, les Etats-Unis et l'Alliance Atlantique, 1958–1969.* Paris: Plon, 1996.

Brady, Anne-Marie. *China as a Polar Great Power.* Cambridge: Cambridge University Press, 2017.

Brands, Hal. *Dilemmas of Brazilian Grand Strategy.* Carlisle, PA: US Army War College, Strategic Studies Institute Monograph, 2012.

Brands, Hal. *What Good Is Grand Strategy? Power and Purpose in American Statecraft from Harry S. Truman to George W. Bush.* Ithaca, NY: Cornell University Press, 2015.

Brands, H.W. "The Age of Vulnerability: Eisenhower and the National Insecurity State." *The American Historical Review* 94, no. 4 (October 1989): 963–89.

Bresser-Pereira, Luiz Carlos. *A construção política do Brasil sociedade, economia e estado desde a independência.* São Paulo: Editora 34, 2016.

Brichs, Ferran Izquierdo, ed. *Political Regimes in the Arab World: Society and the Exercise of Power.* London: Routledge, 2012.

Bronson, Rachel. *Thicker than Oil: America's Uneasy Partnership with Saudi. Arabia.* Oxford: Oxford University Press, 2006.

Brooks, Stephen G., H. John Ikenberry, and William C. Wohlforth. "Don't Come Home America: The Case against Retrenchment." *International Security* 37, no. 3 (Winter 2012/13): 7–51.

Brooks, Stephen G. and William C. Wohlforth. "Hard Times for Soft Balancing." *International Security* 30, no. 1 (Summer 2005): 72–108.

Brooks, Stephen and William Wohlforth. *America Abroad: The United States' Global Role in the 21st Century.* London: Oxford University Press, 2016.

Brzezinski, Zbigniew. *The Grand Chessboard: American Primacy and Its Geostrategic Imperatives.* New York: Basic Books, 1997.

Buchta, Wilfried. *Who Rules Iran?: The Structure of Power in the Islamic Republic.* Washington, DC: Washington Institute for Near East Policy, 2000.

Burges, Sean W. "Consensual Hegemony: Theorizing Brazilian Foreign Policy after the Cold War." *International Relations* 22, no. 1 (March 2008): 65–84.

Buzan, Barry and Ole Waever. *Regions and Powers: The Structure of International Security.* Cambridge: Cambridge University Press, 2003.

Caldwell, Lawrence T. "Russian Concept of National Security." In *Russian Foreign Policy in the Twenty-First Century and the Shadow of the Past*, edited by Robert Levgold, 279–343. New York: Columbia University Press, 2007.

Caporaso, James A. "Across the Great Divide: Integrating Comparative and International Politics." *International Studies Quarterly* 41, no. 4 (December 1997): 563–91.

Cancian, Mark, et al. *Formulating National Security Strategy: Past Experience and Future Choices.* Washington, DC: Center for Strategic and International Studies, 2017.

Cardoso, Fernando Henrique. *Xadrez internacional e social-democracia.* São Paulo: Paz e Terra, 2010.

Cardenas, Sonia. "Norm Collision: Explaining the Effects of International Human Rights Pressure on State Behavior." *International Studies Review* 6, no. 2 (2004): 213–32.

Carlstrom, Gregg. *How Long Will Israel Survive? The Threat from Within.* Oxford: Oxford University Press, 2017.

Carr, William. Arms. *Autarky and Aggression.* New York: Norton, 1973.

Carrillo, Ian R. "The New Developmentalism and the Challenges to Long-Term Stability in Brazil." *Latin American Perspectives* 41, no. 5 (September 2014): 59–74.

Cason, Jeffrey W. and Timothy J. Power. "Presidentialization, Pluralization, and the Rollback of Itamaraty: Explaining Change in Brazilian Foreign Policy Making in the Cardoso-Lula Era." *International Political Science Review* 30, no. 2 (March 2009): 117–40.

Ceaser, James W. "The Origins and Character of American Exceptionalism." *American Political Thought* 1, no. 1 (Spring 2012): 3–28.

Cepik, Marco and Frederico Licks Bertol. "Defense policy in Brazil: bridging the gap between ends and means?" *Defence Studies* 16, no. 3 (July 2016): 229–47.

Cerny, Philip G. *The Politics of Grandeur: Ideological Aspects of De Gaulle's Foreign Policy.* Cambridge: Cambridge University Press, 1993.

Cervo, Amado L. "Political Regimes and Brazil's Foreign Policy." In *Foreign Policy and Political Regime*, edited by José Flávio Sombra Saraiva, 341–61. Brasília: IBRI, 2003.

Chace, James. "The Dilemmas of the City upon a Hill." *World Policy Journal* 14, no. 1 (Spring 1997): 105–7.

Chandrasekhar, Rajeev. "Doklam Heralds the Arrival of a Confident and Assertive India." *The Diplomat*, August 30, 2017, https://thediplomat.com/2017/08/doklam-heralds-the-arrival-of-a-confident-and-assertive-india/.

Charillon, Frédéric. "Hollande and Sarkozy's Foreign Policy Legacy." In *France after 2012*, edited by Gabriel Goodliffe and Riccardo Brizzi, 167–89. New York: Berghan Books, 2015.

Charillon, Frédéric. "Valeurs et intérêts national: le faux dilemme de la politique étrangère française." In *Notre interêt national: Quelle politique étrangère pour la France?*, edited by Thierry de Montbrial and Thomas Gomart, 185–98. Paris: Odile Jacob 2017.

Charmley, John. *Splendid Isolation? Britain and the Balance of Power.* London: Hodder and Stoughton, 1999.

Chase, Robert S., Emily Hill, and Paul M. Kennedy, eds. *Pivotal States: A New Framework for U.S. Policy in the Developing World*. New York: W. W. Norton & Co, 2000.

Chong, Ja Ian. "Popular Narratives Versus Chinese History: Implications for Understanding An Emergent China." *European Journal of International Relations* 20, no. 4 (2014): 939–64.

Christensen, Thomas J. *The China Challenge: Shaping the Choices of a Rising Power*. New York: W. W. Norton & Company, 2015.

Chubin, Shahram. "Extended Deterrence and Iran." *Strategic Insights* 8, no. 5 (December 2009).

Cohen, Stephen P. and Sunil Dasgupta. *Arming without Aiming: India's Military Modernization*. Washington, DC: Brookings Institution, 2010.

Cohen-Tanugi, Laurent. *Euromonde 2015—Une stratégie européenne pour la mondialisation*. Paris: La Documentation française, 2008.

Collard, Daniel. "Le président Sarkozy et l'aggiornamento de la politique étrangère de la France acte 1: 2007–2008." *Arès* 23, no. 3 (2010–2).

Collier, David. "The Comparative Method." In *Political Science: The State of the Discipline II*, edited by Ada W. Finifter. Washington, DC: American Political Science Association, 1993.

Collier, David. "Understanding Process Tracing." *PS: Political Science and Politics* 44, no. 4 (October 2011).

Collins, Gabriel B. and Andrew S. Erickson. "China's S-Curve Trajectory: Structural factors will likely slow the growth of China's economy and comprehensive national power." *China SignPost* (洞察中国), no. 44 (August 15, 2011), http://www.chinasignpost.com/wp-content/uploads/2011/08/China-SignPost_44_S-Curves_Slowing-Chinese-Econ-Natl-Power-Growth_20110815.pdf.

Collins, John M. *Grand Strategy: Principles and Practices*. Annapolis, MD: Naval Institute Press, 1973.

Commins, David. *The Mission of the Kingdom: Wahhabi Power Behind the Saudi Throne*. London: I.B.Tauris, 2016.

Cooper, Andrew F., Richard A. Higgott, and Kim Richard Nossal, eds. *Relocating Middle Powers: Australia and Canada in a Changing World Order*. Vancouver: UBC Press, 1993.

Cordesman, Anthony H. *Saudi Arabia, Guarding the Desert Kingdom*. Boulder, CO: Westview Press, 1997.

Cordesman, Anthony H. *Iran's Military Forces in Transition, Conventional Threats and Weapons of Mass Destruction*. Westport, CT: Praeger, 1999.

Cordesman, Anthony H. *Saudi Arabia: National Security in a Troubled Region*. Santa Barbara, CA: Praeger Security International, 2009.

Corwin, Edward. S. *The President: Office and Powers, 1787–1957*. New York: University Press, 1957.

Couto e Silva, Golbery. *Geopolítica do Brasil*. Rio de Janeiro: José Olympio, 1967.

Coville, Thierry. "The Economic Activities of the Pasdaran." *Revue internationale des études du développement*, no. 1 (2017).

Crabb, Jr., Cecil Van Meter, and Pat M. Holt. *Invitation to Struggle: Congress, the President, and Foreign Policy*, 4th ed. Washington, DC: CQ Press, 1992.

Cross, Mai'a K. Davis. "The EU Global Strategy and Diplomacy." *Contemporary Security Policy* 37, no. 3 (2016): 402–13.

Crossley, Pamela Kyle, Helen F. Siu, and Donald S. Sutton, eds. *Empire at the Margins: Culture, Ethnicity, and Frontier in Early Modern China*. Berkeley: University of California Press, 2006.

Cumings, Bruce. *Dominion from Sea to Sea: Pacific Ascendancy and American Power*. New Haven, CT: Yale University Press, 2010.

Cusumano, Eugenio. "Bridging the Gap: Mobilisation Constraints and Contractor Support to US and UK Military Operations." *Journal of Strategic Studies* 38, no. 5 (2015): 1–29.

Daalder, Ivo H. and I.M. Destler. *In the Shadow of the Oval Office: Profiles of the National Security Advisers and the Presidents They Served—From JFK to George W. Bush*. New York: Simon & Schuster, 2009.

da Costa, Wanderley Messias. *Geografia Política e Geopolítica: discursos sobre o território e o poder*. São Paulo: Editora HUCITEC; Editora da Universidade de São Paulo, 1992.

Dale, Catherine. *National Security Strategy: Legislative Mandates, Execution to Date, and Considerations for Congress*, CRS Report No. RL34505. Washington, DC: Congressional Research Service, July 28, 2008.

Dale, Catherine. *National Security Strategy: Legislative Mandates, Execution to Date, and Considerations for Congress*, CRS Report No. R43174. Washington, DC: Congressional Research Service, August 6, 2013.

Damro, Chad. "Market Power Europe." *Journal of European Public Policy* 19, no. 5 (2012): 682–99.

Danner, Lukas K. "The Debate on China's Grand Strategy." China Policy Institute, University of Nottingham, May 4, 2015, https://cpianalysis.org/2015/05/04/the-debate-on-the-direction-of-chinas-grand-strategy/.

Danner, Lukas K. *China's Grand Strategy: Contradictory Foreign Policy?* New York: Palgrave Macmillan, 2018.

Das, Madhuparna. "Central agencies accuse Bengal of rule breach in Rohingya shelter." *Economic Times*, January 16, 2018. https://economictimes.indiatimes.com/news/politics-and-nation/central-agencies-accuse-bengal-of-rule-breach-in-rohingya-shelter/articleshow/62520123.cms.

Daucé, Francoise. *Être opposant dans la Russie de Vladimir Poutine*. Paris: Le Bord de l'eau, 2016.

Davis, Eric. *Memories of State: Politics, History and Collective Identity in Modern Iraq*. Berkeley: University of California Press, 2005.

de Carvalho, Maria Izabel V. "Estruturas domésticas e grupos de interesse: a formação da posição Brasileira para Seattle." *Contexto Internacional* 25, no. 2 (December 2003): 363–401.

de Castro, Therezinha. "Antártica, o assunto do momento." *Boletim Geográfico* 17, no. 150 (1959): 238–45.

de Castro, Thereziha and Carlos Delgado de Carvalho. "A questão da Antártida." *Boletim Geográfico* 14, no. 135 (1956): 502–6.

De Gaulle, Charles. *Mémoires, vol. 1: Le renouveau, 1958–1962*. Paris: Plon, 1970.

De Gaulle, Charles. *Discours et messages vol. 3: 1958–1962*. Paris: Plon, 1975.

Della Pergola, Sergio. *World Jewish Population: 2016*. New York: the Berman Jewish DataBank, 2017.

de Meira Mattos, Carlos. *Brasil, geopolítica e destino*. Rio de Janeiro: José Olympio, 1975.

de Meira Mattos, Carlos. "Uma geopolítica pan-amazônica." *A Defesa Nacional*, vol. 677 (1978): 5–13.

Demchak, Chris C. and Peter Dombrowski. "Rise of a Cybered Westphalian Age." *Strategic Studies Quarterly* 5, no. 1 (Spring 2011): 32–61.

Desch, Michael C. "Culture Clash: Assessing the Importance of Ideas in Security Studies." *International Security* 23, no. 1 (Summer 1998): 141–70.

Destradi, Sandra. "India and Sri Lanka's civil war: The failure of regional conflict management in South Asia." *Asian Survey* 52, no. 3 (2012): 595–616.

Desuin, Hadrien. *La France atlantiste ou le naufrage de la diplomatie française*. Paris: Les Editions du Cerf, 2017.

Diez, Thomas. "Constructing the Self and Changing Others: Reconsidering 'Normative Power Europe'." *Millennium: Journal of International Studies* 33, no. 3 (2005): 613–36.

Dinan, Desmond. "The Council of the European Union and the European Council." In *Routledge Handbook of European Politics*, edited by José M. Magone, 219–47. London: Routledge, 2015.

"Directors of Policy Planning." U.S. Office of the Historian, accessed August 14, 2018, https://history.state.gov/departmenthistory/people/principalofficers/director-policy-planning.

Djalili, Mohammad-Reza. *Diplomatie Islamique: Stratégie Internationale Du Khomeynisme*. Paris: PUF, 1989.

Dombrowski, Peter and Simon Reich. "Does Donald Trump have a Grand Strategy?" *International Affairs* 93, no. 5 (September 2017): 1013–37.

Dombrowski, Peter and Simon Reich. "Beyond the Tweets: President Trump's Continuity in Military Operations." *Strategic Studies Quarterly* 12, no. 2 (Summer 2018): 56–81.

Donaldson, Robert H., Joseph L. Nogee, and Vidya Nadkarni. *The Foreign Policy of Russia: Changing Systems, Enduring Interests*, 5th ed. New York: M. E. Sharpe, 2014.

Doyle, Richard B. "The U.S. National Security Strategy: Policy, Process, Problems." *Public Administration Review* 67, no. 4 (July–August 2007): 624–9.

Dreyer, Edward L. *Zheng He: China and the Oceans in the Early Ming Dynasty, 1405–1433*. London: Pearson, 2006.

Drezner, Daniel W. "The System Worked: Global Economic Governance during the Great Recession." *World Politics* 66, no. 1 (January 2014): 123–64.

Dror, Yehezkel. *Israeli statecraft: National Security Challenges and Responses*. Abingdon, UK: Routledge, 2011.

Duchêne, Francois. "Europe's Role in World Peace." In *Europe Tomorrow: 16 Europeans Look Ahead*, edited by Richard Mayne. London: Fontana, 1973.

Dudoignon, Stéphane. *The Baluch, Sunnism and the State in Iran*. London: Hurst, 2017.

Dueck, Colin. *Reluctant Crusaders: Power, Culture, and Change in American Grand Strategy*. Princeton, NJ: Princeton University Press, 2006.

Dunlap, Jr, Charles. "Lawfare Today...and Tomorrow." *US Naval War College International Law Studies*, no. 87 (2011): 315–25.

Dutton, Peter. "Three Disputes and Three Objectives: China and the South China Sea." *Naval War College Review* 64, no. 4 (Autumn 2011): 42–67.

Dutton, Peter A. "A Maritime or Continental Order for Southeast Asia and the South China Sea?" Address, Chatham House, London, UK, February 16, 2016; reprinted in *Naval War College Review* 69, no. 3 (Summer 2016): 5–13.

Earle, Edward Mead. "Adam Smith, Alexander Hamilton, Friedrich List: The Economic Foundations of Military Power." In *Makers of Modern Strategy*, edited by Peter Paret, 217–61. Oxford: Clarendon Press, 1986.

Eckstein, Harry. "Case Study and Theory in Political Science." In *Case Study Method*, reprint edited by Roger Gromm, Martyn Hammersley, and Peter Foster, 119–64. London: SAGE Publications, 2009.

Economy, Elizabeth C. *The Third Revolution: Xi Jinping and the New Chinese State*. Oxford: Oxford University Press, 2018.

Egeberg, Morten and Jarle Trondal. "EU-level Agencies: New Executive Centre Formation or Vehicles for National Control?" *Journal of European Public Policy* 18, no. 6 (2011): 868–87.

Ehteshami, Anoushiravan. *After Khomeini: The Second Iranian Republic*. London: Routledge, 1995.

Eisner, Marc Allen. *From Warfare State to Welfare State: World War I, Compensatory State-Building, and the Limits of the Modern Order*. State College, PA: Penn State University Press, 2000.

Elliott, Christopher L. *High Command: British Military Leadership in the Iraq and Afghanistan Wars*. London: Hurst & Co., 2015.

Elliott, Mark. "Frontier Stories: Periphery as Center in Qing History." *Frontiers of History in China* 9, no. 3 (2014): 336–60.

Epstein, Susan B. and Alex Tiersky. *The Quadrennial Diplomacy and Development Review (QDDR)*. CRS Report No. IN10139. Washington, DC: Congressional Research Service, August 27, 2014.

Epstein, Susan B., Marian L. Lawson, and Cory R. Gill. *State, Foreign Operations and Related Programs: FY2017 Budget and Appropriations*. CRS Report No. R44391 Washington, DC: Congressional Research Service, May 26, 2017.

Erickson, Andrew S. "Can China Become a Maritime Power?" In *Asia Looks Seaward: Power and Maritime Strategy*, edited by Toshi Yoshihara and James Holmes, 70–110. Westport, CT: Praeger Security International, 2008.

Erickson, Andrew S. "Beijing's Aerospace Revolution: Short-Range Opportunities, Long-Range Challenges." In *Chinese Aerospace Power: Evolving Maritime Roles*, edited by Andrew S. Erickson and Lyle J. Goldstein, 3–18. Annapolis, MD: Naval Institute Press, 2011.

Erickson, Andrew S. "Through the Lens of Distance: Understanding and Responding to China's 'Ripples of Capability'." *Changing Military Dynamics In East Asia* Policy Brief 3, no. 9 (January 2012).

Erickson, Andrew S. "China's Modernization of Its Naval and Air Power Capabilities." In *Strategic Asia 2012–13: China's Military Challenge*, edited by Ashley J. Tellis and Travis Tanner, 60–125. Seattle, WA: National Bureau of Asian Research, 2012.

Erickson, Andrew S. "Chinese Statesmen and the Use of Air Power." In *The Influence of Airpower upon History: Statesmanship, Diplomacy, and Foreign Policy since 1903*, edited by Robin Higham and Mark Parillo, 237–71. Lexington: University Press of Kentucky, 2013.

Erickson, Andrew S. "China's Military Modernization: Many Improvements, Three Challenges, and One Opportunity." In *China's Challenges*, edited by Jacques deLisle and Avery Goldstein, 178–203. Philadelphia: University of Pennsylvania Press, 2014.

Erickson, Andrew S. "China's Near-Seas Challenges." *The National Interest*, no. 129 (January–February 2014): 60–6.

Erickson, Andrew S. "Rising Tide, Dispersing Waves: Opportunities and Challenges for Chinese Seapower Development." *Journal of Strategic Studies* 37, no. 3 (Summer 2014): 1–31.

Erickson, Andrew S. "Evaluating China's Conventional Military Power: The Naval and Air Dimensions." In *Assessing China's Power*, edited by Jae Ho Chung, 65–90. New York: Palgrave Macmillan, 2015.

Erickson, Andrew S. "Doctrinal Sea Change, Making Real Waves: Examining the Naval Dimension of Strategy." In *China's Evolving Military Strategy*, edited by Joe McReynolds, 99–132. Washington, DC: Jamestown Foundation, 2016.

Erickson, Andrew S. "China's Naval Modernisation, Strategies, and Capabilities." In *International Order at Sea: How it is challenged. How it is maintained*, edited by Jo Inge Bekkevold and Geoffrey Till, 63-92. New York: Palgrave Macmillan, 2016.

Erickson, Andrew S. "China's Maritime Ambitions." In *Asian Security Studies*, 2nd ed. Edited by Sumit Ganguly, Andrew Scobell, and Joseph Chinyong Liow, 100-14. New York: Routledge, 2017.

Erickson, Andrew S. "How Strong Are China's Armed Forces?" In *The China Questions: Critical Insights into a Rising Power*, edited by Jennifer Rudolph and Michael Szonyi, 73-80. Cambridge, MA: Harvard University Press, 2017.

Erickson, Andrew S. "China's Strategic Objectives at Sea." In *Asia-Pacific Regional Security Assessment 2017: Key Developments and Trends*, edited by Tim Huxley and William Choong, 37-50. London: IISS, 2017.

Erickson, Andrew S. "Numbers Matter: China's Three 'Navies' Each Have the World's Most Ships." *The National Interest*, February 26, 2018, http://nationalinterest.org/feature/numbers-matter-chinas-three-navies-each-have-the-worlds-most-24653.

Erickson, Andrew S. and Gabriel B. Collins. "China's Oil Security Pipe Dream: The Reality, and Strategic Consequences, of Seaborne Imports." *Naval War College Review* 63, no. 2 (Spring 2010): 88-111.

Erickson, Andrew S., and Lyle J. Goldstein. "China Studies the Rise of the Great Powers." In *China Goes to Sea: Maritime Transformation in Comparative Historical Perspective*, edited by Andrew Erickson, Lyle Goldstein, and Carnes Lord. Annapolis, MD: Naval Institute Press, July 2009.

Erickson, Andrew S. and Lyle J. Goldstein. "Studying History to Guide China's Rise as a Maritime Great Power." *Harvard Asia Quarterly* 12, no. 3-4 (Winter 2010): 31-8.

Erickson, Andrew S. and Joel Wuthnow. "Why Islands Still Matter in Asia: The Enduring Significance of the Pacific 'Island Chains'." *The National Interest*, February 5, 2016, http://www.andrewerickson.com/wp-content/uploads/2016/02/Island-Chains_Why-Islands-Still-Matter-in-Asia_Erickson-Wuthnow_TNI_20160105.pdf.

Erickson, Andrew S. and Joel Wuthnow. "Barriers, Springboards and Benchmarks: China Conceptualizes the Pacific 'Island Chains'." *The China Quarterly* 225 (March 2016): 1-22.

Erickson, Andrew, Lyle Goldstein, and Carnes Lord. "China Sets Sail." *The American Interest* 5, no. 5 (May/June 2010): 27-34.

Erickson, Andrew, Lyle Goldstein, and Carnes Lord. "When Land Powers Look Seaward." *U.S. Naval Institute Proceedings*, 137, no. 4 (April 2011): 18-23.

Erickson, Andrew, S., Evan Braden Montgomery, Craig Neuman, Stephen Biddle, and Ivan Oelrich. "Correspondence: How Good Are China's Antiaccess/Area-Denial Capabilities?" International Security 41, no. 4 (Spring 2017): 202-13.

Erickson, Jennifer L. "Market Imperative Meets Normative Power: Human Rights and European Arms Transfer Policy." *European Journal of International Relations* 19, no. 2 (2011): 209-34.

"Estrāteji-Ye Jomhuri-Ye Eslāmi-Ye Irān Dar Barobar-E Tahdidat-E Āxir-E Āmrikā." *Rahbord*, no. 24 (Summer 2002): 23-4.

European External Action Service. "EUNAVFOR MED Operation Sophia—Assets." 2016, https://eeas.europa.eu/csdp-missions-operations/eunavfor-med-operation-sophia/12215/assets_en.-072.

European External Action Service. "Ukraine and the EU." https://eeas.europa.eu/headquarters/headquarters-homepage/1937/ukraine-and-eu_en.

European External Action Service. "EU extends sanctions in support of Ukraine's territorial integrity." https://eeas.europa.eu/headquarters/headQuarters-homepage_en/28967/EU%20extends%20sanctions%20in%20support%20of%20Ukraine%27s%20territorial%20integrity.

European Security Strategy. "A Secure Europe in a Better World." December 12, 2003, https://europa.eu/globalstrategy/en/european-security-strategy-secure-europe-better-world.

European Union, Consolidated Versions of the Treaty on European Union and the Treaty on the Functioning of the European Union (2016).

European Union Global Strategy. "Shared Vision, Common Action: A Stronger Europe." June 2016, https://europa.eu/globalstrategy/sites/globalstrategy/files/eugs_review_web.pdf.

Ezrow, Natasha. *Global Politics and Violent Non-State Actors*. London: Sage, 2017.

"Fact Sheet: The 2015 National Security Strategy." https://obamawhitehouse.archives.gov/the-press-office/2015/02/06/fact-sheet-2015-national-security-strategy.

Fact Sheet, The White House. "President Donald J. Trump's 'American Model' Economy." January 30, 2018, https://www.whitehouse.gov/briefings-statements/president-donald-j-trumps-american-model-economy/.

Fair, C. Christine. "Learning to Think the Unthinkable: Lessons from India's Nuclear Test." *India Review* 4, no. 1 (2005): 23–58.

Fair, C. Christine. "US-Indian Army-to-Army Relations: Prospects for Future Coalition Operations?" *Asian Security* 1, no. 2 (2005): 157–73.

Fair, C. Christine. "Lessons from India's Experience in the Punjab, 1978–1993." In *India and Counterinsurgency: Lessons Learned*, edited by Sumit Ganguly and David P. Fidler, 107–26. London: Routledge, 2009.

Fair, C. Christine. "Indo-Iranian Relations-What Prospects for Transformation?" In *India's Foreign Policy: Retrospect and Prospect*, edited by Sumit Ganguly, 132–154. New Delhi: Oxford University Press, 2010.

Fair, C. Christine and Dan Shalmon. "India's Strategic Win: The Upsides of the Lockheed Martin Deal to Produce F-16s In Indian." *Foreign Affairs* (Online), November 3, 2016, https://www.foreignaffairs.com/articles/india/2016-11-01/indias-strategic-win.

Feaver, Peter D. "What Is Grand Strategy and Why Do We Need It?" *Foreign Policy*, April 8, 2009, http://foreignpolicy.com/2009/04/08/what-is-grand-strategy-and-why-do-we-need-it/.

Fedorov, Sergei. "Nicholas Sarkozy's European Policy." *International Affairs* 54, no. 5 (2008).

Feigenbaum, Evan A. "Reluctant Stakeholder: Why China's Highly Strategic Brand of Revisionism is More Challenging Than Washington Thinks." *Macro Polo*, April 27, 2018, https://macropolo.org/reluctant-stakeholder-chinas-highly-strategic-brand-revisionism-challenging-washington-thinks/.

Fedorenko, Vladimir. "The New Silk Road Initiatives in Central Asia." *Rethink Paper*, no. 10 (August 2013).

Fiori, José Luís. *História, estratégia e desenvolvimento: para uma geopolítica do capitalism*. São Paulo: Boitempo Editorial, 2014.

Fiott, Daniel. "European Defence: The Year Ahead." *Policy Brief*, no. 1. Paris: EU Institute for Security Studies, 2017.

Fitzpatrick, Mark. "Iran: A Good Deal." *Survival: Global Politics and Strategy* 57, no. 5 (2015): 47–52.

Fonseca, Pedro Cezar Dutra. *Desenvolvimentismo: a construção do conceito*. Brasília: IPEA, 2015.

Foster, Gregory. "Missing and Wanted: A U.S. Grand Strategy." *Strategic Review* 13, no. 4 (Fall 1985).

France Diplomatie. "Promouvoir la langue française dans le monde", accessed January 1, 2018, https://www.diplomatie.gouv.fr/fr/photos-videos-publications-infographies/publications/enjeux-planetaires-cooperation-internationale/documents-de-strategie-sectorielle/article/promouvoir-la-langue-francaise-114859.

Fravel, M. Taylor. *Strong Borders, Secure Nation: Cooperation and Conflict in China's Territorial Disputes*. Princeton, NJ: Princeton University Press, 2008.

French, David. *The British Way of Warfare, 1688–2000*. London: Unwin Hymen, 1990.

French, Howard. "China's Twilight Years." *The Atlantic* (June 2016), https://www.theatlantic.com/magazine/archive/2016/06/chinas-twilight-years/480768/.

Freilich, Charles D. *Zion's Dilemmas: How Israel Makes National Security Policy*. Ithaca, NY: Cornell University Press, 2012.

Freilich, Charles D. *Israeli National Security: A New Strategy for an Era of Change*. Oxford: Oxford University Press 2018.

Friedberg, Aaron L. *In the Shadow of the Garrison State*. Princeton, NJ: Princeton University Press, 2000.

Friedberg Aaron L. *The Weary Titan: Britain and the Experience of Relative Decline, 1895–1905*. Princeton, NJ: Princeton University Press, 2010.

Friedberg, Aaron L. *A Contest for Supremacy: China, America, and the Struggle for Mastery in Asia*. New York: W. W. Norton & Company, 2011.

Frühling, Stephan and Guillaume Lasconjarias. "NATO, A2/AD and the Kaliningrad Challenge." *Survival. Global Politics and Strategy* 58, no. 2 (March 2016): 95–116.

Gaddis, John Lewis. *Strategies of Containment: A Critical Appraisal of Postwar American National Security Policy*. Oxford: Oxford University Press, 1982.

Gaddis, John Lewis. *The Cold War*. London: Allen Lane, 2005.

Gaddis, John Lewis. "What Is Grand Strategy?" keynote address, American Grand Strategy After War, sponsored by the Triangle Institute for Security Studies and the Duke University Program on American Grand Strategy, February 26, 2009.

Galeotti, Mark. "The 'Gerasimov Doctrine' and Russian Non-Linear War." *In Moscow's Shadows. Analysis and Assessment of Russian Crime and Security* (blog), July 6, 2014, https://inmoscowsshadows.wordpress.com/2014/07/06/the-gerasimov-doctrine-and-russian-non-linear-war/.

Galeotti, Mark. "Putin's Hydra: Inside Russia's Intelligence Services." *European Council on Foreign Relations*, no. 169 (May 2016).

Ganguly, Sumit. "From the Defense of The Nation to Aid to The Civil: The Army in Contemporary India." *Journal of Asian and African Studies* 24, no. 1–2 (1991): 11–26.

Ganguly, Sumit. "India's Pathway to Pokhran II: The Prospects and Sources of New Delhi's Nuclear Weapons Program." *International Security* 23, no. 4 (1999): 148–77.

Ganguly, Sumit. "The Crisis of Indian Secularism." *Journal of Democracy* 14, no. 4 (October 2003): 11–25.

Garcia-Duran, Patricia, Montserrat Millet, and Jan Orbie. "EU Trade Policy Reaction to the BIC: From Accommodation to Entrenchment." In *EU Policy Responses to a Shifting Multilateral System*, edited by Esther Barbé, Oriol Costa and Robert Kissack: 93–114. London: Palgrave Macmillan, 2016.

Gartzke, Erik. "The Myth of Cyber War: Bringing War in Cyberspace Down to Earth." *International Security* 38, no. 2 (Fall 2013): 41–73.

Gautier, Louis *La défense de la France après la guerre froide*. Paris: PUF, 2009.

Gavin, Frank J. *Nuclear Statecraft: History and Strategy in America's Atomic Age*. Ithaca, NY: Cornell University Press, 2014.

Gehring, Thomas, Kevin Urbanski, and Sebastian Oberthür. "The European Union as an Inadvertent Great Power: EU Actorness and the Ukraine Crisis." *Journal of Common Market Studies* 55, no. 4 (2017): 727–43.

Gazeau-Secret, Anne. "Francophonie et Diplomatie d'Influence." *Géoéconomie* 4, no. 55 (2016).

Gelman, Vladimir. *Authoritarian Russia: Analyzing Post-Soviet Regime Changes*. Pittsburg, PA: Pittsburg University Press, 2015.

"General Assembly Votes Overwhelmingly to Accord Palestine 'Non-Member Observer State' Status in United Nations." *UN.org*, November 29, 2012, https://www.un.org/press/en/2012/ga11317.doc.htm.

George, Alexander L. *Forceful Persuasion: Coercive Diplomacy as an Alternative to War*. Washington, DC: United States Institute of Peace, 1992.

Geranmayeh, Ellie. "Towards and Beyond a Final Nuclear Deal with Iran." *The International Spectator: Italian Journal of International Affairs* 50, no. 2 (2015): 1–7.

Gerasimov, Valery. "Cennost' nauki v predvidenii." Voenno-promyšlennyj kur'er" (VPK) 476, no. 8 (February 27–March 5, 2013).

Ghez, Jeremy and Stephen F. Larrabee. "France and NATO." *Survival: Global Politics and Strategy* 51, no. 2 (March 2009): 77–90.

Gholz, Eugene, Daryl G. Press, and Harvey M. Sapolsky. "Come Home America: The Strategy of Restraint in the Face of Temptation." *International Security* 21, no. 4 (Spring 1997): 5–48.

Ghosh, P. K. "Emerging Trends in the Nuclear Triad." *Strategic Analysis* 25, no. 2 (July 2008): 243–70.

Gilderhus, Mark T. "The Monroe Doctrine: Meanings and Implications." *Presidential Studies Quarterly* 36, no. 1 (March 2006): 5–16.

Gilpin, Robert. *War and Change in World Politics*. Cambridge: Cambridge University Press, 1983.

Glaser, Charles L. "What Is the Offense-Defense Balance and Can We Measure It?" *International Security* 22, no. 4 (1998): 44–82.

Global Attitudes and Trends. "Opinion of the United States." *Global Indicator Database*, Pew Research Center, http://www.pewglobal.org/database/indicator/1/survey/all/.

Global Fire Power. "2017 Military Strength Ranking", 2017, https://www.globalfirepower.com/countries-listing.asp.

"Global Investment Trends Monitor." United Nations Conference on Trade and Development (UNCTAD), no. 25 (February 1, 2017), http://unctad.org/en/PublicationsLibrary/webdiaeia2017d1_en.pdf.

Goertz, Gary. *Social Science Concepts: A User's Guide*. Princeton, NJ: Princeton University Press, 2005.

Goldberg, Jeffrey. "The Obama Doctrine." *The Atlantic* (April 2016), http://www.theatlantic.com/magazine/archive/2016/04/the-obama-doctrine/471525/.

Goldman Sachs. "Beyond the BRICs: A Look at the 'Next 11'", accessed April 27, 2018, http://www.goldmansachs.com/our-thinking/archive/archive-pdfs/brics-book/brics-chap13.pdf.

Goldstein, Avery. *Rising to the Challenge: China's Grand Strategy and International Security.* Stanford, CA: Stanford University Press, 2005.

Goodman, Micah. *Catch 67* [Hebrew]. Israel: Kinneret Zmora-Bitan Dvir, 2017.

Gordon, Philip H. *A Certain Idea of France: French Security Policy and Gaullist Legacy.* Princeton, NJ: Princeton University Press, 1993.

Gourevitch, Peter. "The Second Image Reversed: The International Sources of Domestic Politics." *International Organization* 32, no. 04 (September 1978): 881–912.

Gourevitch, Peter. *Políticas estratégicas en tiempos difíciles: respuestas comparativas a las crisis económicas internacionales.* Mexico City: Fondo de Cultura Económica, 1993.

Gomes, Paulo Cesar da Costa. *Geografia e modernidade.* Rio de Janeiro: Bertrand, 2010.

Gray, Colin S. "National Style in Strategy: The American Example." *International Security* 6, no. 2 (Fall 1981): 21–47.

Gray, Colin. *The Strategy Bridge: Theory for Practice.* Oxford: Oxford University Press, 2010.

Gregory, Shaun. *French Defense Policy into the Twenty-First Century.* London: Macmillan, 2000.

Grinberg, Alex. "The Concept of Deterrence in Arab and Muslim Thought—Iran." *The 13th Herzliya conference.* Herzliya, 2013.

Gourlay, Catriona. "Civilian CSDP: A Tool for State-Building?" In *The Routledge Handbook of European Security*, edited by Sven Biscop and Richard G. Whitman, 91–104. New York: Routledge, 2013.

Gwin, Catherine. *U.S. Relations with the World Bank, 1945–92.* Washington, DC: The Brookings Institution, 1994.

Hao, Su. 苏浩. "地缘重心与世界政治的支点" [Geogravitational Centers and World Political Fulcrums], 现代国际关系 *[Contemporary International Relations]*, no. 4 (2004): 54–61.

Haas, Mark L. *The Ideological Origins of Great Power Politics, 1789–1989.* Ithaca, NY: Cornell University Press, 2005.

Haas, Mark, L. *The Clash of Ideologies: Middle Eastern Politics and American Security.* New York: Oxford University Press, 2012.

Hacohen, Gershon. "Israeli Identity: What Has Changed This Year?." BESA Center Perspectives, no. 599 (September 2017), https://besacenter.org/perspectives-papers/israeli-identity/.

Hartz, Louis. *The Liberal Tradition in America.* New York: Harcourt, Brace and World, 1955.

Haesebrouck, Tim and Melanie Van Meirvenne. "EUFOR RCA and CSDP Crisis Management Operations: Back on Track?" *European Foreign Affairs Review* 20, no. 2 (2015): 267–85.

Hagerty, Devin T. "India's Regional Security Doctrine." *Asian Survey* 31, no. 4 (April 1991): 351–63.

Hall, John A. and T. V. Paul. "Preconditions for Prudence: A Sociological Synthesis of Realism and Liberalism." In *International Order and the Future of World Politics*, edited by T. V. Paul and John A. Hall, 67–77. Cambridge: Cambridge University Press, 1999.

Hanson, Victor Davis. "Can Israel Survive?." *The National Review*, January 29, 2015, http://www.nationalreview.com/article/412951/can-israel-survive-victor-davis-hanson.

Haykel, Bernard and Thomas Hegghammer. *Saudi Arabia in Transition: Insights on Social, Political, Economic and Religious Change.* Cambridge: Cambridge University Press, 2015.

"Heads of the NSS in the Past" [Hebrew], The NSS website, accessed December 27, 2017, http://www.nsc.gov.il/he/About-the-Staff/Pages/FormerManagers.aspx.

Heath, Timothy R. "The 'Holistic Security Concept': The Securitization of Policy and Increasing Risk of Militarized Crisis." *Jamestown China Brief* 15, no. 12 (June 19, 2015): https://jamestown.org/wp-content/uploads/2015/06/China_Brief_Vol_15_Issue_12_v2_5.pdf.

Hecht, Eado and Eitan Shamir. "The Case for Israeli Ground Forces." *Survival: Global Politics and Strategy* 58, no. 5 (October–November 2016): 123–48.

Heisbourg, François. "The 'European Security Strategy' is not a Security Strategy." In *A European Way of War*, edited by Steven Everts et al., 27–39. London: Centre for European Reform, 2004.

Hendrix, Cullen S. "Measuring state capacity: Theoretical and Empirical Implications for the Study of Civil Conflict." *Journal of Peace Research* 47, no. 3 (May 2010).

Henökl, Thomas E. "How Do EU Foreign Policy-Makers Decide? Institutional Orientations Within the European External Action Service." *West European Politics* 38, no. 3 (2015): 679–708.

Henökl, Thomas E. and Jarle Trondal. "Unveiling the Anatomy of Autonomy: Dissecting Actor-Level Independence in the European External Action Service." *Journal of European Public Policy* 22, no. 10 (2015): 1426–47.

Henkin, Louis. "Foreign Affairs and the Constitution." *Foreign Affairs* 66, no. 2 (Winter 1987): 287.

Hen-Tov, Elliot and Nathan Gonzales. "The Militarization of Post-Khomeini Iran: Praetorianism 2.0." *The Washington Quarterly* 34, no. 1 (December 2010): 45–59.

Hermann, Tamar. *Religious? Nationalist! The National Religious Camp in Israel* [Hebrew] (Israel: The Israel Democracy Institute, 2014), https://www.idi.org.il/media/6197/the_national_religious_sector_book.pdf.

Hetou, Ghaidaa. *The Syrian Conflict: The Role of Russia, Iran and US in a Global Crisis*. Abingdon, UK: Routledge, 2019.

Herzl, Theodor. *Altneuland*, trans. Shmuel Schnitzer, (Israel: Haifa publishing company, 1961).

Hyde-Price, Adrian. "'Normative' Power Europe: A Realist Critique." *Journal of European Public Policy* 13, no. 2 (2006): 217–34.

Hyde-Price, Adrian. "A 'Tragic Actor'? A Realist Perspective on 'Ethical Power Europe'." *International Affairs* 84, no. 1 (2008): 29–44.

Higgott, Richard and Simon Reich. "Globalisation and Sites of Conflict: Towards Definition and Taxonomy." Working Paper Number 1, Centre for the Study of Globalisation and Regionalisation, Warwick University, Coventry, UK, June 1998. https://warwick.ac.uk/fac/soc/pais/research/researchcentres/csgr/papers/workingpapers/1998/wp0198.pdf.

Hill, Christopher. *The Changing Politics of Foreign Policy*. Hampshire, UK: Palgrave MacMillan, 2003.

Hill, Fiona and Clifford G. Gaddy. *Mr. Putin: Operative in the Kremlin*. Washington, DC: Brookings Institution Press, 2013.

Hill, Ginny. *Yemen Endures: Civil War, Saudi Adventurism and the Future of Arabia*. Oxford: Oxford University Press, 2017.

Hirst, Monica and Maria Regina Soares Lima. "Rethinking Global and Domestic Challenges in Brazilian Foreign Policy." In *Routledge Handbook of Latin America in the World*, edited by Jorge I. Domínguez and Ana Covarrubias, 139–152. New York: Routledge, 2015.

Hitchcock, William I., Melvin P. Leffler, Jeffrey W. Legro, eds. *Shaper Nations: Strategies for a Changing World*. Cambridge, MA: Harvard University Press, 2016.

Hite, Katherine. "Historical Memory." In *International Encyclopedia of Political Science*, edited by Bertrand Badie, Dirk Berg-Schlosser, and Leonardo Morlino, 1078–82. Thousand Oaks, CA: SAGE, 2011.

Hoffman, F.G. "Grand Strategy: The Fundamental Considerations." *Orbis* 58, no. 4 (Fall 2014): 472–85.

Hoffman, Samantha. "Programming China: The Communist Party's Autonomic Approach to Managing State Security." *MERICS China Monitor*, December 12, 2017, https://www.merics.org/en/microsite/china-monitor/programming-china.

Hoffman, Samantha and Peter Mattis. "Managing the Power Within: China's State Security Commission." *War on the Rocks*, July 18, 2016, https://warontherocks.com/2016/07/managing-the-power-within-chinas-state-security-commission/.

Hoffman, Stanley. "De Gaulle, Europe, and the Atlantic Alliance." *International Organization* 17, no. 3 (Winter 1964): 1–28.

Hoffmann, Stanley. "The American Style: Our Past and Our Principles." *Foreign Affairs* 46, no. 2 (January 1968): 362–76.

Holbraad, Carsten. *Middle Powers in International Politics*. London: Macmillan Press, 1984.

Howorth, Jolyon. "Prodigal Son or Trojan Horse: What's in It for France?" *European Security* 19, no. 1 (October 2010): 11–28.

Hoppe, Dominique. "La langue française dans les organisations internationales: le dernier contre-pouvoir?." *HuffingtonPost*, January 4, 2013, https://www.huffingtonpost.fr/dominique-hoppe/langue-francaise-_b_2979045.html.

Hudson, Valerie M., and Christopher S. Vore. "Foreign Policy Analysis Yesterday, Today, and Tomorrow." *Mershon International Studies Review* 39, no. 2 (October 1995): 209–38.

Huntington, Samuel P. "The U.S.—Decline or Renewal?" *Foreign Affairs* 67, no. 2 (Winter 1988/1989): 76–96.

Hughes, David. "Unmaking an Exception: A Critical Genealogy of US Exceptionalism." *Review of International Studies* 41, no. 3 (July 2015): 527–51.

Hussein, Abdulrahman Assad. "The Foreign Policy of the Kingdom of Saudi Arabia, 1979–1991." PhD diss., George Washington University, 1995.

Ibrahim, Itty. *South Asian Cultures of the Bomb: Atomic Publics and the State in India and Pakistan*. Bloomington: Indiana University Press 2009.

Ignatieff, Michael. "Introduction: American Exceptionalism and Human Rights." In *American Exceptionalism and Human Rights* edited Michael Ignatieff, 4–7. Princeton, NJ: Princeton University Press, 2005.

IDF Chief of the General Staff. "IDF Strategy" [English], July 2016, 36–37, 20–21, https://www.idfblog.com/s/Desktop/IDF%20Strategy.pdf.

Inbar, Efraim and Eitan Shamir. "'Mowing the Grass': Israel's Strategy for Protracted Intractable Conflict." *Journal of Strategic Studies* 37, no 1 (February 2014): 65–90.

Inderfurth, Karl F. and Loch K. Johnson, eds. *Fateful Decisions: Inside the National Security Council*. New York: Oxford University Press, 2004.

Isaacson, Walter and Evan Thomas. *The Wise Men: Six Friends and the World They Made*. New York: Simon and Shuster, 1986.

Isenberg, David. *Private Military Contractors and U.S. Grand Strategy*, PRIO Report Oslo: International Peace Research Institute, January 2009.

Jacobs, Bruce and Tonio Andrade, as well as Ruiping Ye. "Colonisation without Exploitation: The Qing Policies in Taiwan during the High Qing Period (1684–1795)." *Journal of the Australasian Law Teachers Association*, no 8 (2013).

James, Charles. *A New and Enlarged Military Dictionary, or, Alphabetical Explanation of Technical Terms*. London: The Military Library, 1805.

Jervis, Robert. *The Logic of Images in International Relations*. Princeton, NJ: Princeton University Press, 1970.

Jervis, Robert. "Cooperation under the Security Dilemma." *World Politics* 30, no. 2 (January 1978): 167–74.

Jervis, Robert. *Perception and Misperception in International Politics*. Princeton, NJ: Princeton University Press, 1978.

Jervis, Robert. *The Illogic of American Nuclear Strategy*. Ithaca, NY: Cornell University Press, 1985.

Jisi, Wang. 王辑思. "苏美争霸的历史教训和美中国的崛起新道路" [The Historic Lesson of the U.S.-Soviet Contest for Hegemony and China's Peaceful Rise], essay in 中国和平崛起新道路 [China's Peaceful Rise: A New Path] (Beijing: 中共中央党校国际战略研究所 [International Strategy Research Institute, Central Party School], April 2004).

Jisi, Wang. "China's Search for a Grand Strategy: A Rising Great Power Finds Its Way." *Foreign Affairs* 90, no. 2 (March/April 2011): 68–79, https://www.foreignaffairs.com/articles/china/2011-02-20/chinas-search-grand-strategy.

Jisi, Wang. "Marching Westwards: The Rebalancing of China's Geostrategy." *International and Strategic Studies* no. 73 (2012).

Jobim, Nelson A., Sergio W. Etchegoyen, and João Paulo Soares Alsina Júnior, eds. *Segurança internacional: perspectivas brasileiras*. Rio de Janeiro: FGV Editora, 2010.

Johnston, Alastair Iain. "Thinking about Strategic Culture." *International Security* 19, no. 4 (Spring 1995): 32–64.

Johnston, Alastair Ian. *Cultural Realism: Strategic Culture and Grand Strategy in Chinese History*. Princeton, NJ: Princeton University Press, 1995.

"Joint Statement of the Inaugural United States-Qatar Strategic Dialogue." U.S. Department of State, January 30, 2018, https://www.state.gov/r/pa/prs/ps/2018/01/277776.htm.

Jones, Peter. "Learning to Live with a Nuclear Iran." *The Nonproliferation Review* 19, no. 2 (July 2012): 197–217.

Jordaan, Eduard. "The Concept of a Middle Power in International Relations: Distinguishing between Emerging and Traditional Middle Powers." *Politikon: South African Journal of Political Studies* 30, no. 1 (2003): 165–81.

Júnior, Alsina and João Paulo Soares. *Política externa e poder militar no Brasil: universos paralelos*. Rio de Janeiro: FGV Editora, 2009.

Kaarbo, Juliet. "A Foreign Policy Analysis Perspective on the Domestic Politics Turn in IR Theory." *International Studies Review* 17, no. 2 (June 2015): 189–216.

Kapstein, Ethan Barnaby. *The Political Economy of National Security*. New York: McGraw-Hill, 1992.

Katzenstein, Peter J. *The Culture of National Security: Norms and Identity in World Politics*. New York: Columbia University Press, 1996.

Katzenstein, Peter J. and Robert O. Keohane. *Anti-Americanisms in World Politics*. Ithaca, NY: Cornell University Press, 2007.

Katzenstein, Peter J. "China's Rise: East Asia and Beyond." *East Asia Institute Working Paper* 12 (April 2008), https://www.files.ethz.ch/isn/137725/2009052018244858.pdf.

Katzman, Kenneth. *The Warriors of Islam: Iran's Revolutionary Guard*. Boulder, CO: Westview, 1993.

Kennan, George F. *Memoirs 1925–1950*. New York: Pantheon, 1983.

Kennedy, Paul. *The Realities Behind Diplomacy: Background Influences on British External Policy, 1865–1980*. London: Fontana, 1981.

Kennedy, Paul. "Grand Strategy in War and Peace: Toward a Broader Definition." In *Grand Strategy in War and Peace*, edited by Paul Kennedy, 1–7. New Haven, CT: Yale University Press, 1991.

Kennedy, Paul. *The Rise and Fall of the Great Powers: Economic Change and Military Conflict from 1500 to 2000*. New York: Vintage Books, 1989.

Kennedy, Paul. "Grand Strategy in War and Peace: Toward a Broader Definition." In *Grand Strategy in War and Peace*, edited by Paul Kennedy. New Haven, CT: Yale University Press, 1991.

Kennedy, Paul. "Grand Strategies and Less-than-grand Strategies: A Twentieth Century Critique." In *War, Strategy and International Politics*, edited by Lawrence Freedman, Paul Hayes, and Robert O'Neill. Oxford: Clarendon Press, 1992.

Kennedy, Paul. "The Rise and Fall of Navies." *New York Times*, April 5, 2007, https://www.nytimes.com/2007/04/05/opinion/05iht-edkennedy.1.5158064.html.

Keukeleire, Stephan and Tom Delreux. *The Foreign Policy of the European Union*. London: Palgrave Macmillan, 2014.

Khan, Saira. *Iran and Nuclear Weapons: Protracted Conflict and Proliferation*. Abingdon, UK: Routledge, 2009.

Khilnani, Sunil, et al. "Nonalignment 2.0: A Foreign and Strategic Policy For India In The Twenty First Century." Centre for Policy Research, February 29, 2012. http://www.cprindia.org/research/reports/nonalignment-20-foreign-and-strategic-policy-india-twenty-first-century.

Kinzer, Stephen. *The Brothers: John Foster Dulles, Allen Dulles, and Their Secret World War*. New York: Times Books, 2013.

Kirshner, Jonathan. *Currency and Coercion: The Political Economy of International Monetary Power*. Princeton, NJ: Princeton University Press, 1995.

Kirshner, Jonathan. "Dollar Primacy and American Power: What's at Stake?" *Review of International Political Economy* 15, no. 3 (August 2008): 418–38.

Kirshner, Jonathan. "Dollar Diminution and New Macroeconomic Constraints on American Power." In *Sustainable Security: Rethinking American National Security Strategy*, edited by Jeremi Suri and Benjamin Valentino. New York: Oxford University Press, 2016.

Kissinger, Henry. *Diplomacy*. New York: Simon and Schuster, 1994.

Knorr, Klaus. *The Power of Nations: The Political Economy of International Relations*. New York: Basic Books, 1974.

Koh, Harold Hongju. "On American Exceptionalism." *Stanford Law Review* 55, no. 5 (May 2003): 1485–986.

Koistinen, Paul A. C. *Arsenal of World War II: The Political Economy of American Warfare, 1940–1945*. Lawrence: University Press of Kansas, 2004.

Koistinen, Paul A. C. *State of War: The Political Economy of American Warfare, 1945–2011*. Lawrence: University Press of Kansas, 2012.

Kolodziej, Edward A. *French International Policy Under de Gaulle and Pompidou.* Ithaca, NY: Cornell University Press, 1974.

Krasner, Stephen. "An Orienting Principle for Foreign Policy: The Deficiencies of 'Grand Strategy'." *Policy Review*, no. 163 (October/November 2010), http://www.hoover.org/research/orienting-principle-foreign-policy.

Krauthammer, Charles. "The Unipolar Moment." *Foreign Affairs* 70, no. 1 (1990/1991).

Krotz, Ulrich, and Richard Maher. "Europe's Crises and the EU's 'Big Three'." *West European Politics* 39, no. 5 (2016): 1053–72.

Kugler, Richard L. *Policy Analysis in National Security Affairs: New Methods for a New Era.* Washington, DC: National Defense University Press, 2011.

Kupchan, Charles. *No One's World: The West, The Rising Rest, and the Coming Global Turn.* Oxford: Oxford University Press, 2012.

Kuhrt, Natasha. "Russia and Asia Pacific: Diversification or Sinocentrism?" In *Russia's Foreign Policy: Ideas, Domestic Politics and External Relations*, edited by David Cadier and Margot Light, 175–88. London: Palgrave Macmillan, 2015.

Ladwig III, Walter C. "A Cold Start for Hot Wars? The Indian Army's New Limited War Doctrine." *International Security* 32, no. 3 (2008): 158–90.

Ladwig III, Walter C. "Indian Military Modernization and Conventional Deterrence in South Asia." *Journal of Strategic Studies* 38, no. 5 (2015): 729–72.

Lake, Anthony. *Laying the Foundation for a New American Century.* Washington, DC: The White House, Office of the Press Secretary, April 25, 1996.

Lake, David A. and Patrick M. Morgan. "The New Regionalism in Security Affairs." In *Regional Orders: Building Security in a New World*, edited by David A. Lake and Patrick M. Morgan, 3–19. University Park, PA: Penn State University Press, 1997.

Lakshmi, Rama and Emily Wax. "India's Government Wins Parliament Confidence Vote." *The Washington Post*, July 23, 2008, http://www.washingtonpost.com/wp-dyn/content/article/2008/07/22/AR2008072200161.html.

Lane, Philippe. *French Scientific and Cultural Diplomacy.* Liverpool: Liverpool University Press, 2013.

Larson, Deborah Welch, T. V. Paul, and William C. Wohlforth. "Status and World Order." In *Status in World Politics*, edited by T. V. Paul, Deborah Welch Larson, and William C. Wohlforth, 33–57. Cambridge: Cambridge University Press, 2014.

Larson, Eric V., David T. Orletsky, and Kristin J. Leuschner. *Defense Planning in a Decade of Change: Lessons from the Base Force, Bottom-Up Review, and Quadrennial Defense Review*, MR-1387-AF. Santa Monica, CA: RAND, 2001.

Layne, Christopher. "The Unipolar Illusion: Why New Great Powers Will Rise." *International Security* 17, no. 4 (Spring 1993): 5–51.

Layne, Christopher. "From Preponderance to Offshore Balancing America's Future Grand Strategy." *International Security* 22, no. 1 (Summer 1997): 86–124.

Layne, Christopher. *The Peace of Illusions: American Grand Strategy from 1940 to the Present.* Ithaca, NY: Cornell University Press, 2006.

Legro, Jeffrey W. "What China Will Want: The Future Intentions of a Rising Power." *Perspectives on Politics* 5, no. 3 (September 2007): 515–34.

Lemke, Douglas. *Regions of War and Peace.* Cambridge: Cambridge University Press, 2002.

Le Monde and AFP. "Commission européenne: la nomination de Martin Selmayr était 'politique', reconnaît un commissaire", accessed March 29, 2018, http://www.lemonde.fr/europe/article/2018/03/27/commission-europeenne-la-nomination-de-martin-selmayr-etait-politique-reconnait-un-commissaire_5277242_3214.html.

Lepgold, Joseph and Timothy McKeown. "Is American Foreign Policy Exceptional? An Empirical Analysis." *Political Science Quarterly* 110, no. 3 (Autumn 1995): 369–84.

Lequesne, Christian. *Ethnographie du Quay d'Orsay*. Paris, CNRS Editions, 2016.

Liddell Hart, *Strategy*. London: Faber and Faber, 1954.

Liddell Hart, Basil H. *The British Way in Warfare*. London: Faber and Faber, 1932.

Lieber, Robert J. "The Rise of the BRICS and American Primacy." *International Politics* 51, no. 2 (March 2014): 137–54.

Lindemann, Thomas. *Causes of War: The Struggle for Recognition*. Colchester, UK: Essex, 2010.

Lindley-French, Julian. "Could Britain respond strategically to Russian aggression." In *Ukraine and Beyond: Russia's Strategic Security Challenge to Europe*, edited by Janne Haaland Matlary and Tormod Heier, 101–28. Basingstoke: Palgrave Macmillan.

Lindsay, James M. *Congress and the Politics of U.S. Foreign Policy*. Baltimore, MD: Johns Hopkins University Press, 1994.

Lindsay, James M. and Ray Takeyh. "After Iran Gets the Bomb: Containment and Its Complications." *Foreign Affairs* 89, no. 2 (March/April 2010): 33–49.

Lionel, Zinsou. *France 2025—Europe et mondialisation*. Paris: La Documentation française, 2008.

Lipset, Seymour Martin. *American Exceptionalism: A Double-Edged Sword*. New York: W. W. Norton & Company, 1997.

Litwak, Robert. "Iran's Nuclear Chess: After the Deal." *Woodrow Wilson International Center for Scholars* (2015): 26–7.

Lo, Bobo. *Axis of Convenience: Moscow, Beijing and the New Geopolitics*. London: Chatham House, 2008.

Lo, Bobo. *Russia and the New World Disorder*. London: Chatham House, 2015.

Lobell, Steven E., Jeffrey W. Taliaferro, and Norrin M. Ripsman. "Introduction: Grand Strategy between the World Wars." In *The Challenge of Grand Strategy: The Great Powers and the Broken Balance between the Wars*, edited by Jeffrey W. Taliaferro, Norrin M. Ripsman, and Steven E. Lobell, 1–36. Cambridge: Cambridge University Press, 2012.

Locher, III, James R. "Has it worked? The Goldwater-Nichols Reorganization Act." *Naval War College Review* 54, no. 4 (Autumn 2001): 95–115.

Locher III, James R. *Victory on the Potomac: The Goldwater-Nichols Act Unifies the Pentagon*, rev. ed. 2002; reprint. College Station, TX: Texas A&M University Press, 2004.

Louër, Laurence. *Chiisme et Politique au Moyen-Orient: Iran, Irak, Liban, Monarchies Du Golfe*. Paris: Autrement, 2008.

Loukianov, Fiodor. "La Russie, une puissance révisionniste?" *Politique étrangère*, no. 2 (Summer 2015): 11–24.

Lukin, Alexander. "What the Kremlin Is Thinking: Putin's Vision for Eurasia." *Foreign Affairs* 93, no. 4 (July–August 2014): 85–93.

Luttwark, Edward N. "From Geopolitics to Geo-Economics: Logic of Conflict, Grammar of Commerce." *The National Interest*, no. 20 (Summer 1990): 17–23.

Luttwak, Edward. *The Grand Strategy of the Byzantine Empire*. Cambridge: Cambridge University Press, 2009.

McDougall, Walter. *Promised Land, Crusader State: The American Encounter with the World Since 1776*. New York: Houghton Mifflin, 1997.

McDougall, Walter A. "Back to Bedrock: The Eight Traditions of American Statecraft." *Foreign Affairs* 76, no. 2 (March–April 1997): 134–46.

McInnis, Kathleen, J. *Goldwater-Nichols at 30: Defense Reform and Issues for Congress* CRS Report No. R44474. Washington, DC: Congressional Research Service, June 16, 2016.

McInnis, J. Matthew. "Iran's Strategic Thinking: Origins and Evolution." *American Enterprise Institute*, May 12, 2015, http://www.aei.org/wp-content/uploads/2015/05/IransStrategic-Thinking.pdf.

Mahan, Alfred Thayer. *The Influence of Sea Power Upon History, 1660–1783*. New York: Dover Publications, 1987.

Maini, Tridivesh Singh. "India-Pakistan Tensions: Why Indian Punjab Is Watching." *The Diplomat*, August 24, 2016, https://thediplomat.com/2016/08/india-pakistan-tensions-why-indian-punjab-is-watching/.

Malashenko, Alexey. "Divisions and Defiance Among Russia's Muslims." Carnegie Moscow Center, November 20, 2015.

Malamud, Andrés. "A Leader Without Followers? The Growing Divergence Between the Regional and Global Performance of Brazilian Foreign Policy." *Latin American Politics and Society* 53, no. 3 (2011): 1–24.

Maloney, Suzanne. *Iran's Political Economy since the Revolution*. Cambridge: Cambridge University Press, 2015.

Mankoff, Jeffrey. *Russian Foreign Policy. The Return of Great Power Politics*. Lanham, MD: Rowman & Littlefield Publishers, 2012.

Marangé, Céline. "Russia's Rapprochement with China: Does Strategy Triumph over Tactics?" *Notes de Recherche Stratégiqueno*, no. 19 Paris: Institute for Strategic Research, 2015.

Marangé, Céline. "Le nucléaire russe: un instrument de dissuasion et d'intimidation." *Revue de Défense nationale*, no. 802 (Summer 2017): 50–7.

Machado, Lia Osório. "A Estratégia Nacional de Defesa, a geografia do tráfico de drogas ilícitas e a Bacia Amazônica Sul-americana." In *Seminário de Defesa e Desenvolvimento Sustentável da Amazônia*, edited by Escola de Comando and Estado Maior do Exército; Secretaria Assuntos Estratégicos, 99–106. Rio de Janeiro: Sá Ribeiro Multimidia, 2011.

Manners, Ian. "Normative Power Europe: A Contradiction in Terms?" *Journal of Common Market Studies* 40, no. 2 (2002): 235–58.

Manners, Ian. "The Normative Ethics of the European Union." *International Affairs* 84, no. 1 (2008): 45–60.

Markovits, Andrei S. and Simon Reich. *The German Predicament: Memory and Power in the New Europe* Ithaca, NY: Cornell University Press, 1997.

Martel, William C. *Grand Strategy in Theory and Practice: The Need for An Affective American Foreign Policy*. New York: Cambridge University Press, 2015.

Massie, Justin and David Morin. "Francophonie et opérations de paix. Vers une appropriation géoculturelle." *Etudes internationales* 42, no. 3 (2011): 313–36.

Mason, Robert. *Foreign Policy in Iran and Saudi Arabia: Economics and Diplomacy in the Middle East.* London: I.B.Tauris, 2015.

Mattelaer, Alexander. "The Empty Promise of Comprehensive Planning in EU Crisis Management." *European Foreign Affairs Review*, vol. 18 (2013): 125–46.

Mattis, Peter. "China Adaptive Approach to the Information Counter-Revolution." *Jamestown China Brief*, June 3, 2011, https://jamestown.org/program/chinas-adaptive-approach-to-the-information-counter-revolution/.

Maxwell, Neville. *India's China War.* London: Jonathan Cape, 1970.

Mead, Walter Russel. "The Jacksonian Tradition: And American Foreign Policy." *The National Interest*, no. 58 (Winter 1999/2000): 5–29.

Mead, Walter Russel. *Special Providence: American Foreign Policy and How It Changed the World.* London: Routledge, 2002.

Mearsheimer, John. *The Tragedy of Great Power Politics.* New York: W.W. Norton & Company Inc., 2001.

Mearsheimer, John J. "Can China Rise Peacefully?." *The National Interest*, October 25, 2014, https://nationalinterest.org/commentary/can-china-rise-peacefully-10204.

Meiser, Jeffrey W. "Ends + Ways + Means = (Bad) Strategy." *Parameters* 46, no. 4 (Winter 2016–17): 81–91.

Metcalf, Thomas R. *Imperial Connections: India in the Indian Ocean Arena, 1860–1920.* Berkeley: University of California Press, 2007.

Meunier, Sophie. "Managing Globalization? The EU in International Trade Negotiations." *Journal of Common Market Studies* 45, no. 4 (2007): 905–26.

Milani Carlos R. S. and Leticia Pinheiro. "The Politics of Brazilian Foreign Policy and Its Analytical Challenges." *Foreign Policy Analysis* 13, no. 2 (April 2016): 278–96.

Milevski, Lukas. *The Evolution of Modern Grand Strategic Thought.* London: Oxford University Press, 2016.

Milani, Carlos R. S., Leticia Pinheiro, and Maria Regina Soares de Lima. "Brazil's foreign policy and the 'graduation dilemma'." *International Affairs* 93, no. 3 (May 2017): 585–605.

Millen, Raymond. "Eisenhower and US Grand Strategy." *Parameters* 44, no. 2 (Summer 2014): 35–47.

Miller, Benjamin. "Explaining Variations in Regional Peace: Three Strategies for Peace-making." *Cooperation and Conflict* 35, no. 2 (June 200): 155–92.

Mills, Melinda, Gerhard G. van de Bunt, and Jeanne de Bruijn. "Comparative Research: Persistent Problems and Promising Solutions." *International Sociology* 21, no. 5 (September 2006): 622–3.

Milne, David. *Worldmaking: The Art and Science of American Diplomacy.* New York: Farrar, Straus and Giroux, 2015.

Mingfu, Liu. *The China Dream: Great Power Thinking and Strategic Posture in the Post-American Era.* New York: CN Times Books Inc., 2015.

"Ministerial Committee on National Security Affairs (Security Cabinet)" [Hebrew], Israel Prime Minster office website, accessed December 24, 2017, http://www.pmo.gov.il/Secretary/ministersCommissions/Pages/cabinetleumi.aspx.

Mintzberg, Henry, and James A. Waters. "Of Strategies, Emergent and Deliberate." *Strategic Management Journal* 6, no. 3 (July–September 1985): 257–72.

Missiroli, Antonio, ed. "The EEAS." In *The EU and the World: Players and Policies Post-Lisbon: A Handbook*, edited by Antonio Missiroli, 27–44. Paris: European Union Institute for Security Studies, 2017.

Missiroli, Antonio, Jan Joel Andersson, Florence Gaub, Nicu Popescu, John-Joseph Wilkins et al. *Strategic Communications: East and South*, no. 30 (Paris: European Union Institute for Security Studies, July 29, 2016).

Meunier, Sophie. "La France face à la mondialisation: se protéger ou se projeter?." Institut de l'entreprise, Working Paper, September 2012, https://scholar.princeton.edu/sites/default/files/france_face_mondialisation_web_0.pdf.

Milani, Carlos R. S., Leticia Pinheiro, and Maria Regina Soares de Lima. "Brazil's foreign policy and the 'graduation dilemma'." *International Affairs* 93, no. 3 (May 2017): 585–605.

Miller, Aaron David. *Search for Security: Saudi Arabian Oil and American Foreign Policy*. Chapel Hill: The University of North Carolina Press, 2017.

Miyamoto, Shiguenoli. "Os Estudos Geopolíticos no Brasil: uma contribuição para sua avaliação." *Perspectivas São Paulo* 4 (1981): 75–92.

Mohan, C. Raja. *Crossing the Rubicon: The Shaping of India's New Foreign Policy*. New Delhi: Penguin/Viking, 2003.

Mohan, C. Raja. "Poised for power: the domestic roots of India's slow rise." In *Strategic Asia 2007–08: Domestic Political Change and Grand Strategy*, edited by Ashley J. Tellis and Michael Wills, 177–207. Seattle: National Bureau of Research, 2007.

Moll-Murata, Christine and Ulrich Theobald. "Military Employment in Qing Dynasty China." In *Fighting for a Living: A Comparative Study of Military Labour 1500–2000*, edited by Erik-Jan Zürcher, 353–92. Amsterdam: Amsterdam University Press, 2013.

Monten, James. "The Roots of the Bush Doctrine: Power, Nationalism, and Democracy Promotion in U.S. Strategy." *International Security* 29, no. 4 (Spring 2005): 112–56.

Moran, Matthew and Christopher Hobbs. "The Iranian Nuclear Dilemma: Light at the End of the Tunnel?" *Defense & Security Analysis* 28, no. 3 (June 2012): 202–12.

Morgenthau, Hans. *Politics Among Nations: The Struggle for Power and Peace*. New York: Knopf, 1973.

Morgenthau, Hans J., and Kenneth W. Thompson. *Politics Among Nations: The Struggle for Power and Peace, Brief Edition*. New York: McGraw Hill, 1993.

Morin, Edgar. *Pour une politique de civilization*. Paris: Arléa, 2002.

Murray, William S. "Revisiting Taiwan's Defense Strategy." *Naval War College Review* 61, no. 3 (Summer 2008): 13–38.

Murray, Williamson and Mark Grimsey. "Introduction: On Strategy." In *The Making of Strategy: Rulers, States, and War*, edited by Alvin H. Bernstein, MacGregor Knox, and Williamson Murray, 1–23. New York: Cambridge University Press, 1994.

Murray, Williamson. "Thoughts on Grand Strategy." In *The Shaping of Grand Strategy: Policy, Diplomacy, and War*, edited by Williamson Murray, Richard Hart Sinnreich, and James Lacey, 1–33. New York: Cambridge University Press, 2011.

Myrdal, Gunnar. *An American Dilemma, Volume 1: the Negro Problem and Modern Democracy*. New York: Harper & Brothers, 1944; sixth printing, New Brunswick, NJ: Transaction, 2009.

Najdi, Youhanni and Mohd Azhari Bin Abdul Karim. "The Role of the Islamic Revolutionary Guards Corps (IRGC) and the Future of Democracy in Iran: Will Oil Income Influence the Process?" *Democracy and Security* 8, no. 1 (2012): 72–89.

Narizny, Kevin. *The Political Economy of Grand Strategy.* Ithaca, NY: Cornell University Press, 2007.

Narlikar, Amrita. *New Powers: How to Become One and How to Manage Them.* Hurst: London, 2010.

Nasr, Vali. "When the Shiites Rise." *Foreign Affairs* 85, no. 4 (July/August 2006): 58–74.

Nathan, Andrew J. and Andrew Scobell. *China's Search for Security.* New York: Columbia University Press, 2014.

Nester, William R. *De Gaulle's Legacy: The Art of Power in France's Fifth Republic.* New York: Palgrave Macmillan, 2014.

Neto, Octavio Amorim. *De Dutra a Lula: a condução e os determinantes da política externa brasileira.* Rio de Janeiro: Campus, Konrad Adenauer Stiftung, 2011.

Nincic, Miroslav. *Democracy and Foreign Policy: The Fallacy of Political Realism.* New York: Columbia University Press, 1992.

Norris, William J. *Chinese Economic Statecraft: Commercial Actors, Grand Strategy, and State Control.* Ithaca, NY: Cornell University Press, 2016.

Norrlof, Carla. *America's Global Advantage: US Hegemony and International Cooperation.* Cambridge: Cambridge University Press, 2010.

Norrlof, Carla and Simon Reich. "American and Chinese Leadership during the Global Financial Crisis: Testing Kindleberger's Stabilization Functions." *International Area Studies Review* 18, no. 3 (March 2015): 1–23.

North Atlantic Treaty Organization. "Bucharest Summit Declaration" press release no. (2008) 049, April 3, 2008, no. 23, https://www.nato.int/cps/us/natohq/official_texts_8443.htm.

"NSC-68, 1950." Milestones: 1945–1952, Office of the Historian, accessed August 14, 2018, https://history.state.gov/milestones/1945-1952/NSC68.

Nye, Joseph S. *Bound to Lead: The Changing Nature of American Power.* New York: Basic Books, 1990.

Nye, Joseph S. *Soft Power: The Means to Success in World Politics.* New York: Public Affairs, 2004.

Nye, Jr., Joseph S. "Public Diplomacy and Soft Power." *The Annals of the American Academy of Political and Social Science* 616, no. 1 (March 2008): 94–109.

Oakes, Tim. "Looking Out to Look In: The Use of the Periphery in China's Geopolitical Narratives." *Eurasian Geography and Economics* 53, no. 3 (2012): 315–26.

O'Donnell, Frank and Yogesh Joshi. "Lost at Sea: The Arihant in India's Quest for a Grand Strategy." *Comparative Strategy* 33, no. 5 (2014).

O'Hanlon, Michael E. "Making the Grade? Assessing John Kerry's Record as Secretary of State." *Order from Chaos* (blog), The Brookings Institution, January 20, 2016, https://www.brookings.edu/blog/order-from-chaos/2016/01/20/making-the-grade-assessing-john-kerrys-record-as-secretary-of-state/.

Onea, Tudor. "Between Dominance and Decline; Status Anxiety and Great Power Rivalry." *Review of International Studies* 40, no. 1 (January 2014): 125–52.

Orenstein, Mitchell A. and R. Daniel Keleman. "Trojan Horses in EU Foreign Policy." *Journal of Common Market Studies* 55, no. 1 (2016): 87–102.

Osnos, Evan. "Trump's Irrational Hatred of the Iran Deal." *The New-Yorker*, October 23, 2017, https://www.newyorker.com/magazine/2017/10/23/trumps-irrational-hatred-of-the-iran-deal.

Ostovar, Afshon P. *Guardians of the Islamic Revolution Ideology, Politics, and the Development of Military Power in Iran (1979–2009)*. Ann Arbor: University of Michigan, 2009.

Owen, John M. "How Liberalism Produces the Democratic Peace." *International Security* 19, no. 2 (Fall 1994): 87–125.

Palissier, Sébastien and Alexandra Crépy. "La France dans les Organisations internationales: quelles influences pour quels projets?." Association AEGE, April 10, 2010, http://bdc.aege.fr/public/La_France_dans_les_organisations_internationales_Quelles_influences_pour_quels_projets.pdf.

Panda, Ankit. "A Slip of the Tongue on India's Once-Hyped 'Cold Start' Doctrine?." *The Diplomat*, January 7, 2017, https://thediplomat.com/2017/01/a-slip-of-the-tongue-on-indias-once-hyped-cold-start-doctrine/.

Pant, Harsh V. "A Rising India's Search for a Foreign Policy." *Orbis* 53, no. 2 (Spring 2009).

Parisot, James. "American Power, East Asian Regionalism and Emerging Powers: in or against empire?" *Third World Quarterly* 34, no. 7 (August 2013): 1159–74.

Paul, G. S. "Centre lets pilgrims visit Pak Sikh shrines." *The Tribune*, October 28, 2017, http://www.tribuneindia.com/news/punjab/centre-lets-pilgrims-visit-pak-sikh-shrines/488393.html.

Paul, T. V. "Soft Balancing in the Age of U.S. Primacy." *International Security* 30, no. 1 (Summer 2005): 46–71.

Paul, T. V. "Regional Transformation in International Relations." in *International Relations Theory and Regional Transformation*, edited by T. V. Paul, 4–6. Cambridge: Cambridge University Press, 2012.

Pavlovsky, Gleb. "Russian Politics Under Putin: The System Will Outlast the Master." *Foreign Affairs* 95, no. 3 (May–June 2016): 10–17.

Peden, G. C. *British Rearmament and the Treasury, 1932–39*. Edinburgh: Scottish Academic Press, 1979.

Peng, Yuan. 袁鹏, "关于新时期中国大周边战略的思考" [Thoughts on China's Great Periphery Strategy in the New Period], 现代国际关系 [*Contemporary International Relations*] 10 (October 2013).

Perkovich, George. *India's Nuclear Bomb: The Impact on Global Proliferation*. Berkeley: University of California Press, 1999.

Perkovich, George and Toby Dalton. *Not War. Not Peace*? New Delhi: Oxford University Press, 2016.

Petrov, Nikolai and Kirill Rogov. "Ispolnitel'naâ vlast' i silovye korporacii" [The executive power and the corporations of force]." in *Političeskoe razvitie Rossii. 2014–2016: Instituty i praktiki avtoritarnoj konsolidacii [Russia's Political Development. 2014–2016: Institutions and Practices of authoritarian consolidation]*, edited by A. V. Kynev, A. G. Kačkaeva, and È. L. Paneâh, 133–53. Moscow: Fond Liberal'naâ Missiâ, 2016.

Pillar, Paul. *Intelligence and U.S. Foreign Policy: Iraq, 9/11, and Misguided Reform*. New York: Columbia University Press, 2014.

Pinkus, Binyamin and Moshe Tlamim. "Atomic Power to Israel's Rescue: French-Israeli Nuclear Cooperation, 1949–1957." *Israel Studies*, 7 (Spring 2002): 104–38.

Pohl, Benjamin. *EU Foreign Policy and Crisis Management Operations: Power, Purpose and Domestic Politics*. London: Routledge, 2014.

"Policy Planning Staff." U.S. Department of State, accessed August 14, 2018, https://www.state.gov/s/p/.

Popescu, Ionut C. "Grand Strategy vs. Emergent Strategy in the Conduct of Foreign Policy." *Journal of Strategic Studies* 41, no. 3 (2018): 438–60.

Portela, Clara. "Member States Resistance to EU Foreign Policy Sanctions." *European Foreign Affairs Review* 20, no. 2 (2015): 39–61.

Posen, Barry. *The Sources of Military Doctrines: France, Britain, and Germany between the World Wars*. Ithaca, NY: Cornell University Press, 1984.

Posen, Barry. "European Union Security and Defense Policy: Response to Unipolarity." *Security Studies* 15, no. 2 (2006) 149–86.

Posen, Barry. "The Case for Restraint." *The American Interest* 3, no. 2 (November/December 2007): 7–32.

Posen, Barry, R. *Restraint: A New Foundation for U.S. Grand Strategy*. Ithaca, NY: Cornell University Press, 2014.

Pouponneau, Florent. "Diplomatic Practices, Domestic Fields, and International System: Explaining France's Shift on Nuclear Nonproliferation." *International Studies Quarterly* 61, no. 1 (March 2017): 123–35.

"President Reuven Rivlin Address to the 15th Annual Herzliya Conference." http://www.president.gov.il/English/ThePresident/Speeches/Pages/news_070615_01.aspx.

"Press Release of the Central Bureau of Statistics in Honor of the 69th Israeli Independence Day" CBS.gov, May 1, 2017, http://www.cbs.gov.il/reader/newhodaot/hodaa_template.html?hodaa=201711113.

"The Process of Assembling a Government" [Hebrew], Parliament 40 (March 2003) https://www.idi.org.il/parliaments/11266/11274.

"Proclamation of Independence", accessed April 20, 2018, https://www.knesset.gov.il/docs/eng/megilat_eng.htm.

Puetter, Uwe. *The European Council and the Council: New Intergovernmentalism and Institutional Change*. Oxford: Oxford University Press, 2014.

Putin, Vladimir. "Munich speech of Vladimir Putin" [in Russian] (speech, Munich Security Conference, Munich, February 10, 2007), http://archive.kremlin.ru/eng/speeches/2007/02/10/0138_type82912type82914type82917type84779_118123.shtml.

Putin, Vladimir. *The Military Doctrine of the Russian Federation* [in Russian] (Moscow: the Kremlin, 2014), rg.ru/2014/12/30/doktrina-dok.html.

Putin, Vladimir. *National Security Strategy* [in Russian](Moscow: the Kremlin, 2015), http://rg.ru/2015/12/31/nac-bezopasnost-site-dok.html.

Putin, Vladimir. *Doctrine of Information Security* [in Russian] (Moscow: the Kremlin, 2016), http://www.mid.ru/en/foreign_policy/official_documents/-/asset_publisher/CptICkB6BZ29/content/id/2563163.

Putin, Vladimir. "Final plenary session: The World of the Future: Moving Through Conflict to Cooperation" [in Russian] (speech, 14th Annual Meeting of the Valdai International Discussion Club, Sochi, October 19, 2017), http://en.kremlin.ru/events/president/news/55882.

Qin, Yaqing. "Continuity through Change: Background Knowledge and China's International Strategy." *The Chinese Journal of International Politics* 7, no. 3 (September 2014): 285–314.

Racz, Andras. *Russia's Hybrid War in Ukraine. Breaking the Enemy Ability to Resist*. Helsinki: The Finnish Institute of International Affairs, June 2015.

Radvanyj, Jean. "Adapter les réseaux de transport eurasien: réussites et défis." *Revue de Défense nationale* no. 802 (Summer 2017): 84–9.

Raghavan, Srinath. "Civil–Military Relations in India: The China Crisis and After." *The Journal of Strategic Studies* 32, no. 1 (February 2009): 149–175.

Raghavan, Srinath. *War and Peace in Modern India*. Bangalore: Orient Black Swan, 2010.

Raik, Kristi. "The Ukraine Crisis as a Conflict over Europe's Political, Economic and Security Order." *Geopolitics* (early view), DOI:10.1080/14650045.2017.1414046.

Rakel, Eve Patricia. "The Iranian Political Elite, State and Society Relations, and Foreign Relations since the Islamic Revolution" (thesis, University of Amsterdam, 2008), https://pure.uva.nl/ws/files/1110757/54677_thesis.pdf; Mehdi Moslem, Factional Politics in Post-Khomeini Iran. Syracuse, NY: Syracuse University Press, 2002.

Ramazani, Rouhollah K. *The Foreign Policy of Iran: A Developing Nation in World Affairs, 1500-1941*. Charlottesville: University Press of Virginia, 1966.

Ratner, Ely, Elbridge Colby, Andrew Erickson, Zachary Hosford, and Alexander Sullivan. *More Willing and Able: Charting China's International Security Activism*. Washington, DC: Center for a New American Security, May 2015, https://s3.amazonaws.com/files.cnas.org/documents/CNAS_ChinaMoreWillingAndAble_Final.pdf.

Reich, Simon and Richard Ned Lebow. *Good-Bye Hegemony! Power and Influence in the Global System*. Princeton, NJ: Princeton University Press, 2014.

Reich, Simon. "Restraining Trade to Invoke Investment: MITI and the Japanese Auto Producers" *Case Studies in International Negotiation*. Philadelphia, PA: Pew Foundation, 1991.

Reich, Simon and Peter Dombrowski. "Has a Trumpian Grand Strategy Finally Stepped into the Light?" *War on the Rocks*, January 29, 2018, https://warontherocks.com/2018/01/trumpian-grand-strategy-finally-stepped-light/.

Reich, Simon and Peter Dombrowski. *The End of Grand Strategy: US Maritime Operations in the Twenty-First Century*. Ithaca, NY: Cornell University Press, 2018.

Reynolds, David. *The Creation of the Anglo-American Alliance, 1937–41: A Study of Competitive Cooperation*. London: Europa, 1981.

Rezaei, Ali Akbar. "Foreign Policy Theories: Implications for the Foreign Policy Analysis of Iran." In *Iran's Foreign Policy: From Khatami to Ahmadinejad*, edited by Anoushiravan Ehteshami and Mahjoob Zweiri, 17–36. Reading, UK: Ithaca Press, 2008.

Richard, Yann, Bernard Hourcade, and Jean-Pierre Digard. *L'iran Au Xxe Siècle*. Paris: Fayard, 1996.

Riedel, Bruce. *Kings and Presidents: Saudi Arabia and the United States since FDR*. Washington, DC: Brookings Institution Press, 2017.

Rieker, Pernille. *French Foreign Policy in a Changing World*. London: Palgrave Macmillan, 2017.

Ripsmam, Norrin M. *Peacemaking by Democracies: The Effect of State Autonomy on the Post-World-War Settlements*. University Park, PA: Penn State University Press, 2002.

Ripsman, Norrin M. and T. V. Paul. "Assessing the Uneven Impact of Global Social Forces on the National Security State: A Framework for Analysis." *International Studies Review* 7, no. 2 (June 2005): 199–227.

Ripsman, Norrin M. "False Dichotomy: Why Economics Has Always Been High Politics." In *Guns and Butter: The Political Economy of International Security*, edited by Peter Dombrowski, 15–31. Boulder, CO: Lynne Reinner, 2005.

Ripsman, Norrin M. and T. V. Paul. *Globalization and the National Security State*. Oxford: Oxford University Press, 2010.

Ripsman, Norrin, M. Jeffrey W. Taliaferro, and Steven E. Lobell. *Neoclassical Realist Theory of International Politics*. Oxford: Oxford University Press, 2016.

Rizvi, M. Mahtab Alam. "Evaluating the Political and Economic Role of the IRGC." *Strategic Analysis* 36, no. 4 (June 2012): 584–96.

Rohani, Hassan. *Amniat-E Melli Va Diplomāsi-Ye Hastéi—Introduction*. Tehran: Center for Strategic Research, 2011.

Rolland, Nadège. *China's Eurasian Century? Political and Strategic Implications of the Belt and Road Initiative*, Seattle, WA: National Bureau of Asian Research, May 2017, http://www.nbr.org/publications/issue.aspx?id=346.

Romer, Jean-Christophe. *La pensée stratégique russe au XXe siècle [Russian strategic thinking in the Twentieth Century]*, Paris: Economica, 1997.

Rose, Gideon. "Neoclassical Realism and Theories of Foreign Policy." *World Politics* 51, no. 1 (October 1998): 144–72.

Rosecrance, Richard N. and Arthur A. Stein. "Beyond Realism: The Study of Grand Strategy." In *The Domestic Bases of Grand Strategy*, edited by Richard N. Rosecrance and Arthur A. Stein, 3–21. Ithaca, NY: Cornell University Press, 1993.

Rosenau, James N. "Comparative Foreign Policy: Fad Fantasy, or Field." *International Studies Quarterly* 12, no. 3 (September 1968): 296–329.

Rosenau, James N. *Along the Domestic-Foreign Frontier: Exploring Governance in a Turbulent World*. Cambridge: Cambridge University Press, 1997.

Rothkopf, David. *Running the World: The Inside Story of the National Security Council and the Architects of American Power*. New York: Public Affairs, 2006.

Rouhani, Hassan. "Enfedjārhā-Ye Amrikā Va Manāfé-Ye Melli-Ye Jomhuri-Ye Eslāmi." *Rahbord*, no. 21 (Autumn 2001).

Rouhani, Hassan. *Andishehā-Ye Siāsi-Ye Eslāmi; Jelv-E Dovvom: Siāsat-E Xareji*. Tehran: Center for Strategic Research, 2009.

Rouhani, Hassan. "Introduction" of *National Security and Nuclear Diplomacy* (Amniat-e melli vā diplomāsi-ye hastéi), Centre for Strategic Research, November 2011, http://www.csr.ir/Pdf/Books241/Nuclear%20Diplomacy.pdf.

Rubin, Lawrence. *Islam in the Balance: Ideational Threats in Arab Politics*. Stanford, CA: Stanford University Press, 2014.

Rudelle, Odile. *Mai 1958: La République*. Paris: Institut Charles de Gaulle, 1988.

Ruiz Palmer, Diego A. "Back to Future? Russia's Hybrid Warfare, Revolutions in Military Affairs, and Cold War Comparisons." In *NATO's Response to Hybrid Threats*, NDC Forum Paper 24, edited by Guillaume Lasconjarias and Jeffrey A. Larsen, 49–72. Rome: NATO Defense College, December 17, 2015.

Russett, Bruce M. *Grasping the Democratic Peace*. Princeton, NJ: Princeton University Press, 1993.

Rynning, Sten. *The Changing Military Doctrine: Presidents and Military Power in Fifth Republic France, 1985-2000*. Westport, CT: Praeger, 2001.

Saghafi-Ameri, Nasser. "New Trends in the EU-US Security Relationship: Implications for the Middle East, Persian Gulf and Iran—Introduction." *CSR*, July 29, 2004, http://www.isrjournals.com/en/monograph/291-new-trends-in-the-eu-ussecurity-relationship-implications-for-the-middle-east-persian-gulf-and-iran.html.

Saghafi-Ameri, Nasser. "The Strategic Interaction between Iran and Europe." Abstract, CSR, May 24, 2006, http://www.isrjournals.com/fa/iran-foreign-policy/848-the-strategicinteraction-between-iran-and-europe.html.

Saghafi-Ameri, Nasser. "Iran and look to the East policy." *CSR*, May 25, 2008, http://www.isrjournals.com/en/experts/295-iran-and-look-to-the-east-policy.html.

Sahebjam, Freidoune. *L'iran Des Pahlavis*. Boulogne-Billancourt, Fra.: Berger-Levrault, 1966.

Samuel-Azran, Tal. *Intercultural Communication as a Clash of Civilizations: Al-Jazeera and Qatar's Soft Power, Critical Intercultural Communications Studies*. Bern, Swiss.: Peter Lang Inc., 2016.

Sartori, Giovanni. "Concept Misformation in Comparative Politics." *The American Political Science Review* 64, no. 4 (December 1970): 1033–53.

Schell, Orville and John Delury. *Wealth and Power: China's Long March to the Twenty-first Century*. New York: Random House, 2013.

Schlesinger Jr., Arthur M. *The Imperial Presidency*. New York: Houghton, Mifflin, Harcourt, 1973.

Schweller, Randall. *Deadly Imbalances: Tripolarity and Hitler's Strategy of World Conquest*. Princeton, NJ: Princeton University Press, 1998.

Seitenfus, Ricardo. *Haiti: dilemas e fracassos internacionais*. Ijuí, Bra.: Editora da Unijuí, 2014.

Shahibzadeh, Yadullah. *Islamism and Post-Islamism in Iran: An Intellectual History*. Berlin: Springer, 2016.

Sharifi, Majid. *Imagining Iran: The Tragedy of Subaltern Nationalism*. Lanham, MD: Lexington Books, 2013.

Shari'tiniâ, Mohsen. "Iran Va Tarh-E Abrisham, Bâzgasht Be Pol-E Sharq Va Qarb." (2016), http://www.csr.ir/fa/news/530/ایران-و-طرح-ابریشم-بازگشت-به-پل-شرق-و-غرب

Shay, Shaul. "Simulation—the Third Lebanon War (Prevention, Warning, Home Front and Subservience)" [Hebrew], IDC, Special Publication for the Herzlya Conference of 2015, last modified June 7, 2015, http://www.herzliyaconference.org/_Uploads/dbsAttachedFiles/SimulasionShaulShay2015.pdf.

Shekhovtsov, Anton. "The Kremlin's marriage of convenience with the European far right." *Open Democracy*, April 28, 2014.

Shekhovtsov, Anton. *Russia and the Western Far Right: Tango Noir*. London: Routledge, 2018.

Shepherd, Alistair, J. K. "'A Milestone in the History of the EU': Kosovo and the EU's International Role." *International Affairs* 85, no. 3 (2009): 513–30.

Siddi, Marco. "German Foreign Policy Towards Russia in the Aftermath of the Ukraine Crisis: A New Ostpolitik?" *Europe-Asia Studies* 68, no. 4 (2016): 665–77.

Silove, Nina. "Beyond the Buzzword: The Three Meanings of 'Grand Strategy'." *Security Studies* 27, no. 1 (January 2018): 27–57.

Silpin, Alon. "UN Resolution 181." *The Virtual Library of Center for Educational Technology* [Hebrew], accessed December 24, 2017, http://lib.cet.ac.il/pages/item.asp?item=10126.

Sil, Rudra and Peter J. Katzenstein. *Beyond Paradigms: Analytic Eclecticism in the Study of World Politics*, London: Palgrave Macmillan, 2010.

Simón, Luis. "Understanding US Retrenchment in Europe." *Survival: Global Politics and Strategy* 57, no. 2 (2015): 157–72.

Singer, Andre. "Cutucando Onças com Vara Curta: O Ensaio Desenvolvimentista no Primeiro Mandato de Dilma Rousseff (2011–2014)." *Novos Estudos* 102 (2015): 42–71.

Singer, André. "A (Falta de) Base Política para o Ensaio Desenvolvimentista." In *As contradições do Lulismo: a que ponto chegamos?*, edited by André Singer and Isabel Loureiro. São Paulo: Boitempo, 2016.

Singer, P.W. *Corporate Warriors: The Rise of the Privatized Military Industry*, updated ed. Ithaca, NY: Cornell University Press, 2008.

Singh, Jaswant. *In Service of Emergent India: A Call to Honor*. Bloomington: Indiana University Press, 2007.

Sinovets, Polina and Bettina Renz. "Russia's 2014 Military Doctrine and Beyond: Threat Perceptions, Capabilities, and Ambitions." *NATO Defense College Research*, Paper no. 117 (July 10, 2015).

"SIPRI Yearbook 2016: Armaments, Disarmament and International Security." Stockholm International Peace Research Institute, 2016, https://www.sipri.org/yearbook/summaries.

SIPRI. "Military Expenditure by Country as Percentage of Gross Domestic Product", accessed April 25, 2017, https://www.sipri.org/sites/default/files/Milex-share-of-GDP.pdf.

SIPRI. "Trends in World Military Expenditures 2016, April 2017, https://www.sipri.org/sites/default/files/Trends-world-military-expenditure-2016.pdf.

SIPRI. "Military expenditure by country as percentage of gross domestic product, 2003–2016." Stockholm International Peace Research Institute, 2017.

Sjursen, Helene. "The EU as a 'Normative' Power: How can this be?" *Journal of European Public Policy* 13, no. 2 (2006): 235–51.

Skocpol, Theda and Margaret Sommers. "The Uses of Comparative History in Macrosocial Inquiry." *Comparative Studies in Society and History* 22, no. 2 (April 1980): 174–97.

Skowronek, Stephen. *Building a New American State: The Expansion of National Administrative Capacities, 1877–1920*. Cambridge: Cambridge University Press, 1982.

Smith, Karen E. "The EU, human rights and relations with third countries: 'foreign policy' with an ethical dimension?" In *Ethics and Foreign Policy*, edited by Karen E. Smith and Margot Light, 185–204. Cambridge: Cambridge University Press, 2001.

Smith, Michael. "EU Diplomacy and the EU-China Strategic Relationship: Framing, Negotiation and Management." *Cambridge Review of International Affairs* 29, no. 1 (2016): 78–98.

Smith, Steve and Michael Clarke, eds. *Foreign Policy Implementation*. London: Unwin & Allen, 1985.

Snyder, Jack L. *The Soviet Strategic Culture: Implications for Limited Nuclear Operations*. Santa Monica, CA: RAND Corporation, September 1977, https://www.rand.org/content/dam/rand/pubs/reports/2005/R2154.pdf.

Snyder, Jack. *Myths of Empire: Domestic Politics and International Ambition*. Ithaca, NY: Cornell University Press, 1991.

Soares de Lima, Maria Regina. "Instituições Democráticas e Política Exterior." *Contexto Internacional* 22, no. 2 (2000): 265–303.

Soares de Lima, Maria Regina. "Brasil e Polos Emergentes do Poder Mundial: Rússia, Índia, China e África do Sul." In *O Brasil e os demais BRICS – comércio e política*, edited by Renato Baumann, 155–76. Brasília: CEPAL/IPEA, 2010.

Soares de Lima, Maria Regina. "A agência da política externa brasileira (2008-2015): Uma análise preliminar." In *Crise sistêmica e inserção internacional: A política externa brasileira de 2008 a 2015* edited by W. Desiderá and H. Ramanzini Jr. Brasília: IPEA, FUNAG, 2017.

Soares de Lima, Maria Regina, et al. *Atlas of Brazilian Defence* Policy. Buenos Aires: CLACSO, 2018.

Soares de Lima, Maria Regina, and Rubens Duarte. "Diplomacia Presidencial e Politização da Política Externa: Uma Comparação dos Governos FHC e Lula." *Observador On-Line* 8, no. 9 (2013): 1-24.

Soares de Lima, Maria Regina, and Monica Hirst. "Brasil como poder intermediário e poder regional." In *Os Brics e a ordem global* edited by Andrew Hurrell, 43-73. Rio de Janeiro: FGV Editora, 2009.

Soares de Lima, Maria Regina, and Carlos R. S. Milani. "Política Externa Brasileira: Campo de Estudos e Principais Avanços." In *A ciência política no Brasil: 1960-2015*, edited by Leonardo Avritzer, Carlos R. S. Milani, and Maria do Socorro Braga, 393-422. Rio de Janeiro: FGV, 2016.

Sokolski, Henry and William Tobey. "A Poorly Negotiated Saudi Nuclear Dear Could Damage Future Regional Relationship." *The National Interest*, February 5, 2018, http://nationalinterest.org/feature/poorly-negotiated-saudi-nuclear-deal-could-damage-future24367.

Solingen, Etel. *Regional Orders at Century's Dawn: Global and Domestic Influences on Grand Strategy*. Princeton, NJ: Princeton University Press, 1998.

Sonntag, Albrecht. "The Burdensome Heritage of Prestige Politics." In *France on the World Stage: Nation State in the Global Era*, edited by Mairi Maclean and Joseph Szarka, 77-90. Basingstoke: Palgrave Macmillan, 2008.

Spector, Leonard S. and Avner Cohen. "Israel's Airstrike on Syria's Reactor: Implications for the Nonproliferation Regime." *Arms Control Today* 38 (July-August 2008): 15-21.

Spektor, Matias. "Brazil: Shadows of the Past and Contested Ambitions." In *Shaper Nations: Strategies for a Changing World*, edited by William I. Hitchcock, Melvyn P. Leffler, and Jeffrey Legro, 17-35. Cambridge, MA: Harvard University Press, 2016.

Spence, David. "The Evolving Role of Foreign Ministries in the Conduct of European Union Affairs." In *Foreign Ministries in the European Union: Integrating Diplomats*, edsited by Brian Hocking and David Spence. London: Palgrave Macmillan, 2005.

Stanzel, Angela, Nadège Rolland, Jabin Jacob, and Melanie Hart. *Grand Designs: Does China Have a 'Grand Strategy'?* European Council on Foreign Relations, October 18, 2017, http://www.ecfr.eu/publications/summary/grands_designs_does_china_have_a_grand_strategy.

Steindler, Chaira. "Mapping Out the Institutional Geography of External Security in the EU." *European Security* 24, no. 3 (2015): 402-19.

Stent, Angela E. *The Limits of Partnership. US-Russian Relations in the Twenty-First Century*. Princeton, NJ: Princeton University Press, 2014.

Stevenson, Charles A. "Underlying Assumptions of the National Security Act of 1947." *Joint Forces Quarterly* no. 48. (First Quarter 2008): 129-30.

Stevenson, Charles A. "The Story Behind the National Security Act of 1947." *Military Review* 88, no. 3 (May/June 2008): 13-20.

Stockholm International Peace Research Institute. *Trends in World Military Expenditure, 2017*, SIPRI Fact Sheet, https://www.sipri.org/sites/default/files/2018-05/sipri_fs_1805_milex_2017.pdf.

Stockholm International Peace Research Institute. *Trends in International Arms Transfer*, Stockholm International Peace Research Institute, 2014.

Stolberg, Alan G. *How Nation-States Craft National Security Strategy Documents*, enlarged ed. Carlisle Barracks, PA: Strategic Studies Institute, U.S. Army War College, October 2012.

Strachan, Hew. *The Direction of War: Contemporary Strategy in Historical Perspective.* Cambridge: Cambridge University Press, 2013.

Swaine, Michael D. and Ashley J. Tellis, *Interpreting China's Grand Strategy: Past, Present, and Future.* Santa Monica, CA: RAND, 2000, 74–6; maps, 87–92, https://www.rand.org/pubs/monograph_reports/MR1121.html.

Swaine, Michael D. "Chinese Views and Commentary on Periphery Diplomacy." *China Leadership Monitor* 44, no. 3, July 28, 2014. https://www.hoover.org/sites/default/files/research/docs/clm44ms.pdf.

Sweijs, Tim, et al. *Why are Pivot States So Pivotal? The Role of Pivot States in Regional and Global Security.* The Hague: The Center for Strategic Studies, 2014, https://hcss.nl/sites/default/files/files/reports/Why_are_Pivot_States_so_Pivotal__The_Role_of_Pivot_States_in_Regional_and_Global_Security_C.pdf.

Tabatabai, Ariane. "Presidential Elections and Nuclear Policy in Iran." *Arms Control Today* 43, no. 5 (2013): 15–20.

Taliaferro, Jeffrey W., Norrin M. Ripsman, and Steven E. Lobell. "Introduction: Grand Strategy between the World Wars." In *The Challenge of Grand Strategy: The Great Powers and the Broken Balance between the Wars*, edited by Jeffrey W. Taliaferro, Norrin M. Ripsman, and Steven E. Lobell, 1–36. Cambridge: Cambridge University Press, 2012.

Talbot Stobe, *Engaging India: Diplomacy, Democracy, and the Bomb.* Washington, DC: The Brookings Institution, 2010.

Talbott, Ian. "Pakistan and Sikh Nationalism: State Policy and Private Perceptions." *Sikh Formations* 6, no. 1 (2010): 63–76.

Tanham, George K. *Indian Strategic Thought: An Interpretative Essay*, R-4207-USDP. Santa Monica, CA: RAND Corporation 1992.

Tammen, Ronald, et al. *Power Transitions: Strategies for the 21st Century.* New York: Chatham House Publishers, 2000.

Tammen, Ronald L. and Jacek Kugler. "Power Transition and China-US Conflicts." *Chinese Journal of International Politics* 1, no. 1 (July 2006): 35–55.

Telhami, Shibley Z. and Michael Barnett. *Identity and Foreign Policy in the Middle East.* Ithaca, NY: Cornell University Press, 2002.

Tellis, Ashley J. *India's Emerging Nuclear Posture: Between Recessed Deterrent and Ready Arsenal.* Santa Monica, CA: RAND Corporation, 2001.

Tellis, Ashley J. *India as a New Global Power: An Action Agenda for the United States.* Washington, DC: Carnegie Endowment for International Peace, 2005.

Tellis, Ashley J. "The Merits of Dehyphenation: Explaining U.S. Success in Engaging India and Pakistan." *The Washington Quarterly* 31, no. 4 (2008): 21–42.

Tellis, Ashley J. *Nonalignment Redux: The Perils of Old Wine in New Skins.* Washington, DC: Carnegie Endowment for International Peace, 2012.

Tertrais, Bruno. *L'arme nucléaire.* Paris: PUF, 2008.

Tertrais, Bruno. "Leading on the Cheap? French Security Policy in Austerity." *The Washington Quarterly* 36, no. 3 (Summer 2013): 47–61.

Tertrais, Bruno. "Russia's Nuclear Weapons: Worrying for the Wrong Reasons." *Survival: Global Politics and Strategy* 50, no. 2 (April–May 2018): 33–44.

Tessler, Itzchak. "In the Next Generation, US Jews Will Disappear." *YNET*, February 15, 2014, https://www.ynetnews.com/articles/0,7340,L-4488219,00.html.

The International Institute for Strategic Studies. *The Military Balance 2018*. London: Routledge, 2018.

The National Security Staff Law [Hebrew], 2008 (Israel), law number 2178, https://www.nevo.co.il/Law_word/law14/law-2178.pdf.

The World Bank. "The World Bank in Islamic Republic of Iran", accessed April 15, 2018, http://www.worldbank.org/en/country/iran/overview.

Thomas, Hugh. *The Suez Affair*, London: Weidenfeld and Nicolson, 1957.

Thurston, Alexander. "Islamic Universities and their Global Outreach." *Oxford Islamic Studies Online*, accessed February 10, 2017, http://www.oxfordislamicstudies.com/Public/focus/essay1009_Islamic_Universities.html.

Tian, Nan. Aude Fleurant, Pieter D. Wezeman, and Siemon T. Wezeman. "Trends in World's Military Expenditure, 2016." *SIPRI Fact Sheet*, April 2017.

Tilly, Charles. *Coercion, Currency, and the European States, AD 990–1990*. Cambridge, MA: Blackwell, 1990.

Tocci, Nathalie. "The Making of the EU Global Strategy." *Contemporary Security Policy* 37, no. 3 (2016): 461–72.

Toje, Asle. *America, the EU, and Strategic Culture: Renegotiating the Transatlantic Bargain*. New York: Routledge, 2008.

Toje, Asle. "The 2003 European Union Security Strategy: A Critical Appraisal." *European Foreign Affairs Review* 10, no. 1 (2005): 117–33.

Tomes, Robert R. "American Exceptionalism in the Twenty-First Century." *Survival: Global Politics and Strategy* 56, no. 1 (January 2014): 27–50.

Tömmel, Ingeborg. "The Presidents of the European Commission: Transactional or Transforming Leaders?" *Journal of Common Market Studies* 51, no. 4 (2013): 789–805.

Tønnesson Stein, and Hans Antlöv, eds. *Asian Forms of the Nation*. New York: Routledge, 1996.

Torbat, Akbar E. "Impacts of the US Trade and Financial Sanctions on Iran." *The World Economy* 28, no. 3 (March 2005): 407–434.

Towell, Pat and Lynn M. Williams. *Defense: FY2017 Budget Request, Authorization, and Appropriations*, CRS Report No. R44454. Washington, DC: Congressional Research Service, April 12, 2016.

Trachtenberg, Marc. *The Craft of International History: A Guide to Method*. Princeton, NJ: Princeton University Press, 2006.

Travassos, Mário. *Projeção Internacional do Brasil*. São Paulo: Companhia Editora Nacional, 1931.

"Trump Davos speech: 'America First policy is not America alone'." *BBC*, January 26, 2018, http://www.bbc.com/news/world-us-canada-42835934.

Turner, Fredrick Jackson. *The Frontier in American History*. New York: Henry Holt and Company, 1928.

Tziarras, Zenonas. "Israel-Cyprus-Greece: a 'Comfortable' Quasi-Alliance." *Mediterranean Politics* 21, no. 3 (February 2016): 407–27.

U.S. Department of State. "Town Hall on the Quadrennial Diplomacy and Development Review at the Department of State." July 10, 2009, https://2009-2017.state.gov/secretary/20092013clinton/rm/2009a/july/125949.htm.

Vahabi, Mehrdad. "A Positive Theory of the Predatory State." *Public Choice* 168, no. 3-4 (June 2016): 153-75.

Vahabi, Mehrdad and Thierry Coville. "L'économie Politique De La République Islamique D'iran." *Revue internationale des études du développement*, no. 1 (2017): 11-31.

Vaïsse, Maurice. *La Grandeur: Politique étrangère du général de Gaulle*. Paris: Fayard, 1998.

Vaïsse, Maurice. *La puissance ou l'influence: la France dans le monde depuis 1958*. Paris: Fayard, 2008.

Valeriano, Brandon, and Ryan C. Maness, *Cyber War Versus Cyber Realities: Cyber Conflict in the International System*. New York: Oxford University Press, 2015.

Vaziri, Mostafa. *Iran as Imagined Nation: The Construction of National Identity*. New York: Paragon House, 1993.

Védrine, Hubert. *Rapport pour le Président de la République sur la France et la mondialisation*. Paris: Fayard, 2007.

Vélez, Álvaro Uribe, et al. *Iran's Strategic Penetration of Latin America*. Lanham, MD: Lexington Books, 2014.

Vennesson, Pascal. *Politique de défense: institutions, innovations, européanisation*. Paris: L'Harmattan, 2001.

Vigevani, Tullo and Gabriel Cepaluni. *Brazilian Foreign Policy in Changing Times: The Quest for Autonomy from Sarney to Lula*. Lanham, MD: Lexington Books, 2012.

Wachman, Alan M. *Why Taiwan? Geostrategic Rationales for China's Territorial Integrity*. Stanford, CA: Stanford University Press, 2007.

Wade, Geoffrey, ed., *China and Southeast Asia*. vols. 1-6. New York: Routledge, 2009.

Wade, Geoffrey. "The Zheng He Voyages: A Reassessment." *Journal of the Malaysian Branch of the Royal Asiatic Society* 78, no. 1 (288) (2005): 37-58.

Wade, Robert Hunter. "US Hegemony and the World Bank." *Review of International Political Economy* 9 no. 2 (May 2002): 215-43.

Wagner, Wolfgang. "Liberal Power Europe." *Journal of Common Market Studies* 55, no. 6 (2017): 1398-414.

Walt, Stephen M. *The Origin of Alliances*. Ithaca, NY: Cornell University Press, 1987.

Walt, Stephen M. "The Renaissance of Security Studies." *International Studies Quarterly* 31, no. 2 (1991): 211-39.

Waltz, Kenneth N. *Foreign Policy and Democratic Politics, the American and British Experience*, Boston: Little, Brown, 1967.

Waltz, Kenneth. *Theory of International Politics*. New York: Addison-Wellesley, 1979.

Waltz, Kenneth N. "Why Iran Should Get the Bomb: Nuclear Balancing Would Mean Stability." *Foreign Affairs* 91, no. 4 (July/August 2012): 2-5.

Wang, Zheng. "National Humiliation, History Education, and the Politics of Historical Memory: Patriotic Education Campaign in China." *International Studies Quarterly* 52, no. 4 (December 2008): 783-806.

Watts, Barry, Andrew F. Krepinevich. *Regaining Strategic Competence*. Washington, DC: Center for Strategic and Budgetary Assessments, September 1, 2009, http://csbaonline.org/research/publications/regaining-strategic-competence.

Wang, Yuan-kang. *Harmony and War: Confucian Culture and Chinese Power Politics*. New York: Columbia University Press, 2011.

Weinberger, Kathleen. "Russian Anti-Access and Area Denial (A2AD) Range." Institute for the Study of War, August 29, 2016, http://www.understandingwar.org/backgrounder/russian-anti-access-and-area-denial-a2ad-range.

Weiss, Linda. *America Inc.? Innovation and Enterprise in the National Security State.* Ithaca, NY: Cornell University Press, 2014.

Wehrey, Frederic. *The Rise of the Pasdaran: Assessing the Domestic Roles of Iran's Islamic Revolutionary Guards Corps.* Santa Monica, CA: RAND Corporation, 2009.

Wessels, Wolfgang, Peter Valant, and Tobias Kunstein. "The EU Council(s) System and Administrative Fusion." In *The Palgrave Handbook of the European Administrative System,* edited by Michael W. Bauer and Jarle Trondal, 265–80. London: Palgrave Macmillan, 2015.

Wilkinson, Steven I. *Army and Nation: The Military and Indian Democracy Since Independence.* Cambridge, MA: Harvard University Press, 2015.

Williams, William Appelman. "The Frontier Thesis and American Foreign Policy." *Pacific Historical Review* 24, no. 4 (November 1955): 379–95.

Williamson, John. "A Short History of the Washington Consensus." *Law and Business Review of the Americas* 15, no. 1 (Winter 2009): 7–23.

Wilson, Andrew R. "The Maritime Transformation of Ming China." In *China Goes to Sea: Maritime Transformation in Comparative Historical Perspective,* edited by Andrew S. Erickson, Lyle J. Goldstein, and Carnes Lord. Annapolis, MD: Naval Institute Press, 2009.

Wohlforth, William C. "The Stability of a Unipolar World." *International Security* 24, no. 1 (Summer 1999): 5–41.

Wohlforth, William C. "Unipolarity, Status Competition, and Great Power War." *World Politics* 61, no. 1 (January 2009): 28–57.

Wolfers, Arnold. *Discord and Collaboration: Essays on International Politics.* Baltimore, MD: Johns Hopkins University Press, 1962.

Woolcock, Stephen. *European Union Economic Diplomacy: The Role of the EU in External Economic Relations.* Farnham, UK: Ashgate, 2012.

Wu, Guo. "New Qing History: Dispute, Dialog, and Influence." *The Chinese Historical Review* 23, no. 1 (2016): 147–69.

Wuthnow, Joel. *Chinese Diplomacy and the UN Security Council: Beyond the Veto.* New York: Routledge, 2013.

Wuthnow, Joel. *Chinese Perspectives on the Belt and Road Initiative: Strategic Rationales, Risks, and Implications, China Strategic Perspectives* 12 Washington, DC: National Defense University, September 27, 2017, http://inss.ndu.edu/Media/News/Article/1326963/chinese-perspectives-on-the-belt-and-road-initiative-strategic-rationales-risks/.

"X." "The Sources of Soviet Conduct." *Foreign Affairs* 25, no. 4 (July 1947): 575–6.

Xi, Tianyang. "All the Emperor's Men? Internal Conflicts and Bureaucratic Selection in Late Imperial China." *Comparative Political Studies,* 2018 (forthcoming): 12–15, http://www.xitianyang.com/uploads/1/8/7/3/18733898/qing_feb2017.pdf.

Xi Jinping. "Secure a Decisive Victory in Building a Moderately Prosperous Society in All Respects and Strive for the Great Success of Socialism with Chinese Characteristics for a New Era." Delivered at the 19th National Congress of the Communist Party of China, October 18, 2017, http://english.qstheory.cn/2018-02/11/c_1122395333.htm. Unless otherwise specified.

Xuefeng, Sun, M. Taylor Fravel, and Liu Feng, eds. *Understanding China's Foreign Policy Transformation: A Chinese Journal of International Politics* (CJIP) Reader, https://academic.oup.com/cjip/pages/understanding_china_foreign_policy_transformation_reader.

Xuetong, Yan and Sun Xuefeng, eds. 阎学通, 孙学峰等著, 中国崛起及其战略 *[The Rise of China and its Strategy].* 北京 [Beijing]: 北京大学出版社 [Beijing University Press], 2005.

Ya'alon, Moshe. "Intelligence from the Standpoint of the Decision-Maker" [Hebrew]. In the *Challenges of the Israeli Intelligence Community*, edited by David Siman-Tov and Shmuel Even. Tel-Aviv: INSS, 2017.

Yablokov, Ilya. "Conspiracy Theories as a Russian Public Diplomacy Tool: The Case of Russia Today (RT)." *Politics* 35, no. 3-4 (2015): 301-15.

Yihu, Li. 李义虎, "从海陆二分到海陆统筹—对中国海陆关系的在审视" *[Sea and Land Power: From Dichotomy to overall Planning—A Review of the Relationship Between Sea and Land Power]*, 现代国际关系 [Contemporary International Relations] (August 2007).

Zagare, Frank C. and D. Marc Kilgour. "Asymmetric Deterrence." *International Studies Quarterly* 37, no. 1 (March 1993): 1-27.

Zakaria, Fareed. "Realism and Domestic Politics" *International Security* 17, no. 1 (Summer 1992): 177-98.

Zamecnick, Julia. "Obama's European Missile Defense Strategy: Will France Play Nice?" *The Monitor: Journal of International Studies* 16, no. 1 (Winter 2010): 31-42.

Zarif, Mohammad Javad. "What Iran Really Wants: Iranian Foreign Policy in the Rouhani Era." *Foreign Affairs* 93, no. 3 (May/June 2014): 49-54, 55-9.

Zavadski, Katie. "Putin's propaganda TV lies about its popularity." *The Daily Beast*, September 17, 2015.

Zegart, Amy B. *Flawed by Design: The Evolution of the CIA, JCS, and NSC*. Stanford, CA: Stanford University Press, 1999.

Zhengyu, Wu. "Toward 'Land' or Toward 'Sea'? The High-Speed Railway and China's Grand Strategy." *Naval War College Review* 66, no. 3 (Summer 2013): 53-66.

Zinn, Howard. *A People's History of the United States, 1492–Present*. Revised and updated 1980; repr., New York: HarperPerennial, 1995.

Zoltán, Kalmar. "Theodor Herzl's National Answer to the Misery of the Jewish People." *European and Regional Studies* vol. 1 (2010). http://www.acta.sapientia.ro/acta-euro/C1-2/eur12-4.pdf.

Zonis, Marvin. *The Political Elite of Iran*. Princeton, NJ: Princeton University Press, 1971.

Zonis, Marvin and Daniel Brumberg. *Khomeini, the Islamic Republic of Iran, and the Arab World*. Cambridge, MA: Center for Middle Eastern Studies, Harvard University, 1987.

INDEX

9/11 terrorist attacks on US 36, 123, 136, 243–4, 251

Abdul Aziz Al Saud, King 246
Acheson, Dean 29
Adams, Gordon 35
Adams, John Quincy 36
Adamsky, Dima 290
agency, role of 9–10
Ahmadinejad, Mahmoud 192–3, 196–7, 200–2, 206–7
aims, goals and objectives
  behaviours, and 7, 286
  economic 292–3
  hard security 291
  ideational/ideological 291–2
  long-term objectives, GS and 9–10
  prestige, recognition and status 291
  variety of 290–1
  see also ends, ways, and means
al-Assad, Bashar 59
al-Qaeda 37, 251
America First doctrine *see* United States
Amidror, Yaakov 221–2
Art, Robert J. 6, 26
Ashton, Catherine 275
Aspin, Les 36
Attlee, Clement 132

Bajpai, Kanti 181–2
balance of power, GS and 287
Balci, Bayram 206
Banerjee, Mamata 185–6
Barnett, Michael 240
Bastrykin, Alexander 289–90
Bazargan, Mehdi 193
Begin, Menachem 228–9
behaviours
  aims, goals and objectives, and 7
  plans, and 8–9
Belt and Road initiative (BRI) *see* China
Ben Gurion, David 217–19, 232
Betts, Richard 34, 38
Bhaba, Homi 174
Blair, Tony 138

Brands, Hal 6–12
Brazil
  aims, goals and objectives 155–6
  authors' analytical approach 149
  conception of GS 285–6
  concept of GS 149
  Constitution of 1988 149, 151–2, 156–7
  cooperative strategy 296
  defence and military capacity, policies and activities
    budgetary assymetries 152–3
    Higher School of War (*Escola Superior de Guerra*: ESG) 150
    Ministry of Defence (MD) 149
    regional dominance 152–3
    separation from civil sphere 149
    separation from foreign policy 149
    United Nations Stabilization Mission in Haiti (MINUSTAH) 154–5
    World War 2 150
  documentary sources 285–6
  domestic politics
    development strategies 156–63
    neo-developmentalist coalition 161
    rentist coalition 161
    Workers' Party (*Partido dos Trabalhadores*: PT) 17, 153, 156
  economic capacity, policies and activities 293
    critical junctures 157
    development cooperation in Latin America 154–5
  foreign policy
    assertiveness 156
    autonomy 152, 157–8
    global priorities 154
    regional priorities 153
    revisionism 155
    separation from defence policy 149
  France, and 151, 153
  geographical factors 288
  geopolitical thought 150–1
  implementation of GS
    domestic political and economic factors 156–63

Brazil (*cont.*)
    military 152–3
    resource factors 152–5
    separation of foreign and defence
        policies 149, 151–2
    India compared 13
    institutions, processes, and instruments
        Brazilian Association of Defense Studies
            (ABED) 152
        documentary sources 152
        integration of foreign and defence
            policies 152
        Ministry of Defence (MD) 149
        separation of foreign and defence
            policies 149, 151–2
    international institutions, and 153, 155–6,
        293–4, 296–7
    Iran, and 207
    opportunities 292
    prestige, recognition and status
        global power aspiration 13
        regional power status 13, 150, 295
    regional factors 287–8
    security environment 296
    summary overview 17, 163–6
    US, and 162, 287
Bronson, Rachel 239–40
Brooks, Stephen 5–9
Brzezinski, Zbigniew 56
Bush, George H. W. 37
Bush, George W. 40, 55–6

'calibrated strategies' 38–9
Cameron, David 139
Cardoso, Fernando Henrique 149, 158
Carter, Jimmy 56
Centenary Goals *see* China
Cerny, Philip 102
Chase, Robert 208
Chavez, Hugo 207
China
    aims, goals and objectives
        Centenary Goals 75–6, 81–2
        contemporary context 77–81
        global power aspiration 85
        historical continuities 76–7
        ideational/ideological 292
        New Historic Missions 81–2
        overseas projection of power 81–2
        prestige, recognition and status 291
        prioritisation of 76–82
    Belt and Road initiative (BRI) 37, 62,
        83–7, 293

Centenary Goals 75–6, 81–2
Communist Party 77–9, 82–3, 292
concept of GS 73–4, 285–6
contemporary context of GS 77–81
cultural factors 289–90
decision-making 74, 288–9
defence and military capacity, policies and
    activities 78, 80
documentary sources 285–6
domestic reforms 87–9
economic capacity, policies and activities
    Belt and Road initiative (BRI) 293
    Centenary Goals 75
    economic power 80
    fiscal flexibility 80
    state-owned enterprises 293
geographical factors 76, 79–80, 288
great power status 2, 12–13, 295
history, identity and collective memory
    exceptionalism 81
    historical continuities of GS 76–7
    no overseas imperialism 81
implementation of GS
    Belt and Road initiative (BRI)
        83–7
    Communist Party control 82–3
    domestic reforms 87–9
    independent strategy 296–7
    institutions, processes, and
        instruments 82–3
Iran, and 199
Korean War 78
'March West' concept 85
Ming Dynasty realist GS 289–90
New Historic Missions 81–2
nonstate actors 294
North Korea, and 141
overseas projection of power 81–2
political constraints 76, 79
public relations 294
Russia, and 50–1, 60, 62–3, 65, 297
Saudi Arabia, and 239, 244–5
sea power 80–2
security environment 76
soft power 75
state-owned enterprises 294
summary overview 16–17, 89–90
Taiwan, and 77–8
technological factors
    Centenary Goals 75
    cyber warfare 288, 293–4
traditional great-power strategy 295
UK, and 141

US, and 37, 78, 87, 141, 287
  Xi Jinping's GS 73–6
Churchill, Winston 127
classicist approach 6–7, 11–12, 50
Clausewitz, Carl von 247
Clinton, Bill 36
Clinton, Hillary 33
Cohen, Avner 230
Cohen, Stephen P. 177
collective memory *see* history, identity and collective memory
comparative approach 10
  emergence 284
  obstacles 285–7
  reasons 11–14
conceptual approaches 3, 9–11
constructivism, interpretative approach, and 10–11
contextual approach 15
Cook, Robin 138
cooperative strategy 296–7
Cordesman, Anthony 248
Corwin, Edward 288–9
Coville, Thierry 197
critical junctures, theory of 157
cultural factors 289–90
Curzon, George Curzon, 1st Marquess 171, 183

Daesh *see* ISIS
Dalton, Toby 184
Dasgupta, Sunil 177
deductive approach 11
deep engagement 8–9
defence and military capacity, policies and activities 50, 287–8, 293
definitions of grand strategy 5–6, 284
de Gaulle, Charles 99–103, 107, 208–9
de Lima, Maria Regina Soares 157
Deng Xiaoping 74
domestic factors, neglect by IR scholarship 4
Dulles, John Foster 133

economic capacity, policies and activities
  critical junctures 157
  importance 293
  industrialization 158
economic goals *see* aims, goals and objectives
Eden, Anthony 133
Ehteshami, Anoushiravan 198–9
Eisenhower, Dwight 31, 37
Eisenkot, Gadi 222

ends, ways, and means
  alignment of 128
  balancing of 50
  contextual approach to 15
  definitions of GS 9, 11, 284–5
  indeterminacy of 10
  objectives, and 9–10
  values, and 123
  see also aims, goals and objectives
Erdoğan, Recep Tayyip 227
European Union (EU)
  aims, goals and objectives 14, 269–72
  authors' analytical approach 263–4
  Common Foreign and Security Policy (CFSP) 263
  Common Security and Defence Policy (CSDP) 263
  conception of GS 262–4
  Council of the EU 262
  democratic principles 263
  economic integration 293
  European External Action Service (EEAS) 262
  European Political Cooperation (EPC) 262–3
  European Security Strategy (ESS) 262
  European Union Global Strategy (EUGS) 262
  former Soviet Bloc countries, and 55, 61
  global strategy aspiration 14
  history, identity and collective memory
    Cold War legacy 262–3
    democratic principles 263
    World War II legacy 262–3
  implementation of GS 273–6
  institutions, processes, and instruments
    decision-making 264–9
    multiplicity of institutions and actors 263–4
  Iran, and 201–2
  NATO, and 262–3
  resource factors 14
  security environment 296
  summary overview 17, 277–9
  Syria, and 271, 276
  uniqueness of GS 297–8
  see also France; United Kingdom

Falkland Islands 134–5, 139
Feaver, Peter 8, 38
Fedorov, Sergei 107–8
foreign policy, analysis of 15

France
  Africa, and 100
  aims, goals and objectives
    ideational/ideological 291–2
    prestige, recognition and status 291
  authors' analytical approach 100
  Brazil, and 151, 153
  China, and 111, 114–15
  defence and military capacity, policies and activities
    force de frappe 99
    military power and alliances 109–11
    multilateralization 114–15
    nuclear deterrence 102–3
  defensive realism 108–9
  diplomacy 112–16
  economic capacity, policies and activities 111–12, 115
  EU, and 99, 102, 110, 112, 294, 296–7
  Francophonie
    Alliances françaises 115–16
    Constitutional foundation 113
    cultural influence 115
    deployment 113–14
    economic diplomacy 115
    education support 115–16
    French language business use 115
    French language training 114
    international security issues 114
    liberal engagement, and 113
    multilateralization of military action 114–15
    new members 115
    Parliamentary Assembly of the Francophonie 112
    public relations 294
    strategy of 294, 296
  grandeur
    continuance 99, 107, 290
    elements 99
    exceptionalism 101–2
    historical foundations 100–3
    independence 102
    liberalism, and 103
    multipolar balance of power 103
    offensive realism 101
    shift to liberal engagement 99, 107–16, 292
    strategy of 291, 294
  history, identity and collective memory
    exceptionalism 99, 101–2
    Gaulish resistance to Roman Empire 101
    grandeur 100–3
  great power status 102–3
  independence 102–3
  institutions, processes, and instruments
    decision-making 106–7, 288–9
    Defence Council 105
    Defence Minister 105
    documentary sources 107
    grand strategic system 104–7
    hierarchical principles 104
    president's exclusive domain (*domaine réservé*) 99, 104
    prime minister 104
    reorientation under liberal engagement 109–16
  international institutions, and 100, 108–9, 294
  Iran, and 193
  liberal engagement
    adoption 99–100, 107
    defensive realism 108–9
    elements 99–100, 107
    foundational assumptions 107–8
    Francophonie, and 113
    international institutions, and 108–9
    reorientation of GS instruments 109–16
    strategy 108
  liberal hegemony 100, 291–2
  NATO, and 55–6, 99, 109–10
  neoconservatism 99
  'Occidentalism' 99
  prestige, recognition and status
    grandeur 99
    great power status 12–13
    regional power status 295–6
    UN Security Council permanent seat 108
  realism 108–9
  regional factors 287–8
  Russia, and 63
  security environment 296
  'soft balancing' 100
  summary overview 16–17, 116–17
  US, and 99, 102, 107–8, 111–12, 114–15, 287, 297
  World War II 101
Francophonie see France
Fravel, M. Taylor 77

Gandhi, Indira 174–5, 177
Gandhi, Rajiv 177, 185–6
geographical factors
  influence of 288
  technological factors in relation 288

Gerasimov, Valery 291
global system stability, assumptions as to 2–5
goals *see* aims, goals and objectives
Goertz, Gary 10
Goldstein, Avery 10–11
Gordon, Philip 101
Gourevitch, Peter 157
grandeur see France
grand strategy (GS)
  agency, and 9–10
  analytical pitfalls 149
  attributes 9–10
  authors' analytical approach 1, 14–15
  balance of power, and 287
  categorisation 8–9
  conceptual approaches 3, 9–11
  cooperative strategy 296–7
  countervailing assumptions 3–5
  debate on definition 2
  definitions 5–6, 173, 284
  empirical conceptualisation 9
  focus on external environment 2
  future study 295
  independent strategy 296–7
  integrated analytical framework 4
  makers 288–9
  powers able to implement 2–3, 12–13
  prevailing assumptions 2–3
  process 9–10, 288–9
  purpose 5
  research programme 8–9
  sources 287–90
  theoretical foundation 38
  tools 293–5
  traditional great-power strategies 295
  unipolarity 287
  uses 8–9
  varieties of states and strategies 295–6
Gray, Colin S. 6–9, 16
Great Britain *see* United Kingdom
great power status *see* prestige, recognition and status
GS *see* grand strategy

Haiti 158
Hekmatyar, Gulbuddin 179
Henkin, Louis 28
Herzl, Theodor 217
Herzog, Chaim 217
high strategy *see* grand strategy
Hill, Emily 208

Hirst, Monica 157
history, identity and collective memory 9–10, 289–90
Hitchcock, William I. 12
Hoffman, Stanley 102
Hollande, François 108
Hoppe, Dominique 113–14
Hudson, Valerie 15
Hu Jintao 74, 81–2, 85–6
Hussein, Abdulrahman Assad 239–40

ideational/ideological goals *see* aims, goals and objectives
Ikenberry, John 8–9
implementation of GS 38
independent strategy 296–7
India
  Afghanistan, and 179
  authors' analytical approach 172
  Brazil compared 13
  British Raj 171
  China, and 176, 178, 187
  conception of GS 171–2
  cultural factors 173
  defence and military capacity, policies and activities
    British legacy 175–6
    civilian control 183
    Cold Start doctrine 183–4, 187
    interservice rivalry 183–4
    nuclear weapons 174, 179–80, 187
    procurement process 184–5
    war with China 1962 176
    war with Pakistan 1965 178
  documentary sources 173
  domestic politics
    democratic constraints on GS decision-making 185
    federal democracy 171–2, 174
    federalisation of politics 185
  economic capacity, policies and activities
    democratic constraints on decision-making 186
    reforms of 1990s 179
    'self-reliance' strategy 171–2, 174
    statist centralised planning 174
  foreign policy of nonalignment 171–2, 174
  geographical factors 288
  institutions, processes, and instruments
    democratic constraints on GS decision-making 185
    documentary sources 173
  Iran, and 179

India (*cont.*)
  Nehruvianism
    conception of GS 171–2
    debates on (dis)continuance 178–80
    debates on successor GS 181–2
    implementation and legacy 173–7
    incremental transition from 187
    obstacles to transition from 183–6
    'strategic restraint' 177
  Pakistan, and 178–80, 183–4
  regional power status 13, 295
  Russia, and 179
  security environment 296
  Soviet Union collapse, and 179
  summary overview 17
  technological factors
    'indigenous production' strategy 184–5
    nuclear weapons 293–4
    'self-reliance' strategy 171–2, 174
  threat perception 13
  UK, and 174–5
  US, and 174, 177, 187
inductive approach 11
international institutions
  ability to have GS 297
  GS tool, as 294
international relations approach to grand strategy 7–8, 11–12
international relations theory (IR theory)
  systemic approaches to GS, and 15
interpretative approach
  constructivism and 10–11
  use of 16
Iran
  Afghanistan, and 179
  aims, goals and objectives
    Conservative (Imam's) line (*Hefz-e Mahvar*) 198–201
    factional articulation of 198
    hard security 291
    ideational/ideological 291–2
    preservation of independence 193
    Progressive line (*Pishraft-e-Mahvar*) 198–200
  authors' analytical approach 193–4
  Brazil, and 207
  China, and 199
  conception of GS 192–4
  cultural factors
    anti-Western culture 195
    cultural integrity as national priority 195
    cultural understanding of Iranian GS 192
    government expenditure on cultural heritage 207–8
    revolution of 1979 195
  defence and military capacity, policies and activities
    Iraq war (1980–88) 202–3, 243–5, 252
    nuclear weapons 224, 288, 293–4
    overview of 202–4
  domestic politics
    Conservative (Imam's) line (*Hefz-e Mahvar*) 198–201
    factionalism 198
    informal networks 195
    Progressive line (*Pishraft-e-Mahvar*) 198–201
    revolution of 1979 194–5
  economic capacity, policies and activities
    cooperation with China 205–6
    IRGC control 205
    Islamic socialism 205
    oil and gas resources 204
  'equilibrium' (*tavāzon*) principle
    aim of 193
    continuance 193
    Iran's pivotal character 193
  EU, and 201–2
  foreign policy, eastward/westward debate 201–2
  France, and 193
  geographical factors 288
  geopolitical factors 192–3
  Hamas, and 294
  Hezbollah, and 294
  history, identity and collective memory
    historical foundations of GS 194–5
    independence narratives 290
    Persian past 17
  Holocaust controversy 192–3, 200–1
  implementation of GS
    continuity and change 208–10
    eastward/westward debate on foreign policy 201–2
    economic instruments 204–6
    military capability 202–4
    priorities 201
    Progressive line (*Pishraft-e-Mahvar*) 201
    social power 206–8
  independent strategy 296–7
  India, and 179
  institutions, processes, and instruments
    constitutional foundation 196
    factional decision-mking 195–6, 288–9
    informal networks 195

INDEX 345

Islamic Revolutionary Guard Corps (IRGC) 195-8, 288-9
Supreme Leader of Iran (*Rahbar*) 196
Supreme National Security Council (SNSC) 196
Iraq, and 200, 203-4, 206, 224, 243-4, 251, 253-4
Israel, and 13-14, 200-1, 224, 228-30
Israel compared 13-14
Latin America, and 207
militant organisations 294
nonstate actors 294
political factionalism 192-3
prestige, recognition and status
  negative image worldwide 207-8
  pivotal status 193
  regional power status 13, 295-6
Russia, and 65, 193
Saudi Arabia, and 13-14, 200, 243-5
security environment 296
Shia revolution 291-2
social power 206-8
structural understanding of Iranian GS 192
summary overview 17
Syria, and 198, 203-4, 243-4, 251, 253-4, 256
technological factors
  cyber warfare 293-4
  nuclear weapons 224, 288, 293-4
UK, and 193-5
US, and 193-5, 200-1, 229, 254, 287, 291, 293-4
Iran-Iraq war (1980-88) 202-3, 243-5, 252
Iraq
  Iran, and 200, 203-4, 206, 224, 243-4, 251, 253-4
  Islamic revolution 206
  Israel, and 224-5, 228-9
  Kuwait, and 252-3
  Qatar, and 253-4
  Russia, and 59
  Saudi Arabia, and 244-5, 250-1, 255-7
  Soviet Union, and 252
  Turkey, and 254
  UK, and 126-7, 133, 137, 140
  US, and 86-7
  see also Iran-Iraq war (1980-88); ISIS
Iraq War (1991) 138-9, 179
Iraq War (2003) 123, 133-8, 270-1
ISIS 37, 39, 59, 136, 198, 203, 229, 251, 271, 293-4
Islamic Republic of Iran (IRI) *see* Iran
Islamic State in Syria and Iraq *see* ISIS

Ismay, Hastings Ismay, 1st Baron 131-2, 176-7
Israel
  aims, goals and objectives
    hard security 291
    ideational/ideological 292
    independence 223
    legitimacy 223
    prestige, recognition and status 291
  conception of GS 217-19
  cooperative strategy 296
  cultural diversification 226
  defence and military capacity, policies and activities
    'Begin Doctrine' 228
    covert operations ('MABAM') 228
    Defence Ministry 220
    defence technology exports 230-1
    'Deterrence, Early-Warning, Decision' concept 219
    Directorate of Military Intelligence (*Agaf HaModi'in*: Aman) 221
    Independence War 1948 217-18
    'Iron Wall' concept 218
    Israel Defence Forces (IDF) 218, 220-1, 227-8, 291
    NATO links 227
    nuclear weapons 229-30
    US military aid 227
  documentary sources 218, 222
  domestic politics
    Palestinian situation 231
    parliamentary democracy 220
  economic capacity, policies and activities
    European links 227
    technology exports 230-1
  Egypt, and 224
  foreign policy
    Ministry of Foreign Affairs 222
    objectives 223
    Palestinian situation 230-1
  geographical factors 288
  Hamas, and 224-5, 228
  Hezbollah, and 224, 228
  history, identity and collective memory
    diaspora 217-18
    Holocaust 217-18, 290
    Masada Complex 11, 218, 290
    Zionism 217
  institutions, processes, and instruments
    alliances 227
    civil society actors 222
    Defence Ministry 220

Israel (*cont.*)
  Directorate of Military Intelligence
    (*Agaf HaModi'in*: Aman) 221
  documentary sources 218, 222
  government 220
  hard power instruments 227
  integrated GS approach 227
  intelligence agencies 221
  Israel Defence Forces (IDF) 220-1
  Israeli Atomic Energy Commission
    (IAEC) 221-2
  Meridor commission 222
  Ministry of Foreign Affairs 222
  National Security Staff (Hamatah
    leBitachon Leumi) 221-2
  Parliament 220
  security doctrine 227-8
  soft power instruments 227
  US military aid 228
Iran, and 13-14, 200-1, 224, 228-30
Iraq, and 224-5, 228-9
NATO, and 227
Palestine, and 225, 230-1
public relations 294
regional factors 287-8
regional power status 13
Russia, and 228
Saudi Arabia, and 229
Saudi Arabia compared 13-14
security environment 296
success of GS 231-3
summary overview 17
Syria, and 224-5, 228-9
technology
  exports 230-1
  nuclear weapons 293-4
threat perception 223-6, 292
Turkey, and 227
US, and 227, 229, 287, 296
Ivanov, Serguey 290

Jabotinsky, Vladimir 218
Jackson, Andrew 40
Jiang Zemin 74
Johnson, Lyndon 37

Kaarbo, Juliet 15
Kabir, Amir 192-3
Kennan, George 29, 33, 35-6
Kennedy, Paul 7, 130-1, 173, 208
Kerry, John 33-4
Khamenei, Sayyid Ali Hosseini 196-7,
  200-1, 206

Khashogji, Jamal 255
Khatami, Seyyed Mohammad 196, 201-2
Khomeini, Rouhollah M. 195-6, 199,
  201, 206
Kipling, Rudyard 26-7
Koh, Harold 27
Korean War 37, 39, 77-8
  see also North Korea; South Korea
Krasner, Stephen 5
Kugler, Richard 34
Kuwait 135, 138-9, 244, 252-3, 255-6

Lavrov, Sergei 276
Lew, Jack 33
liberal engagement, strategy of *see* France
Liddell Hart, Basil 130-1
Li Ruogu 87
Liu Mingfu 86
Locher, James, III 30
Louis XIV 100-1
Lukianov, Fyodor 56
Lula da Silva, Luiz Inácio 149, 153-6,
  158-61
Luttwak, Edward 231-2, 239-40

Macmillan, Harold 133
Macron, Emmanuel 107
Manmohan, Singh 185-7
Mao Zedong 74
'March West' concept *see* China
Marshall, George 33
Martel, William 7, 38
Mason, Robert 241
May, Theresa 137
McCloy, John 29
Mead, Walter Russell 40
means *see* ends, ways, and means
Mearsheimer, John 34, 77
Metternich, Klemens Wenzel, Prince von 50
Milevski, Lukas 5-6
militant organisations *see* nonstate actors
Mitterrand, François 103
Modi, Narendra 172, 187
Mohammad bin Salman, Prince 246, 248,
  251, 254-5
Mohammad bin Zaid Al Nahayan 246
Montebourg, Arnaud 111-12
Morgenthau, Hans 294-5
Morin, Hervé 111
Mosaddegh. Mohammad 193-4
multilateral institutions *see* international
  institutions
Murray, Williamson 11

Najibullah, Mohammad 178–9
Napoleon (Bonaparte) 50, 54–5
Narizny, Kevin 8–9
Nasser, Gamal abd' al 133
Nathan, Andrew J. 85
national factors *see* domestic factors
NATO
  former Soviet Bloc countries, and 55
  foundation 25
  Mediterranean Dialogue 227
  military command structure (IMCS) 110
  Russian perception 57
Nehru, Jawaharlal
  China, and 178
  conception of GS 171–2
  leadership of India 172
  legacy of his GS 173–8
  statist economic planning 179
Nester, William 103
Netanyahu, Benjamin 221, 230–1
New Historic Missions *see* China
Nitze, Paul 33, 35
Nixon, Richard 37
non-linear warfare *see* Russia
nonstate actors as GS tool 294
North Korea 4–5, 39, 58, 79–80, 137, 141, 179–80, 207–8, 288, 293–4, 296
  see also Korean War
Nye, Joseph, Jr 34, 67

Obama, Barack 32–4, 37, 39, 245, 254
objectives *see* aims, goals and objectives
O'Hanlon, Michael 33–4
opportunities
  choice to pursue 292
  response to 38

Pahlavi, Reza Shah 194
Palmerston, Henry John Temple, 3rd Viscount 125
Pant, Harsh V. 180
Perkovich, George 184
plans
  behaviours, and 8–9
  principles, and 8–9
Posen, Barry R. 5–9, 34
prestige, recognition and status
  goal, as 291
  great power status 2, 12–13, 295
  powers able to implement GS 2–3, 12–13
  smaller powers' GS capability 3
  superpower status 2
principles, plans and 8–9

private military institutions (PMIs) *see* nonstate actors
public relations as GS tool 294
Putin, Vladimir
  doctrinal statements 57
  foreign policy 53
  NATO, and 55
  personalization of power 51
  Ukraine, and 62
  US, and 60–1

Qatar 244, 252–7
Qin Yaqing 86–7

Rabin, Yitzhak 231
Rafsanjani, Hashemi 197–9, 201
Raghavan, Srinath 177–8
rationalism
  advantages 10–11
  authors' rejection 3
  bias towards 287
  disadvantages 10–11
Reagan, Ronald 26, 40
realism
  agency, and 9
  Ming Dynasty China 289–90
recognition *see* prestige, recognition and status
regional factors 287–8
resource factors 9–10
restraint 8–9
Riedel, Bruce 248
Rivlin, Reuven 225–6
Rogozin, Dmitri 276
Roosevelt, Franklin 26, 29
Roosevelt, Theodore 26–7
Rosecrance, Richard 4
Rosenau, James 15
Rostow, Walt 33
Rouhani, Hassan 192–3, 198–9, 201
Rousseff, Dilma 149, 155–6, 158, 160–1
Russia
  aims, goals and objectives
    prestige, recognition and status 53–4, 60–2, 291
    security and foreign policy objectives 59–64
  Armenia, and 62
  authors' analytical approach 50
  China, and 50–1, 60, 62–3, 65, 297
  Cold War 50–1
  conception of grand strategy 285–6
  Crimea annexation 62

Russia (cont.)
  cultural factors 52, 290
  decision-making 51, 288-9
  defence and military capacity, policies and activities
    imbalance of economic and military power 60-2
    military capability 65-6
    non-linear warfare 289-90
    nuclear deterrence 66-7
    strategic deterrence and intimidation 66-7
  defensive approach to GS 50
  documentary sources 56-9, 285-6
  economic power imbalance with military power 60-2
  EU, and 55, 61
  France, and 63
  Georgia, and 55-6, 61-2, 65
  Gerasimov doctrine on non-linear warfare 289-90
  global balance of power, and 53
  history, identity and collective memory
    difference between real power and perceived power 50
    fear of encirclement 54-5
    fear of surprise attack 54-5
    invasions by Mongols, Napoleon and Hitler 54-5
  implementation of GS 64-8
  independent strategy 296-7
  India, and 179
  influence strategy 67-8
  institutions, processes, and instruments 51-2
  international institutions, and 60
  Iran, and 65, 193
  Iraq, and 59
  ISIS, and 59
  Islamic-inspired instability, and 59
  Israel, and 228
  Kyrgyzstan, and 55-6
  Moldova, and 62
  NATO, and 50-1, 53, 55, 57, 61
  non-linear warfare 289-90
  political approaches 67-8
  prestige, recognition and status
    goal of 53-4, 291
    great power status 2, 12-13, 53-4, 60-1, 295
    imbalance of economic and military power 60-2
    regional power status 53-4, 56, 61-2
  realism 53-4
  Saudi Arabia, and 239, 244-5
  security environment 296
  soft power 67
  Soviet-Iraq relations 252
  Soviet Union collapse 56, 179
  strategic thinking 52-3
  summary overview 16-17, 68-9
  Syria, and 59, 65-6, 69, 228, 296
  technological factors
    cyber warfare 288, 293-4
    Gerasimov doctrine on non-linear warfare 289-90
  threat perception
    characterization of threats 56-9
    instability risks 58-9
    NATO military power 57
    selective focus 50-1
    strategic challenges 55-6
    Western subversive capabilities 57-8
  traditional great-power strategy 295
  Ukraine, and 50-1, 55-6, 61-2
  US, and 53, 55-8, 60-1, 63, 65, 287
  WTO, and 60

Salman, King 246, 251
Sarkozy, Nicolas 108-11
Sartori, Giovanni 9-10
Saudi Arabia
  Afghanistan, and 179
  aims, goals and objectives 246, 291-2
  authors' analytical approach 240
  China, and 239, 244-5
  conception of GS 239-41
  Cooperation Council of the Arab States of the Gulf (GCC), and 252-6
  cooperative strategy 296
  decision-making 245-6
  defence and military capacity, policies and activities 248-50
  economic capacity, policies and activities 246-8
  Egypt, and 244-5
  geographical factors 288
  history, identity and collective memory 17
    exceptionalism 242
    national unification 241-2
    oil wealth 243
    Salafism 242
  implementation of GS
    aims, goals and objectives 246

defence and military 248–50
economic 246–8
mobilisation of state power 256–7
social power 250–2
Iran, and 13–14, 200, 243–5
Iraq, and 244–5, 250–1, 255–7
Israel, and 13–14, 229
mobilisation of state power 256–7
Oman, and 253
Pakistan, and 256–7
Qatar, and 253–7
regional factors 287–8
regional power status 13, 295–6
Russia, and 239, 244–5
Salafism 291–2
security environment 296
social power 250–2
summary overview 17, 257–8
Syria, and 246–7, 250–1
threat perception 243–5, 292
US, and 239, 245, 254, 256, 287, 296
Schlesinger, Arthur 28
Scobell, Andrew 85
security
aims, goals and objectives 291
stable environment 296
unstable environment 296
Shah, Mohammad Reza 194–5
Shi Yinhong 86
Silove, Nina 8–9
Singh, Manmohan 185–7
Skockpol, Theda 15
smaller powers *see* prestige, recognition and status
Snyder, Jack 241
soft power, concept of 67
Sommers, Margaret 15
South Korea 63, 115, 273
see also Korean War
Soviet Union *see* Russia
state-based threats *see* threat perception
state-owned enterprises as GS tool 294
status *see* prestige, recognition and status
Stein, Arthur 4
Stent, Angela 60–1
Stone, Oliver 58
strategic culture *see* cultural factors
structuralism, agency and 9
Subrahmanyam, K. 173–4
Suez crisis 133–4
superpower status *see* prestige, recognition and status
Swaine, Michael 76

Syria
EU, and 271, 276
Iran, and 198, 203–4, 243–4, 251, 253–4, 256
Israel, and 224–5, 228–9
Qatar, and 253–4
Russia, and 59, 65–6, 69, 228, 296
Saudi Arabia, and 246–7, 250–1
US, and 256
see also ISIS
systemic approaches
authors' rejection 4
focus on 2
IR theory, in 15

Taiwan 77–8
Taliaferro, Jeffrey W. 7
Talleyrand, Charles-Maurice, Prince de 50
Tanham, George K. 173, 181
technology
cyber warfare 293–4
geographical factors in relation 288
nuclear weapons 288, 293–4
Telhami, Shibley Z. 240
Tellis, Ashley 76, 173
Temer, Michel 162
terrorism *see* 9/11 terrorist attacks on US; al-Qaeda; ISIS; War on Terror
Tertrais, Bruno 108
theoretical foundation of GS 38
threat perception 38
choice to respond to threats 292
focus of classicist GS on military threats 50
state-based threats 2–3
Truman, Harry 132
Trump, Donald
Afghanistan, and 256
'America First' doctrine 270–1, 291–2, 297
continuity and change in US GS 25
emphasis on reform 30, 37, 39–40
EU, and 278–9
Iran, and 229
National Military Strategy, and 32
Saudi Arabia, and 239, 245, 256
Syria, and 256
US as worldwide exemplar 26
Turkey 65, 132–3, 223, 227, 230, 244, 249–50, 253–8
Turki al-Faisal, Prince 256
Turner, Frederick Jackson 27

United Kingdom (UK)
9/11 terrorist attacks on US, and 123, 136
Afghanistan, and 136, 140–1

United Kingdom (UK) (*cont.*)
   aims, goals and objectives
      balance of power in Europe 126
      clarity of key interests 124
      independence 125
      reconfiguring after 9/11 terrorist attacks 136
      'special relationship' with US 132
   Atlantic regionalism 141
   authors' analytical approach 123, 125
   balance of power in Europe, and 126
   Brexit 141–2, 294
   China, and 141
   Cold War, and 127, 132
   conception of GS 123–5, 285–6, 288–9
   continuing challenges and constraints
      Atlantic regionalism 141
      Europe post-Brexit 141–2
      forward projection of defence 142
      global interconnectedness 140
      new kinds of warfare 140–1
      new nuclear capability 140
      reserve forces funding 140
      shift in geostrategic balance of power 141
      terrorism 139
   cooperative strategy 296–7
   decolonisation 126–7, 132
   defence and military capacity, policies and activities
      advantages 126
      Afghanistan 136, 140–1
      constraints 126
      contraction after World War 2 125, 134
      Falklands War 134–5
      former Soviet Bloc countries 136
      forward projection of defence 142
      Iraq Enquiry 138
      Iraq War 133–4
      ISIS 136
      military successes 126–7
      new nuclear capability 140
      nuclear deterrence 133
      Suez crisis 133–4
      War on Terror 136
      world wars 125–7, 130–2
   documentary sources 285–6
   domestic politics
      debates on GS 130–2
      influence on GS 124
   economic capacity, policies and activities
      advantages 126
      constraints 126
      decline after World War 2 132
      international aid 135
      'soft power' sources 129–30
      trade with Europe 136
   EU, and 135–8, 141–2, 294, 296–7
   Falklands War 134–5
   foreign policy
      alliances 125
      international law, commitment to 135
      success 125
   France, and 127
   geographical factors 126
   history, identity and collective memory
      Brexit 137–8
      influence of history on GS 123–4
      influence of world wars 125–7, 130–2
      Iraq War 133–4
      perceptions of world role 124
      Suez crisis 133–4
      War on Terror 138–9
   implementation of GS
      continuing challenges and constraints 139–42
      economic 130
      gradual adaptation approach 124
      'indirect approach' 127, 131
      instruments of GS 125
      international law, commitment to 124
      problem areas 138–9
      reconfiguring after 9/11 terrorist attacks 136
      regional factors 287–8
      'soft power' sources 129–30
      'special relationship' with US 124, 132
      ways 124
   India, and 132, 171, 174–5
   'indirect approach' to GS 127
   institutions, processes, and instruments
      decision-making 127–30
      documentary sources 134–5
      Foreign and Commonwealth Office (FCO) 129
      governmental bodies 127–9
      National Security Council (NSC) 128
      non-governmental advisory bodies 129
      'soft power' sources 129–30
   international institutions, and 133, 294
   international law, commitment to 124, 135
   Iran, and 193–5
   Iraq, and 126–7, 133, 137, 140
   Iraq War 133–4
   ISIS, and 136
   Israel, and 138–9

NATO, and 132, 135–6, 294, 297
PMIs 140
prestige, recognition and status
  decline after World War 2 127, 131–2
  great power status 12–13
  regional power status 295
security environment 296
'special relationship' with US 124, 132
Suez crisis 133–4
summary overview 16–17, 142–3
technology 140
US, and 36, 124, 126–7, 132–3, 138, 141, 287, 296–7
United States (US)
9/11 terrorist attacks 36, 123, 136, 243–4, 251
Afghanistan 39
aims, goals and objectives 36, 291–2
'America First' doctrine 40, 270–1, 291–2, 296–7
American Creed 26
authors' analytical approach 25
Brazil, and 162, 287
China, and 37, 78, 87, 141, 287
Cold War 30, 35–6
comparative studies 12
conception of grand strategy 285–6
containment of Soviet expansion 36–7
continuity and change 39–40
cultural factors 290
decision-making 29
defence and military capacity, policies and activities 28, 30, 34, 36–9
Department of Defense (DOD) 32–3
Department of State (DOS) 33–4
diplomacy 34, 40
documentary sources 29, 31–9, 285–6
economic capacity, policies and activities
  global economic power 34–5
  liberal hegemony 293
  sanctions 34–5
foreign policy 28, 33–4
France, and 99, 102, 107–8, 111–12, 114–15, 287, 297
geographical factors 288
great power status 12–13, 295
history, identity and collective memory
  exceptionalism 26–7
  foundational myths 25, 290
  frontierism 27–8
  'Shining City on the Hill' 26
ideational/ideological goals 291–2
independent strategy 296

India, and 174, 177, 187
institutions, processes, and instruments
  GS outputs 35–9
  implementation 38–9
  institutions 29, 31–4
  instruments 29, 34–5
  legislative parameters 28–30
  overview 30–5
international institutions, and 294
Iran, and 193–5, 200–1, 229, 287, 291, 293–4
Iraq, and 39, 86–7
ISIS, and 39
isolationism 38–9
Israel, and 40, 227, 229, 287, 296
Korean War 37
liberal hegemony 291–2
Monroe Doctrine 37
National Defense Strategy (NDS) 32
National Military Strategy (NMS) 32
National Security Council (NSC) 31–2
National Security Strategy (NSS) 29, 31–2, 37–8
NATO, and 25, 55–6
neo-isolationism 38–9
nonstate actors 294
North Korea, and 39
NSC-68 35–6
opportunities 292
other states' GS in relation 287
overview of postwar grand strategies 36–7
PMIs 294
prestige, recognition and status
  preeminent global power 25, 37
  superpower status 2, 25
  unipole status 25
prevailing assumptions about grand strategy 2
Quadrennial Defense Review (QDR) 32–3
regional factors 287–8
Russia, and 53, 55–8, 60–1, 63, 65, 287
Saudi Arabia, and 239, 245, 254, 256, 287, 296
security and GS in relation 28
security environment 296
Solarium project 31
Soviet Union, and 36–7
'special relationship' with UK 124, 132
studies of GS 25
Suez crisis, and 133
summary overview 16–17
Syria, and 39, 256
threat perception 32, 34–5, 37, 39

United States (US) (*cont.*)
   traditional great-power strategy 295
   UK, and 36, 124, 126–7, 132–3, 138, 141, 287, 296–7
   unipole, as 287
   Vietnam War 36
   War on Terror 37
   'Washington Consensus' 28
   World War I 36
   World War II 28–9, 36

Vaïsse, Maurice 101
Vietnam 37, 80
Vore, Christopher S. 15

Walt, Stephen 243
Wang Huning 75–6
Wang Jisi 85–6
War on Terror 138, 223
Warsaw Pact, dissolution 55
Washington, George 36
ways *see* ends, ways, and means
Williams, Cindy 35
Williams, William Appleman 27
Wilson, Andrew 82

Wilson, Woodrow 26
Winthrop, John 26
Wohlforth, William 5–9, 291
Wolfers, Arnold 292
Wolfowitz, Paul 33
World War I 28–9, 36, 125–7, 130–2, 171
World War II 28–9, 36, 125–7, 131–2, 150, 171, 217–18, 262–3, 296

Xi Jinping
   Belt and Road initiative (BRI) 62, 83–7
   Centenary Goals 81–2
   doctrinal statements 74
   domestic reforms 87–9
   grand strategy 73–6
   leadership of China 74, 82–3
   peripheral expansion 78

Yanukovych, Viktor 62
Yan Xuetong 86
Yuan Peng 84–5

Zarif, Mohammed Javad 192–3
Zheng He 82
Zia-ul-Haq, Muhammad 178